YOUNG GIFTED AND BLACK

THE STORY OF TROJAN RECORDS

Copyright © 2018 Omnibus Press
(A Division of Music Sales Limited)
Originally published by Sanctuary Publishing Ltd in 2003

Original cover illustration courtesy of Mystery Design
Discography by Marc Griffiths and Andy Lambourn

ISBN: 978.1.78760.117.8
Order No: OP57838

Exclusive Distributors
Music Sales Limited
14/15 Berners Street
London, W1T 3LJ

Music Sales Pty. Ltd
(Australia and New Zealand)
Level 4, 30–32 Carrington Street
Sydney
NSW 2000
Australia

Every effort has been made to trace the copyright holders of the photographs in this book but one or two were unreachable. We would be grateful if the photographers concerned would contact us.

Typeset by Evolution Design & Digital Ltd (Kent)
Printed in Malta.

A catalogue record for this book is available from the British Library.

Visit Omnibus Press on the web at www.omnibuspress.com

YOUNG GIFTED AND BLACK

THE STORY OF TROJAN RECORDS

Michael de Koningh & Laurence Cane-Honeysett

Discography by Marc Griffiths and Andy Lambourn

OMNIBUS PRESS

London / New York / Paris / Sydney / Copenhagen / Berlin / Madrid / Tokyo

Contents

Acknowledgements And Thanks

This book was very much a team effort and I have to offer my great thanks to the following people:

First and foremost Laurence Cane-Honeysett, who provided interviews and discographical information and acted as a contact with Trojan Records.

Mike Atherton for his endless pertinent snippets of information and enlightening tables of '25 Soul Covers/R&B Covers' etc. He also attempted to edit my rather peculiar style of English into literate sentences, something for which all readers will no doubt thank him as they progress through the book.

Marc Griffiths for the mass of various label discographies, an unenviable task, but now we all have the information in print. He also contributed to the whole with odds and ends which I for one certainly wasn't aware existed.

Very special thanks to my wife Kathy, who, to her great surprise, became chief researcher and added structure to the whole project. She selflessly devoted many hours of the limited time with which a very busy job left her to wring facts and figures from all manner of sources. Her brother (my brother-in-law) Neil Davies also has to be thanked for his out-of-hours research material.

All the people who gave interviews and put up with my endless questions have my heartfelt gratitude. This, after all, is their story and I hope I've got it right. In particular I would like to thank Bob Andy, Rob Bell, Joe Sinclair, Bruce White, Janis at I-Anka, Sid Bucknor, Dandy, Vic Keary, Clive Crawley, Colin Newman, Graeme Goodall, John Reed, David Betteridge, Dave Hendley, Nick Bourne and the Trojan Museum Trust. I've no doubt missed somebody out and offer my profound apologies as it wasn't intentional.

I also want to thank the 'old timers' who offered memories and sparked my ageing brain into action: Danny Hatcher, Reg Stanley, Trevor and Denny Ball, Dave Sandford, Pete Fontana, Rob Faulconbridge and Mike Pealing.

Acknowledgement must also be paid to three seminal archivists of Jamaican music: Steve Barrow, Roger Dalke and Chris Prete. Without these guys, we wouldn't know half what we do today.

Michael de Koningh
April 2003

Preface

So the Trojan story will be told. This I learned from Michael, who has taken on the project. How pleasantly surprised I was that he asked me to involve myself by contributing a preface.

Trojan and I go back over 30 years – in fact, as far back as when Marcia Griffiths and yours truly discovered that we had a single running up the UK charts. 'Young, Gifted And Black' was on its way to becoming a memorable hit and would eventually place itself firmly in the history of the birth, development and growth – in a word, the evolution – of Jamaican music in all its genres.

Marcia and I were completely taken by surprise when we were told to get our passports and pack our bags hurriedly. This was like a dream – until then, we'd never even remembered that we had recorded this particular work together!

Nina Simone, who originally sung the song, had always been a favourite performer; I appreciated the melodic and lyric content and the message that the song was sending out. But the cover of the song was not done expressly because we related to those sentiments; it was just one of those things.

The title has endured the test of time, made the transition from vinyl to the CD format, and now also to this book.

Writing this piece reminded me of how shocked I was to see throngs of young white people chorusing to the tune of 'Young, Gifted And Black'. I am still amazed!

The financial rewards from the record were not great. However, it opened up a brand new world to me. I had the privilege of getting a glance into the different culture and lifestyles of Europe. The United Kingdom also became a second home for me. Some of my favourite people who are currently active in my life reside in the UK. I have also done a great deal of work at various times in my career in British recording studios and live venues. My record label, I-Anka (Annville Ltd), and my publishing company, Andisongs, to this day are still registered in the United Kingdom.

This book tells the story of how a famous record label contributed to the marketing, promotion and selling of the early Jamaican music. It should give fans of Jamaican music everywhere an insight into the workings, the behind-the-scenes machinations and the development of a truly unique music.

Bob Andy
April 2003

Foreword

The name of Trojan Records is synonymous with Jamaican music the world over.

Between its formation in 1968 and the demise of reggae music in the public consciousness in 1975, prior to Bob Marley's assault on the bastions of white rock, Trojan led the way.

It had competitors, such as the Pama group of labels and Melodisc Records' Fab imprint, but no one moved units and created a brand identity in the marketplace like Trojan Records. Trojan had the know-how, or maybe just the luck, to be in the right place at the right time and, with the right staff and the right musicians behind it, to capture the musical moment.

It rose on the crest of the skinhead youth culture wave of the late 1960s and maintained a presence after the demise of that culture, with a swansong of major pop hits from Ken Boothe and John Holt in 1974.

It championed a minority music initially imported for the swelling West Indian population of London, Birmingham, Bristol and many other cities across the UK and carried it far from home and into the bedroom of many a teenage record buyer. But, just as importantly, Trojan Records created a fertile ground for UK-based Jamaicans to grow their own brand of reggae music. The Shrowder/Bryan/Sinclair partnership, later known as both Bush and Swan Productions, produced some of the most satisfying club sounds of the early 1970s. Their collective work with powerhouse groups such as The Rudies vied with Jamaican productions week after week as the most sought-after tunes of the moment. London-based Joe Mansano's heavyweight work with DJ Dice The Boss shook up the dancehalls with the same force as any Kingston sound by

King Stitt. And let's not forget the most prolific artist and producer of all, Dandy, whose chuckling 'Reggae In Your Jeggae' must have filled every dancefloor in every club across the British Isles as the new sound of reggae broke.

That's not to discount the input of Jamaica, from one of whose top producers, Duke Reid The Trojan, the company took its very name. The demand for his swinging, jazzy and mellow rocksteady inspired Island Records to move further into the UK market, and they accordingly dedicated a label to his work. Initially little more than an overspill from the parent Island label, 35 years later the name Trojan is as strongly associated with reggae as Biro with ballpoint pens, Hoover with vacuum cleaners and Motown with soul.

Lee Perry, the madcap 'Scratch The Upsetter', established his own label within the Trojan confines and poured out his patented idiosyncratic music, helped no end by the studio band that Bob Marley would filch as his own after their collaboration on the *Soul Rebel* sessions. 'Return Of Django' by that studio band The Upsetters, with its catchy heavyweight rhythm topped with Val Bennett's raucous saxophone, helped put reggae on the popular-music map. It also put Trojan on the financial map as it shot into the hallowed Top 10 in October 1969.

Trojan picked up Bob Marley and The Wailers long before anyone outside the reggae community had heard of them and released some of their finest compositions, major songs that Bob would revisit many times during his tragically short career. Sadly for the Trojan coffers, Mr Marley had moved on before superstardom struck, but few would deny that the Marley/Perry/ Trojan work has a sullen brilliance which Bob would never recapture.

Trojan Records championed the new 'toasting' (DJing or rapping) phenomenon, from the formative work of U Roy over sublime Duke Reid rocksteady rhythms to the harsh and prophetic warnings of Big Youth and I-Roy as the Rastafarian '70s moved on. Artists like these felt the pulse of the Kingston dancehall and ran with the flow of new lyrics, keeping ever abreast of the changes that influenced US rap, which it pre-dated by some ten years.

There is no doubt that luck played a big part in the rise of Trojan Records, but there's no doubt either that the company guided the UK reggae market rather than being guided by it. Even when Trojan was losing ground to the roots-and-culture brigade and floundering in the string-laden swamp in which it would finally drown, the label still managed to pull musical rabbits out of the hat – not once but twice, as Ken Boothe and John Holt both tickled the Top 10 and gave the media image of reggae one last flash.

Even at the very end of the '70s, Trojan surfaced for air, releasing a handful of superb contemporary albums and 12" singles, their last thrash at issuing the 'now' sounds of Jamaica before apparently slipping from view for good, only to break the surface once again as a 'revive' label.

The last 20 years have seen the rise and rise of what's commonly called 'revive music', a retrospective scene playing the reggae of yesteryear. Maybe this burgeoning scene arose as a backlash against the current brash ragga and dancehall, engendering a desire to return to the mellower styles of former times. Maybe it was fostered by the numerous 30-somethings who yearned for their misspent youth and found solace in their old friends of sound.

Whatever the reason, thanks to employing some of the most knowledgeable connoisseurs of the music as compilers and annotators, Trojan Records have gained an enormous market share in this growth area. Under the guidance of their new owners, they are finally mining the cavernous depths of their massive back catalogue.

So this book is the story of a record company. It does not attempt to be the story of Jamaican music, though of course the two are tightly intertwined. It is the story of a name that has passed through various hands, with each new owner looking for that magic ingredient for his acquisition: money!

Trojan Records was set up to release Jamaican music in Britain. But let us not think for a moment that this was an altruistic venture; it has always been a business, and as with all businesses the bottom line is to make hard cash, in this instance from the sale of vinyl records and, latterly, compact discs. This was true for Island Records in 1967, and it holds equally true for the Sanctuary Group, who now own the mighty name and its equally mighty back catalogue. Bear this in mind as you voyage through the book: artistic creativity is a wonderful gift, but unless it is properly channelled and marketed, it does not put food on the table.

Lee Gopthal, the first owner of Trojan after its split from Island in 1968, was a professional accountant who sought to organise a company that would feed him and his employees. He was a shrewd man, and much criticism has been levelled at him and his successors regarding artists' rights, royalties and general financial workings. Thirty-odd years on, Mr Gopthal is no longer with us to present his side of the story; all we have are scant paperwork and the fallible memories of staff, singers and players. Any commentary in this area is either from government and press sources, to which anyone can freely gain access, or a direct quotation from a protagonist.

12

In putting out records at such a rapid rate in the late '60s and early '70s, Lee Gopthal and his Trojan staff unwittingly created an important musical legacy. They were selling records to make a living and could not have imagined the extensive monument of sound which they were building. It is only now, with the benefit of hindsight, that we see the contents of Sanctuary's vast vaults as history – history which was often laughed at and reviled at the time but which is now revered and enjoyed by music fans the world over.

Whatever they may think of Trojan's working practices, no one can deny that the company created one of the richest and most varied collections of the art form that is Jamaican music, utilising both the guys across the Atlantic and those trying to make their mark on this side of the ocean. I doubt that, beyond Clement Dodd, Duke Reid and Prince Buster, any producer or label can offer as much variety and supreme quality as the Trojan catalogue.

This book is a testament to all those artists and their endeavours, but it is also dedicated to a veritable host of backroom boys, from producers to chart compilers. They were part of one great whole, a creative process that came under the banner of Trojan Records and whose spark of ignition sent reggae music on a fast path to *Top Of The Pops* and into the hearts of millions of listeners across the globe.

Michael de Koningh
April 2003

1 Early Years

The long and winding story of Trojan Records did not start, as you would expect, in a hot and dusty recording studio in downtown Kingston, but much nearer to home in suburban Croydon.

The building boom of the 1930s had turned this pleasant town on London's southern outskirts into a sprawling mass of overspill centred around Britain's first commercial airport. Industry grabbed greenfield sites to cater for the ever-increasing demands of the consumer.

Into this climate came a small but well-established and successful motor-vehicle manufacturer which sited its engineering works in Purley Way, just beside Croydon Airport. The company, Trojan Ltd, had been producing cars and light commercial vehicles since Leslie Hounsfield had founded it in the 1920s. The 1950s were particularly good years for the firm as they built not only vans but that icon of the age, the bubble car.

Trojan specialised in fitting their basic and sturdy chassis with all manner of back bodies, from flatbed to security boxed, while their customers ranged from one-off buyers to fleet purchasers such as the Royal Mail, the RAF and, most famously, Brooke Bond Tea. With the post-World War II export boom, they started exporting vehicles to many overseas countries, particularly the then still-numerous British colonies, including the small Caribbean island of Jamaica. These exports would consist of chassis, engine and cab only, and the lucky new owner would then fit his truck out to his own specification.

One such Jamaican owner was Arthur 'Duke' Reid.

Reid was born in 1915 and, after leaving school, spent ten years serving as a police officer in the island's capital, Kingston. Of necessity, he developed an aggressive and hard-faced approach in dealing with the dangerous situations that a hot Saturday night in the city's poorer areas could produce. Of necessity too, he became a crack pistol shot. His dexterity with firearms stood him in good stead during his time as a policemen, and a gun would never be far from his side for the rest of his life.

In the early '50s, Reid's wife, Lucille, won a substantial lottery prize, which she invested in their future by buying a business, an off-licence called the Treasure Isle Liquor Store, which was located in the same run-down ghetto area that the Duke had patrolled for a decade. The store was such a success that, in 1958, they relocated to larger premises at 33 Bond Street.

It was normal practice around Kingston for shopkeepers and bar owners to play recorded music as a tactic to attract customers. Not to be outdone, Reid rigged up a 78rpm record player in the shop, with a speaker outside the front door, and discovered a formula for increasing his turnover. Nothing drew in the music-hungry local people like a Wynonie Harris record rocking out through the speaker and carrying right across the street.

But Reid went a step further than most of his rivals. On 9 July 1950, Jamaica's first radio station, RJR (Radio Jamaica Rediffusion), had commenced broadcasting. So that as much of the population as possible could hear its programmes, even though most of them couldn't afford their own radios at that time, the station installed wirelesses in local gathering points like schools and shops.

On this fledgling network, Reid took his first steps into showbusiness by sponsoring and presenting a programme called *Treasure Isle Time*. Using alto saxophonist Tab Smith's 'My Mothers Eyes' as his theme tune, he would catch the listeners' ears with the driving R&B of Amos Milburn and Rosco Gordon or the tear-stained ballads of Johnny Ace, then regale them with news of the latest booze bargains available in his off-licence. He had an excellent knowledge of and taste in American R&B, which was all the rage in '50s Jamaica, and soon found himself presiding over a highly successful show. Still, Reid was ambitious, and he decided to launch a sound system.

Sound systems – the Jamaican equivalent of the mobile disco – had risen with the demise of live big bands as the 1940s had turned into the 1950s. These live bands, such as Eric Dean's and River Cook's, had played a mixture of mento (the Jamaican equivalent of calypso) and replicated US swing in the Count Basie mould. However, there was one problem with such bands: their predilection to break for half an hour for refreshments, leaving the dance patrons in silence. Dance promoters therefore favoured recorded music because of its ability to keep their patrons entertained all evening, making them less likely to wander off to a rival dance and more likely to stay and consume rum and beer, which was where the profits were made. So the sound system was born.

Enterprising dance organisers favoured sound systems also because to hire one cost much less than paying the musicians of a big band. Although primitive, with only one record deck, a 'sound' could keep the music flowing and the revellers dancing all night. The inevitable gaps between records were bridged by slick DJ patter copied directly from the New Orleans jocks whose radio shows beamed across the Caribbean to eager Jamaican listeners. A sound system had to be powerful, as most dances took place outdoors with the dance arena, or 'lawn', bounded by temporary, rough corrugated-iron fencing.

The sound system also became important in the structure of working-class Jamaica, particularly for the city dwellers of Kingston, as it provided much-needed escape and relaxation from the trials of everyday living: for them, it was as much a meeting place as any bar or liquor store. The audience at any dance consisted mainly of poorly-paid working people and the even poorer ghetto underclass.

The mainly white ruling and upper echelons of society had always swung to a different beat; they liked a more refined sound and didn't like voyaging to the seedier parts of town. The arrival of US R&B – with the powerhouse sounds of BB King, the great blues shouter Big Joe Turner and raucous instrumentalists like Big Jay McNeely – polarised the social groups still further.

Swiftly, Duke Reid moved forward by constructing his first 'set' (so called because the first sound systems were little more than radiogram sets with extra speakers) and took his music and his money-spinning liquor out to the evening dancers. That slow but hardy van which he had purchased to carry the bulky equipment to locations around his area gave the set its name. As it approached, fans would shout 'Here comes the Trojan!', and so he became known as Duke Reid The Trojan, playing out around his territory in the Bond Street and Pink Lane area of Kingston.

The slot on RJR was providing a great advertising place for both Reid's store and his sound system, and it also created a demand for those tough R&B records which he played. By the mid '50s the Duke was unstoppable, with the might of radio and his exclusive R&B records – dredged from dusty locations in the nearby continent – rocking him to the top, supplanting rival sound owner Thomas 'Tom The Great Sebastian' Wong.

Prince Buster credits Thomas Wong as the original sound-system champion and the man responsible for pioneering the modern Jamaican dancehall. With Count Machuki, his DJ, playing the latest R&B sent over from the USA by his brother, Tom moved from playing out of the front of his hardware store to building the formative sound system and taking it to the dancehall. Known as a gentleman, as competition grew fiercer he resigned from the race and later opened the Silver Slipper club further uptown. Eventually, he mysteriously committed suicide by gassing himself in his car.

Seasonal cane-cutting in the USA was a major source of employment for lower class Jamaicans throughout the post-war years, and whilst away working they would be introduced to the smoky inner-city R&B music via bars and the radio. Many of them supplemented their meagre cane-cutting wages by returning with a pile of the latest R&B 78s, which they would then sell to various sound-system operators, sometimes for a substantial profit. One such cane-cutter was a young man by the name of Clement Seymour Dodd.

As a youth, Dodd had been a promising cricketer, so much so that he was nicknamed 'Coxson' after Bill Copson, a Derbyshire fast bowler who had greatly impressed cricket-loving Jamaicans by taking five wickets against the West Indies in a test match at Lord's. Coxson picked up the hottest R&B and jazz discs and initially sold them on his return to Jamaica. Apparently Duke Reid purchased some of his latest finds to use on his newly founded Trojan sound system.

In 1954, Clement Dodd launched his own sound, named Sir Coxson The Downbeat (*Down Beat* was America's leading jazz and swing magazine), and put his vast knowledge and collection of R&B and jazz to good use. He rose rapidly to become a direct challenger to Duke Reid, and alongside Vincent Edwards – with his mammoth 'King Edwards The Giant' – he became the third member of the ruling elite of operators.

So by the late 1950s there were three major sounds vying for premiership, with other fast-rising systems like Count Smith and V-Rocket snapping at their heels. Competition was fierce and each new sound system would try to outclass its rivals with incredibly obscure American records and increasingly powerful amplifiers. Proven hit makers like Fats Domino or Louis Jordan no longer impressed the punters; a hip DJ had to spin a

Clifton Chenier, Big Mike Gordon or Zu Zu Bollin platter if he wanted to be at the cutting edge.

Despite the competition, Duke Reid proved how enduringly popular his Trojan sound was. He was crowned King Of Sounds And Blues in 1956 at the Success Club, in 1957 at the Foresters' Hall, and in 1958, again at the Success Club, by his appreciative and ever-growing army of followers.

Without doubt, it wasn't just his musical ear that gave him this meteoric success; equally it was his muscular arm, backed up by a crew of henchmen recruited from the underworld of the Back o' Wall ghetto, which he had patrolled a few years earlier. The Duke's vicious way of literally beating down other sounds is legendary, with tactics including cutting speaker cables, throwing stones into the midst of the dancers and flashing knives in their faces. He would use every method he could to subdue and overrun the opposition so that many smaller operators simply relocated to more hospitable areas outside the ghetto territories in order to escape injury and destruction.

Although Reid's henchmen were the most feared and notorious, all the sound system operators had to be seen to be tough. Doctor Bird label owner and sound engineer Graeme Goodall recalls that they could all be violent if they had to be: 'You had to be tough, albeit in those days, remember, no firearms *per se* – firearms hadn't permeated society – and so the smashing up was bottles, bricks, pieces of iron pipe, two-by-fours, maybe an occasional knife. But it was the old bar-room brawl type of violence.'

Singer, producer and former sound-system DJ Lee Perry agrees: 'In those days you had to be a toughie, and to make it you had to be monster tough. In those days Duke Reid and all those people were the toughest guys. It was like those guys... all the time they wanted power.'

Due to Reid's fearsome ways of (sometimes literally) flattening a rival sound, the other rigs had to employ tough roadies to counteract his henchmen. Among Coxson's muscle was a certain Cecil Bustamente Campbell (aka Prince Buster), an ex-boxer and a well known figure in the rough ghetto quarter where he had been born in 1938. In 1960, Buster left Coxson's employ to set up his own sound system, Voice Of The People, whose title reflected his position absolutely, as his roots were in the ghetto and he was now playing especially for his downtrodden brothers. No one was ever to be more 'from the people and for the people' than Prince Buster, who was justly proud of his impoverished pedigree.

But the Duke, Coxson and King Edwards were at the top of the music pile when it came to exclusive, driving R&B discs, for which they had scoured out-of-the-way record shops on their many trips throughout the southern United States. These discs would be used against all comers in sometimes violent sound clashes (competitions between two rival sound systems).

The object was to play records which would get the crowd moving, thereby ensuring their support and 'killing' or 'flopping' the other sound. The more exclusive the sound – usually via the use of one-off special recordings – the more likely it was to gain the support of the crowd, who would declare the winner as the purveyor of the best tunes, and also the one who managed to deafen his patrons with the loudest set-up. What did a little loss of hearing matter when Dodd was playing tunes like 'Coxson's Hop' and 'Coxson's Shuffle'?

These were actually US R&B discs whose labels had been blanked, by Willis Jackson ('Later For Gator') and Harold Land ('San Diego Bounce') respectively. These Downbeat 'exclusives' kept the rivals at bay. With no indication of the real title of the dance-buster visible, even if you could get close enough to see it (which the roadies made sure you couldn't), the others would have to find even more underground sounds to fight back.

This practice of scratching all the details from a record's label was necessary to keep tunes exclusive to the one sound system, as the minute a rival held the same piece of shellac, its drawing power was over. In that climate of intense rivalry, the instant that you lost the best sounds, you lost everything. Crowds were as fanatical as any football supporter, but far less loyal: they would switch their fickle allegiance to another player in a flash.

By the mid '50s, Bill Haley and Elvis Presley were unwittingly creating a major problem in Kingston as, much to Mom and Pop's displeasure, blue-jeaned, white middle-class America found out how to rock 'n' roll. The Kingstonian's staple diet for a rousing night out at his favoured sound system dance was a chilled bottle of Red Stripe and an earful of driving R&B. However, new R&B records were in short supply as American studios rushed to record every clean-cut, clean-shaven white singer they could find. The old hands found themselves out of a job, and the sound systems found themselves running out of music.

Rock 'n' roll was fine for the children of the Land of the Free, with their newly slicked-back hair, but in Kingston it was a disaster. Dancers simply did not like the new hillbilly bop purveyed by Carl Perkins *et al* and thirsted for the greasier shuffle of Bill Doggett or Nappy Brown. Suddenly, the pickings became slim: sound men returned almost empty-handed from their record-buying trips to North America. There wasn't enough old stock to go round, and little new music that fitted the bill was being recorded.

So Coxson and Duke Reid, in particular, had an acute need to replenish their steadily dwindling stocks of new records if they were to stay top dogs in the sound system stakes. In the late '50s, these two – along with lesser lights such as Simeon L Smith of Little Wonder Sound – found a simple answer: try out some local talent.

Kingston was full of aspiring Little Richards and Nat 'King' Coles eager to wow crowds as their idols did on a Saturday night via the pumping sound systems. Foundation singers like Owen Gray, Wilfred 'Jackie' Edwards, Derrick Morgan and Laurel Aitken all ran the gauntlet of the crowd at Vere Johns Junior or Victor Sampson's volatile talent contests, where the patrons would launch anything to hand at the stage should the performer displease.

'My first recording,' recalls Derrick Morgan, 'was in 1959, but the first time I sang in public was 1957 in the Vere Johns contest, and I came first that night. I was imitating Little Richard at the time, singing "Long Tall Sally" and "Jenny Jenny Jenny", and I came ahead of Monty Morris, Owen Gray, Wilfred Edwards and Hortense Ellis.'

So it was that, among the puppet shows, comedians, contortionists and jugglers, the sound men sought out singers with enough ability to convince an audience, via records, that they were gritty Kansas City blues shouters or dreamy balladeers. King Edwards, Coxson Dodd, Prince Buster and Duke Reid became talent scouts and formative producers who, almost by chance, kick-started the whole Jamaican recording industry.

Prior to their involvement, only one recording studio existed on the island. Motta's Recording Studio was run by radio and electrical dealer Stanley Motta. The studio was behind his shop and was primitive in the extreme, with only two microphones and with the walls draped with old carpets and sacking to deaden the sound – the spitting image of Joe Von Battle's Hastings Street studio, in which a young John Lee Hooker had kicked off the Detroit recording industry a few years earlier.

The enterprising Motta had started to record traditional mento folk singers in around 1951 or 1952. As there were no mastering and pressing facilities on the island, he had to send his recordings to England, where major label Decca manufactured the discs, via Emil Shallit's Melodisc company. The fragile 78s were then exported back to Jamaica.

But it was Coxson, Duke Reid, Buster and King Edwards – alongside Australian-born sound engineer Graeme Goodall, aided by future Island Records boss Chris Blackwell – who would really found the island's recording industry proper. The four sound-system men needed a plentiful supply of new, exciting R&B sounds to keep their demanding dancers happy. Their records would be especially for use on their sounds and were not initially issued for public consumption.

The Blackwell-Goodall partnership, on the other hand, started to make records after Blackwell gained six jukeboxes in a business deal. In typical Jamaican fashion, he decided to make his own records to stock his jukeboxes, rather than buying them from elsewhere. When he first met Goodall (who was then working for RJR) at a wedding reception, they mooted this plan, and in 1958 the pair were sneaking into RJR's studio afterhours to record local musicians. At about the same time, future Jamaican Prime Minister Edward Seaga formed WIRL (West Indies Records Limited) to record local talent approximating that authentic R&B music.

The band on these pioneering RJR sessions was built around four Australians who had come to Jamaica to work at Tilly Blackman's Glass Bucket Club: guitarist Denis Sindrey, pianist Pearce Doddard, drummer Lol Morris and a clarinettist whose name no one can remember but who soon left anyway, according to Graeme Goodall. Local nightclub musicians like double bassist Lloyd Brevett (who would find fame a few years later as a member of The Skatalites) and guitarist Ernest Ranglin would augment the Aussies. They needed to be night owls, for sessions would run from late evening, after RJR had closed down, until five in the morning.

'It went from there,' remembers Graeme Goodall. 'My term was up at Radio Jamaica, and after putting in at JBC – Jamaican Broadcasting Corporation – we built their transmitters for them, shared facilities, shared transmitter sites. So I was involved in that, establishing the FM links through the island, but the music was the love, while the engineering was paying the bills. Mind you, I loved the engineering side of it too. However, I was not an RF [Radio Frequency] man. Deep down, I was an audio man.

'But during this time I met Ken Khouri. Ken had gone up to Miami to buy a car, evidently, and he was wandering around and I think next to the car dealership he wandered into a pawnshop. A guy – a musician – had just come in and pawned a Presto portable disc recorder, with a supply of 20 blank discs, and so Ken asked me, "What's this?" And I explained it to him, and I think he had, like, a half an hour with this musician who had pawned this thing, and he packed it all up in the back of this Ford Fairlane which he'd bought and brought it back to Jamaica, the idea being that he was going to record people and teach Stanley Motta a thing or two.

'But of course he'd forgotten – or at least nobody bothered to tell him – that in the meantime disc recording had been bypassed and there was tape recording. So Ken and I were talking and we became firm friends – Papa Khouri, as we called him; Papa Kool. And so he went back up and bought a Magnecord recorder and a box of tapes, and he said, "Well, when can we do this?" By this time, he was pressing 78 records from stampers for Mercury Records that were sent down from America.

'We went out the back of his record-pressing plant which was in Upper King Street, and we found an old building. It was like a ramshackle sort of outhouse, with termites running up and down the wall and everything, but I got the bright idea that I'd strengthen the walls by pouring sand down them to give me some sort of isolation.

'We poured sand in there and it went well until I got about six feet up the wall and the whole wall collapsed. So I thought I'd better go back and re-examine the engineering of this thing. We filled it up with fibreglass and anything else we could find – carpets, dead dogs, you know – and so we had this Magna with a three-channel mixer. Ken went on recording calypsos and things like that. But it was an attempt. It was a start.

'When I decided to leave Radio Jamaica, I went to see Ken, 'cos he really wanted to get into it, and he'd already started building Federal Records. So he said, "Let's build a studio," and I went in there. He had an Ampex, I believe, and a four-channel mixer, and we worked out of two rooms. We had air conditioners, wall units that we used to switch off during recordings. Then we'd record for 2 minutes 45 seconds, switch the recorder off and switch the air conditioning back on!

'I modified the mixer and got another two channels out of it, plus three feeds for echo. Ken and I built an echo chamber, a physical echo chamber out of cement blocks. We begged an old RCA amplifier and speaker from Alec Durie, who was one of the original investors in Federal Records. We installed those and a Neumann microphone, and then I tried to get some Jamaican masons to build a room without any parallel surfaces.

'They couldn't understand this crazy white guy who spoke funny telling them to build a room like they'd never built before, where nothing was parallel, everything was angled. Anyway, it worked quite good.

'But there was one occasion when I heard a noise in the mixer and I couldn't figure out what it was. This was night time and I was recording Byron Lee, I think. There was this terrible chirping noise. It took me about an hour to track it down, and eventually I found that a cricket had got up inside the speaker and he was singing along with the music.

'Of course, when I went in to check it, he thought, "Oh-oh, human being approaching, I've got to keep quiet now," and he'd keep quiet till we started recording again, and then he'd start chirping again.

'So we had one tape recorder and a Neumann microphone. We'd record from Monday through Thursday, then Friday was dub day.'

At those early sessions, the real job of producing was down to the bandleader and the studio engineer, who would take the basic song and shape it to fit. Dodd, Reid and others certainly financed the formative sessions, but they offered minimal input into the actual recording process. This was to change as they gained experience, discovering what the people wanted to hear and which records moved the most copies. Consequently they took a greater interest in their investments as time rolled on.

The sound system would play a new recording on a dub plate (a soft wax one-off pressing) for as long as it drew the crowds. Sometimes a year would pass before the dancers' passion for it cooled. Then it was a quick trip down to the Federal Records pressing plant with the master tape to gain maximum benefit from the recording as it was made commercially available to an eager public.

The success of his home-grown recordings gave Duke Reid the impetus to build his own recording studio of wood in 1962, above his Treasure Isle off-licence. Now, with his new resident engineer Byron Smith, he could achieve a high quality of production and experiment with new sounds and rhythms, as Graeme Goodall remembers: 'Smithy eventually went to work for Duke Reid when Duke built his own studio above the liquor store. It was incredible: it was right up on the roof of his place, built of wood, with pigeons and God knows what up there.'

Coxson Dodd followed suit soon afterwards, in late 1962, and opened his Studio One recording set-up in a former nightclub at 13 Brentford Road, Kingston, where one of his first employees was the future Upsetter Lee Perry, along with esteemed engineer and producer Sid Bucknor.

Derrick Morgan witnessed Duke Reid's tough tactics in the studio: 'He was all right, but he always went around with his two guns. It's true that, if you were singing in a session and he didn't like it, he would shoot his gun and the musicians would get timid. That's why the music was so good!' It does sound like a powerful incentive to do your best.

'Yes, he used his gun during recording sessions,' agrees Graeme Goodall, 'but he was one of the nicest men in the world. But remember, niceness you could not show: too much niceness, to a lot of people there in the music business, would be seen as a sign of weakness!' Engineer and producer Sid Bucknor agrees with Goodall and also recalls that, although Reid was fond of guns, he was a perfectly reasonable employer.

Before you climbed the starry ladder of success as a recording artist, you had to pass the audition. These were crowded affairs, with flocks of aspiring young singers hoping to grab the dream and launch themselves out of the ghetto and into the nation's hearts. One of those young hopefuls in 1959 was a 19-year old Derrick Morgan: 'I went to Duke Reid and sang four songs for him and he picked two which we then recorded. The first song was "Lover Boy", which got the alias of "South Corner Rock", and then "Oh My". The first song I heard on the radio was "Oh My" on *Treasure Isle Time*, Duke Reid's radio programme. I recorded the song Wednesday, and Saturday I heard it on the radio. You can imagine the first time on radio – I was so excited, I started jumping around all over the place. It was so nice, you know? Well, Duke used to keep those songs for his sound system and he never wanted to release them for the public.' Both tunes saw release the following year.

Earl Morgan of vocal trio The Heptones remembers auditioning for the Duke some seven years later: 'We checked Duke Reid and sang "Fatty Fatty" and "Only Sixteen" and all them tunes. There'd be lots of people in a line to do recording. We'd probably be about number 59 or 60 in the line, and by the time you reached him, you'd be a little bit shocked, 'cos the man was an old police officer and he had a big gun over his shoulder.' The Duke turned them down that time and they moved to Ken Lack and then Coxson, where they finally waxed 'Fatty Fatty' and 'Only Sixteen', along with some of their most endearing and enduring love songs.

The very first Jamaican records – those pressed by Decca for Stanley Motta – were 10" 78rpm shellac discs, but by the time of the birth of Jamaican R&B at the end of the '50s they were the new and (comparatively) unbreakable 7" platters, spinning at 45rpm, resplendent with labels bearing the names of the producer and/or his sound system. There could be little doubt as to who produced these early 45s, as label names like Coxsone, Duke Reid's, Prince Buster – Voice Of The People and Smith's proudly announced their provenance.

In keeping with the other players in the island's new recording industry, Duke Reid founded his own imprints. He first issued a handful of 78s bearing the Trojan imprint after his powerhouse sound system, calypsos by Lord Power And The Calypso Quintet, but founded his Duke Reid's label for his productions from 1959 onwards. Later he added Dutchess (*sic*), named after his beloved wife Lucille, and the renowned Treasure Isle, named obviously after his studio. The last-named, along with a revived Trojan, would establish his name in the UK.

While Reid and Coxson concentrated on making records which sounded right on their sound systems, other non-system-owning producers were also gaining footholds in the music business in 1959. In reality, Chris Blackwell and Edward Seaga (more of a financier than a producer) were chiefly responsible for taking recorded sound into people's homes. Although both men supplied the occasional special (exclusive recording) for sounds, their releases were made for jukeboxes and home record players.

In 1959, Blackwell hit big "with Cuban-born Laurel Aitken's 'Boogie In My Bones' on his R&B label and Seaga matched him with (Joe) Higgs And (Roy) Wilson's 'Manny Oh' on WIRL. These records were very much instilled with the sound of mid-'50s black America, with walking bass lines and raucous brass, as on Owen Gray's paean to the Downbeat sound 'On The Beach' or singer/pianist Theophilus Beckford's easy-rocking boogie 'Easy Snapping', with piano chords that pre-dated the ska pattern by a couple of years.

Other strands of black American music influenced those pioneering Jamaican recording artists. Some essayed doo-wop, one as sublimely as Derrick Harriott and His Jiving Juniors on intricately harmonised finger-snappers such as 'Over The River' and 'Sugar Dandy', and sentimental R&B ballads as purveyed by Keith and Enid on their hit 'Worried Over You' and the honey-coated tones of Wilfred 'Jackie' Edwards, who scored with 'Your Eyes Are Dreaming', 'Tell Me Darling' and other seductive late-night sides before becoming an in-demand songwriter in the 1960s.

As the '60s dawned, the sound of R&B was being reinvented by Jamaican musicians such as Coxson's studio crew Clue J And The Blues Blasters, with a less harsh edge and a more shuffling beat. The shuffle was the direct precursor of the rousing ska rhythms that would shake the island for the next five years. Inspired largely by Rosco Gordon, the Memphis-based singer/pianist who played in a 'back-to-front' style – stressing the second and fourth beats of each bar – and who played live shows in Kingston about this time, the music began its long journey away from its American origins and towards a uniquely Jamaican identity.

2 Windrush To 1974

Lee Gopthal And The Growth Of British Trojan

Among the numerous passengers alighting from the SS *Empire Windrush* at Tilbury Docks on 21 June 1948 was 28-year-old Indian-Jamaican Sikarum Gopthal. Giving his address as 'the International Club, East Croydon', and his occupation as 'mechanic', he started a new life in post-war Great Britain. According to his son Leichman (or Lee for short), he made the move 'to escape the consequences of a life of heavy spending'.

A few years later, Sikarum, by now a tailor, set himself up in commercial premises at an address which would later become familiar to the first generation of British R&B and blue-beat fans: 108 Cambridge Road, London NW6. Lee followed him over from Jamaica in November 1952, stayed with his father in the flat above the shop and entered into the employ of a firm of certified accountants. An ambitious young man, he further studied the profession in the evenings.

Sometime in the early '60s, Sikarum decided to return to the Isle of Springs, leaving his son as the sole occupant of number 108, which, as a fast-rising accountant, he was soon able to buy. To help him with the mortgage payments, he advertised the empty basement to let and promptly found a prospective lessee in fellow West Indian immigrant Sonny Roberts, who wished to turn it into a nightclub.

It was probably Lee's desire to sleep at nights that led him to refuse this suggestion. Undaunted, Sonny came back with a plan that would put the humble building on the music map. Still with music in mind, he now wanted to turn the basement into a recording studio. Lee agreed, doubtless thinking that sessions would take place during the day and thus not disturb his sleep, and so in 1962 Sonny Roberts constructed Britain's first black-owned recording studio, a primitive affair with old egg-trays lining the walls to dampen the sound. In this basement, he recorded early UK ska and operated his Planetone and Sway labels. One of his most notable visitors was trombonist Rico Rodriguez, who cut some formative R&B sides at the studio.

At this time, the ground-floor shop was empty, as it had been since Gopthal Sr decamped back to Jamaica, although a group of men who hoped to get a betting shop licence for it were paying the rent. In the autumn of 1962, as the unsuccessful turf accountants pulled out, opportunity literally rang as a young man named David Betteridge called to say that his boss, Chris Blackwell, would like to come and see the place.

Blackwell had been licensing work to jazz label Esquire's Starlite offshoot, run by Carlo Krahmer, but had recently moved to London to pioneer the West Indian market. He had arrived after being shown unlicensed UK pressings of his productions and decided to stay in the city as there appeared to be a ready market for his recordings of Owen Gray, Jackie Edwards and others. He formed the UK version of his Island Records label with his girlfriend Esther Anderson, his future sister-in-law Francine Winman and Australian sound engineer Graeme Goodall.

The original idea was for Jamaican producer Leslie Kong of Beverley's Records to supply the material, and for Island to market it in the UK. Sadly, this idea did not work; as David Betteridge says of Kong, 'He was a talented man, but *so* laid back!' With Blackwell as the driving force, this lack of material forced a change of plan. More recordings were urgently needed to satisfy the growing market. Luckily, Chris Blackwell, a white Jamaican, could deal with the island's producers with ease, as he could slip into the patois at will when the time came to cut a deal. Among the producers who provided sounds for Island was Duke Reid.

David Betteridge, Blackwell's right-hand man in the fast-growing company, had started his career working for Lugton's, an old-established record distributor which had commenced business in 1910. His father had worked there for 50 years, gaining a good reputation as a sales manager. David recalls those early years: 'I was a buyer for a company called Lugton's, which in around 1962 – along with Thompson, Diamond and Butcher, Selecta and EMI – were mainstream distributors of all sorts of things. EMI didn't just distribute EMI; it distributed Decca, and Decca distributed EMI. Everybody distributed everyone else. Lugton's was independent, and two of the lines I dealt with were Melodisc and Esquire, which was basically a jazz label, but it had also developed West Indian music on its Starlite label.

'So one day I got this phone call, and later Chris Blackwell came in. He was charming, tall, and he was with a Chinese-Jamaican called Leslie Kong. So Chris played me "Hurricane Hattie" [by Jimmy Cliff] and "Independent Jamaica" [by Lord Creator]. So I went up to see my director, the head of the record department, and he said, "Well, we don't really want any more lines. We've got a lot." It was a time when there was a lot of uncertainty around.

'So I rang Chris and said, "Look, I'm sorry, I can't help," and he asked me what I could suggest. I gave him the names of one or two people to get in touch with. He rang me two or three weeks later and said, "You know, every time I go and talk to someone, you seem to be the guy who knows about distributing and selling these things. Would you be interested in coming to talk to us?"'

So David Betteridge went from a steady, safe position to selling records from the back of his mini-van and Blackwell's Mini Cooper, operating from their base at Chris's flat at 4 Rutland Gate Mews, off Connaught Square. To begin with, resources were slim.

'It was one of those circle things,' explains David. 'When you've got some cash, go to the plant and buy the records, sell the records to the retailer and come back with the cash and start again, so the circle gets bigger and bigger as you take on more records.'

By late 1962, Island was outgrowing Cris's flat and was looking for larger premises. Enter Lee Gopthal and his roomy shop to let. So Blackwell and Betteridge set up an office in the rented shop and began to distribute West Indian music from there. Blackwell was keen to get his landlord involved, but in those early days Gopthal could see no incentive that would tempt him to give up accountancy. 'Eventually, however,' he recalled years later, 'he started having a lot of trouble selling his records and he asked me if I'd be interested in setting up a mail-order business. I told him that I thought the only way we could get to the potential buyers was to go to their homes, because a lot of West Indians were too google-eyed by the television to go out much.'

Lee Gopthal and his new partners advertised for agents to go around the West Indian areas of London, selling records from door to door. 'The biggest problem we had,' he recalled, 'was to persuade customers to pay for their records before they got them, since we didn't have the finance to risk losing money.'

Eventually, Lee and four old school friends – Jim Flynn, Barry Creasy, Alan Firth and Fred Parsons – controlled a squad of 16 salesmen from his bedroom at 108 Cambridge Road. (All the remaining rooms were either occupied by Island or let out to others from necessity, as cash was short.) By early 1963, the enterprising Lee, along with future Charisma label owner Tony Stratton-Smith, formalised this *ad hoc* selling operation into a proper record-distribution company, which they called Beat & Commercial Records ('because records had a beat and somebody talked about being commercial'). B&C became a limited company – Beat & Commercial Records Limited – on 19 April 1963.

This was just before Island, via a licensing deal with major label Fontana, cracked the national pop consciousness with 'My Boy Lollipop', by diminutive ska singer Millie Small. As soon as 'Lollipop' was recorded, Blackwell realised that it was not only a catchy pop record but a sure-fire chart hit. As Island were still basically operating out of the back of a van, he placed the record with a major label who had the financial and marketing push which he, as yet, didn't.

His hunch was right, and 'My Boy Lollipop' rocketed up the charts, coming to rest at the Number Two spot in March 1964. It was the first record based on a Jamaican rhythm to crack the magic Top 20. It also convinced Lee Gopthal that this was the time to quit his accountancy career to focus fully on the music business. Along with Blackwell and Betteridge, he went out looking for a retail shop in a suitable location.

Thus was the Musicland chain born. The first shop was in Willesden Lane, off Kilburn High Rqad, where Lee himself stood behind the counter, serving the music-hungry buyers. From this point, he concentrated on the retail side of the business, leaving Blackwell and Island to license and press the product. So successful was he that within two years he had four shops, plus a stall in Shepherd's Bush Market. He bought this with some trepidation (the asking price of £60 was a considerable sum at the time) and installed one of his former salesmen, Webster Shrowder, behind the counter. After almost forty years, Webster's Record Shack was still trading.

Another former salesman, Desmond Bryan, stepped off the street to run another of the shops, and a young man named Joe Sinclair was hired as manager of another. Future producer and skinhead hero Joe Mansano also learned his shopcraft under Sinclair's wing before opening his own Joe's Records in Brixton, south London. Of Gopthal's original partners, Barry Creasy and Alan Firth moved over to Musicland while Jim Flynn and Fred Parsons threw in their lot with B&C.

So many of the key players who would shape British reggae over the next decade were learning their trade at Musicland, a chain that sold all types of modern popular music. Sister chain Muzik City, which started in around 1970, grew as some of the Musicland shops were converted to Muzik City outlets and catered more specifically for the West Indian community by purveying the latest in soul, reggae and calypso. Although basically owned by Trojan, Muzik City stocked a veritable host of other labels' product too. The Muzik City Record Shops chain became a limited company on 21 August 1972.

A certificate of change of name (no 758078) is lodged with Companies House showing that Beat & Commercial Records Limited changed their name to Musicland Record Stores Limited on 29 July 1970. Musicland Record Stores Limited, meanwhile, is recorded as being dissolved on 14 February 1977. (Beat & Commercial Records Limited is not to be confused with B&C Recordings Limited, which has continued to exist up until today.)

Lee Gopthal would carry on running Musicland until late in 1972, when he sold out to rival dealership Scene & Heard, giving the new owners some 20 branches in total.

(The April 1972 Companies Act return for Musicland Record Stores lists the directors as Lee Gopthal, with 352 shares; James Sydney Flynn, with 154; Fredrick William Parsons, with 100; Barry Creasy, with 124; Alan Fredrick Frith, with 100; David Joseph Charles Betteridge, with 70; and Christopher Gordon Blackwell, with 100, giving a total of 1,000 shares.)

By the mid '60s, Island Records was well established at 108 Cambridge Road, which was now listed as the registered address of the 'gramophone record wholesalers' business. Every time someone moved out, Blackwell would commandeer the vacant room until his empire had engulfed almost the entire premises. Even the rat-infested cellar-cum-recording studio that had been vacated by Sonny Roberts was in use as a storeroom for the ever-expanding business.

Official documents from 1975 reveal the Muzik City Record Shops directors to be Lee Gopthal, Webster Shrowder, Joe Sinclair and Desmond Bryan, with Gopthal holding 60 per cent of the share capital, Shrowder 14 per cent and Sinclair and Bryan 13 per cent each. Muzik City Record Shops went into voluntary winding-up on 22 January 1976 (Desmond Bryan signed the notice of 'Extraordinary Resolution' in his capacity as director), with a final winding-up meeting of members and creditors on 1 December 1978.

* * *

31

A devout blues fan, Rob Bell joined Island in 1966 and recounts his years there: 'I called Island in September of 1965 to see if they had any openings. I was 18 and in London for the day with my father, who had set me up with an interview earlier that day with Leslie Perrin, publicist to The Rolling Stones and many others. I left that interview with some time to spare before catching up with my father for the journey back to Winchester, my hometown. Thus I called Island, thinking I might get to work for Sue Records, Island's R&B label, run by Guy Stevens. Little did I know that Sue was a small money-losing division of Island!

'I went to their offices at Kilburn and met with David Betteridge, who was looking for a van salesman. Realising I wouldn't get the job if I told him I didn't have a driving licence, I fudged the issue by saying I was taking lessons and expected to pass any day. Actually, I had never driven a car in my life. David, who I am proud to say is still a very good friend, told me to report for work the following Monday. So I had a job; I just had to learn to drive! After a few days I had to confess to David that my driving career wasn't quite as advanced as I had intimated, but he, taken I imagine with my youthful *chutzpah*, laughed and said he had by now guessed as much, and that I could carry on doing telephone sales and working in the stores with Tim Clark, who had started a few weeks before me. Tim and I are still great buddies. He now manages Robbie Williams.

'Those days were wild. Ska permeated London and the clubs. Nights we'd go to Count Suckle's Cue Club in Paddington, or the Scotch of St James. Soul music was hot, too; Island imported albums from the US – Otis Redding, Garnett Mimms, Joe Tex, Don Covay. Down in the stores, which were in the basement below Island's offices, Tim and I pulled orders for the two London van reps, Tom Hayes and Bob Glynn, and the Midlands rep, whose name I now forget. He was later replaced by Dave Bloxham. Island then had the Island label (WI 209 "Go Whey"/"Shelter the Storm" by Jackie Opel was released the week I joined); Black Swan, which was by then pretty much discontinued; and Aladdin, Island's pop label.

'Albums were the Island series. Then of course there was the Sue series, and Surprise, which were risqué LPs of the Rusty Warren/Belle Barth variety. The two biggest sellers were *Rugby Songs Volumes 1 & 2* by the Jock Strapp Ensemble. In fact, those two albums probably provided a very decent chunk of Island's total income back then.

'Around May of 1966, David called Tim and myself into the office and tearfully told us we would have to go, that Island was in a bad state and that the company had to cut back on its employees. I think at that point there were seven or eight people employed there: Tim, myself, David, Tom, Bob, the midlands rep, Neville the accountant, Charles someone or other, who was a phone sales guy, and Deidre Meehan, the receptionist. I believe Neville had a part-time assistant. So Tim and I split. I went to Transatlantic Records and Tim went to Saga.'

The company weathered the storm and continued to grow. Then, one day in 1968, a different kind of panic set in. Out of the blue, Lee Gopthal received a letter from the local council informing him that the house was to be demolished to make way for a new roundabout.

Lee, along with David Betteridge (now marketing manager of Island), had little option but to set out to find new premises for their expanding businesses. One of their discoveries was the former premises of mail-order traders New Fairway House Ltd, a large and now deserted warehouse at 12 Neasden Lane in the north London suburb of Harlesden. As Gopthal and Betteridge considered the possibility of the place as their new premises, a discarded pair of pink bloomers flapped gently and ominously high up in the draughty interior.

One thing was clear: it was too big for Island and too big for B&C. But as a shared site, it was just right. After Chris Blackwell agreed to the move, the new joint occupancy was cemented and the lease signed. The rather ramshackle building was promptly and somewhat grandiosely named Music House, the address that would be synonymous with Trojan Records during its glory years,

Inspired by Island's example, Lee Gopthal began to strike deals with Jamaican producers, and he aimed high. Indeed, his initial agreements were with the island's top two. The mighty Clement Dodd saw his myriad productions issued in Britain on the Studio One, Coxsone and Tabernacle labels. Duke Reid's primary releases were on the label named after his off-licence, Treasure Isle, but its overspill label, Trojan, was part of the expanding Gopthal empire. Its first release, on 28 July 1967, was titled 'Judge Sympathy' b/w 'Never To Be Mine' (TR001) and credited to Duke Reid, although the top side was actually by The Freedom Singers and The Duke Reid All Stars, and saxman Roland Alphonso took care of the flip. However, Trojan was not established as a household name until later that year.

Gopthal also established a new label for the London-grown product of artist/ producer Robert 'Dandy Livingstone' Thompson. When they first met, in early 1967, Dandy was working for R&B Discs, helming their Giant label, but in the following year he established a lucrative partnership with Lee, working as a freelance producer and recording artist. He was given his own Downtown label, the original imprint being deep red with black text, although this was quickly revised to a more striking two-colour design. The prolific Dandy would later have a second Trojan label, J-Dan, dedicated to his productions.

Lee also saw the lucrative opportunity of radio advertising. As there weren't any legal commercial stations in Britain at that time, he decided to advertise on Radio Caroline and Radio London, the infamous offshore pirate stations. This was evidently a very lucrative decision. 'People thought I was mad to advertise on London and Caroline,' he later said, 'but I was selling a hell of a lot of records and making a lot of money over a couple of years.' It obviously paid off as Desmond Dekker reached Number 14 in the UK charts on 12 July 1967 with '007' (his song about Jamaican rude boys) on the Pyramid label, in which Gopthal had an interest.

All the early Trojan-related single releases had TMX matrices stamped into the vinyl, irrespective of the label on which they were issued. 'Tunes would sometimes get mastered before a label was decided upon or, more accurately, a catalogue number was assigned,' explains Rob Bell. 'That actually is the real purpose behind the whole concept of having matrix numbers in the first place. Matrix is Latin for master. Assigning a master number and then recording the master numbers in a book means that one is able to keep track of masters at the plant. A master is a metal plate used to grow stampers from. Having a number on it keeps everything organised – or so we always hoped!

'Vic [Keary] at Chalk Farm did all our UK sessions, overdubs, all that kind of stuff. Tony down at Pye, at Marble Arch, did all our mastering – all those dubs from discs! Many is the time I'd take something to Pye, waiting for the lacquers to be cut, and then take them to Orlake, in Dagenham, filling up all the space in my car, or sometimes my old 1943 jeep with boxes of whatever was hot off the press for the return journey to Music House.'

In such a fast-moving market, the need to turn a record around rapidly was paramount – and Trojan were equal to the task: 'Oh man, we could be fast! If a tune was really hot, and the clamour for its release deafening, we could, and would, get the thing mastered at 9am – or whenever we could persuade Tony to open up Pye in the morning – have it at Orlake by 11am, and they would then start processing the lacquers. I think they called it "silvering".

'A lacquer is a wax master – an acetate, if you like, a record cut by the cutting lathe. It is the final master. Upon arrival at the pressing plant, it is suspended in a tank of chemicals and electroplated. After a certain period of time – an hour or several, I can't remember exactly how long – a metal father is formed, or grown. A reverse record, if you like. From that father, mothers are then grown, and from the mothers, stampers are made. Stampers are, like the fathers, reverse records. It is these stampers that are put upon the press and that are used to press the records.

'It is possible that Orlake could be pressing records by mid-afternoon, and a few hundred could be back at Music House by the end of the day. If a record was really hot, we'd have it up on several presses, and if it was charting, we'd have it being pressed at perhaps Phillips' Croydon plant and/or at one of the EMI plants. Thus then I would have to deal with three separate stocks of labels, product and pressing plants.

'This was exactly what was happening when I first started production at Trojan, when we had four Top 10 records. I was dealing with three plants and potential stock problems on four catalogue numbers – times the three plants! Plus the regular dozen or so new releases each week.

'John Rooks was the general manager at Orlake – great guy, fantastic manager. Of course, we were the big customer, so we had some very real clout. There would be times we would take over Orlake's entire capacity, 24 presses. I'd call John, get a pressing figure on a particular number, tell him that would get me through the next two days, have him take that one off the press and put up in its place such-and-such a number and so on. This would go on all day long, week after week, month after month. The pressure we put on him was tremendous, but he always came through. Very exciting days.

'We had constant hassles with Lee Gopthal about the amount of money we'd spend on having cabs bringing over product at the end of the day. Orlake would deliver by truck every day, of course, but that truck would basically bring what had been pressed the day and evening before. Lee would grumble about the amount we spent on cabs, but at the same time he would rant and rave if such-and-such a title wasn't in stock for his Musicland stores to sell. So we cabbed 'em over and to hell with the expense.

'So we could turn stuff around really fast. It was a strange business – a tune could be hot one week and dead if you released it a week later. So there was always this pressure to get things out quickly if they were being asked for. And if we got wind that Producer X or one of the more, shall we say, free-wheeling producers might have given one of "our" titles to Pama, then of course we rushed things.'

*   *   *

35

Mainstream DJs working for that bastion of British broadcasting, the BBC, refused to programme Jamaican singles in their shows and only reluctantly gave them airplay once they had finally broken through to the general consciousness (except, that is, the ribald Judge Dread, whose early-'70s discs would be forever banned from BBC radio). Accusations of being boring and monotonous, with incomprehensible lyrics – even though many records were to all intents and purposes instrumentals – and the skinhead/bovver connection were all levelled at reggae music as reasons for its dismissal by the nation's hit-pickers.

So it was left to the pirates – who, on the other hand, had picked up on the new youth culture way back in the swinging '60s – to slip into their playlists exotic gems such as bandleader Baba Brooks's rolling 'Girls Town Ska' and The Skatalites' rousing 'Guns Of Navarone', which both gained very healthy sales outside the West Indian market. The trendy, hip pirate-radio listeners, the club DJs and the skinheads were much more in touch with the grass-roots sounds that set the reggae ball rolling.

John Peel, an influential ex-pirate-ship DJ now working for the BBC and specialising in non-mainstream music, declared that he quite liked reggae, and later in the '70s he would champion notable roots-reggae groups such as Misty In Roots and Culture, but he was still too hungover from the psychedelic '60s to get really involved. Tony Blackburn, the breakfast-time DJ of BBC's new pop station Radio 1 and the man people loved to hate, was against it right from the start and sided with the 'boring and monotonous' lobby, so it was left to champions like Mike Raven and the grandly named Emperor Rosko to drop the new music in the public's lap.

Raven started out on Pirate Radio 390 before becoming the first presenter to have an R&B show on the newly inaugurated Radio 1. On his pioneering hour-long Sunday evening show, Raven would always slip in two or three 'blue beat' records alongside the rousing US rhythm-and-blues and soul releases.

The high-profile Emperor Rosko, meanwhile, was born Michael Pasternak in Los Angeles, California, on 26 December 1942, and his first radio experience was on the aircraft carrier USS *Coral Sea*'s station, KCWA. He then moved to France and, later, to England, where he arrived in 1965. A stint on Radio Caroline followed before he went to Radio Luxembourg's French-language station, where, as Le President Rosko, he started a successful pirate-style show called *Minimax* ('Minimum de bla-bla, maximum de musique'). In late 1967, BBC Radio 1 beckoned, and Rosko was to take the hot seat there for some ten years.

Rosko produced his own shows and thus was not bound by the conventions to which the BBC held. Consequently he was not confined to playing the hits of the day and featured a much broader width of music. His patronage of an unknown record could turn it into a hit, so strong was his following. He programmed a whole lot of soul and, alongside it, the bright new sound of reggae.

Reggae artists saw Rosko as such a champion of their music that not only did he have a record dedicated to him – Dice The Boss's eerie 'Tea House From Emperor Rosko', released on Trojan's Joe subsidiary – but he even got to enter the hallowed Chalk Farm Studio to recut Prince Buster's 'Al Capone' to a reggae beat. (It was issued on Trojan with a limited-edition picture sleeve, but it didn't manage to set the charts alight.) He also graced the sleeve of the Trojan compilation LP *Club Reggae Volume 4* and, aside from Judge Dread, is one of the few white males to make it onto a reggae album's cover shot.

Almost as soon as Island and B&C moved into Music House, David Betteridge and Lee Gopthal started to discover the advantages of working so close together. As at this time the two companies were in fact rivals, the Jamaican producers started to play one off against the other. The hopeful producer would phone and offer the self-same 'exclusive' new recordings to both companies, little knowing that they were sitting almost face to face in the roomy London warehouse.

David and Lee compared notes and soon realised what was going on. They turned the tables on the wily producers by each offering less for a new recording than the other had done. In the end, the pair decided to fly out to Jamaica to regain control of the situation, and they also cut a few new deals while they were there.

Chris Blackwell, meanwhile, had discovered the financial advantages of rock music after signing The Spencer Davis Group, who became a significant force within the pages of the *NME* and *Melody Maker* and chalked up a string of pop hits between 1964 and '67. Blackwell had signed them to Island's great advantage and was determined to lead Island along the golden path of white rock. The cash injection to the small company from just one successful pop group was already showing its significance, compared with their numerous Jamaican releases. At the same time, Blackwell was losing faith in Jamaican music, apparently due to difficulties with the producers and their 'soon come' attitude, so in 1968 he decided to sell his subsidiary labels to Lee Gopthal.

In conjunction with Island, B&C then formed Trojan Records Ltd, which was in fact a partnership between Lee Gopthal, Alan Firth and Graham Walker, but unfortunately no official records survive to give an exact date for the formation, although the first singles issued by the company officially saw issue in July of that year. The previous Trojan, the Duke Reid subsidiary label from a year earlier, had been quickly deleted, and it was with this new company that the brand known to reggae lovers throughout the UK was formed. After all, the situation had become silly, as Gopthal recalled in a 1973 interview: 'Both Island and ourselves were chasing around Jamaica after the same producers, so, as we were already operating from the same premises, we decided to form Trojan as a joint label.'

Dandy Livingstone remembers the original Trojan staff as Lee Gopthal, Graham Walker, Alan Firth, Fred Parsons, Jim Flynn, Tilly the secretary and a familiar face who had returned to the fold: Rob Bell, who came back in 1968 to run the distribution side of the business. 'I joined Trojan – you will recall Island owned 50 per cent of Trojan and worked out of the same building – in 1969, as production manager. I became general manager when Graham Walker left to start the US end of the operation in 1970.'

Returning to Trojan was a definite shock for Rob: 'I can't remember the date but most definitely recall that we had four 45s on the charts, all in the Top 10: "Elizabethan Reggae", "Liquidator" and probably a Desmond [Dekker] and a [Jimmy] Cliff... It was the only time Trojan had such a concentrated chart showing.

'It was baptism by fire! I am proud to say that we never went out of stock of any of those titles... I do recall waking up in the middle of the night many times wondering if I was going to run out of labels on a particular number, of having nightmares of endless catalogue numbers, a mad dreamscape of numbers and prefixes.'

Rob goes on to give an outline to the Trojan US operation: 'Graham left for the US around the end of 1970, or possibly early in 1971. The idea was to set up Trojan in the US. I really can't recall that much, but I do remember he was there for about six months, mainly in New York City. Brooklyn, as you probably know, had – as it still does – a sizeable Jamaican population. I don't know if he actually released anything, or what happened, except that Trojan USA never got off the ground. It is possible that Jamaican producers already had outlets there, or that they shipped finished product and that was more profitable.

'I do remember much ribald laughter over the fact that Trojan in the US is the leading condom manufacturer, and that *Trojan* was then synonymous with *rubber*. I believe this came as a surprise to Graham.'

A small series of 7" singles was in fact pressed in the USA with the familiar Trojan label design turned to black and white and the catalogue prefix CATTR. These were the product of Graham Walker's unsuccessful mission to convert the USA to Trojan reggae. It was normal practice for the record-pressing plant to print single-colour labels for their smaller releases, as opposed to paying a high price to a printer for a full colour version.

Rob Bell was left in charge of the British end of Trojan: 'Until Graham's departure, I had been production manager, scheduling and organising the releases, which meant getting 45s and albums mastered, labels printed, sleeves printed and records pressed. When Graham left, I became general manager, assuming many of the duties he obviously couldn't handle from New York City. When he returned, he wanted his old job back. Also, there was talk of the company being sold to Marcel Rodd, of Saga. Under the circumstances, I split and returned to work for Island.

'Shortly thereafter, I moved to Island's other offices, the Basing Street/ Lancaster Road complex just off the Portobello Road. There I worked with international director Tom Hayes and spent a lot of time working in Europe, especially Scandinavia.'

Rob also recalls the 7" pre-release singles, which would be pressed with blank white labels and bearing the matrix GPW (signifying Graham P Walker) plus a numbering system in the vinyl: 'They were pre-release. Graham and Lee [Gopthal] would press between 50 and 200 white labels and Lee would sell them through his Musicland stores at a hefty price.' These were very desirable items for the top-flight DJs as the music was fresh and unavailable elsewhere, hence the high premium that could be charged for the discs. Other labels, such as Pama, put out similar pre-release singles at the same time. Some of the GPWs would find general release later, after the input from the Musicland stores and DJs was taken in to account, while others would disappear into obscurity.

Rob recounts a story to make all of today's record collectors weep: 'I hadn't been back at Island for long in 1968 before I realised that no one there really had an eye for the company's Jamaican history. Everyone there worked in the here and now, with no thought for the likes of folks like you and I, trying to reconstruct things... Often we dubbed from disc in the absence of having master tapes, so there was not much of a tape archive to begin with.

Thus, around 1969, I instituted a policy whereby three or four of every new release was put aside in a corner of the stores. (You will recall that Trojan released anywhere from 6 to 16 singles every week.) Every now and then, I would box these up into a large box and store them at home, in order to avoid pilferage.

'When I left Island at the end of 1972, I very conscientiously returned these boxes – which probably numbered seven or eight two-by-two-by-two-foot boxes full of 45s – to the then store manager for safe keeping. I remember my words: "Look after these. These boxes are the company's archives, and thus the company heritage. Put 'em in a safe place!" I think they were stolen within a month.'

There are many factors which contribute to the rarity of certain Trojan releases on the collectors' market: 'Maybe once a year we'd dump – literally – tens of thousands of records. This is an amazing story... but first a little background. This was in the days before VAT. Items sold at retail then were liable to what was known as Purchase Tax. On a 45, it was I think about 1/9d, nearly ten pence in decimal money. As wholesale price to a store was about four shillings and sixpence, this tax represented a fairly large sum of money. And it was charged upon all the inventory.

'Thus one could not sell the records for less, because the Purchase tax remained the same. One couldn't get it reduced. It was calculated from the factory delivery notes/invoices. The only way not to pay this tax was to have the records certified as being destroyed.

'We first achieved this by hiring a large box van and filling it with dead stock. Once a record stopped selling, it was dead. If it had been a strong seller at time of release, it might have a decent life for a few years, but given the sheer amount of product we put out, there were inevitably those that were dead on arrival. They took up valuable warehouse space, which was obviously finite. So we'd clean out the warehouse, take all the dead stuff and load it into the hired truck and then drive it to the municipal dump in St Albans. We'd meet the tax man there – I think it would be a guy from Customs and Excise – and give him the list of what we were dumping. He'd watch as my cohort and I slung box after box out of the back of the van, until we had an empty van and a mountain of 45 boxes. Then a bulldozer would bury the lot, the tax guy would be satisfied they were destroyed and the tax liability was lifted.

'After a couple of these adventures, 45s started showing up in stores around St Albans – word was obviously getting out, and the stuff was getting unearthed and offered for sale. Big problem, as far as the tax men were concerned. So of Island. It was from this pool that we promoted guys to other jobs within the company. They were proven and had some expertise by then. On the B&C side, there were more West Indian guys, mainly through the Musicland stores... but really, there was no percentage in being discriminatory. Making money was the name of the game, not keeping people down. To be sure, I can recall small store owners coming in to buy product. Those that were on a cash basis would sometimes call us, or even me, racist, because they didn't have credit. They didn't have credit because, if we gave it to them, we simply wouldn't get paid – because they had no money, not because they were black. All of them had track records of having had credit in the past that they had fucked up. Basic capitalistic theory put into practice.'

By 1970, it was all go for reggae. Major labels entered the market: MCA UK, with Count Prince Miller guiding them through the murky waters, and an EMI production deal with an R&B Production Co (apparently unconnected with the R&B Discs record label in existence at the time) and Pye, and later Decca, to distribute Charles Ross's hopeful Sugar label. However, Sugar would dissolve after a handful of singles and albums failed to entice the cash from buyers' pockets, and R&B Production Co appear to have produced no records.

Trojan was growing fast, and so was its label roster. David Betteridge explains: 'If you had six releases, you couldn't put them all out on the same label. The culture in Jamaica is such that a shop in Orange Street will have its own label, rather like Our Price having its own label. Because we had an inflow, we needed to have different channels for different products, especially when we merged Island and B&C/Trojan, and before that Rio and Doctor Bird, which Graeme Goodall had. If we had six or eight records, we couldn't put them all on the same label.'

Each new label needed its own design, as David recalls: 'I remember Alan Smith, who in those days had CCS Advertising Associates Ltd, which was our design company, coming up every other week with new designs for labels, some of which were quite nice when I look back, primitive but quite fun. They had to be bright and simple.'

Most producers in Jamaica had their own labels, such as Joel 'Joe Gibbs' Gibson's Amalgamated and, obviously, Duke Reid's Treasure Isle. To enter the burgeoning UK market, Trojan Records decided to duplicate these labels, feeling that a familiar label would quicken the sales of records, so Harry J (for

Harry Johnson's productions), Song Bird (for the work of Derrick Harriott) and Upsetter (for Lee Perry) all came into being early in 1969.

'In the UK, we had labels printed by Harrisons, in High Wycombe,' says Rob Bell. 'Harrisons also printed postage stamps and other high-quality work. They would print, say, 100,000 backgrounds and then would overprint the label copy for each individual release. The labels would be shipped to the pressing plant, or, if the title was selling very fast, I would leave my house in Hemel Hempstead at 5am, go to Harrisons and collect the labels, and then drive to Dagenham, to Orlake, our principal pressing plant, drop off the labels and pick up whatever product they might have ready for us, and then be at Music House at perhaps 9am. A mad frenzied time.'

Another significant move in that year was the appointment of St Kitts-born Joe Sinclair. Joe had been with the Musicland shop at 23 Ridley Road since 1965 (no official documentation can be found to substantiate that this branch was trading as early as that, but much paperwork of this age has now been destroyed by Companies House) and had elevated the premises to be the number-one retail outlet of the chain. He was rewarded with an appointment as the manager of Trojan Records.

Joe was an accomplished keyboard player and, as well as being responsible for the day-to-day running of the office, moved into playing on and producing records. He founded the Grape label in late 1969 as 'a take on Apple' and started to record UK-based group The Rudies on crunching skinhead-friendly numbers like the revamped 'Guns Of Navarone'. Some of their records were covers of other artists' tunes, such as 'Shanghai', which was similar to the Lloyd Charmers original, already released by Pama. 'That was just to make some money,' chuckled Joe in an interview, adding that it was standard practice in Kingston, if someone had a hit, to version it to oblivion, with many people avidly pulling together every variation on the theme. Trojan did the same, as did all the reggae labels vying for hits as the new decade dawned.

The other problem that confronted Sinclair, and that had caused headaches far back for Chris Blackwell, was the producers' philosophy of getting as much mileage out of a record as possible. Sometimes Trojan were offered a brand-new recording from Jamaica; they would buy the master tape from the producer and issue it on one of their labels. Pama would have gone through a mirror-image situation with the same producer, who would have two or even three copies of his 'exclusive', which he would proceed to sell to rival companies before jetting back to the sunshine with a maximum profit.

Sometimes two rival companies' labels would release a record almost simultaneously – such as Marley's 'Lively Up Yourself', which appeared on Trojan's Green Door imprint and Pama's Punch label – or, if one unfortunate owner saw it already out on the street, they would just shelve their release. Trojan Records own a considerable number of recordings that they have never released due to this problem, and one can conjecture that the other labels active at the time also had a box of unusable master tapes. Rob Bell and Joe Sinclair were astute and tried to be alert to competitors' releases so that Trojan would not fall into this trap, but alas some did slip through their net.

'Big problem,' recalls Rob of the double-selling practice. 'Folks like Producer X would fly over, come see us and sell us a bunch of tunes, and then drive up to Neasden High Road, to Pama's place, and sell them the same songs. And then fly back to Jamaica. The next week, the new releases would come out and the phone would start ringing, either Harry Palmer calling us or us calling him: "What the *fuck?*" And Producer X would be back in Jamaica. It was a good game, and several producers played it. A short-term advantage was gained, in that the producer got a quick bit of extra cash but rapidly gained a shocking reputation. We liaised with Pama fairly closely with some guys in order to stop the confusion... Advances were constantly being adjusted and contracts rewritten to reflect duplicity by these guys.'

Bell and Sinclair were also very much aware of the musical needs of the new crop-headed public. Joe, aside from producing some exemplary sides himself, hired skinhead favourite Laurel Aitken to record and produce some tracks. Aitken had his finger on the youth-market pulse and, under the guise of King Horror, cut some classic talk-over or DJ sides such as 'Loch Ness Monster' and the ribald 'The Hole'.

Although not directly under Sinclair's control in the studio, south London record-shop owner turned producer Joe Mansano recorded some crunching numbers aimed directly at the skinhead market, moonstompers such as his own 'Skinhead Revolt' and Laurel Aitken's (in his King Horror guise) 'Dracula, Prince Of Darkness', which were received very well by the new audience. Mansano was rewarded early on with his own Trojan offshoot label, Joe, and proceeded to entice money from both West Indians and white skinheads, so popular were his records

Joe Mansano had come to the UK in 1963 to study in a London college. In May 1965 he found a job with two Jamaicans setting up a new cosmetics shop, Len Dyke and Dudley Dryden. Alongside their cosmetic wares Dyke & Dryden became one of the only places to buy the latest imported records from Kingston.

Mansano was soon treading the streets with the records as he sold them door to door and enticed many buyers in clubs and house parties. This was aside from the booming trade in vinyl at Dyke & Dryden's store. News of his aptitude as a record salesman reached back to Jamaica and Graeme Goodall came over to launch his UK Doctor Bird label at the Dyke & Dryden shop in 1966. Late in 1967, Island MD David Betteridge visited Joe Mansano and offered him his own record shop, which was to be called Joe's Records and would fall under the control of the new Trojan Records company that was just being formed.

Joe soon progressed from selling records to producing them, and one of his first, 'The Bullet' from trombone player Rico, was a strong seller. 'Brixton Cat' came a little later and encouraged Trojan to issue an album of the same name featuring Mansano productions and then set up his own imprint.

Two main bands carried out the session work for the majority of Trojan's UK-related recordings. Joe Sinclair favoured The Rudies, with Freddie Notes as lead vocalist (Joe Sinclair says that no one can remember what Freddie's real surname was to this day), Earl Dunn on lead guitar, Trevor Ardley White on bass, Danny Bowen Smith on drums and with Sonny 'SS' Binns normally ensconced behind the Hammond organ. Formed in the mid '60s, this London-based five-piece band soon gained a formidable reputation on the local West Indian scene with their powerful live performances. They were soon in the studio, recording under a number of different guises as well as Freddie Notes & The Rudies, and scored a major chart hit in 1970 with a reworking of the Barry Bloom pop hit 'Montego Bay'.

The other Joe, Mansano, looked to The Cimarons as his main players. The band comprised Maurice Ellis (drums and percussion), Locksley Gichie (guitar/ vocals), Franklyn Dunn (bass guitar/guitar/percussion), Carl Levy (keyboards/ harmonies/percussion) and Winston Reid (lead vocal/percussion). The first four members noted here formed the band in 1967 without any finance or knowledge of the music business. Initially The Cimarons backed visiting Jamaican artists, with Reid joining a little later, but after a considerable number of years serving with the group he took a solo career move which hit paydirt

The quality control of the releases has always been something of a mystery, as some discs were obviously losers and yet still gained issue. Rob explains how these rogues appeared: 'There was no quality control at all, really. I don't think either Graham [Walker] or Lee [Gopthal] had a huge amount of artistic appreciation. The majority of the folks involved saw the whole thing merely as a business, which of course it was.

'Here is the core explanation. Trojan was the major UK – read international – player. In order to maintain that position, the label tried to corner the market and sign up every producer. They had already been giving Kong, Reid, Coxson Dodd, Mrs Pottinger, Joel Gibson etc their own labels. Each new signee wanted his own label *and* a guaranteed amount of releases a year. Thus Trojan was obliged to put out a certain amount of records on each producer, and sometimes that meant we put out shit just to keep the quotas current. Stupid, of course, but it is what happened. I know that, when I was production manager, I never put out less than eight 45s in a week, and I remember putting out 16 releases one week.'

Dandy recalls that Lee Gopthal often called him into the office to listen to some new Jamaican music that Gopthal was interested in purchasing. On one occasion in 1971, when The Pioneers were actually staying around the corner from Dandy's house in Leyton, east London, Lee asked him to pop round and chat to Sidney Crooks. The pair hit it off, and a week later the group were in Chalk Farm studios recording the song 'Let Your Yeah Be Yeah', although it took Dandy to persuade them to record it, as they did not like the number. History shows their dislike was wrong, and the song gave them a Number Five hit in the pop charts.

Each Trojan release was afforded little marketing, and the ones which succeeded did so on merit or just plain luck, such as getting on the playlist at Count Suckle's Cue Club in Paddington, which could literally make a reggae hit in a weekend. By this time, Chris Blackwell at Island had discovered, via its progressive rock acts, the art of promotion and the rewards that could be reaped from the correct marketing of an artist. Island were to follow this path with Bob Marley in 1973, pushing him to the white music press and to great long-term success.

A constant problem for the administration of Trojan was the matter of artists' royalty payments. David Betteridge on payment and royalties: 'The interesting thing about the ownership of a lot of the material from the late '50s and

with 'Dim The Lights', a particularly smooth reggae love song which took the renamed Winston Reedy to the top of the reggae charts in 1983. The Rudies' keyboard player, Sonny Binns, was also a member of The Cimarons early on in their career.

Like The Rudies, The Cimarons can be heard on a considerable number of UK-recorded discs from the late 1960s through to the early 1970s, under many spelling variations of the band name. They also found fame as The Hot Shots, with producer Clive Crawley on lead vocals, and their 'Snoopy Vs The Red Baron' single – released on the B&C-owned Mooncrest label – hit Number Four in the national charts in June 1973. An album was soon issued, named after the hit single, along with further singles, such as 'Yesterday Man', but the band failed to follow up on their run of good fortune.

Brixton-based Hot Rod sound-system operator Lambert Briscoe also made use of The Cimarons' tight sound when he formed the Torpedo label, with the aid of The Equals' Eddie Grant, in 1970. Renaming the group after his sound as The Hot Rod All Stars he proceeded to record and release some choppy, fast, semi-instrumental sides aimed squarely at the white skinhead contingent, such as 'Skinheads Don't Fear' and 'Moon Hop In London'.

Trojan also rewarded Briscoe with his own brand, Hot Rod, where the majority of the recordings were by The Cimarons, under their alias, where they recorded some straight-to-the-jugular skinhead sides like 'Skinhead Speaks His Mind'.

Neither the Torpedo nor the Hot Rod singles sold particularly well. Very few enthusiasts of the time recall any of the titles beyond Winston Groovy's 'Please Don't Make Me Cry', which was Torpedo's only real hit with the reggae public and also found release (as a slightly different recording) on Trojan's Explosion label.

In its early days, the way in which Trojan was run was vital to its success, as Rob Bell explains: 'First of all, nearly all the sales came from product that originated in Jamaica. UK-produced things usually died a death. If a record was a success in Jamaica, it was just about certain to be a success in the UK. The degree of that success was, of course, unknown. A good seller sold 2,500 to 5,000 in the West Indian market. Perhaps it might go pop, and then it could do 40,000 to 200,000 or more. The two things that made Trojan a happening label were the facts that its two owners, Island and B&C, had the following going for them: Island had the distribution and the clout in Jamaica (i.e. contacts with the producers) and B&C had the retail outlets.

'Island's van reps called on all the West Indian stores in the UK. B&C owned several stores in the lucrative London market. Record buyers would ask the stores if such-and-such record was available yet, a record they knew about from reading the *Jamaica Gleaner* [a newspaper published in London for ex-pat West Indians], or from a visiting relative, or because they heard it at a sound system on an import from Jamaica.

'The stores in turn asked the van reps about this record or, if they were Musicland stores, phoned Music House. One way or another, we – Island, B&C, Trojan – knew very quickly indeed which records had the potential to be hot or not. The demand for some tunes would be at a fever point; we'd get the tape, if it was a quality producer like Leslie Kong, or dub from a 45 if it was Bunny Lee or one of those guys, who only occasionally sent us tapes. The trick was to get the record out ASAP, while the demand was there. A delay of a week or so could often kill a record.

'We rarely got test pressings on a record. If it was a potential pop thing, then of course we did, but a regular shot at the West Indian market didn't usually require a test. However, we did occasionally press up pre-release – the GPW matrices. This killed two birds with one stone. Firstly, a few copies – a very few – were circulated to a few key sound systems. This was to either gauge reaction, or more likely to build demand. The sound systems in Jamaica had a long tradition of scratching off the labels of US releases to confuse the opposition. This morphed into the white-label system of pre-release, whereby only the initiated knew the identity of the disc. However, while some white labels did indeed help promote a future official release; the majority were pressed for very simple capitalistic reasons. Graham and Lee sold them to stores and sound-system operators at a high price – say 7/6 to 15/-.'

At the start of the '70s, two other successful shop managers, Webster Shrowder and Desmond Bryan, joined Joe Sinclair to form one of the best-known UK production teams, Shrowder/Bryan/Sinclair, with Joe describing himself as the driving force. The team recorded under different name groupings, depending on who was in the studio with the artists. Records can be found with just plain 'Sinclair', and also 'Shrowder/Bryan', as well as 'Shrowder/Bryan/Sinclair' as the producers.

The group also used Bush Productions and Swan Productions as their joint production-house name, the latter of which was taken from the revived Black Swan label (originally an Island subsidiary), which carried their production work, such as the hit Steel Pan version of Montego Bay, 'Mo' Bay', by

Selwyn Baptiste in 1970. According to Joe Sinclair, the label's revival was due to a desire to have a brand that was already familiar with record buyers.

Along with Joe Mansano and Dandy, Shrowder/Bryan/Sinclair were responsible for nearly all of the London reggae released on Trojan labels, including Judge Dread's big pop hits 'Big Six' and 'Big Seven', major breakthroughs for the company's Big Shot label. 'I bought the two Judge Dread rhythms in from GG's – Alvin Ranglin – and Bunny Lee for £500 each,' recalls Joe. 'I also played keyboards on "Big Seven" and recorded the rhythm track for Ken Boothe's "(That's The Way) Nature Planned It" in London, which I later sold on to Lloyd Charmers.'

Joe paid £7,000 for Ken Boothe's recording of 'Everything I Own' to producer Lloyd Charmers in 1974. The money was well spent, as it was a major chart success for all concerned, becoming a Number One pop hit. Aside from these major hits, Sinclair played with The Deltones and the London version of The Uniques. 'It would be me on piano and Sonny Binns on organ, or the other way round,' he explains.

Early in the '70s, Trojan had a plethora of labels catering for a prolific number of artists and producers. The sheer amount of vinyl released was summed up by a former Trojan employee: 'Throw enough records at the wall and some of them will stick. Those that did stick, we'd press up a few more.' It was said – somewhat facetiously – that anyone with sufficient prestige and with a record soon to be released by Trojan could demand a label of their own and the company would oblige.

The figures are startling. In 1970, the year of its heyday, the company issued 500 singles across its many labels, with sales of over 1.5 million discs to West Indians (and skinheads) and with pop-market sales (i.e. discs that made the national charts) of roughly half a million. In the same year, major rival Pama Records managed 300 single releases, with sales in excess of two million, mainly selling to the West Indian market and the skinheads.

'Pama was Trojan's main rival, really the only rival,' says Rob Bell, 'so we did our best to stay on top, keep producers happy and coming to us. On a day-to-day basis, we were friendly. No reason not to be. I'm sure their presence in the market kept us on our toes, made us more competitive and probably helped lead to the policy that Trojan adopted of attempting to monopolise the market, and thus ultimately led to its demise. Of course, I do have to interject here that I was never privy to the company's finances, so the preceding is simply an assumption based on rational observations.'

certainly the '60s and early '70s is, in many cases, people just don't know who owns them. Because it really wasn't catalogues; it was somebody who just came along that had some tracks of songs – it might be a retailer in Jamaica – who would do some productions on the side.

'Apart from Duke Reid and Coxson Dodd, there were about 20-30 people, perhaps ten of which were regular, and the difficulty is [the way in which] a lot of those deals were done. I mean, we've all heard the famous stories about a T-shirt and bottle of coke [for payment for material]. Well, that's not dissimilar to what happened, because there were certainly times I can remember in the early days where proof of contract was the returned cheque, signed by the person who cashed it.

'A lot of the time there wasn't royalties; it was an outright purchase, which is of course absolutely unknown today, really. There was no copyrighting ownership, who owned what, in Jamaica for many years, so it wasn't ratified. There wasn't a contract, we didn't have renewals, options. You bought the music not off the artist but straight from the producer.'

With the company paying the Jamaican producer for the recording, the onus was on him to pay the singer – that is, if the performance hadn't been bought for a flat one-off fee. Another means of forming a deal with an artist would be to mail out a contract along with cheque made out to the performer, and if the cheque was cashed then the contract would be deemed in force.

In an interview between Dave Barker and Rob Randall in the 15 January 1972 edition of the *NME*, where Barker is complaining of being paid only £1,000 for his contribution to the smash hit 'Double Barrel', Lee Gopthal is quoted as saying: 'In fact, Barker and Collins aren't legally entitled to any share at all of the proceeds of the record's sales... You see, Ansel Collins had sold the backing tapes to Winston Riley [the producer] outright and Dave Barker was simply brought in as a session singer and paid a straight session fee.

'This is one of those deals, common in the record business, when the producer takes the gamble of laying out cash on an untried product. If, as is the frequent case, the disc fails to sell enough to cover production costs, the producer bears the loss and doesn't ask the artists or technicians to return their fees. So if, on the other hand, the gamble pays off and the record makes a lot of money, those same artists and technicians can hardly reasonably expect a share of the profits. In this case, Riley has given the boys £1,000 each out of the goodness of his heart.'

Rob Bell remembers Dave and Ansel and their Jamaican-style relaxed attitude: 'Dave and Ansel... two great guys who didn't have a clue [about promoting themselves]. Our promo guy, Dave Bloxham, set up a *Top Of The Pops* for them. Getting an act on *TOTP* meant a hit record, meant selling probably 10,000–40,000 copies after the show. Dave and Ansel never bothered to show. "Soon come, mon." Of course, they should have had someone to busy them along, but it didn't happen. Lost opportunity.'

But Trojan could not believe their luck as the minority music of reggae sidled up the glittering Top 20 and filled the coffers of a company that, not long before, had been peddling its wares out of the back of a minivan. Every record label owned a van or car that would travel around the record shops selling their particular brand of reggae. This small-man-and-a-van syndrome had originated in Kingston, where it had sometimes been taken to extremes with a guy on a pushbike hawking half a dozen singles from shop to shop.

The surprising buying power of the skinheads had taken Trojan and, marginally, its rivals Pama and the Melodisc offshoot Fab Records into the big time. This was no longer a little company just ticking over – it was big business, and so was reggae. Even the hallowed pages of the *NME* and *Melody Maker* were forced to pay respect, with exotically named experts like Henderson Dalrymple and the amalgam Brutus Crombie pronouncing judgement on the latest sounds from Music House. The end of the '60s and the beginning of the new decade were indeed Trojan's halcyon days.

The problem of publicity was always high on the agenda with little or no help from the Jamaican producers whose work Trojan were anxious to promote as their main interest was in the song not the singer. Rob Bell again: 'One of the problems was that reggae was pigeonholed, just like blues is today... One paper – *NME,* I think – had a reggae columnist for a while, Rob Randall. Thus a photo [of an artist] might get published there. Also, we only got what was sent us from JA, and it was hard enough to get master tapes, let alone publicity stuff! So it was an uphill struggle from every aspect. And of course, the producer situation being what it was, there was often great confusion as to even who the artists were sometimes. Indeed, I myself was responsible for one cock-up, and that was calling toaster U Roy on his early UK releases Hugh Roy. As you know, Jamaicans tend to drop Hs, and to add them sometimes, *viz* Marley's line in "Trench Town Rock" "an 'ungry man is a hangry man".

'So little old middle-class Rob Bell, one of whose tasks it was to prepare label copy, very carefully typed Hugh Roy on the copy for those releases... As I did all the label copy for at least two years, I am sure I am responsible for many cock-ups! However, in my defence, I took the details from the Jamaican label, or got the info from the producer – both sources being, of course, absolutely infallible!'

(If it's any consolation to Rob, the toaster's debut LP, *Version Galore*, was issued by Duke Reid in Jamaica in a sleeve proclaiming the artist to be I-Roy!)

'Sometimes I would correct spellings – Hugh Roy again! – or insert better composer info. But by and large I used the information I was given. To return to a by now well-worn theme, the producers just weren't too bothered about the artists – and to be fair, it was the sound that sold records, not really the name.'

Rob then goes on to give an overview of the pitfalls of the artist riding on the crest of a hit to the UK and then being stranded: 'In JA, it was the producer, rather than the artist, that really called the shots. Thus when something went pop in the UK, there was pressure to come up with a follow-up that was equally commercial. Often by that time the artist was living in the UK, and his producer was in JA.

'His producer obviously wanted to capitalise on the UK success, but at that point Trojan UK was also in the mix, and there were, to some extent, conflicting points of view as to just what the follow-up was to be, and also how it was to sound. The focus was on a follow-up single, rather than really developing the artist long term. And by that I mean developing the artist with material which brings out his or her creativity.

'The most obvious example of the right way to do this was Blackwell's involvement with Marley and The Wailers. The freedom to be creative without record company meddling is just one aspect. A degree of financial autonomy is another... But it was that second factor that Blackwell supplied to The Wailers... letting them spend time in the studio and paying them, too. (I know that all those monies would be treated as advances against royalties, but that is the record business – the fact is that he made it happen.) Thus one had the scenario of a JA artist moving to the UK upon achieving UK chart success, thus kind of divorcing themselves from their original source of creativity – their JA producer – being promoted as a pop act and concentrating on 45s rather than a rock act and concentrating on more profitable albums. I dig that this was in many ways a kind of self-fulfilling situation in that these acts came to success via a 45, and also that 45s were proven in the reggae/pop market and that albums were not. Nevertheless, with hindsight, had Trojan been able to spend more on developing these artists, perhaps they would have lasted longer. It is a subject that one can speculate upon endlessly.'

In interviews of the time (1969–71), many visiting artists commented on their versatility and ability to sing and play a far wider scope of music than just the reggae. They regarded the UK pop industry as a far more attractive proposition than the limited reggae market and were anxious, through the interviews, to make the point that they were happy with the commercial angle taken on their work with string arrangements being added. They would be very happy, they said, to sing pure pop songs or reggae-tinged chart music.

With the relocation to London, many did branch out, while resident London performers who had always incorporated soul and blues numbers within their repertoire continued to expand on that base. Due to a number of these artists now, in interviews, reversing their views of wanting and liking the commercial wash added to their work, few names can be mentioned. However, in the 28 August 1971 issue of *Disc*, Jackie Robinson of The Pioneers commented, 'We'd like people to stop calling us reggae singers. That makes it sound like we can only sing reggae... We can sing a lot of other things, styles, besides. We do a lot of soul in our act. Music is just music.'

This quote highlights the fact that many artists were very keen to be seen as just singers and were prepared to drop reggae and retune to pop and supper-club work in the expectation of making a far better living.

Rob Bell on the way Trojan marketed its product to the new skinhead audience: 'Trojan had its "Hot Shot" series. This was a marketing ploy to differentiate records that had pop potential as opposed to strictly ethnic appeal.

'The skinheads were seen as the pop end of the market. If they bought it, we loved them. At that point, the skinhead movement hadn't been co-opted by the National Front and the racist right. It was just another British teenage fad fuelled by Britain's mass-circulation papers. For some strange reason... the British music fans have always seemed to form clubs or movements, *viz* the Teds, Mods, etc.'

The 'Hot Shot' sleeve, with a bright orange target design, was overprinted in black with the record title, artist and catalogue number. Rob Bell: 'Thus we'd sleeve the first, say, 5,000 of a new Pioneers release, with the idea that the retailers and the public at large would get the idea that this particular release was "special."' Jimmy Cliff was even given the prestige of a full-colour picture sleeve for the 'Wonderful World, Beautiful People' chart single.

On the 'Maxi single' series, Rob says, 'The Maxi singles were, as I remember, a little gimmick to make them stand out from the clutter. The retail price was the same as for a regular single. An evolution from the "Hot Shot" concept, if you like.'

Trojan also instigated the 'Trojan Target' logo on album sleeves at this point, and produced T-shirts and other odd advertising merchandise. 'Trojan Target' was the album version of the 'Hot Shot' single sleeves, aiming for higher awareness of certain releases in the pop/skinhead market.

Thanks to Rob, we can at last answer the age-old question as to why a producer-dedicated label such as Harry J or Song Bird would suddenly release work from other sources: 'The obvious answer would be that Trojan and the producer went their separate ways, and Trojan was left with a useable quantity of label backgrounds sitting at Harrisons, the printers. Or that sales were so low on that producer's product that a decision was made to make that label a general-release type of label, handling product from various producers who didn't have their own designated label.'

One quite out-of-the-ordinary singer arrived at Trojan's door one day in 1970. Rob: 'Here's one artist probably no one in the world knows had a Trojan connection – Clyde McPhatter, lead singer of The Drifters in the early '50s, who then branched out to a solo career by around 1955 or '56. Huge influence on R&B – you can listen to thousands of R&B or doo-wop recordings from the '50s and hear Clyde's influence. Enormous.

'He was in London for a while around 1971 [the master index shows that Clyde recorded in 1970 for Trojan], down on his luck. I don't know how he showed up at Trojan, but he did. We cut a session with him and The Rudies, with ex-Pioneer Sydney Crooks as producer. Four tunes, assigned Song Bird matrices. Somewhere around SB 1027 to 1032 A and B, as far as I can recall... For some reason, Graham [Walker] and Lee [Gopthal] hated him, and I remember having to tell Clyde that we had no bread for him on the one occasion that I met him.

'It is not a moment that I recall with relish. He seemed like a nice man and was certainly a singer for whom I had a very high regard. As far as I know, these titles have never been issued.' In fact, one single, 'Denver', was released on the pop-slanted B&C label, and was one of the great vocalist's last records before alcoholism killed him prematurely in 1972.

In November 1969, Lee Perry and a small group of his Upsetters comprising Aston 'Family Man' Barrett on bass, his brother Carlton on drums, Alva

'Reggie' Lewis on guitar and Glen Adams on keyboards arrived at Heathrow Airport for a six-week string of dates set up on the success of 'Return Of Django'. A pre-recorded appearance on *Top Of The Pops* was also scheduled and recorded while the band were in Europe. The tour was organised by Commercial Entertainments, run by Bruce White and Tony Cousins. Bruce White gives some background to the company: 'Commercial Entertainments was started by myself and Tony Cousins in the mid '60s, and our first office was at 4 Denmark Street, aka Tin Pan Alley. We started booking artists to clubs and ballrooms throughout the UK and most of Europe. It was not too long before 50 per cent of our artists were of Jamaican origin when Delroy Williams – a nine-piece band at the time, with dancers [The Soul Explosion] – became one of our most in-demand bands.

'Not long after this, we met Graeme Goodall, who owned the Doctor Bird label. He had just released 'Israelites' by Desmond Dekker, on the Pyramid Label, and asked for our assistance on the promotion side. We agreed to help and decided we would service Radio 1 and other stations throughout England in the hopes of getting radio play.

'We contacted Leslie Kong of Beverley Records, JA, and arranged to bring Desmond Dekker and The Aces over to England for a promo tour. Our hard work on the radio stations paid off, and when we collected Desmond from the airport his record had reached Number One. We had approximately five bookings per week for Desmond, and he played Mecca Clubs such as Hammersmith Palais and the Orchid Ballroom, Purley, and also the Bailey's Clubs up north. He consistently broke box-office attendances. Desmond was an immediate success, and we'd often have to sneak him into the venue as there were queues of screaming fans encircling the building.

'We negotiated with Desmond and Leslie Kong to become his managers, which continued for approximately ten years. After this initial success we arranged promotional tours for many JA artists and we also became their managers.'

The Upsetters' tour took in a number of dates all around the UK but was subject to Lee Perry's erratic behaviour, although the tour was considered a success. Further Trojan/Upsetter singles – 'Night Doctor', 'The Vampire' and the suggestive 'Live Injection' – all did well, thanks, no doubt in part, to the tour.

Trojan Records assembled an Upsetters album titled *Return Of Django*, complete with a quality art-board gatefold sleeve. The album was issued in

January 1970 and comprised the skinhead sound of tight rhythms and pumping organ. Three of the tracks, 'Night Doctor', 'Soulful I', and 'Man From MI5', had actually been issued on Trojan's debut Lee Perry album, *The Upsetter*, in November the previous year, although the company marketed *Django* as Perry's first album.

As the tour finished, Lee Perry's profile as a hit-maker had expanded and he had deals going with both Trojan Records and their main rival, Pama Records, and he spent much of his time jetting back and forth across the Atlantic. The four UK Upsetter band members – the two Barrett brothers, Reggie Lewis and Glen Adams – were left somewhat stranded in London, and Bruce White and Tony Cousins under the alias of Bruce Anthony (Bruce-and-Tony) offered to finance and produce an album with them. As Bruce White recounts, 'We liked the group and their music. Also, we were their managers and wanted to progress their career and felt they needed an album release.' He continues, regarding the recording sessions, 'Both myself and Tony were joint producers, involved musically, and we paid for the sessions. This was all recorded at Chalk Farm studios with engineer Vic Keary.'

The resulting album, *The Good, The Bad And The Upsetters* saw issue on Trojan Records, resplendent with a sleeve shot of a group of West Indians in cowboy outfits and toting pistols, while a single from the album, 'Family Man' b/w 'Mellow Mood', found issue on Trojan's main label early in May 1970.

Rumour had it that some of the tracks were not by The Upsetters but instead by UK-based session players. This was not the case, however, and the album really did feature the four Kingston players, with the confusion possibly coming from the fact that the recording took place in London.

The end of the swinging '60s and the beginning of the new decade were to be the halcyon days for Trojan, with artists like Lee Perry's Upsetters hitting Number Five in October 1969 and Bob and Marcia making Number Five in March 1970 with Nina Simone's black pride anthem 'Young, Gifted And Black'. Although sung and made famous by Simone, she wrote only the music; the lyrics were penned by J Irvine Jr. Producer Harry Johnson already had the backing track recorded at Byron Lee's Dynamic Studio when he invited Bob Andy to voice the Nina Simone song over the top. Bob then invited his childhood sweetheart, Marcia Griffiths, to duet with him.

Although a gifted songwriter, as a creature of vibe and impulse Bob just felt like doing a recording at the time Harry J happened to approach him and was happy to cover such an outstanding piece of work. 'I didn't have any above-average expectations for the record's performance before it was released, and as far as I know neither did Harry J,' said Bob of the recording in an interview.

When asked about the overdubbed string arrangement, Bob said, 'I didn't know about the strings until we got to England, but I liked them; I always wanted to see greater attention paid to arrangements in reggae.' The first Bob and Marcia knew of the success of 'Young, Gifted And Black' was when producer Harry J asked them to ensure their passports were in order and to have their bags packed. The song was a smash hit in the UK and they were booked to appear on the hallowed *Top Of The Pops*.

In the interview, Bob was asked if he was surprised that 'Young, Gifted And Black' sold into the white market and that reggae music in general was supported massively by the skinhead youth culture over here. 'It was overwhelming' he replied. 'I didn't know anything about this angle [the skinheads] before I came. Bob Marley must have felt the same when he came. We knew that the majority of the country was white but couldn't have anticipated the avalanche of interest from the white fans. It was a head-spinner. It was a perfect example of how music can transcend all barriers and cultural differences.'

When asked of his first visit to the UK and how Trojan treated him in comparison to Coxson or Harry J back in Kingston, Bob replied, 'It was exciting. [Trojan] were excited to have another set of artists in the charts, and prospects looked good. But I soon discovered they were excited about records rather than artists – they didn't think in terms of artist development.'

In the 17 July 1971 edition of *Record Mirror*, Simon Burnett interviewed Bob and Marcia and asked the pair how they saw their music. Bob's thoughtful reply underlined the power struggle in all aspects of Jamaican life and culture: 'I don't think that there is a real classification to put our music into. I suppose it could be called sunshine music. Jamaican music is crying out for social and economic freedom and for justice and it all involves politics. That's not because music is involved with politics but because politics is involved with everything.'

The follow-up to 'Young, Gifted And Black', 'Pied Piper', and an album of the same name, were recorded at London's Chalk Farm Studio as Bob started to divide his time between the UK and Jamaica.

* * *

The engineer at Harry Johnson's session at Dynamic Studios on the day that 'Young, Gifted And Black' was recorded was Sid Bucknor. A first cousin to Clement 'Coxson' Dodd, Bucknor started his recording career at Studio One in around 1963. He was with Lee Perry when the youthful Wailers first auditioned for the studio and was impressed by their sound. History vindicates his opinion.

Sid estimates that, by the end of the decade, his hand was present in around 70 per cent of all the recordings coming from the small island, so great was the demand for his talents as a freelance producer and engineer. He estimates that the average number of recordings he would undertake in a normal day was a staggering 12. He never had to look for work as his reputation preceded him and most producers looked to him to turn a song into a hit.

As a professional engineer and producer at Dynamic Studios (after leaving Studio One and his freelance career), he recorded work for, among others, Bunny Lee, Harry Mudie, Alvin GG Ranglin and Leslie Kong. He was the engineer on Johnny Nash's smash 'I Can See Clearly Now', engineered the formative DJ work of producer Keith Hudson with Big Youth on 'Ace 90 Skank' and worked on the first three Marley Island albums. He has also remixed both Duke Reid's and Coxson's work at various times to give 'a more up-to-date sound'.

Sadly, much of Sid's work has been unrecognised, and it is only in the last decade or so that account has been taken of his vast input to Jamaican music. He recalls that, in the reggae heyday of the start of the '70s, 'I would be asked to do two mixes of a tune, one for Jamaica and a lighter one for the UK,' which is indicative of the increasing awareness of the producers of the UK as a new burgeoning market for their products and their need to retune the sound accordingly.

With the reggae boom in full swing, Sid was enticed to relocate to London, where he worked freelance at Chalk Farm Studio from 1974 until its closure. As a freelance, the more work you did, the more you were paid, and he recalls working from 8:30am right through to starting a session at 3:30am the next morning with 'just a little sleep on the studio carpet'. He recorded 16 sessions a day as normal, so in-demand was he and the studio, with all the minor and major UK reggae players booking time either to voice-over pre-recorded Jamaican rhythms, overdub strings or lay down fresh home-grown reggae.

The technology was 'like from a different planet' Sid says with regard to the primitive Jamaican studios in comparison to Chalk Farm's more up-to-date controls. It says much for his skill that he was able to coax such marvellous sound from Studio One and Dynamic, despite the basic nature of their equipment.

One visitor to Chalk Farm, rock artist Wild Willie Barrett (quite often paired with John Otway), commented to Sid that the studio looked like an upturned dustbin, but the sound they got was great, and of course that was what counted. Of Chalk Farm, Sid recalls, 'I enjoyed my days there,' and of Trojan, for whom he cut many later sessions, 'They deserve credit for getting reggae music out there which no other reggae company could do.'

The man responsible for the string arrangement on 'Young, Gifted And Black' was Clive Crawley, in conjunction with Chalk Farm Studio owner and engineer, Vic Keary. Clive recounts how the inspiration came about: 'We used to get the masters over from Jamaica and I decided to put brass and strings on them, and the first one I did was "Young, Gifted And Black". That was in 1970. The reason why I did it was that reggae was considered dance music at the time – the radio stations wouldn't play the music because they felt it was more for discos and parties – so I was just trying to make the records radio-friendly. I was wearing my record plugger's hat and wanted to get the records aired. Anyway, I remember after that we did "Love Of The Common People", by Nicky Thomas, and The Pioneers' ["Let Your Yeah Be Yeah"]. I arranged for the overdubs to go on those all those.

'Johnny Arthey did that arrangement. [Arthey was an experienced bandleader and arranger but was more used to working in mainstream pop. His other claims to fame included producing hits for Vince Hill and acting as musical director for the 1970 and 1971 British entries in the Eurovision Song Contest.] It was the funniest thing, actually. I phoned up Johnny and I said, "I'm gonna send you down a tape of a song called 'Young, Gifted And Black'," 'cos Johnny was at the height of his fame in those days. He'd just done "Eloise" with Paul and Barry Ryan, which was an enormous hit. It was a wonderful arrangement, a fantastic arrangement.

'And so I sent him this record down and I said, "Now, what I want you to imagine Johnny is, listen to this record and imagine the strings on it. They don't have to be technically brilliant, but they must be fantastically rhythmic." He said, "I understand." So he got tape and he made the arrangement and that was that. So that was an enormous hit, as you know.'

Many of the Trojan master tapes bear Crawley's name as producer, but the finished record often has a different name on the label. 'That's life,' says Clive. 'But if you just look at the realities... if the rhythm track and the vocals for a record were laid down by a guy in Jamaica – i.e. 'Young, Gifted And Black'

– and I've picked up the tape over here and added to it [with overdubs], you don't really know the reason the record was aired on radio.' In other words, who should be given credit for the record's success at getting radio play – the Jamaican originator or Clive Crawley, who created a different soundscape with the overdubs?

Clive continues, 'But I was quite happy. They gave me the money for doing it, and all I was interested in was pound notes in those days. But what I didn't realise, what I should have realised, was the credit was worth more than the money. But at that time, I was a novice – I didn't understand – so I was enjoying myself so much, I didn't give a monkey's, really.'

Crawley's background had been originally in sales, and then record promotion for B&C and Trojan Records. 'I got into the music business as a result of a £10 bet, funnily enough,' he recalls. 'I was in a pub one night having a drink with Lee Gopthal and I asked him how business was. He had some [Musicland] retail shops as well as the record company, and he said the record shops were doing great but the record company was a bit slow. So I asked him, "Why is that?" and he said, "Well, we're not getting exposure on the records."

'"What do you mean?" I asked.

'"Well," he said, "we send them to the BBC but they never play them."

'"What do you mean, 'send them'?"

'"We post them."

'"No, that's not the way to do it. I don't know anything about it, but would imagine they call that 'plugging'."

'"Yeah, I suppose they do," said Lee, "but I couldn't do that." So I said, "Well, I bloody well could!" So I had a bet with him. I bet £10 I could get his record played on the radio.

'The next one he had coming out was a song called "Kansas City", sung by Joya Landis. I went down and played the record, but I thought, "This is going to be tricky," 'cos, although it was a good record, it wasn't really a radio record, more a dancing record. But I went home and got a copy of the *Radio Times* – I've a £10 bet on this, this was half a week's wages, you know? So I go off down to the BBC, having looked up the names of these record shows, and the very first play I got was by a guy called Ian Fenner, who produced a show called *Late Night Extra*, which was hosted by Terry Wogan.

'This was in 1968, and it went on every night of the week, Monday to Friday, from ten o'clock till midnight. And he's the first guy I go and see, this guy Fenner, and I gave him a lot of nonsense, you know, told him a few stories, a few dirty jokes, whatever, and eventually he said, "Are you going to play me something else?" I said yeah, and he said, "What have you got?"

'"Well, it's a new kind of music from the West Indies called reggae, and if you put it between a Frank Sinatra and an Ella Fitzgerald, it might sound half tidy."

'He quite liked that. "I'll play it Wednesday night, just before the 10:30 news," he said. I thought, "Christ, this is easy!"

'So anyway, Wednesday night comes along and I'm sitting indoors with *News at Ten* on, transistor down one side of the armchair, and sure enough at about 10:25 Wogan comes on and says, "Now we got a new kind of music from the West Indies called reggae, and here to sing 'Kansas City' is Joya Landis."

'Well, you can imagine! I leaped out the chair and the following day I was down there [at Trojan], collecting my tenner. And then [Lee Gopthal] said, "Clive, why don't you carry on doing this? I'll give you a fiver for every play you get." And that was the start of my career. That led to 30 years in the record business.'

Crawley and the other UK-based producers would make use of the aforementioned Chalk Farm Studio, located in north London, as the normal place to lay down tracks and overdub string sections onto imported Jamaican rhythms with the assistance of engineer Sid Bucknor. The studio was owned and run by south Londoner Vic Keary, who gives an insight to his career up to opening Chalk Farm: 'The [first] studio was just an amateur thing. It must have been about 1957, but it was in a cow shed and the cows were still downstairs, so we were in the upstairs bit – it was quite a tall barn. We were recording local rock bands – it was the days of Cliff Richard and The Shadows. Having got my certificate from the college, first of all I went to Lansdowne [Studios], which is still one of the biggest three studios in London. It's in Lansdowne Road, in Notting Hill Gate.

'I got involved, oddly enough, with Adam Faith, because I also used to run a club in Farnborough, just a little thing while I was studying, and [Faith] used to come down to the club. He got involved with Larry Parnes [a leading pop impresario] and he said, "So why don't you go down to Lansdowne and see if they have anything going?" So I did, and they didn't.

'I then went on to do some work in television and didn't like it, and then I got a call from Lansdowne, and they said they had a place available and would

I like to come down for an interview? I did and I got the job. That was 1960, when Joe Meek left, 'cos he was the chief engineer there and he went on to produce his own things.'

The shift into Jamaican music happened almost by chance: 'I got a bit fed up with Lansdowne because I wasn't getting paid enough – as usually happens in studios in this country – and managed to start my own place. I managed to borrow some money and I worked in the old Radio Atlanta studios that then had become Radio Caroline. That was the top floor of 47 Dean Street, in the West End, and in fact we had a pirate flag on the roof because of the pirate-radio connection. We were on the top floor and there were nine flights of stairs and it was a bit of a job carrying a Hammond organ up nine flights of stairs and no lift. And having bands coming in and out was a bit hairy. That was '64 and '65. So we had Sugar and Dandy coming in...'

The recordings were issued on the small independent label Carnival: 'The one that really did well at this time was the Mel Turner single "White Christmas", on Carnival. That was brilliant. I got some television on that. Of course, the thing was, the distribution of Carnival was absolutely rubbish. There was a great demand for the thing, but nobody could buy it.'

The Carnival label was run by Alan Crawford, an Australian, recalls Vic: 'He also had a label called Cannon Records, and they did a sort of *Top Of The Pops* thing: they had a six-track EP with cover versions of all the hits. And that was pretty good practice for a sound engineer, to be frank, as you had to copy all the hits of the day. Old Ross McManus, who's Elvis Costello's father, used to come in and do a lot of the vocals – he just changed his voice on different records.

'Anyway, then I got involved with Dandy Livingstone, who sort of stuck with me for a long time, because we left the West End because Alan Crawford's company went bust, and we were kicked out so we started another studio in the Old Kent Road, in what is now the Workhouse. [This was the famous Maximum Sound.] We had Prince Buster and Rico, the trombone player, in there. These things came out on Blue Beat. In fact, I used to work for both Blue Beat/Melodisc and R&B/Ska Beat. I used to sell records for them around 1967/68... I decided to take a break from making music and went on the road, selling. I used to drive a van up and down the north of England – Leeds, Birmingham, Manchester, Liverpool and about as far as Leicester.'

Vic remembers the main nucleus of the studio band and an embarrassing moment for The Cimarons: 'It used to be The Cimarons plus Trevor Starr.

Trevor is now the boss at Theorum Music – he was a bloody good guitarist. The other band was of course Greyhound, aka The Rudies. They used to do quite a few backing tracks.

'The Cimarons once said to me, "You'll never get a Jamaican sound here. You have to be in Jamaica to get the right sound." They used to get annoyed, as they felt it was my fault that they could never get the right sound at Chalk Farm.

'Then Sly and Robbie came over and Trevor was also on the session, and they used The Cimarons' drum kit, but Robbie had his own bass and he said, "Just plug the bass in, man. Don't do anything to it. It'll sound perfect." So I did that, and it did. And Sly just sort of retuned the drums a bit, and it was the way he played them. He played them much quieter than The Cimarons did, and it sounded just like it came out of Kingston – exactly the Jamaican sound. Of course, The Cimarons were really brought down by that.'

Chalk Farm Studio, although not tied to Trojan, suffered badly with the latter's downfall in 1975, having been in operation since 1968, and found it a struggle after their departure. About 70 per cent of the studio's work in the early '70s was for Trojan.

'We used to do a lot of work for Bunny Lee,' remembers Vic. 'Bunny would come over with a lot of tapes, and he had a guy called Ken Elliott, who played synthesiser, and we had this band that recorded as The Vulcans. Bunny did an awful lot with Ken. But about every six months, Bunny would turn up totally unannounced and say, "Hey man, I just want a couple of hours in the studio to do some voicing." And he'd turn up with all these guys – Scratch Perry would go around with him as well. I got used to this, as he'd ask for a couple of hours and spend about 12 hours – that was his usual average. So he'd ring around, either Trojan or Pama or Creole, and say he was at the studio and ask them if they'd pay for studio time, and almost always they'd say yes. So that was it. He'd ask for a couple of hours and stay all night.'

Sadly, the Chalk Farm Studio is now an off-licence. Vic describes the final days of the studio: 'It wasn't just the money that Trojan owed us when they went in to liquidation, which was quite a lot in those days; it was also the fact that the whole reggae thing died. The studio was mainly geared to reggae and we really put most of our eggs in one basket – Trojan was our biggest client by far, although we did quite bit with Creole and Pama. So after Trojan went down, the studio was a struggle until about 1982, and then the rent went up to about triple what it was before, as Chalk Farm became a very desirable area and we were sort of forced out. We just couldn't afford it, so we packed up.'

The first major Reggae Festival, held at the Empire Pool, Wembley, on Sunday 26 April 1970, found Bob and Marcia performing their hit, with Desmond Dekker, The Pioneers, The Maytals and John Holt in the line-up and with backing from Byron Lee's band and The Pyramids. The show was compered by Count Prince Miller, who also belted out a lively rendition of his current smash, 'Mule Train'. 'What a guy!' enthuses Rob Bell. 'A big, big man with an equally big sense of humour.' The appreciative audience was a mixed bag of West Indians, hippies, the curious and, of course, those new appreciators of the sound, the skinheads.

The event was captured on film by director Horace Ové in a documentary called simply *Reggae,* which cut the concert performances in between interviews with leading figures in the music of the day. DJ Mike Raven provided a very succinct and insightful progression of the music and the trials of getting mainstream airplay. He also commented that the newer UK sound wasn't to his taste and he preferred the 'real Jamaican stuff'.

Trojan Records' Lee Gopthal and Graham Walker concurred on the difficulties of getting daytime radio play, providing illustrations of the vast numbers of units sold with still no help from the BBC. Gopthal went on to say that general record buyers did not classify music; they just bought what they liked.

Meanwhile, UK producer Dave Hadfield, along with Doctor Bird group owner Graeme Goodall, confirmed just how hard it was for non-Jamaicans to pick up the beat. They predicted that they saw reggae as the next big thing, albeit in a more commercialised style.

Reggae saw a very limited release into specialist cinemas at the time. Sadly, it has now not been aired for over thirty years and is unavailable on any video or DVD format. This is a great pity, as it is one of the only professional films covering the UK side of reggae development as the '60s turned to the '70s and has some sparkling concert footage.

Rob Bell recounts a story regarding The Maytals which may well have taken place at the time they were performing at the Reggae Festival in Wembley: 'I remember a buddy of mine being asked to find some grass for The Maytals for a very early UK tour of theirs. He managed to find a pound, which back then – even in those euphoric days – was a heck of a lot of marijuana. The story went that The Maytals smoked it all in two days and returned to JA on the third day complaining about the dire English winter weather and the absolute dearth of smokeable pot. Whether this is really true, I don't know, but it is a fine story.'

By 1971, Bruce White and Tony Cousins' Commercial Entertainments agency had made significant inroads into the Jamaican music business. 'We managed, or were agency for, most major Jamaican artists,' affirms Bruce. 'It was at this stage that we were approached by Graham Walker of Trojan Records to see if we were interested in them buying 50 per cent of Commercial Entertainments. Meetings were subsequently set up with Lee Gopthal and Dave Betteridge, directors of Trojan Records. We negotiated a deal between us for £7,000 and formed Trojan Artistes Management Ltd between us. The directors were myself, Tony Cousins, Lee Gopthal and Dave Betteridge.

'Myself and Tony Cousins moved the company into Music House, Neasden Lane – Trojan's base – so that we could work closer together with the record company. More hits followed, and Tony and I handled the booking and management of the artists. By now, Tony and I had become very interested in the record side of the business and sold our 50 per cent of Trojan Artistes Management Ltd to the other directors and moved on to pursue our record career.

'About six months later, we were asked to attend a meeting with Lee Gopthal and Graham Walker where they asked us if we would consider managing Desmond Dekker again. This we did, and not long after many other artists followed. Commercial Entertainments became active again! It was total coincidence that Lee's company was called Beat & Commercial, and it was in no way connected to Commercial Entertainments.'

In March 1971, a new sound captured the coveted Number One spot: the sound of 'Double Barrel' by Dave and Ansel Collins. Dave Barker's enthusiastic DJ work over a rolling rhythm was the first many people had heard of the new craze sweeping the Kingston dancehalls. The track's producer Winston Riley, in an interview published in *NME*, said of the track, 'The approach to "Double Barrel" was a conscious attempt to create something different, an unusual song with an unusual treatment in a bid to knock down a great deal of the competition back home.'

'Double Barrel' appeared on a UK version of Riley's Techniques label, which Trojan had formed to carry his production work in the UK. The backing rhythm track had been recorded by keyboard player Ansel Collins, who then sold it on to Riley, as he was unable to finance its progression on to vinyl. This was standard practice, as Collins had previously recorded and sold the 'Night Doctor' recording to Lee Perry, who achieved considerable success with it under his alias as The Upsetters.

Riley decided to spice up the organ-based sound of 'Double Barrel' and employed vocalist Dave Barker to strut his DJ stuff over the top (in every sense) prior to its release. So Dave and Ansel were not a duo in the accepted sense of the term. 'When "Double Barrel" was already a best selling single, Ansel Collins and I hadn't even met,' revealed Dave in an *NME* interview of 15 January 1972. By this time, Ansel Collins and Winston Riley had returned to the Kingston studios to cut more rhythm tracks and Dave had opted to stay on in London and 'make it on my own as Dave Barker'.

Lee Gopthal was justifiably proud of the success of 'Double Barrel', as he recounted in an interview for *Melody Maker* conducted by Rob Randall: 'I spent months trying to encourage our pluggers to push it for me, but they said, "Look, we'll be laughed out of the Beeb." Our promotions man was a DJ before he joined us. [I said], "We've got a very good plugger in Clive Crawley. I feel we've got fantastic promotion and that, once we see a little bit of action, we can make a record. All we need is the right response from, say, the airplay situation."'

The airplay was at first grudgingly given until the mainstream retailers reported a growing demand, and Radio 1 then started programming it into their prime-time shows. The fact that 'Double Barrel' made it out of the reggae clubs at all says a lot for Gopthal's faith in his staff and product.

While on the Double Barrel tour, Dave Barker spoke to *Record Mirror*'s Lon Goddard about the music scene back home: 'Reggae is the big thing back in Jamaica. Reggae is the big monster beat – it swings with a down-to-earth soul feeling. There aren't any heavy blues bands there; most people like a lot of reggae and most of the Tamla records.

'I would love to see some of the other bands back home have some success. People like Delroy Wilson and John Holt make reggae records that could do very well here. Sometimes the English reggae records are a little more like rock 'n' roll to be the real thing.'

As reggae gained a firm hold in the charts and minds of Mr Average Record Buyer, the stars of rock took notice, including The Rolling Stones, who had championed black music since their early days. Under the headline 'Rudies

Play At Mick Jagger's Wedding', the 10 June 1971 issue of US music magazine *Rolling Stone* reported, 'At the slightly seedy Cafe des Arts, where the reception was held, a local band opened the show and flopped. Next came The Rudies, a thumping reggae group big in their own scene in Britain. They lifted up plenty of souls ready for a set by Terry Reid and his band.'

The traditional way a Jamaican bought his music was on a 7″ single. This accepted norm was the result of the original sound-system culture of the late '50s, after the passing of the fragile shellac 78rpm records. DJs would play 7″ singles or one-off soft wax dub plates. Also, the major producers' first forays into record retailing to the general public were mainly singles, with only the odd LP, which usually collected the producer's work with a variety of artists. In general, the album format was restricted to more traditional folk songs or mento recordings of local groups, which big-spending tourists could buy and take home. For Kingston residents, a quick fix of The Skatalites or Jackie Opel, running in sometimes at little over two minutes, was the desired way to hear the music.

In Britain, Island had tried out the long-playing format as early as 1963, with albums by their top signings such as Derrick Morgan's *Forward March* and the uplifting two-part harmonies of *The Blues Busters*, while R&B Discs issued collections of The Maytals and Delroy Wilson, but none had succeeded in selling in appreciable quantities. Island had also issued, in 1967, the *Duke Reid Rock's Steady* LP, with the Island ILP prefix, but on a deep-orange 'Trojan' label specifically designed for Reid's UK releases. It too had sold poorly, even though the music contained in its bands was some of the finest of the age and many of the tracks had been good sellers as single releases.

In 1968, Trojan tried their hand at the album market and issued their first three long-players. Two were at full price and marked with the TRL (Trojan Records Long-player) prefix: 'single-artist collections *Follow That Donkey* from The Brother Dan All Stars' (alias the ubiquitous Dandy) and *Dandy Returns* (also from Mr Thompson, *sans* pseudonym). The third was a budget various-artists album of Dandy productions, with the TBL (Trojan Budget Long-player) prefix, entitled *Let's Catch The Beat*. None of these titles made any appreciable impact on the scene and instead merely served to emulate what Island and R&B had already discovered.

Undeterred by this, Lee Gopthal commissioned a market-research survey to find out what the problem with albums was and why so few were purchased, at a time when the LP was overtaking the single in the pop and rock markets. The results threw up two facts. Firstly, they were considered too expensive. Secondly, the overall sound of a single-artist album made for uninteresting listening. Buyers wanted a variety of sounds: different tempos, different rhythms and, above all, different voices, just as they would hear at a sound-system dance.

With this in mind, the astute Gopthal decided to launch a series of budget albums, but at such a low price that sacrifices had to be made. To cut costs, he decided to use existing material that had already seen the light of day on singles (and which had therefore amortised its original costs). The first LP to roll off the presses was *Tighten Up*, which consisted mainly of previous Trojan singles and was identified as a budget release by its TTL prefix (although no one can now recall what these initials stood for).

Rob Bell remembers, 'Full-price ska/reggae albums sold in minute quantities. The *Tighten Up* series did sell well, but that was because they consisted of compilations of singles that had already sold very well indeed. Trojan wanted to piggyback other titles... hence the ambitious TTL reissue project.'

Priced at just 14/6d – the cost of two singles – this album moved units, and its first pressing on the original all-orange Trojan label sold out quickly. It was repressed with a slightly altered sleeve design using the new orange-and-white label design, which was introduced in 1969.

The other side of the rock-bottom-priced TTL series was to be a lavish reissue programme of previous Island albums from notable artists like Derrick Harriott and Derrick Morgan, alongside early collections of singles like 'Club Ska 67'.

Rob Bell again: 'You will recall Island owned half of Trojan, with B&C owning the other half. Island formed Trojan in order that Island focus on pop. Island still wanted to market its Jamaican masters, and old product was reissued through Trojan. The entire Island Jamaican LP catalogue was scheduled to be reissued on the TTL series. I think everything got mastered, but possibly not everything got released.

'There was always a market for oldies. Singles, for instance, had a fairly long life – providing, of course, they had been good sellers to begin with. So the reissuing of old product made some sense. It may perhaps have been a way for Trojan to physically get its hands on catalogue that was previously owned by Island. Also, we exported a modest amount of stuff to Africa, especially older stuff. Also, it may well be that, when the expansion of the TTL series – using the old Island albums – was planned, it was also the time of the anticipated Trojan invasion of the USA. There is always good money to be made from exporting finished product. I recently came across a Beverley's Jamaican pressing of *Forward March* in a TTL jacket with "Copy For Trojan" handwritten across the front.' No doubt this was the master copy to be dubbed from to create the Trojan issue. In actual fact, a considerable number of ex-Island TTL album titles were advertised but never found their way to the high street.

By this time, the skinheads had got involved in reggae and, as many of them were too short of cash to buy all the singles as they were released, a budget-price collection suited them just right. They didn't mind the time lapse between the various tracks' issue on 7″ and the arrival of the album, and pushed high street retailers into opening new 'Reggae' sections in their racks. Even so, that time lapse could be quite considerable, with a record sometimes gaining a release in London six months behind Kingston, with the *Tighten Up* album series collecting the tracks together a few months after that.

Tighten Up Volume 2 appeared quickly afterwards and was not only much more up to date in its tracks; it was also a sizzling selection of recordings. It really hit the spot with both West Indians and the skinheads, who flocked to every record store to grab a copy. Gone was the Caribbean BOAC picture of a happy West Indian girl and in came a bare female midriff with the album title written in what looked like lipstick on her stomach. *Tighten Up Volume 2* was Trojan's all-time best-selling album and would remain available for many years, such was its enduring popularity. It even scored in the pop-album charts, the entry rules for which were promptly revised to exclude budget records!

Tighten Up Volume 3, issued in 1970, took the pretty girl off the sleeve and on to the bedroom wall with a splendid double-album-sized poster nestled in a die-cut sleeve. The young lady peeped through the central hole and, when the poster was opened out, revealed the titles of all the album's tracks painted on her finely toned body. It may have been a gimmick, but because of the poster *Tighten Up Volume 3* became legendary in every school classroom and extremely popular on the skinheads' walls.

The *Club Reggae* and *Reggae Chartbusters* series of albums followed the *Tighten Up* lead in the budget-album racks. Trojan, in their desire to enlighten the music world to the delights of reggae, duplicated many tracks across the three series of LPs, although a cynic might say that this was done to derive maximum profit from their recordings.

Single-artist sets, like The Ethiopians' superb *Reggae Power*, which was a favourite with West Indians and skinheads alike, and single-producer sets like *Hot Shots Of Reggae*, showcasing Leslie Kong's bouncing board work, soon appeared, still at budget prices.

Many of these compilations were nothing more than a collection of singles placed together by Trojan. Joe Sinclair remembers pulling together The Maytals' *From The Roots* LP from some of their currently popular singles, alongside working out which titles would go on the *Tighten Up* series from Volume 5 onwards. (The previous four had been compiled by Rob Bell.) Joe and Rob also compiled the superb 1972 triple-album set *The Trojan Story*, the first retrospective collection of Jamaican music (the *History Of Ska* album had been issued by Bamboo Records but covered only the R&B to the ska-beat periods), most of whose vintage tracks were dubbed directly from Jamaican vinyl copies in Joe's collection.

Trojan's album sleeves were a mix of re-using Jamaican graphics, the 'pretty girl' image (some of the early *Tighten Up* series were graced by professional models) and contrived shots taken around the area of the Trojan offices. Rob Bell recalls the *Liquidator* album cover: 'My secretary, whom I inherited from Graham [Walker], was Bertilia someone or other. Everyone called her Tilly. She was on the *Liquidator* cover, together with Henry Glasgow, who was a contractor – he did odd jobs around Music House sometimes. She may be on other covers.' In fact, she also appeared on the front cover of the *Soul Rebels* LP.

The sleeve of the debut TRL album, *Follow That Donkey*, shows Musicland shop managers Webster Shrowder and Desmond Bryan along with Desmond's brother, 'Lenky'. Anyone available was drafted in to form a picture, whether it be relevant or not, should there be no available graphics from the Jamaican counterpart.

Shortly after compiling *The Trojan Story*, Rob Bell, tired of the London rat race, left Trojan and moved to Wales, where he spent some years as a shepherd. He returned to the music business in around 1980 to manage a hot new US band called Roomful Of Blues, a post he held until 2002.

Many high-street retailers disliked stocking reggae singles due to their poor sound quality. Joe Sinclair explains the reason: 'Apart from the big producers like Leslie Kong and Byron Lee, who provided us with master tapes, we always had to dub off a record for our releases.' In other words, a normal Jamaican-pressed record would be used as the master copy for the Trojan release. All the inherent faults of the none-too-special JA pressing would thereby be transferred to the UK issue, along with a second step away from master-tape sound quality.

As the expansion of the reggae market took hold, individual producers were allotted their own singles labels by Trojan, as we have already seen. In addition, a few albums were issued with distinctive producer branding. Sonia Pottinger's production on The Hippy Boys, *Reggae With The Hippy Boys*, appeared on her High Note label in 1969, the same year that Clancy Eccles' *Fire Corner* set – featuring King Stitt and The Dynamites – appeared on Clan Disc. Lee Perry had a whole host of long-players issued on his Upsetter brand, including The Wailers' moody *Soul Rebels* set, which reappeared a few months later on the main Trojan label. 'That was probably because it made the distribution set-up easier,' opines Rob. 'Phillips distributed Trojan – at least the "Hot Shot" series – but not all the other labels. Thus having all the albums on Trojan, rather than Amalgamated, Big Shot or what have you, meant we could sell more product.

'Trojan really got under way in 1969. The first Trojan 45 series [issued in 1967] was an Island label, 100 per cent. Then Island and B&C formed the joint venture called Trojan. The new Trojan 45 series then started at TR601. After a few weeks or months, product that was previously Island now was switched to Trojan, and then it became gradually apparent that it made sense to have more LP titles on Trojan in order to get them distributed through Phillips.'

Despite Trojan's efforts to make buyers aware of the benefits of the LP format, albums accounted for only one-ninth of the total sales for 1970, and the majority of those were various-artists compilations. The single was, and would always remain, the dominant force in Jamaican music, a situation which continued even after heavy pressure by the major labels to relocate all music to CD, SACD and DVD.

By the early 1970s, local radio had at last arrived in the UK. Even the BBC had to take notice of the number of chart placings afforded to reggae records and, as the trend appeared to be continuing, Auntie Beeb looked to set up minority music shows on those local stations thought to cover the inner-city areas where the music had its core audience. Unfortunately, by the time the behind-the-scenes machinations of the BBC got the shows in place, the skinhead cult was waning, and basically the corporation missed the boat, as far as peak audiences for reggae were concerned.

Nevertheless, tight one-hour slots were allocated to 'ethnic' broadcasting. One such programme was *Reggae Time*, hosted by Steve Barnard and transmitted every Sunday lunchtime from 1pm to 2pm on BBC Radio London. Steve, in his inimitable, slightly haphazard manner, would play some of the latest releases, and the oddly named Tony Fish would scale the list of notable London-area dances at lightning speed.

It was an all-too-brief show. Radio London latterly elongated *Reggae Time* to two hours at the tail end of the '70s and installed Tony Williams as presenter, soon to be joined in 1978 by one David Rodigan, a white actor-turned-presenter who quickly gained his own show, alternating week by week with Williams.

Capital Radio, London's new independent station, latched onto the black music scene much more quickly than the grand old BBC and, from its inception, quickly filled its time slots with the best club music around. Its *TV On Reggae* was aired on Saturday nights, with ex-pirate DJ and hard rocker Tommy Vance somewhat out of his league in attempting to present a reggae show. Luckily, he had a sidekick by the name of Cliff St Lewis, who knew his stuff and was an occasional Trojan recording artist. And as the hard roots era moved across from Jamaica, London was lucky enough to have two legal reggae radio shows.

The stumbling *TV On Reggae* did not last too long, and in 1979 David Rodigan was installed at Capital Towers with his own Saturday late-night show *Roots Rockers*, which initially went out from 11pm to 1am and then moved to an earlier slot, while Tony Williams was left with the BBC show.

Rodigan was to host the show for 11 years before moving across to the newly legalised Kiss FM, where Joey Jay was already running a roots reggae show on Sunday evenings. Rodigan was to concentrate more on the modern dancehall business while Jay took the listeners through new and old roots classics. London sound system Menassah also ran a show on Kiss FM, running through Saturday night to early Sunday morning, playing the latest in UK dub alongside exemplary roots-reggae sides.

The music press of the mid '70s continued to report frustration that chart success was not an easy thing for a reggae artist to achieve, due to the vicious circle of 'no hit, no airplay; no airplay, no hit'. The problem remained the same – the specialist soul and reggae shops were not included in the sales-charting process. 'These early sales are important,' noted Lee Gopthal. 'Once a record shows at the bottom of the chart, most shops will stock it, Radio 1 will start to play it and the pop fans will pick up on it.'

A reggae record could sell a staggering 35,000 copies and still not reach the national Top 50. Many artists felt disillusioned about trying to change their musical style to get commercial success. In 1972, when 'Have A Little Faith' by Nicky Thomas had shot to the Number One position in the Jamaican charts and sold a massive 50,000 copies out there, its UK Trojan pressing was given no airplay on the BBC. By this stage, Trojan was exploiting every possible promotional outlet. Clubs and discos received promo releases, as did a network of over 100 reggae and soul shops and even hospital and factory radio stations.

In 1972, Island and B&C ended their joint ownership of the Trojan group due to what they described at the time as 'policy differences', and B&C took full control. Island, utilising their newly inaugurated Blue Mountain label, decided to concentrate on developing specific artists, such as The Wailers and Toots and The Maytals, as opposed to tying in with particular producers. Lee Gopthal recognised the wisdom of this move.

The palatable, easy-listening sound of strings dubbed over reggae rhythms proved to make a narrow pathway to the Top 20 and the odd spot on *Top Of The Pops* in the early '70s, although these were still almost token appearances to appease the many underground-reggae fans. In 1973, Trojan, under the guidance of Joe Sinclair, issued two volumes of *Reggae Strings*, with top rhythms of the day awash with sweeping and diving string arrangements by Johnny Arthey. 'This was my pet project,' observed Joe Sinclair, 'a kind of driving music, as I had a Jensen at the time with an eight-track stereo, and I thought it would sound good.'

In that same year, also through Joe's inspiration, the Shrowder/Bryan/Sinclair set-up instigated the first album of reggae tracks overdubbed with synthesiser, courtesy of Ken Elliott, masquerading as 'The Vulcans'. Taking space and, more pointedly, the *Star Trek* TV series as its theme, the album of that name carried some well-loved rhythms from producers like Bunny Lee and redesigned them for the '70s easy-listening crowd. It was an inspired release and remains one of the highlights of Trojan's LP back catalogue.

By 1973, the sound of British reggae was well established and some record companies had decided to end their involvement with the Jamaican producers. The *NME* of 27 January that year carried an article by Danny Holloway catchily entitled 'Suddenly Reggae Is Up After Being Almost Booted To Death By The Skins'. In it, Jeffrey Palmer of Pama Records was quoted as saying, 'I have stopped dealing with the Jamaican scene because it is too hard to control. You never know what the producers are up to behind your back. They have been known to sell the same record both to me and to Lee Gopthal at Trojan. When that happens, neither one will sell because the record shops don't like it.' This reiterates the problem recounted earlier with Joe Sinclair and Trojan.

'We've had too many problems dealing with Jamaica,' continued Jeffrey Palmer, explaining Pama's new policy. 'Our future is now with reggae in England. We've got our own artists and facilities, and our reggae is different anyway.'

'I don't dislike the fact that the music has become anglicised,' said David Betteridge, by now the MD of Island. 'It needs to have strings and horns at times, like any music. I tend to lean towards pop reggae more than ethnic reggae. To me, a band like Greyhound are capable of playing good ethnic reggae, but a lot of people in Jamaica would disagree with me.'

The pop reggae produced in the UK was by now very different from its Jamaican counterpart, particularly as the JA style was evolving into the Rasta-roots sound. In a perceptive article in *The Times* on 19 March 1973, Richard Williams glimpsed the future: 'Sometime during the coming summer, reggae will become a vital force in pop music – perhaps, for a while at least, *the* force. For those who have not heard, reggae is the Jamaican version of rhythm and blues, black popular music based on a highly individual swaying, clip-clopping beat in which the musicians subtly imply as much as they actually play.

'Among British rock snobs, reggae has been a dirty word for the last couple of years. They have called it dull, crude and monotonous, entirely missing the point that this is functional dance music, still close to its people and a total stranger to sophistication. It is the story of the blues all over again. That attitude is changing, led by top white rock musicians. Paul Simon, The Rolling Stones, Cat Stevens and Elton John have all recorded in Jamaica, savouring its loose, relaxed atmosphere, while Paul McCartney's Wings and the J Geils Band have adapted the reggae beat to their own ends – with not entirely successful results.

'The next step is an album called *Catch A Fire* by a long-established Jamaican group called The Wailers. This record is the one which will snare rock fans, making them aware of reggae's inherent beauty and vast potential. Bob Marley, the group's leader and chief songwriter, has added slide guitar, electric piano and synthesiser to the basic rhythm section, thus spicing up the sound, but sparingly so that the funky essence remains.'

In actual fact, Marley had not instigated the overdubs to *Catch A Fire*, and The Wailers did not play the overdubbed instruments; these were provided by

London-based session musicians hired by Chris Blackwell, who at that time had his eye firmly set to break Marley and co into the white rock arena. The Basing Street Studio overdubs had definitely done their job and caught the ear of the white-music press, as illustrated by Richard Williams' comments in the same *Times* article: 'He is a marvellously flexible lead singer, stitching breathtaking little ornamental phrases on to memorable melodies – like the slow, sensual "Stir It Up", a magnificent love song – and his arrangements for the background vocals are quite the equal of, say, The Impressions. His bassist and drummer lie right back on the beat, keeping decoration to a minimum, and I defy you not to dance to it.'

Rob Bell had seen Marley's potential when his work was being issued by Trojan prior to the Island deal: 'I loved Lee Perry's Marley stuff: "Small Axe", "Duppy Conqueror" *et al...* really very different, very soulful. Riveting sounds. His singles on Upsetter sold very well, and it was no surprise to me when Blackwell got behind him.'

3 1975 To Date

Fall And Rise

By 1974, Joe Sinclair had left the employ of Trojan Records and his former producing partner, Webster Shrowder, had taken over the managing directorship of the mighty empire. By this time, Trojan were the UK market leaders by a country mile, controlling 75 per cent of the reggae market and with their records available across the counter in every high street store, something that their former rivals, Pama – who were taking a temporary break at this time – never managed.

Smaller, recently launched labels like Count Shelley, Lord Koos, Larry Lawrence's Ethnic and Ethnic Fight, Mr Coke's Magnet, Dennis Harris' DIP and the Creole/Cactus/Rhino set-up, as well as a much-diminished Melodisc, competed for the other 25 per cent. As well as the reggae labels, Shrowder also controlled the People and Action soul labels at this stage, with hopes for a disco floor-filler like Don Downing's 'Lonely Days, Lonely Nights' always to the fore.

As MD of Trojan, Shrowder swung into action with a number of changes. He reduced the number of releases per week from ten to four, yet maintained the same level of sales as previously. He also streamlined the number of producers with whom Trojan had deals in Jamaica, ensuring too that new deals were made in conjunction with the artist as well as the producer. He explained his methods to *Black Music* magazine: 'Producers don't really look after the artists in Jamaica, so it's up to us to ensure that there's fair treatment, otherwise it will reflect on us. You see, there are only two companies in Jamaica, Dynamic and Federal. Most of the others are just little labels, one-man things. They hire an artist, produce a record, get it pressed and take it around on a scooter and flog it to the shops. Too much of it is amateurish, and that's why the artists get robbed. So we like to deal with producers who do their business properly. We do everything legally. We don't issue records unless a particular artist or product is contracted to us, and we only deal in royalties.'

With nationwide distribution through B&C, and as many records being sold through Muzik City shops, Trojan seemed to be at the top of the musical food chain with no natural predators. But an unfortunate remark from the aforementioned *Black Music* article gives an indication that Shrowder did not see the growing threat that was undermining Trojan's position. 'I don't know what these small labels are doing,' he said. 'I'd like them to be successful, but there's really no competition.' He was apparently oblivious to the threat that was creeping up on the giant.

By 1974, an underground reggae scene was thriving at clubs such as Bluesville in Wood Green, the Cobweb in Hornsey, the Crypt in Deptford, the Four Aces in Dalston and larger venues, such as the Pama-owned London Apollo in Willesden and the All Nations in Hackney. Even Ronnie Scott's, one of London's leading jazz clubs, ran specific reggae nights that attracted a different crowd from their usual bearded clientele.

The younger audiences at these clubs were dissatisfied with the pop reggae that Trojan was producing. They felt that the emotion that was the very soul of the music had been removed, and although the new music was popular with the older generation, their children couldn't relate to it. The youth market was struggling to find worthwhile Trojan releases to buy as the company's output focused tighter and tighter on desperate cover versions of happy pop songs. The smaller labels, however, had recognised that the so-called ethnic reggae was selling not only to the West Indian population of the UK but also to young white fans who wanted to hear of struggle and torment.

By late 1973, there were very few radio shows playing reggae music and music magazine reviews had succinctly divided reggae into two opposing styles: in one corner nestled the chart-hopeful soft-and-cheery commercial product, while in the other stood bass-heavy, uncompromisingly raw reggae with firebrand lyrics of revolution and Rasta. This was ethnic reggae, which would evolve into the roots-and-culture sound of a couple of years later, taking reggae from the ghetto to *Top Of The Pops*.

Speaking to *Black Music* magazine in February 1974, Dandy Livingstone explained the need to change his musical image to a new and deeper sound: 'I changed labels from Trojan to B&C/Mooncrest because I wanted to change my musical direction. I believe I wouldn't have been able to do that if I had stayed with Trojan.' Dandy did swing about, both in lyrics and in general sound, and made a handful of exemplary roots singles in the latter part of the '70s, but sadly his name was to be forever associated with the cheery 'Suzanne, Beware Of The Devil' and he found few listeners.

In a 1974 interview, Nicky Thomas reflected, 'I'm not interested whether the BBC want to play my songs or not. I lost £3,000 trying to make a song to please the BBC. I could have made down-to-earth ethnic reggae and the black people would have bought it. In future I'll make songs for the black market only.' Sadly, Nicky never regained his chart success, either in the pop mainstream or with ethnic West Indian buyers, and had faded from view by the end of the decade.

Old Trojan comrades like Lee Perry were enticed to sell their new, harder-sounding product to minor labels like Ethnic, who released some outstanding Upsetter material, such as 'Fist Of Fury', in the middle of the decade.

An indication of the mounting financial problems was the closure of various sub-labels like Upsetter, which ceased to exist in 1973. The use of cheap, plain, single-colour labels replaced the far more expensive multicolour designs in an effort to reduce costs. Harry J, Bread and Explosion, to name but three surviving labels, took to the monochromatic cover designs between 1973 and the sale of Trojan two years later.

White sound-system operator and independent producer Tony Ashfield recorded some one-off 'specials' with ex-Paragons vocalist John Holt in the early 1970s. The success of the records in the dancehall was spectacular and, based on that triumph, a Trojan employee suggested adding strings and orchestra to Holt's work in order to make it more smooth and palatable, in typical pursuit of the ever-sweetening reggae sound recorded in London.

The resulting *1,000 Volts Of Holt* album, released by Trojan Records in 1973 and awash with sweeping banks of strings and bittersweet melodies orchestrated by Ashfield, was a huge success. Based on this achievement, Trojan hired Ashfield as an in-house producer, with *carte blanche* to sign whomever he felt worthy, both in the UK and on trips to Jamaica.

Holt's 1974 chart smash 'Help Me Make It Through The Night' only furthered the Ashfield sound of sweetness. The collaboration between Holt and producer/arranger Keith Bonsoir continued the lush Ashfield tradition with the *2,000 Volts Of Holt* album, which was issued in 1976, just as the divide between JA roots-reality songs and London super-smooth supper-club reggae widened. Once again the nattily dressed Holt won new hearts with his exemplary crooning, aided by the full might of a horn-and-string section.

By the end of 1976, the suave John Holt orchestration had run its course, and when producer Bunny Lee delivered a no-frills Jamaican-recorded album of John singing reggae ballads Trojan decided to stay with the title, in keeping with the previous volumes. *3,000 Volts Of Holt* hit the streets early in 1977 and, although lacking the elaborate sophistication of its predecessors, still managed to become one of the label's all-time best-selling albums.

By this time, the new, harder-sounding product was starting to take hold both in the dancehalls and with the general reggae record-buying public. At the same time, Trojan had complacently stocked the high street with sweet non-sellers and the little man was creeping into the market and moving his wares to the core audience that the crumbling giant courted.

At odds with their normal view of the current reggae sound, in March 1975 Trojan issued – somewhat surprisingly – the Dadawah album *Peace And Love*, featuring the unmistakable voice of Ras Michael Henry. *Peace And Love* was four long Nyahbinghi tracks spiced up with funky dub effects courtesy of the finest Kingston sessionmen. Producer Lloyd Charmers had captured the moving sound of the Rasta element in Jamaican music and combined it to perfect effect with the now sound of dub mixing.

The album charmed the reviewers (Carl Gayle gave it a four-star review in the April issue of *Black Music*) and the younger record-buying public, but Trojan failed to take the hint and continued to pursue the pop charts, although they did release some more 'roots'-orientated albums in May of the same year, such as Augustus Pablo's *Ital Dub* and the somewhat lacklustre Ras Michael album *Nyahbinghi*.

The particularly UK-based Lovers Rock scene was also just breaking out as 1975 moved along, with Louisa Mark's 'Caught You In A Lie' single on the tiny Safari Records imprint selling a staggering 10,000 copies in the first week of its release in June. Trojan almost missed the emerging sweet swinging new sound that was to sell an amazing amount of records as the decade moved on, with only the occasional record released, such as Matumbi's 'After Tonight', which was issued in 1977 after the Saga purchase. It was a style at odds with the harsh social commentary pouring from Kingston, with love and heartbreak the staples of the shrill-voiced teenage girl singers.

Black Music journalist Carl Gayle wrote a comprehensive piece on the fall of Trojan and the rise of the underdog small labels in the magazine's October 1975 issue. He also commented intriguingly on the success of Trojan sales to Europe, Australia and Japan, the latter of which had apparently pressed and issued 30 Trojan albums just prior to the label's collapse and the Saga purchase. Sadly, no confirmation of these pressings has ever come to light.

So, despite releasing a couple of sizeable pop hits, the overall situation continued to worsen for Trojan as more strong-selling product was diverted from their door. The decline can be charted from the tail end of 1973 until 1975, when the company was taken over.

The details of this transfer are sketchy, but a report in the October 1976 issue of *Black Music* aimed to clarify the story. Trojan Records had made various allegations of professional misconduct against the magazine, and the article is summarised here in the absence of any other source of material facts.

Marcel Rodd, a Jewish businessman, had taken early retirement after a successful career in printing and publishing but had soon ended his self-imposed retirement to set up a pressing and distribution plant, specialising in children's records, in Kensal Rise, London W10. He had also licensed the Leisure Arts catalogue of classical albums from the USA. Frustrated by the monopolisation of high-street shops by HMV and Decca – the two leading classical-music labels in the 1950s – Rodd set up the mail-order company World Record Club. This flourished, and in 1960 he bought the Saga company, which specialised in budget-priced LPs of various types of music on its labels such as Saga and Fidelio.

By 1973, Rodd had built up a thriving and self-contained record company, complete with its own pressing plant, at the Kensal Rise premises and was seeking to expand his Saga empire. Indeed, he placed an advert in the trade paper *Music Week*, seeking to buy another record company as a going concern. Nothing came of this scheme at the time, but before long, and quite by chance, he became aware of Trojan Records.

In 1974, Trojan, frantically fulfilling orders for Ken Boothe's Number One hit 'Everything I Own', had used Saga's pressing capacity to manufacture £20,000 worth of records. They had difficulty paying for these, which of course brought them to the attention of Saga's chief accountant. This worthy, doubtless mindful of his boss's expansionist plans, duly told Mr Rodd about the company.

81

Wasting no time, Rodd attended a meeting with Trojan directors Lee Gopthal and the company's accountant, Brian Gibbon, to offer them a deal. According to *Black Music,* this deal would give Saga a ten-per-cent share of B&C/Trojan. In return, they would loan B&C/Trojan £150,000, which would be secured against the latter's audited assets of £600,000. However, the sagacious chief accountant then spent a week auditing the accounts himself and found that B&C/Trojan was grossly in deficit, with the result that Saga hurriedly pulled out of the deal.

Trojan then allegedly approached Saga and offered themselves for sale at a price of £25,000, valid for 48 hours only. The astute Rodd, not wishing to take on the company's liabilities, proposed that two new companies should be set up: B&C Recordings Ltd and Trojan Recordings Ltd. These firms would have the same directors as the previous companies and the same assets in terms of stock, record contracts, etc, but the financial liabilities of the previous companies would not be transferred to them. This 'what's in a name?' syndrome is a perfectly legal move for companies with cashflow problems, although for those workers involved whose jobs are on the line the procedure does not treat them particularly fairly.

So it was that these two 'new' companies were immediately sold to Saga for £30,000. The article then reports that the funds received by the directors of B&C/Trojan should have been used to refloat the previous companies. Instead, the money was allegedly used to pay off overdrafts personally guaranteed by the B&C/Trojan directors. All the staff were dismissed and the companies went into voluntary liquidation. The latter part of this story seems to be somewhat supported by notices that appeared on 10 June 1975 in the *London Gazette.*

TROJAN RECORDS LIMITED

Notice is hereby given pursuant to Section 293 of the Companies Act, 1948, that a meeting of the Creditors of the above-named Company will be held at the Westbury Hotel, New Bond Street, Piccadilly, London W1, on Friday 20 June 1975 at 3:30 o'clock in the afternoon, for the purposes mentioned in Sections 294 and 295 of the said Act.

Dated this 4 June 1975. By order of the board (952).

L Gopthal, Director.

B&C RECORDS LIMITED

Notice is hereby given pursuant to Section 293 of the Companies Act, 1948, that a meeting of the Creditors of the above-named Company will be held at the Westbury Hotel, New Bond Street, Piccadilly, London W1, on Friday 20 June 1975 at 2 o'clock in the afternoon, for the purposes mentioned in Sections 294 and 296 of the said Act.

Dated this 4th June, 1975. By order of the board (954).

L Gopthal, Director.

These notices were followed in the same publication on 19 June 1975 by this one:

In the High Court of Justice (Chancery Division).
Companies Court No 001980 of 1975.
In the matter of TROJAN RECORDS Limited and in the matter of the Companies Act, 1948.

Notice is hereby given that a petition for the winding-up of the above-named Company by the High Court of Justice was on the 10th day of June 1975 presented to the said Court by Mechanical Copyright Protection Society Limited, whose registered office is situated at Elgar House, 380 Streatham High Road, London SW16 3HR, and that the said petition is directed to be heard before the Court sitting at the Royal Courts of Justice, Strand, London WC2, on the 7th day of July 1975 and any Creditor or Contributary of the said Company desirous to support or oppose the making of an Order on the said petition may appear for that purpose and a copy of the petition will be furnished by the undersigned to any Creditor or Contributory of the said Company requiring such copy on payment of the regulated charge for the same.

Joynson-Hicks & Co, St Martins House, 140 Tottenham Court Road, London W1, Solicitors for the Petitioner.

NOTE: Any person who intends to appear on the hearing of the said Petition must serve on or send by post to the above-named notice in writing of his intention so to do. The notice must state the name and address of the person, or, if a firm, the name and address of the firm, and must be sent by post in sufficient time to reach the above named not later than 4 o'clock in the afternoon of the 4th day of July 1975.

An identical notice was also printed regarding B&C Records.

The later notices seem to imply some inability to pay royalties (the MCPS was, and is, the body responsible for their distribution), and this would certainly be supported by the negative feelings and reactions that have been encountered during the preparation of this book. The full details of the events that took place on these dates may never come to light; in researching this book, we have tried various official and unofficial sources of information and have come up with nothing but speculation. Even the MCPS are unable to assist, as their records have been destroyed after the passing of over a quarter of a century.

It appears that Saga thought that they were buying the rights to an extensive rock-music catalogue. However, by the date of the transaction, the B&C/Mooncrest (a B&C rock offshoot) contracts had expired and rock label Charisma had changed their distribution from B&C to Island. Marcel Rodd was therefore left with only an extensive catalogue of which he had no knowledge whatsoever. He recognised that Webster Shrowder would be a useful general manager, but soon this arrangement had to end as Shrowder had conflicting interests – he had formed his own reggae company, Vulcan, in association with former Bamboo label owner Junior Lincoln.

By the time of that *Black Music* article, the pressing plants were once again whirring into action, bringing Trojan back to life. As well as advertising on the full back cover of the magazine, Trojan was signing new acts and re-signing the popular acts from its former existence. Rodd was seen as a respectable and honest businessman with the initiative and professionalism to make reggae a money-spinner for those artists. But the circumstances surrounding that change of ownership have tarnished the name of Trojan to this day.

A number of artists had received little or no payment for their services when the original Trojan went into liquidation, and they turned to the new Rodd-owned company for reimbursement. As far as they were concerned, Trojan was Trojan, and Trojan owed them money, although of course all the outstanding debts were with the Official Receiver and Trojan Recordings Ltd was under no obligation to pay anyone for their previous efforts.

After the departure of Webster Shrowder, Bill Ross – previously the chief accountant of Saga – became a co-director of Trojan, along with Clive Stanhope, who was the ex-managing director of Dart Records. Stanhope knew very little about reggae music but had an extensive knowledge of record sales and distribution. Trojan hoped that his expertise would bring them back onto the marketplace.

Black-music journalist Tony Cummings filled the new company's A&R position, along with his assistant Floyd Lloyd Seivright, who also had an understanding of the reggae field. Floyd left after a short time, and noted reggae photographer and former Island Records A&R man Dave Hendley applied for the vacancy after a tip-off by distributor, DJ and label owner Mo Claridge. Dave recalls his lunchtime introductory interview with Marcel Rodd: 'We sat in his office – no windows, right down in the centre of the factory, with pipes all round the walls, nowhere near the Trojan offices on the top floor – and in comes this woman like a school dinner lady with a plate of dry ham sandwiches. That was the lunch!

'Marcel Rodd was a small wizened old man with a slightly sinister feel to him. He always wore a cream linen jacket, like out of *Casablanca*, and he had a slight air about him. The rumour that everyone in the reggae community knew was that he was supposed to have been Al Capone's driver and then a spy in the last war. I dunno why; I suppose just the way he acted and looked.'

With the departure of Tony Cummings, Dave Hendley was elevated to the A&R position, which was extremely well paid in comparison to similar jobs at other record companies. The good wages were strangely at odds with Marcel Rodd's 'penny pinching', as Dave called it, his determination not to pay the going rate for new work offered by various Jamaican producers.

So in the late '70s, Trojan was drifting, as the only product which producers would offer them was rejects from other deals or substandard work. Due to the company policy of not paying to the same level as their competitors, such as the rapidly expanding Greensleeves Records, Trojan's reputation in the marketplace had taken a dive. Marcel Rodd was determined to reverse this trend. And so February 1979 saw Dave Hendley, Mo Claridge and fast-rising reggae DJ David Rodigan heading out to Kingston. Dave's brief was to raise the Trojan flag in Kingston and sign up some acts – although the company had provided no contacts for him to visit.

Due to Dave's resourcefulness, the outcome was Sugar Minott's *Ghettology* album and The Morwells' 12" disco 45 'Kingston 12 Tuffie', with a stunning remix courtesy of Prince Jammy. It wasn't much to show for the trip; the main problem was that Trojan, with their low money offers and poor contractual terms, just weren't competitive in the marketplace, as Dave explains: 'Trojan would pay £300 max for a disco 12" single, while the going rate was £400, and they would only pay up to £2,500 for an album, when up to £4,000 was the normal price. I badly wanted a Freddie McGregor album that Niney had and, give him his due, Rodd went to four grand, but Niney wouldn't let it go for that. Freddie was just so big back then. I tried for the 'Hard Time Pressure' 12" single from Sugar Minott but couldn't get it due to the money. In the end I put it out on my own Sufferers' Heights label. I offered Sugar a good deal and he took it.'

Neither were Trojan competitive contractually. They often offered low royalty rates and 'in perpetuity' contracts, which basically meant that they owned the rights to an artist's work for ever. Their rivals offered better royalty payments and a three-year contract, after which the artist's work was open to negotiation. Not surprisingly, Trojan found it hard to entice acts to sign on the dotted line.

Nevertheless, thanks mainly to Dave Hendley, Trojan did issue some excellent contemporary albums, such as a strong roots set by The Viceroys. In July 1979, Dave met Michael 'Mikey Dread' Campbell in New York and gained the rights to an LP that became one of Trojan's best-sellers of the late '70s, *Dread At The Controls*, which achieved significant sales in the white-student and new-wave markets. This was a rapidly-growing new area, leading on from the interest shown by the punks a couple of years earlier – when, for example, punk rebels The Clash had released a version of 'Police And Thieves' – for the outspoken reggae with which they could identify, albeit only in spirit.

Island had been issuing LPs of Lee Perry productions such as the superb *Police And Thieves* set by Junior Murvin, which had been well received in the new-wave press, and they had put Marley well on the road to rebel-rock superstardom. Virgin's Front Line offshoot offered DJ Tapper Zukie, the supercool Gregory Isaacs and The Mighty Diamonds to the interested new listeners, while other names who drew large crowds at new-wave gigs included dub poet Linton Kwesi Johnson, Prince Hammer and the gruff-voiced Prince Far I.

These were established artists who had already tasted moderate success, but with the new white audience taking reggae and, more specifically, them to their hearts, major-label interest in reggae was rewarded. However, a couple of years into the 1980s, and after Marley's death, all the majors would drop their reggae rosters as the music swung into the dancehall era.

Before Dave Hendley's arrival at Trojan, Marcel Rodd had dropped the old orange-and-white album label and recoloured it to a pale blue or pale green, although the established brown Trojan shield design which had been in use since the early 1970s remained for the singles. The company then ran a series of reissues of what they thought to be popular albums of their time. In some cases, original album sleeves which had languished in the warehouse were restocked with new pressings of their accompanying vinyl albums.

Other old albums were wholly revamped, with new sleeves showing the new company address, such as the 1973 *Presenting I-Roy* LP, although in this case, according to Dave, 'There was absolutely no market for a five-year-old DJ album.' No one now remembers who was responsible for this reissue programme, but, judging by some of the albums which they chose to revive, whoever it might have been was aware of buyers' tastes of the time.

At the same time, music appeared on a completely redesigned version of the long-serving Attack offshoot. There was a series of 12" singles, a highlight being a reissue of Black Uhuru frontman Michael Rose's harsh 'Born Free', resplendent with a wild Prince Jammy's dub mix at the end. No more than 1,000 copies of each single were pressed, and while some fell by the wayside, others quickly sold out and are now sought-after collectors' items.

In August 1979, due to personal reasons, Dave Hendley left Trojan, although he was back by special request by the following spring. By this time, the Trojan offices were relocating from Saga HQ to Harlesden, an area of London that was a fertile breeding ground for reggae, with seemingly a small label operating out of every street.

The label slowly began to assemble a catalogue of new music, like the *Kamakazi Dub* LP. This actually came from Lloyd 'Prince Jammy' James, who sent it to the Trojan offices as an unnamed master tape with no track titles. Dave Hendley, who was in his kung-fu period at the time, proceeded to title the package and its tracks in martial-arts style and commissioned an appropriate sleeve design.

Dave also put together a definitive collection of earlier reggae entitled *Rebel Music,* which he described as 'purely self-indulgent – there was no market for this sort of collection and I just put together records that I really liked'. Much to Dave's surprise, the double album was a great success and moved many units for Trojan. That first tentative and surprisingly successful step took Trojan towards what would become their main profit area: the revival and repackaging of old ska and reggae recordings. Based on the achievement of *Rebel Music*, Dave Hendley set to work once more and compiled the six-volume *Creation Rockers* series. This was a truly groundbreaking set; for the first time since the triple-LP *Trojan Story* in 1972, a series traced the progress of Jamaican music from the formative early ska days to the present. Unknowingly, but without doubt, Dave had sparked the whole retrospective scene within the reggae-music industry and had set Trojan on the lucrative course that it has pursued this day. His stay at Trojan, however, was less lucrative for him, and in 1982 he became A&R man for another ex-Trojan employee, Clive Stanhope, at the latter's new CSA (Clive Stanhope Associates) label.

After the departure of Dave Hendley, Trojan began a period of comparative inactivity, seemingly reissuing the same few dozen golden oldies in as many permutations as possible, until it was sold to Sharesense Ltd in 1985.

Former chairman Colin Newman offers the background to his company's interest in the record label: 'As a business manager, I represented Chas Chandler, a former member of The Animals who was a very famous producer of artists such as Jimi Hendrix and Slade. He had a record label with Frank Lea – brother of Slade's Jim Lea – called Cheapskate Records, and when it started Frank worked out of our basement offices. And then Chas and Frank fell out and because Frank was actually working in our offices, we'd started to form some kind of friendship, and basically we started a new separate label, which was essentially a singles label, and then that progressed into an album-based compilation label.

'We spent about a year putting together about 15 compilation albums, for which we licensed product from different companies, which was in 1984/85. One of the albums that we licensed was a reggae album from Trojan... and we were quite pleased because we got a big order in from Woolworth's.

'About a week after the order went in, the distributor went bust, and we spent about a year extricating ourselves from the mess that we'd got ourselves into with that label. But it was a fantastic lesson of dealing with the majors and it set me and Frank Lea working together. And so at that point, I thought we needed to get a catalogue. Doing all this and going out doing compilation albums, licensing from the majors, was a complete nightmare. We'd have a rock album that had 15 tracks on it with 15 different licences, because it was a kind of 'rock best of', and I think we were a little bit ahead in terms of timing

– the industry wasn't doing it; people weren't going around doing that kind of thing.

'So as I said we'd licensed one album almost completely from Trojan, which had in fact been the easiest of all of them, because it was one source. There was a chap who was loosely the managing director of Trojan, so we talked to him and then he introduced me to Marcel Rodd, the actual owner of Trojan and B&C.

'At our acquisition point, it was a label that was languishing. I mean, it had literally an accounting executive, who was loosely the MD. It had a pretty poor distribution agreement and it had a label manager. The label manager was in charge of putting together the first Lee Perry box set, and that was a work-in-progress item at the time of our acquisition. If you go back in history, there is one album within that box set which was an unreleased dub album. Essentially, it was two Lee Perry albums and an unreleased dub album. There was a lot of research went into that, and it was one of the first Trojan box-set releases.

'A lot of people initially actually thought we were fronting for Mr Rodd, but in fact that wasn't the case at all, and I found basically that he was a very tough businessman to deal with. Although at that time he was in his 70s, he didn't actually want to sell Trojan. It wasn't for sale.

'The reality was that I went to him and formed a good relationship with him, and I'd like to actually think that he liked me. He thought I was a man in business and knew what records were, old records in particular, and when it eventually came down to it I got the feeling he wanted me to buy it, and again it was interesting because obviously a lot of people come up with the question "How much did you pay?" Obviously, that's a piece of confidential information, but my final negotiating ploy with him was, "Well Mr Rodd, I really want to go ahead with this deal but can't afford it." It was a little ploy, really, on my part to try and get something off the purchase price. [And then he did] something I'll never forget: he put his arm around me and said, "Colin, I'll lend it to you!" And I knew at that point that I was snookered. It was over and done with, and we actually wrote all the contracts out ourselves, without the cost and expense of going to a major law firm, and completed the transaction in which we acquired Trojan.

'Obviously, we'd satisfied ourselves to an extent that it was a proper catalogue and there were tapes and so on and so forth. That was the beginning of it; that gave us what we saw as a catalogue that we could package, and we could market and deal with the people. Then we went through the rather tortuous first 18 months of an onslaught of visitors and artists/producers who came in with the comment, "We never gave any rights, we've never been paid any money," etc.

'Basically, our policy has always been to be very artist-orientated. My whole career had been working for artists. We wanted to be helpful and sympathetic to people, and so we made a policy decision at that point that, if people came, we would do our best to research what their position was. We'd go try to find royalty statements, contracts, and we'd try and essentially make new deals with people so they weren't left with royalties in old pennies.

'We had a very early relationship with Lee Perry in 1986, and our policy then was also to try to talk to people and get them to make new records for Trojan. We had a vision at that point that Trojan should expand by making new recordings. We were probably hampered, looking back on it, by the fact that we had good knowledge of the record industry – good knowledge of the back catalogue, but not specifically at that time good knowledge of the reggae market.

'That's something that we acquired and built up over the years. My background to all this started with my hobby as a record collector. So I went out and basically trod the boards of the country, looking for – and finding – old records that were part of the Trojan catalogue so I could a) educate myself on it and b) build myself a library that would constitute the Trojan library of music.'

Colin goes on to describe the formative Newman-Trojan days: 'In that early time period, around '86, it started purely and simply as Frank Lea and myself and two other staff. Then we got a warehouse and a warehouse manager that we inherited from somebody else who had been distributing records, and we then had Enzo Hamilton, who was essentially an old-style record man but somebody who had an understanding of records and distribution and overseas sales.

'What really happened was that, when we took on Trojan, we found that they had deals in place with overseas distributors where they were really being exploited badly, and we would have situations whereby people would come on and say, "Well, we bought your records for £1 each from your distributor in Holland." And so over the first few years we embarked on a policy which just came about because of this problem, rather than being the result of any clever pre-planning, of actually terminating all licences and manufacturing agreements everywhere in world on the basis that, if you wanted Trojan, the only place in the world you could buy it was from one of our newly appointed distributors or from our warehouse in London. We would distribute directly from our warehouse in London to an overseas distributor, but you couldn't buy the Trojan label from so-called third parties, who were in fact people that we hadn't then started doing business with. I think that helped to control things and gave us sort of quality control and also price control. Our policy had always been to sell less copies at a proper price, rather than job out loads of copies at silly or cheap prices.

'At that time, Enzo Hamilton was our overseas sales person, basically being multilingual and able to communicate with overseas distributors. When we first took on the label, there was a label manager, Patrick Meads, who was employed by the old Trojan, and he was the one label employee who came on with us. There was a warehouse manager as well, but Patrick essentially came over and he was the compiler at that time, and eventually he left. He was so entrenched in calling himself "Patrick from Trojan" that he released a record on his new label, which was Big One Records, and he [stated that it was] "produced by Patrick T Rojan".

'Then, I don't recall exactly how, we came across Steve Barrow, because I was out meeting reggae experts and buying records. I built up a fantastic knowledge and collection of records across all the labels that had been owned and represented by Trojan and Steve Barrow came on board at that point. He had a deep and intimate knowledge of the music and the people.'

One of the first projects Steve instigated was the *Producer* series of albums, with each volume training the spotlight on one particular worthy creative Jamaican producer. They were a great success and solidified Trojan's position as a force to be reckoned with in revival reggae.

Steve Barrow stayed with Trojan for a comparatively short time before moving on to set up the Blood And Fire imprint. B&F continues Steve's meticulous dedication to detail in presenting fine collections of Jamaican music from the 1970s, both as single-artist albums and superb collections.

Chris Prete, another extremely knowledgeable Trojan and reggae enthusiast, was recruited on a freelance basis to replace Steve Barrow and began to assemble an excellent catalogue of compilations and reissues of past Trojan glories. Compilation albums put together by Chris such as *Babylon A Fall Down* once again took Trojan to the forefront of revival reggae by unearthing long-forgotten work and crisply presenting it to a new audience. Alongside Chris came long-time reggae scribe Penny Reel and Lionel Young, who both contributed excellent collections of work in a freelance capacity.

* * *

In 1990, Laurence Cane-Honeysett began freelancing for Trojan Records and brought his enthusiasm and expertise to bear on their vast catalogue.

Laurence gives an insight to his background and how he came to join Trojan: 'My first memory of hearing Jamaican music is back in the '60s, when my older brother, Tony, used to take me to Stamford Bridge to watch Chelsea play. We went to most home games from around 1968 onwards, standing at the infamous Shed end, although very much on the outskirts of the main area. At the time, Chelsea had one of, if not the largest skinhead followings in the country, and they used to play reggae and ska records over the tannoy before the game. Of course, "Liquidator" and all the other big reggae hits of the day were played, but every now and then they also used to play less well-known records. I remember on one occasion "Sammy Dead" by Eric Morris blared out over the tannoy. It was fantastic and left an indelible impression on me.

'I grew up in Fulham, which was quite a working-class area in those days, and I remember at the local junior school all the boys of a certain age tried to emulate their elders and adopt a hard look. I had a pair of Tonik trousers and wore Ben Sherman shirts and the like, but of course we were just wannabes – too young to understand or appreciate the fashion. Of course, at the time everyone in the country was exposed to reggae – the hits were riding high in the charts and just about every home had at least a few reggae singles in their collections. My family was no different, and while my brother wasn't a great fan of reggae, my elder sister, Julia, had some of the records, which I played to death. Although my brother didn't much like the style, he did, however, introduce me to R&B and doo-wop, which eventually led me back to Jamaican music a few years later.

'As the '70s progressed, Jamaican music changed, and to be honest, it really put me off for a while – I was a young, white teenager growing up in London, and I just couldn't identify with all the roots and dub music that was coming out of Jamaica. So my musical tastes developed in other directions – I really got into '50s and '60s R&B and doo-wop in a big way, and by the late '70s I had a huge collection of the stuff, although most of the records I had were reissues. In fact, by this time my collection had grown to such an extent that I really ran out of things to buy, and I suppose it was this that made me look back to the Jamaican music I had loved as a kid, so I picked up a few old albums and soon began to realise the similarities of the styles. I remember one album that had a big influence was the *Wailing Wailers* LP on Studio One. Even the look of it was like an old Impressions album. I played it and thought, "This is fantastic." So it picked up from there and then, I suppose.

'Just a little after, there was the big Two-Tone thing, and suddenly ska was in the charts, although obviously a somewhat bastardised version. But nonetheless, I thought it was great. I loved 'Gangsters' and all the early Madness and Specials stuff, and it really spurred me on to dig deeper. Then, thanks to Dave Hendley, Trojan released *Rebel Music* and *Monkey Business,* and it all came flooding back – this was the real McCoy, really great music, great songs, great rhythms and great performances. Who could ask for more?

'I started to buy the records in earnest, and when the ska-revival bubble burst, I just carried on. I remember picking up a lot of great little collections from people who had briefly embraced ska as a fad, on the back of Two-Tone. I started hunting down records all over the place, and when record fairs started I began to go to all of those in the London area; in those days, you really could pick up reggae records for a song. It was at these fairs that I eventually became aware of Colin Newman, who, after acquiring Trojan in 1985, began to buy all the Trojan stuff. He became a major rival as a collector.

'Around this time, I also befriended a number of other serious reggae collectors, people like Bob Brooks and Dave Home, and we used to meet up at Bob's flat, off Ladbroke Grove, and exchange and play records. Bob was a good friend of Steve Barrow, who was working for Trojan at the time, and on a few occasions he asked if I'd help out with releases by lending some of my records, but I don't think I ever did, as, like most collectors, I wouldn't let my records out of my sight.

'But when Steve Barrow left Trojan, around 1990, I thought I wouldn't mind giving this compiling lark a go. At the time I was freelancing as an illustrator, after briefly trying my hand as a record dealer. Actually, I think by this time I'd already started doing the odd job for *Record Collector* magazine, after John Reed, who was one of the main editors there, had contacted me with a number of ideas about reggae articles and information. He'd got my name from a fellow collector, Jim Silles, who was, and still is, a very good friend. Of course, at this time I had no idea how important John would become in terms of Trojan and that, a decade or so later, we'd be working together, overseeing releases on the label.

'Anyway, back then, Chris Prete, Penny Reel [aka journalist Scotty Bennett] and Lionel Young had all begun to do stuff for Trojan following Steve Barrow's departure, and I was keen to give it a try – I was also trying to make a few bob, at the same time, of course. So I spoke to Colin Newman and convinced him to give me a go. The first releases I worked on were compilations of Desmond Dekker and Derrick Morgan's early recordings in around 1991.

'I can't remember who I mainly dealt with at the beginning, but I know Zep Gerson was there, doing sales. Arthur Sharp, a lovely bloke who had been the lead singer of The Nashville Teens in the '60s and had later gone on to work for Jet Records, dealt with the production side of things, and Dorothy Howe dealt with PR, although she left after a while and a very nice young woman called Hedge [Heather] filled her role.

'They all worked from the Camden office, while in Walthamstow the company had a warehouse run by Lars Gredal where, aside from the stock, there was a little studio and where the master tapes were kept. Of course, Colin was the head of the whole operation, but the MD was Frank Lea, the brother of Jimmy Lea from Slade.

'For the next few years, I carried on working for Trojan in a freelance capacity – I'd submit ideas for releases, with Frank and, to a lesser degree, Colin selecting what was issued. Once they gave the go-ahead, I'd get on with compiling the releases and writing the sleeve notes. This was all well and good, but after a while I began to get a little frustrated with the situation. To be honest, I wanted more control over what was issued, and since nobody had filled the void left by Steve Barrow, I thought that, if I began to work for the company in some capacity, my chance would eventually come.

'I knew that the master tapes had never been properly logged and was desperate to know what was available for release, and so I told Colin that I should do the job and he agreed. So from around the mid '90s I worked for the company full time, commuting to the warehouse every day. It was quite a trip, two hours each way, and to be honest it wore me out. Also, after a while I was given other duties and found I had less and less time to devote to the things I wanted to do, which was basically to manage the releases. In fact, I ended up getting involved with pretty much everything *but* that!

'My other roles at this time included dealing with certain licensing jobs, by liaising with Clive Wills, who had formerly worked for Island and who single-handedly ran Business Affairs; working with Patsy Kennedy, who oversaw the [songwriting] publishing side of things; listening to all new reggae product that was submitted by producers; compiling lists of recordings for any new contract schedules; seeking out tapes for new Trojan releases; liaising with the royalties department, run by Graeme Lamb; filling out the MCPS and PRS forms for new releases; and dealing with all the press and promo stuff following Hedge's departure. This was on top of trying to sort out the tapes and compiling and writing sleeve notes, as by now only myself and Chris Prete were doing all the Trojan releases.

'Anyway, after a few years, I found I hadn't really progressed in terms of managing the releases in the way I wanted to, and of course that had been my initial aim. In fact, many of the releases I worked on were someone else's concept – often Frank's – so I decided to go back to freelancing. Other than the press and promo side of things, I still did all the other stuff, but without having to do the horrible commute five days a week.

'By this time, Del Taylor had been brought in to be the label manager for Trojan. His initial position had been running the Indigo label, which was a blues-oriented imprint Sharesense owned, but his role had widened since joining the company and he was made the general label manager for most of Trojan's releases, regardless of the genre.

'This situation carried on for the next few years. Although officially I was freelance, in effect I was pretty much full-time. And then, of course, in the summer of 2001, Sanctuary came in and bought Trojan from Colin Newman. By this time, I'd actually done a few jobs on the sly for Sanctuary, using pseudonyms – in truth, I'd done the same for a few other companies, most notably Westside, under Tony Rounce's management. Of course, by this time John Reed was at Sanctuary, after they'd bought the Sequel imprint in September 2000, and under the general management of Roger Semon and Joe Cokell he was given the job of overseeing the releases, exploiting all the new product that had come in from Trojan.'

Between Chris Prete and Laurence, a vast amount of music was unearthed and reissued for the first time, following on from Dave Hendley's groundbreaking collections and Steve Barrow's knowledgeable assemblies.

The new business had its humorous moments as well, as Colin Newman recalls: '[Once] we picked up an old file and found an old note of a meeting that Bill Ross, Mr Rodd's accountant, had with a particular artist, and it said that this particular artist thumped the desk and said, "You've got no contract with me, you've never had any contract with me and you've never paid me any money!" And so Mr Ross, who was a chartered accountant, pulled out a contract and some receipts, whereupon the artist leaped across the table and ripped the contract to pieces. And, in fact, in the file was an envelope with the pieces of this contract, and I always thought of that as a jigsaw. I'd try and piece this contract together again, but it got lost with the passage of time.

'But that summed it up, in a way. I think that many people don't understand the modern techniques of the music business, that we give advances, we sell records, the advance is against the royalty and that they would think that they're not being paid until recoupment. And I think it's an endemic view that the artist will always think that you've sold more records that you've actually sold and that you've used his creative process to feather your nest.

'Our whole policy with Trojan was, we had a lot of releases, we didn't sell in great quantity and we also had a lot of compilation releases – a producer series – which we developed. We produced these multi-artist compilations, and at the end of the day, if you know anything about royalty accounting, one track on a multi artist compilation record that's likely to sell 3,000 to 5,000 units isn't going to attract a great royalty. But, understandably, artists think you owe them more than you do, and we understood that and tried to form new relationships with people. We tried to see them; we tried to bring in more people to be available to meet artists and producers.'

Colin also notes that some things never change in the reggae industry: 'We know on some occasions that we'd sign a contract with somebody for a worldwide right, and as soon as they could get out of our offices they'd be down to somewhere else and possibly deposit some of the same records elsewhere. On one occasion, we signed an album and we thought, "Oh, that's good, we'd better get it out quick," and a week later the actual released version of the album was out on import and available at Jet Star.

'No matter what some people want to say about the period in which we ran Trojan, we think we acted in a manner that was fair and reasonable. We think we gave care and attention to the music, care and attention to the artwork, care and attention to the way the music was presented to the public. We enjoyed doing it and, as you know, we built up other labels which had other genres of music – again, all built up with direct artist relationships – with very few problems. We built up a big chart list of British singles charts, tracks that had individually been in the charts, and we mixed the benefit of those releases with Trojan's expertise, in terms of the ability of putting tracks on compilations and things like that. And we had some success with some TV ads, probably the most famous was 'Israelites' by Desmond Dekker for a TDK ad, with 'My Ears Are Alight', which we thought was great and very funny.

'Young, Gifted And Black', Bob (Andy) & Marcia (Griffiths), 1970, used on TBL122.

Bob Andy, 2002 (Picture: 'Spinello').

Trojan single 'all orange' design, first (Duke Reid) series, 1967.

Trojan single 'orange and white' design, 1971.

Trojan single 'brown' label design, Kensal Road sleeve, 1978.

Trojan single 'brown' label design, 1971.

'Hot Shot' sleeve design, 1969.

Demo single aimed at the pop charts, 1971.

GPW pre-release single with the centre pushed out for use on a sound system (GPW77 is 'Java' by Augustus Pablo, which, alhough a sizable hit on import, Trojan never issued). Issued on 16 February, 1971.

Reggae Party sleeve shot, taken at Chalk Farm Studio, used on TBL172, 1971. Clockwise from top left: Sonny 'SS' Binns (cigar), The Rudies/Greyhound (keyboards), Errol Denver (Greyhound, guitarist), Dandy Livingstone, George Decker (head only), Bruce Ruffin, Danny Bowen Smith (Greyhound, drummer). Centre: Honey Boy (Keith Williams, stout hand), Alex Hinds (Marvels), unknown guy in black and Maurice Ellis (wearing tam), Cimarons drummer. Front: Nicky Thomas, Franklyn Dunn (Cimarons, bass), Locksley Gichie (Cimarons, guitar).

NICKY THOMAS

KIETH HUDSON

JOHN HOLT

THE PIONEERS

JUDGE DREAD

A selection of Trojan publicity pictures from 1972.

Shot taken outside Music House, used on TBL170, 1971.
L-r: unknown, Webster Shrowder, Desmond Bryan, Dandy Livingstone.

Magazine ad from 1973.

Skinhead Moonstomp album sleeve, TBL102, 1970.

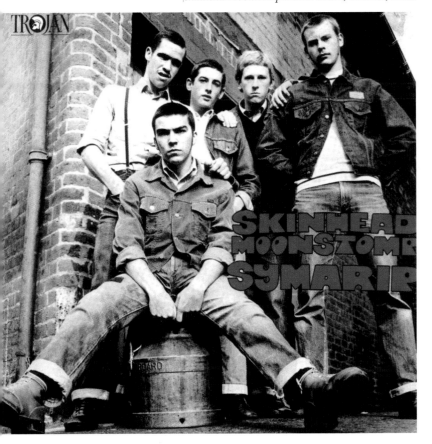

Dalston Market, January 1973.

London sound system, 1973.

Trojan staff outing, 1968, used on TRL1. L-r: 'Lenky' Bryan, Webster Shrowder, Desmond Bryan.

Producer Derrick Harriott's studio band, The Crystalites, used on TBL114. The musicians were from a relatively small pool of session men who would work for a variety of producers. They would work under a different group name for each producer. Back row (l-r): Wallace Wilson, Paul Douglas, Derrick Harriott, Jackie Jackson, Winston Wright, Larry McDonald, Gladstone Anderson. Front (l-r): Hux Brown (pushing), Les Davis ('Bongo Les'), Heman Davis ('Bongo Herman').

Producer Clancy Eccles' studio band The Dynamites, used on TBL124.
Back (l-r): Hux Brown, Paul Douglas, Winston Wright, Gladstone Anderson.
Centre: Jackie Jackson. Front: Clancy Eccles.

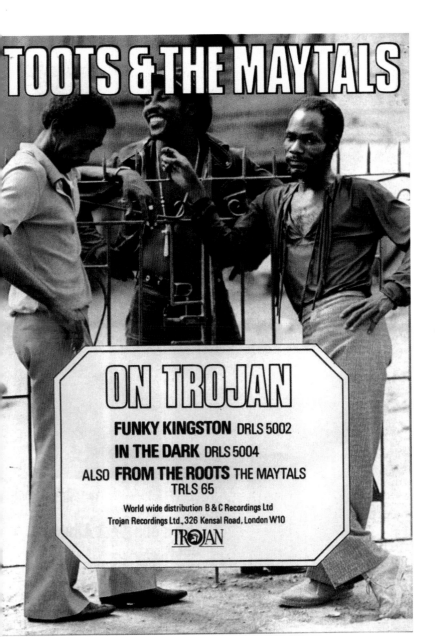

Magazine ad, March 1976.

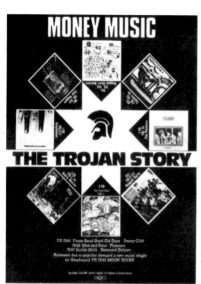

Advert from 11 December 1971.

Rico Rodriguez, London, January, 1973

Dandy Livingstone, 1972, used on TRLS45.

The Maytals, 1970, used on TBL107.

Ken Boothe, 1974, photographer unknown.

Ad from April 1973.

TR⊕JAN **TOP 50 & New Releases.**

W/E 10th MARCH 1972
****

LAST WEEK	THIS WEEK				
1	1	TR	7848	MOON RIVER	GREYHOUND
3	2	TR	7852	MOTHER AND CHILD REUNION	THE UNIQUES
2	3	TRM	9001	CHOPSTICKS/I'VE GOT IT/PUT IT ON	THE DELTONES
6	4	GD	4020	HYPOCRITE	THE HEPTONES
7	5	GD	4022	LIVELY UP YOURSELF	BOB MARLEY
4	6	TE	915	KARATE	DAVE AND ANSEL COLLINS
5	7	DYN	428	JUST A DREAM	SLIM SMITH
8	8	US	380	BET YOU DON'T KNOW	SHENLEY DUFFUS
20	9	SUM	8535	STORY BOOK CHILDREN	SIDNEY, GEORGE AND JACKIE
10	10	DYN	427	ALCAPONE GUNS DON'T BARK	DENNIS ALCAPONE
11	11	TR	7850	YESTERDAY MAN	NICKY THOMAS
18	12	PB	5510	SKANKY DOG	BUNNY FLIP
9	13	BR	1107	JOHNNY GUNMAN	JACKIE EDWARDS
16	14	BI	598	A SOMETIMES GIRL	THE CABLES
15	15	US	377	ALPHA AND OMEGA	DENNIS ALCAPONE
14	16	SUM	8533	NEVER YOU CHANGE	THE MAYTALS
19	17	US	381	WONDER MAN	THE UPSETTERS
12	18	SB	1065	HAVE YOU SEEN HER	DERRICK HARRIOTT
17	19	JP	786	I NEED YOUR LOVING	SLIM SMITH
13	20	RAN	521	IT'S NOW OR NEVER	JIMMY LONDON
32	21	GD	4021	RIOT	SOUL SYNDICATE
22	22	GG	4530	DONKEY FACE	THE MAYTONES
41	23	TR	7854	BUT I DO	BOB AND MARCIA
26	24	DU	129	ONLY LOVE CAN MAKE ME SMILE	GABY AND THE CABLES
31	25	US	376	GIVE ME POWER	THE UPSETTERS
24	26	HS	057	ONE NIGHT OF SIN	JACKIE BROWN
39	27	HS	058	PRAY FOR ME	MAX ROMEO
45	28	TI	7068	MIGHTY REDEEMER	JUSTIN HINDS
29	29	GD	4008	FLYING MACHINE	TEDDY MAGNUS
30	30	DU	127	LAST CALL	SIR HARRY
25	31	PB	5509	THEM A FI GET A BEATIN	PETER TOUSH
21	32	SB	1068	OVER THE RIVER	DERRICK HARRIOTT
-	33	DYN	430	I BELEIVE IN MUSIC	THE JAMAICANS
34	34	DU	125	MEDLEY VERSION	DENNIS ALCAPONE
43	35	SUM	8532	MY LIFE, MY LOVE	THE MELODIANS
36	36	GG	4529	KEEP IT UP	JOHN HOLT
49	37	BI	600	IT'S NOT WHO YOU KNOW	TWINKLE BROTHERS
38	38	GD	4019	BREAKING YOUR HEART	THE SCORPIONS
27	39	BI	595	DANCING WITH MY BABY	LAUREL AITKEN
40	40	GD	4017	I'M SORRY	THE MATADORS
23	41	TRM	9000	SONGS OF PEACE	BRUCE RUFFIN
-	42	JP	787	COME ON	THE CABLES
35	43	US	375	EARTHQUAKE	THE UPSETTERS
44	44	GD	4015	LIVING IN SWEET JAMAICA	JACKIE BROWN
28	45	TR	7846	GIVE AND TAKE/PRIDE AND PASSION	THE PIONEERS
46	46	BI	602	I'M TRYING	ALTON ELLIS
47	47	GD	4007	MISS LABBA LABBA	TWINKLE BROTHERS
48	48	JP	772	STICK BY ME	JOHN HOLT
37	49	GD	4016	JAMAICAN HILITE	THE GAYTONES
50	50	BI	601	YOU DON'T CARE	LLOYD SPARKS

Trojan Top 50, week ending 10 March 1972.

'Young, Gifted And Black' sheet music, 1970.

'We had Lord Tanamo with 'I'm In The Mood For Ska', again for a TV ad [for Paxo stuffing], we got one of the Toots tracks ['Broadway Jungle'] into the Adidas TV ad over the Euro 2000 football tournament and we had one or two others. And again, we worked the label. We finished up doing well out of it, financially, but that's the reward for effort in life. We feel we had a great time with it.

'The point I'm making here is that the Trojan label was not 100 per cent of our business; it finished up being probably about half of our business. The other half was a complete mix of rock, pop, blues, jazz and other genres of music, which, with all respect to the Jamaican music, was in the main more commercially viable for European tastes. So a lot of the Trojan pop reggae we were able to do well with, because it went alongside a lot of our other pop and different genres of music activity. But when you look at our actual Trojan releases themselves, very few attained huge volumes.

'Obviously some of them were better than others. I think we can also take some credit for the *Trojan Histories* that were beautifully packaged in digipacks with very impressive artwork, and I think also the Trojan box-sets packages were brilliant – great value for money, three CDs in a box and well compiled. At the end of the day, I do genuinely believe we did something for the music, and we've still kept some relationships going with those who we felt were genuinely nice people.

'When Sanctuary came along, we felt that they were the right home, in that they understood the concept of a back-catalogue release and how to present music to the public. And we also thought that they would be able to achieve greater sales volumes than we could ever achieve – selling was not one of our strong points – and that if they achieved greater sales levels it would be beneficial all round, because it would increase the artist royalties, and so everyone would be happier.'

Aside from Trojan Records, Sharesense owned an array of other labels: Action Replay Records, which specialised in 'best of' collections; the old Mooncrest imprint (mainly folk); Morgan Blue Town (psychedelic); Clay (new wave); and Receiver Records (punk, pop and new wave). They also reactivated the old-style Yellow Attack label for a series of albums and formed the Trojan World label in order to offer South African township sounds to the world.

In 1987, the Burning Sounds imprint, which issued singles, 12" singles and albums in the mid to late 1970s and was owned by former Trojan employee Clive Stanhope, was up for sale and Trojan purchased it. Sharesense had noted its excellent releases, and it was thought that the albums would sell well in the mid-price arena.

Along with further establishing the brand of Trojan at the forefront of reissue reggae, Chris Prete also reformed the Trojan Appreciation Society. Originally, the TAS had appeared in 1970 as a newsletter informing members of forthcoming tours and releases by their favourite Trojan artists. Two enthusiasts named only as Helen and Rose, working from a private address in Kingsbury, north London, gave the low-down on all things Trojan and ran the society. By 1973, only Rose Barrie was still running the society and the address had changed to 8 Neasden Lane, very close to Music House at number 12. A little later in the year, Rose's name disappeared and the signature 'Titch' could be found on TAS letters.

After paying the vast sum of 72p, the new member would receive 'a full year's membership of the TAS, a bright shining Trojan medallion, a copy of the latest catalogue, a short history of reggae, postcard pics of your favourite Trojan artists and 12 monthly newsletters', according to the application form. 'Be the envy of all your friends – join the reggae people...' boasted the ad on the joining letter.

Initially, the monthly newsletter, although slightly erratic in its arrival, was full of interesting titbits, news and reviews of Trojan. It advertised posters of Trojan artists for sale and ran a 'Record Sales And Wants' page beside the pen-pal column. The last newsletter was dated May/June 1973.

In October of the same year, a new newsletter dropped through the letterboxes of all TAS members. The grandly named West Indian Music Appreciation Society, run by one E Denham from Berkhamsted, Hertfordshire, welcomed all to the newly formed society. The WIMAS newsletter proposed to cover not only Trojan releases but all reggae issued in the UK, as well as other West Indian styles like steel band and calypso. It was a jolly A4 stapled-together affair comprising a main feature, such as 'The Roots Of Reggae'; some reviews of (mainly Trojan-related) reggae records; a competition; a Trojan merchandise sales page; record sales and swaps; and a pen-pals correspondence page.

The seventh issue, dated September 1974, was accompanied by a photocopied letter announcing that this was to be the last newsletter. 'When I amalgamated my own society with the Trojan society, I was given to understand that help would be given with regard to the financial side,' ran the explanation. It went on to say that the subscription charge did not cover the actual production costs and postage stamps and that the majority of the costs had been borne by the writer. The letter continued, 'As no money has been received from Trojan Records, I will be sending the mailing lists and all correspondence back to them.' And that was the end of any form of Trojan newsletter for some quarter of a century.

Chris Prete revived the society in 1989 and proceeded to produce thick labour-intensive magazines bearing the new name of 'The Official Trojan Appreciation Society' (TOTAS). The magazine was named *Let's Catch The Beat*, after Dandy's debut album, and the A5-sized magazine became synonymous with superbly researched, in-depth articles, so much so that the magazines have become collectable in their own right and bear testament to Chris Prete's painstaking work.

In June 2001, the Sanctuary Group paid a massive £10.3 million for Trojan Records, thus becoming the curators of this renowned reggae label in the new millennium.

Sanctuary was founded in 1976 by Rod Smallwood and Andrew Taylor and was originally intended to be a music-management business. In 1979, Taylor discovered the heavy rockers Iron Maiden, whose gigantic international record sales (they chalked up five platinum-selling albums in a row in the USA) gave the company an ever-increasing income from mainstream rock throughout the '80s and into the '90s.

In December 1997, a company called Burlington paid £15 million for Sanctuary – good news for Smallwood and Taylor, who each had a 20 per cent stake in their company. Burlington, which had previously been known as Gold & Base Metal Mines, changed its name to the Sanctuary Group after the deal. Their empire has continued to expand, and as well as Trojan's massive repository of Jamaican music they now own the Castle label, which has issued many excellent oldies CDs and has a very enviable soul back catalogue. They also own the entire Pye label, a giant of '60s pop music.

Laurence Cane-Honeysett of Trojan Records states 'After the sale went through, I was given the job as the Jamaican-music consultant. In fact, among the regular staff at the old owners of Trojan, I ended up being the only employee working for the company's new owners, but knowing and being a friend of John Reed's was obviously a great help, and he made sure I felt at home straight away. Soon I got to know everyone there, and I can say in all honesty, without exception, they're a genuinely lovely bunch of people.

'But back at the beginning of Sanctuary's ownership, it was all a little daunting and I wasn't sure how things would progress. Thankfully, we soon developed a workable system, which has worked well ever since. Now, John – who soon after the sale of Trojan to Sanctuary was made head of the whole Mid-Price division – and myself sort out the schedule together and deal with the day-to-day situations that need to be addressed, which can mean all manner of things, from the promotion of a certain release to working with a producer or artist.

'While John is in overall charge of everything that we release, he's obviously involved in all number of releases on the various Mid-Price – or Special Markets, as it's now termed – labels. So, in terms of getting new Trojan releases out, on a practical level it's up to me to manage things, from a creative perspective. I still do a large percentage of the compiling, although we're very keen to keep the appeal of the releases as broad as possible, so we do use freelancers to write liner notes and occasionally come up with new angles for releases, and of course I have to oversee their contributions.

'Among those who have recently undertaken work on Trojan releases are some really knowledgeable and respected people, including Dave Hendley, Noel Hawks, Stephen Nye, David Katz, Jeremy Collingwood, Mike Atherton and some bloke called Michael de Koningh. But of course, as you can imagine, after all these years, every obvious idea under the sun has been submitted to Trojan for release. I myself have put forward hundreds of ideas, of which a small percentage have seen release to date.

'Aside from compiling and working with contributors, there are other aspects of getting the releases together, and these include helping Richard Jaskeran and Mike Mastragelo in Archives find the best sources for the necessary recordings, coming up with all the information regarding label copy, sorting out the visual material for the booklets, briefing the designers and of course checking the final product, both in terms of the artwork and aurally.

'This is just to give you an idea of what's involved creatively from my point of view. There are, of course, other aspects, such as mastering and design, and the work of those who co-ordinate and oversee things in terms of the production – most notably Joe Smith and Nick Bourne – is essential in getting the releases together.

'Apart from the releases, there are other sides to my work, including liaising with Business Affairs, Contracts and Licensing and writing monthly sales sheets on all the Trojan releases. Other than that, I'm also there to assist, when necessary, [former Trojan employee] Dorothy Howe and Coalition, who handle all the PR for the releases, while I also check out and report on any new repertoire that's offered to us. So it's a pretty varied role, and while it's certainly hard work sorting out five CD releases and at least an additional three vinyl releases each month, it can be hugely rewarding. It's still early days, really, but I like to think that we can maintain the momentum and that, through our work, Trojan will continue to be arguably the world's greatest classic-reggae label.'

Nowadays, most of the production work for Trojan releases is done at external specialist studios, who are able to run the source through a Cedar unit, which can identify and remove the clicks and pops which are inherent in old vinyl records. The production process has come a long way since Joe Sinclair dubbed from Jamaican vinyl records to master Trojan's UK singles.

Laurence Cane-Honeysett gives a quick run-through of the procedure: 'First, we decide on a release and compile a track listing, and that needs to be checked, in terms of the rights of usage. Then they are submitted to the MCPS for clearance. This ensures that the right people are paid royalties for their work. At this stage, each recording is given an individual code. In the meantime, the best sources are located, whether it's master tape, CD, exabyte, DAT [Digital Audio Tape] or vinyl.'

Sound engineer Nick Bourne explains the process for non-boffins: 'The new album will usually be recorded onto an exabyte. An exabyte is essentially a digital tape, bigger than a DAT and much better to use as a CD master than any other format. The reason is that you can encode it accurately, with PQ points and ISR codes, which is vital for CD masters. A DAT would only be able to hold less accurate ID points.

'PQs are literally pauses and cues, the times when the album has breaks in it and so on, and the ISR (Internatonal Standard Recording) codes are basically track identities. Each track, even different versions and variations, will have its own code to identify it. The code is on the label copy which gives the publisher, artist, composer and title, etc, so it is needed for royalties, in particular. If a track was played on the radio, for example, the code would be registered and royalties duly paid.

'The exabyte is sent up for a glass master to be made. A glass master is what a CD is made from, and this is in fact an extremely complicated process.'

'If we don't possess a clean digital copy of a recording,' adds Laurence, 'we either try to buy the original record or ask a collector if we can borrow his copy. Once all the sources are assembled, the release goes to mastering. It's at this stage that all the Cedaring – de-clicking, de-hissing and de-crackling – is done. We're then sent a CD-R of the mastered release for approval, which I will check along with the compiler.

'In the meantime, the sleeve notes need to be written, pictures sourced and the designer briefed. With Trojan, I sort out images and brief the designers. They then design a cover and, once it's approved by John and myself, it's used for the sales sheets, which also contain a blurb about the release (which I write for the Trojan releases), and this is then sent to the appropriate sales people at Sanctuary and subsequently on to all the retailers and distributors around the world who stock our releases.

'Once the liner notes and all the pictures are in, they're submitted to the designer, who sets about designing the rest of the package: booklet, liner tray and on-body label. He liaises with the product manager and consultant – in Trojan's case, Joe Smith and me respectively – and to a lesser extent with John Reed, the overall manager.'

A particular gripe that collectors have levelled at the past three owners of Trojan is their continual reissuing of the work of the most prominent artists, such as Bob Marley and Lee Perry. But the hard fact is that, whenever another collection of work by one of these seminal artists hits the streets, it promptly outsells every other Trojan release. Long-term collectors, of course, know these works inside out, but it must be remembered that reggae is one of the few musical styles that has a continuing influx of eager young, new appreciators, and it is to them that Trojan offer these compilations. For the die-hard specialist collector, expert compilers like David Katz, Dave Hendley, Noel 'Harry Hawk' Hawks and Trojan's own Laurence Cane-Honeysett offer their authoritative knowledge in bringing together outstanding releases. Thus the Sanctuary/Trojan label aims to cover all markets with their release programme, with something for all levels of Jamaican music collectors.

John Reed, who managed the Special Markets division of which Trojan was a part, appreciated the value of the reggae label: 'Trojan Records is a rare thing. Like Blue Note, Motown, Factory, Elektra and all the other great labels, it crystallises an era and is synonymous with a type of music from that era. In Trojan's case, they dominated the reggae explosion from 1968 to 1975 – a quick look at the reggae charts at the time reveals that they sometimes boasted 80 per cent of the best-sellers in any given week. Trojan, in short, was the Jamaican Motown.

'But unlike many other great labels, Trojan had never benefited from proper marketing. While many of their individual packages were strong and several initiatives over the years – like those cute three-CD box sets – were inspired, there was a feeling that the quality of the concepts and the packaging wasn't always as strong. And somehow, Trojan had failed to tap into that wider heartland of people who either grew up listening to it or belatedly discovered it. So our first priority was to prune the existing catalogue back, hence a major deletions programme in the first few months. Meanwhile, we worked on a schedule of releases which aimed at the various types of reggae fan. And finally, we searched high and low for a design house who could capture the rough-and-ready appeal of Trojan – and that company was Mystery Design, who have played a crucial part in rebranding the label.'

John explains the various categories into which modern Trojan releases fall:

Artist Anthologies

'Whether one- or two-CD sets, or more, these single out artists who are poorly represented or who needed a one-stop release for the casual buyer. So Bob Marley, Max Romeo, Horace Andy, Augustus Pablo and many others have been given this treatment.'

Artist 'Best Ofs'

'A quick look down the hit artists within Trojan revealed that they were poorly served with basic entreés – introductions – so all the hit artists are being treated to single-CD collections: Desmond Dekker, The Upsetters, Bob and Marcia, Toots and The Maytals, The Pioneers, etc.'

'Genre Collections'

'One of the backbones of the new Trojan thus far has been a series of mainly two-CD various-artists collections that aim to define a given era or style within Jamaican music. So we did *Rough & Tough* (ska), *Let's Do Rocksteady*, *Punky Reggae Party* (late '70s), *A Place Called Africa* ('70s roots), *Flashing Echo* (dub), *Funky Kingston* (funky reggae), *Work Your Soul* ('60s soul), *Dancehall '69* (skinhead reggae), *High Explosion* (DJ) and so on.

'Part of the appeal here is the attractive and evocative artwork, with the generic slipcases featuring various Trojan labels across the top and the masking tape, which gives them a kind of DIY feel. Partly inspired by the superb artwork of companies like Soul Jazz and partly by the original Trojan look, this has managed to capture the appeal of the music, thereby introducing it to new audiences, as well as coming as a welcome surprise to older, perhaps more jaded fans.'

CLASSIC ALBUMS
'From the legendary *Tighten Up* series to landmark LPs by the likes of Jimmy Cliff, The Wailers, U Roy, Prince Buster, John Holt, The Maytals and Lee Perry, another facet of the new Trojan is to draw out classic LPs and re-present them as deluxe editions – often two-CD sets – with numerous bonus tracks. Part of the reason for this is that the Trojan catalogue was swamped with a plethora of various artist sets which, collectively, seemed to have no rhyme or reason – of course, they did individually, but not necessarily as a whole. Also, there was no sense of the "classics", so in a way, we're applying a rock-music approach to Trojan in a way which other record companies, post-Island, have done.'

THE TROJAN BOX SETS
'Despite all these initiatives, it was clear from the sales figures we inherited that we'd be insane not to continue the wonderfully simple three-CD box sets. Retail chains loved them, punters collected them – the only problem has been coming up with new concepts to keep the series alive! We've had some fun with projects like *Mod Reggae*, *X-Rated* and *Calypso* while also serving up real rarities on my favourite from 2002, *Reggae Revive*, and others. Long may this series continue! *Trojan Sisters* was given five stars in *Mojo*, so we still seem to be getting it right. But we can also dig deeper with something like the *Nyahbinghi* box set. Let's face it, outside hardcore reggae circles, no one's ever heard of Nyahbinghi!'

TV-ADVERTISED PROJECTS
'Aah, now we're talking. Part of Sanctuary's development in the last two years has been to enter the shark-infested waters of TV advertising, and so far, so successful. When Trojan was purchased, we knew we had a reggae hits package to rival anyone's, but none of us really expected *Young, Gifted And Black* to sell so well. A Top 5 compilation album that went gold within a couple of months, it wiped the floor with the competition to become the must-have classic reggae compilation.

'Comforted by this success, we lined up a companion follow-up, *Reggae Love Songs*, to try to crack the bearpit that is the Valentine's market. Every major record company hits this hard, and yet *Reggae Love Songs* got to Number Two – beaten only by the *8 Mile* soundtrack – outselling the competition, going silver week one, gold week two and significantly ruffling the feathers of those major record-company executives involved in back-catalogue TV-advertised projects. We have no doubt *Reggae Love Songs* will go platinum – it's already the fastest selling album that Sanctuary or Castle have ever released. And there'll be more to come, including *Young, Gifted And Black II* and possible joint ventures with other record companies.'

AND NOW FOR THE COLLECTORS...

'There has been much criticism of the new Trojan's willingness to revisit the tried and tested. First reason: the best-sellers are still the best-sellers. John Holt's *1,000 Volts* outsold pretty well everything else last year, other than the mighty three-CD box sets and the TV albums. Also, the initial feedback from UK retail was pessimistic – a lot of Trojan material had been licensed out to third parties, including many budget labels, and the feeling was that the racks were full. Oh, how wrong they were, in terms of sales potential of new product. But it's taken time to build retail's confidence, and that process started by revamping the titles they knew had a solid sales history.

'BUT! We have also tried to cater for collectors. If year zero for new Trojan was January 2002, then we kicked off with *Jamaican Memories*, the legendary Blue Cat collectable. *The Birth Of Trojan* included all the As and Bs from the original 1967 Trojan label. And Mark Lamarr's new collection, *Nuclear Weapon*, boasts rare or previously unissued Duke Reid productions from way back in 1962. Meanwhile, Dave Hendley re-presented his classic *Rebel Music* title, and many of the compilations boast rare tracks.

'As we roll through 2003, expect more albums aimed squarely at the reggae collector's market as other series kind of run their course. Albums might be devoted to individual producers, artists, labels and eras. It doesn't matter how it's compiled, Trojan has room for everything.'

4 Music History – Part 1

1950s To 1967 – R&B To Rocksteady

As the rockin' and rollin' US R&B sounds progressed into their Kingston equivalent at the tail end of the 1950s, other forces were afoot within the confines of music creation. The Jamaican beat was loping forward into the first true sound of the West Kingston ghetto as shuffle beat took hold and became the staple diet of the dancehalls. Many dancefloor heroes' light twists across the floor gained them recognition in the social ranking of the ghetto. It was also a tentative step towards escape from the grinding tedium of the slum, with the hope of making their own music for the dance one day.

As those dancers shuffled their moves across the lawns, one day in 1959 Prince Buster was taking a revolutionary step himself. In Kingston's studio, he had ensconced three brothers with a song, plus a group of the blackheart men – those men who were shunned by all mothers, who berated their children to stay away lest the men's twisted locks should touch them and cause them to have chill dreams in the hot night.

These were the Rastamen, the outcasts of society whom no self-respecting citizen would be seen dead talking to, men who lived in the distant hills or in the dankest of ghetto townships. Chief Rasta Elder, Count Ossie, was laying down a drumbeat for Buster that was so different from the norm it could have been crafted in a different country – a beat closer to dusty Ethiopia than to colonial Britain, closer to Mother Africa than to Uncle Sam. Into this framework, the three Folkes Brothers – John, Meko and Junior – wove a simple, hauntingly sung song of love for a girl called Carolina.

In 1960, society was still trying to forget the black history which the Rastafarians spoke of with hot biblical references. This was the time when budding record producers still rejected the swelling mass feelings of the lower classes which the Rastas imbibed along with their communal chalice of herb. Yet here was a major player in the 'sound' stakes, not only accepting Count Ossie and his brethren but encouraging them to break new ground by committing the very sound of Rasta to vinyl.

Time has shown that the Rasta-percussive 'Oh Carolina' made headway both in Kingston and, more surprisingly, in London, where the newly formed Melodisc Records subsidiary Blue Beat took it up in early 1961. It was a song and sound way ahead of the times, and rarely would the Rasta Nyahbinghi (drumming and chanting) break through the wall of negative oppression that society had built around it until the red, gold and green 1970s. Buster himself would record many gospel-slanted gospel sides in the early '60s, but it would be a long time before he opened up the heartland of Rasta-Afrika in the studio again.

Jamaican independence, on 8 August 1962, was called from the very rooftops of Kingston as the city and the whole country celebrated their freedom from a distant motherland. A young Jimmy Cliff recorded an anthem of love for both his girl and his country, 'Miss Jamaica', for Leslie Kong, using the new ska sound to propel his cheery lyrics. The loping shuffle beat had moved up a notch by then and, with an input from the jazz masters of JA, such as guitarist Ernest Ranglin and trombonist Don Drummond, had snapped into place as ska.

A rough-and-ready rhythm from the poor quarter, dominated by former Alpha Boys' School musicians slotting jazz and blues riffs into the hypnotic framework, ska blew away all that had gone before it as it injected the dancehalls with an electric power to move you until you dropped.

In particular, the short-lived band The Skatalites had no rivals as they tore through mighty instrumentals for producers like Coxson, Buster and Justin Yap, to name but three lucky recipients of their combined talents. Yap's Top Deck, Tuneico and Sound Deck labels never made the big time, but with the likes of Jackie Opel on vocals and the mighty Skatalites blazing behind him, there was no better music to be heard in the hot city in 1965.

In 1963, Prince Buster released the loping ska of 'Madness', a title that would be remembered not just because of its compelling call to dance but as an echo of the future, when the best Two-Tone band of the late '70s adopted it as their name. Then, prophetically, in 1965 he issued the gangster-themed 'Al Capone', complete with tommy-gun fire and screeching car tyres. The record's theme was too close for comfort, however, and the ska era faded with the hot summer of 1966 as the angry ghetto youths known as Rude Boys took to the streets.

The 'Rudies' had grown from the impoverished rural folk who had moved to the city, hoping for work, as the new dawn of independence had risen. In reality, that dawn broke over hundreds of hapless people confused by the city and unable to find work or shelter. They gravitated to the poor areas and scratched out livings there, seething with discontent as the promise of a brave new world was not fulfilled.

The complete antithesis of their impoverished background resulted in their sharply dressed, coolly shaded sons frequenting the dancehalls and bars, almost denying in their manner and clothes the very essence of where they lived. The Rudies were rough and tough, ruling their areas, running around town, causing disturbance and drawing comment from newspapers and singers alike.

That summer of 1966 was too hot to dance to ska, and a tryst between the musicians (who also came from the rough end of town) and the Rudies saw the musical pace dropping from a gallop to a walk. The Ethiopians' recording 'Train To Skaville' was ska in name only, with its insistent chugging beat and catchy peep peep vocals. This was the new sound of rocksteady, the cool Rudies' music.

Violence was rife and ever-worsening at that time, as the Rudies ripped up the town. Desmond Dekker's '007 Shanty Town', resplendent with its shimmering rocksteady beat, commented on the situation and gave Dekker a taste of things to come as his record reached the UK charts in the summer of 1967.

Not to be outdone, Jamaican London saw the Rudies carving up their native city (and each other), and the fragile-voiced Dandy penned and sang 'Rudy A Message To You', a view from afar which was still pertinent in its comment. This gentle berating of the Rude-Boy culture was later recut in 1979 by The Specials, using the same trombonist from the original version, that stalwart of the London scene Rico Rodriguez.

But rocksteady wasn't all about the Rudies and their wayward habits; it could be the essence of beauty, with majestically sweeping horns gently driving the incomparable tight harmonies of groups such as The Paragons and The Techniques, who modelled themselves on wonderful US soul acts like Curtis Mayfield and his Impressions. The sound was all about sweet harmonies and haunting melodies, something Mayfield knew inside out. He became the musical icon of the age in Kingston, with every street corner collective trying to capture that sweet bitterness. There were instrumentals, too, by sultry horn masters like Roland Alphonso and Lester Sterling which graced many a dance and echoed through the balmy nights on RJR.

Duke Reid was the past-master of rocksteady. He did little production work personally, but his funds lured the exemplary talents of Tommy McCook and The Supersonics to create such gentle dreams as 'The Tide Is High', written and sung by a pre-solo John Holt and The Paragons. A decade and a half later, the song became a hit for both punk-poppers Blondie and UK girl group Atomic Kitten.

Rocksteady had a brief but illustrious life, flitting across the dancehalls and airwaves for no more than a couple of summers before a new, brasher rhythm made Kingston's dancers sweat again. It was the new sound of the reggay.

5 Music History – Part 2

1968 To 1972 – Reggay To Strings

The Maytals' blasting 'Do The Reggay' from 1968 kicked the dancers back to wild abandon after the shimmer of rocksteady. You just couldn't shimmer when Toots Hibbert started ripping out his lines. The song, such as it was, was interspersed with wild yelps of fervour from his cohorts and aided by a pounding rhythm so intense that it was literally a pulsating wall of sound.

Toots's gospel-drenched voice had long graced superior discs, from ska masterpieces like 'Hallelujah' and 'Mathew Mark' to crunching rocksteady gems such as the ganja-rap '54-46, That's My Number' and the howling call-and-response of 'Struggle'. Now he dropped like no other onto the new sound of the reggay, reggie or reggae.

'Bangarang', by singer Stranger Cole and alto-saxman supreme Lester Sterling, was another early reggie piece that made a big impression. In a TV interview, its producer, Bunny Lee, cited it as the very first record with the new beat, but many others also claim that coveted first, and we shall probably never know whose claim is true. A chugging non-entity of a song with a slightly ribald slant, 'Bangarang's rhythm did it all as it spun across the Atlantic to London and found eager new listeners keen to hear more of this new rhythmic structure.

By 1969, the musical iceberg was floating in, and this was reggae time in the truest sense, with the latest generation of producers finding new variations on the sound almost every day. London was basking in the freshest rhythms and, bolstered by the new white appreciation of the music, swiftly became a greedy market for reggae, whether flown in from Kingston or concocted by new local producers such as Dandy. Old-established labels like Doctor Bird, Studio

One and Coxsone were given the boot by the new buyers, with only Blue Beat's resurgence as Fab really taking on the reggae and dropping into vacant slots in collectors' boxes. Discerning fans of more mellow tastes were going for Clement Dodd's new UK label, Bamboo, with its burbling Jackie Mittoo organ rhythms, but the big two who were squaring up for the marketplace battle in 1969 were Trojan and Pama.

Max Romeo's smutty 'Wet Dream' took London by storm in May 1969, slipping up to Number Ten and hanging in the charts for 24 weeks without a single play on national radio. Adopting the 1968 rhythm utilised by old hand Derrick Morgan for his 'Hold You Jack' and new, cheeky lyrics, it sold an astounding 250,000 non-chart return copies. This delighted its label owners, Pama, on whose Unity offshoot it appeared, along with the pirate radio stations that did play it and the kids who smirked at Max's near-the-knuckle lyrics. But it didn't delight the BBC or the music press, which derided its rude lyrics and repetitive rhythm.

Desmond Dekker was luckier with his (to some) lyrically incomprehensible 'Israelites'. 'Get up in the morning, baked beans for breakfast' was the playground chant of school kids. Little did they know of the painful reality: Dekker was actually singing, 'Get up in the morning, slaving for bread, Sir'! Nevertheless, the disc kicked Marvin Gaye's 'I Heard It Through The Grapevine' from the top spot in March 1969, only to be busted a week later by The Beatles' 'Get Back'.

Dekker's choppy follow-up, 'It Mek', grabbed a very respectable Number Seven position in June the same year, while 'Pickney Girl' only touched the 42nd slot during a brief chart run post-Christmas. All three records appeared on the familiar yet soon-to-disappear Pyramid label, which was resurrected by Trojan a few years later.

Trojan moved into the chart stakes with ace producer Lee Perry, whose spaghetti western spoof 'Return Of Django', on his dedicated Upsetter label, rocked its way to Number Five in October, causing a spate of reggae records referring to Clint Eastwood and his outlaw Mexican buddies. Spaghetti was big in Jamaica – not the edible kind but master film director Sergio Leone's out-of-lip-sync flicks, which transfixed the small island with their reckless gunplay and dauntless heroes.

Trojan must have loved this offshoot label, for such was 'Scratch' Perry's prestige with the fervent new appreciators that any new Upsetter single would fly out of the shops unheard. One of Scratch's most loved records was called

'Live Injection', but Trojan saw it as a very healthy cash injection and a stab at Pama, who also juggled Perry's product on various imprints, notably their flashy Punch label.

A well-reggae-documented scientific wonder of the age was 1969's US moon landing. Almost as soon as Neil Armstrong's foot had pushed up the dust and made one small step, 'Moon Hop' landed. Recorded in London by old hand Derrick Morgan (who had relocated there to be closer to his new-found fan base) and premier UK band The Rudies, it was a dancer of sheer wanton enjoyment. A throbbing walking bass line aided by a yeah-yeah-yeah chorus and Derrick's exhortations added up to a skinhead delight, a moon-stomper *par excellence*. Indeed, it was so good that it scraped into the charts at Number 49 in January the following year, after selling by the cartload to all and sundry for months.

Such was the popularity of 'Moon Hop' that a replica recording entitled 'Skinhead Moonstomp' was hastily issued on the Doctor Bird subsidiary label Treasure Isle. The very capable outfit Symarip, who were the Pyramids more or less spelled backwards, had already made their mark in the soul and blue-beat field on the President label with their 'Train Tour To Rainbow City', which had reached a very respectable Number 35 in 1967. 'Skinhead Moonstomp' became a club anthem, with lead-singer/boss skinhead Caleb announcing that he had the biggest boots and encouraging listeners to give it some of that 'old moonstompin'' across a mighty can't-keep-still rhythm.

Excited by its success, Trojan knocked together an album on the back of the single's popularity. The band shot was relegated to the back cover, while the front threatened any potential buyer with a full-cover photo of trying-to-look-tough skinheads, giving an obvious indication of the market at which the LP was aimed. Schoolkids everywhere pranced around with the LP – the ultimate status symbol of the moment if you could afford it – but very few actually played the thing, with its slightly hopeful sounds that didn't quite capture the spirit of reggae at its British best. The album's allure was similar to that of the trashy *Skinhead* novels written by Richard Allen: great cover, shame about the contents.

The sound of reggae – as it had become universally known, although the odd news piece still tried variants on the spelling, while some out-of-date scribes still called it by its old mod name of blue beat – now ruled London's dances. Every session was full of foot-moving gems of the new beat, alongside Tamla and Atlantic classics and some fresh soul nuggets. But it was the reggae, with its sweaty bass and pounding piano, that rocked the place. Some of the best records were now home-grown, like Dandy's cheerful 'Reggae In Your Jeggae'. No one had the faintest idea what a jeggae was, but they grooved along to this London-recorded sound anyhow. They grooved so hard, in fact, that many thought it would touch the national charts. As it turned out, due to heavy sales in shops that didn't file sales returns to the all-important BBC, it soared unnoticed.

Dandy did, however, nibble the nationals with his buddy Tony Tribe and a take on an old Neil Diamond song, 'Red Red Wine', on Trojan's new Downtown imprint. It hit the big five-oh for one week in July 1969, then resurfaced in August for one more week, this time finding its final resting place at Number 46. Tony was kitted out in the latest trendy gear of boots and braces for his debut (and only) *Top Of The Pops* appearance, paying homage to the new appreciators who eagerly snapped up the reggae.

As they had done with Mr Upsetter Perry, Trojan had inaugurated a label specially for Dandy's work, both as a singer and for his rhythmic London reggae productions. Kicking off in 1968, Downtown became synonymous with strong organ-led pumps aimed equally at the shaven-headed masses and West Indian buyers. After a run of productions that excelled in power, Dandy discovered sweet-voiced singer Audrey Hall and skipped off to MOR-reggae balladeering, much to the disgust of his many fans, who required a decent throb to their beat.

Jamaican vocal trio The Pioneers raced into the Top 40 with their paean to a racehorse that died in service. The wonderfully titled 'Long Shot Kick The Bucket' told the sorry tale of the horse that gave its all in a race at Caymanas Park, Kingston, and expired. The subject matter may have been sad, but Trojan Records were jumping up and down with joy as the tune cracked the national charts and stuck there for ten weeks, hitting Number 21 in October 1969.

At the same time that poor Long Shot's death was being musically exploited, 'Liquidator', a searing Hammond workout by the ubiquitous Harry J All Stars, clicked in at Number Nine during an amazing 20-week chart run through the tail end of 1969. It was a *tour de force* of instrumental reggae funded by Harry Johnson and played by crack sessioners led by Winston Wright, riding the mighty B3. It was held back from climbing higher by The Archies' prophetic-for-UK-reggae 'Sugar Sugar', which hovered at the Number One slot.

Another rhythmic rider into the charts was The Melodians' 'Sweet Sensation', recorded for ace producer Leslie Kong and grabbed by Trojan

Records as a sure-fire club favourite. It managed Number 41 for just one week in January 1970. The Melodians also created the musical template for the disco-pop favourite 'Rivers Of Babylon', as used by Boney-M to infiltrate the nation in April 1978, when they grabbed Number One with the supposedly pious piece.

A talented young singer and songwriter, James Chambers, reinventing himself as Jimmy Cliff, had made his mark way back as Independence and ska had boogied across Jamaica. By the time most of Great Britain came to hear of him, he had notched up minor hits with Trojan's then masters Island Records. Come 1969, his star rose far above the white-rock grooming that Island had planned for him as the bright and hopeful 'Wonderful World, Beautiful People' took him to Number Six in October, its cheery overtones belying a message of profound hope.

Jimmy's follow-up, 'Vietnam', cut straight to the jugular, although still retaining a smile in its sound, popping in at Number 47 in February 1970 and then popping out again before slipping back in the following week to better its placing by just one position. No doubt the climb of the single was hampered by the political message in its lyric content.

Returning to the Island label, Cliff then issued a Cat Stevens cover, 'Wild World', the backing on which was considerably slanted towards the white-rock world. He was rewarded with a pleasing Number Eight hit in August as 'Wild World' hung around in the charts for 12 weeks.

A month after the incisive 'Vietnam' came Bob (Andy) and Marcia (Griffiths)'s supercharged cover of the black-rights anthem 'Young, Gifted And Black'. Hit-making producer Harry J had scored again – the disc reached Number Five in March 1970. Nina Simone's epic cry had been overlaid with a string section and beefed up by The Harry J All Stars to create a swinging, harmonious joy, so reggae that many were surprised to find an American song hidden beneath the Caribbean sun. Pama Records issued the self-same recording untouched by the London-dubbed string arrangement, but it gained little ground as the Trojan version grappled the ladder of success.

Bob and Marcia's follow-up single release was 'Pied Piper', a jolly nonsense affair first recorded by US group Changin' Times in 1965 and later a British hit for Crispian St Peters. Jolly nonsense it may have been, but it was serious business for Trojan as it reached Number 11 and filled their coffers as it hovered around for 13 weeks. Gone but not forgotten by Bob was the angry social comment that hid in 'Young, Gifted And Black''s grooves. Bob Andy was to emerge as one of Jamaica's finest songwriters as the soon-to-be-dread decade moved on, and his accomplished works and words still echo alongside Marley's as a prophetic judgement on those times.

Toots and The Maytals also courted the glittering chart in April 1970, first on the bottom rung at Number 50 and then again in May, when they re-entered and clambered up to Number 47 with the song 'Monkey Man', which had Toots regaling the world with the tale of a past girlfriend who had taken up with a man who was such an oaf that he must surely be part ape. Aided by producer Leslie Kong's finest bouncing rhythm, 'Monkey Man' scored well for the soulful Toots, and Trojan gathered together some Maytals/Kong gems on an album of the same name.

The Maytals never gained chart superstardom, but their uplifting belters like 'Pressure Drop', 'Sweet And Dandy' and the revamped '54-46 Was My Number' absolutely wrecked many a dancefloor with their impassioned power. To black and white alike, Frederick 'Toots' Hibbert was one of the finest voices ever to come out of Jamaica – or anywhere else, for that matter – and his records slid into the boxes of every DJ and collector.

As The Maytals were monkeying around, ex-Technique Bruce Ruffin was first tasting the big time with a moody version of Jose Feliciano's 'Rain' which took Trojan and him to Number 19 in May. His only other mainstream success would come on a different label, Rhino, with the lightweight sugar-reggae of 'Mad About You', which gave him a Number Nine.

As Mungo Jerry chugged 'In The Summertime' to Number One in June 1970, the distinctively voiced Cecil 'Nicky' Thomas called to mind the less fortunate people of the world with the melodic 'Love Of The Common People'. This gave Trojan a Number Nine and would give Paul Young a second hit over a decade later in 1983, after he had pinched a Marvin Gaye song for his first triumph.

Desmond 'Israelites' Dekker attacked the charts in a big way through August 1970 with the Jimmy Cliff-penned 'You Can Get It If You Really Want' and was kept from the crest only by Elvis, whose 'Wonder Of You' stayed at Number One for six weeks. Hovering in the second spot, 'You Can Get It' pushed hard during a 15-week chart run but couldn't quite crack the Presley barrier. Even now, the song is one of the all-time favourite reggae tracks at any oldies get-together.

Freddie Notes and The Rudies took singer Bobby Bloom's 'Montego Bay' – a song in praise of the paradise beach inhabited by the wealthy of Jamaica

115

– to Number 45 in October 1970 with one of their customary reggae romps. The Rudies, being a highly versatile band, took rock, soul and reggae in their stride, but unfortunately for them their fans wanted only their best pulsing London-to-JA beat. Mr Notes would decamp a little while later to travel a more expressive path than that offered by a reggae session band. In keeping with many artists, Notes had no wish to be pigeonholed as 'just a reggae singer' and saw the glittering lights of rock, soul and pop as his street paved with gold.

Beneath the glittering sea of the national chart swam a multitude of supercharged reggae records as the new decade slid into its second year. For those in the know and with full enough pockets, a voyage to Joe's Record Shack or Desmond's Hip City on a Saturday afternoon was the highlight of the week. It was then that the new and eminently desirable discs would be aired to the public.

You could hear the rhythmic thump way up along the pavement before your destination was in sight, and gaudy album sleeves would line the shop window, with smiling half-naked girls vying for space with the gospel according to country giant Jim Reeves. The West Indian love of ballads, country music and the odd sacred sound were almost at odds with the ribald chant to dance from such masters as Lee Perry, whose new record(s) of the week would get continual plays until all the copies were sold.

Most people had heard of Perry The Upsetter and his 'Django' hit, but it was his powerhouse rhythms, which the national-chart-lovers never heard, that really got the shop on its toes. Sticky, grinding sounds like the western-inspired 'Sipreano', who always shoots first were bought avidly. The Reggae Boys' chant-like 'Ba Ba' and its flipside organ version, 'Power Cut' (courtesy of the Upsetter's Hammond man, Glen Adams) rocked the very foundations of the shop on Pama's garish Gas label. ('Power Cut' was actually Perry's 'Cold Sweat' without the spoken introduction, which Pama rival Trojan had licensed from Mr Upsetter, but who cared? You bought them both anyway. That way you had both versions to confound your friends with that evening.)

Names like Lloyd Charmers and Derrick Harriott brought an instant grin when a new disc was brought forth over the shop counter and very rarely failed to gain approval. Both producers were old hands at the game and had retuned their output to the rocking reggae of the day. Charmers' '5 To 5' and 'In The Spirit', with their fast-heartbeat bass lines and breathy exhortations, instantly hit the spot, while Harriott and his Crystalites band organned up The Kingstonians' mighty 'Sufferer' rhythm and retitled it 'Splash Down', to the immense approval of the dancers' feet. He also whipped out the intense Whitfield-Strong social conscience of 'Message From A Black Man', reggae-tuned to hypnotic effect and reggae-funked with John Shaft.

Not only was Kingston rocking the shop but the UK guys were having a ball as well. Organ-led instrumentals like The Rudies' 'The Split', which was hidden away on the flipside of a mediocre reggae cover of Clarence Carter's soul gem 'Patches', got the shop play and audience fever. 'The Split' was reused some two years later as 'Dread' and graced the flip to Judge Dread's 'Big Seven'.

London soundmen also had a go, such as Clancy 'Sir' Collins, who had already tried his hand at the rocksteady sound and who now went for the reggae. His few releases ranged between sentimental love songs aimed squarely at his West Indian clientele and fearsome, moody organ-fests directed at the new appreciators of the sound. His best, though, had to be the in-your-face 'Black Panther', with an unnamed DJ and eerie organ running over a bass to bust up the place.

Lambert Briscoe and his London-based Hot Rod Sound moved from speaker boxes to vinyl and zeroed in on the skinheads with sharp, bright instrumentals. Unfortunately, his records on the Trojan Hot Rod and Torpedo labels were so obscure that, even if you wanted one, the chances were that you would never find a copy to buy.

Laurel Aitken had climbed aboard the 'Skinhead Train' before most and knew just what buttons to push to gain a super-seller in the new market. Pama favoured him with the Nu Beat label, in return for which he favoured them with cash from such skinhead staples as 'Woppi King', 'Jesse James' and 'Pussy Price'. Even his commentary on politician Enoch Powell's chilling 'rivers of blood' speech on immigration control, 'Run Powell Run', received hefty sales and nightspot plays.

Trojan also enticed him, and he growled his way through some DJ work for them – like the ever-popular 'Dracula Prince Of Darkness' title – under the name of his alter-ego, King Horror. By 1970, Laurel was in his James Brown soul phase and funked out 'Reggae Popcorn' and 'Sex Machine' alongside some reggae balladeering on the newly restyled Pama New Beat label.

As 1970 turned to winter, the chattering Kingston DJ work of such absurd names as Dennis Alcapone and U Roy were breaking new ground and giving the old-time singers plenty of trouble when it came to staying afloat in the charts. Everyone liked the DJs, or *toasters* – black, white or indifferent all rushed to grab hot tracks like Hugh 'U' Roy's 'Tom Drunk'. The new-style DJ records' popularity started to rise as the skinhead numbers peaked.

March 1971 saw one of Kingston's most distinctive voices making a break for the national charts. Dave (Barker) and Ansel Collins' 'Double Barrel' whipped up a storm as Dave rapped Yankee-style over keyboardist Ansel's running-bass-led track. The sound was deliberately different, the sound of now, then. The brash DJ had ridden in as he had in Jamaica, talking up rhymes and rocking the public. The song shot to Number One and stayed in the charts for 15 weeks, making a mint for Trojan, on whose Techniques subsidiary label it had appeared. The United States were also receptive to the new DJ sound and 'Double Barrel' hit Number 22 in the *Billboard* Hot 100.

In June, the two non-brothers came again with 'Monkey Spanner' and secured the Number Seven spot before Ansel Collins headed back home. Dave dropped anchor in London, using the stage name Dave Collins to get a little work. Meanwhile, Trojan whipped out the *Double Barrel* LP full of organ workouts and Dave's yelping vocals, and even managed to license it Stateside, where it appeared on the Big Tree label. However, US citizens weren't as broad-minded as London dwellers, and a mirror-image nude girl residing in the cartoon gun barrels on the sleeve front had to be sent home as American tastes obviously couldn't take such a beauty.

After Mr Notes' departure, London's premier moonstomp band, The Rudies, reconfigured as Greyhound and promptly nabbed a smash hit on Trojan with 'Black And White', which hit Number Six in June 1971. Then, in 1972, they raided the charts twice, first with a smooth version of Danny Williams' 1961 favourite 'Moon River', which pushed up to Number 12 in January, and then with the jaunty 'I Am What I Am', which reached the bottom rung of the Top 20 in March.

'Moon River' came in the three-track maxi Trojan format, with a different mix to the standard brown-shield-design label. The final track on the flip was 'The Pressure Is Coming On', which was a foretaste of the angry commentary that would follow in the harsh mid 1970s and was well ahead of its time for 1972 British reggae.

Meanwhile, The Pioneers, by now relocated to these shores, issued the ultimate pop-reggae singalong tune 'Let Your Yeah Be Yeah', a song which, once heard, stuck in the grey matter all day and moved enough units for Trojan to propel the tune to Number Five in July 1971. The hits were starting to

118

come thick and fast for Trojan Records. But The Pioneers had by now begun to turn the corner into Stringsville, a path which the majority of London-based reggae performers would take over the next year. What was at first perceived as salvation would see the hits wither and desperation set in.

The last man who really flew the Trojan flag for a while was a nightclub bouncer from Snodland in Kent. Alex Hughes, or Judge Dread to his legion of fans, took his 'Big Six' to Number 11 in August 1972, and 'Big Seven' hit the Number Eight spot in December of the same year. But then, his next record – surprisingly titled 'Big Eight' – crept in unloved by the BBC to peak at Number 14 in April 1973 before the Judge changed court to the Cactus/Creole set-up and provided them with more Top 50 hits (although only one more Top Tenner, 'Je T'Aime', which reached Number Nine in July 1975) up until 1978.

As the hits switched off, the Rasta switched in across Jamaica, and although lacking in national hits, Trojan persisted in issuing some of the most accomplished Kingston recordings. These were so much at odds with their London sugar sounds that many either bought one style or the other.

The UK side, after The Gable Hall School Choir's 'Reggae Christmas' from late 1972, slipped increasingly towards the desperately happy face of string-orchestrated pop reggae. By 1973, you had on one hand The Pioneers chortling out 'At The Discotheque', a happy song of nothingness, and on the other Ken Boothe recalling Syl Johnson's epic 'Is It Because I'm Black', coupled with his own harsh 'Black, Gold And Green', two songs of majestic black pride and hope.

Meanwhile, in the same year, DJ I-Roy took the deep rhythm track of 'Black, Gold And Green', recoloured it to the Rasta 'Red, Gold And Green' and cut one of the most succinct raps of black awareness ever laid to wax for youthful producer Augustus 'Gussie' Clarke. I-Roy's *Presenting I-Roy* album, issued by Trojan in 1973, has become a benchmark for all aspiring social-commentary DJs to aspire to, and of his contemporaries only Big Youth could stand even close to his sharp, perceptive lyrics.

At this time, the divide between London and Kingston was ever widening, with new and not-so-new names offering views about the society in which they lived. Big Youth, I-Roy, Keith Hudson, Burning Spear, Bob Andy, The Abyssinians and the most well known, Robert Marley, all spoke of their observations. Marley's Upsetter-produced work from 1970 had been one of

119

the few proto-Rasta-roots type recordings which hit a chord on both sides of the Atlantic, but as 1973 rolled in it was definitely the sound of now.

Producer Perry was to go from strength to strength, his work culminating in the Black Ark sound by the turn of the decade. Trojan actively issued his work with tough new singers like Junior Byles and DJ providers like the stalwart Dennis Alcapone, along with some of his most beloved skanks in the shape of tunes like 'Jungle Lion' and the mad 'Cow Thief Skank'.

The final issue on the UK Upsetter label also took place in the spring of 1973. The top side was David Isaacs singing 'Stranger On The Shore', which was originally an instrumental Number Two hit for clarinet-playing Acker Bilk in 1961, while the flip was the side everyone wanted: 'John Devour' by a young fresh DJ named after US gangster Dillinger. Lester Bullocks was his real name and he was to progress through the 1970s to rise to the top of the DJ pile with seminal sets for Studio One and their near-namesake Channel One.

Album sleeves turned from showing pretty faces to depicting dreadlocked freedom fighters by the mid '70s as the grooves bore witness to the new roots sound, although quality singers would never be out of place and the likes of Delroy Wilson, Ken Boothe and John Holt released some exemplary work, such as Ken's album *Let's Get It On*, on which he performed new compositions and soul gems with equal ease. Indeed, 1974 found Ken riding to the top with the David Gates composition 'Everything I Own', solidly produced by veteran Lloyd Charmers, which hit the pop Number One spot in September and hung in the charts for 12 weeks. His follow-up, 'Crying Over You', gave Trojan another cash injection as it peaked at Number 11 in December of the same year.

Then, just before Christmas 1974, John Holt took Kris Kristofferson's 'Help Me Make It Through The Night' to the Number Six slot, just slipping above label-mate Ken Boothe. By then, however, running underneath the glitz of the national chart was a new-style roots rhythm courtesy of producer Bunny Lee and top youth singer Johnny Clarke. The 'flying cymbal' sound was exemplified by Johnny's stepping 'Move Out Of Babylon', issued in the UK on the Trojan Harry J imprint.

The charts might have been rocking to Ken Boothe, but the dancehalls on both side of the Atlantic were stepping to this latest bright rhythm structure, and a veritable host of variations were to follow in best Jamaican style.

The DJs were also doing the business in the better clubs for Trojan. One of the best tracks was Big Youth and youthful superstar Dennis Brown's 'Ride

On, Ride On', using Dennis' own vocal hit 'Cassandra' as its basis. Issued on what was now a free-for-all sub-label, Harry J, the Winston 'Niney' Holness production carried the swing, as Jah Youth had been doing for a couple of years with rolling chants like 'Screaming Target', 'Cool Breeze' and his formative 'Ace 90 Skank'.

Trojan then had a long wait for their next chart attack, which wasn't until April 1976, when Pluto Shervington of 'Dat' fame carried the jolly 'Ram Goat Liver' to Number 43. Still, some exemplary records were slipping out from the Trojan warehouse almost unnoticed, such as 'African Dub' by vocal group The Silvertones. A revamp of the Lee Perry-produced 'Rejoice Jah Jah Children' from a couple of years earlier, complete with militant double drumming, this shot right into any roots collector's box. It was Maytals member Jerry McCarthy who, in one of his few excursions in the producers chair, really caught the dread sound of 1977.

Other reggae hits were still occasionally infiltrating the national charts through the latter part of the 1970s, but for Trojan there was no reward, despite some fine music being issued. Althea and Donna, Barry Biggs, Dennis Brown and, of course, Bob Marley and The Wailers all scored, but sadly not for Trojan.

The revamped Attack label, in 12" form, had some heavy gems hidden between the more average items, including joys such as Jimmy Riley's harsh 'Give Thanks And Praise' and Barry Brown's tough rocker 'Mr CID'. But beyond the reggae charts little was heard of these records, as there was such a plethora of 12" vinyl scattered across every record-shop counter come the end of the decade.

It was to be the Two-Tone and ska-revival scene, which sparked in 1979 and was up and running by 1980, that gave Trojan their next hit. The old Pioneers favourite 'Long Shot', backed with 'Liquidator' from Harry J and the boys, managed a Number 42 hit in March as Madness, The Specials and a host of others rediscovered not only Jamaican music but the whole skinhead style. With the style came the reggae music of a decade earlier, and from then on Trojan divided their resources between up-to-date 1980s dancehall business and retro-reggae compilations. They had already tested the retro-water in 1979 with a series of 14 maxi Trojan four-track EPs and found success with the new fans. Available for the roots fan was the garishly sleeved *Rebel Music* double album full of early-'70s sensations, with some tracks very few people actually knew.

As Two-Tone faded in the early '80s, so did Trojan's active involvement with new Jamaican product – the die was cast for delving back rather than looking forward. The two decades that followed saw Trojan move from Rodd to Newman to Sanctuary, with each proud new owner rediscovering marvellous recordings, many thought lost forever or only to be found on scratch-ridden (and often very expensive) vinyl.

The techno-brilliance of digital cleaning has sometimes given a new lease of life to a much-played disc for both the die-hard vinyl lover who is happy to clutch a repress and the quick-stop CD-rack buyer. Through the long-play CD and the understanding of the needs of a vinyl lover, Trojan brought much of the music to life again. It has made it available to the mass market buyer and reggae lover alike. Of course the real collector elements still crave the one and only original pressing, but at least even they can hear tracks they may never have known had it not been for a Trojan compilation CD.

Bob Marley's work, for example, has seen a multitude of CD covers, with each revamped issue selling well to eager new converts, while the marketplace for Jamaican – and, let's not forget, UK-based Jamaican – music compilations has never been stronger.

The British Trojan label has been with us for 50 years at the time of writing and has seldom been in better health. In that time, the company has issued literally thousands of ska, rocksteady and reggae performances on 7" single, 12" single, LP and CD. Who knows how the reggae fans of the future will buy their music? One thing's for sure, though: whether, as U Roy advised, they play the musical disc with a flick of their wrist or, as Freddie Notes once asserted, it comes from out of the sky, you can bet that a goodly proportion of it will be on Trojan and selling by the vanload.

Leslie Hounsfield would surely approve.

6 The Mods And The Skinheads

White Appreciators Of The Jamaican Sound

The youths known as the Mods were the first British appreciators of both American soul and Jamaican ska music, and they also sparked some of the most influential home-grown bands of the 20th century, such as The Who and Small Faces.

The original Modernists appeared crisply dressed in Italian suits and clutching modern jazz albums in their manicured hands just as the '60s had dawned. Their group name was derived from their fondness for hip modern jazz, as purveyed by the likes of The Modern Jazz Quartet and Dave Brubeck, whose work they would endlessly discuss in steamy coffee bars around Soho.

This appreciation was a backlash against traditional – or 'trad' – jazz fever that was sweeping the country, with Kenny Ball and Acker Bilk heading up swinging New Orleans-style bands and drawing huge crowds in the pre-Beatles era. With the jazz came the cool image of the laid-back dude, suited in the finest continental fashion, with supple suede shoes gracing his feet.

There were few members at first, mainly because of their expensive tastes, but by 1962 the cult had grown from its small London beginnings. Shops such as His Clothes in Carnaby Street were discovered with their stocks of fine Italian and French fashions. The clothes were bold and statement-making, something that the emerging Mod desperately required. What's more, for the first time such clothes were cheap enough for those on middle incomes to afford.

Mod music, via the TV, was provided by Independent Television's trend-setting *Ready, Steady, Go!* show, hosted by Cathy McGowan, which supplied the Mod with not only the latest hip sounds but, by providing panning shots around the studio, the hippest fashions were displayed, as worn by the invited audience. Many of the audience were chosen because they were the top trend-setting 'faces' that hung around Soho and Carnaby Street and were instrumental in instigating the latest twist to the sharp fashion. With their faces on *Ready, Steady, Go!*, the programme was sure to be a winner, week in and week out.

On the day after each programme's transmission, record and clothing shops would be inundated with fashion-conscious Mods after the striped jacket 'that bloke wore on *Ready, Steady, Go!*' and the latest Motown pre-hit that had been aired for the first time.

Marc Bolan – or Mark Feld, as he was still known back then – was interviewed with a group of teenagers for *Town* magazine in 1962 and expounded about all things Mod in the first newspaper article on the growing cult, giving a new horizon for all teenagers reading his youthful words. As a 15-year-old fashion guru, he snobbishly recommended Bilgorri of Bishopsgate as a fine tailor – 'All the faces go to Bilgorri' – and moved on to comment on finding good clothes at Burton's and C&A.

The Mod preoccupation with clothes and looks was summed up in a colour feature in *The Sunday Times Magazine* of 2 August 1964. Denzil from Streatham, southwest London, commented, 'American styles are out, like madras cotton jackets... It's suits now and basket shoes... You need £15 a week to be a leader... Most Mods make between £8 and £10 a week and spend about £4 on clothes.'

'It's pure dress now,' said another face in the same interview.

The Mods had sprung up as the youth culture of the 1960s, much like the Teddy Boys of the previous decade, and like the Teds they adopted certain brands and a look as their own. Soon quality mohair suits, short neat hair, parkas (to keep the suits clean) and the all-important Lambretta scooters were pre-requisites for well-appointed clan members.

In the late 1950s, Lambretta Concessionaires Ltd, the sole distributors of Lambretta scooters in the UK, purchased commercial vehicle manufacturer Trojan Ltd as a going concern. At first, completed scooters were distributed through Trojan, but later, in order to reduce costs, they were imported in component form and assembled at the Trojan works.

Trojan Ltd continued to develop its own products, which included a Lambretta scooter sidecar. The agile Lambretta was an all-important Mod accessory for travelling around town, attracting the opposite sex and the infamous bank-holiday outings to coastal towns like Hastings and Brighton.

The difference between this time and the era of Teddy Boys was that rationing, spivs and the war were all way back in time for the Mods. While the Teds were the first generation not forced into National Service or to have ration-hungry bellies and inner-city bomb sites to wreck, the Mods had all-night cafes and the burgeoning concrete-jungle rebuilds of the same inner cities to roam around. And the Mods had new neighbours, the immigrants – mainly Jamaican West Indians – who had settled into all the major cities by the time the scooter ruled the road.

As the Modernists moved in, released from the constraints of being mini-grown-ups as their fathers had had to be, they embraced the growing club culture, both the existing London scene and the new Anglo-Jamaican sounds that were moving the feet of those in the know. It was just so trendy to mix into one of the new inner-city clubs with rocking R&B sounds shaking the grimy floor and snake-hipped Jamaicans wowing the patrons with their agile steps.

The Mods moved quickly from standing on the sidelines to picking up the young West Indian fashion epitomised by the rise of the wayward Rudie in Kingston and, more importantly, gaining a taste for the sounds of the Caribbean in the form of the new ska or blue-beat music that was shaking the Jamaican nation.

The Rude Boy problems had started in Jamaica after independence dawned in 1962, with promises of a new world of plenty for all. A multitude of rural youths and young men flocked to its capital, Kingston, searching for this promised work. The reality of the new dawn shone across hungry and homeless masses swirling round Kingston with no skill and no job. They gravitated to the only areas of the capital that could, or would, accommodate them: the ghettos.

The heat was turned up in the swollen ghettos and flashpoints ignited, with violence, injury and death commonplace. This harsh living produced the dissatisfied ghetto youth who adopted his own stance against this forced way of life: the Rude Boy, whose image was that of being cool, deadly and sharply dressed – the complete antithesis of their grinding, poverty-stricken background. Every penny they could muster was spent on dense black shades and supple patent-leather shoes to enable them to strut their stuff in the dancehall.

Soon the young UK-based Jamaicans picked up on this cool style. Word was spread via relatives still in Kingston; via *The Gleaner*, which carried daily lurid stories of their vicious antics; and via the increasingly numerous records highlighting the problem that were being played by the sound systems.

The Rude Boys' white counterparts, the Mods, who were investigating these new and exciting inner-city clubs, soon took to the snappy new West Indian dress style and adapted some of the elements into their wardrobes. Almost as quickly, they started to fill their record boxes with the records they heard played in the clubs. The obligatory pork-pie hat was closely followed by the equally mandatory Prince Buster blue-beat record into the annals of Mod must-haves, along with a cut of Jimmy Smith's grooving Hammond B3 and a Small Faces album.

Prince Buster's blazing ska recording 'Al Capone' was somewhat belatedly hoisted to Number 18 in the UK national charts in February 1967 due to the demand created by none other than the Mods, who heard it in the clubs they frequented and on pirate radio. The power of the underground consumer was starting to have teeth, and further on in the decade that same subterranean system would be the instrument that prompted the rise of reggae and Trojan Records.

But all was not well in the Mod camp early in 1967. The cult had continued to evolve into increasingly flowery thinkers and the whole thing was becoming impossibly elitist and imploding, with only the very best suits bought at Savile Row considered to be correct and supple patent-leather Italian shoes gracing the most immaculate pedicured feet. It was almost a return to the Modernist beginnings of the first years of the decade, with only the privileged few able to compete in the increasingly dandy stakes. This was fine for the well-heeled (or rich-parented) Modernist, but the ordinary guy or gal on the street didn't have much chance of joining the ranks. Many a hopeful would suffer derision for having had the misfortune to turn out in what the group perceived as the wrong shirt for an event.

Fragmentation soon appeared within the ranks. The working-class, lower-funded would-be Mods rejected the dandy paisley almost-hippy shirt-wearers and spent their limited cash in basic army-surplus and work-wear emporia, rebounding from the over-indulgence of their brothers. And so from curtained changing rooms across the country emerged the complete antithesis of the cultured highbrow, with tough weatherproof donkey jackets, army fatigues and solid work boots adopted as normal daywear. The beloved Levis hung on as the number-one jean and a quality shirt still graced the newly christened Hard Mod's back, but gone was the expensive soft, crisp and luxurious tailoring as hard denim took the brunt of the chill weather.

By the spring of 1967 the two contingents happily sat side by side, but it was obvious that a new thinking was moving the youth culture forward as more joined or changed sides, with workwear-clothed individuals infiltrating the traditional Mod groups more and more.

As the Hard Mods increased in presence, they gained the nickname of 'Peanuts' as their hair slowly became cropped even shorter. As if to mirror the tough, no-nonsense attitude to clothing, their outlook on life became very much more down to earth, no doubt a trait inherent in the very struggle of their working-class background.

By late 1968, old-school Mods had retired to art colleges and hippy communes, leaving the streets of Britain's towns open to a new group of angry young men. At first they wore army fatigues, but, like all fashions, skinhead clothing evolved. By the end of the year, every skinhead wanted a Harrington jacket and a Crombie overcoat for Christmas. The old Mod way of thinking still ran through the cult, and quality clothing was always respected, particularly for eveningwear, for which the boots and braces were tucked away and sharp two-piece suits took the floor.

It was now easier on the pocket to achieve that quality look, as the rag trade zeroed in on the new youth money-maker, whipping out racks of Fred Perry T-shirts and crisp Levi's Sta-Prest trousers to every branch of John Collier's throughout the land. More dissatisfied working-class youths joined the new movement, more clothes hastened their way out of basement sweatshops and more eager ears listened to the equally underground sound of reggae.

Among the skinheads' inheritance from their Mod older brothers was a love of black music. They lapped up the soul sounds of Tamla-Motown, Atlantic and Stax eagerly enough, but the emergent reggae music was the real deal.

Quite why skinheads took reggae as their own music has been much debated over the years, learnedly but inconclusively, but it's a simple fact that the more kids listened to the music, the more they bought the records, which they then played to their friends, and so more and more people heard it. This ever-increasing circle would soon spiral out of the underground and make obscure Kingston artists into national stars, if only for a few short months, in some cases.

The Mods, although majoring on soul and Small Faces, had always had time for ska – or 'blue beat', as it was commonly known to white Britons right up to the advent of the skinheads – so there was a background of appreciation of driving, exotic rhythms. However, quite why skinheads and reggae became so closely linked by the end of the '60s is pure conjecture. Some say that, just as white kids borrowed a few fashion ideas from their black friends whom they considered hip, such as the half-mast trousers and the shaved-in 'razor' parting, so they also appropriated their music. Another theory is that the skinheads' musical tastes were a reaction against the bloated, album-orientated progressive rock with which middle-class kids were currently boring the flares off each other; the raw spontaneity of reggae, perhaps heard at school discos or through friends' record collections, was more honest and immediate. It usually came on 45rpm singles, too, so you could afford to take more music home for your money.

Whatever the reason or reasons, by the time The Pioneers were climbing the glittering ladder of mainstream chart success with 'Long Shot Kick The Bucket' in October 1969, skinheads and reggae were inextricably intertwined.

The skinheads' passion for reggae music was invaluable in pushing the music out of the smoky clubs and independent record shops and into the mainstream of popular music. The buying power of the mods had moved Prince Buster and The Skatalites into the nation's consciousness for a few months, and Millie's throw-away ska bouncer 'My Boy Lollipop' had invaded British homes way back in March 1964, hitting Number Two in what was then called the Hit Parade. But it was the massive buying power of the boots-and-braces brigade at the tail end of the decade that really moved reggae units and elevated unknown Jamaican artists to transient stardom.

'The whole skinhead thing played a big role,' comments Robert 'Dandy' Thompson, a major player with Trojan during the late '60s. 'They were the ones who went out and bought "Red Red Wine" and "Reggae In Your Jeggae" when Trojan was on its face.'

Dandy produced one of the most collectable 45s of the era, 'Skinheads: A Message To You' by Desmond Riley, issued on Trojan's Downtown subsidiary in 1969, just as the skinhead cult was sweeping the country. But what were his friend Desmond's motives in making that record?

'I would say, to capitalise on the craze,' Dandy replies frankly, 'but also to quench the little violence that was around.'

In the public perception, skinheads and violence did indeed go hand in hand, as evidenced by this typical letter to *The Times* from a Mr DJ Chadwick of Keble College, Oxford, published on 22 November 1969: 'At 9:30pm last

Sunday, a graduate colleague of mine was assaulted by "skin-heads" whilst walking the few yards across Oriel Street from his college middle common room to the porter's lodge. Eight of these vicious teenagers used their hobnailed boots to such an extent that hospital treatment was required.

'Unfortunately, this is not an isolated incident, for, to my knowledge, one person has lost an eye and another has been injured about the face through being struck with a bicycle chain in the past weeks of this term.

'It is a sad reflection on the moral standards of some teenagers that it is no longer possible for members of the University to walk the streets in safety. I hope that your readers will join with me in a vigorous condemnation of such senseless violence and will encourage the police to do all in their power to bring young hooligans to justice.'

The very sight of a gang of booted youths entering a record shop would dissuade the proprietor from stocking their beloved moonstomping reggae records.

The 27 January 1973 issue of the *NME* carried an article by Danny Holloway entitled, 'Suddenly Reggae Is Up... After Being Almost Bottled To Death By The Skins'. In it, Harry Palmer of Trojan's main rivals Pama Records confirms the extent of the problem: 'When reggae began to establish itself in the charts, the skinheads came along and ruined it. We lost half our accounts because shops refused to stock reggae.'

'It just gave us another battle to fight,' confirms Trojan's Lee Gopthal in the same article.

Island Records' David Betteridge, meanwhile, wasn't so worried; he acknowledged that skinheads drew attention to reggae and recognised the good of a mix of skinheads and West Indian culture, although he didn't like the bad publicity that skinheads attracted.

The skinhead/reggae combination kicked off with Desmond Dekker's often lyrically misunderstood 'Israelites', released on the Pyramid label. This was Dekker's second UK chart climber, as his Rude Boy commentary '007' had managed to reach the respectable Number 14 position in 1967. Issued in 1968, 'Israelites' became an underground club smash before climbing the glittering ladder of success the following year.

While Pyramid wasn't owned by Trojan, being an offshoot of the Doctor Bird group of labels, owned by Graeme Goodall, the progress of 'Israelites' is a perfect example of the formative buying power of the skinheads and of their influence on a record's fortunes. Originally titled 'Poor Me Israelite' and issued in Jamaica on Leslie Kong's Beverley's Records, the track's catchy tune and Desmond's heavy patois-drenched lyrics won it instant dancehall success in Kingston. Jamaican-pressed copies hit the UK, impressing Goodall, who picked up the rights to the recording and issued it, retitling it simply 'Israelites', with an eye on selling a few thousand copies to the West Indian and club-going communities. But Goodall had reckoned without the skinheads' invasion of black nightspots and their appreciation of reggae music, which ensured a whole new audience for the record. As expected, West Indians asked for the record in their local independent record retailers, but meanwhile on the other side of town the skinheads were requesting their copies in the mainstream high-street shops – which filed chart returns.

Under this pressure from their shaven-headed clientele, the major stores stocked the record. The offshore pirate station Radio Caroline plugged it heavily, and was soon copied by BBC Radio 1. 'Israelites' was soon on the move and reaching far beyond its target audience, as one long-serving fan remembers: 'I was a student at Birmingham University at the time, certainly not a skinhead. One morning at breakfast I heard "Israelites" on Tony Blackburn's show and it just hit me like a missile. It was so damned catchy that it picked me up and carried me along with it. I reviewed my finances and calculated that I could afford either to eat lunch that day or go and buy the record. It was a no contest: I high-tailed it down to the Diskery in Hurst Street and returned to my digs clutching the record, hungry but happy. I must have driven my landlady mad by playing it six times in a row!'

Skinheads were very fashion conscious, and fashions extended beyond clothing. A copy of The Upsetters' 'Live Injection' clutched tightly to your Harrington jacket was as much a fashion statement as any pair of highly polished oxblood Dr Marten's boots. As the skinheads bought more and more reggae records, their appreciation grew, along with their collections.

Lists

25 COVERS OF US RHYTHM & BLUES HITS ON TROJAN LABELS (PLUS ORIGINAL ARTISTS AND LABELS)

Most of these originate from the days when sound systems played US tunes and show the enduring influence of R&B on musicians a decade or more later.

HUBERT LEE: Something On Your Mind (Downtown DT520) (Big Jay McNeely, Swingin', 1959)

THE RAVING RAVERS: Rock And Cry (Big Shot BI-507) (Clyde McPhatter, Atlantic, 1957)

THE SILVERTONES: Endlessly b/w Kiddyo (Upsetter US309) (Brook Benton, Mercury, 1959/1960)

LEE PERRY: Yakety Yak (Upsetter US328) (Coasters, Atlantic, 1958)

DERRICK MORGAN: Let Them Talk (Jackpot JP793) (Little Willie John, King, 1959)

JACKIE ROBINSON: Let The Little Girl Dance (Amalgamated AMG824) (Billy Bland, Old Town, 1960)

JOYA LANDIS: Kansas City (Trojan TR620) (Wilbert Harrison, Fury, 1959)

TOOTS AND THE MAYTALS: Louie Louie (Trojan TR7865) (Richard Berry And The Pharaohs, Flip, 1957)

TOOTS AND THE MAYTALS: Fever (Dragon DR1021) (Little Willie John, King, 1956)

TOOTS AND THE MAYTALS: Daddy's Home (Dragon DRLS5002) (Shep and The Limelites, Hull, 1961)

AL T JOE: Prisoner's Song (Dynamic DYN429) (Warren Storm, Nasco, 1958, although originally a US pop hit in 1925 for Vernon Delhart)

MARVELS: CC Rider (Trojan TRLS67) (Chuck Willis, Atlantic, 1957, although originally recorded by Ma Rainey in the 1920s)

WINSTON WRIGHT: Silhouettes (Duke DU111)

DENNIS BROWN: Silhouettes (Song Bird SB1074) (The Rays, Cameo, 1957)

THE RUDIES: Night Train (Downtown DT424) (Jimmy Forrest, United, 1952)

NEVILLE GRANT: Sick And Tired (Downtown DT509) (Chris Kenner, Imperial, 1957)

VAL BENNETT: Baby Baby (Trojan TR640) (Ruth Brown, as '5-10-15 Hours', Atlantic, 1952)

DERRICK MORGAN: Hey Little Girl (Downtown DT520) (Dee Clark, Abner, 1959)

JIMMY LONDON: Shake A Hand (Randy's RAN514) (Faye Adams, Herald, 1953)

OWEN GRAY: Lavey Dovey (Trojan TR632) (Clyde McPhatter, Atlantic, 1959)

LASCELLES PERKINS: English Chicken (Big Shot B1618) (Louis Jordan, as 'Ain't Nobody Here But Us Chickens', Decca, 1946)

DERRICK MORGAN AND PAULETTE: Lee's Dream (Harry J HJ6697) (Shirley And Lee, Aladdin, 1955)

JACKIE BROWN: One Night Of Sin (High Note HS057) (Smiley Lewis, Imperial, 1956)

JOHN HOLT: It May Sound Silly (Moodisc MU3513) (Ivory Joe Hunter, Atlantic, 1955)

25 TAMLA-MOTOWN COVER VERSIONS ON TROJAN LABELS

Not surprisingly, the sound of young America provided a fertile source of songs for Jamaican artists.

DELROY WILSON: Put Yourself In My Place (High Note HS011) (The Elgins, VIP, 1966)

DELROY WILSON: The Same Old Song (Jackpot JP795) (The Four Tops, Motown, 1965)

DELROY WILSON: Ain't That Peculiar (Green Door GD4060) (Marvin Gaye, Tamla, 1965)

DELROY WILSON: This Old Heart Of Mine (Jackpot JP800) (The Isley Brothers, Tamla, 1966)

DAVID ISAACS: Place In The Sun (Trojan TR616) (Stevie Wonder, Tamla, 1966)

THE PARAGONS: Left With A Broken Heart (Duke DU-7) (The Four Tops, Motown, 1965)

MAXINE: Everybody Needs Love (Smash SMA2301) (Gladys Knight and The Pips, Soul, 1967)

ALTON ELLIS: What Does It Take To Win Your Love (Duke Reid DR2501) (Jr Walker and The All Stars, Soul, 1969)

JOHN HOLT: The Further You Look (Horse, HOSS 22) (The Temptations, Gordy, 1963)

THE PIONEERS: Get Ready (Summit SUM 8517) (The Temptations, Gordy, 1965)

DERRICK HARRIOTT: Since I Lost My Baby (Song Bird SB1071) (The Temptations, Gordy, 1965)

DERRICK HARRIOTT: Let Me Down Easy (Explosion EX2071) (GC Cameron, Motown, 1973)

LLOYD CHARMERS: Come See About Me (Song Bird SB1002) (The Supremes, Motown, 1965)

ERIC DONALDSON: The Way You Do The Things You Do (Dragon DR1018) (The Temptations, Gordy, 1964)

THE TECHNIQUES: I Wish It Would Rain (Duke DU1) (The Temptations, Gordy, 1968)

KEN BOOTHE: You Keep Me Hanging On (Coxsone CS7043) (The Supremes, Motown, 1966)

ERNEST WILSON: If I Were A Carpenter (Studio One SO2057) (The Four Tops, Motown, 1968, although previously a pop hit for Bobby Darin, 1966)

FREDDIE NOTES AND THE RUDIES: Yester-Me Yester-You (Grape GR3010) (Stevie Wonder, Tamla, 1969)

GLEN ADAMS: Never Had A Dream Come True (Upsetter US 367) (Stevie Wonder, Tamla, 1970)

THE GAYLADS: Stop Making Love (Trojan TTL 48) (The Four Tops, as 'It's The Same Old Song', Motown, 1965)

SIDNEY, GEORGE AND JACKIE: Papa Was A Rolling Stone (Attack ATT8077) (The Temptations, Gordy, 1972) ·

DARKER SHADE OF BLACK: Ball Of Confusion (Jackpot JP758) (The Temptations, Gordy, 1970)

PAT RHODEN: Boogie On Reggae Woman (Horse HOSS59) (Stevie Wonder, Tamla, 1974)

RANDY'S ALL STARS: War (Randy's RAN505) (Edwin Starr, Gordy, 1970)

LLOYD PARKS: Stop The War Now (Trojan TRLS 109) (Edwin Starr, Gordy, 1970)

25 SERIOUSLY OBSCURE COVER VERSIONS ON TROJAN LABELS

All of these selections are either obscure in their own right or versions of obscure (and sometimes unlikely) American songs, demonstrating just how keenly Jamaicans followed US music in the 1950s and 1960s. In some cases, the cover version has become far better known than the original recording. Sometimes a change in song title increases the obscurity factor!

THE ETHIOPIANS: Good Ambition (Song Bird SB1047) (Roy C, as 'High School Dropout', Jameco, 1966)

JIMMY SHONDELL: Snake In The Grass (Horse HOSS35) (Paul Martin, Ascot, 1967)

WINSTON WRIGHT: Moon Invader (Trojan TR7715) (The Meters, as 'Look-ka-py-py', Josie, 1969)

ALTON ELLIS: Willow Tree (Treasure Isle TI7044) (Chuck Jackson, as 'My Willow Tree', Wand, 1962)

BORIS GARDINER: Elizabethan Reggae (Duke DU39) (Gunther Kallman Choir, as 'Elisabeth Serenade', German Polydor, 1964)

UNIQUES: Watch This Sound (Trojan TR619) (Buffalo Springfield, as 'For What It's Worth', Atco, 1967)

JOHN HOLT: I Had A Talk With My Woman (Smash SMA2303) (Mitty Collier, as 'I Had A Talk With My Man', Chess, 1964)

JOHN HOLT: Sometimes (Trojan TRLS 37) (Gene Thomas, as 'Sometime', Venus, 1961)

NICKY THOMAS: Doing The Moonwalk (Trojan TR7862) (Joe Simon, as 'Moon Walk', Sound Stage 7, 1970)

JUDY MOWATT: Way Over Yonder (Trojan TR7900) (Carole King, Ode LP track, 1971)

PAT KELLY: Just For A Day (Jackpot JP 764) (Chuck Jackson, as 'The Prophet', Wand, 1963)

JOHN HOLT: Stick By Me (Jackpot JP772) (Shep and The Limelites, as 'Stick By Me And I'll Stick By You', Hull, 1963)

THE TECHNIQUES: You Don't Care (Treasure Isle T17001) (Major Lance, as 'You'll Want Me Back', OKeh, 1966)

JUSTIN HINDS: Here I Stand (Treasure Isle T17002) (The Rip Chords [a surfing group!], Columbia, 1963)

TROPIC SHADOWS: Our Anniversary (Big Shot BI603) (Shep and The Limelites, Hull, 1962)

SIR LORD COMIC AND HIS COWBOYS: Ska-ing West (Trojan TTL48) (Billy Hope and The Badmen, as 'Riding West', Savoy, 1958)

THE TECHNIQUES: Queen Majesty (Treasure Isle TI7019) (The Impressions, as 'Minstrel And Queen', ABC-Paramount LP track, 1963)

LLOYD PARKS: Mighty Clouds Of Joy (Upsetter US395) (BJ Thomas, Scepter, 1971)

BOB MARLEY AND THE WAILERS: African Herbsman (Upsetter US392) (Richie Havens, as 'Indian Ropeman', Verve-Forecast LP track, 1969)

DELROY WILSON: It Hurts (High Note HS011) (Ray Whitley and The Tams, as 'I've Been Hurt', ABC-Paramount, 1965)

THE BABA BROOKS BAND: King Size (Trojan TTL51) (Eddie Cantor, as 'Making Whoopee' in the film *Whoopee*, 1930)

ROLAND ALPHONSO: El Pussy Cat (Trojan TTL16) (Mongo Santamaria, Columbia, 1965)

THE MARVELS: Voice Your Choice (Trojan TRLS67) (The Radiants, Chess, 1965)

NICKY THOMAS: New Morning (Trojan TBL208) (Bob Dylan, Columbia LP track, 1970)

NICKY THOMAS: Love Of The Common People (Trojan TR7750) (The Everly Brothers, Warner Bros, 1967)

25 COVERS OF US POP HITS ON TROJAN LABELS

Of course, many soul records crossed over to hit the pop charts, but this list concentrates on records by pop acts (i.e. generally white bands or singers) that received the Jamaican treatment. Once again, in some cases the cover version has become better known than the original – who, for example, remembers The Joe Reisman Orchestra these days?

HONEYBOY MARTIN : Have You Ever Seen The Rain (HarryJ HJ6643) (Creedence Clearwater Revival, Fantasy, 1971)

HOPETON LEWIS: Grooving Out On Life (Dragon DRA1011) (The Newbeats, Hickory, 1968)

THE SKATALITES: Guns Of Navarone (Trojan TTL16) (The Joe Reisman Orchestra, Landa, 1961)

SLIM SMITH: Just A Dream (Dynamic DYN428) (Jimmy Clanton, Ace, 1958)

JOHN HOLT: You Baby (Trojan TR7953) (The Turtles, White Whale, 1966)

JOHN HOLT: It May Sound Silly (Moodisc MU3513) (The McGuire Sisters, Coral, 1955)

BRENT DOWE AND HORTENSE ELLIS: Put Your Hand In The Hand (Summit SUM8525) (Ocean, Kama Sutra, 1971)

BRUCE RUFFIN: Rain (Trojan TR7814) (Jose Feliciano, RCA , 1969)

BRUCE RUFFIN: Candida (Summit SUM8516) (Dawn, Bell, 1970)

BRENT DOWE: Knock Three Times (Summit SUM8521) (Dawn, Bell, 1971)

BOB AND MARCIA: Pied Piper (Trojan TR7818) (Changin' Times, Phillips, 1965)

BARBARA JONES: Changing Partners (Attack ATT8077) (Kay Starr, RCA, 1954)

THE GAYTONES: Joy To The World (High Note HS054 (Three Dog Night, Dunhill, 1971)

THE GAYLADS: Love Me With All Your Heart (Studio One SO2017) (Steve Allen, as 'Cuando Caliente El Sol', Dot, 1963)

THE GAYLADS: Fire And Rain (Trojan) (Simon and Garfunkel, Columbia, 1965)

LLOYD CHARMERS: California Dreamin' (Explosion EX2041) (The Mamas and The Papas, Dunhill, 1966)

THE PIONEERS: Storybook Children (Summit SUM8535) (Billy Vera and Judy Clay, Atlantic, 1967)

DAVID ISAACS: He'll Have To Go (Upsetter US311) (Jim Reeves, RCA, 1959)

ALTON ELLIS: You Made Me So Very Happy (Duke Reid DR2512) (Blood, Sweat And Tears, Columbia, 1969)

JOE WHITE: If It Don't Work Out (Gayfeet GS203) (The Casinos, as 'Then You Can Tell Me Goodbye', Fraternity, 1967)

THE HEPTONES: I Shall Be Released (Studio One SO2083) (The Box Tops, Mama, 1969)

THE UPSETTERS: Na Na Hey Hey (Upsetter US332) (Steam, Fontana, 1969)

STRANGER COLE: Crying Every Night (Spinning Wheel SW 109) (The Guess Who, as 'These Eyes', RCA 1969)

WINSTON FRANCIS: The Games People Play (Studio One SO2086) (Joe South, Capitol, 1969)

NICKY THOMAS: If I Had A Hammer (Trojan TR7807) (Peter, Paul And Mary, Warner Bros, 1962)

25 COVERS OF UK POP HITS ON TROJAN LABELS.

You might expect this section to be crammed with London-recorded pop reggae of the kind which Trojan increasingly churned out in the mid '70s. In fact, more than half of the selections here are Jamaican recordings.

AL T JOE: Hitching A Ride (Dynamic DYN408) (Vanity Fare, Page One, 1969)

HOPETON LEWIS: Going Back To My Home Town (Dynamic DYN436) (Hal Paige and The Whalers, Melodisc, 1960 – recorded by Fury of New York, but a hit in Britain only)

DERRICK HARRIOTT: Eighteen With A Bullet (Trojan TR7973) (Pete Wingfield, Island, 1975)

WAYNE HOWARD: All Kinds Of Everything (Explosion EX2042) (Dana, Rex, 1970)

NORMA FRASER: The First Cut Is The Deepest (Coxsone CS7017) (PP Arnold, Immediate, 1967)

THE THREE TOPS: A Groovy Kind Of Love (Coxsone CS7033) (The Mindbenders, Fontana, 1966)

ROB WALKER: Puppet On A String (Jackpot JP761) (Sandie Shaw, Pye, 1967)

CYNTHIA RICHARDS: United We Stand (Pressure Beat PB5507) (Brotherhood Of Man, Deram, 1970)

ALTON ELLIS: A Whiter Shade Of Pale (Coxsone CSL8008) (Procol Harum, Deram, 1967)

VAL BENNETT: Stranger On The Shore (Upsetter US321)

DAVID ISAACS: Stranger On The Shore (Upsetter US400) (Mr Acker Bilk, Columbia, 1961)

JOHN HOLT: The Last Farewell (Trojan TRLS160) (Roger Whittaker, EMI, 1975)

JOYCE BOND: Ob-la-di Ob-la-da (Trojan TTL1) (Marmalade, CBS, 1968)

JACKIE MITTOO: Norwegian Wood (Coxsone CS7040) (The Beatles, Parlophone LP track, 1965)

137

NICKY THOMAS: Let It Be (Amalgamated AMG860, 1970) (The Beatles, Apple, 1970)

THE RUDIES: My Sweet Lord (Spinning Wheel SW106) (George Harrison, Apple, 1971)

BUSTY BROWN: To Love Somebody (Upsetter US308) (The Bee Gees, Polydor, 1967)

MARCIA AND JEFF: Words (Studio One SO2047) (The Bee Gees, Polydor, 1968)

DAVE BARKER AND THE WAILERS: Don't Let The Sun Catch You Crying (Upsetter US347) (Gerry and The Pacemakers, Columbia, 1964)

DANDY: What Do You Want To Make Those Eyes At Me For? (Trojan TR7854) (Emile Ford and The Checkmates, Pye, 1959)

THE MUSIC DOCTORS: In The Summertime (J-Dan JDN 4414) (Mungo Jerry, Dawn, 1970)

THE GAYLETS: Son Of A Preacher Man (Big Shot, BI516) (Dusty Springfield, Phillips, 1968)

THE PIONEERS: Blame It On The Pony Express (Trojan TRLS64) (Johnny Johnson and The Bandwagon, Bell, 1970)

DENNIS BROWN: Black Magic Woman (Explosion EX2068) (Fleetwood Mac, Blue Horizon, 1968)

PAT KELLY: He Ain't Heavy, He's My Brother (Jackpot 764) (The Hollies, Parlophone, 1969)

Musicland And Muzic City Chronology

1963

Beat and Commercial Records Ltd incorporated on 19 April, ref 758078

1966

Musicland outlets:
  13 High Road, Willesden Green

1967

Additional Musicland Outlets:
  13 High Road, Willesden Green (head office)
  42 Willesden Lane, NW6 (mail order)
  5a Extension Market, Shepherds Bush, W12
  230 Portobello Road
  20g Atlantic Road
  53 Watling Avenue, Burnt Oak
  256a North End Road

1968

Additional Musicland Outlets:
  44 Berwick Street (Mail Order)
  23 Ridley Road
(Note: 42 Willesden Lane no longer shown as Musicland mail-order outlet)

1969

Additional Musicland outlets:
  21 High Street, SE8

153 Kilburn High Road
96 High Street, Watford
11a Church Street, Kingston
153 High Road, Hounslow

1970

Notice in June issue of *The London Gazette* regarding the possible winding up of Musicland Ltd

Additional Musicland Outlets:
12 Neasden Lane (head office)
12a Extension Market, Shepherds Bush
297 Portobello Road
4 Soho Street, W1

Dropped Musicland outlets:
20g Atlantic Road
(Note: 12 Neasden Lane becomes Musicland head office; directory records show Musicland as 'Proprietors: B&C' for the first time)

1971

Additional Musicland Outlets:
135 High Street, Watford
226 High Road, Hounslow
44 Lewisham High Street

Dropped Musicland outlets:
21 High Street, SE8
96 High Street, Watford
153 High Road, Hounslow

Musicland outlets converted to Muzik City outlets:
5a Extension Market, Shepherds Bush
12a Extension Market, Shepherds Bush
23 Ridley Road, Dalston, E8
42 Willesden Lane, NW6
297 Portobello Road

New Muzik City outlets:
   21 High Street, Deptford
   30 Station Parade, Kensal Rise, NW1O
   32 Goldhawk Road, W9
   72 Granville Arcade, Brixton, SW9
   94 Granville Arcade, Brixton, SW9
   530 Harrow Road, W9
   Balham Kiosk, Balham High Street, SW12

1972

Ref 1074876 – Music City Ltd set up
Ref 1066926 – Muzik City Records Shops Limited set up
Ref 1042071 -Trojanland Ltd set up
Reference to Companies House Certificate of Incorporation
Musicland (unknown which company) is sold

Additional Musicland outlets:
   66 The Broadway, Ealing
   Incredible Department Store, 94a Brompton Road
   Ravels, 44 Kings Road, SW3

Dropped Musicland outlets:
   256a North End Road
   4 Soho Street, W1

1973

Ref 43178 – Musicland Ltd dissolved
Musicland Head Office no longer shown as 12 Neasden Lane

Dropped Musicland outlets:
   53 Watling Avenue, Burnt Oak
   135 High Street, Watford
   11a Church Street, Kingston
   226 High Road, Hounslow
   Ravels, 44 Kings Road, SW3

Additional Muzik City outlets:
   Music House, 11 Neasden Lane

11a Model Market, Lewisham, SE13

96 Granville Arcade, Brixton, SW9

(Note: At this stage Music House is not shown as head office)

Dropped Muzik City outlets:

32 Goldhawk Road

94 Granville Arcade, Brixton, SW9

297 Portobello Road

(Note: Adverts also show 55 Atlantic Road – Desmond's Hip City – as an outlet, although this address is not noted in the Post Office Directory as Musicland or Muzik City)

1974

Dropped Musicland outlets:

66 the Broadway, Ealing

94a Brompton Road

44 Lewisham High Street

(Note: Music House is shown as head office)

1975

Dropped Musicland outlets:

230 Portobello Road

44 Berwick Street

(Note: The only Musicland outlet remaining in this year is 153 Kilburn High Street, which did not survive into 1976)

Dropped Muzik City Outlets:

21 High Street, Deptford

530 Harrow Road

Balham Kiosk

42 Willesden Lane

Muzik City record shops went into voluntary winding-up on 22 January 1976, with a final winding-up meeting of members and creditors taking place on 1 December 1978. Musicland Record Stores Ltd was dissolved on 14 February 1977.

Suggested Listening

This section is intended as nothing more than a snapshot of some excellent albums that are out at the time of writing to give an idea of what is available. There are literally hundreds of other worthy releases out there, both reissues of old albums and modern compilations of earlier work.

BOB ANDY: SONG BOOK (COXSONE)

This album deserves to be in every music lover's collection with its heartfelt songs of hope, love and oppression, recorded at Studio One at the turn of the '60s into the '70s. Most of the rhythms, and the songs themselves, have become standards within the Jamaican music scene.

BOB ANDY: RETROSPECTIVE (I-ANKA RECORDS)

Following on from Bob Andy's stay at Studio One, this album collects together his work for a variety of producers between 1970 and 1975. As with *Song Book*, this collection further cements his reputation as one of the key figures of Jamaican music.

BOB MARLEY AND THE WAILERS: SOUL REBELS (TROJAN)

A pre-hit and, you could say, un-electrified Marley at his best from 1970. The songs are aided by Lee Perry's dense and mystical production, which only highlights the almost ethereal quality of tracks like the title cut and Peter Tosh's angry '400 Years'. To many connoisseurs, his later, over-orchestrated work for Island isn't a patch on the raw soul recorded here.

143

BOB MARLEY AND THE WAILERS: CATCH A FIRE (ISLAND)

The latest variant of this release is a double-CD set with disc one being the normal Island issue complete with London overdubs, as issued in 1973. It is the second disc which is of interest here, as it is the raw Jamaican mix of the album before Island got their heavy hands on it, and it is far superior. 'Concrete Jungle' is particularly chilling, with Marley bringing to the fore a sparse hopelessness completely lost in the Basing Street reworking.

I-ROY: PRESENTING/HELL & SORROW (TROJAN)

Alongside Big Youth's *Screaming Target* set, this two-for-one CD epitomises the art of roots-reality DJ chat. Enhanced no end by the tough new rhythm structures produced by Gussie Clarke on *Presenting* (he also produced the Big Youth set) and by I-Roy on *Hell & Sorrow*, this is the new (1973), no-nonsense, tough-talking rapper at his best.

KEITH HUDSON: PICK A DUB (BLOOD AND FIRE)

Produced by Hudson and Wailers bass player Family Man Barrett, this album deconstructs some of Keith's finest rhythms. Released in 1974 alongside Augustus Pablo's *King Tubby's Meets The Rockers Uptown* and Perry's *Black Board Jungle Dub*, both of which were mixed by King Tubby, *Pick A Dub* offers some of dub's finest moments.

KEN BOOTHE: ANTHOLOGY (TROJAN)

A double-CD set of one of the most unmistakeable voices of Jamaica, covering the majority of his hits, both on the local scene and across the Atlantic.

THE SKATALITES: SKA BOO-DA-BA (WEST SIDE)

Producer Justin Yap's Top Deck and Tuneico labels issued some of the most satisfying ska sessions from The Skatalites. It is said that they gave some of their best performances for him, as he paid them not only well but also on time.

U ROY: VERSION GALORE (TROJAN)

Version Galore is an album of such popularity that it is rarely unavailable in some form or another. The most recent Trojan issue combines the original DJ album with all the respective original tracks that U Roy used as his base for the groundbreaking raps.

VARIOUS ARTISTS: DANCEHALL '69 (TROJAN)

A double-CD set of the rarer recordings enjoyed in the clubs at the time, not necessarily aimed at the skinhead audience by the artists but adopted by them all the same. One CD is of UK recordings while the other is all Jamaican.

VARIOUS ARTISTS: DARKER THAN BLUE – SOUL FROM JAMDOWN 1973–1980 (BLOOD AND FIRE)

Eighteen cuts of reggae with a funk or soul twist. A style derided at the time but which has now found its own market – very deservedly.

VARIOUS ARTISTS: FOUNDATION SKA (HEARTBEAT)

Sumptuous double LP/CD of the best ska band (The Skatalites) at the best studio (Brentford Road). Features rip-roaring instrumentals plus top ska vocals like Jackie Opel's 'Old Rocking Chair', with the unbelievable sound of Ernest Ranglin's guitar.

VARIOUS ARTISTS: SKINHEAD REGGAE (BOX SET) (TROJAN)

A bargain three-CD box set highlighting the more popular skinhead club tunes of the day.

VARIOUS ARTISTS: THE BIGGEST DANCEHALL ANTHEMS, 1979–82 (GREENSLEEVES)

When Trojan stumbled in the later part of the '70s, Greensleeves took the reins and proceeded to release a large proportion of the then-current new music being recorded in Kingston. This double CD collects all their major triumphs in an age when dancehall was just starting to usurp the Rasta-roots style and DJs like Yellowman were coming to prominence.

VARIOUS ARTISTS: THE COMPLETE UK UPSETTER SINGLES COLLECTION VOLS 1–4 (TROJAN)

Four double-CD sets with integral books chronologically charting Lee Perry's Trojan/Upsetter label with each A and respective B side from start to finish. All of the triumphs (and the few failures) are present and the series provides an excellent way to collect all of the Upsetter singles without paying an arm and a leg.

VARIOUS ARTISTS: THE FRONT LINE (VIRGIN)

Virgin, alongside Island, were grabbing all and sundry performers as reggae rose to prominence in the mid 1970s. This four-CD set with integral book collects many of the best moments from the label, with such roots artists as The Abyssinians, Culture and The Mighty Diamonds, while DJs like I-Roy, Big Youth and U Roy all get a look-in. A superb overview of 1970s roots reggae.

VARIOUS ARTISTS: THE HARDER THEY COME (ISLAND)

Perry Henzell's 1972 feature film captured the reggae moment in time, with Jimmy Cliff starring as a country boy who moves to Kingston and turns to crime via the record industry. The story may be a little well-worn now, but the sight of such luminaries filmed in the studio as The Maytals and DJ Scotty, plus the soundtrack itself, make this essential for any reggae lover. Available on CD, vinyl, video, DVD and download.

VARIOUS ARTISTS: HISTORY OF TROJAN RECORDS 1968–1971 VOL 1 (TROJAN)/1972–1995 VOL 2 (TROJAN)

Two double CDs tracing not only Trojan's progression but also the ever-changing style of Jamaican music. *Volume One* is slightly misleading, as it starts off in the ska era of Island, prior to Trojan Records being formed, but both volumes combined provide an excellent musical ride through the years.

VARIOUS ARTISTS: REBEL MUSIC (TROJAN)

This album was revamped in 2002 by the original compiler, Dave Hendley, who replaced a couple of the more easily found tracks with some of equal quality but much higher scarcity. A definite must-have for anyone interested in where Kingston was at in the 1970s.

VARIOUS ARTISTS: STUDIO ONE DJs (SOUL JAZZ)

All of the Soul Jazz *Studio One* collections are well worth picking up, but the *DJs* set shows the roots of many of the US rap superstars of today, and the rhythm tracks are sublime as well.

VARIOUS ARTISTS: STUDIO ONE STORY (SOUL JAZZ)

An exemplary musical overview of the famous recording studio through the years, made even more desirable by a four-hour DVD featuring Mr Dodd in Kingston, plus live band/studio footage. The set comes with a 100-page book.

VARIOUS ARTISTS: THE BIRTH OF TROJAN – DUKE REID ROCKSTEADY 1967 (TROJAN)

Where it all began for Trojan Records, this album features the first 11 single releases on the then Island/B&C-owned Trojan label, mainly comprising sublime Tommy McCook-led rocksteady. It's easy to see why Duke Reid has always been regarded as the finest producer of the beat.

VARIOUS ARTISTS: TIGHTEN UP VOL 1/VOL 2/VOL 3/VOL 4/ VOL 5 (TROJAN)

The highly successful *Tighten Up* series sold extremely well at the time, and the Trojan reissues with bonus tracks are even better value. As an overview and progression of what was happening on the reggae scene of the late '60s and early '70s they are invaluable, aside from being full of first-rate music.

VARIOUS ARTISTS: TOUGHER THAN TOUGH – THE STORY OF JAMAICAN MUSIC (ISLAND)

This four-CD set traces the progression of Jamaican music from its early beginnings to the dawn of the '90s. Steve Barrow compiled the set and wrote the text for the excellent integral book.

Suggested Reading

In the early '70s, books on Jamaican music just didn't exist. Thankfully, their number has been steadily growing, and now there are quite a few available. Below are some recommendations which are felt to be of particular use and interest to anyone requiring further reading.

BISHTON, DEREK: *Blackheart Man* (Chatto & Windus)
Subtitled 'A Journey Into Rasta', which is just what this is, with evocative pictures and an easily accessible text taking the reader from the beginnings of the religion to the present day.

GRIFFITHS, MARK: *Boss Sounds – Classic Skinhead Reggae* (STP Publishing)
The only book of its kind, as it focuses on just the 'skinhead' years of reggae music, checking out both UK and JA recordings. A detailed overview of the scene is complemented by a label-by-label description and record-buying recommendations.

REEL, PENNY: *Deep Down With Dennis Brown* (Drake Brothers)
A superbly presented book full of colour and black-and-white plates illustrating the (mainly London) reggae scene of the '70s and offering a snapshot of the then young (but now late) Dennis Emanuel Brown. Penny Reel writes evocatively and knowledgeably of his life and times.

KATZ, DAVID: *People Funny Boy – The Genius of Lee 'Scratch' Perry* (Payback Press)
Dave Katz offers an exhaustive (460-page) progression of the life and works

of Lee Perry from his birth to the present day. Along the voyage, the reader is treated to biographies of a legion of other singers, players and producers, so the book far transcends its title as just a view of Perry's life and work.

DAVIS, STEPHEN and SIMON, PETER: *Reggae International* (Thames & Hudson)
Reggae International is a sumptuous large-format book and has recently reached its 35th anniversary. As a guide to the genre, from the music's African roots to the then-new sounds of dancehall, it is good, but when you add the superb colour and black-and-white plates, the book comes into its own. It is a volume well worth searching out.

BARROW, STEVE and DALTON, PETER: *The Rough Guide To Reggae* (Rough Guides/Penguin)
Without the slightest doubt, *The Rough Guide To Reggae* is the definitive book for any enthusiast. Alongside a very readable progression of the music and biographies of just about every individual involved from its formative R&B roots to ragga, the book offers commentary on over 1,000 LP/CD releases.

LARKIN, COLIN: *The Virgin Encyclopaedia Of Reggae* (Virgin)
A handy reference overview to reggae artists, but beware that there are occasional mistakes, such as Dave and Ansel Collins being cited as brothers in one entry.

Sources

CHAPTER 1: EARLY YEARS

Trojan Lorries website (with permission)

The Rough Guide To Reggae – Steve Barrow and Peter Dalton (Rough Guides/ Penguin)

Derrick Morgan interview – LCH

Graeme Goodall interview – LCH

Earl Morgan interview – LCH

Mike Atherton

CHAPTER 2: WINDRUSH TO 1974

Public Records Office

Empire Windrush passenger list (PRO)

Companies House

The Guild Hall

Keep On Moving: The Windrush Legacy – Tony Sewell (Voice Enterprises Ltd)

The Rough Guide To Reggae – Steve Barrow and Peter Dalton (Rough Guides/ Penguin)

David Betteridge interview – LCH

Lee Gopthal interview – Rob Randall (*Melody Maker*, 30 December 1972)

Joe Sinclair interview – MdK

Rob Bell interview – MdK

Robert Thompson interview – LCH

Greyhound CD sleeve notes – LCH (courtesy Trojan Records)

The Cimarons interview – Carl Gayle (*Black Music* magazine, July 1976)

'Reggae' – Mark Plummer (*Melody Maker*, 22 May 1971)

Dave Barker interview – Rob Randall (*NME*, 15 January 1972)

Jackie Robinson interview – unknown (*Disc*, 28 August 1971)

Bruce White interview – MdK

Bob Andy interview – MdK

Bob and Marcia interview – Simon Burnett (*Record Mirror*, 17 July 1971)

Clive Crawley interview- LCH

Vic Keary interview – LCH

Notes taken for the film *Reggae*, produced and directed by Horace Ové

Winston Riley interview – unknown (*NME*, March 1971)

Dave Barker interview – unknown (*NME*, 15 January 1972)

Dave Barker interview – Lon Goddard (*Record Mirror*, 1971)

'Rudies Play At Mick Jagger's Wedding' – unknown (*Rolling Stone*, 10 July 1971)

Jeffrey Palmer interview- Danny Holloway (*NME*, 27 January 1973)

Times article – Richard Williams (*The Times*, 19 March 1973)

CHAPTER 3: 1975 TO DATE

The Guild Hall

Companies House

Webster Shrowder interview – Carl Gayle (*Black Music* magazine, July 1974)

Club Scene – Carl Gayle (*Black Music* magazine, 'UK Reggae' feature, July 1974)

Dandy interview – Carl Gayle (*Black Music* magazine, February 1974)

Sid Bucknor interview – MdK

Nicky Thomas interview – Carl Gayle (*Black Music* magazine, February 1974)

Tony Ashfield/Keith Boviour – Trojan press release

Louisa Mark, Safari single sales – *Black Music* magazine, July 1975

Marcel Rodd interview – Carl Gayle (*Black Music* magazine, October 1976)

Notices – *The London Gazette*, 10 June 1975

Dave Hendley interview – MdK

Colin Newman interview – LCH

Laurence Cane Honeysett interview – MdK

Trojan Appreciation Society documents – MdK

Sanctuary financial information – various 'city' reports

John Reed interview – LCH/MdK

CHAPTERS 4 & 5: MUSIC HISTORY – PARTS 1 & 2

Trojan release sheets and charts – MdK

Black Music magazine charts – MdK

The Guinness Book Of Hit Singles – Paul Gambaccini, Tim Rice, Jonathan Rice (Guinness)

The Complete Book Of The British Charts Singles And Albums – Tony Brown, Jon Kutner and Neil Warwick (Omnibus Press)

CHAPTER 6: THE MODS AND THE SKINHEADS

Sunday Times Magazine feature 'Changing Faces' by Kathlene Halton (2 August 1964)

Mods – Richard Barnes (Plexus)

Marc Bolan interview – unknown *(Town* magazine, 1962)

Robert Thompson interview – LCH

Times letter November 1969

Harry Palmer interview – Danny Holloway (*NME*, 27 January 1973)

Lee Gopthal interview – Danny Holloway (*NME*, 27 January 1973)

David Betteridge interview – Danny Holloway (*NME*, 27 January 1973)

Rob Bell interview – MdK

Mike Atherton

Label Profiles

AMALGAMATED

This label was set up by B&C in 1968 to issue the productions of Joel Gibson, otherwise known as Joe Gibbs. Unusually, there is absolutely nothing among its 72 issues that can be described as a bum cut, although the flipside of AMG 804, 'We Are Not Divided', was a Sacred effort and possibly originally destined for the short lived Amalgamated Sacred series. The Pioneers crop up most on the label and their 'Jackpot', 'Catch The Beat' and 'Gimme Little Loving' are classics, also to be found on their *Greetings From The Pioneers* set. Other goodies are 'El Casino Royale' (Lyn Tait and The Jets), 'Good Time Rock' (Hugh Malcolm), 'On The Move' (The Soul Mates) and 'Man Beware' (The Slickers). Another superb track is The Immortals' 'Red Red Wine' (flipside of AMG 869), which has nothing to do with its more famous namesake. Some of the best sides from 1968 and 1969 were collected on Amalgamated's *Jackpot Of Hits* compilation.

As is the case with a number of these producer-dedicated Trojan subsidiaries, it is now being discovered that not all of the issues were the work of the producer in question, and the sides by The Cobbs are believed to be Ken Jones productions. The Victor Morris sides (AMG 813) are also from elsewhere and saw issue on the Double D label as well, where the production credits went to Bobby Aitken. All in all, though, Amalgamated really was a solid-gold Trojan subsidiary. The Pressure Beat label was created for Gibbs' productions in 1970 and Amalgamated was retained alongside it until the early part of 1971, when it was scrapped entirely.

ATTACK

Started in 1969 by Graeme Goodall's Doctor Bird group, Attack was initially concerned with productions from Philip Chen's Philligree stable, which pretty much consisted of The Pyramids in their various guises (mainly as Family Circle) and the male vocalist Pat Sandy. With the exception of The Soul Directions' excellent 'Su Su Su', which was recorded in Jamaica and featured some, if not all, of The Pioneers, the label featured average-to-superior British reggae fare. The label folded at some point in 1970, when Doctor Bird went into liquidation. Trojan then took up the reins, possibly around the time of ATT 8013, as for this release the label format and pressing type changed and a couple of Laurel Aitken releases were put out.

However, the label fared no better under Trojan's wing and the plug was pulled before the dawn of 1971. Things didn't stay that way, though, and the company later resurrected Attack – with original label design intact – in 1972 to deal with the material of a variety of producers. It was to become a real survivor, lasting until 1979, when a 12" series was issued. Particularly strong titles include U Roy Junior's 'This A Pepper', Pat Satchmo's 'What's Going On' (and he doesn't do his customary Louis Armstrong impression, either), Gregory Isaacs' 'Love Is Overdue' and, from the later period, Michael Dyke's 'Saturday Night Special', although the pressings are absolutely diabolical on this one. During the 1974–5 period, the label changed to a plain black-and-white design, in common with other Trojan economy measures of the time, and there is relatively little of real quality from this era.

BIG

This subsidiary was initiated by Trojan for productions from Rupie Edwards, although it came to light later that the occasional non-Edwards track found its way in here and there. Without a doubt, the two strongest releases on the label are Dave Barker's 'Love Is What I Bring' and Errol Dunkley's 'Deep Meditation', although many fans find little to recommend on the label. The Gaylads' 'Can't Hide The Feeling' is an exception, however, as is the aforementioned Dave Barker track, itself a cut of The Uniques' classic 'Out Of Love'.

The label was wrapped up at the very end of 1972 with the release of the monstrous 'Christmas Parade', after which Rupie had product out on other Trojan subsidiaries like Harry J (particularly for The Ethiopians).

BIG SHOT

Launched by Trojan/B&C in the closing months of 1968, Big Shot lasted seven years and spanned a massive 120 issues. From the outset, there was some excellent early reggae from The Tennors ('Reggae Girl' and 'Another Scorcher'), Rudy Mills ('John Jones'), The Crystalites ('Biafra'), Ken Boothe ('The Old Fashioned Way'), Dennis Alcapone ('El Paso') and Niney ('Blood And Fire'). There are also three highly sought-after compilation albums on Big Shot, namely *Live It Up*, *Once More* and *Reggae Girl*. The 1968–71 era includes barely a duff release.

The label ran until 1975 and included almost all of Judge Dread's 'Big' series of records. With so many releases by so many artists and producers, it's difficult to form a definitive view of this long-running label. Worth seeking out, however, is the Shrowder/Bryan/Sinclair material from 1970 – much of which was collected together for the *Queen Of The World* compilation – and the Winston Riley productions from the same year. Album-wise, Big Shot bowed out with a handful of albums which either sold poorly or were of decidedly limited press, namely *Turntable Reggae* (various artists) and *Ready Or Not* Johnny Osbourne and others).

BLACK SWAN (TROJAN SERIES)

Another old imprint revived briefly by Trojan/B&C, the second series of Black Swan issued productions in the main from Webster Shrowder, Des Bryan and Joe Sinclair, who were calling themselves Swan Productions at this time. The label's output is generally above-average British reggae for its time (1970) and worth a listen, particularly The Lowbites' 'I Got It' (featured on *Tighten Up Volume 4*), Selwyn Baptiste's steel-pan cut of 'Montego Bay' and Rad Bryan's super-smooth 'Girl You Rock My Soul'.

BLUE CAT

This label seems to have become a legend, largely through the *Jamaican Memories* album. It was launched by Island/B&C in around April 1968, and followed Trojan a few months later, when it became a separate company. The 1968 releases numbered around 50, which is something in the region of about six issues per month. The label was wrapped up in 1969, with the last eight or so releases having a different-coloured label design.

Without a doubt, the only tracks which turn up on anything like a regular basis are Dermott Lynch's 'I've Got Your Number', The Uniques' 'Girls Like Dirt', The Slickers' 'Nana', The Maytones' 'Billy Goat' and 'Loving Reggae', and Vernon Buckley's '2,000 Tons Of TNT'. There was a lot of very good Studio One music issued on Blue Cat during 1968 – titles such as The Hamlins' 'Sugar And Spice', The Thrillers' 'Last Dance' and The Righteous Flames' 'Seven Letters' – that seems to have been shunted away from the usual Studio One and Coxsone subsidiaries for some reason.

All of the most common releases mentioned earlier are worth hearing, as are Dennis Walks' 'Belly Lick', The Sparkers' 'Dig It Up' and 'Israel', and Ranfold (Ranny) Williams's 'Code It'. Probably 70 per cent of Blue Cat's output – but certainly not everything – is top notch.

BREAD

Launched by Trojan in 1970 as a subsidiary label for Jackie Edwards and his productions, Bread is perhaps one of the least known of the company's many labels. The music was pretty commercial, but not altogether bad, and was clearly aimed at the 30-something Jamaican market. The most popular sides were Danny Ray and Jackie's 'Your Eyes Are Dreaming', Jackie's 'Johnny Gunman' (also on *Club Reggae Volume 3*) and 'I Do Love You'.

Almost exactly halfway through Bread's 20-issue existence, Jackie's output seemed to have been switched to Trojan and Horse, with other producers taking over. Of these, notable releases include Lee Perry's 'Station Underground News', The Maytones' Rasta-inspired 'All Over The World People Are Changing' and Dennis Alcapone's 'Musical Liquidator'. The label crumbled at the end of 1973.

Finally, there is a 'does it exist?' release, namely Bobby Foster's 'Tell Me Why You Said Goodbye', on either BR 1101 or BR 1102.

CLANDISC

Trojan established Clandisc in 1969 as the UK counterpart to Clancy Eccles' back-a-yard operation, and there is undoubtedly some truly superb music among the run of around 30 releases, including The Dynamites' moody 'Skokiaan (Mr Midnight)', Clancy's own 'The World Needs Loving', Andy Capp and King Stitt's 'Herbsman Shuffle' and The Silvertones' 'Teardrops Will Fall'. There's hardly a release that won't get your dancing feet on the move. Alongside the singles, there were albums by Clancy Eccles (*Freedom*) and three various-artists compilations: *Cynthia Richards And Friends*, *Herbsman Shuffle* and *Fire Corner*. Most of the compilations have a healthy proportion of instrumentals by Clancy's session band, The Dynamites.

Clandisc ground to a halt early in 1972 and Clancy seemed to disappear from the recording scene pretty much overnight. Trojan put out the *Top Of The Ladder* compilation on Big Shot late in 1973, but this seemed to include a bunch of discarded outtakes from a couple of years earlier, and while it featured the odd gem, it was a poor testament to Clancy's talents.

DOCTOR BIRD

Just three issues from this revived label. Of these, the most notable is Al Barry's 'Morning Sun', which is regarded as one of the best pieces of UK reggae from the time and, until its reissue on the Trojan *British Reggae* box set, remained for many years a forgotten classic.

DOWNTOWN

A label set up exclusively for Dandy (aka RL Thompson, RLT and Bobby Thompson, among other pseudonyms) soon after Trojan was formed, in the summer of 1968. As himself, Dandy really did have some wonderful music issued on it, such as 'Move Your Mule', 'Tell Me Darling', 'Pushwood' (appearing as by 'Mr Most'), 'Reggae In Your Jeggae' and 'I'm Your Puppet'. Dandy's session outfits included The Brother Dan All Stars, The Israelites and The Music Doctors, the line-ups of which were ever-changing, while featured vocalists were Desmond Riley, Lyndon Johns, Tony Tribe and Gene Rondo (also known as Winston Laro). All told, just over two-thirds of Downtown's 115 releases were produced by Dandy. The remainder were issued in the 1972–3 period, by which time Dandy had reinvented himself as Dandy Livingstone and was recording more commercially biased material on Horse and the main Trojan label.

Not everything on Downtown is worth checking out, however, as there are a few run-of-the-mill efforts by Audrey (some of which are admittedly good), Soul Explosion, The Megatons and Boy Friday. The albums, however – two volumes of *Red Red Wine*, The Music Doctors' *Reggae In The Summertime* and Dandy's own *Your Musical Doctor* – are all worth obtaining.

After around DT 491, Downtown dealt with all manner of producers and issued some very heavy-duty material from Big Youth ('S90 Skank' and 'Dock Of The Bay'), Hubert Lee ('There Is Something On Your Mind'), The Starlites ('You Are A Wanted Man'), Glen Brown ('Two Wedden Skank') and I-Roy ('Blackman Time' and 'Clapper's Tail'). Trojan finally scrapped the imprint late in 1973.

DUKE

Trojan originally initiated Duke in late 1968 to handle output from Duke Reid but, for reasons best known to the company, discarded this idea after only the second issue and gave it over to many different producers.

This really is a wonderful label with so much variety. The first release to make an impact was Herbie Carter's (actually Keble Drummond's) 'Happy Time', followed by Lloyd Charmers' excellent 'Cuyah', Clancy Eccles' 'Auntie Lulu' and The Beltones' 'Home Without You'. As outlined in the Joe label profile, there were around 11 issues from Brixton kingpin Joe Mansano with Duke numbers and Joe labels. Continuing with the London scene, Clancy Collins (aka Sir Collins) has seven of his productions on the label, including the thrilling 'Brother Moses' and 'Black Panther'. Freddie Notes and The Rudies, through ace Trojan producer Joe Sinclair, had a decent showing on Duke with 'The Bull' and 'Chicken Inn'.

The label hit paydirt with Boris Gardiner's 'Elizabethan Reggae', which reached the UK Top 20 early in 1970. Following this, there was a fair amount of material from Byron Lee, Duke Reid, Lloyd Charmers, JJ Johnson and back to British again – Domino Johnson and Larry Lawrence. Unusually, The Ethiopians' 'My Girl' (DU 35) was soul, and there were two calypso sides by Emile Straker and Mighty Sparrow on 113 and 114 respectively.

Trojan wrapped up Duke late in 1973, when the label was top of the company's sales lists with 'Children Of The Night' by Norman Brown and Lloyd Charmers, masquerading as The Chosen Few – a brilliant marketing ploy. Presumably, with the scaling-down of operations in full swing, Trojan didn't need the label any longer.

DUKE REID

Twenty-four issues from the Mighty Duke, including all of U Roy's then-current (1970) hot favourites like 'Wake The Town', 'Rule The Nation', 'Wear You To The Ball' and 'You'll Never Get Away'. In fact, a third of the label's entire output came from Mr Beckford and it pretty much seemed to be a vehicle to raise his profile, with a few other current Duke Reid bits thrown in for good measure. Other notables include Hopeton Lewis's 1970 Song Festival success 'Boom Shacka Lacka', Justin Hinds' 'Say Me Say' and The Tennors' 'Hopeful Village', which is a truly wonderful sound. The label seemed to run out of steam four releases from the end, perhaps signalling Reid's diminishing status in the reggae-production world. There were no further issues after mid 1973.

DYNAMIC

This Trojan subsidiary dealt with releases from Byron Lee's Jamaican Dynamic Studio (formerly WIRL, or West Indies Records Limited) and spanned some 55 releases between 1970 and 1972. Aside from Lee's productions, Dynamic also put out material from a variety of other producers recording at Dynamic at the time, most notably Sid Bucknor, Lee Perry, Bunny Lee and Tommy Cowan. The Jamaican counterpart was a real one-stop recording organisation, with releases coming out on various Dynamic subsidiaries like Panther, Top Cat and Jaguar (a definite feline connection here!). As such, determining who was responsible for the various productions is often difficult, as almost everything was labelled as 'A Dynamic Sounds Production'. The bulk, however, did come from Byron Lee and was at the commercial end of Jamaican Reggae, although it really is worth checking out, as some of it is pretty good. Among the best cuts are Junior Byles' 'Pharaoh Hiding', Eric Donaldson's 1971 Festival song winner 'Cherry Oh Baby' (the biggest seller on the label), Barry Biggs' 'Got To Be Mellow' and Tesfa MacDonald's 'Life Is The Highest', which uses a strong rocksteady backing.

Quite a lot of Dynamic's output was conveniently spread across both volumes of Trojan's *Sixteen Dynamic Reggae Hits* compilation, with the second of these easily being the better. After Trojan scrapped the label late in 1972, Island's Dragon imprint continued as the main UK issuing outlet for Byron Lee until 1976, when Creole established a second series of Dynamic, with Barry Biggs' 'Sideshow' becoming a UK Top 3 hit in that year.

EXPLOSION

Started in 1969, Explosion's first few releases were from Derrick Harriott, following which his output was moved over to Song Bird. The label was then given over to material from a multitude of producers. There are a few particularly good British productions from Laurel Aitken (Trevor Lloyd's 'Chinee Brush' and Dice The Boss's 'Funky Duck') and Nat Cole (Billy Jack's cover of 'In The Summertime'). JA-wise, there was The Slickers' wonderful 'Gold On Your Dress' (flipside of 'Man From Carolina'), Lloyd Robinson's 'Death A Come' (Explosion's first release), The Hippy Boys' 'Vengeance' and Audley Rollen's 'Whisper A Little Prayer'.

There was a more commercial thread running through some of the 1971–2 releases with productions from Neville Willoughby and Federal Records. Before Trojan pulled the plug in 1974, the most notable releases were Carl

Dawkins' 'I Feel Good', Dennis Brown's 'Black Magic Woman', Slim Smith's 'The Time Has Come' and The Tennors' 'Weather Report'. Interestingly, in the hardly memorable last gasp of Explosion's final 12 releases, eight were cover versions! This label certainly had its moments, but there was no real consistency of quality on it.

GAYFEET

The UK counterpart of Sonia Pottinger's JA imprint and a sister label to High Note, this imprint never really got off the ground. Only Junior Soul's 'Slipping' (by the artist later known as Junior Murvin) is really recommended.

GG

Trojan's main issuing outlet for Alvin Ranglin's productions, GG has a fair amount of very undervalued music, with The Maytones just about the most featured artists on it. Among the biggest and best releases are Cornell Campbell and The Eternals' 'Music Keep On Playing', Verne and Son's 'Little Boy Blue' (which provided the rhythm track for Judge Dread's 'Big Six'), Gerald McKleish's overlooked 'False Reaper', Cynthia Richards' 'Is There A Place In Your Heart For Me' and The Maytones' heavy cut of 'Black And White'.

Some of the best Ranglin music was released across a number of Trojan compilations, namely *Man From Carolina* (actually the only Trojan album pressed with a GG label), *Reggae Flight 404*, the second volume of *Reggae Reggae Reggae* and the scarce but less thrilling *Pipeline*. GG was wrapped up in 1973 as part of Trojan's rationalisation exercise, but Ranglin still had product released on some of the company's other outlets, notably Attack and Horse.

GPW

Not a formal issuing label but one which was used for blank pre-release discs containing sides that may or may not have been ultimately released by Trojan. (The GPW stands for Graham P Walker, who was Trojan's manager at the time.) These discs would be sold through the Musicland record stores at a hefty mark-up as the music was unavailable elsewhere and very valuable to sound systems and DJs.

GRAPE

This was started by Trojan in 1969 as an issuing outlet for Joe Sinclair's UK productions, although its first release was a Jamaican-recorded effort by little-known singer Carlton Alphonso. There were some fine skinhead-reggae things on this part of the label from Freddie Notes and The Rudies, King Horror (actually Laurel Aitken, who produced for Grape) and Nyah Shuffle. Around the middle of 1970, Joe shelved his Grape productions set-up and formed Swan Productions with Webster Shrowder and Des Bryan, with whom he was increasingly working. This effectively resulted in the ending of the first phase of the Grape label.

In 1972, Trojan reactivated Grape as another ragbag label. Some of the output from this time was excellent, particularly Big Youth's 'Foreman Versus Frasier', Delroy Wilson's 'Can I Change My Mind' and Freddy McKay's 'Our Rendezvous'. The label was not a stand-out Trojan subsidiary by any means. The company discontinued it late in 1973 and the final issue had a very plain label design in appropriate purple, in contrast with the previous garish yellow and green one.

GREEN DOOR

Not a label to be overlooked as it featured some of the best of Trojan's early-'70s music, spanning as it did 1971 to early 1974, issuing some high-quality sounds from the likes of Bob Marley ('Lively Up Yourself' and 'Trench Town Rock'), The Charmers ('Rasta Never Fail'), The Wailing Souls ('Harbour Shark'), The Hoffner Brothers ('The King Man Is Back') and The God Sons ('Merry Up').

Trojan may have established Green Door to handle its more rootsy output from Jamaica, as a lot of what emanated from it is certainly in a pretty cultural vein. Particularly of note on the label are the aforementioned 'The King Man Is Back' and Shorty's 'President Mash Up The Resident' (on the 'My Conversation' rhythm). Sadly, the last dozen Green Door releases were a mixed bag of pleasant love songs, cover versions of a few current hits and a couple of Jimmy London's more mediocre efforts. Trojan seemed to have switched the heavy stuff somewhere else.

HARRY J

Most famous for its two chart hits 'Liquidator' and 'Young, Gifted And Black', Harry J was established by Trojan for Harry Johnson productions early in 1970, although a few sides pressed with a Harry J label were released on the Trojan 600 series. The bulk of the releases in the first year were given over to The Jay Boys, aka The Harry J All Stars, and collected together for the *Liquidator* compilation. The Cables, Bob Andy and Marcia Griffiths (either individually or collectively) were the other prominent artists on the label at this time. For reasons unknown, there were only four issues in 1971 and six in 1972.

The superior Harry Johnson-produced music resumed again in 1973 with The Ethiopians, Joe White and The Geoffrey Chung All Stars. Something clearly went awry just after this, however, as no more of his music was released on the imprint. It may have been that Johnson was giving his material to Island (for Blue Mountain) at this time.

So what of the rest of the music? It coincided with the 1974/5 struggling Trojan and could not be relied on for any real quality music. There was an abundance of covers of current pop hits – 'Walking Miracle', 'Rock Your Baby', 'Kung-Fu Fighting', 'Homely Girl', etc – and a few (literally) really decent offerings like Delroy Wilson's 'What Happen To The Youth Of Today', Bob Andy's 'Fire Burning' and The Ethiopians' 'Big Splish Splash'. There was also a plethora of relatively weak UK-recorded product from the likes of Sidney Crooks, Kush (The Cimarons) and Ellis Breary. When many early reggae fans are asked why they eventually went off reggae, they often point the finger at the Harry J label from specifically around this period. The label went out with a bang, however, with Johnny Clarke's superb 'Move Out A Babylon'.

HIGH NOTE

One of the formative Trojan/B&C subsidiaries, High Note was the company's main outlet for Sonia Pottinger productions and put out around 60 singles between 1968 and 1972. Most everything is worth picking up here, with the exception of the releases by The Creary Sisters and Otis Wright (which were Sacred) and Nora Dean (which was mento). There's plenty of really good music on here from the likes of Delroy Wilson (notably 'It Hurts' and 'Put Yourself In My Place'), Delano Stewart ('Dance With Me' and 'Got To Come Back') and The Hippy Boys ('Reggae Pressure' and 'Chicken Licken'). Perhaps the very best are Patsy's 'We Were Lovers' and the Victors' 'Reggae Buddy'. High Note was also responsible for three highly collectable LPs: Roland Alphonso's *ABC Rock Steady*, the various-artists compilation *Dancing Down Orange Street* and The Hippy Boys' *Reggae With The Hippy Boys*.

HORSE

Initiated by Trojan in 1971 as a pop/soul label, Horse was very much aimed at the middle-of-the-road punter. It was successful almost immediately, with white singer Scott English's 'Brandy' breaking into the UK charts. Then Dandy Livingstone hit the Top 20 with 'Suzanne Beware Of The Devil' and, later, the Top 30 with 'Big City'/'Think About That'. The label eventually stretched to over 150 releases, finishing in 1978.

There is little about Horse which is really commendable to the reggae connoisseur, although exceptions are Judy Mowatt's 'Mellow Mood', Marcia Griffiths' 'Sweet Bitter Love' and Carl Malcolm's 'No Jestering'. It tended to get tarred with the 'commercial' brush when some of the product issued on the label was, in retrospect, quite credible. Nicky Thomas was a Horse regular and his work is now highly regarded by some collectors. Similarly, Tito Simon's time will surely come; his 'Easy Come, Easy Go' is truly excellent. Add to these Jackie Robinson (one-third of The Pioneers), Lloyd Charmers, Barrington Spence and Owen Gray.

Bunny Lee productions seemed to dominate the label from 1975 through to 1976 and Johnny Clarke seems to proliferate. In truth, there were some pretty ropey items being released at this time, however, and the label really seemed to lose what little direction it had. Without doubt, an essential Horse release from 1975 was Joe White's 'Skank Indigo' (HOSS 85).

HOT ROD

Just 12 releases on this label, which Trojan established to showcase productions by Lambert Briscoe, who operated the Hot Rod sound system in the Brixton area of south London. The most highly prized record on the label is The Hot Rod All Stars' 'Skinhead Speaks His Mind'. Others include the very commercial 'I Wish You Well' (Delroy Dunkley) and 'Keep On Trying' (Tony Nash) and the much rougher 'Dog Your Woman' (Patsy and Peggy) and 'Remember Easter Monday' (Peggy and Jimmy). The latter was based on Alton Ellis's 'Remember That Sunday'.

Like the Joe label, almost everything on Hot Rod is collectable these days, in some cases undeservedly so, such as Josh's 'Leaving Everything', which is basically just an organ version of 'All Kinds Of Everything'. On the other hand, 'Prison Sentence' by Winston James is one of the most credible British-produced efforts from the period. Eddy Grant's Torpedo label also issued quite a lot of Briscoe's material but, given the absence of specific release dates, it is not known whether this appeared directly after Trojan had shut down Hot Rod. It should also be mentioned that a couple of Hot Rod productions appeared on the main Trojan 7700 series and on Duke. Again, it is never clear at all why they weren't issued on the producer-dedicated subsidiary.

JACKPOT

A UK version of Bunny Lee's Jamaican Jackpot label, but a huge wedge of the early releases contained a whole host of British material from producers Laurel Aitken, Clancy Collins, Nat Cole, Roy Smith and Larry Lawrence. Most people prefer the Lee offerings to the bulk of this, although Nat Cole's cover of 'Sugar Sugar' is a pretty credible reggae cover, if you can stand the song in the first place. Of the Lee material, The Twinkle Brothers' 'You Can Do It Too', Winston Williams's 'DJ Choice' and 'The People's Choice', Dave Barker's 'Girl Of My Dreams', and Delroy Wilson's 'Better Must Come' and 'Cool Operator' are very worthy releases. Some very solid rhythms, too. However, beware of some of the 1970-era pressings, which are woefully poor and seem not to have originated from the usual Trojan sources.

After Jackpot was concluded in 1973, Trojan switched Bunny Lee's output to other Trojan labels, including Horse and Attack. Never a person to put all his eggs in one basket, Bunny also had product being issued on Count Shelly's labels and Lord Koos during this time.

J·DAN

With some 17 releases, J-Dan lasted just over a year (early 1970 to around April 1971) and was intended to be a sister label to Downtown, which had been launched to highlight Dandy productions. Without a doubt, the biggest sellers were The Music Doctors' stepping 'Bush Doctor' and 'In The Summertime'. Apart from other Music Doctors titles, the rest is pretty run-of-the-mill stuff by the likes of Roy Gee and Boy Friday (another pseudonym for Dandy).

JOE

Joe catered exclusively for productions by Joe(l) Mansano, who owned and managed Joe's Record Shack in Brixton's Granville Arcade for some 15 years. Prior to Trojan giving him his own subsidiary, 11 of Mansano's productions had appeared on special Joe labels in amongst the main Duke catalogue numbers. Even before then, he had product out on Revolution (Clive Williams and The Heatwave's 'In Loving Memory Of Don Drummond') and Blue Cat ('Life On Reggae Planet' and 'The Bullet'). 'Brixton Cat' was one of those issued on the Duke numbering system with great success.

The main Joe label was very much directed at the burgeoning skinhead market, with the release of tracks like 'Trial Of Pama Dice' (Lloyd, Dice And Mum), 'Son Of Al Capone' and 'Skinhead Revolt' (Joe Mansano as Joe The Boss), 'Small Change' (Girlie) and 'The Informer' (Dice The Boss). One of the most popular releases on the label, and one with real lasting appeal, is the mournful 'She Caught The Train' by Ray Martell, who also recorded under the names Martel Robinson and Mike Robinson. After the 'Mansano sound' had run its course and skinheads had begun to decline, Trojan took no more product from Joe and pulled the plug on the label.

JJ
Only two known issues on this revived label. Originally a Doctor Bird group offshoot with the records carrying the DB matrix numbering system – the Trojan version carries the JJ matrix.

JUMP-UP
Was calypso making a comeback in 1971? Trojan seemed to think so, putting out a few re-releases on Duke and just two on this revived Island subsidiary from the 1962–5 period. Actually, to be fair, they did select probably the two most topical issues for the time.

MOODISC
After producer Harry Mudie's sojourn with Pama, Trojan put out a first series of his Moodisc label during 1970/1. This short run of just 15 issues was notable for Cornel Campbell and The Eternals' 'Let's Start Again', Lloyd Charmers' organ workout 'Back Door' and The Eternals' soulful 'Push Me In The Corner', along with some worthy but unnoticed early sides from I-Roy. There were two albums put out on the imprint, namely Joe Joe Bennett's *Groovy Joe Joe* (issued on the back of his big-selling 'Leaving Rome' 45) and the first-rate *Mudie's Mood* compilation.

Curiously, however, by the close of 1971 Mudie had switched to Rita and Benny King's R&B Discs set-up, which issued another series of Moodisc (with a plain all-red label and HM prefix).

PRESSURE BEAT
Pressure Beat more or less carried on from where Joe Gibbs' Amalgamated label left off and put out just 15 releases between 1970 and 1973. (Gibbs also

had a Pressure Beat label in JA.) Highlights include Lord Comic's 'Jack Of My Trade', Desi Young's cut-and-paste proto-dub 'News Flash', The Soul Brothers' 'Pussy Catch A Fire', Cat Campbell's punchy 'Hammering Version' and Peter Tosh's angry 'Them A Fi Get A Beatin''. Oddly, there were no releases on the label in 1971, suggesting perhaps that Gibbs was putting the bulk of his UK-issued product with Pama at this time. Pressure Beat certainly wasn't a bad label, but neither was it a particularly memorable one. Quite a lot of Gibbs' 1971–3 output was usefully spread over two volumes of Trojan's *Heptones And Friends* albums, which were essentially various-artists sets containing a relative smattering of Heptones material.

PYRAMID (SECOND SERIES)

Amazing how Trojan resurrected these old labels without any apparent commitment to identity or longevity. Not a bad run of a dozen or so issues on this one during 1973–4, with highlights from I-Roy ('Tip From The Prince'), Gregory Isaacs ('Innocent People Cry') and Johnny Clarke ('My Desire'/'Lemon Tree'), but the quality didn't match the earlier Doctor Bird-administered imprint.

Q

Probably the Trojan label you're least likely to see, ever, and home to probably the worst record ever issued on a Trojan label, 'Tribute To Jimmy [*sic*] Hendrix'. Its four-issue output came courtesy of legendary soundman Count Suckle, and the label name came directly from his Q Club, in Paddington's Praed Street, which he ran for 20-odd years. There was one other Suckle production put out on the Duke label, namely 'Chicken Scratch' (apparently the Q Club's in-house dance), which also appeared on the *Funky Chicken* compilation.

RANDY'S

Trojan started this label in 1970 to issue productions from the late Vincent Chin's Jamaican Randy's and Impact labels. It's one that has few real goodies, although The Ethiopians' 'Mr Tom', Rocking Horse's 'Hard Time', Jimmy London's 'A Little Love' and Dennis Brown's 'Cheater' are all recommended. Probably the best-known release was Jimmy London's version of 'Bridge Over Troubled Water', which saw inclusion on the fifth volume of the *Tighten Up* series. There were a few superb Chin-less productions late in the series, with notable offerings from Lee Perry, Keith Hudson and Derrick Harriott.

In conclusion, there was a huge amount of wonderful music from the Randy's stable, but you'll have difficulty finding much of it on here.

SMASH

As Bunny Lee had a Smash label in JA, this was probably intended as its counterpart, although, like most other Trojan imprints, its focus drifted as time went on. From 1971, there are some noteworthy tunes from Clancy Collins, among which are Merlene Webber's heavyweight 'Hard Life' and Delroy Wilson's 'Satisfaction'. Otherwise, there is John Holt's best-ever cut of 'My Heart Is Gone' for Phil Pratt, which has a cracking bubbling bass line, and an early effort from Dennis Alcapone with 'Ball Of Confusion'. The label was eventually wound up by Trojan in 1973, after running for three years.

SONG BIRD

The first dozen or so issues on Song Bird (beginning in 1969) were given over to productions by Lloyd Charmers, Ken Jones, Stranger Cole and Trojan's own Joe Sinclair. Among these formative releases, Bruce Ruffin and The Techniques' 'Long About Now' was a solid-gold classic, while The Megatons' 'Memphis Reggae' is a belting organ instrumental in the Glen Adams style. Later in the year, however, Song Bird became dedicated to the productions of Derrick Harriott and his JA Crystal and Move & Groove outlets. For a reggae subsidiary, the label was consistent in its excellent-quality music and in having Harriott as the main man right through to 1973, when it was wrapped up. The bulk of Song Bird's output is by just a handful of acts, including The Crystalites (Harriott's house band), The Kingstonians, Scotty, The Ethiopians, The Chosen Few and Derrick's own super-smooth vocal talents.

Harriott was responsible for a quite staggering series of instrumentals, including the western-inspired 'The Undertaker', 'Undertaker's Burial', 'Ghost Rider', 'The Overtaker' and 'True Grit' (with Bongo Herman and Les Chen). Almost without a doubt, though, the biggest seller was The Chosen Few's cover of 'Shaft', which had some success in crossing over to the white market.

Song Bird was discontinued in 1973, after a few non-Harriott productions, with the man subsequently having some of his product out on Harry J (and of course he had nothing to do with Harry Johnson!).

SPINNING WHEEL

Named after a particular Lee Perry track (Melanie Jonas and Dave Barker's 'Spinning Wheel'), this subsidiary label issued half a dozen or so highly sought-after Perry productions. It is believed that Melanie Jonas, Perry's girlfriend at the time, peddled the tracks to Trojan as her own work during a visit to London, but they really emanate from Perry himself. Following these, the last handful were by Jimmy (Martin) Riley, The Cimarons, The Rudies and Stranger Cole. Stranger's 'Crying Every Night' is a most worthwhile issue, which also saw release on Pama's Camel subsidiary.

SUMMIT

Bar the last few issues, Summit focused on productions from Leslie Kong's Beverley's Records set-up in Jamaica. Kong's work with The Maytals, The Pioneers, Bruce Ruffin and The Melodians has never really been as eagerly collected in comparison with the likes of Perry, Dodd, Reid, *et al*, possibly because of its tendency towards the commercial end of reggae and its generally 'international' appeal.

Of Summit's 43 issues between 1970 and 1973, 37 were provided by Kong, and some, like Tony Brevett's 'Staircase Of Time', Glen Brown's 'Collie And Wine' and Delroy Wilson's 'Got To Get Away' are really scarce. The biggest seller was undoubtedly The Melodians' 'Rivers Of Babylon', and the most neglected nugget is Brent Dowe's excellent 'Freedom Train'.

Following Kong's death in August '71, Summit continued to issue his productions posthumously, but after these had dried up Trojan put out a few oddities from other producers. Keep an eye out for some rogue issues with different B sides, as these seemed to be pretty common the label.

TECHNIQUES

Started by Trojan in 1970, Techniques showcased the productions of Winston Riley, who had hitherto seen some of his material issued on Big Shot. It is best known for Dave (Barker) and Ansell Collins' 'Double Barrel' and 'Monkey Spanner', but generally the label doesn't seem to include really top-drawer Riley sides. Winston Wright's moody 'Top Secret' is probably the finest, barring the aforementioned.

The last ten releases were given over to producers other than Riley and highlights include Prince Jazzbo's 'Mr Harry Skank', The Silvertones' 'That's When It Hurts', The Eagles' 'Rub It Down' and KC White's elusive

'Anywhere But Nowhere'. In fact, one could go as far to say that the end of Techniques was an improvement on the beginning. The plug was pulled at the start of 1974.

TREASURE ISLE

The position on this one – at least, for part of it – is a bit unclear. Island issued the Treasure Isle label between 1967 and 1968, following which it was discontinued in around summer 1968. Almost exactly a year later, the label was revived by Graeme Goodall's Doctor Bird group for a handful of issues, including Andy Capp's 'Pop A Top', Symarip's 'Skinhead Moonstomp', a few other Symarip sides and an odd one from Boris Gardiner. It's not known, however, whether Trojan had a part to play in this relaunch, particularly since some pressings – such as 'Skinhead Moonstomp' – seemed to have been pressed by the same source used by Trojan. And then there was the *Skinhead Moonstomp* album, which appeared on Trojan. But whatever was going on, midway through 1970 Treasure Isle was scrapped yet again. Whether this coincided with the liquidation of the Doctor Bird group is also as yet unknown.

From issue TI7058 onwards, Treasure Isle was definitely in the hands of Trojan. The label reverted to dealing with Duke Reid product, just as it had during the period when it was administered by Island. As with the Duke Reid imprint, numerous U Roy recordings appear, with the DJ teamed with the likes of Hopeton Lewis and The Melodians, and with Phyllis Dillon for the wonderful 'Midnight Confession'. One to look for is the great Justin Hinds' 'Botheration'. This run of 17 issues ended with Dennis Alcapone's 'Wake Up Jamaica'.

Trojan wound up Treasure Isle in 1973, since the Duke was by then producing very little in the way of new music.

TROJAN

Trojan issued product over four main series: the first short Duke Reid-oriented-run during 1967 and 1968; the 600 run from 1968–9; the 7700s from 1969–76; and finally, from 1976 through to the mid '80s, the TRO series, which pretty much continued the 7700 series.

There is some nice rocksteady in the first series, but the 600s really came into their own with some excellent Dandy material (prior to the launch of Downtown), some early Lee Perry and Lynford Anderson offerings and a batch of top-notch Duke Reid sides. There is a smattering of more average fare from Owen Gray, Federal, The Merrymen and Byron Lee, but the rest can generally be relied on.

The 7700s led directly on from the 600s, with more top-quality music, notably from Leslie Kong and Duke Reid, but the label's commercial success with Desmond Dekker, Nicky Thomas, Bruce Ruffin *et al* in 1970 and 1971 had led to an overall sweetening of its output, with the addition of strings and an orchestra, courtesy of Johnny Arthey. The familiar orange-and-white label changed to a brown shield design.

The reasons behind the old Trojan's reversal of fortunes within a matter of years appear to be manifold. Sure, the hits had become few and far between, but there was more to it than that, and the core of the problem appears to have been a series of poor management decisions, as succinctly summarised by David Betteridge: 'Personally, I think that basically the company was under-funded. They had a big staff and when, in 1972, Island and Trojan went their separate ways, they just didn't have the revenue to maintain the company. To be honest, by the time we pulled out, Trojan was a bit of a pain. Island was having [pop] hits all over the place and a lot of the money earned from these went into Trojan. So when Trojan and Island went their separate ways, the money just wasn't there any more. Lee [Gopthal] really should have brought in someone else to act in the same way that Island had done, but he decided to go it alone, which I think was a mistake. Also, the UK-[produced] reggae recordings were a bit of a mistake. When you look at Trojan's early success, it was with Jamaican product, and of course the overheads were much lower for those. We didn't have to pay for any production costs, and so we could budget much more effectively. And so the costs just spiralled and that of course had a big effect on the company's finances. I'm sure there's more to it than that, but I think that was basically the problem.'

Following Saga's takeover of Trojan, the TRO series never really established itself or the company. It appears that Saga thought that they were buying the rights to an extensive rock-music catalogue...

UPSETTER

As Trojan subsidiaries go, this must be the most extensively reissued. In fact, every known release from it has been reissued as part of Trojan's *Complete Upsetter Singles Collection*. The label was launched in 1969 to issue Lee Perry productions and issued a high proportion of Upsetters instrumentals such as

'Night Doctor', 'Man From MI5' and 'Soulful I', although the big one was, of course, 'Return Of Django'. Other regulars were Dave Barker and Bob Marley and The Wailers, while perennial connoisseurs' favourites are The Ravers' 'Badam Bam' (the vocal cut to 'Live Injection'), The Bleechers' 'Check Him Out' and The Upsetters' 'Cold Sweat'.

Trojan Singles Discography

Due to the nature of Jamaican music, it would be impossible to produce a discography that is 100% accurate. While this discography is considerably more accurate than the previous edition, new information is still arriving at a steady pace. There will also always be record credits which are debated and disputed between dedicated reggae collectors and the singers, players and producers involved in creating Jamaican music.

ACTION (PREFIX ACT)

101   Knotty No Jester/Knotty No Jester (Instrumental) – Big Youth (Prod: Clive Chin and Victor Chin for Randy's) (1975) [ALSO PRESSED WITH ATTACK LABEL BUT USING SAME MATRIX NUMBER]

102   Natty Dread In A Greenwich Farm/Natty Version – Cornel Campbell (Prod: Edward 'Bunny' Lee) (1975)

103   Natty Dread Girl/Natty Dread Girl (Version) – Linval Thompson/The Aggrovators (Prod: Edward 'Bunny' Lee) (1975)

Note

Action had always been a soul-oriented label but Trojan revived it for a few reggae releases at the end of its run.

AMALGAMATED LABEL (PREFIX AMG)

800   Please Stop Your Lying/Feel So Fine – Errol Dunkley/Tommy McCook and The Supersonics (1968)

801   Hope Someday/Just Like A River – The Leaders/Stranger [Cole] and Gladdy [Anderson] (1968)

802   Just Can't Win/Sometimes – The Versatiles/The Leaders (1968)

803   That's The Way You Like It/The Big Takeover – The Overtakers (1968)

804   Tit For Tat/You Take So Long To Know [SACRED] – The Leaders (actually
      by Neville Hinds)/The Marvettes (1968)

805   I'm Not Your Man/I'm Going Home – Errol Dunkley (1968)

806   Seeing Is Knowing/Music Is The Key – Stranger [Cole] and Gladdy
      [Anderson]/Roy Shirley (1968)

807   The Scorcher/Do It Right Tonight – Errol Dunkley (1968)

808   The Upsetter/Thank You Baby – Lee Perry (1968)

809   Girl You Rough/Wooh Oh Oh – The Overtakers/Keith Blake (1968)

810   El Casino Royale/Dee's Special – Lyn Taitt's Band (actually with Count
      Machuki) (1968)

811   Give Me Little Loving/This Is Soul – The Pioneers/Lyn Taitt's Band (1968)

812   Fat Girl In Red/Trust The Book – The Mellotones/The Versatiles (1968)

813   Now I'm All Alone/Fall And Rise – Victor Morris (Prod: Bobby Aitken)
      (1968)

814   Long Shot/Dip And Fall Back – The Pioneers (1968)

815   The World Needs Love/Dance The A Ups (actually 'Dance The Arena') – Roy
      Shirley (1968)

816   Having A Party/Day By Day – Dennis Walks/The Groovers (1968)

817   Feel Good/Soulful Mood – The Mellotones (actually by The Bleechers)/The
      Mellotones (actually by Tommy McCook and The Supersonics) (1968)

818   Holding Out/Get On Up – The Creations (1968)

819   Over And Over/Woman Of Samaria – Jackie Robinson/Jackie Robinson
      (actually by The Spanishites with The Blenders) (1968)

820   Love Brother/I Spy – Errol Dunkley/Errol Dunkley (actually by Lyn Taitt and
      The Jets) (1968)

821   Jackpot/Kimble – The Pioneers/The Creators (actually by Lee Perry) (1968)
      [SEE ALSO AMALGAMATED CSP SERIES]

822   People Grudgeful/Sharpen Ya Machete – Sir Gibbs (actually by Joe Gibbs and
      The Pioneers)/The Pioneers (1968)

823   No Dope Me Pony/Great Great In '68 – The Pioneers/Lord Salmons (1968)

824   Let The Little Girl Dance/I Want To Go Home – Jackie Robinson/Derrick
      Morgan (1968)

825   Train To Soulsville/Cinderella – Cool Sticky [Count Sticky]/Errol Dunkley
      (1968)

826   Tickle Me/The Time Has Come – The Pioneers/The Versatiles (1968)

827   Good Time Rock/Sleepy Ludy (actually titled 'Sleepy Lady') – Hugh
      Malcolm/Lyn Taitt's Band (1968)

828   Catch The Beat/Janan (actually 'Jane Anne') – The Pioneers/Sir Gibbs All Stars
      (actually by The Immortals) (1968)

173

829   Man About Town/Mortgage – Cannonball Bryan [Karl Bryan]/Hugh
      Malcolm (1968)
830   Sweet Dreams/Caterpillar Rock – The Pioneers/Vincent Gordon (1968)
831   Never See Come See/Jumping Jack – The Royals/Cannonball Bryan [Karl
      Bryan] Trio (1968)
832   Secret Weapon/Jumpy Jumpy Girl – The Conquerors (actually by Ansell
      Collins)/The Conquerors (actually by The Viceroys) (1968) [A SIDE
      REISSUED ON PRESSURE BEAT PB 5506B. B SIDE REISSUED ON
      AMALGAMATED AMG 842B]
833   Don't You Know/Me Naw Go Believe You (actually titled 'Me Naw Go A
      Bellevue') – The Pioneers (1968)
834   Hurry Come Up/Off Track – The Crashers (actually The Ethiopians) (1969)
835   Mama Look Deh/Decimal Currency – The Pioneers (actually by Alva Lewis
      and Glen Adams)/The Blenders (1969)
836   Them A Laugh And A Ki Ki/The Hippys Are Here – The Soul Mates (actually
      The Pioneers)/The Hippy Boys (1969)
837   Private Number/She's So Fine – Ernest Wilson/Glen Adams (Prod: Derrick
      Morgan/Bunny Lee) (1969)
838   What Moma No Want She Get/We Two – Stranger Cole (1969) [SEE ALSO
      AMALGAMATED CSP SERIES]
839   Wreck A Buddy/Push It In – The Soul Sisters/The Versatiles (1969)
840   I'm Moving On/Who The Cap Fits – The Pioneers (1969)
841   Me No Born Ya/The Wicked Must Survive – The Reggae Boys (1969) [B
      SIDE REISSUED ON PRESSURE BEAT PB 5502B]
842   On The Move/Jump It Up (actually titled 'Jumpy Jumpy Girl') – The
      Soulmates (actually by Count Machuki and Joe Gibbs' All Stars)/The
      Soulmates (actually by The Viceroys) (1969) [B SIDE ALSO ISSUED ON
      AMAGAMATED AMG 832B]
843   The Reggae Train/Dolly House On Fire – The Reggae Boys (1969)
844   Why Did You Leave?/Man A Wail – The Young Souls (1969)
845   Hot Buttered Corn/It Is I – The Cobbs/Count Machuki (A side produced by
      Jackson Jones) (1969)
846   Apollo 11/Love Love Everyday – The Moon Boys/The Pioneers (1969)
847   It's Alright/One Love – Ken Parker/The Cobbs (B side produced by Jackson
      Jones) (1969)
848   Professor In Action/Reflections Of Don D – The Scientists/The Supersonics
      (actually by Johnny Moore) (1969)
849   Space Doctor/Baby Reggae (actually titled 'Baby Let's Reggae Now') – The
      Cobbs/Lloyd [Robinson] and Devon [Russell] (Prod: Jackson Jones) (1969)

850   Alli Button/Death Rides (actually titled 'Bangalang Shangalang') – The Pioneers/The Hippy Boys (B side produced by Lloyd Deslandes) (1969)

851   Bongo Jah/My Last Walk – The Immortals/Ansel Collins (1969)

852   Man Beware/Mother Matty – The Slickers (1969) [A SIDE REISSUED ON AMALGAMATED AMG 866B]

853   Only Yesterday/Joe Gibbs Mood – Ken Parker/Ansel Collins (1969)

854   Lu Lu Bell/Long Long Time – The Versatiles (1969)

855   Nevada Joe/Straight To The Head – Johnny Lover/The Destroyers (1969)

856   Niney Special/Danger Zone – The Destroyers (actually by Niney)/The Destroyers (actually by Lloyd Willis) (1970)

857   Take Back Your Duck/Nothing For Nothing – The Inspirations (1970)

858   Franco Nero (Version 1)/Franco Nero (Version 2) – Joe Gibbs and The Destroyers (actually by Count Machuki)/The Destroyers (1970)

859   Rock The Clock/Rock The Clock (Version) – The Destroyers (1970)

860   Let It Be/Turn Back The Hands Of Time – Nicky Thomas (1970)

861   La La/Reggae Fever – The Inspirations (1970)

862   The Train Is Coming/Man Oh Man – The Inspirations (1970)

863   Danzella/Danzella (Version) – Nicky Thomas/Joe Gibbs' All Stars (1970)

864   Not Yet Traced (NYT)

865   Hi Jacked/Life Is Down In Denver – Joe Gibbs' All Stars (1970) [B SIDE ALSO ON AMALGAMATED AMG 866B]

866   Money Raper (actually plays 'Turn Back The Hands Of Time (Version)')/Mother Matty – The Slickers (actually by Joe Gibbs' All Stars)/The Slickers (1970) [A SIDE ALSO ON AMG 865B. B SIDE REISSUED FROM AMG 852A]

867   Movements (The Joe Gibbs Way)/Caesar – Count Machuki/Joe Gibbs All Stars (1970)

868   Gift Of God/The Raper – Lizzy/The Joe Gibbs' All Stars (1970)

869   Perfect Born Yah/Red Red Wine – Joe Gibbs All Stars (actually by The Immortals) (1970)

870   Seeing Is Believing/Ghost Capturer – Charlie Ace/Joe Gibbs' All Stars (1970)

871   Pumpkin Eater/Pumpkin Eater (Version) – Johnny Lover/Joe Gibbs' All Stars (1970)

872   Ghost Walk/Joy Stick – Caly Gibbs [Carlton Gibbs]/Joe Gibbs' All Stars (1971)

873   Two Edged Sword/Two Edged Sword (Version) – Johnny Lover/Joe Gibbs' All Stars (1971) [A SIDE REISSUED ON GREEN DOOR GD 4020B UNDER DIFFERENT TITLE]

AMALGAMATED (PREFIX AMG CSP)

003   What Moma No Want She Get/Jackpot – Stranger Cole/The Pioneers (1969)

Note

This was a one-off issue and quite why it came out is a mystery. The 'CSP' prefix was used by Trojan only once, on the Coxsone label compilation album *Reggae Special* issued in 1969. It may have been intended as a promotional vehicle for Amalgamated (i.e. a double A side featuring two of the labels' top sellers) but the link with Coxsone is tenuous.

AMALGAMATED 'SACRED' SERIES (PREFIX AMGSS)

001   We Are Not Divided/He Is So Real To Me – The Marvettes (1968)
002   We Shall Have A Grand Time/Let The Power Fall On Me – The Marvettes (1968)
003   I Was Once Lost In Sin/What A Wonderful Thing – The Marvettes (1968)

Note

All issues on Amalgamated were produced by Joel Gibson [Joe Gibbs] except where stated otherwise. The three releases on the 'Sacred' series all saw issue on his JA 'Testimony' imprint.

ATTACK (FIRST SERIES: 1969–70): PREFIX ATT

8000   Gentle On My Mind/Music Box – Pat Sandy/Big L (actually George Lee) (Prod: Philligree) (1969)
8001   Phoenix Reggae/Music Box – Family Circle [Symarip]/Big L (actually George Lee) (Prod: Philligree) (1969)
8002   Reggae Krishna/Official – Family Circle [Symarip]/Family Circle [Symarip] with Rico Rodriguez (Prod: Philligree) (1969)
8003   Consider Me/Family Man – Pat Sandy/Big L (actually George Lee) (Prod: Philligree) (1969)
8004   By The Time I Get To Phoenix/Hungry Man – Family Circle [Symarip] and Carl Griffiths/Big L (actually George Lee) (Prod: Philligree) (1969)
8005   Stagger Back/The Show Boat – Family Circle [Symarip]/Big L (actually George Lee) (Prod: Philligree) (1969)
8006   NYT
8007   NYT
8008   NYT
8009   NYT
8010   NYT
8011   Su, Su, Su/Better Herring – The Soul Directions (actually The Pioneers) (Prod: Byron Lee) (1969)
8012   NYT

8013   I'm A Puppet/Vindication – The Pyramids (Prod: Philligree) (1970)

8014   Hey Little Girl/Why Don't You Try Me? – Dave King Reggae Band (Prod: Philigree) (1970)

8015   Loving Lover/Cora – Ray Martell (Prod: Philligree) (1970)

8016   Nyah Bingewe/Message – Nyah Earth (Prod: Philligree) (1970)

8017   Dual Heat/Night Of The Long Knives – Nyah Earth (Prod: Philligree) (1970)

8018   I Can't Go On/Only You – Winston Groovy/Winston Groovy (actually by unidentified male vocalist) (Prod: Laurel Aitken) (1970)

8019   You Can't Turn Your Back On Me/The Worm – Winston Groovy/Pama Dice (Prod: Laurel Aitken) (1970)

8020   Let Me Out/I Belong To You – Concorde (Prod: Philligree) (1970)

8021   Get Lost Boss/I'll Be There – The Prodigal Sons with The Cimarons/Theresa and Catherine with The Cimarons (Prod: Philligree) (1970)

8022   You, Yes You/Version Be There – The Reaction/The Cimarons (Prod: Philligree) (1970)

8023   I'm A Drifter/Drifting Version – Tubal Caine [The Cimarons]/The Cimarons (Prod: Philligree) (1970)

Note

Most, or all, of the above releases were put out during the time Attack was administered by Doctor Bird. Trojan took over the label at some point but it is not clear exactly when, particularly given that Philligree productions continued to be released on it. Attack had slightly changed its label design and was using 'standard' B&C/Trojan pressings by the time ATT 8013 was put out, so the switch to Trojan may have occurred at that point.

ATTACK (SECOND SERIES: 1972–78): PREFIX ATT

8024   What's Going On – Pat Satchmo/Tubby's In Full Swing – Lloyd and Kerry (actually Lloyd Young and Carey Johnson) (Prod: Tony Robinson [Prince Tony]) (1972)

8025   This Beautiful Land/Beautiful Version – The Melodians/Melodious Rhythms (Prod: Tony Brevett) 1972)

8026   Feel Good (actually 'Feel Good All Over')/Feel Good Version – H Handy (actually Horace Andy)/Phil Pratt All Stars (Prod: Phil Pratt) (1972)

8027   Fine Style/On The Track – Dennis Alcapone/Winston Scotland (Prod: Tony Robinson [Prince Tony]) (1972) [B SIDE ALSO ISSUED ON GREEN DOOR (GD 4023B)]

8028   Sylvia's Mother (Reggae)/Sylvia's Mother (Soul) – John Jones and The Now Generation (Prod: Richard Khouri for Federal Records) (1972)

8029   Scorpion/Hands And Feet – Lloyd [Young] and Carey [Johnson] and GG All Stars/The Maytones (Prod: Alvin Ranglin) (1972)

177

8030   This A Pepper/Justice – U Roy Junior/John Holt (Prod: Phil Pratt) (1972)

8031   Without You (What Would I Do)/Instrumental – The Melodians/The Dynamites (Prod: Tony Brevett) (1972)

8032   Blue Moon/After Midnight – The Platonics/Sidney, George and Jackie [The Pioneers] (Prod: Sidney Crooks and Ted Lemon [Judge Dread]) (1972)

8033   Do It Again/Watch It – Lloyd [Young] and Carey [Johnson]/Gary Ranglin (Prod: Alvin Ranglin) (1972)

8034   Take It Easy/How I Want To Love – The Reggae Boys (actually The Pioneers)/Sidney, George and Jackie [The Pioneers] (Prod: Sidney Crooks) (1972)

8035   Starting All Over Again/Instrumental Version – Hopeton Lewis/The Dynamites (Prod: Tommy Cowan and Warwick Lyn) (1972)

8036   Save The Last Dance For Me/Be The One – The Heptones (Prod: Joel Gibson [Joe Gibbs]) (1972) [ALSO ISSUED ON DUKE DU 143]

8037   Ganja Free/Ganja (Version) – Clancy Eccles/The Dynamites (Prod: Clancy Eccles) (1972)

8038   Don't Believe Him Donna/Beyond The Reef – Johnny Lynch (Prod: Sonny Roberts) (1972)

8039   Bound In Chains/Chains Version – The Clarendonians/Stud All Stars (Prod: Ernest Wilson and Peter Austin) (1972)

8040   Standing In The Rain/Stand Up (Version) (actually 'Rain (Version)') – Rad Bryan (actually Neville Grant)/Rad Bryan (actually by The Thoroughbreds) (Prod: Rad Bryan) (1972)

8041   Feel Nice (Version)/Quick And Slick – Bongo Herman, Les [Chen] and Bunny/Winston Scotland (Prod: Tony Robinson [Prince Tony]) (1972)

8042   It Was Written Down/Sweet And Dandy – The Maytals (Prod: Warwick Lyn/Leslie Kong) (1972) [B SIDE IS 1969 VERSION]

8043   Musical Goat/Stinging Dub – Shorty Perry/Winston Grennon and J [Jackie] Jackson (Prod: Alvin Ranglin) (1972)

8044   This World/Same Thing – The Soulettes/The Soulettes (actually by the Upsetters) (Prod: Lee Perry) (1973)

8045   Time And The River/Time And The River (Version) – John Holt (Prod: Arthur 'Duke' Reid) (1973)

8046   Da Doo Ron Ron/Da Doo Ron Ron (Instrumental) – Winston Heywood (Prod: Tony King) (1973)

8047   Aily I/Aily I (Version) – Cynthia Richards/Reid's All Stars (Prod: Arthur 'Duke' Reid) (1973)

8048   Derrick's Big Eleven/My Ding-a-Ling – Derrick Morgan (Prod: Edward 'Bunny' Lee) (1973)

8049   Multiplication/Morning Rises – The Thoroughbreds (Prod: Lloyd Coxsone
        [Lloyd Blackford]) (1973)

8050   Space Flight/Burning Wire – I-Roy/Jerry Lewis (Prod: Lee Perry) (1973)

8051   Nice One Cyril/Nice One Cyril (Version) – The Breadcrumbs (Prod: Henry
        Bowen) (1973)

8052   People Got To Be Free/Come Together – Denzil Dennis (Prod: Pat Rhoden)
        (1973)

8053   Give Me A Chance/King Of Zion – The Cables/Jah Fish (Prod: Keble
        Drummond) (1973)

8054   Papa Was A Rolling Stone/Feeling High – Sidney, George and Jackie [The
        Pioneers] (Prod: Sidney Crooks, George Agard and Jackie Robinson) (1973)
        [PRESSED WITH TWO DIFFERENT MIXES BUT WITH IDENTICAL
        LABELS ON EACH: JA MIX HAS MATRIX ATT 8054 A1/ATT 8054 A2;
        UK MIX HAS MATRIX ATT 8054+2/ATT 8054 B]

8055   Live To Love/Heart's Desire – Sid Cook (actually Sidney Crooks)/Sid Cook
        (actually by The Pioneers) (Prod: Sidney Crooks) (1973)

8056   Brown Baby/Brown Baby (Version) – Derrick Harriott/The Crystalites (Prod:
        Derrick Harriott) (1973)

8057   Crowded City/Thula Thula – The Messengers (Prod: Lloyd Charmers) (1973)

8058   Baby Don't Get Hooked On Me/Harry Hippy – Neville Grant (Prod: Sidney
        Crooks) (1973)

8059   One Of A Kind/Ace Blank – Happy Junior and The IQs/The Shondell All
        Stars (Prod: Sidney Crooks) (1973) [UNISSUED]

8060   Without You In My World/It's Flowing (actually 'It's Growing') – Audley
        Rollins (Prod: Sonia Pottinger) (1973)

8061   Thinking Of You/Thinking Of You (Version) – King Sporty (Prod: Noel
        Williams) (1973)

8062   Girl I've Got A Date/We've Got To Make Love – King Sporty (Prod: Noel
        Williams) (1973)

8063   Kiss An Angel In The Morning/Inez – Ken Parker/Lester Sterling (actually
        with Tommy McCook and The Supersonics) (Prod: Arthur 'Duke' Reid)
        (1974) [B SIDE IS REMIXED VERSION OF 1967 ORIGINAL]

8064   At The Club/Reggae Fever – Sidney, George and Jackie [The Pioneers] (Prod:
        Dandy Livingstone/Agard, Crooks, Robinson) (1974)

8065   I See You/Pass It On – The Henneseys (actually The Pioneers) (Prod: Sidney
        Crooks) (1974)

8066   Love Is Overdue (Part 1)/Love Is Overdue (Part 2) – Gregory Isaacs (Prod:
        Alvin Ranglin) (1974)

179

8067   Heartaches/P.E.O 111 – Annetta Jackson and Bobby Stephen (actually by Ornell Hinds and Bobby Davis)/Annetta Jackson and Bobby Stephen (actually by Des All Stars [Ken Elliott and The Cimarons]) (Prod: Webster Shrowder, Des Bryan and Joe Sinclair) (1974)

8068   All On The House/Cold Blood – Boy Wonder (actually Eugene Paul)/Boy Wonder (actually by unidentified instrumental outfit, possibly The Cimarons) (Prod: Sidney Crooks) (1974) [B SIDE IS INSTRUMENTAL VERSION OF THE VICEROYS' 'WHEEL AND JIG']

8069   Frankie And Johnny/Frankie And Johnny (Version) – Al Cook (actually Eugene Paul) (Prod: Sidney Crooks) (1974)

8070   Hold My Hand/Hold My Hand (Part 2) – The Starlites/GG All Stars (Prod: Alvin Ranglin) (1974)

8071   Duppy Gunman/Duppy Gunman Version – Ernie Smith (Prod: Ernie Smith) (1974) [A SIDE REISSUED ON TROJAN (TR 9048A)]

8072   Living For The City/Just Wanna Live – Pat Rhoden (Prod: Trojan) (1974)

8073   Count Your Blessings/Count Your Blessings (Version) – Ken Parker (Prod: D C Anderson) (1974)

8074   Labour Day/Labour Day (Version) – Tropic Sunlight (Prod: D C Anderson) (1974)

8075   Atlantic One (Part 1)/Atlantic One (Part 2) – Ansel Collins/GG All Stars (Prod: lvin Ranglin) (1974)

8076   NYT

8077   Changing Partners/Changing Partners (Part 2) – Barbara Jones/GG All Stars (Prod: Alvin Ranglin) (1974)

8078   Sweet Rebel Woman (Vocal)/Sweet Rebel Woman (Instrumental) – Sonny Popkiss (actually Danny Ray) (Prod: Dandy Livingstone) (1974)

8079   Oh Carol (Vocal)/Oh Carol (Instrumental) – Freddy McKay (Prod: Lloyd Campbell) (1974)

8080   A Noh Me Trouble You/A Noh Me Trouble You (Instrumental) – The Willows/GG All Stars (Prod: Alvin Ranglin) (1974)

8081   Don't Go/Dub Wise – Gregory Isaacs/GG All Stars (Prod: Alvin Ranglin) (1974)

8082   The Same Folks/Dubwise – Ronnie Davis/GG All Stars (Prod: Alvin Ranglin) (1974)

8083   I'm Gone/I'm Gone (Instrumental) – Derrick [Morgan] and Hortense [Ellis] (Prod: Edward 'Bunny' Lee) (1974)

8084   Love Vibration/Rock A Bye Woman – The Uniques (actually by Freddy McKay) (Prod: Sidney Crooks) (1974)

8085   Arise Selassie I Arise/(Sitting On) The Dock Of The Bay – Freddy McKay (Prod: Sidney Crooks) (1974)

8086 I Feel Sorry/I Feel Sorry (Instrumental) – Brad Lundy (Prod: Sidney Crooks) (1974)

8087 The Monkey/110th Avenue – Count Prince Miller/Love Children Band (Prod: R D [Dandy] Livingstone) (1974)

8088 I Lost My Lover/Bula Dub – Ronnie Davis/Matador All Stars (Prod: Lloyd Campbell) (1975)

8089 NYT

8090 Kiss Me Neck/Da Ba Day – The Upsetters (Prod: Lee Perry) (1975)

8091 Share The Good Times/Share The Good Times (Version) – Brent Dowe and The Gaytones (Prod: Sonia Pottinger) (1975)

8092 How Glad I Am/How Glad I Am (Part 2) – The Tidals (Prod: Alvin Ranglin) (1975)

8093 Dread Out Deh/Dread Dub – Joy White (Prod: Lloyd Campbell) (1975)

8094 Ok Carol/Dub – Lennox Brown/Spiderman (actually by Matador All Stars) (Prod: Lloyd Campbell) (1975)

8095 Bad Da/Ad Dab – Gregory Isaacs (Prod: Winston Holness [Niney]) (1975)

8096 House Of Dreadlocks/Tangle Locks – Big Youth/The Groove Master (Prod: Tony Robinson [Prince Tony]) (1975)

8097 Nothing Is Impossible/Black Out – The Interns/The Hardy Boys (Prod: Winston Riley) (1975)

8098 I'm Falling In Love/Love – Dub – Ranchie [McLean]/Skin, Flesh And Bones (Prod: Panschly) (1975)

8099 Walk Through This World/Instrumental – Barbara Jones/GG All Stars (Prod: Alvin Ranglin) (1975) [A SIDE REISSUED ON ATTACK ATT 8114B]

8100 Rock With Me Baby/A Crabit Version – Johnny Clarke/King Tubby's and The Aggrovators (Prod: Edward 'Bunny' Lee) (1975)

8101 Don't Cut Off Your Dreadlocks/Don't Cut Off Your Dreadlocks (Instrumental) – Linval Thompson/King Tubby's (Prod: Edward 'Bunny' Lee) (1975)

8102 Outformer Parker/Natty Down There – I-Roy (Prod: George Agard and Sidney Crooks) (1975)

8103 NYT

8104 Mummy Hot And Daddy Cold/Some Like It Dread – Big Youth/The Groovemaster (Prod: Tony Robinson [Prince Tony]) (1975)

8105 Just Be Jolly/Dub With I – U Roy (Prod: Edward 'Bunny' Lee) (1975)

8106 Fly Little Silver Bird/Fly Little Silver Bird (Dub) – Gregory Isaacs (Prod: Tony Robinson [Prince Tony]) (1975)

8107 Bushweed Corntrash/Callying Butt – Bunny and Ricky/The Upsetters (Prod: Lee Perry) (1975)

8108 Jah Jah Bless The Dreadlocks/Jah Jah Version – The Diamonds/The Aggrovators (Prod: Edward 'Bunny' Lee) (1975)

8109 Too Bad Bull/Bad Cow – Bunny and Ricky/The Upsetters (Prod: Lee Perry) (1975)

8110 Natty Dread Don't Cry/The Medusa – Tapper Zukie/Tommy McCook (Prod: Edward 'Bunny' Lee) (1975)

8111 Seven Letters/Seven Letters Version – Delroy Wilson/The Aggrovators (Prod: Edward 'Bunny' Lee) (1975)

8112 Saturday Night Special/Saturday Night Version – Michael Dyke/Chinna [Earl Smith] (Prod: Earl 'Chinna' Smith) (1975)

8113 Just Can't Figure Out/Just Can't Figure Out (Version) – The Diamonds (Prod: Edward 'Bunny' Lee) (1975)

8114 Slim Boy/Walk Through This World – Barbara Jones (Prod: Alvin Ranglin) (1975) [B SIDE REISSUED FROM ATTACK ATT 8099A]

8115 NYT

8116 Tradition/Tradition (Version) – Ronnie Davis (Prod: Edward 'Bunny' Lee) (1975)

8117 Nice And Easy/Nice And Easy (Version) – Horace Andy (Prod: Edward 'Bunny' Lee) (1975)

8118 Cold I Up/Cold I Up (Version) – Johnny Clarke (Prod: Edward 'Bunny' Lee) (1975)

8119 Rainbow/Rainbow (Version) – Michael Dyke (Prod: Earl 'Chinna' Smith) (1975)

8120 Honey Child (aka 'You Won't See Me')/Time Is Running Out – Delroy Wilson (Prod: Bob Andy) (1975)

8121 World Class/World Class (Version) – Jah Lloyd (Prod: Glen Lee) (1976)

8122 The Wormer/The Great Pablo – Prince Jazzbo/Prince Jazzbo (actually by Augustus Pablo) (Prod: Edward 'Bunny' Lee) (1976)

8123 The Voice Of The Father/The Voice Of The Father (Version) – Glen Washington (Prod: Alvin Ranglin) (1976)

8124 I'm Alright/Skin Him Alive – Jah Woosh/Dino Perkins (Prod: Keith Hudson) (1976)

8125 I Will Never Change (actually titled 'Undying Love')/I Will Never Change (Version) (actually 'Undying Love (Version)') – Cornel Campbell (Prod: Edward 'Bunny' Lee) (1976)

8126 Scorpion/Scorpion Version – Nora Dean (Prod: Edward 'Bunny' Lee) (1976)

8127 Niah Dread/I Man Free – Lester Lewis (Prod: Harry Johnson) (1976)

8128 White Bird Come Down/White Bird Come Down Version – Thunderball (Prod: Jerry Maytal [Jerry Morris]) (1976)

8129 Show I The Way/Show I The Way (Version) – Jah Woosh (Prod: Neville Beckford [Jah Woosh]) (1976)

8130 Fight Down/Jah Jah Bless I – Lizzard [Clive Hunt] (Prod: Clive Hunt) (1976)

8131 Another Moses/I Can't Understand – The Ethiopians/Sylford Walker (Prod: Clive Hunt) (1976)

8132 A Weh We A Go Do/A Weh We A Go Do (Part 2) – Eric Donaldson (Prod: Eric Donaldson) (1977)

8133 Stranger In Love/Babylon Bridges – Eli Emmanuel (Prod: Eli Emmanuel) (1977)

8134 Christmas Time/Santa Claus – Wain Nelson (Prod: Wain Nelson) (1977)

8135 I Love Marijuana/Jamaica Collie (Version) – Linval Thompson (Prod: Edward 'Bunny' Lee) (1978)

8136 Tubby At The Controls/Dignity And Principle – Big Joe (Prod: Linval Thompson) (1978) [B SIDE ALSO ISSUED ON HORSE HOSS 138A]

8137 Marcus Say/Take Heed – Jah Woosh (Prod: Neville Beckford [Jah Woosh]) (1978)

ATTACK

ACT 101 Knotty No Jester/Knotty No Jester (Instrumental) – Big Youth (Prod: Clive Chin and Victor Chin for Randy's) (1975) [THIS ISSUE USES SAME CATALOGUE NUMBER AS ACTION LABEL RELEASE BUT IS PRESSED ON ATTACK LABEL]

BIG (PREFIX BG)

301 This Is The Time/Since The Other Day – Joe White (1970)

302 When You Go To A Party/Good Morning Mother Cuba – The Meditators (1970)

303 That Wonderful Sound/I Wasn't Born Yesterday – Dobby Dobson (1970)

304 Everytime/Everytime Version 2 – The Itals/Rupie Edwards All Stars (1970)

305 Music Alone Shall Live/Music Alone Shall Live (Version 2) – Rupie Edwards All Stars (actually by The Meditators)/Rupie Edwards All Stars (1970)

306 Dip Dip (probably titled 'Vena')/Too Much Of One Thing – The Slickers (Prod: Sidney Crooks) (1970) [PROBABLY UNISSUED]

307 Oh Me Oh My/Staccato – Pam Brooks (some copies credit 'D Brooks')/ Ansell Collins (Prod: credited to 'G Robinson' but more likely to be Sidney Crooks) (1970)

308 NYT

309 Baby I Care/Ain't Misbehaving – Joe White (Prod: Rupie Edwards) (1970)

310 Halfway To Paradise/Utopia – Dobby Dobson (Prod: Hyland [Dobby] Dobson) (1970)

311 If You Don't Mind/Lenore – Bruce Bennett (actually by The Gaylads)/ Bruce Bennett (actually by Dobby Dobson) (Prod: Howard McGraw) (1970) [PROBABLY UNISSUED]

312   Burning Fire/Fire Burn (Version) – Joe Higgs/Rupie Edwards All Stars (1970)

313   Uncle Charlie/Socialise (When You Go To A Party (Version)) – Froggy
       Ray (actually U Roy Junior) (Prod: Rupie Edwards) (1970) [PROBABLY
       UNISSUED]

314   Half Moon/Full Moon – Froggy Ray (actually U Roy Junior)/Rupie
       Edwards All Stars (1971) [PROBABLY UNISSUED. B SIDE ALSO ISSUED
       ON EXPLOSION LABEL (EX 2030A)]

315   Musical Attack/Shack Attack – Keith Cole/Rupie Edwards All Stars (1971)

316   Music Alone Shall Live Version 3/Behold Another Version – Keith Cole/
       Rupie Edwards All Stars (1971)

317   You Must Believe Me/You Must Believe Version – Dennis Alcapone and
       Niney/The Observers (Prod: Rupie Edwards) (1971) [UNISSUED]

318   Jamaican Boy/Brainwash – The Conscious Minds (Prod: BB Seaton) (1971)

319   Can't Hide The Feeling/Can't Hide The Feeling (Version 2) – The Gaylads
       (Prod: Gaylads) (1971)

320   Soulful Stew/Soulful Stew Version 2 – Rupie Edwards All Stars (1971)

321   Weary Version 3/Hills And Valleys – Glen Adams/Tony Brevett (1971)

322   Ain't Misbehavin'/Genuine Love – Ken Parker (1971)

323   Love Is What I Bring/Love Version – Dave McClaren (actually by Dave Barker
       and The Uniques)/Rupie Edwards All Stars (actually by U Roy Junior) (1971)

324   Deep Meditation/Meditation Version – Errol Dunkley/Rupie Edwards All
       Stars (1971)

325   Ba Da Doo Ba Dey/Ba Da Doo Ba Dey Version – The Itals/Rupie Edwards
       All Stars (1971)

326   Girl You Are Too Young/Too Young Version – The Diamonds/Rupie Edwards
       All Stars (1971)

327   Three In One (Medley)/One In Three – Errol Dunkley/Rupie Edwards All
       Stars (1971)

328   NYT

329   Papacito/I'm Gonna Live Some Life – U Roy Junior/Rupie Edwards (1972)

330   Solid As A Rock/Solid (Version) – The Ethiopians/Rupie Edwards All Stars
       (1972)

331   Three Tops Time/Tops (Version) – Dion Cameron and The Three Tops/
       Underground People (1972)

332   Eternal Drums/Darling Ooh Wee – Bongo Herman and Les [Chen] (actually
       with U Roy Junior)/Errol Dunkley (actually with U Roy Junior) (1972)

333   Press Along/Press Along (Version) – Rupie Edwards All Stars (actually by Max
       Romeo)/Rupie Edwards All Stars (1972)

334   Are You Sure/Are You Sure (Version) – Max Romeo/Rupie Edwards All Stars
       (1972) [PROBABLY UNISSUED]

335   Jimmy As Job Card (actually titled 'Jimmy Has A Job Card')/Riot – Rupie
       Edwards All Stars (1972)
336   I Want Justice/Justice (Version) – BB Seaton/Rupie Edwards All Stars (1972)
337   Christmas Parade/Santa – Rupie Edwards All Stars/Underground People
       (1972)

Note

All issues produced by Rupie Edwards except where stated otherwise.

BIG SHOT (PREFIX BI)

501   Reggae Girl/Donkey Trot – The Tennors/Clive's All Stars (Prod: Albert Gene
       Murphy) (1968)
502   If You Can't Be Good Be Careful/Something About My Man – The Gaylets
       (Prod: Ken Khouri for Federal Records/Lynford Anderson) (1968)
503   Chattie Chattie/Magic Touch – Junior Soul [Junior Murvin] (Prod: Derrick
       Harriott) (1968)
504   It's Reggae Time/The Clamp Is On – Don Tony Lee (actually with Roy
       Richards)/Errol Dunkley (Prod: Edward 'Bunny' Lee) (1968) [REISSUE
       FROM ISLAND LABEL WI 3160]
505   Standing In/Bumble Bee – Derrick Harriott/The Crystalites (Prod: Derrick
       Harriott) (1968)
506   Shower Of Rain/It Might As Well Be Spring – Derrick Morgan/Val Bennett
       (Prod: Edward 'Bunny' Lee) (1968)
507   Forest Gate Rock/Rock, Rock And Cry – Lester Sterling/The Raving
       Ravers (Prod: Edward 'Bunny' Lee) (1968)
508   Sufferer/Kiss A Finger – The Kingstonians (Prod: Derrick Harriott) (1968)
509   John Jones/Place Called Happiness – Rudy Mills (Prod: Derrick Harriott)
       (1968)
510   Biafra/Drop Pon – The Crystalites (Prod: Derrick Harriott) (1969) [B SIDE
       REISSUED ON SONG BIRD SB 1030B]
511   Another Lonely Night/Been So Long – Derrick Harriott (Prod: Derrick
       Harriott) (1969)
512   You're My Girl/Ooh-Pa-Pa-Py (actually titled 'Let Them Say') – Eddie
       Lovette (Prod: Federal Records) (1969)
513   Deportation/Say I'm Back (aka 'He Is Back') – Eric 'Monty' Morris (Prod:
       Albert Gene Murphy) (1969)
514   You're No Good/Do The Reggae – The Tennors (Prod: Albert Gene Murphy)
       (1969)
515   Is It Because?/Take Life Like It Is – Sugar Simone (Prod: Les Foster) (1969)
       [SOUL]

185

516   Son Of A Preacher Man/That's How Strong My Love Is – The Gaylets (Prod: Ken Lazarus and Richard Khouri for Federal Records) (1969)

517   Another Scorcher/My Baby – The Tennors (actually with Jackie Bernard)/ The Tennors/The Tennors (actually by The Harmonians) (Prod: Albert Gene Murphy) (1969)

518   Parapinto/Cool Hand Luke – Cannonball King [Karl Bryan] and Johnny Melody [Johnny Moore] (Prod: Albert Gene Murphy) (1969)

519   You're My Girl/Let Them Say – Eddie Lovette (Prod: Federal Records) (1969) [ESSENTIALLY REISSUE OF BI 512 WITH B SIDE SAME BUT WITH CORRECT TITLE]

520   Worries A Yard/Hound Dog Special – The Versatiles/Val Bennett (Prod: Lee Perry and Enid Barnett) (1969)

521   Suzy Wong/Deebo – Keelyn Beckford/The Swinging Kings (Prod: Enid Barnett) (1969)

522   Windy/Windy Part 2 – The Saints (Prod: Les Foster) (1969)

523   You Belong To My Heart/Bless You – The Demons (Prod: Melmouth Nelson) (1969)

524   Make It Easy On Yourself/I've Tried Before – The Impersonators (Prod: Melmouth Nelson) (1969) [PROBABLY UNISSUED]

525   Old Man Dead/Reggae Me – Verne [Vernon Buckley] and Alvin [Ranglin]/ GG Rhythm Section (Prod: Alvin Ranglin) (1969)

526   Nice Nice/I'll Be Around – The Kingstonians (Prod: Derrick Harriott (1969)

527   The Hustler/Magic Touch – Junior Murvin [Junior Soul] (Prod: Derrick Harriott) (1969) [B SIDE REISSUED FROM BI 503B]

528   Mr Tambourine Man/Old Fashioned Way – Keith Hudson (actually by Ken Boothe) (Prod: Keith Hudson) (1969)

529   Do It Nice/Because You're Mine – Les Foster (Prod: Les Foster) (1969)

530   NYT

531   NYT

532   Sweeter Than Honey/Son Of Reggae – Sylvan Williams (Prod: Hawk) (1969)

533   This Old Man/When The Morning Comes – Sylvan Williams (Prod: Hawk) (1970)

534   Dirty Dog/Round And Round The Moon – Amor Vivi (Prod: Vivian Comma [Vee Coma]) (1969)

535   I'm So Afraid Of Love/Mother Nature – The Escorts (actually The Sensations) (Prod: Winston Riley) (1970)

536   He Who Keepeth His Mouth/One Day (You'll Need My Kiss) – Johnny Osborne and The Sensations (Prod: Winston Riley) (1970)

537   Sweet Soul Special/Memories Of Love – Boris Gardner and The Love People (Prod: Winston Riley) (1970)

538 Darkness/Watch This Music (actually 'Lamb Chops') – Boris Gardner (actually by Ansel Collins and The Love People (Prod: Winston Riley) (1970)

539 Hot Shot/Watch This Music – Boris Gardner and The Love People (Prod: Winston Riley) (1970)

540 Let Me Hold You/London Bridge – Sir Washington [Norman Washington] (Prod: unidentified) (1970)

541 NYT

542 NYT

543 Come Back Darling (actually 'Who You Gonna Run To (Version)'/Move Over – (actually 'Look Who Is Back' aka 'Hi There')/Techniques All Stars/Techniques All Stars (actually by Karl and The Aces) (Prod: Winston Riley) (1970)

544 NYT

545 Elfrego Bacca/Iron Joe – Techniques All Stars (actually by Dave Barker and Ansell Collins)/The Techniques (actually by Dave Barker) (Prod: Winston Riley) (1970)

546 Queen Of The World/Top Of The World – Lloyd and Claudette/The Prophets (Prod: Des Bryan and Webster Shrowder) (1970)

547 I Don't Want To Love You/Love Is Pure – Errol English [Junior English] (Prod: Larry Lawrence) (1970)

548 Once In My Life/Rabbit In A Cottage (actually titled 'In A Cottage In A Wood') – Errol English [Junior English] (Prod: Larry Lawrence) (1970)

549 See And Blind/Scar Face – Johnny Osbourne/The Techniques (actually by Boris Gardner and The Happening) (Prod: Winston Riley) (1970) [B SIDE REISSUED ON TECHNIQUES TE 916B]

550 Return Of The Pollock/Concorde – Patrick and Lloyd/The Prophets (Prod: Des Bryan and Webster Shrowder) (1970) [B SIDE REISSUED ON TROJAN TR 7763B. A SIDE REISSUED ON HORSE HOSS 18B]

551 Unidentified track/Sycidilic – Sir Collins' All Stars (Prod: Charles [Clancy] Collins) (1970) [UNISSUED]

552 African Train/unidentified track – Sir Collins All Stars (Prod: Charles [Clancy] Collins) (1970) [UNISSUED]

553 Bush Beat/Please Come Home – Lloyd and The Prophets with The Cimarons/Patrick (actually Locksley Gichie) and The Prophets with The Cimarons (Prod: Grape) (1970)

554 Crystal Blue Persuasion/Crystal Blue Persuasion (Version 2) – The Prophets and The Cimarons (Prod: Grape) (1970)

555 Tumble Time (Version 1)/Tumble Time (Version 2) – The Prophets and The Cimarons (actually with Claudette)/The Prophets (with The Cimarons) (Prod: Grape) (1970)

556   Jaco/Soul Reggae – Lloyd and The Prophets (Prod: Grape) (1970) [A SIDE
       REISSUED ON BIG SHOT BI 611B]

557   Revenge Of Eastwood (Version 1)/Revenge Of Eastwood (Version 2) – The
       Prophets and The Cimarons (Prod: Grape) (1970)

558   Once A Man/Soul Mood – Billy Jack (actually Winston Groovy) and The
       Cimarons/Candy (actually Eugene Paul) and The Cimarons (Prod: Swan)
       (1970)

559   Ace Of Hearts (aka 'You're Gonna Need Somebody')/Bet Yer Life I Do –
       Candy (actually Eugene Paul) and The Cimarons/Billy Jack (actually Winston
       Groovy) and The Cimarons (Prod: Grape) (1970)

560   Lonely Boy/unidentified instrumental – The Cimarons (Prod: Carl Levy)
       (1970) [HAS 'CIM 1' IN RUN-OUT]

561   Put It On/Rasta Isies – The Hi-Tals (Prod: Swan) (1970)

562   Funky Fight/You Turned Me Down – The Cimarons (Prod: Carl Levy) (1970)
       [LABELLED COPY STATES 'CIM 3'. ALSO ISSUED ON BLANK LABEL
       WITH 'CIM +3' IN RUN-OUT]

563   Unidentified instrumental/unidentified instrumental – The Cimarons (Prod:
       Carl Levy) [UNISSUED – PUT OUT ERRONEOUSLY ON CLANDISC
       CLA 227 INSTEAD. MOST LIKELY INTENDED AS 'CIM 4']

564   NOT ISSUED. ACTUALLY PUT OUT AS 'CIM 4A/CIM 4B ON
       CLANDISC CLA 227 – SEE ALSO BI 563]

565   Shades Of Hudson/Spanish Amigo – Dennis Alcapone (Prod: Keith Hudson)
       (1970)

566   Freedom Sound/Last Love – Lloyd Sievright and Barry Howard (Prod: Bruce
       White for Creole productions) (1970)

567   Bongo Man/Creation Version – The Linkers/Fud Christian All Stars (Prod:
       Fud Christian for La-Fud-Del productions) (1971)

568   Blood And Fire/Mud And Water – Niney (Prod: Winston Holness [Niney])
       (1970)

569   He's Not A Rebel/Rebel Version – The Ethiopians/JJ All Stars (Prod: Karl 'JJ'
       Johnson) (1971)

570   Perseverence/Perseverence Version – Carl Dawkins/JJ All Stars (Prod: Karl 'JJ'
       Johnson) (1971)

571   Never Fall In Love Again (actually 'I'll Never Fall In Love With You
       Again')/Never Fall Version – Fud Christian All Stars (actually with Winston
       Heywood)/Fud Christian All Stars (Prod: Fud Christian for La-Fud-Del
       productions) (1971)

572   Out The Light Baby/Mosquito One – El Paso (actually by Dennis Alcapone)
       (Prod: Byron Smith) (1971)

573　El Fishy/Nightmare (actually 'In The Spirit') – Herman Chin-Loy/Herman's All Stars (actually by Lloyd Charmers) (Prod: Herman Chin-Loy/Winston Lowe) (1971)

574　The Selah/Don't Let Me Go – The Ethiopians (Prod: Karl 'JJ' Johnson) (1971)

575　Brimstone And Fire/Lightning And Thunder – The Observers (Prod: Winston Holness [Niney]) (1971)

576　Wig Wam/Peace And Love – Sonny Bradshaw and Young Jamaica (Prod: Premiere) (1971)

577　Tar Baby (actually 'Crazy Baby')/Archie [version of A side] – Herman Chin-Loy (actually by U Roy Junior)/Tommy McCook (Prod: Herman Chin-Loy) (1971)

578　New Love/The Mood – Herman Chin-Loy/Augustus Pablo (Prod: Herman Chin-Loy) (1971)

579　East Of The River Nile/River Nile Version – Augustus Pablo and Herman's All Star (Prod: Herman Chin-Loy) (1971)

580　Hard Fighter/Voodoo – Little Roy/The Hippy Boys (Prod: Lloyd Daley) (1971)

581　I'm Moving On/I'm Moving On Version Two – Cynthia Richards/The Hippy Boys (Prod: Lloyd Daley) (1971)

582　Two In One (actually titled 'Send Requests')/Rock A Boogie – The Teardrops (actually by The Viceroys)/Larry's All Stars (actually by Morgan's All Stars) (Prod: Derrick Morgan) (1971) [TRACKS ARE REISSUES FROM 1968]

583　Worried Over You/Worried Over You (Version) – Ruby and Gloria (actually by TT Ross)/Lloyd's All Stars (Prod: Lloyd Campbell) (1971)

584　Lonely Man/Lonely Man Version – Gregory Isaacs/Rupie Edwards All Stars (Prod: Rupie Edwards) (1971)

585　Psalm 9 To Keep In Mind/Mood Of The Observers – Tommy McCook and The Observers/The Observers (Prod: Winston Holness [Niney]) (1971)

586　Message To The Ungodly/Isiah Version – Niney and The Observers (Prod: Winston Holness [Niney]) (1971)

587　Sister Big Stuff/Free Man – Danny Raymond (actually by Danny Ray and Dandy)/Boy Friday [Dandy] (Prod: R Thompson [Dandy]) (1971)

588　Keep Pushing/Hot Tip – The Observers (actually by The Heptones)/The Observers (Prod: Winston Holness [Niney]) (1971)

589　Be True To Yourself/Be True To Yourself Version – Alton Ellis and Luna Funk (Prod: Spider [possibly Sylvan Williams and Des Bryan]) (1971)

590　So Nice/So Nice (Version) – Ken Boothe (Prod: Herman Chin-Loy) (1971)

591　I'll Be Right There/Hot Pants Rock – Rad Bryan (actually by Bobby Davis and The Sensations)/The Playboys (actually by Kirk Redding and The Cimarons) (Prod: Rad Bryan for Bush Productions/Des Bryan and Webster Shrowder for Bush Productions) (1971)

592   My Best Girl/My Best Girl (Version) – Rad Bryan (actually by by unidentified male vocalist)/Rad Bryan (Prod: Rad Bryan for Bush Productions) (1971) [TWO DIFFERENT PRESSINGS EXIST: ONE WITH A STRAIGHT VERSION OF THE B SIDE, AND ANOTHER THAT HAS AN ORGAN OVERLAID]

593   You Took Me By Surprise/You Took Me By Surprise Version (actually unidentified instrumental) – Twinkle Brothers (actually by Tony Brevett)/ Twinkle Brothers (actually by unidentified artist) (Prod: Marshalleck) (1971)

594   Nyah Festival/Brixton Serenade (actually 'What Am I Living For?') – The Matador (actually by Lloyd the Matador [Lloyd Campbell])/The Matador (actually by Derrick Morgan) (Prod: Lloyd Campbell) (1971)

595   Dancing With My Baby/Do The Boogaloo – Laurel Aitken (Prod: Laurel Aitken for Bush Productions) (1971) [SOME COPIES DATED 1972]

596   Know Your Friend/Know Your Friend (Version) – Sketto (actually Sketto Richards)/Three Sevens (Prod: Bush Productions) (1971)

597   Waterloo Rock (aka 'Jericho Rock')/Walls Soul – Don Reco (actually Rico Rodriguez and Lloyd Campbell's All Stars)/Lloyd Campbell's All Stars (Prod: Lloyd Campbell for Bush Productions) (1971)

598   A Sometime Girl/Sometime Girl Version – The Cables/The In-Crowd Band (Prod: Hugh Madden) (1971)

599   Just Do The Right Things/Corporal Jones – Rad Bryan (actually by Lloyd Parks) (Prod: Rad Bryan for Bush Productions) (1971)

600   It's Not Who You Know/I Need Someone – The Twinkle Brothers/The Twinkle Brothers (actually by The Ethiopians) (Prod: Lloyd Campbell and Glen Brown) (1971)

601   You Don't Care/Must Care (Version) – Lloyd Sparks (actually Lloyd Parks)/ Prince Tony's All Stars (Prod: Tony Robinson [Prince Tony]) (1972)

602   I'm Trying/Luna's Mood – Alton Ellis/Luna Funk (Prod: Sylvan Williams and Des Bryan/Sylvan Records) (1972)

603   Our Anniversary/Anniversary Version – Tropic Shadow (Prod: Phil Pratt) (1972)

604   Va Va Voom/Rebel – Carl Masters/The God Sons (Prod: Glen Brown and M Mahtani) (1972)

605   Take Me In Your Arms/Two Timing Woman – Laurel Aitken/Laurel Aitken (actually by Tiger) (Prod: Laurel Aitken for Bush Productions) (1972)

606   Tubby's Control/More Music – Tommy McCook and Ron Wilson (Prod: Glen Brown) (1972)

607   Hiding By The Riverside/The Red Sea – Niney/The Observers (Prod: Winston Holness [Niney]) (1972)

608   Big Six/One Armed Bandit – Judge Dread (Prod: Bush Productions) (1972)

609   Beg In The Gutter/Beg In The Gutter (Version) – Niney (Prod: Winston
       Holness [Niney]) (1972)

610   Everyday Music/Observing The AV – The Observers/Niney (Prod: Winston
       Holness [Niney]) (1972)

611   Night Food Reggae/Jaco – Nora Dean/Lloyd and The Prophets (Prod: Bush
       Productions) (1972) [B SIDE REISSUED FROM BI 556A WHERE IT WAS
       CREDITED AS A GRAPE PRODUCTION]

612   Dr Spock/Joe Kidd – The Vulcans (Prod: Bush Productions) (1972)

613   Big Seven/Dread – Judge Dread (Prod: Bush Productions) (1972)

614   Are You Sure/I Don't Know Why – Dave Barker/Dave Barker (actually by
       The Sensations) (Prod: Larry Lawrence for Bush Productions) (1972)

615   Red Herring/Vulcanised – The Vulcans (Prod: Joe Sinclair, Des Bryan and
       Webster Shrowder) (1973) [PROMO COPIES HAVE A SIDE ON BOTH
       SIDES]

616   Ain't It Groovy/My Children Favourite – Buster Pearson (Prod: Buster
       Pearson for Bush Productions) (1973) [PROMO COPIES HAVE A SIDE
       ON BOTH SIDES]

617   Housewives Choice/Don't You Worry – Derrick Morgan and Hortense Ellis
       (Prod: Edward 'Bunny' Lee for Bush) (1973)

618   English Chicken/Material – Lascelles Perkins (Prod: Lloyd Coxsone [Lloyd
       Blackford] (1973) [A SIDE TITLE ON JAMAICAN ISSUE WAS 'AIN'T
       NOBODY HERE BUT US CHICKENS']

619   Big Eight/Mind The Doors – Judge Dread (Prod: Des Bryan, Webster
       Shrowder and Joe Sinclair) (1973) [PROMO COPIES HAVE A SIDE ON
       BOTH SIDES]

620   Ding-A-Ling, Ting-A-Ling/Run Rhythm Run – Steve Collins (Prod: Charles
       'Clancy' Collins for Bush) (1973)

621   Don't Throw Stones/Toughness (actually titled 'Lucifer') – Sidney Rodgers
       and The Fighters/The Fighters (actually by Winston Wright) (Prod: Larry
       Lawrence) (1973) [A SIDE ALSO ISSUED ON TECHNIQUES TE 923]

622   La La At The End/Sound Track La La La – Norman Brown/Prince Tony's All
       Stars (Prod: Tony Robinson [Prince Tony]) (1973)

623   Stop Baby/Stop Baby Version – Millie and Winston/The Gaytones (Prod:
       Sonia Pottinger) (1973)

624   White Rum And Salvation/Jam Dung – Lloyd Charmers/Lloyd Charmers
       (actually by Murphy Romeo) (Prod: Lloyd Charmers) (1973)

625   Jill's On The Pill/Pill Control – Gary and Ken (Prod: unidentified) (1974)

626   Big Nine/Nine And A Bit Skank – Judge Dread (Prod: Des Bryan and Webster
       Shrowder for Bush) (1974)

627   You Can't Get/Showcase – Kingston Four Combo (Prod: Dandy and Shady
       Tree) (1974)

628   Grandad's Flannelette Nightshirt/Dance Of The Snods – Judge Dread (Prod:
       Alted [Judge Dread]) (1974)

629   Mama Dee/Mama Dee (Part 2) – The Starlites/GG All Stars (Prod: Alvin
       Ranglin) (1975)

630   If You're Ready, Come Go With Me (The People's Champion)/ If You're
       Ready, Come Go With Me (Dub Ali Dub) – Vin Gordon/Skin, Flesh and
       Bones (Prod: Lloyd Parks) (1975)

BLACK SWAN (TROJAN SERIES – PREFIX BW)

1401   Bongo Bongo/Ramba – Young Satch [Ferdinand Dixon]/The Boys (Prod:
       Swan) (1970)

1402   Mo'Bay (Montego Bay)/Going West – Selwyn Baptiste/Rico's [Rodriguez]
       All Stars (actually Rico and The Rudies) (Prod: Bryan, Shrowder and Sinclair
       for Grape productions) (1970) [B SIDE REISSUED ON BS 1407B]

1403   I Got It/I Got It Version – The Low Bites (Prod: Swan) (1971)

1404   Dawn Patrol/Whisky Bonga – The Itals (Prod: Swan) (1971)

1405   Love You The Most/Love You The Most Version 2 – Lloyd Clarke/The
       Low Bites (actually by Morgan's All Stars) (Prod: Derrick Morgan for Swan
       Productions) (1971)

1406   Tomorrow's Dreams/Hot Pants Reggae – Lee Bogle/The Swans (Prod: Bryan,
       Shrowder and Sinclair) (1971)

1407   Judgement Rock (actually titled 'Musical Sorrow')/Night West (actually
       'Going West') – The Itals (actually by DJ Sparrow)/The Itals (actually by
       Rico Rodriguez and The Rudies) (Prod: Max Romeo/Bryan, Shrowder and
       Sinclair) (1971) [B SIDE REISSUED FROM BS 1402B]

1408   If It's Hell Down Below (We're All Gonna Go)/Just A Little Bit Of Loving –
       Laurel Aitken (Prod: Laurel Aitken) (1971)

1409   Talk To Me Baby/Talk To Me Baby (Version 2) – Ruby and Gloria (actually
       by TT Ross)/Lloyd's All Stars (Prod: Lloyd Campbell) (1971)

1410   Girl You Rock My Soul/Rock My Soul (Version) – Rad Bryan (Prod: Rad
       Bryan) (1971)

BLUE CAT (PREFIX BS)

100   Shake It Up/Goodies Are The Greatest – The Pioneers with The Lyn Taitt
       Band (Prod: Joel Gibson [Joe Gibbs]) (1968)

101   I've Got Your Number/Hot Shot – Dermott Lynch (Prod: Charles Ross)
       (1968)

102 Musically/I'm Moving On – Keith Blake with The Lyn Taitt Band (Prod: Joel Gibson [Joe Gibbs]) (1968)

103 Give It To Me/Someday Someway – The Pioneers and Lyn Taitt and The Jets/ The Leaders (Prod: Joel Gibson [Joe Gibbs]) (1968)

104 Soul Glide/My Friends – Neville Hinds/The Dynamics (Prod: Joel Gibson [Joe Gibbs]) (1968)

105 Whip Them/Some Having A Bawl – The Pioneers with The Lyn Taitt Band (Prod: Joel Gibson [Joe Gibbs]) (1968)

106 Get Right/If I Did Look – The Wrigglers with The Caribbeats (Prod: Bobby Aitken) (1968)

107 7-11 (Part 1) (actually 'The 7-11 To The Go-Go Club'/7-11 (Part 2) (actually 'The 7-11 To The Go-Go Club (Part 2)' – The Rudies (Prod: Charles Reid) (1968)

108 Way Of Life/I'm So Proud – Karl Bryan and Lyn Taitt's Band/Joe White (actually with Glen Brown and Trevor Shield) (Prod: Charles Ross) (1968)

109 Cupid/Wise Message – The Rudies/Rico's [Rodriguez] All Stars (Prod: Charles Reid) (1968)

110 Go Away/Julie On My Mind – The Gaylads/The Soul Vendors (Prod: Coxsone Dodd) (1968)

111 Letter To Mummy And Daddy/Letter To Mummy And Daddy (Instrumental) – Duke All Stars (actually with Roy Ellis)/Duke All Stars (Prod: Charles Reid) (1968)

112 Seven Letters/To Sir With Love – The Righteous Homes (actually The Righteous Flames)/The Soul Vendors (Prod: Coxsone Dodd) (1968)

113 Pretty Blue Eyes/Pretty Blue Eyes (Instrumental) – Roy [Ellis] and Duke All Stars (Prod: Charles Reid) (1968)

114 I Love The Way You Are/I Can't Stand It – Dermott Lynch (Prod: Charles Ross) (1968)

115 Sugar And Spice/Mercy, Mercy, Mercy – The Hamlins/The Soul Vendors (Prod: Coxsone Dodd) (1968)

116 Zigaloo/Wiser Than Solomon – Lester Sterling (Prod: Coxsone Dodd) (1968)

117 The Train (Vocal)/The Train (Instrumental) – Roy [Ellis] and Duke All Stars/ Duke All Stars (Prod: Charles Reid) (1968)

118 Bye Bye Baby/Heart For Sale – Zoot Sims/Al Campbell and The Thrillers (Prod: Coxsone Dodd) (1968)

119 Try A Little Tenderness/Tender Arms – Joe White/Cannonball [Karl Bryan] and Lyn Taitt (Prod: Charles Ross) (1968)

120 Good Girl/Musical Fever – Ed Nangle/The Enforcers (Prod: Coxsone Dodd) (1968)

121   Fat Fish/You're Gonna Lose – The Viceroys/The Octaves (Prod: Coxsone Dodd) (1968)

122   I've Got Everything/Echo – Dermott Lynch (Prod: Charles Ross) (1968)

123   These Foolish Things/This I Promise – Owen Gray (Prod: Charles 'Clancy' Collins) (1968)

124   Always/Big Man – The Gray Brothers (Prod: Charles 'Clancy' Collins) (1968)

125   The Fiddle/Shook (actually 'Something About My Man') – Leroy [Nehemia] Reid/The Untouchables (actually by The Gaylettes) (Prod: Nehemia Reid/ Lynford Anderson) (1968)

126   Girls Like Dirt/She's Leaving – The Uniques/Glen Adams (actually by Alva Lewis) (Prod: Harry Robinson) (1968)

127   Khaki/Great Surprise – The Untouchables (actually by The Tennors)/Leroy [Nehemia] Reid (Prod: Nehemia Reid) (1968)

128   The Last Dance/Unworthy Baby – The Thrillers (actually with Al Campbell)/ The Delta Cats (Prod: Coxsone Dodd) (1968)

129   Tender Arms/Something Is Worrying Me – Trevor [Shields], Joe White and Glen Brown/Dermott Lynch (Prod: Charles Ross) (1968) [A SIDE IS VOCAL CUT TO BS 119B]

130   Pretty Girl/You Went Away – Trevor [Shields], Joe White and Glen Brown/ Dermott Lynch (Prod: Charles Ross) (1968)

131   Way Of Life/I'm So Proud – Trevor [Shields], Joe White and Glen Brown/ Carl Bryan and Lyn Taitt (Prod: Charles Ross) (1968) [A SIDE IS VOCAL CUT TO BS 108A. B SIDE IS INSTRUMENTAL CUT TO BS 108B]

132   Intensified Girls/Jump And Shout – Anderson's All Stars (Prod: Gladstone Anderson) (1968)

133   Wala Wala/Super Special – The Slickers/Lester Sterling (Prod: Enid Barnett/ Edward 'Bunny' Lee) (1968)

134   Nana/I May Never See My Baby – The Slickers/Martin Riley (Prod: Slickers/ Edward 'Bunny' Lee) (1968)

135   You Can Never Get Away/La La La Bamba – Enos McLeod/Enos and Sheila (Prod: Enos McLeod) (1968)

136   Young Love/Wall Flower – Lloyd Clarke/Ken Rose (Prod: Enid Barnett) (1968)

137   Prisoner In Love/True Love – The Untouchables/Edward Raphael (Prod: Enos McLeod) (1968)

138   Tonight You're Mine/Your Love – Enos and Sheila/The Untouchables (Prod: Enos McLeod) (1968)

139   Reggae Beat/Miss Eva – The Pioneers (Prod: Joel Gibson [Joe Gibbs]) (1968)

140   Uncle Joe/I Am Losing You – Austin Faithful (Prod: Nehemiah Reid/Ranny [Ronnie] Williams) (1968) [B SIDE REISSUED ON BS 151B UNDER TITLE 'CAN'T UNDERSTAND']

141   I Want It Girl/She Is Gone – Teddy Charmes [Roy Willis] (Prod: Tony Shabazz) (1968)

142   ISSUED ON BLANK LABEL ONLY – OFFICIAL RELEASE ON TROJAN TR 628

143   Mullo Reggae/Life Line – Amiel Mudie (Prod: Amiel Mudie) (1968)

144   Belly Lick/The Game Song – Dennis Walks/Drumbago and The Blenders (Prod: Joel Gibson [Joe Gibbs]) (1968)

145   Reggae Jeggae (actually titled 'Royal Reggae Jeggae')/Delilah – Drumbago and The Blenders/Tyrone Taylor (Prod: Joel Gibson [Joe Gibbs]) (1968)

146   I Know A Place/I Dangerous – The Dee Set (actually by Tony Scott)/Roy Bennett (Prod: Tony Shebazz) (1968)

147   You Stole My Money/Tell Me The Reason – Blue and Ferris/George Ferris (Prod: Charles Organaire) (1968) [PROBABLY UNISSUED]

148   Read The News/Return Of The Bullet – Lance Hannibal [Tito Simon]/Rico [Rodriguez] and The Rhythm Aces (Prod: Joe Mansano) (1968)

149   Billy Goat/Call You Up – The Maytones (Prod: Alvin Ranglin) (1968)

150   Life On Reggae Planet/ZZ Beat – Joe Mansano/Rico [Rodriguez] and The Rhythm Aces (Prod: Joe Mansano) (1968)

151   Out Of The Fire/Can't Understand – Lloyd and Devon/Austin Faithful (Prod: Joel Gibson [Gibbs]/Ronnie [Ranny] Williams) (1968) [B SIDE REISSUED FROM BS 140B]

152   Loving Reggae/Musical Beat – The Maytones/Roy Samuel (Prod: Alvin Ranglin) (1969)

153   Everyday Is Like A Holiday/Have You Time – Trevor and The Maytones (Prod: Alvin Ranglin) (1969)

154   Frying Pan/Code It – The Slickers/Ranfold [Ranny] Williams (Prod: Ronnie [Ranny] Williams) (1969)

155   Dig It Up/This Life Make Me (actually 'This Life Make Me Wonder') – The Sparkers/Delroy Wilson (Prod: Ronnie [Ranny] Williams) (1969)

156   I Can't Stop Loving You/Tell Me Darling – Owen Gray (Prod: Owen Gray) (1969)

157   Drumbago's Dead/Song Of The Year – Sam Sham/The Sparkers (Prod: Nehemia Reid) (1969)

158   What A Sin Thing/Short Up Dress – Devon and Sedrick (Prod: Nehemia Reid) (1969)

159   Want It, Want It/Israel – Samuel Edwards/The Sparkers (Prod: Nehemia Reid) (1969)

160   The Bullet/Rhythm In – Rico [Rodriguez] and The Rhythm Aces (Prod: Joe Mansano) (1969) [MATRIX NUMBER IS JRS 1 A/JRS 1 B]

161   Vietcong/Me Want Man – Al Reid/Max Romeo (Prod: Nehemia Reid) (1969)

195

162   Leave Me To Cry/Warning – Carlton Reid (Prod: Nehemia Reid) (1969)

163   It's Not The Way/Darling – Maxie [Max] Romeo/Al Reid (Prod: Nehemia Reid) (1969)

164   Ratchet Knife/Bend The True – Amiel Moodie (Prod: Amiel Mudie) (1969)

165   2,000 Tons Of TNT/Botheration – GG Rhythm Section (actually by Vernon Buckley and The GG All Stars)/The Maytones (Prod: Alvin Ranglin) (1969)

166   Copper Girl/Love – The Maytones (Prod: Alvin Ranglin) (1969)

167   Everybody Reggae/Another Fool – Verne and Alvin (actually by GG All Stars)/Verne and Alvin (actually by David and Bonnie) (Prod: Alvin Ranglin) (1969)

168   Wickeder/Stay In My Arms – Alove and Paxton (actually Laxton [Ford] and Oliver [St. David]) (Prod: Alvin Ranglin) (1969)

169   The Magnificent Seven/Long Lost Love – The Soul Twins (actually by Winston Wright)/Rupie Edwards (Prod: Rupie Edwards) (1969)

170   Buttoo/I Need Your Loving – The Concords (Prod: Rupie Edwards) (1969)

171   Strange/Your New Love – Dobby Dobson (Prod: Rupie Edwards) (1969)

172   Judas/World Come To An End – Gladstone Adams and The Followers (Prod: Alvin Ranglin) (1969)

173   Mi Nah Tek You Lick/DD Money (actually 'Dig Away De Money') – The Maytones (Prod: Alvin Ranglin) (1969)

174   If I Could Hear My Mother/Satan Can't Prevail – The Righteous Twins (Prod: Sonny Roberts) (1969) [BADGED AS 'SACRED SERIES']

BREAD (PREFIX BR)

1101   Susanne/I Need Your Love – Del Davis/Gene Laro (actually Gene Rondo) (Prod: Jackie Edwards) (1970)

1101   Tell Me Why You Said Goodbye/I'll Make Them Believe In You – Bobby Foster (actually Tito Simon)/Youth [actually I Jah Man Levi] (Prod: Jackie Edwards) (1970)

1102   NYT

1103   Your Eyes Are Dreaming/Yes I Will – Danny [Ray] and Jack [Jackie Edwards]/Victor Scott (Prod: Jackie Edwards) (1970)

1104   Cum-Ba-Laa/I Want You Beside Me – Jackie's Boys/Jackie Edwards (Prod: Jackie Edwards) (1971) [A SIDE REISSUED ON BREAD BR 1110B]

1105   Baby Don't Wake Me/Wishing And Hoping – Del Davis (Prod: Jackie Edwards) (1971) [B SIDE REISSUED ON TROJAN TR 7870B]

1106   NYT

1107   Johnny Gunman/Johnny Gunman (Version) – Jackie Edwards/Jackie's Boys (Prod: Jackie Edwards) (1971)

1108   I Do Love You/Who Told You So? – Jackie Edwards (Prod: Jackie Edwards) (1972)

1109 Don't Stop/Your Eyes Are Dreaming – Danny Ray/Danny Ray and Jackie
Edwards (Prod: Jackie Edwards) (1972) [B SIDE REISSUED FROM BR 1103A]

1110 Bewildered/Cum-Ba-Laa – Count Prince Miller/Jackie's Boys (Prod: Jackie
Edwards) (1972) [B SIDE REISSUED FROM BREAD BR 1104A]

1111 Station Underground News/Better Days – Lee Perry/The Carltons [Carlton
and The Shoes] (Prod: Lee Perry) (1973)

1112 The Youth Of Today/Close Observation – The Coolers/Tyrone Taylor (Prod:
Clancy Eccles) (1973)

1113 Pray For The Wicked/Pray For The Wicked (Version) – The Untouchables
(Prod: Alvin Ranglin) (1973)

1114 All Over The World, People Are Changing/Changing World (Dubwise) – The
Maytones/The Mayones (actually by GG All Stars) (Prod: Alvin Ranglin) (1973)

1115 You Need Love/Love (Dub) – Billy Dyce and The Millions/GG All Stars
(Prod: Alvin Ranglin) (1973)

1116 Cherry Baby/Summertime – The Messengers/BB Seaton (Prod: Lloyd
Charmers) (1973)

1117 Mama/Man A Walk And Talk – Nora Dean (Prod: Edward 'Bunny' Lee) (1973)

1118 Just Enough/We Are Neighbours – David Isaacs (Prod: Lee Perry) (1973)

1119 I Who Have Nothing/I'm Not Home – Derrick Morgan (Prod: Edward
'Bunny' Lee) (1973)

1120 Don't Try To Use Me/Goddess Of Love – Horace Andy/Horace Andy
(actually by Cornel Campbell) (Prod: Edward 'Bunny' Lee) (1973)

1121 Musical Liquidator (aka 'Shake It Up')/Lorna Banana – Dennis Alcapone/
Dennis Alcapone and Prince Jazzbo (Prod: Edward 'Bunny' Lee) (1973)

CLANDISC (PREFIX CLA)

200 Mr Midnight (Skokiaan)/Who Yeah – The Dynamites/King Stitt (1969)

201 The World Needs Loving/Dollar Train – Clancy Eccles and The Dynamites
(1969)

202 Vigorton 2/Mount Zion – King Stitt/Clancy Eccles and The Dynamites (1969)

203 Foolish Fool/On The Street – Cynthia Richards/King Stitt (1969) [A SIDE
REISSUED ON CLA 220A]

204 Soul Power/Rub It Down – Barrington Sadler (1969)

205 NYT

206 The Ugly One/Dance Beat – King Stitt/King Stitt and Clancy Eccles (1970)
[B SIDE REISSUED ON CLA 220B]

207 Herbsman Shuffle/Don't Mind Me – King Stitt and Andy Capp/Higgs and
Wilson [Joe Higgs and Roy Wilson] (1970) [B SIDE REISSUED ON CLA
218A. A SIDE REISSUED ON TROJAN TRO 9064A]

208   Mademoiselle/Lion – Joe Higgs/The Dynamites (1970)

209   Open Up/Again – Clancy Eccles/Higgs and Wilson [Joe Higgs and Roy
       Wilson] (1970)

210   Conversations/Conversations (Version 2) – Cynthia Richards/The Dynamites
       (1970)

211   Promises/Real Sweet – Cynthia Richards/Clancy Eccles and The Dynamites
       (1970) [A SIDE REISSUED ON CLA 216B]

212   Black Beret/Love Me Tender – The Dynamites/Barry [Barrington Clarke] and
       The Affections (1970)

213   Phantom/Skank Me – The Dynamites/Barry [Barrington Clarke] and The
       Affections (1970)

214   Africa/Africa Part 2 – Clancy Eccles and The Dynamites (1970)

215   False Nyah (actually 'See Me')/Sound Of '70 – Barry [Barrington Clarke]
       and The Affections (actually by Earl Lawrence [Earl] George)/King Stitt with
       Clancy Eccles and The Dynamites (1970)

216   Can't Wait/Promises – Cynthia Richards (1970) [B SIDE REISSUED FROM
       CLA 211A]

217   Zion (actually 'Zion We Want To Go')/Revival – The Westmorelites/Clancy
       Eccles and The Dynamites(1970)

218   Don't Mind Me/Angel – Higgs and Wilson [Joe Higgs and Roy Wilson]/Glen
       and Roy (actually by The Vibrators) (1970) [A SIDE REISSUED FROM
       CLA 207B]

219   Sha La La La/Pop It Up – The Dynamites (1970) [B SIDE REISSUED ON
       CLA 239B]

220   Foolish Fool/Dance Beat – Cynthia Richards/King Stitt and Clancy Eccles
       (1970) [A SIDE REISSUED FROM CLA 203A, B SIDE REISSUED
       FROM CLA 206B]

221   Unite Tonight/Uncle Joe – Clancy Eccles and The Dynamites (1970)

222   Swanee River/The Past Time (actually titled 'Feeling Inside') – The Baugh All
       Stars (actually Gladstone Anderson)/The Baugh All Stars (actually by Alton
       Ellis) (Prod: C Baugh) (1970)

223   King Of Kings/Reggaedelic – King Stitt/The Dynamites (1970)

224   Holly Holy/Kingston Town – The Fabulous Flames/Lord Creator (1970)

225   I Was Just Thinking About You/I Was Just Thinking About You Version – Cynthia
       Richards/The Dynamites (1970) [ISSUED ON BLANK LABEL ONLY]

226   NYT

227   Credit Squeeze (actually unidentified instrumental)/Credit Version (actually
       unidentified instrumental) – Clancy Eccles/The Dynamites (both sides actually
       by the Cimarons) (Prod: Carl Levy) (1970) [SEE ALSO BIG SHOT BI 564]

228 Name Of The Game (aka 'Ife L'Ayo')/Holly Holy Version 2 – Larry Macdonald and Denzil Laing/The Fabulous Flames (1970)

229 Stand By Your Man/Stand By Your Man (Version 2) – Cynthia Richards (actually by Merlene Webber)/The Dynamites (1970)

230 Tomorrow (actually 'Where Will You Be Tomorrow')/Tomorrow Version 2 – Clancy and Cynthia (actually by Stranger Cole and Gladstone Anderson)/The Dynamites (actually with Gladstone Anderson) (1971)

231 Sweet Jamaica/Going Up West – Clancy Eccles/The Dynamites (1971)

232 NYT

233 Rod Of Correction/Rod Of Correction Version – Clancy Eccles/The Dynamites (1971)

234 Teardrops Will Fall/Teardrops Version – The Silvertones (1971)

235 John Crow Skank/Merry Rhythm – Clancy Eccles (with uncredited female DJ, possibly Cynthia Richards or Merlene Webber)/King Stitt and The Dynamites (1971)

236 Power For The People/Power For The People (Version) – Clancy Eccles/The Dynamites (1971)

237 Hello Mother/Hi-Di-Ho – The Dynamites/The Fabulous Flames (1971)

238 Don't Call Me Nigga/Joe Louis – The Soul Twins/The Dynamites (1971)

239 Hallelujah Free At Last/Sha La La La – Clancy Eccles/The Dynamites (1972) [REISSUED FROM CLA 219A]

Note
All tracks produced by Clancy Eccles unless otherwise stated.

DOCTOR BIRD (SECOND SERIES – PREFIX DB)

1501 Just Wait And See/Message To Mary – Al Barry/The Markonians (Prod: Al Barry) (1970) [POSSIBLY UNISSUED]

1502 Morning Sun/Over And Over – Al Barry and The Cimarons/The Markonians with The Nyah Shuffle (Prod: Al Barry) (1970)

1503 Rum Bum A Loo/Drummer Bird – The Message (Prod: Philigree) (1970)

1504 This Little Light/Lover – Ray Martell with The Cimarons and The Reactions/Ray Martell and The Cimarons (Prod: Al Barry and Philigree/Philigree) (1970) [UNISSUED – RELEASED ON TROJAN TR 7787 INSTEAD]

DOWNTOWN (PREFIX DT)

401 Move Your Mule/Reggae Me This – Dandy (1968) [SOME COPIES PRESSED WITH A AND B SIDES REVERSED]

402 Come Back Girl/Shake Me Wake Me – Dandy (1968)

403 Dream (actually 'All I Have To Do Is Dream')/Sincerely – Denzil [Dennis] and Pat [Rhoden] (1968)

404 Tell Me Darling/Cool Hand Luke – Dandy/Brother Dan All Stars (1968) [ISSUED 10/1/69]

405 Copy Your Rhythm/Lovely Lady – Dandy/Brother Dan All Stars (1968)

406 Doctor Sure Shot/Put On Your Dancing Shoes – Dandy (1968)

407 Sweet Chariot/Let's Go Downtown – The Dreamers (1968) [ISSUED 7/1/69]

408 I Second That Emotion/Dear Love – Audrey [Hall] and The Dreamers (1968) [ISSUED 14/2/69]

409 Pushwood/Reggae Train – Mr Most [Dandy] (1968) [ISSUED 7/2/69]

410 Reggae In Your Jeggae/Reggae Shuffle – Dandy/The Dreamers (1969)

411 You Don't Care/Tryer – Dandy and Audrey [Hall] (1969)

412 NYT

413 Moma Moma/Melody For Two – The Israelites (1969)

414 Love Me Tonight/Shoot Them Amigo – Audrey [Hall]/Brother Dan All Stars (1969)

415 Rock Steady Gone/Walking Down Easy Street – Dandy (1969)

416 I'm Your Puppet/Water Boy – Dandy (1969)

417 Quando Quando/Reg 'A' Jeg – Rico [Rodriguez] (actually with The Rudies) (1969)

418 Lover's Concerto/Along Came Roy – Audrey [Hall]/Herbie Grey and The Rudies (1969)

419 Red Red Wine/Blues – Tony Tribe/The Rudies (actually with Rico Rodriguez) (1969) [SOME COPIES CREDIT A SIDE TO 'TONY TRIPE']

420 The Untouchables/Lazy Boy – Sonny Binns and The Rudies/The Rudies (1969)

421 Games People Play/One Fine Day – The Israelites/Audrey [Hall] (1969)

422 Lover's Question/Blue Moon – Gene Rondo/Herbie Grey and The Rudies (1969)

423 Groovin'/These Memories – Owen Gray/Herbie Grey and The Rudies (1969)

424 Wheels/Night Train – Sonny Binns and The Rudies (1969)

425 NYT

426 Everybody Feel Good/Downtown Jump – Downtown All Stars/The Rudies (1969)

427 I Don't Wanna Lose That Girl/Train From Vietnam – Freddie [Notes] and The Rudies (1969)

428 Lovey Dovey/Kitty Wait – Owen [Gray] and Dandy/Herbie Grey and The Rudies (1969) [PROBABLY UNISSUED]

429 People Get Ready/Near East – Dandy/The Rudies (1969)

430 NYT

431 Sentimental Reasons/Then You Can Tell Me Goodbye – Gene Rondo (1969)

432 Tear Them/Chaka Grind – Desmond Riley/George Lee and The Rudies (1969)

433 Seven Books/Chuka Beat – The Israelites (1969)

434   Be Natural, Be Proud/Who You Want To Run To – Dandy (1969)

435   Tears On My Pillow/Man Pon Spot – Desmond Riley/The Rudies (1969)

436   You'll Lose A Good Thing/If I Had Wings – Audrey [Hall]/Desmond Riley (1969)

437   Come On Home/Love Is All You Need – Dandy (1969)

438   Out Your Fire/No Return – Desmond Riley (1969)

439   Gonna Give Her All The Love I Got/Why Wait – Tony Tribe/Herbie Grey (1969)

440   Boss Sound/Everything Is Alright – Dessie [Desmond Riley] and John (actually Lyndon Johns) (1969)

441   Burial Of Longshot (Part 1)/Burial Of Longshot (Part 2) – Prince Of Darkness [Dandy]/George Lee (1969)

442   Everybody Loves A Winner/Try Me One More Time – Dandy (1969)

443   Talking Boss/Jungle Fever – George Lee (actually with Prince Of Darkness [Dandy])/George Lee (1969)

444   Don't Gamble With Love/Songbird – Lyndon Johns (1969)

445   Come Together/Music Fever – Dandy and The Israelites/Jake Wade (1969)

446   Give Me Love/Daddy's Home (actually 'Ghost Rider') – The Emotions/Horace Faith (actually by Music Doctors) (1969)

446   Give Me Love/Daddy's Home – The Emotions/Horace Faith (1969) [DUPLICATE ISSUE OF DT 446 WITH CORRECT B SIDE BUT EXISTENCE UNCONFIRMED]

447   Music Doctor Chapter 1/Music Doctor Chapter 2 – Music Doctors (1969)

448   Meeting Over Yonder/Ghost Rider – Prince Of Darkness [Dandy]/Music Doctors (1969) [SEE ALSO DT 446B]

449   Pop Your Corn/Pledging My Love – Audrey [Hall] (1969)

450   Skinhead A Message To You/Going Strong – Desmond Riley/Music Doctors (1969)

451   Oh Mama, Oh Papa/Bring Back The Night – Lyndon Johns (1969)

452   Sweeter Than Sugar/The Way You Move – Audrey [Hall] (1969)

453   Won't You Come Home/Baby Make It Soon – Dandy (1969)

454   Oh I Was Wrong/Let's Try Again – Audrey [Hall]/Dandy and Audrey [Hall] (1969)

455   Gumption Rock/Bounce Down – Soul Explosion (1970) [UNISSUED]

456   Raining In My Heart/First Note – Dandy/Dandy (actually by Music Doctors) (1970)

457   Someday We'll Be Together/Sunset Rock – Audrey [Hall]/Music Doctors (1969)

458   Build Your Love On A Solid Foundation/Baby, Let's Talk It Over – Dandy (1970) [SOME COPIES ISSUED IN PICTURE SLEEVE]

459   Spreading Peace/Guitar Riff – Gene Rondo/Music Doctors (1970)

460   I'm Gonna Keep On Trying ('til I Win Your Love)/Girl I Need You – Count Prince [Miller] (1970)

461   Goodnight My Love/I Don't Want To Be Hurt – Winston Laro (actually Gene Rondo)/Boysie (actually Ansel Collins) (1970)

462   Morning Side Of The Mountain/Show Me Baby – Dandy and Audrey [Hall]/Audrey [Hall] (1970)

463   How Glad I Am/I'm So Glad – Audrey [Hall]/Dandy and Audrey [Hall] (1970)

464   Take It Easy/Funk The Beat – The Megatons (1970)

465   What's Your Name/Mr Lockabe – Dennis Lowe (actually by Gene Rondo)/Music Doctors (1970)

466   Grindin' Axe/Unknown instrumental – Music Doctors (1970) [ISSUED ON BLANK LABEL ONLY]

467   Red Red Wine Version/Sound Of Today – Prince Of Darkness/Music Doctors (1971) [RELEASE ANNOUNCED FOR 22/1/70 BUT POSSIBLY UNISSUED]

468   Standing Up For The Sound/Old Man Trouble – Dennis Lowe (actually by Dandy)/Owen and Dennis (actually by Owen Gray and Dandy) (1970)

468   Walk The World Away/unidentified instrumental – Dandy/Music Doctors [DUPLICATE ISSUE ON BLANK LABEL ONLY] (1971)

469   Militant Man/Reggae Jeggae Version – The Megatons/Music Doctors (1970) [POSSIBLY UNISSUED]

470   Version Girl/Grumble Man – Boy Friday [Dandy] (1970)

471   Music So Good/Right Track – Boy Friday [Dandy] and The Groovers/The Groovers (actually with Boy Friday [Dandy]) (1970)

472   Sound I Remember/Reconsider Our Love – Boy Friday [Dandy]/Joan Long (actually TT Ross) (1971)

473   Take A Message Ruby/Second Note – Boy Friday [Dandy] (1971)

474   NYT

475   NYT

476   There'll Always Be Sunshine/Sunshine Track – Boy Friday [Dandy] (1971)

477   Hot Pants Girl/El Raunchy – Boy Friday [Dandy] (1971) [UNISSUED]

478   NOT ISSUED – ISSUED ON TROJAN TR 7828

479   The Vow/Bank Raid – Tammi Dee/Music Doctors (1971) [UNISSUED]

480   The Pliers/The Pliers (Version) – Music Doctors (actually with Ansel Collins) (1971)

481   El Raunchy/Making Conversation – Boy Friday [Dandy] (1971)

482   Only The Strong Survive/Survival – Dave Barker/Committee All Stars (Prod: Patrick Harty) (1971)

483   Could It Be True/B Side – Dandy and Jackie [Edwards]/The Conthos (1971)

484   Daddy's Home/Everyman – Dandy (1971)

485   Under The Boardwalk/Barrel – Down To Earth/Ansel Collins and Riley's All
       Stars (Prod: Dandy/Mulby for Bush/Downtown Productions/Winston Riley)
       (1971)

486   Oh Mammy Blue/Oh Mammy Blue Version – The Cimarons (1971)

487   Holy Christmas/Silent Night/White Christmas (Medley) – The Cimarons
       (1971) (Prod: R Thompson/Mulby and House Production)

488   Forever Music/The Boy I Love – John Shaft/Blossom Johnson (1971)
       [UNISSUED]

489   Give Me Some More/Some More Version – Studio Sound (1972)

490   Wanna Be Like Daddy/A Little More – Gene Rondo/Studio Sound (1972)
       [B SIDE IS STRAIGHT VERSION OF A SIDE AND UNRELATED TO
       EITHER SIDE OF DT 489]

491   Herb Tree/Holy Poly – Family Man [Aston Barrett]/Studio Sound (1972)

492   True True To My Heart/Ace 90 (actually titled 'S90 Skank') – Keith Hudson
       (actually with Hudson's All Stars)/Big Youth (actually with Hudson's All Stars)
       (Prod: Keith Hudson) (1972)

493   Meet The Boss/Musical Right – Sir Harry (Prod: Kenneth Wilson) (1972)

494   Get Out Of My Life/Get Out (Version) – Niney (actually with The
       Observers) (Prod: Winston Holness [Niney]) (1972)

495   Hi Diddle (actually 'Beardedmen Feast')/Hi Diddle (actually titled 'Episode')
       – Niney (actually with Max Romeo)/Niney All Stars (actually by The
       Observers) (Prod: Winston Holness [Niney]) (1972)

496   Swinging Along/My Baby Is Gone – Dennis Alcapone/Delroy Wilson (Prod:
       Bush Productions (Edward 'Bunny' Lee for Bush Productions) (1972)

497   Dock Of The Bay/Bass And Drum Version – Big Youth/The Crystalites (Prod:
       Derrick Harriott) (1973)

498   There Is Something On Your Mind/Something On Your Mind (Version) –
       Hubert Lee/Impact All Stars (Prod: Randy's) (1973)

499   Black Ipa/Black Ipa Skank – The Upsetters (actually with Lee Perry) (Prod:
       Lee Perry) (1973)

500   Dreadlocks Man/Rasta Want Peace – The Aggrovators (actually by Twin
       Roots, aka The Rasta Twins) (Prod: Edward 'Bunny' Lee for Bush Productions)
       (1973)

501   Pretty Girl/Face Girl (Version) – Delroy Wilson/Joe Gibbs and The
       Professionals (Prod: Joel Gibson [Joe Gibbs]) (1973)

502   You Are A Wanted Man/Back To Dubwise – The Starlites/GG All Stars (Prod:
       Alvin Ranglin) (1973)

503   Black Man Time/Hi Jacking – I-Roy (Prod: Augustus 'Gussie' Clarke) (1973)

504 Apollo 17/Uptown Rock – Sir Harry (actually with the Cables) (Prod: Hugh Madden) (1973)

505 Why Do People Have To Cry/Why Do People Have To Cry (Version) – Brenton King (Prod: Frank Campbell) (1973)

506 Sunshine Showdown/Sunshine Showdown Version – The Upsetters (actually with Lee Perry)/The Upsetters (Prod: Lee Perry) (1973)

507 Two Wedden Skank/Daughter A Whole Lotta Sugar Down Deh! – Glen Brown/Berry Simpson [Prince Hammer] (Prod: Glen Brown and M Miller) (1973)

508 What Did You Say/What Did You Say (Version) – Dennis Alcapone/Prince Tony's All Stars (Prod: Tony Robinson [Prince Tony]) (1973)

509 Sick And Tired/Hot Tip – Neville Grant/Prince Django (Prod: Lee Perry) (1973)

510 The Meaning Of One/Let Me In Your Heart – Prince Jazzbo/Suzanne Prescod (Prod: Glen Brown and M Miller) (1973)

511 Rastafari Ruler/Yesterday – The Twins (actually the Rasta Twins)/Tyrone Taylor (Prod: Clancy Eccles) (1973)

512 Tighten Up Skank/Mid East Rock – The Upsetters (actually with Dillinger) (Prod: Lee Perry) (1973)

513 Bucky Skank/Yucky Skank – The Upsetters (actually with Lee Perry) (Prod: Lee Perry) (1973)

514 Sugar Plum/Sugar Plum (Dub) – Bellfield (Prod: Alvin Ranglin) (1973)

515 The Meaning Of Life/The Meaning Of Life (Version) – The Heptones/Morwell Esq. (Prod: Maurice Wellington) (1973)

516 Love Of Jah Jah Children/Jah Jah Children (Version) – The Millions/GG All Stars (Prod: Alvin Ranglin) (1973)

517 Dedicated To Illiteracy/Illiteracy Dub – Stranger [Cole] and Gladdy [Anderson] with Shorty Perry/GG All Stars (Prod: Alvin Ranglin) (1973)

518 Try Me/Rhythm Style – Roman Stewart/Simplicity People (Prod: Augustus 'Gussie' Clarke) (1973)

519 Clapper's Tail/Live And Learn – I-Roy (Prod: Augustus 'Gussie' Clarke) (1973)

520 Hey Little Girl/Don't Blame The Man – Derrick Morgan (Prod: Edward 'Bunny' Lee) (1973)

Note

All releases produced by Dandy unless otherwise stated: issues 401 to 481 inclusive were all produced by him but it then becomes a very mixed-bag affair. Just to clarify, the production credits 'Brother Dan', 'Thompson/Mulby', 'Downtown Music', 'R Thompson' and 'Shady Tree' are all him. Note that some early issues carry a 1968 date but were issued early in 1969.

DUKE (PREFIX DU)

1   I Wish It Would Rain/There Comes A Time – The Techniques (Prod: Arthur 'Duke' Reid) (1968)

2   Those Guys/I'll Never Fall In Love Again – The Sensations (Prod: Arthur 'Duke' Reid) (1968)

3   One Dollar Of Music/I'll Make It Up – Carl Dawkins (actually by JJ All Stars)/Carl Dawkins (Prod: Karl 'JJ' Johnson) (1968)

4   Happy Time/Smashville – Herbie Carter (actually Keble Drummond)/The Boys (actually The Jay Boys) (Prod: Harry Johnson) (1968)

5   Cuss Cuss/Lavender Blue – Lloyd Robinson (Prod: Harry Johnson) (1968) [B SIDE REISSUED ON HARRY J HJ 6601B]

6   Man Of My Word/The Time Has Come – The Techniques (Prod: Winston Riley) (1968)

7   Left With A Broken Heart/I've Got To Get Away – The Paragons (Prod: Winston Riley) (1968)

8   Penny Reel/Soul Tonic – Whistling Willie [Neville Willoughby] (Prod: Neville Willoughby) (1969)

9   Auntie Lulu/Bag-a-Boo (actually titled 'Don't Brag, Don't Boast') – The Slickers (actually by Clancy Eccles)/Clancy Eccles (Prod: Clancy Eccles) (1969)

10   What A Botheration/Stand By Me – The Upsetters (actually with Lee Perry)/The Upsetters (actually by The Inspirations) (Prod: Lee Perry) (1969) [A SIDE ALSO ISSUED ON TROJAN TR 612B]

11   Eight For Eight/You Know What I Mean – The Upsetters/The Inspirations (Prod: Lee Perry) (1969) [UNISSUED – RELEASED ON UPSETTER US 300]

12   Reggae Dance/I Know – Owen Gray (Prod: Owen Gray) (1969)

13   Soul Pipe/Overproof – King Cannon [Karl Bryan] (actually with Anderson's All Stars) (Prod: Lynford Anderson) (1969)

14   Diana/Personality – Alton Ellis with Tommy McCook and The Supersonics (Prod: Arthur 'Duke' Reid) (1969)

15   Cuyah/Forever – Lloyd Tyrell [Lloyd Charmers]/The Uniques (Prod: Winston Lowe)

16   Follow This Sound/Love In Summer – Lloyd Tyrell [Lloyd Charmers] (actually with The Hippy Boys) (Prod: Winston Lowe) (1969)

17   Home Without You/Why Pretend – The Beltones (Prod: Harry Johnson) (1969)

18   Life/I Like Your Smile – Roy Shirley (Prod: Karl 'JJ' Johnson) (1969)

19   Freedom Sound/Easy Sound – The Afrotones/The Boys (actually The Jay Boys) (Prod: Harry Johnson) (1969)

20   Suffering Stink/The Break – Band of Mercy And Salvation/Bob Melody (actually Winston Francis) (Prod: Coxsone Dodd for Disclick Productions) (1969)

21   Never My Love/The Bold One – Boris Gardner (actually with The Love
      People) (Prod: Sam Mitchell) (1969)

22   You're My Everything/What Am I To Do – The Techniques (Prod: Winston
      Riley) (1969)

23   Friends And Lovers (actually 'Friends And Lovers Forever')/Hot Line – Patti
      La Donne/Joe's All Stars (Prod: Joe Mansano) (1969) [JOE LABEL]

24   Hey Jude/Musical Feet – Joe's All Stars (Prod: Joe Mansano) (1969) [JOE
      LABEL]

25   Five To Five/Come See About Me – Lloyd Charmers (actually with The
      Hippy Boys)/The Soul Stirrers (Prod: Winston Lowe/Lloyd Charmers) (1969)
      [B SIDE ALSO ISSUED ON SONG BIRD SB 1002B]

26   Hear Ya/Live Life – The Scorchers/The Vibrators (Prod: Karl 'JJ' Johnson)
      (1969)

27   Glad You're Living/Help Wanted – Stranger Cole (Prod: Karl 'JJ' Johnson)
      (1969)

28   Battle Cry Of Biafra/Funky Reggae Part 1 – Joe's All Stars (Prod: Joe
      Mansano) (1969) [JOE LABEL]

29   Never Gonna Give You up/Don't Mix Me Up – The Royals (Prod: L
      Edwards) (1969)

30   Fire Corner/John Public – Clancy Eccles (actually by King Stitt)/The
      Dynamites (Prod: Clancy Eccles) (1969)

31   I Don't Care/Shoo Be Doo – The Dynamites (actually by The Dingle
      Brothers)/Clancy Eccles (Prod: Clancy Eccles) (1969)

32   Mother Hen/Chastise Them – The Harmonisers/Winston Sinclair (Prod: Joel
      Gibson [Joe Gibbs]) (1969)

33   Seven Lonely Days/He Didn't Love You Like I Do – Owen Gray (Prod:
      Owen Gray) (1969)

34   Dracula, Prince Of Darkness/Honky – King Horror/Joe's All Stars (Prod: Joe
      Mansano) (1969) [JOE LABEL]

35   Bigger Boss/My Girl – Ansel Collins (actually with Count Sticky)/The
      Ethiopians (Prod: Karl 'JJ' Johnson) (1969)

36   Safari/Last Laugh – Lloyd Charmers (Prod: Winston Lowe) (1969)

37   Everybody Bawlin'/Come Look Here – Don Drummond Junior [Vincent
      Gordon]/The Silvertones (Prod: Arthur 'Duke' Reid) 1969

38   Dream Baby/Stagger Lee – Anonymously Yours (Prod: Bart Sanfilipo) (1969)

39   Soul Serenade/Bond In Bliss – Byron Lee and The Dragonaires (actually
      with Winston Wright) (Prod: Byron Lee) 1969 [FIRST PRESSING WITH
      DIFFERENT B SIDE. FEW COPIES EXIST. B SIDE ALSO RELEASED
      ON TROJAN TR 7747A AND REISSUED ON HORSE HOSS 56B]

39   Soul Serenade/Elizabethan Reggae – Byron Lee and The Dragonaires (actually with Winston Wright)/Byron Lee and The Dragonaires (actually by Boris Gardner) (Prod: Byron Lee/Junior Chung) (1969) [SECOND PRESSING. A SIDE REISSUED ON HORSE HOSS 56A (ALSO APPLIES TO OTHER ISSUES OF THIS PARTICULAR TITLE ON THIS NUMBER)]

39   Elizabethan Reggae/Soul Serenade – Byron Lee and The Dragonaires (actually by Boris Gardner)/Byron Lee and The Dragonaires (actually with Winston Wright) (Prod: Junior Chung/Byron Lee) (1969) [THIRD PRESSING]

39   Elizabethan Reggae/Soul Serenade – Byron Lee and The Dragonaires featuring Boris Gardner (actually by Boris Gardner)/Byron Lee and The Dragonaires (actually with Winston Wright) (Prod: Junior Chung/Byron Lee) (1969) [FOURTH PRESSING]

39   Elizabethan Reggae/Soul Serenade – Boris Gardner/Byron Lee and The Dragonaires (actually with Winston Wright) (Prod: Junior Chung/Byron Lee) (1969) [FIFTH PRESSING]

39   Soul Serenade/Elizabethan Reggae – Byron Lee and The Dragonaires (actually with Winston Wright)/Byron Lee and The Dragonaires (actually with Boris Gardner) (Prod: Byron Lee/Boris Gardner and Byron Lee) (1969) [SIXTH PRESSING ON WHICH SOME COPIES CORRECTLY CREDIT 'ELIZABETHAN REGGAE' TO BORIS GARDNER. A SIDE REISSUED ON HORSE HOSS 56A]

40   Organism/Itch – Anonymously Yours (Prod: Bart Sanfilipo) (1969)

41   The Judge/Soul Of Joe – Josh [Roberts]/Ron (Prod: Joe Mansano) [JOE LABEL] (1969)

42   African Meeting/Higher And Higher – Girlie and Jomo [Denzil Dennis]/Josh [Roberts] (Prod: Joe Mansano) (1969) [JOE LABEL]

43   NYT

44   NYT

45   NYT

46   Black Panther/I Want To Be Loved – Sir Collins and The Black Diamonds (Prod: Charles 'Clancy' Collins) (1969)

47   Black Diamonds/I Remember – Sir Collins and The Black Diamonds/The Black Diamonds (Prod: Charles 'Clancy' Collins) (1969)

48   Bye Bye Love/It's Love – The Dials (Prod: Charles 'Clancy' Collins) (1969)

49   Love Is A Treasure/I Want To Be – The Dials/The Black Diamonds (Prod: Charles 'Clancy' Collins) (1969)

50   Brixton Cat, Big And Fat/Solitude – Dice The Boss/Joe's All Stars (Prod: Joe Mansano) (1969) [JOE LABEL]

51   Gun The Man Down/The Thief – Dice The Boss/Joe Mansano (Prod: Joe Mansano) (1969) [JOE LABEL]

207

52   But Officer/Reggae On The Shore – Dice The Boss/Joe's All Stars (Prod: Joe Mansano) (1969) [JOE LABEL]

53   It's Not Impossible/Dynamite Line – Joe's All Stars (actually by Tito Simon)/Joe's All Stars (Prod: Joe Mansano) (1969) [JOE LABEL]

54   Pair Of Wings (actually titled 'Muriel')/I Can't Stop Loving You – The Earthquakes/Sir Collins and The Earthquakes (Prod: Charles 'Clancy' Collins) (1969)

55   Brother Moses/Funny Familiar Forgotten Feelings – Sir Collins and The Earthquakes (Prod: Charles 'Clancy' Collins) (1969)

56   Earthquake/Simmering – Sir Collins and The Earthquakes/The Earthquakes (Prod: Charles 'Clancy' Collins) (1969)

57   Your Boss DJ/Read The News – Dice The Boss/Joe's All Stars (actually by Lance Hannibal [Tito Simon]) (Prod: Joe Mansano) (1969) [JOE LABEL]

58   My Girl/You Were To Be – The Gladiators (actually by Glen Adams)/The Gladiators (Prod: Arthur 'Duke' Reid) (1969)

59   Lick A Pop/Treasure – Hot Rod All Stars (Prod: Hot Rod [Lambert Briscoe]) (1970)

60   Where Were You (When The Lights Went Out)/Just One Smile – The Techniques (Prod: Winston Riley) (1969)

61   Mek You Go On So/Neck Tie – The Ethiopians/Winston Wright and The JJ All Stars (Prod: Karl 'JJ' Johnson) (1970)

62   Poppy Cock/This World And Me (aka 'Satisfaction') – Winston Wright and The JJ All Stars/Carl Dawkins (Prod: Karl 'JJ' Johnson) (1970) [A SIDE ALSO ISSUED ON TROJAN TR 7765A]

63   The Bull/The River Ben Come Up – Freddie Notes and The Rudies (Prod: Joe Sinclair) (1970)

64   NYT

65   Paint Your Wagon/Organ Man – The Setters (actually by The Hot Rod All Stars) (Prod: Hot Rod [Lambert Briscoe]) (1970)

66   Return Of The Bad Man/Cayso Reggae – Hot Rod All Stars (Prod: Hot Rod [Lambert Briscoe]) (1970)

67   Drink Milk/Everywhere I Go – Justin Hinds and The Dominoes (Prod: Arthur 'Duke' Reid) (1970)

68   Chicken Inn/Scratching Chicken (actually titled 'Chicken Scratch') – Freddie Notes and The Rudies/Count Suckle with Freddie Notes and The Rudies (Prod: Joe Sinclair/Count Suckle) (1970)

69   The Law (Part 1)/The Law (Part 2) – Andy Capp/Winston Wright and The Dragonaires (Prod: Byron Lee) (1970)

70   It's A Shame/Desertion – Al T Joe (Prod: Byron Lee) (1970)

71   Poppy Show/Pop A Top (Part 2) – Andy Capp (Prod: Byron Lee) (1970)

72   Remember That Sunday/Last Lick – Alton Ellis (actually with Phyllis Dillon)/
      Tommy McCook (actually with The Supersonics) (Prod: Arthur 'Duke' Reid)
      (1970)

73   Stealing Stealing/Stealing (Instrumental Version) – John Holt/Winston Wright
      (actually with The Supersonics) (Prod: Arthur 'Duke' Reid) (1970)

74   Funky Reggae/I Love You My Baby – Dave Barker/Tommy McCook and The
      Supersonics (actually by The Yard Brooms) (Prod: Arthur 'Duke' Reid) (1970)

75   NYT

76   The Rooster/Walk Through This World – Tommy McCook and The
      Supersonics (actually with Jeff Barnes)/Phyllis Dillon (Prod: Arthur 'Duke'
      Reid) (1970)

77   Open Jaw/Working Kind – Tommy McCook/John Holt (actually with
      Tommy McCook and The Supersonics) (Prod: Arthur 'Duke' Reid) (1970)

78   The Key To The City/Give It To Me – Tommy McCook and The Supersonics
      (actually with Family Man [Aston Barrett]/Dorothy Reid (Prod: Arthur 'Duke'
      Reid) (1970)

79   I Can't Hide/Kansas City – Ken Parker (actually with Tommy McCook and
      The Supersonics)/Tommy McCook (actually with The Supersonics) (Prod:
      Arthur 'Duke' Reid) (1970)

80   Geronimo/Feel Alright – The Pyramids (Prod: Bruce Anthony) (1970) [B
      SIDE REISSUED ON B SIDE OF SECOND PRESSING OF TROJAN
      TR 7814]

81   Ooh Wee/Hold It Baby – Al Barry (Prod: Bruce Anthony) (1970)

82   Death Rides/Destruction – The Good Guys (Prod: Byron Lee) (1970)

83   Wreck It Up/Dynamic Groove – The Good Guys (Prod: Byron Lee) (1970)

84   Happiness/Latissimo – The Good Guys (Prod: Byron Lee) (1970)

85   Hard On Me/Please Don't Stop The Wedding – Tommy Cowan and The
      Jamaicans (actually featuring Norris Weir)/Tommy Cowan and The Jamaicans
      (Prod: Tommy Cowan) (1970)

86   Going In Circles/Doggone Right – Bobby Blue (actually Bobby Davis) (Prod:
      Lloyd Charmers) (1970) [A SIDE REISSUED ON EXPLOSION EX 2054A
      AND TROJAN TR 7936B]

87   Colour Him Father/Colour Him Father (Version 2) – The Charmers (Prod:
      Lloyd Charmers/The Charmers) (1970)

88   You Can't Wine/Bee Sting – The Kingstonians/Rupie Edwards All Stars
      (Prod: Rupie Edwards) (1970)

89   Broke My Heart/Tell Me The Reason – Domino Johnson and The
      Champions (Prod: Larry Lawrence) (1970)

90   Eye For An Eye/Broke My Heart (Version 2) – Tony and The Champions
        (does not in fact feature Tony [Sexton])/The Champions (Prod: Larry
        Lawrence) (1970)

91   Cashbox/Strolling In Hyde Park – Byron Lee and The Dragonaires (actually
        with Winston Wright) (Prod: Byron Lee) (1970)

92   Cloudburst/Message From A Black Man – The Hippy Boys/Lloyd Charmers
        (Prod: Lloyd Charmers) (1970)

93   Get Together/Instalment Plan – Carl Dawkins/Family Man [Aston Barrett]
        (Prod: Karl 'JJ' Johnson) (1970)

94   Collecting Coins/Cabbage Leaf – JJ All Stars (Prod: Karl 'JJ' Johnson) (1970)

95   This Land/Land Version – JJ All Stars (actually by Carl Dawkins)/JJ All Stars
        (Prod: Karl 'JJ' Johnson) (1970)

96   Surprise Package/I'm Sorry – Rico [Rodriguez] and Satch [Ferdinand
        Dixon]/P Johnson [Pete/Domino Johnson] (Prod: Larry Lawrence) (1970)

97   Come Along/Try To Be Happy – The Clarendonians (Prod: Karl 'JJ' Johnson)
        (1970)

98   Funny/Sugar Cane – Rupert Cunningham (Prod: Flame) (1970)

99   Sometimes/Girl Like You – Errol English [Junior English] and The Champions
        (Prod: Larry Lawrence) (1970)

100   NYT

101   Coolie Man/Coolie Version – The Cambodians/JJ All Stars (Prod: Karl 'JJ'
        Johnson) (1970)

102   Drop Him/Version Drop – The Ethiopians/JJ All Stars (Prod: Karl 'JJ' Johnson)
        (1970)

103   Pharoah's Walk/Little Caesar – Exodus/Exodus (actually by Sammy Jones)
        (Prod: Jack Price) (1970)

104   Single Girl/Together We'll Be – Silkie Davis [TT Ross]/Silkie Davis (actually
        by Les Foster) (Prod: Les Foster) (1970)

105   Love I Tender/When The Lights Are Low – U Roy/Joya Landis (Prod: Byron
        Smith) (1970)

106   Donkey Skank/Skank Version – Delroy [Jones] and The Tennors/The Mules
        (Prod: Albert Gene Murphy) (1971)

107   To The Fields/Fields Version – Herman [Chin-Loy]/Herman's Version Men
        (Prod: Aquarius) (1971)

108   Rim Bim Bam/Rim Bim Bam (Version) – The Ethiopians/Randy's All Stars
        (Prod: Victor Chin for Randy's) (1971)

109   Be Loving To Me/Judgement Rock – The Tillermen (Prod: Big 'G') (1971)
        [THE TILLERMEN BECAME GREYHOUND SHORTLY AFTER
        THESE RECORDINGS]

110 One Bad Apple/Poop-A-Poom – Barry Biggs with Byron Lee and The Dragonaires/Byron Lee and The Dragonaires (Prod: Byron Lee) (1971)

111 Silhouettes/That Did It – Winston Wright (Prod: Carl Blake) (1971)

112 Grooving Out On Life/Fire Fire – Hopeton Lewis with Byron Lee and The Dragonaires/ Byron Lee and The Dragonaires (Prod: Byron Lee and Winston Blake/Byron Lee) (1971)

113 Big Bamboo/King Ja Ja – Emile Straker and The Merrymen (Prod: George Benson) (1971) [1968 CALYPSO REISSUE FROM TROJAN TR 692]

114 Maria/Only A Fool (Breaks His Own Heart) – Mighty Sparrow with Byron Lee and The Dragonaires (Prod: Byron Lee) (1971) [CALYPSO REISSUE FROM 1969. REISSUED ON TROJAN TRO 9046]

115 Dr Kitch/Love In The Cemetery – Lord Kitchener (Prod: Telco Records, Trinidad) (1971) [CALYPSO REISSUES FROM 1963 AND 1962 RESPECTIVELY]

116 Babylon A Fall/Version Buggy – The Maytones/Tony King (Prod: Alvin Ranglin) (1971)

117 NYT

118 Put It Good/Good Good Version – The Bleechers/JJ All Stars (Prod: Karl 'JJ' Johnson) (1971)

119 Bend Down/Heaven Help Us All – Ernie Smith (Prod: Federal Records) (1971)

120 Remember/Madhouse – The Sensations/Larry's All Stars (Prod: Larry Lawrence) (1971)

121 What Are You Doing Sunday?/Sweet Dream – The Sensations/The Ruffians (Prod: Larry Lawrence) (1971)

122 Reggae In The Fields/Aquarius 2 – Augustus Pablo/Augustus Pablo (actually by Tommy McCook) (Prod: Herman Chin-Loy for Aquarius) (1971)

123 Come On Home Girl/You Are Mine – Bill and Pete Campbell (Prod: Tyrone Patterson) (1971)

124 Mixing/In Orbit – The Cables/The In Crowd Band (Prod: Hugh Madden) (1971)

125 Medley Version (Part 1)/Medley Version (Part 2) – Dennis Alcapone and The Gaytones (Prod: Sonia Pottinger) (1971)

126 Lion's Den/Lion's Den Version – The Kingstonians/JJ All Stars (Prod: Karl 'JJ' Johnson) (1971)

127 Last Call/Hot Call – Sir Harry/Organ D (Prod: Maurice Wellington) (1972)

128 The Sensational Melodians (Medley)/Part 2 – The Melodians (Prod: Sonia Pottinger) (1972) [UNISSUED AND RELEASED ON DU 130 – DIFFERENT TITLES BUT SAME TRACKS]

211

129 Only Love Can Make You Smile/Only Love Version – Gaby and The Cables (actually Gaby Wilton and The Rebels)/The Cables (Prod: Glen Brown and M Mahtani) (1971)

130 The Mighty Melodians (Part 1)/The Mighty Melodians (Part 2) – The Melodians (Prod: Sonia Pottinger) (1972)

131 The Sky's The Limit/Limit Version – Dennis Alcapone/Hudson's All Stars (Prod: Keith Hudson) (1972)

132 Bald Headed Teacher/Bald Headed Teacher (Version) – Trevor Lambert (actually Max Romeo)/The Headmasters (Prod: Trevor Lambert [Max Romeo]) (1972) [PROBABLY UNISSUED]

133 My Whole World/How Can You Mend A Broken Heart? – Carl Dawkins (Prod: Karl 'JJ' Johnson) (1972)

134 Rebel Train/Babylon Version – Jago (Prod: Maurice Wellington) (1972)

135 Soup/Soup (Version) – JJ All Stars (actually with Lloyd Young)/JJ All Stars (actually with Ron Wilson) (Prod: Karl 'JJ' Johnson) (1972)

136 Apples To Apples/Good Life – Sir Harry/Drumbeat All Stars (Prod: Glen Brown and M Miller) (1972)

137 Live It Up/Baby Don't Do It – U Roy Junior/Dennis Brown (Prod: Lloyd Daley) (1972)

138 NYT

139 What About The Half/Version – Dennis Brown (Prod: Phil Pratt) (1972)

140 Wheel And Tun Me/Hey Mama – Whistling Willie [Neville Willoughby] (Prod: Neville Willoughby) (1972)

141 Boat To Progress/Boat To Progress (Version) – Richard [Macdonald] and Glen [Brown]/Glen Brown (Prod: Glen Brown and M Miller) (1972)

142 I Forgot To Be Your Lover/I've Got To Settle Down – Denzil Dennis (Prod: Pat Rhoden) (1972)

143 Save The Last Dance For Me/Be The One – The Heptones (Prod: Joel Gibson [Joe Gibbs] (1972) [ALSO ISSUED ON ATTACK ATT 8036]

144 Reggae Limbo/Broken Contract – Hudson All Stars/Zap Pow (Prod: Keith Hudson) (1972)

145 Satan Side/Evil Spirit – Keith Hudson/Don D Junior [Karl Bryan] (Prod: Keith Hudson) (1972)

146 Runaway Child/Wedding March – Roy Bailey (Prod: Lloyd Campbell) (1972)

147 Get In The Groove/Get In The Groove (Version) – Dennis Alcapone and Dennis Brown/The Dynamites (Prod: Dynamic) (1972)

148 Vision/Young And Unlearned – Al T Joe (Prod: Byron Lee) (1972)

149 Headquarters/Black Girl In My Bed – Dillinger/Shenley Duffas (Prod: Lee Perry) (1973)

150   Rastaman Going Back Home/Barble Dove Skank – [Lloyd] Flowers and Alvin
       [Ranglin]/Little Youth (Prod: Alvin Ranglin) (1973)
151   Africa Want Us All/Liberation – Allan King/Joe Gibbs All Stars (Prod: Joel
       Gibson [Joe Gibbs]) (1973)
152   Wipe Them Out/Go Back Home – Matumbi (Prod: Dennis Bovell) (1973) [A
       SIDE ALSO ISSUED ON HORSE HOSS 39B]
153   Words Of My Mouth/Words Of My Mouth (Version) – The Gatherers/The
       Upsetters (Prod: Lee Perry) (1973)
154   Murmuring/Murmuring (Version) – The Millions/Tommy McCook and
       Bobby Ellis (Prod: Alvin Ranglin) (1973)
155   Suspicion/Suspicion (Version) – Jimmy Green (actually Jimmy London)/
       Lloyd's All Stars (Prod: Lloyd Campbell) (1973)
156   Buck And The Preacher/Buck And The Preacher (Version) – I-Roy/Pete
       Weston All Stars (Prod: Pete Weston) (1973) [UNISSUED]
157   The Higher The Mountain/Higher Mountain (Version) – U Roy/Old Boys
       Incorporated (Prod: Augustus 'Gussie' Clarke) (1973)
158   Shotgun Wedding/Girl Of My Dreams – Cornel Campbell (Prod: Edward
       'Bunny' Lee) (1973)
159   The Very Best I Can/Heading For The Mountains – Cornel Campbell (Prod:
       Edward 'Bunny' Lee) (1973)
160   Blackbird/Always – Roslyn Sweat and The Paragons (Prod: Arthur 'Duke'
       Reid) (1973)
161   Love Is A Treasure/Love Is A Treasure (Version) – Lizzy (actually with Freddy
       McKay)/Tommy McCook All Stars (actually by Freddy McKay) (Prod: Arthur
       'Duke' Reid) (1973) [B SIDE IS 1967 VERSION]
162   Children Of The Night/For The Good Times – The Chosen Few/Lloyd
       Charmers (Prod: Lloyd Charmers) (1973)
163   Stoned In Love With You/Stoned In Love (Version) – The Chosen Few/
       Micky Chung and The Now Generation (Prod: Lloyd Charmers) (1973)
164   It's Too Late/It's Too Late (Version) – The Chosen Few/Micky Chung (Prod:
       Lloyd Charmers) (1973)
165   Beef Sticker/Ten Commandments – Fud and Del/Prince Heron (Prod: Fud
       Christian for La-Fud-Del) (1973)

DUKE REID (PREFIX DR)

2501   What Does It Take To Win Your Love/Reggae Merengue – Alton Ellis/
       Tommy McCook and The Supersonics (1970)
2502   Hopeful Village/The Village (actually titled 'White Rum') – The Tennors/
       Tommy McCook (actually by Earl Lindo) (1970)

2503   Sunday Gravy/Write Her A Letter – Neville Hinds/John Holt (1970)

2504   Sugar Pantie/Ballafire – Tommy McCook and The Supersonics (actually by Andy Capp and Ken Parker)/Tommy McCook and The Supersonics (1970)

2505   Boom Shacka Lacka/Dynamite – Hopeton Lewis (actually with The Chosen Few)/Tommy McCook Quintet (1970)

2506   Come Out Of My Bed/Hide And Seek – John Holt (actually with Tommy McCook and The Supersonics)/Winston Wright (actually with Tommy McCook and The Supersonics) (1970)

2507   Mother's Tender Care/Soldier Man – The Ethiopians/Tommy McCook (1970)

2508   This Is Me (actually titled 'If Your Name Is Andy')/Skavoovie – Phyllis Dillon (actually by Dorothy Reid) (1970)

2509   Wake The Town/Big Boy And Teacher – U Roy (1970)

2510   Rule The Nation/Ay Ay Ay Ay (probable title 'Angle La-La') – U Roy (actually with The Tommy McCook Quintet)/Nora Dean (actually with The Tommy McCook Quintet) (1970)

2511   Say Me Say/I Want It – Justin Hinds (1970)

2512   You Made Me So Very Happy/Duke's Reggae (actually titled 'Continental') – Alton Ellis/The Supersonics (actually with Tommy McCook) (1970)

2513   Wear You To The Ball/The Ball – U Roy and John Holt (actually The Paragons)/Earl Lindo (1970)

2514   You'll Never Get Away/Rock Away – U Roy (actually with The Melodians)/Tommy McCook Quintet (1970)

2515   Version Galore/Nehru – U Roy (actually with The Melodians)/Tommy McCook (actually with The Supersonics) (1970)

2516   Testify/Super Soul (actually titled 'Superman') – U Roy (actually by Hopeton Lewis)/Tommy McCook (actually by Hopeton Lewis with Tommy McCook and The Supersonics) (1970)

2517   Tom Drunk/Wailing – U Roy and Hopeton Lewis/Tommy McCook (1971)

2518   True True/On The Beach – U Roy (actually with Ken Parker and Tommy McCook and The Supersonics)/U Roy (actually with The Paragons and Tommy McCook and The Supersonics) (1971)

2519   Flashing My Whip/On The Beach – U Roy and The Paragons (1971) [DUPLICATE ISSUE – HAS 'DR 2519A1/DR 2519A2' RESPECTIVELY IN RUNOUT GROOVES]

2519   Flashing My Whip/Do It Right – U Roy (actually with The Paragons and Tommy McCook and The Supersonics)/U Roy (actually with The Three Tops and Tommy McCook and The Supersonics) (1971) [DUPLICATE ISSUE – HAS 'DR 2519B1/DR 2519B2' RESPECTIVELY IN RUNOUT GROOVES]

214

2520   Rock To The Beat (actually titled 'Number One Station')/Love Is Not A
       Gamble – U Roy (actually by Dennis Alcapone and The Duke Reid All
       Stars)/U Roy (actually by Dennis Alcapone and The Techniques) (1972)
2521   Jimmy Brown/Jimmy Brown (Version) – Ken Parker/Ken Parker (actually by
       The Duke Reid All Stars) (1972)
2522   Hurt (actual title 'Your Enemy Can't Hurt You')/Hurt (Version) – Reid's All
       Stars (actually by The Eagles)/Reid's All Stars (1973)
2523   Guess I This Riddle/Riddle (Version) – Eddy Ford/Reid's All Stars (1973)
2524   You're The One I Love/You're The One (Version) – Dorothy Russell/Reid's
       All Stars (1973)

Note

All releases produced by Arthur 'Duke' Reid.

DYNAMIC (PREFIX DYN)

401   Got To Be Mellow/Love Grows – Barry Biggs (Prod: Byron Lee) (1970)
402   Out Of Time/Love For Everyone – Henry III [Henry Buckley] and Hubcap
       and Wheels/The Viceroys with Hubcap and Wheels (Prod: Byron Lee) (1970)
403   One Pound Weight/Come Dance – Henry III [Henry Buckley] and Hubcap
       and Wheels (Prod: Byron Lee) (1970)
404   Commanding Wife/Band Of Gold – Boris Gardner Happening/Boris
       Gardner (Prod: Byron Lee) (1970)
405   Hitching A Ride/Ride Version – Al T Joe/Byron Lee and The Dragonaires
       (Prod: Byron Lee) (1970)
406   Johnny Too Bad/Saucy Hoard (actually 'Saucy Horn') – The Slickers/Roland
       Alphonso (Prod: Sid Bucknor) (1971)
407   634-5789/Warm And Tender Love – Austin Faith [Faithful]/The Dynamic
       Boys (Prod: Byron Lee) (1971)
408   Each One, Teach One/Thinking Of You – The Blues Busters (Prod: Byron
       Lee) (1971) [SOME COPIES SHOW 'THINKING OF YOU' AS A SIDE
       AFTER TROJAN DECIDED TO FLIP IT]
409   My Sweet Lord/Shock Attack – Byron Lee and The Dragonaires (actually
       with Keith Lyn)/Byron Lee and The Dragonaires (actually by The Dynamic
       Boys) (Prod: Byron Lee) (1971)
410   Love Uprising/My Love For You – The Jamaicans (Prod: Byron Lee) (1971)
411   Hallelujah/Trying To Reach My Goal – Ken Boothe (Prod: Byron Lee) (1971)
412   NYT
413   Never Gonna Give You Up/Never Give Up – The West Indians/Rebellious
       Subjects (Prod: Sid Bucknor) (1971)

414   Way Back Home/Way Back Home (Version) – Byron Lee and The
       Dragonaires (Prod: Winston Blake) (1971)
415   Bed Of Roses/Forgive Me – Jo Spencer (actually Hortense Ellis) (Prod: Byron
       Lee) (1971)
416   NYT
417   Mary/Soldier Boy – The Jamaicans/The Conscious Minds (Prod: Tommy
       Cowan) (1971)
418   You Don't Know/Rich Man, Poor Man – The Dingle Brothers/The Cables
       (Prod: Sid Bucknor) (1971)
419   You Can't Win/Don't Fight The Law – The Slickers (Prod: Sid Bucknor) (1971)
420   Cherry Oh Baby/Sir Charmers Special – Eric Donaldson (Prod: Edward
       'Bunny' Lee) (1971)
421   Horse And Buggy/Buggy And Horse – Dennis Alcapone/Roland Alphonso
       and Denzil Laing (Prod: Edward 'Bunny' Lee) (1971)
422   Ripe Cherry/Red Cherry – Dennis Alcapone/Inner Circle (Prod: Edward
       'Bunny' Lee) (1971)
423   Love Of The Common People/The Dragon's Net – Eric Donaldson/The
       Dragonaires (actually with Denzil Laing) (Prod: Dynamic Sounds) (1971)
424   Bam Sa Bo/Bam Sa Bo (Version) – Winston Heywood and The Hombres
       (Prod: Winston Heywood) (1971)
425   Just Can't Happen This Way/Just Can't (Version) – Eric Donaldson/The
       Dragonaires (Prod: Dynamic Sounds) (1971)
426   Carry That Weight/More Weight – Dobby Dobson/Dobby Dobson (actually
       by The Dragonaires) (Prod: Dynamic Sounds) (1971)
427   Al Capone's Guns Don't Bark/Guns Don't Bark (Version) – Dennis Alcapone/
       Dennis Alcapone (actually by The Dynamites) (Prod: Edward 'Bunny' Lee)
       (1971)
428   Just A Dream/Send Me Some Loving – Slim Smith (Prod: Edward 'Bunny'
       Lee) (1972)
429   What A Price/The Prisoner's Song – Al T Joe (Prod: Byron Lee) (1972)
430   I Believe In Music/Music (Version) – The Jamaicans/The Jamaicans (actually
       by The Dynamites) (Prod: Tommy Cowan) (1972)
431   I'm Indebted/I'm Indebted (Version) – Eric Donaldson/Eric Donaldson
       (actually by The Dynamites) (Prod: Tommy Cowan) (1972)
432   Pharaoh Hiding/Hail To Power – Junior Byles/The Upsetters (Prod: Lee
       Perry) (1972)
433   Geraldine/Reverend Leroy – Tommy (actually Tommy Cowan) (Prod: Tommy
       Cowan) (1972)
434   Man No Dead/Man No Dead (Version) – K C White/K C White (actually by
       The Boris Gardner Happening) (Prod: Boris Gardner) (1972)

435 Make It Reggae/Go Johnny go – Byron Lee and The Dragonaires/Dennis Alcapone (Prod: Dynamic Sounds) (1972)

436 Come Together/Going Back To My Home Town – Hopeton Lewis (Prod: Lee Perry) (1972)

437 Everybody Needs Help/Everybody Needs Help Version – Derrick Morgan/Derrick Morgan (actually by The Dynamites) (Prod: Edward 'Bunny' Lee) (1972)

438 Redemption Song/Redemption Version – The Maytals/The Dynamites (Prod: Dynamic Sounds) (1972)

439 Miserable Woman/The Lion Sleeps – Eric Donaldson (Prod: Dynamic Sounds) (1972)

440 Kenyatta/Kenyatta (Version) – Joe White/Joe White Recording Band (Prod: Joe White) (1972)

441 Stop The War/Stop The War (Version) – Winston Heywood and The Hombres/The Hombres (Prod: Winston Heywood) (1972)

442 Are You Sure/Are You Sure (Version) – The Jamaicans/The Dynamites (Prod: Warwick Lyn) (1972)

443 Throw Away Your Gun/Sad Song – Busty Brown and The Warners/The Twinkle Brothers (Prod: Sid Bucknor) (1972)

444 We Love Jamaica/We Love Jamaica (Version) – Max Romeo/Soul Rhythms (Prod: Max Romeo) (1972)

445 Blue Boot/Blue Boot (Version) – Eric Donaldson/Eric Donaldson (actually by The Dynamites) (Prod: Dynamic Sounds) (1972)

446 My Confession/Confession (Version) – Cornel Campbell/The Aggrovators (Prod: Edward 'Bunny' Lee) (1972)

447 Good Together/Good Together (Version) – Hopeton Lewis/The Dynamites (Prod: Dynamic Sounds) (1972)

448 Festival Wise/Festival Wise Part 2 – U Roy (Prod: Dynamic Sounds) (1972)

449 Family Man/Family Man (Version) – Ricky Slick [Richard Grant] (Prod: Dynamic Sounds) (1972)

450 (Last Night) I Didn't Get To Sleep At All/Last Night (Version) – Chris Leon/The Dynamites (Prod: Dynamic Sounds) (1972)

451 Peace/Peace (Version) – Shenley Duffas and The Soul Avengers/The Upsetters (Prod: Lee Perry) (1972)

452 Little Did You Know/Version – Eric Donaldson/Eric Donaldson (actually by The Dynamites) (Prod: Dynamic Sounds) (1972)

453 Tears From My Eyes/Version – Ken Boothe/The Conscious Minds (Prod: Ken Boothe) (1972)

454 Talk About Love/Don't Forget To Remember – Adinah Edwards (Prod: Tommy Cowan) (1972)

217

455 Life Is The Highest/Reincarnate – Tesfa Macdonald (Prod: Tesfa Macdonald) (1972)

456 Sunshine Love/Sunshine (Version) – The Jamaicans (Prod: Dynamic Sounds) (1972)

457 Seek And You'll Find/Version – Winston Heywood and The Hombres/The Hombres (Prod: Winston Heywood) (1972)

EXPLOSION (PREFIX EX)

2001 Death A Come/Zylon – Lloyd Charmers (actually by Lloyd Robinson)/Lloyd Charmers (Prod: Lloyd Charmers) (1969)

2002 Doctor Who (Part 1)/Dr Who (Part 2) – Bongo Les and Herman (actually Bongo Herman and Les Chen) (Prod: Derrick Harriott) (1969)

2003 Barefoot Brigade/Slippery – Winston Wright and The Crystalites/The Crystalites (actually with Winston Wright and Bobby Ellis) (Prod: Derrick Harriott) (1969)

2004 NYT

2005 Slippery/Bag A Wire – The Crystalites (actually with Bobby Ellis) (Prod: Derrick Harriott) (1969) [B SIDE REISSUED FROM EX 2003B]

2006 A Fistful Of Dollars/The Emporer – The Crystalites/The Crystalites (actually with Bobby Ellis) (Prod: Derrick Harriott) (1969)

2007 Lemi Li/Goody Goody – Rudy Mills (Prod: Derrick Harriott) (1970)

2008 Tighten Up Your Gird (actually 'Tighten Up Your Guard' aka 'Run To The Rocks')/Look To The Sky – Keith and Tex and The Crystalites (Prod: Derrick Harriott) (1970)

2009 She's Gone/Old Old Song – Tinga [Stewart] and Ernie [Smith] (Prod: Derrick Harriott) (1970)

2010 The Bad (Version 1)/The Bad (Version 2) – The Crystalites (Prod: Derrick Harriott) (1970)

2011 Flight 404/Gawling Come Down – Winston Wright/Lloyd and Robin (Prod: Alvin Ranglin) (1970)

2012 Funny Man/Champion – The Maytones/The Maytones (actually by GG All Stars) (Prod: Alvin Ranglin) (1970)

2013 Sentimental Reason/Lover Girl – The Maytones (Prod: Alvin Ranglin) (1970)

2014 Barabus/This Kind Of Life – The Maytones (Prod: Alvin Ranglin) (1970)

2015 Funny Girl/Funny Girl (Version 2) – Winston Wright (Prod: Alvin Ranglin) (1970)

2016 Higher Than The Highest Mountain/Musical Shot – Monty [Eric] Morris/GG All Stars (Prod: Alvin Ranglin) (1970)

2017 Funky Monkey/Funky Monkey (Part 2) – Dice The Boss (Prod: Laurel Aitken) (1970)

2018 Chinee Brush/Real Collie – Trevor Lloyd/Dice and Cummie (Prod: Laurel Aitken) (1970)

2019 Give Me Back Your Love/Hold Me – Trevor Lloyd (Prod: Laurel Aitken) (1970)

2020 Funky Duck/Funkier Than Duck – Dice The Boss (Prod: Laurel Aitken) (1970)

2021 NYT

2022 In The Summertime/Apollo Moon Rock – Billy Jack (actually Winston Groovy)/Nat Cole (Prod: Nat Cole) (1970)

2023 Man From Carolina/Gold On Your Dress – GG All Stars/GG All Stars (actually by The Slickers) (Prod: Alvin Ranglin) (1970)

2024 African Melody/Serious Love – GG All Stars/GG All Stars (actually by The Maytones) (Prod: Alvin Ranglin) (1970)

2025 Ganga Plane/Deep River – GG All Stars/GG All Stars (actually by Aston Barratt) (Prod: Alvin Ranglin) (1970)

2026 Can I Get Next To You/Big Five – The Charmers (actually Lloyd Charmers and Busty Brown) (Prod: Lloyd Charmers) (1970) [A SIDE REISSUED ON HARRY J (HJ 6618B)]

2027 Cecilia/Chariot Without Horse – The Maytones/The Maytones (actually by Nyah Hunter and GG All Stars) (Prod: Alvin Ranglin) (1970)

2028 Too Late/Each Day – Joel Marvin (actually Gregory Isaacs) (Prod: Rupie Edwards) (1970)

2029 Mudie Jo Jo (actually 'Groovy Jo Jo')/Ten Steps To Soul – Jo Jo Bennett and Mudie's All Stars (Prod: Harry Mudie) (1970)

2030 Full Moon/Baby (actually titled 'Why Can't We Learn') – Rupie Edwards All Stars/Rupie Edwards All Stars (actually by Hughroy Henry) (Prod: Rupie Edwards) (1970) [A SIDE ALSO ISSUED ON BIG LABEL BG 314B]

2031 Love At First Sight (actually unidentified title)/I Need Your Care – Rupie Edwards (actually by unidentified male vocalist)/Rupie Edwards (actually by unidentified male vocalist) (Prod: Rupie Edwards) (1970)

2032 Vengeance/Look A Py-Py – The Hippy Boys (actually with Lloyd Charmers)/ The Hippy Boys (Prod: Lloyd Charmers) (1970)

2033 Another Festival/Happy Time – The Maytones (Prod: Alvin Ranglin) (1970)

2034 Ready Talk (actually titled 'Jamaica Reggae')/There Is Something About You (actually titled 'I Love You Madly') – Lloyd Charmers/Lloyd Charmers (actually with Busty Brown) (Prod: Lloyd Charmers) (1970)

2035 Sweet Back/Music Talk – The Charmers (actually with Karl Walker) (Prod: Lloyd Charmers) (1970)

2036 Ring The Bell/Ring The Bell (Version 2) – Trevor and Keith (Prod: Alvin Ranglin) (1970)

2037   Blue Moon/Oh Me Oh My (Version) – Guts McGeorge (actually Lloyd
        Charmers) (Prod: Lloyd Charmers) (1970)

2038   NYT

2039   Revelation Version/Marka Version – Hugh Roy (actually Dennis Alcapone)
        (Prod: Keith Hudson) (1970)

2040   Whisper A Little Prayer/Rain A Fall – Hugh Roy (actually by Audley
        Rollen)/Melanie (actually Merlene Webber) (Prod: Keith Hudson) (1970)

2041   California Dreaming/One Woman – Hugh Roberts (actually Lloyd Charmers)
        (Prod: Lloyd Charmers) (1970)

2042   All Kinds Of Everything/Cool And Easy – Wayne Howard (actually Lloyd
        Charmers) (Prod: Lloyd Charmers) (1970)

2043   Delivered/Especially For You – Neville Hinds/Neville Hinds (actually by
        Blake Boy [Winston Blake]) (Prod: Lloyd Daley) (1971)

2044   Love I Madly/Musical Shower – Tony [Binns] and The Charmers (Prod: Lloyd
        Charmers) (1971)

2045   Skinhead Train/Ever Strong – The Charmers/Tony Binns (Prod: Lloyd
        Charmers) (1971)

2046   Humpty Dumpty/Got To Get A Message To You – Tony Binns/Dave Barker
        and The Charmers (Prod: Lloyd Charmers) (1971) [UNISSUED]

2047   Back To Africa/Born To Lose – Lloyd and Joy (actually by Alton Ellis)/Lloyd
        and Joy (Prod: Lloyd Daley) (1971)

2048   Never Fall In Love With You Again (Version 3)/Jet 747 (Version 4) – Glen
        Adams/ The Jet Scene (Prod: Fud Christian for La-Fud-Del) (1971)

2049   Love Brother/Uganda – Herman [Chin-Loy] (Prod: Herman Chin-Loy)
        (1971)

2050   Starvation/Version 2 – The Ethiopians/The Trojan All Stars (actually the JJ All
        Stars) (Prod: Karl 'JJ' Johnson) (1971)

2051   I Feel Good/I Feel Good Version 2 – Carl Dawkins/JJ All Stars (Prod: Karl 'JJ'
        Johnson) (1971)

2052   Hold On Girl (actually titled 'Oh No Girl')/Hold On Girl (Version) (actually
        titled 'Oh No Girl' (Version)') – Randy's All Stars (actually by The Lyrics)/
        Randy's All Stars (Prod: Victor Chin for Randy's) (1971)

2053   Oh Lord/Raindrops (actually titled 'My Baby') – Errol Dunkley and The
        Impact All Stars/Keith [Poppin] and The Impact All Stars (Prod: Keith Chin
        for Randy's) (1971)

2054   Going In Circles/Just My Imagination – The Charmers (actually with Bobby
        Blue [Bobby Davis])/The Charmers (actually with Dave Barker) (Prod:
        Lloyd Charmers) (1971) [A SIDE REISSUED ON DUKE DU 86A AND
        TROJAN TR 7936B]

220

2055   Reggae In Wonderland/Wonder (Version) – The Charmers (actually by Lester Williams from Byron Lee and The Dragonaires) (Prod: Lloyd Charmers) (1971)

2056   Girl/Sister Big Stuff – Ken Lazarus/Tomorrow's Children (Prod: Federal Records) (1971)

2057   I Love Jamaica/Marry Me Marie – Neville [Willoughby] (Prod: Neville Willoughby) (1971)

2058   Life Is Rough (actually titled 'Rough Life')/Life Is Rough (Version) (actually titled 'Rough Life (Version)') – Shout (actually by Laxton Ford) (Prod: Federal Records) (1971)

2059   Make It Great/What A Day – Carl Dawkins/Stone (actually Selvin 'Stone' Stewart) (Prod: Federal Records) (1972)

2060   Stagger Lee/Musical Version – John Lee (actually by John Holt)/The Aggrovators (Prod: Edward 'Bunny' Lee for Federal Records) (1972)

2061   Bounce Me Johnny/Bounce Me Version (actually not a version and titled 'Say You') – The Slickers (Prod: Stare McCallum for Federal Records) (1972)

2062   Repatriation/Repatriation Version – Audley Rollen/U Roy Junior (Prod: Lloyd Daley) (1972)

2063   Samba Gal/Samba Version – England 'Sam' Cook [Sam Cargill]/Now Generation (Prod: Lloyd Daley) (1972)

2064   Hail The Man/Where Do I Go? – Ken Lazarus (Prod: Federal) (1972)

2065   Not Another Woman/Don't Go Wrong – Carl Dawkins (Prod: Edward 'Bunny' Lee) (1972)

2066   Soul And Inspiration/Trying My Faith – Paddy Corea/The Stags (possibly The Versatiles) (Prod: Bush) (1972)

2067   Sprinkle Some Water/Howdy And Tenky – Shorty Perry/Lloyd [Flowers] and Alvin [Ranglin] (Prod: Alvin Ranglin) (1972)

2068   Black Magic Woman/Black Magic Woman (Version) – Phil Pratt (actually by Dennis Brown)/Phil Pratt All Stars (Prod: Phil Pratt) (1972)

2069   Long Long Road/Long Long Road (Version) – Milton Hamilton and The Classics (actually with Denzil Dennis)/The Classics (Prod: Pat Rhoden) (1972)

2070   The Killer Passing Through/Show Some Loving (actually titled 'Treat Me Good') – The Swans (actually by Roy Bailey)/The Swans (actually by Al Barry and The Aces) (Prod: Barry Howard [Al Barry]) (1972)

2071   Let Me Down Easy/Easy (Version) – Derrick Harriott/Derrick Harriott (actually by The Crystalites) (Prod: Derrick Harriott) (1972)

2072   Memories Of Love/In Peace – The Orbitones/Sonny Earl [Sonny Roberts] (Prod: Sonny Roberts) (1972)

2073   Chirpy Chirpy Cheep Cheep/Instrumental – The Jay Boys (actually by The Fabulous Five)/The Jay Boys (Prod: Harry Johnson) (1972)

221

2074   The Time Has Come/Blessed Is Man (actually 'The Time Has Come (Version)') – Slim Smith/Slim Smith (actually by Rico Rodriguez and The Aggrovators) (Prod: Edward 'Bunny' Lee) (1972)

2074   The Time Has Come/The Time Has Come (Version) – Slim Smith/Slim Smith (actually by Rico Rodriguez and The Aggrovators) (Prod: Edward 'Bunny' Lee) (1972) [SECOND PRESSING WITH CORRECTED B SIDE CREDITS]

2075   Forward Up/Forward (Version) – The Stingers/The Upsetters (Prod: Lee Perry) (1972)

2076   Brown Girl/Halfway Tree Rock – The Maytones/Shorty Perry (Prod: Alvin Ranglin) (1972)

2077   Rhythm Pleasure (actually 'Rhythm Of Pleasure')/Doctor Seaton – Jerry Lewis/The Aggrovators (Prod: Edward 'Bunny' Lee) (1972)

2078   Stand Up And Fight/Sunny Side Of The Sea – Slim Smith/Slim Smith and Dennis Alcapone (Prod: Edward 'Bunny' Lee) (1973)

2079   Weather Report/Weather Report (Version) – The Tennors (Prod: Arthur 'Duke' Reid) (1973)

2080   I'll Never Find Another You/Another You (Version) – Jimmy London/Impact All Stars (Prod: Randy's) (1973)

2081   Seven Little Girls (Sitting In The Back Seat)/Give A Little Love – The Peaches (actually Winston Groovy and The Marvels) (Prod: Sidney Crooks) (1973)

2082   Sha La La La Lee/No Matter What You Do – The Clem Bushay Set/Clement Bushay (Prod: Clement Bushay) (1973)

2083   I'm A Believer/You'll Be Mine – Winston Groovy [Winston Tucker] (Prod: Winston Tucker [Winston Groovy]) (1973)

2084   My Island/My Island (Version) – Paulette Williams/GG All Stars (Prod: Alvin Ranglin) (1973)

2085   That Lady/Sonia – The Paris Connection (actually featuring Jackie Paris) (Prod: Carlton Troutt) (1973)

2086   Nose For Trouble/Same Thing Version – Winston Groovy/Rhythm Rulers (Prod: Winston Tucker [Winston Groovy]) (1973)

2087   Single Girl/Single Girl (Version) – Barbara Thompson (Prod: Shady Tree [Dandy]) (1974)

2088   Please Don't Make Me Cry/So Easy – Winston Groovy (Prod: Sidney Crooks/ Winston Tucker [Winston Groovy]) (1974)

2089   None Shall Escape The Judgement/Every Rasta Is A Star – Johnny Clarke (Prod: Edward 'Bunny' Lee) (1974)

2090   The Man Who Sold The World/The Man Who Sold The World (Instrumental) – The Wally Brothers/Wally's All Stars (Prod: Webster Shrowder and Des Bryan) (1974)

2091   Mockingbird/Mockingbird (Instrumental) – The Tulips (actually The
        Marvels)/Des All Stars (Prod: Webster Shrowder and Des Bryan) (1974)

GAYFEET (PREFIX GS)

FIRST SERIES

201   Fatty/Landlord – Bim and Bam (1969)
202   If It Don't Work Out (actually titled 'Then You Can Tell Me Goodbye')/
        Ki- Salaboca – Joe White/Baba Brooks Recording Band (1969) [1966
        RECORDINGS]
203   By The Time I Get To Phoenix/Lover Boy – Lou Sparkes/Roland Alphonso
        (1969)
204   Little Donkey/Hope And Joy – Lou Sparkes and Maxine/Lou Sparkes (1970)
205   Jennifer/Slipping – Junior Soul [Murvin] (1970)
206   NYT
207   You Are Not My Kind/You Are Not My Kind (Version 2) – Naomi/The
        Gaytones (1970)
208   We Will Make Love/Sticker – Lou Sparks/Roland Alphonso and The
        Gaytones (1970)

SECOND SERIES

206   Medicine Doctor/Facts Of Life – Big Youth (1973)
207   Emergency Call/Emergency Call (Version) – Judy Mowatt/Judy Mowatt
        (actually by The Gaytones) (1973) [REISSUED ON TROJAN TR 7912]
208   You Make Me Cry/You Make Me Cry (Version) – Winston Jones (actually
        with The Gaytones)/Winston Jones (actually by The Gaytones) (1973)
209   My Baby Just Cares For Me/Jah Jah Me No Horn Yah – Cornel Campbell
        (Prod: Edward 'Bunny' Lee) (1973)
210   Hard Feeling/Regular Style – U Roy (Prod: Alvin Ranglin) (1973)

Note

All issues produced by Mrs Sonia Pottinger unless otherwise indicated.

GG (PREFIX GG)

4501   Music Keep On Playing/Keep On Playing Version – GG All Stars (actually by
        The Links)/GG All Stars (1970) (Prod: Sid Bucknor)
4502   NYT
4503   NYT
4504   It's Been A Long Time/Feel It More And More – Winston Wright/Paulette
        and Gee (1970)
4505   I Don't Like To Interfere/I Don't Like To Interfere (Version 2) – GG All Stars
        (actually by The Maytones)/GG All Stars (1970)

4506   Hold On Tight/Tight Version – Paulette and Gee/GG All Stars (1970)
4507   Ontarius Version/Ontarius Version Part 2 (actually 'All One Nation (Version)')
        – Charlie Ace/Winston Wright (actually by Clifton Smith) (1970)
4508   Cleanliness/Cleanliness Version – The Maytones/GG All Stars (1970)
4509   NYT
4510   Rocking On The GG Beat/Rocking On The GG Beat (Version 2) – GG All
        Stars (actually by Clifton Smith and Winston Wright)/Winston Wright (1971)
4511   Lonely Nights/Let The Version Play – GG All Stars (actually by Eric
        Donaldson)/The Maytones (1971)
4512   Mr Brown/Minna Hear Me Now – Trevor Brown/Winston Wright and
        Clifton [Smith] (1971) [PROBABLY UNISSUED. A SIDE RELEASED ON
        GG 4522B]
4513   All One Nation/Judgement Warrant – GG All Stars (actually by Clifton
        Smith)/Val Bennett (1971)
4514   Groove Me/Groove Version – Keelyn Beckford/Keelyn Beckford (actually by
        Winston Wright) (1971)
4515   Shock And Shake (Version 3) (actually titled 'Shook, Shimmy And Shake
        (Version 3)')/Roll On Version 2 (actually 'Reaping Version') – Charlie [Ace],
        Paulette and Gee/Winston Wright (1971) [B SIDE ALSO ON GG 4516B]
4516   False Reaper/Reaping Version – Gerald Mckleish/GG All Stars (actually by
        Winston Wright) (1971) [B SIDE ALSO ISSUED ON GG 4515B]
4517   Lover's Affair/My Love And I – Charlie [Ace] and The Maytones/Winston
        Wright (1971)
4518   Do Something/Groove Me – Grooving Charlie [Charlie Ace]/The Maytones
        (1971)
4519   Sounds Of Our Forefathers/Love Bug – The Ethiopians (1971)
4520   Jordan River/Version 2 – Maxie [Max Romeo] and Glen [Adams]/Glen
        Adams (1971)
4521   Devil's Angel/Devil's Angel Version – Bunny and The Kiemanaires (1971)
4522   Black And White/Mr Brown – The Maytones/Trevor Brown (1971)
4523   Little Boy Blue/Little Boy Blue Version – Verne [Vernon Buckley] and Son
        [Gladstone Grant] (actually The Maytones)/Typhoon All Stars (1971)
4524   Oh My Baby/Change Of Love Version (actually 'Oh My Baby') – The
        Slickers/Winston Wright (actually by The Slickers) (1971) [SAME TRACK
        ON BOTH SIDES]
4525   Bongo Man Rise/Remember – The Maytones/Roy and Bim (1971)
4526   Rod Of Righteousness (actually titled 'Stretch Forth His Hand')/King
        Of Kings (actually titled 'King Of Glory') – GG All Stars (actually by Jah
        Huntley)/Dennis Alcapone (1971)

4527   Got To Go Home/How Long Will You Stay – The Invaders/Paulette and Gee (1971)

4528   Place In My Heart (actually titled 'Is There a Place In Your Heart For Me')/ You've Got A Friend – Cynthia Richards/Irving [Al Brown] and Cynthia Richards (1971)

4529   Keep It Up/A Love Like Yours – John Holt (1972)

4530   Donkey Face/Donkey Face (Version) – The Maytones/GG All Stars (1972)

4531   As Long As You Love Me (Side 1)/As Long As You Love Me (Side 2) – The Maytones (1972) [B SIDE IS SLOW VERSION OF A SIDE]

4532   Be My Guest/Way Down South – Billy Dyce/U Roy (1972)

4533   Israel Want To Be Free/Israel (Version) – The Ethiopians/Typhoon All Stars (1972)

4534   Take Warning/Warning (Version) – Billy Dyce/Typhoon All Stars (1972)

4535   Is It Really Over?/Born To Be Loved – Max Romeo/The Maytones (1972)

4536   Undying Love (actually 'Unity Is Love')/Version (actually 'The Harder They Come') – Billy Dyce/Typhoon All Stars (actually by Charlie Ace) (1972) [B SIDE ALSO ISSUED ON GREEN DOOR GD 4040A]

4537   Time Is Still Here/Time Is Still Here Version – Billy Dyce/Typhoon All Stars (1972) [B SIDE ALSO ISSUED ON GREEN DOOR GD 4040B]

4538   Musical Alphabet/Things Gonna Change (actually 'I'm Feeling Lonely') – Dennis Alcapone/Buckley All Stars (actually by Vernon Buckley) (1972)

4539   Bad Cow Skank/Drummer Roach – Tommy McCook and Bobby Ellis/ Gladstone Anderson (1973)

4540   Brother Louie/Brother Louie (Version) – Matumbi/Blackbeard All Stars (1973)

Note

All issues produced by Alvin Ranglin except 4501 (Sid Bucknor), 4521 (Keimanaires) and 4540 (Dennis Bovell).

GRAPE (PREFIX GR)

3000   Belittle Me/Keep Your Love – Carlton Alphonso (Prod: Carlton Alphonso) (1969)

3001   Moon Walk/Think – Sprong and The Nyah Shuffle (Prod: Joe Sinclair) (1969)

3002   Darling It Won't/Moon Train – Johnny Youth (actually Trevor Sutherland) and The Nyah Shuffle/The Hip City Boys (Prod: Joe Sinclair) (1969)

3003   Cutting Blade/The Vampire – King Horror (Prod: Laurel Aitken) (1969)

3004   Casa Boo Boo/My Girl (actually 'Casa Boo Boo (Instrumental)') – Tony (actually by Count Sticky and The Hippy Boys) (Prod: unidentified) (1969)

3005   Leaving Me Standing/Little Girl – Winston Groovy (Prod: Laurel Aitken) (1969)

3006   The Hole/Lover Come Back – King Horror/Winston Groovy (actually by Lloydie [Lloyd Deslandes] and The Mellotones) (Prod: Laurel Aitken/Lloyd Deslandes) (1969)

3007   Lochness Monster/Zion I – King Horror (actually with Rico Rodriguez)/ The Visions (Prod: Laurel Aitken/Winston Riley) (1969)

3008   Merry Xmas/I Am Lonely – Winston Groovy/Winston Groovy (actually by Barry Bailey) (Prod: Laurel Aitken/Lloyd Deslandes) (1969)

3009   Captain Hook/Girl I Love – The Visions (Prod: Winston Riley) (1969)

3010   Guns Of Navarone/Yester-me, Yester-you, Yesterday – Freddie Notes and The Rudies (Prod: Joe Sinclair) (1969)

3011   Babylon/Girl I've Got A Date – Freddie Notes and The Rudies (Prod: Joe Sinclair) (1969)

3012   True Love (actually titled ('If You Cry True Love, True Love')/Another Saturday Night – Terry, Carl and Derrick/Roy [Junior] Smith (Prod: Calva L [Les] Foster) (1970)

3013   See Through Craze/I'm The One – Roy [Junior] Smith/Terry, Carl and Derrick (Prod: Calva L [Les] Foster) (1970)

3014   Night Food Reggae/Walk With Des – Des All Stars (Prod: Des Bryan and Webster Shrowder) (1970)

3015   If I Had A Hammer/Hammer Reggae – Des All Stars (Prod: Des Bryan and Webster Shrowder) (1970)

3016   Henry The Great/Black Scorcher – Des All Stars (Prod: Des Bryan and Webster Shrowder) (1970)

3017   Ace Of Hearts (aka 'You're Gonna Need Somebody')/Bet Yer Life I Do – Candy (actually Eugene Paul and The Cimarons)/Billy Jack (actually Winston Groovy and The Cimarons) (Prod: Grape) (1970) [UNISSUED – RELEASED ON BIG SHOT BI 559]

3018   Let's Work Together/Jam Monkey – Billy Jack (actually Winston Groovy)/The Corporation (Prod: Grape) (1970)

3019   Boot Lace (actually titled 'Simmer Down')/Honey Won't You Stay (actually titled 'Sylvie You're No Good') – Nyah Shuffle (Prod: Grape) (1970)

3020   Skinhead A Bash Them/Walking Through Jerusalem – Claudette and The Corporation/The Corporation (Prod: Grape) (1970) [B SIDE REISSUED ON GR 3022B]

3021   Stingray (actually titled 'Get Up Edina')/Paradise – Nyah Shuffle (Prod: Grape) (1970)

3022   Sweet Musille (actually titled 'Sweet Mademoiselle', aka 'Corner Hop')/ Walking Through Jerusalem – The Corporation (actually by The Dynamites)/ The Corporation (Prod: Clancy Eccles/Grape) (1970) [A SIDE REISSUED ON TROJAN TR 7852B. B SIDE REISSUED FROM GR 3020B]

3023 NOT USED

3024 NOT USED

3025 Come Down (Part 1)/Come Down (Part 2) – Carey [Johnson] and Lloyd [Young]/The Dynamites (Prod: Warwick Lyn and Tommy Cowan) (1972)

3026 On Top Of The Peak/Rack-A-Tack – U Roy/Typhoon All Stars (Prod: Alvin Ranglin) (1972)

3027 Searching For Your Love/Searching (Version) – Dell Williams/GG All Stars (Prod: Alvin Ranglin) (1972)

3028 If Loving You Is Wrong (I Don't Want To Be Right)/In A De Pum Pum (Version) (actually not the Version side) – The Maytones/[Lloyd] Flowers and Alvin [Ranglin] (Prod: Alvin Ranglin) (1972)

3029 Big Bad Boy/Big Bad Version – Alton Ellis/Hudson's All Stars (Prod: Keith Hudson) (1972)

3030 The Exile Song/In The Burning Sun (Ya Ho) – Skiddy and Detroit/Bunny Gayle (Prod: Keith Hudson) (1972)

3031 Sincerely/Sincerely (Version) – Shenley Duffus/Shenley Duffus and The Upsetters (Prod: Lee Perry) (1972)

3032 Send A Little Rain (aka 'I'm Just A Sufferer')/A Little Rain (Version) – Derrick Morgan/Derrick Morgan's All Stars (Prod: Derrick Morgan) (1972)

3033 You're A Big Girl Now/Version 2 – The Chosen Few (Prod: Derrick Harriott) (1972) [A SIDE ALSO ISSUED ON TROJAN TR 7882B]

3034 Vampire Rock/El-Sisco-Rock – Jah Fish/The Mod Stars (Prod: Keble Drummond) (1972)

3035 Rasta Dub/Rasta Version – Dennis Alcapone/The Upsetters (Prod: Lee Perry) (1973)

3036 Be Faithful Darling (actually titled 'Remember You're Mine')/Faithful Version (actually titled 'Remember You're Mine (Version)' – Clancy Eccles All Stars (actually by Leon Hyatt)/Clancy All Stars (Prod: Clancy Eccles) (1973)

3037 Babylon Gone/Speak No Evil – Zeddie Bailey/King Tony (Prod: Fud Christian for La-Fud-Del) (1973)

3038 Can I Change My Mind?/Just Because – Delroy Wilson (Prod: Edward 'Bunny' Lee) (1973)

3039 Why Did You Do It?/One Love – Errol Dunkley (actually with Freddy McGregor)/ Errol Dunkley (Prod: Edward 'Bunny' Lee for Bush Productions) (1973)

3040 Foreman versus Frasier/Round Two – Big Youth (Prod: Joel Gibson [Joe Gibbs]) (1973)

3041 Warrika Hill/Battlefield – Love Generation/Third and Fourth Generation (Prod: Joel Gibson [Joe Gibbs]) (1973)

227

3042 Let Me Dream/Let Me Dream (Version) – The Hoffner Brothers/The Hoffner Brothers (actually with unidentified DJ) (Prod: Larry Lawrence) (1973)

3043 Change Partners/Pleading For Your Love – Cynthia Richards/The Selectors (Prod: Larry Lawrence) (1973)

3044 JA To UK/JA To UK Version – Big Youth (Prod: Frank Campbell) (1973)

3045 Dear Lonely Hearts/I Tried To Love You – Lloyd [Banton] and Barbara/Lloyd Banton (Prod: Lloyd Bantam) (1973)

3046 Money Raper/The Magnificent Heptones Three In One (Baby/Why Must I/Why Did You Leave) – The Love Generation/The Heptones and The Love Generation (Prod: Joel Gibson [Joe Gibbs]) (1973)

3047 Free From Chains/Papa Do It Sweet – Prince Jazzbo/Lloyd and Patsy (Prod: Tony Robinson [Prince Tony]) (1973)

3048 George Foreman/George Foreman Version – Bacca (Prod: N Harvey and Harry Johnson) (1972)

3049 Backslider/Mosquito Dub – The Untouchables/GG All Stars (Prod: Alvin Ranglin) (1973)

3050 Blacula/Blacula Version – The Crystalites (Prod: Derrick Harriott) (1973)

3051 Opportunity Rock (Midnight In Moscow)/Double Attack (Midnight In Moscow) – Big Youth (Prod: Glen Brown and M Miller) (1973)

3052 Abusing And Assaulting/Food Control – Shorty Perry (Prod: Alvin Ranglin) (1973)

3053 Old Time/Dub – The Heptones/GG All Stars (Prod: Alvin Ranglin) (1973)

3054 One Wife/One Wife (Version) – Junior Soul [Murvin]/The Crystalites (Prod: Derrick Harriott) (1973)

3055 Morning Has Broken/Don't Take Love For A Game – You and I (actually Bobby Davis and Ornell Hinds) (Prod: Carlton Troutt) (1973)

3056 Be True/Navajo Trail – Tony Gordon (actually by Alton Ellis) (Prod: Stanley Pemberton, Sylvan Williams and Des Bryan) (1973)

3057 Mr Softhand/Mr Softhand (Version) – Vernon Buckley (actually by The Starlites)/GG All Stars (Prod: Alvin Ranglin) (1973)

3058 Ital Queen/Ital Queen Dub – Vernon Buckley/GG All Stars (Prod: Alvin Ranglin) (1973)

3059 People Got To Be Free/Ups And Downs – Denzil Dennis (Prod: Pat Rhoden) (1973)

3060 Our Rendezvous/Our Rendezvous (Version) – Freddy McKay/Soul Dynamites (Prod: Warwick Lyn) (1973)

3061 Concrete Jungle/Screaming Target – Big Youth and Simplicity People (Prod: Augustus 'Gussie' Clarke) (1973)

3062 Murderer/The Killer – Simplicity People/Big Youth (Prod: Augustus 'Gussie' Clarke) (1973)

GREEN DOOR (PREFIX GD)

4000   Rasta Never Fails/Rasta Version – The Charmers [Ken Boothe and Lloyd
       Charmers])/Charmers All Stars (Prod: Lloyd Charmers) (1971)
4001   One Big Unhappy Family/Africa Is Paradise – The Charmers/The Conscious
       Minds (Prod: Lloyd Charmers) (1971)
4002   Medley (Version 1)/Medley (Version 2) – Ken Boothe (Prod: Herman Chin-
       Loy) (1971)
4003   Carroll Street/Carroll Street Version – The Winstons [Winston Wright and
       Winston Blake] and The M Squad/Ansel Collins and The M Squad (Prod:
       Winston Blake) (1971)
4004   Drums Of Passion/Love And Emotion Version – B Leggs (actually by Bongo
       Les [Chen])/B Leggs (actually by Morgan's All Stars) (Prod: Derrick Morgan)
       (1971)
4005   Trenchtown Rock/Grooving Kingston 12 – Bob Marley and The Wailers
       (Prod: Bob Marley and Tuff Gong) (1971) [A SIDE REISSUED ON
       TROJAN TR 7979A]
4006   You've Got A Friend/Cheep – Zimm and Dee Dee (actually Winston Francis
       and Donna Dawson)/The Groovers (Prod: Bush) (1971)
4007   Miss Labba Labba/Best Is Yet To Come – Twinkle Brothers (Prod: Three
       Sevens) (1971)
4008   Flying Machine/Machine Version – Teddy Magnus/The Version Boys (actually
       by Hux Brown) (Prod: KG Productions) (1971)
4009   Seven In One (Medley)/Medley (Continued) – The Clarendonians (Prod: L
       Hanson and Kenneth Wilson) (1971)
4010   Chopsticks/Belmont Street – The Deltones (Prod: Bush Productions) (1971)
4011   Heads Or Tails/Raunchy – Winston Wright/The Roasters (Prod: Lynford
       Anderson) (1971)
4012   Girl Called Clover/Girl Called Clover (Version) – Young Al Capone (possibly
       Dillinger) (Prod: Tony Robinson [Prince Tony]) (1971)
4013   NYT
4014   Harbour Shark/Harbour Shark Version – Wailing Souls (Prod: Keith Cole)
       (1971)
4015   Living In Sweet Jamaica/Sweet Jamaica Version – Jackie Brown/Tony's All
       Stars (Prod: Tony Robinson [Prince Tony]) (1971)
4016   Jamaican Hi-Lite (Part 1)/Jamaican Hi-Lite (Part 2) – The Gaytones (Prod:
       Sonia Pottinger) (1971)
4017   I'm Sorry (actually titled 'So Ashamed')/Sorry Version – The Matadors
       (actually by Tony Brevett)/The Rhythm Rulers (Prod: Lloyd Campbell for
       Bush) (1972)

4018   NYT

4019   Breaking Your Heart/Breaking Your Heart (Version) – The Scorpions/The In
Crowd (Prod: Hugh Madden) (1972)

4020   Hypocrite/Straight To The Head (aka 'Two Edged Sword') – The Heptones/
Johnny Lover (Prod: Joel Gibson [Joe Gibbs]) (1972) [REISSUED FROM
AMALGAMATED AMG 873A WHERE IT WAS CREDITED UNDER
'TWO EDGED SWORD' TITLE]

4021   Riot/Smoke Without Fire – Soul Syndicate (actually with Johnny Moore)
(Prod: Keith Hudson) (1972)

4022   Lively Up Yourself/Live – Bob Marley and The Wailers/Tommy McCook
(Prod: Bob Marley and Tuff Gong) (1972)

4023   High School Serenade/On The Track – Lennox Brown/Winston Scotland
(Prod: Tony Robinson [Prince Tony]) (1972) (B SIDE ALSO ISSUED ON
ATTACK ATT 8027B]

4024   Merry Up/Merry Up (Version) – God Sons (Prod: Glen Brown and M
Miller) (1972)

4025   Guava Jelly/Redder Than Red – Bob Marley and The Wailers (Prod: Bob
Marley and Tuff Gong) (1972)

4026   A Sugar/A Sugar (Part 2) – Altyman Reid (actually with Roy Shirley)/Roy
Shirley (Prod: Lloyd Charmers) (1972)

4027   My Little Filly/My Girl – Winston Scotland/Bunny Brown (Prod: Tony
Robinson [Prince Tony]) (1972)

4028   I Can't Forget/I Can't Forget (Version) – Lloyd Robinson/Lloyd Robinson
and The Now Generation (Prod: Lloyd Daley) (1972)

4029   Jamaican Skank/Bings Comes To Town – Pomphey (actually Lizzy)/G Moore
(possibly Johnny Moore) (Prod: The Rohoism) (1972)

4030   Hot Bomb/The Bomb (Version) – I-Roy and The Jumpers/The Jumpers
(Prod: Bush Productions) (1972)

4031   Have I Sinned/Sinned (Version) – Ken Boothe (actually with Lloyd
Charmers)/Ken Boothe (actually by The Charmers Band) (Prod: Lloyd
Charmers) (1972)

4032   Breezing/Breezing Version – Mickie Chung and The Now Generation/The
Now Generation (Prod: Lloyd Charmers) (1972)

4033   Loving You/Loving You Version (Prod: Glen Brown and M G Mahtani) (1972)

4034   Hudson Affair/Hot Stick Version – U Roy/Keith Hudson (Prod: Keith
Hudson) (1972)

4035   Bringing In The Sheaves/Bringing In The (Version) – Hortense Ellis and
Stranger Cole/Bunny Lee's All Stars (Prod: Edward 'Bunny' Lee) (1972)

4036   Cheer Up/Cheer Up (Version) – Rue Lloyd (Prod: Glen Brown and M G
Mahtani) (1972)

4037 Shalimar Special/Shalimar (Version) – Lloyd Young/G Mahtani All Stars (Prod: Glen Brown and M G Mahtani) (1972)

4038 Night Owl/Version – Lee [Hubert Lee] and The Clarendonians/Tony's All Stars (Prod: Tony Robinson [Prince Tony]) (1972)

4039 The King Man Is Back/King Man (Version) – The Hoffner Brothers/Shalimar All Stars (Prod: Glen Brown and M G Mahtani) (1972)

4040 The Harder They Come/Time Is Still Here (Version) – The Carifta All Stars (actually by Charlie Ace)/Typhoon All Stars (Prod: Alvin Ranglin) (1972) [A AND B SIDES ALSO ISSUED ON GG LABEL (GG 4536B AND 4537B RESPECTIVELY)]

4041 Rub Up A Daughter/Daughter (Version) – Dennis Alcapone/Tony's All Stars (Prod: Tony Robinson [Prince Tony]) (1972)

4042 Dearest Darling/Stardust – Cornel Campbell (Prod: Edward 'Bunny' Lee for Bush Productions) (1972)

4043 President Mash Up The Resident/President Mash Up Version – Shorty [The President] (Prod: Rupie Edwards) (1972)

4044 Make Love/Tic Toc Bill – I-Roy/The Stags (Prod: Pete Weston for Bush Productions) (1972)

4045 Summertime/Grazing – Domino Johnson/The Swans (Prod: Bush Productions) (1972)

4046 Big Boy/Version – Junior Soul [Murvin] (Prod: Derrick Harriott) (1972)

4047 Life/Life (Version) – Bob Andy/Harry J All Stars (Prod: Bob Andy) (1972)

4048 Honey Baby/Chalk Farm Special – Niney and Ken Elliott (Prod: Winston Holness [Niney]) (1972)

4049 African Breakfast/Chairman Of The Board – Bongo Herman/Bongo Herman, Les Chen and Bingy Bunny (Prod: Harry Johnson) (1972) [A SIDE ALSO ISSUED ON HARRY J HJ 6642B]

4050 High School Dance/Dance Version – Hubert Lee/Tony's All Stars (Prod: Tony Robinson [Prince Tony])(1972) 4051 Cool Breeze/Wind Storm – Big Youth/The Crystalites (Prod: Derrick Harriott) (1972)

4052 King Tubby's Special/Here Come The Heartaches – U Roy/Delroy Wilson (Prod: Edward 'Bunny' Lee) (1972)

4053 Silver Words/Rasta God Version – Ken Boothe/Now Generation (Prod: Lloyd Charmers) (1973) [A SIDE REISSUED ON TROJAN TRO 9003A]

4054 Lonely Soldier/Lonely Soldier (Version) – Gregory Isaacs/Impact All Stars (Prod: Randy's) (1973)

4055 Alone Again Naturally/My Part – The Now Generation/Mind, Body and Soul (Prod: Federal Records) (1973)

4056 The First Cut Is The Deepest/No Good Girl – K C White (Prod: Frank Campbell) (1973)

4057   Give Me Love/Help Them Oh Lord – Cornel Campbell (Prod: Edward 'Bunny' Lee) (1973)

4058   Let Me Love You/If It Don't Work Out (actually titled 'Then You Can Tell Me Goodbye') – Slim Smith (Prod: Edward 'Bunny' Lee) (1973)

4059   You Don't Know/The Border Song (Holy Moses) – Bob Andy (Prod: Harry Johnson) (1973) [BOTH SIDES RECORDED 1970]

4060   Ain't That Peculiar/What Is Man? – Delroy Wilson (Prod: Douglas Williams) (1973)

4061   Reggae Makossa/Reggae Makossa (Version) (actually 'No Nola') – Brent Dowe/The Gaytones (actually by The Melodians) (Prod: Sonia Pottinger) (1973) [B SIDE REISSUED FROM HIGH NOTE LABEL HS 044B]

4062   I'll Be Standing By/I'll Be Standing By (Version) – Jimmy Green [Jimmy London]/Lloyd's All Stars (Prod: Lloyd Campbell) (1973)

4063   Yearful Of Sundays/Yearful Of Sundays (Version) – King Sporty (Prod: King Sporty) (1973)

4064   Save The People/Salvation Train – Lloyd Charmers/Scotty (Prod: Lloyd Charmers) (1973)

4065   Rock And Roll Lullaby/Rock And Roll Version – Jimmy London (Prod: Lloyd Campbell) (1974)

HARRY J LABEL (PREFIX HJ)

6601   Big Three/Lavender (actually 'Lavender Blue') – Harry J All Stars/Harry J All Stars (actually by Lloyd Robinson) (1970) [B SIDE REISSUED FROM DUKE LABEL DU 5B]

6602   The Dog (Part 1)/The Dog (Part 2) – Harry J All Stars (1970)

6603   Feel A Little Better/I'll Be A Man – Lloyd Parks (1970) [B SIDE REISSUED ON TROJAN TR 7974B AND TR 7985B]

6604   Fire (Part 1)/Fire (Part 2) – The Jamaicans (1970)

6605   Young, Gifted And Black/Young, Gifted And Black (Instrumental) – Bob [Andy] and Marcia [Griffiths]/The Jay Boys (1970) [REISSUED ON TROJAN TR 7925A]

6606   NYT

6607   Jack The Ripper/Don't Let Me Down – Harry J All Stars (1970)

6608   Reach For The Sky/Interrogator – Harry J All Stars (1970)

6609   Jay Moon Walk/Elcong – The Jay Boys (1970)

6610   Je'Taime/It Ain't Me Babe – The Jay Boys (1970)

6611   Hang My Head And Cry/Hang My Head And Cry (Instrumental) – Bob Andy/The Jay Boys (1970) [UNISSUED]

6612   Peace Of Mind (actually titled 'Peace In Your Mind')/Weep – Bob Andy (1970) [A SIDE REISSUED ON TROJAN TR 7809B]

6613 Put A Little Love In Your Heart/Bah Oop Ah – Marcia Griffiths/The Jay Boys (actually by Des All Stars) (1970) [A SIDE ALSO ISSUED ON TROJAN TR 693A WITHOUT STRINGS]

6614 Didn't I Blow Your Mind This Time/Tilly (titled 'Mellow Mood' on JA issue) – The Cables/The Jay Boys (1970)

6615 We've Got To Get Ourselves Together/Festival Spirit (actually 'Feel It Festival Spirit') – Bob [Andy] and Marcia [Griffiths]/The Jay Boys (actually by The Jamaicans) (1970)

6616 Salt Of The Earth/Name Ring A Bell – The Cables (1970) [UNISSUED. RELEASED ON TROJAN TR 7792 INSTEAD]

6617 Del Gago/Killer Version – The Jay Boys (1970)

6618 I Can't Get Next To You/I Can't Get Next To You (Part 2) – The Jay Boys (actually by Lloyd Charmers and Busty Brown) (1970) [A SIDE ALSO ISSUED ON EXPLOSION EX 2026A]

6619 Cambodia/Cambodia Version – The Blake Boy [Winston Blake]/The Jay Boys (1970)

6620 Feel Alright/Equal Rights – The Cables (1970)

6621 Return Of The Liquidator (titled 'Tons Of Gold' on JA issue)/All Day – Harry J All Stars (actually with Val Bennett)/Harry J All Stars (1970)

6622 NYT

6623 Band Of Gold/Cowboy (Version 2) – Marcia Griffiths/The Jay Boys (actually by Ranny Williams and The Upsetters) (1970)

6624 The Same Old Life/Life Version – Roy Panton/The Jay Boys (1970)

6625 More Heartaches/More Heartaches Version – Lizzy/The Harry J All Stars (1970)

6626 Holy Moses (The Border Song)/Version – Bob Andy/The Jay Boys (1970) [PROBABLY UNISSUED]

6627 NYT

6628 The Arcade Walk/The Arcade Walk (Version 2) – The Jay Boys (1971)

6629 NYT

6630 NYT

6631 NYT

6632 NYT

6633 NYT

6634 Set Me Free/Free Version – Uriel Aldridge/Lloyd Willis (1971)

6635 NYT

6636 NYT

6637 NYT

6638 NYT

6639 ISSUED ON EXPLOSION EX 2073

6640　Come Back And Stay/Come Back And Stay Version – Fabulous Five Inc./The Peter Ashbourne Affair (1972)

6641　Down Side Up/Down Side Up (Version) – Harry J All Stars (actually by Carey [Johnson] and Lloyd [Young])/Harry J All Stars (1972)

6642　Skank In Bed/African Breakfast – Scotty/Bongo Herman (1972) [B SIDE ALSO ISSUED ON GREEN DOOR GD 4049A]

6643　Have You Ever Seen The Rain?/Spanish Harlem – Honey Boy Martin (1972)

6644　The Lament of African People/Instrumental (Part 2) – The Jay Boys (actually by Funky Brown and Inner Circle)/Harry J All Stars (actually by Inner Circle) (1972)

6645　U.F.O/U.F.O (Version) – Geoffrey Chung and Harry J All Stars (actually with Gayman)/Geoffrey Chung and Harry J All Stars (1972)

6646　The Word Is Love/The Word Is Love (Version) – The Ethiopians (1973)

6647　Zion Iah/Zion Iah Version – Giginri (1973)

6648　Me And Mrs Jones/Mrs Jones (Version) – Joe White (1973)

6649　Time Is Getting Harder/Hardest Version – Simplicity People (1973)

6650　Lottery Spin/Lottery Spin Version – Zap Pow (1973)

6651　Treasure Isle Skank/Words Of Wisdom – U Roy (Prod: Duke Reid) (1973)

6652　Yim Mas Gan/Crankshaft Version – The Abyssinians/The John Crow Generation (Prod: Lloyd Daley) (1973)

6653　Deliver Us To Africa [Lord Deliver Us/Back To Africa Medley])/Nyah Medley – Alton Ellis/Little Roy (Prod: Lloyd Daley) (1973)

6654　What's Your Name/What's Your Name Version – Audley Rollins/The Now Generation (Prod: Lloyd Daley) (1973)

6655　Musical Drum Sound/Musical Drum Sound (Version) – I-Roy/The Now Generation (Prod: Lloyd Daley) (1973)

6656　Glitter (And Not Gold)/Glitter (And Not Gold) (Version) – Big Joe/Matador All Stars (Prod: Lloyd Daley) (1973)

6657　Musical Splendour/Musical Drum And Bass – Neville Hinds/John Crow Generation (Prod: Lloyd Daley) (1973)

6658　Chucky/Chucky (Version) – The Viceroys (Prod: Sidney Crooks) (1973)

6659　NYT

6660　Pussy Cat/Skanky Pussy – Lloydie [Charmers] and The Lowbites (Prod: Lloyd Charmers) (1973)

6661　Country Living/Country Living (Version) – The Jamaican Eagles (Prod: Federal) (1973)

6662　I'm Gonna Love You Just A Little Bit More/Have I Sinned – Lloyd Charmers (Prod: Lloyd Charmers) (1974)

6663　Buy You A Ring/Pray Muma – The Ethiopians (Prod: Rupie Edwards) (1974)

6664   Brighter Days Will Be Coming (titled 'Stop Yu Criticism' on JA issue)/
       Brighter Days (Version) – Clancy Eccles (Prod: Clancy Eccles) (1974)

6665   Big Splish Splash/Hail Rasta Brother Hail – The Ethiopians (Prod: Rupie
       Edwards) (1974)

6666   Sorry Harry/Party Time – Dennis Alcapone (Prod: Sidney Crooks) (1974)
       [REISSUED ON TROJAN LABEL (TR 9042) BUT WITH A AND B
       SIDES REVERSED]

6667   What Happen To The Youth Of Today/Baby Don't Do It – Delroy Wilson
       (Prod: Edward 'Bunny' Lee) (1974)

6668   Eddie My Love/What Is Your Plan? – Nora Dean/Jackie Brown (Prod:
       Edward 'Bunny' Lee) (1974)

6669   Wheel And Jig/Version – The Viceroys (Prod: Sidney Crooks) (1974)

6670   Butter Fe Fish/Bammie Fe Fish – Skin, Flesh and Bones (Prod: Dickie Wong)
       (1974)

6671   Why Do Fools Fall In Love?/Why Do Fools Fall In Love? (Version) – Derrick
       Harriott (Prod. Derrick Harriott) (1974) [A SIDE REISSUED ON TROJAN
       LABEL TR 7981A]

6672   Let's Get It On/Let's Get It On (Version) – Lloyd Tyrell [Charmers] (Prod:
       Lloyd Charmers) (1974)

6673   Keep Those Records Playing (Having A Party)/Star Apple – Al Cook (actually
       Eugene Paul and The Cimarons)/Al Cook (actually by The Cimarons) (Prod:
       Sidney Crooks) (1974)

6674   Homely Girl/Thunderball (Beard Man) – Jackie Robinson/Jackie Robinson
       (actually by Des All Stars [Ken Elliott and The Cimarons]) (Prod: R Thompson
       [Dandy]/Des Bryan and Webster Shrowder) (1974)

6675   Some Guys Have All The Luck/Version – Derrick Harriott (Prod: Derrick
       Harriott) (1974)

6676   Burning Fire/Burning Drums – Bob Andy (Prod: Keith Anderson [Bob
       Andy]) (1974)

6677   Skanking Monkey/Skanking Monkey (Version) – Ken Parker (actually by
       Stranger [Cole] and Gladdy [Gladstone Anderson]) (Prod: D C Anderson)
       (1974)

6678   Lord A Massie Massie (titled 'Hard Times' on JA issue)/Lord A Massie Massie
       (Version) – Danny D and The Shadows (Prod: D C Anderson) (1974)

6679   Let's Ride On/Let's Ride On (Version) – Bobby Lawrence (Prod: Ellis Breary)
       (1974)

6680   Please Don't Make Me Cry/So Easy – Winston Groovy (Prod: Sidney Crooks)
       (1974) [ALSO ISSUED ON EXPLOSION EX 2088]

6681   I Need Your Love/I Need Your Love (Version) – Gregory Isaacs (Prod: Alvin
       Ranglin) (1974)

6682 Ride On, Ride On/Wild Goose Chase – Dennis Brown and Big Youth/ Observer All Stars (Prod: Winston Holness [Niney]) (1974)

6683 Rock Your Baby/Rozey Dozey – The Maroons [Cimarons] (Prod: Des Bryan and Webster Shrowder/The Cimarons) (1974)

6684 Sitting On The Sidewalk/Sitting On The Sidewalk (Version) – Ansell Linkers/ GG All Stars (Prod: Alvin Ranglin) (1974)

6685 Drift Away/Upside Down – George Dekker (Prod: Sidney Crooks) (1974)

6686 A Walking Miracle/A Walking Miracle (Version) – Baby Bertie [Bertie Chin] (Prod: Bertie Chin) (1974)

6687 Saturday Night/Saturday Night (Instrumental) – Lorenzo [Laurel Aitken] (Prod: Laurel Aitken) (1974) [TRACKS RECORDED IN 1969]

6688 Irie Festival/Instrumental – Turnell McCormack and The Cordells/Fabulous Five Inc. (Prod: Ed Wallace) (1974)

6689 Black Pepper/Pepper Rock – Heavy Jeff (Prod: Dickie Wong) (1974)

6690 Solitary Man (Vocal)/Solitary Man (Instrumental) – Skin, Flesh and Bones/ Skin, Flesh and Bones (featuring Beverley and Ranchie) (Prod: Dickie Wong) (1974)

6691 Together (Vocal)/Together (Instrumental) – Jimmy London (Prod: Lloyd Campbell) (1974)

6692 Oh Pa Pa/Bone Yard Skank – The Drifting Blenders/Lloyd's All Stars (Prod: Lloyd Charmers) (1974) [B SIDE ALSO ISSUED ON HORSE HS 052B]

6693 I'm Leaving It Up To You/Teach The Children – Winston [Reedy] and The Zion Boys/L Gitchie [Locksley Gitchie] and The Zion Boys (Prod: Kush) (1974)

6694 Kung Fu Fighting/The Teacher – The Maroons [Cimarons] (Prod: Des Bryan for Kush/Des Bryan and Webster Shrowder for Kush) (1974)

6695 My Love For You/Smokey Mountains – Jackie Robinson/R.D.L All Stars (Prod: R D Livingstone [Dandy] for Trojan/R D Livingstone [Dandy] for Shady Tree) (1974)

6696 Nosey Parker (Vocal)/Nosey Parker (Instrumental) – George Dekker (Prod: G Agard [George Dekker]) (1974)

6697 Lee's Dream/So Long Baby – Derrick Morgan and Paulette (Prod: Edward 'Bunny' Lee) (1974)

6698 Country Boy/Give The Little Man A Great Big Hand – Cornel Campbell (Prod: Edward 'Bunny' Lee) (1974)

6699 Lonely Woman/Lonely Woman (Instrumental) – Horace Andy/Horace Andy (actually by The Crystalites) (Prod: Derrick Harriott) (1974) [SAME VERSION AS THAT RELEASED ON SONG BIRD LABEL (SB 1085) BUT WITHOUT HORNS]

6700   Why Don't You Do Right (Oh Yeh)/Why Don't You Do Right (Oh Yeh)
        (Instrumental) – Dimples Hinds (Prod: Shady Tree [Dandy]) (1974)
6701   Natty Dread/Collie Burning – Sambo Jim (actually by The Cimarons) (Prod:
        Kush) (1974)
6702   Lee Goofed (So Long Baby)/Ruff Ready – Love Children (Prod: R D
        Livingstone [Dandy] for Shady Tree) (1974)
6703   Feel So Good/Feel So Good (Instrumental) – Derrick [Morgan] and Hortense
        [Ellis]/Derrick [Morgan] and Hortense [Ellis] (actually by The Aggrovators)
        (Prod: Edward 'Bunny' Lee) (1974)
6704   A Message To Martha/Tears Won't Help – Treasure Boy (actually Freddie
        McKay) (Prod: Sidney Crooks) (1974)
6705   Take These Chains From My Heart/If You Want To Be Happy – Bill Walker
        (actually by Freddy McKay) (Prod: Sidney Crooks) (1974)
6706   Move Out A Babylon/Move Out A Babylon (Instrumental) – Johnny Clarke/
        Johnny Clarke (actually by The Aggrovators) (Prod: Edward 'Bunny' Lee)
        (1974) [REISSUED ON HORSE HOSS 86]
6707   NYT
6708   Blue Moon/Greensleeves – George Larnyoh and Love Children/Love
        Children (Prod: R D Livingstone [Dandy]/Shady Tree) (1975)

Note

With the exception of HJ 6613B (a Des Bryan and Webster Shrowder production),
HJ 6623B (a Jackson Jones production) and HJ 6646 (a Keith Anderson [Bob Andy]
production), all tracks from HJ 6601 to HJ 6650 were produced by Harry Johnson.
After this, productions were varied and are credited accordingly.

HIGH NOTE (PREFIX HS)

001   ABC Rock Steady/Soul Drums – The Gaylads/Leslie Butler and Count Ossie
       (1968) [EARLY PRESSINGS ON 'HI-NOTE' LABEL]
002   NOT USED
003   Lady With The Starlight/Gay Drums – Ken Boothe/Leslie Butler and Count
       Ossie (1968)
004   Dance With Me/Let's Have Some Fun – Delano Stewart (1968)
005   Check Up/I'll Come Back – Al and The Vibrators (actually with Boris
       Gardner and The Gaysters)/Al and The Vibrators (actually with Byron Lee and
       The Dragonaires) (1968)
006   POSSIBLY ISSUED ON HS 015
007   Fire In Your Wire/Move Up Calypso – Patsy with Byron Lee and The
       Dragonaires/Al and The Vibrators (1968)

008   Top Cat/Stars Above – Leslie Butler/The Webber Sisters (1968)

009   Revival/Over The Rainbow's End – Leslie Butler/The Gaylads (1968)

010   Lucky Is The Boy/Bobby Socks To Stockings – Boris Gardner (1968)

011   Put Yourself In My Place/It Hurts – Delroy Wilson (1968)

012   We Were Lovers/Give Me A Chance – Patsy/Patsy and Delano Stewart (1968)

013   National Lottery/Round Seven – The Soul Rhythms (1969)

014   Rocking Sensation/One Look – Delano Stewart (actually with The Soul
       Rhythms)/The Gaysters (1969)

015   I'm The One Who Loves You/If I'm In A Corner – Delroy Wilson/The
       Afrotones (1969)

016   If You Can't Beat Them Join Them/Anywhere You Want To Go – The
       Conquerors (1969)

017   Mary, Mary/Going Away – The Beltones (1969)

018   The Storm/You Can't Stop Me – The Emotions (actually with The Hippy
       Boys) (1969)

019   Reggae Buddy/Easy Squeeze – The Victors (1969)

020   Oh What A Glory/The Morning In The Sky – The Creary Sisters (1969)
       [NOTED ON LABEL AS 'GLORY SACRED SERIES']

021   Dr No Go/Sailing (actually titled 'Faberge') – The Hippy Boys/The Hippy
       Boys (actually by Baba Brooks and His Recording Band) (1969) [B SIDE IS
       REISSUE FROM 1967]

022   I've Tried My Best/Your Number One – Delroy Wilson (1969)

023   Broken Heart/All For One – The Beltones/The Afrotones (1969)

024   Wailing Festival/Me And My Baby (actually titled 'By The River') – The
       Federals (1969)

025   Mr DJ/National Dish – The Conquerors (1969)

026   Rumbay Rumbay/I Held Your Hand – The Emotions/Patsy (1969)

027   Got To Come Back/Don't Believe Him – Delano Stewart (1969)

028   Good To Me/What Do You Want Me To Do – Delroy Wilson (1969)

029   Talk (actually titled 'Toil')/Talk (Part 2) (actually 'Toil (Part 2)') – Marcia
       Griffiths (1969) [A SIDE ALSO CREDITED AS 'MY AMBITION' ON JA
       ISSUES]

030   Chicken Lickin' (aka 'Night Fall')/Our Man Flint – The Hippy Boys/Baba
       Brooks (actually with His Recording Band) (1969) [B SIDE IS REISSUE
       FROM 1966]

031   NYT

032   Rasta (actually titled 'Rasta No Like Pork')/Like Dirt – The Tadpoles (1969)★

033   The Man Of Galilee/Take Up The Cross – Otis Wright (1969) [NOTED ON
       LABEL AS 'SACRED SERIES']

034   Hallelujah/I Wish It Could Last – Delano Stewart (1969)

035 Reggae Pressure/It Hurts (Instrumental) – The Hippy Boys (1969)

036 NYT

037 Target (actually titled 'Musical Fight')/Find Someone (actually titled 'True Love') – The Gaytones (actually by The Crashers)/Patsy (1970)

038 Piccadilly Hop/Nigeria (aka 'Drum Song') – The Hippy Boys (1970)

039 Wherever I Lay My Hat/Don't Believe Him – Delano Stewart (1970) [B SIDE REISSUED FROM HS 027B]

040 Soul Pressure/Seed You Sow [SKA] – Winston Wright and The Gaytones/Winston Wright and The Gaytones (actually by Bonnie Frankson) (1970) [B SIDE IS REISSUE FROM 1966]

041 Stay A Little Bit Longer/Stay A Little Bit Longer (Version 2) – Delano Stewart/Delano Stewart (actually by Gladstone Anderson and The Gaytones) (1970)

042 Praise Far I/Cherrie, Part 2 – The Ethiopians/The Gaytones (1970)

043 Little Suzie/Cherrie – The Soul Twins (1970)

044 Love Is A Good Thing/No Nola – The Melodians (1970) [B SIDE REISSUED ON GREEN DOOR GD 4061B]

045 When/Chapter – First Generation (actually with Judy Mowatt)/The Gaytones (1970)

046 Your Destiny/Lock Love Away – The Gentiles (1970)

047 Natural Woman/Woman Version – Naomi/The Gaytones (1970)

048 Ten To One/Another Version – The Gaytones (actually with Busty Brown)/The Gaytones (1970) [B SIDE IS NOT ACTUALLY A VERSION OF THE A SIDE]

049 She Want It/Give Him Up – Dave Barker (actually with The Gaylads)/First Generation (1970)

050 Must Get A Man/The Valet – Nora Dean (1970) [BOTH SIDES CALYPSO]

051 Creation Version/Version 3 – Charlie [Ace] and The Melodians/The Gaytones (1970)

052 Run To The Rock/Run to the Rock (Version) – The Righteous Flames/The Gaytones (1971)★★

053 Home Bound/Chapter 3 – Teddy and The Conquerors/The Gaytones (1971)

054 Joy To The World/Joyful – Julie Anne [Judy Mowatt] and The Chosen Few with The Gaytones/The Gaytones (1971)

055 Heart Of The Knights/One Toke Over The Line – The Gaytones (actually by Lennox Brown)/The Gaytones (actually by Stranger Cole and Gladstone Anderson) (1971)

056 NYT

057 One Night Of Sin/One Night (Version) – Jackie Brown (actually with The Gaytones)/The Gaytones (1971)

239

058   Pray For Me/Pray For Me (Version) – Max Romeo and The Gaytones/The
       Gaytones (1972)

059   She Kept On Talking/Talking (Version) – Julie Anne [Judy Mowatt] and The
       Gaytones/The Gaytones (1972)

060   Last Dance/Version – Jackie Brown and The Gaytones/The Gaytones (1972)
       [UNISSUED]

061   Skavito/Savito – The Undergrounds (1972) [CALYPSO]

Notes

All tracks produced by Sonia Pottinger except ★ which was a D Anderson production
and ★★ which was produced by Lee Perry.

HORSE (PREFIX HOSS)

1   I Must Go Back/I Want To Be Near You – Jackie Edwards (Prod: Andrew
       Heath/Jackie Edwards and Andrew Heath) (1971) [SOME COPIES IN
       PICTURE SLEEVE]

2   Summer Is The Season/Riding My Bicycle – Riverbank (Prod: R Thompson
       [Dandy]) (1971)

3   Bouncing All Over The World/Tell Me – Tony Gregory (Prod: C Miller
       [Count Prince Miller] for Seashells Productions) (1971)

4   Chick-A-Boom (Don't Ya Jes' Love It)/Sunflower Wine – Big Gee (Prod:
       Kool Records) (1971) Sandy Roberton for September Productions) (1971)

5   Jesus Is Just Alright/You Knew How To Hurt A Man – Bourbon Street
       Mission (Prod: Sandy Roberton for September Productions) (1971)

6   Sunday Morning/One Three (actually 'One Dream') – Ernie Smith (Prod:
       Federal Records) (1971)

7   Brandy/Lead Me Back – Scott English (Prod: Dave Bloxham) (1971)

8   Skinny Dippin'/Sweet Bread – The Zooms (Prod: Ken Howard and Alan
       Blakely) (1971)

9   Act Like A Man/Back On My Feet – Roger Holman (Prod: Holman and
       May) (1971)

10   Hey Mama/Ride Baby Ride – Rick Whitehead (Prod: Kris Ife) (1971)

11   Who Turned The World Around?/I Love You So – Tony Gregory (Prod: A
       Christine Production) (1972)

12   I Feel So Bad/I'll Make Them Believe In You – Danny Ray (Prod: Jackie
       Edwards) (1972)

13   Love Sweet Love/Open The Door – Del Davis (Prod: Jackie Edwards) (1972)

14   Willie Come Home/Heaven Knows – Chris Parie (Prod: Trojan Production)
       (1972)

15   Baby Don't Wake Me/A Little Story – Jackie Edwards (Prod: Jackie Edwards)
       (1972)

16   Suzanne Beware Of The Devil/Right On Brother – Dandy Livingstone (Prod:
      Shady Tree [Dandy]) (1972)

17   Tchaikovsky Piano Concerto No. 1/Cool Shade – Neasden Connection [The
      Cimarons] (Prod: Shady Tree [Dandy]) (1972)

18   Struggling Man/Return Of The Pollock – The Cimarons/The Prophets
      (actually by Patrick and Lloyd) (Prod: Bush/Des Bryan and Webster Shrowder)
      (1972) [B SIDE REISSUED FROM BIG SHOT BI 550A]

18   Struggling Man/Struggling Man (Version) – The Cimarons (Prod: Bush)
      (1972) [DUPLICATE ISSUE]

19   I'll Be True To You/Easy Come, Easy Go – Tito Simon (Prod: Clancy Eccles)
      (1972)

20   Nose For Trouble/Times Have Changed – Pat Rhoden (Prod: An RMI
      Production [Pat Rhoden]) (1972)

21   White And Wonderful, Black And Beautiful/Peace And Love – Danny Ray
      (Prod: Joe Sinclair, Webster Shrowder and Des Bryan for Bush Productions)
      (1972) [A SIDE REISSUED ON HORSE HOSS 33A]

22   The Further You Look/I Wanna Dance – John Holt (Prod: Tony Ashfield and
      Mike Berry) (1972) [PROMO COPIES HAVE A SIDE ON BOTH SIDES]

23   How Could I Let You Get Away/How Could I Let You Get Away (Version)
      Barry Biggs/The Dynamites (Prod: Dynamic Sounds) (1972) [PROMO
      COPIES HAVE A SIDE ON BOTH SIDES]

24   Lord Pity Us All/Beautiful Feeling – Martin Reilly [Martin Riley] (Prod:
      Mike Berry and Tony Ashfield) (1973)

25   Big City/Brand New Day – Dandy Livingstone (Prod: Shady Tree [Dandy])
      (1972) [FIRST PRESSING]

25   Big City/Think About That – Dandy Livingstone (Prod: Shady Tree [Dandy])
      (1972) [SECOND PRESSING – PROMOTED AS DOUBLE A SIDE]

26   World Without Love/Bucket – Del Davis/Del Davis (actually by Des All Stars)
      (Prod: Joe Sinclair, Des Bryan and Webster Shrowder for Bush Productions)
      (1973)

27   NYT

28   Come Back Liza/Got To Say I'm Sorry – Dandy Livingstone (Prod: D
      Livingstone) (1973) [PROMO COPIES HAVE A SIDE ON BOTH SIDES.
      ALSO ISSUED IN PICTURE SLEEVE]

29   Images Of You/Doing The Moonwalk – Nicky Thomas (Prod: Nicky Thomas/
      Joe Gibbs) (1973) [PROMO COPIES HAVE A SIDE ON BOTH SIDES]

30   Build It Up/You Can't Be Serious – Tito Simon (Prod: Clancy Eccles) (1973)

31   One Woman/No Secondhand Love – Bob Andy (Prod: Bob Andy and Clive
      Crawley/Bob Andy) (1973) [REISSUED FROM TROJAN TR 7840]

32   Loving Her Was Easier/Ling Tong Ting – Lloyd Charmers (Prod: Lloyd
      Charmers/Winston Lowe) (1973) [B SIDE REISSUED FROM SONG
      BIRD SB 1001A]

33   White And Wonderful, Black And Beautiful/On The Run With A Gun –
      Danny Ray (Prod: Joe Sinclair, Webster Shrowder and Des Bryan for Bush
      Productions)/Jackie Edwards) (1973) [A SIDE REISSUED FROM HORSE
      HOSS 21A]

34   Loop-de-Loop/In Style – Happy Junior and The I.Qs (Prod: Sidney Crooks)
      (1973)

35   Snake In The Grass/Snake In The Grass (Part 2) – Jimmy Shondell (actually
      Eugene Paul)/Ron Stewart (actually Roman Stewart) (Prod: Sidney Crooks)
      (1973) [B SIDE IS ACTUALLY ANOTHER VOCAL VERSION OF THE A
      SIDE ON THE SAME RHYTHM]

36   Build Me Up/Close To You – Brent Dowe and The Gaytones (Prod: Sonia
      Pottinger) (1973)

37   Lonely For Your Love/Message To Maria – Nicky Thomas (Prod: Sidney
      Crooks) (1973) [B SIDE REISSUED ON HORSE HOSS 155B]

38   She Ain't Nothin' But The Real Thing/Oh What A Feeling – Tito Simon
      (Prod: Clancy Eccles/Joe Sinclair) (1973)

39   (I Can't Get Enough Of That) Reggae Stuff/Wipe Them Out – Matumbi
      (Prod: Dennis Bovell) (1973) [B SIDE REISSUED FROM DUKE DU 152A]

40   Mellow Mood/Mellow Mood (Version) – Judy Mowatt (actually with The
      Gaytones) (Prod: Sonia Pottinger) (1973)

41   We Can Make Sweet Music/Stoned Out Of My Mind – Winston Groovy
      (Prod: Winston Tucker [Winston Groovy]) (1974) [UNISSUED]

42   I Shall Sing/Close (Instrumental) – Judy Mowatt and The Gaytones/The
      Gaytones (Prod: Sonia Pottinger) (1974) [A SIDE REISSUED FROM
      TROJAN TR 7817A]

43   Love Is A Hurting Thing/Gladness – Brent Dowe/The Gaytones (Prod: Sonia
      Pottinger) (1974)

44   For The Good Times/You Are Everything – Lloyd Charmers/Lloyd Charmers
      (actually with Hortense Ellis) (Prod: Lloyd Charmers) (1974)

45   Caribbean Rock/All Strung Out On You – Dandy Livingstone (Prod: Shady
      Tree [Dandy] (1974)

46   Life Is Just For Living/To Be With You – Lloyd Charmers (Prod: Lloyd
      Charmers) (1974)

47   Sweet Harmony/Sweet Organ (Version) – Lloyd Charmers (Prod: Lloyd
      Charmers) (1974)

48   I'm Only Here For The Beer (In Heaven There Is No Beer)/Sober Up – The
      Artistic League (Prod: Shady Tree [Dandy]) (1974)

49   Black Oppressor/Black Oppressor (Version) – Leo Simpson (Prod: Leo Simpson) (1974)

50   Personality/Stone Cold – Jackie Robinson/The All Stars (Prod: Sidney Crooks for Trojan Productions) (1974)

50   Stone Cold – The All Stars (Prod: Sidney Crooks for Trojan Productions) (1974) [ONE-SIDED TEST PRESSING – DUPLICATE ISSUE]

51   It's Not Who You Know/I Need Someone – The Twinkle Brothers/The Ethiopians (Prod: Lloyd Campbell and Glen Brown) (1974) [UNISSUED]

52   Sweet Bitter Love/Sweet Bitter Love (Version) (actually 'Bone Yard Skank') – Marcia Griffiths/Marcia Griffiths (actually by Lloyd's All Stars) (Prod: Lloyd Charmers) (1974) [B SIDE ALSO ISSUED ON HARRY J LABEL (HJ 6692B)]

53   Warm And Tender Love/Love Is A Game – Jackie Robinson (Prod: Sidney Crooks) (1974)

54   Something's Gotten Hold Of My Heart/Tenod – Jenny Taylor/Des All Stars (Prod: Webster Shrowder, Des Bryan and Steve Barnard/Webster Shrowder and Des Bryan) (1974)

55   Rock The Boat/Curfew – The Circles [The Inner Circle] (Prod: Tommy Cowan) (1974)

56   Soul Serenade/Bond In Bliss – Winston Wright and The Dragonaires (Prod: Byron Lee (1974) [A SIDE REISSUED FROM DUKE DU 39A. B SIDE REISSUED FROM TROJAN TR 7747A]

57   This Monday Morning Feeling/Count The Hours – Tito Simon (Prod: Keith Foster [Tito Simon]) (1974)

58   The Best Time Of My Life/What Am I To Do – Pat Kelly (Prod: Winston Riley) (1974)

59   Boogie On Reggae Woman (Vocal)/Boogie On Reggae Woman (Instrumental) – Pat Rhoden/Des All Stars (Prod: Webster Shrowder) (1974)

60   When Will I See You Again/When Will I See You Again – Marcia Griffiths/Onika (Prod: Geoffrey Chung and Ossie Harvey) (1974)

61   Do It 'Til Your Satisfied/Collie Dub – Soul Messengers [The Cimarons] (Prod: Kush) (1974)

62   (Hey There) Lonely Girl/Grasshopper – J D Alex [Judge Dread] (Prod: Alted) (1974)

63   Marie's Song/Marie's Song (Dub) – Fitz Major/GG All Stars (Prod: Alvin Ranglin) (1975)

64   Bongo Natty/Look What You Done – Owen Gray (Prod: Edward 'Bunny' Lee) (1975)

65   Never Fall In Love Again/Hey Girl, Don't Bother Me – Johnny Clarke (Prod: Edward 'Bunny' Lee) (1975)

66   Rasta Don't Fear/Version – Derrick Morgan (Prod: Edward 'Bunny' Lee) (1975)

67   Black Superman (Muhammed Ali)/Black Superman (Muhammed Ali)
      (Instrumental) – Derrick Morgan (Prod: Edward 'Bunny' Lee) (1975)
68   Duke Of Earl/Instrumental – Cornel Campbell (Prod: Edward 'Bunny' Lee
      and Delroy Wilson) (1975)
69   In My life/In My Life (Instrumental) – Jackie Robinson (Prod: Jackie
      Robinson) (1975)
70   Let Locks Grow/Natty Locks – Barrington Spence (Prod: Tony Robinson
      [Prince Tony]) (1975)
71   Nyah Nyah/Nyah Nyah (Version) – Jerry Morris (Prod: Toots and The
      Maytals) (1975)
72   Face Dog/Face Dog (Part 2) – Derrick Harriott (Prod: Derrick Harriott) (1975)
73   Bump Me Baby/Kush Maroons – The Maroons [The Cimarons] (Prod: The
      Cimarons) (1975)
74   No Jestering/Part 2 Dub – Carl Malcolm/Carl Malcolm (actually by Skin,
      Flesh and Bones) (Prod: Randy Chin for Randy's Productions) (1975)
75   Nine Pound Steel/Money Day (Part 2) – Sidney [Crooks], George [Dekker]
      and Jackie [Robinson] [The Pioneers] (Prod: Sidney Crooks) (1975)
76   At The End Of The Rainbow/At The End Of The Rainbow (Version) –
      Johnny Clarke/Rupie's All Stars (Prod: Rupie Edwards) (1975)
77   Jah Jah Train/Move Jah – Barrington Spence/Skin, Flesh and Bones (Prod:
      Tony Robinson [Prince Tony]) (1975)
78   I Hear My Train/I Hear My Train (Instrumental) – Junior English (Prod: Ellis
      Breary) (1975)
79   God Bless Jamaica/God Bless Jamaica (Instrumental) – Max Romeo (Prod:
      Randy Chin for Randy's Productions) (1975)
80   Talking Blues/Talking Blues (Instrumental) – The Maroons [The Cimarons]
      (Prod: Des Bryan and The Cimarons) (1975)
81   Dr Honey/Honey Dub – Norris Weir (Prod: Tommy Cowan) (1975)
82   NYT
83   Je'taime Moi Non Plus/Look A Pussy – Judge Dread (Prod: Alted) (1975)
      [ALSO ISSUED ON CACTUS LABEL]
84   The End Of The World/Escape From The Planet Of The Apes – Jason Sinclair
      [Judge Dread]/The Baboons (Prod: Alted) (1975)
85   Skank Indigo/Expression In Dub – Harry J All Stars (actually with Joe
      White)/Harry J All Stars (Prod: Harry Johnson) (1975)
86   Move Out A Babylon/Move Out A Babylon (Instrumental) – Johnny Clarke/
      Johnny Clarke (actually by The Aggrovators (Prod: Edward 'Bunny' Lee)
      [REISSUED FROM HARRY J HJ 6706]
87   On The Beach/On The Beach (Instrumental) – Owen Gray (Prod: Edward
      'Bunny' Lee) (1975)

88   Soldering/Soldering Part 2 – The Starlites/GG All Stars (Prod: Alvin Ranglin)
      (1975)
89   I'm Your Puppet/Up Town Skank – Jimmy London/Skin, Flesh and Bones
      (Prod: Lloyd Campbell) (1975)
90   Who Knows I Love You/Who Knows I Love You (Version) – Dimples Hinds
      (actually with The Marvels)/Dimple Hinds' All Stars (Prod: Shady Tree
      [Dandy]) (1975)
91   Mama/Mama (Version) – The Soul Syndicate (Prod: G O'Sullivan) (1975)
      [UNISSUED]
92   You Are Mine/You Are Mine (Version) – Johnny Clarke and Paulette [Morgan]/
      Bunny Lee All Stars (Prod: Edward 'Bunny' Lee) (1975) [UNISSUED]
93   I Don't Want To See You Cry/I Don't Want To See You Cry (Version) –
      Cornel Campbell/Bunny Lee All Stars (Prod: Edward 'Bunny' Lee) (1975)
      [UNISSUED]
94   I Shall Not Remove/I Shall Not Remove (Version) – Cornel Campbell/
      Bunny Lee All Stars (Prod: Edward 'Bunny' Lee) (1975) [UNISSUED]
95   Heavenly/Heavenly (Instrumental) – The Starr Bounds (Prod: Trevor Brown
      [Trevor Starr]) (1975)
96   Wherever I Lay My Hat/Wherever I Lay My Hat (Version) – Cornel
      Campbell/Bunny Lee All Stars (Prod: Edward 'Bunny' Lee) (1975)
      [UNISSUED]
97   NYT
98   Say You/Say You (Instrumental) – Jackie Robinson (Prod: Jackie Robinson)
      (1975)
99   Darling Dry Your Eyes/Darling Dry Your Eyes (Dub) – Barrington Spence
      (Prod: Tony Robinson [Prince Tony]) (1975)
100   Too Much War/War Version – Johnny Clarke (Prod: Edward 'Bunny' Lee) (1975)
101   I Want To Stay Here (And Love You)/I Want To Stay Here (Version) – Derrick
      and Paulette [Morgan]/Bunny Lee All Stars (Prod: Edward 'Bunny' Lee)
      (1975)
102   Back In My Arms/Back In My Arms (Version) – Jackie Edwards/The
      Aggrovators (Prod: Edward 'Bunny' Lee) (1975)
103   Since I Fell For You/Since I Fell For You (Version) – Johnny Clarke/The
      Aggrovators (Prod: Edward 'Bunny' Lee) (1975)
104   Behold/Behold (Version) – Derrick Morgan and Johnny Clarke/The
      Aggrovators (Prod: Edward 'Bunny' Lee) (1975)
105   Some Woman Must Cry/Some Woman (Version) – Derrick Morgan/The
      Aggrovators (Prod: Edward 'Bunny' Lee) (1975)
106   Move Out/Dance With Me – Tommy McCook (Prod: Edward 'Bunny' Lee)
      (1975)

107   Rebel Soldering/Rebel Soldering (Version) – Johnny Clarke (Prod: Edward
       'Bunny' Lee) (1975)
108   Do You Love Me/Do You Love Me (Version) – Johnny Clarke (Prod: Edward
       'Bunny' Lee) (1975)
109   Everybody Needs Love/In The Middle Of The Night – Honey Boy (Prod:
       Keith Williams [Honey Boy]) (1975)
110   Let's Have Some Fun/'Cos I Love You – Honey Boy (Prod: Keith Williams
       [Honey Boy]) (1975)
111   Fatty Bum Bum Gone To Jail/Fatty Bum Bum Gone To Jail (Version) – Laurel
       Aitken (actually with The Trojans) (Prod: Laurel Aitken) (1975) [B SIDE
       REISSUED ON TROJAN TR 9005B]
112   Sounds Of A Good Song/Dansak Home (Version) – Clinton Taylor and
       Dansak/Dansak (Prod: Sonny Binns and Trevor Starr) (1975)
113   How Could You Do This?/Album Of My Life – Nora Dean and Dansak
       (Prod: Sonny Binns and Trevor Starr) (1975)
114   Moving Away/Moving (Version) – Dennis Brown/Observer (Prod: Winston
       Holness [Niney]) (1975)
115   Tell Me Baby/You Keep Me Hanging On – Mike Dorane (Prod: Mike
       Dorane) (1975)
116   Your Cheating Heart/News For My Baby – Winston Groovy (Prod: Winston
       Groovy) (1975)
117   Rock Away (aka 'Rock On')/Rock Away (Version) – Gregory Isaacs (Prod:
       Winston Holness [Niney]) (1975)
118   NYT
119   Free Up Jah Jah Children/Free Up Jah Jah Children (Version) – Owen Gray
       (Prod: Owen Gray) (1975)
120   Take A Little Time To Know Me/Side Show – Junior Tucker (Prod: Earl
       Smith) (1976)
121   Sha-La-La/Sha-La-La (Version) – The Maytones/GG All Stars (Prod: Alvin
       Ranglin) (1976)
122   I Say Super Jaws/I Say Super Jaws (Version) – Owen Gray (Prod: Eddie Airey)
       (1976)
123   Everybody's Got A Song To Sing/We've Got To Part – The Cables/Trevor
       Shield and The Beltones (Prod: Harry Johnson) (1976)
124   Cool Rasta/Dreadlocks – The Heptones (Prod: Harry Johnson) (1976)
125   Oh Patricia/Read The News – Tito Simon (Prod: Keith Foster [Tito Simon]/
       Clancy Eccles) (1976) [ALSO ISSUED ON TROJAN TRO 9002. B SIDE
       REISSUED FROM TROJAN TR 7964B]
126   My Love For You Is Over Now/My Love For You Is Over Now (Version) –
       Doreen Murray (Prod: Jerry Maytal [Jerry Morris]) (1976)

127   I Don't Want To Be A Beggar/Lyndia – Rudolph [Rudy] Mowatt (Prod: Harry Johnson) (1976)

128   Peacemaker/Mellow Up Yourself – Jam Now Generation/Bonnie [Bunny] Gayle (Prod: Clive Hunt) (1976)

129   My Sweet Ceceile/He'll Have To Go – Lloyd Banton (Prod: Lloyd Banton) (1976)

130   Ching Lue/Ching Lue (Version) – Cliff St Lewis (Prod: Cliff St Lewis) (1976)

131   Everybody Needs Love/Everybody Needs Love (Version) – Lloyd Parks/ Bunny Lee All Stars (Prod: Edward 'Bunny' Lee) (1976)

132   Run Joe/Mr Bojangles – Lloyd Charmers (Prod: Lloyd Charmers) (1977)

133   Change Your Style/(Sitting On) The Dock Of The Bay – Dennis Brown (Prod: Sidney Crooks) (1977)

134   Mr Fixit/Version – Max Romeo (Prod: Edward 'Bunny' Lee) (1977)

135   Let The World Unite/Version – Paulette Walker (Prod: Barry Gruber) (1977)

136   Banana/Banana (Version) – Cliff St Lewis (Prod: Cliff St Lewis) (1977)

137   Slow Down/Version – Floyd Lloyd Seivreight (Prod: Floyd Lloyd Seivreight and Lenny Kool) (1977)

138   Dignity And Principle/Version – Big Joe (Prod: Cecil Clarke) (1977) [A SIDE ALSO ISSUED ON ATTACK ATT 8136B]

139   Jah Jah Forgive You/Version – Jah Stitch (Prod: Cecil Clarke) (1977)

140   Lead On Jah Jah/Jah Jah Version – Cecil 'Guitar' Smith (Prod: C S Smith) (1977)

141   I'm Still In Love With You Girl/Muriel – Alton Ellis (Prod: Alton Ellis) (1977)

142   NYT

143   Opportunity/Version – Earl George [George Faith] (Prod: Barry [Barrington] Dunn) (1977)

144   Up Park Camp/Version: Up Park Dub – John Holt/John Holt (actually by The Aggrovators) (Prod: Edward 'Bunny' Lee) (1977)

145   Mother And Father/Songs Of Distress – Michael Robinson and XLR (Prod: XLR) (1977)

146   No Chance/No Chance (Version) – Johnny Orlando (Prod: Al Vassell [Johnny Orlando]) (1977)

147   Going Over Yonder/Going Over Yonder (Version) – Rocky Delvar [Les Foster] (Prod: Les Foster) (1977)

148   Wailing Of Black People/Dubbin' An' Wailin' (Version) – Velvet Shadows (Prod: Velvet Shadows) (1977)

149   Some Helping Up/Some Helping Up (Version) – Owen Gray (Prod: Alton Ellis) (1978)

150   Don't Stay Away/Don's Stay Away (Instrumental) – Dudley Houston [Winston Groovy] (Prod: Winston Groovy) (1978)

151   Sweet Memories/Sweet Memories (Version) – Winston Groovy and Sandra Brightly (Prod: Winston Tucker [Winston Groovy]) (1978)

152   Babylon A Fall Down/Down Fall Rock – Velvet Shadows (Prod: Velvet Shadows) (1978)

153   Segregation/Segregation Version – Tony Sexton/[Ranking] Superstar (Prod: Clement Bushay) (1978)

154   Love Plea/Rocker's Plea – Pancho Alphonso (Prod: Pancho Alphonso) (1978)

155   Message From Maria/I'll Be Waiting – Nicky Thomas (Prod: Sidney Crooks/Nicky Thomas) (1978) [A SIDE REISSUED FROM HORSE HOSS 37B. B SIDE REISSUED FROM TROJAN LABEL TR 7885B AND TRO 9026B]

156   Just Like A River/The Same One – Danny Ray (Prod: J O Christie/Jackie Edwards) (1978)

157   Walk Away/Walk Away (Version) – Marie Pierre (Prod: Dennis Bovell) (1978) [REISSUED ON TROJAN TRO 9066]

158   Like I Used To Do/Heavy Reggae Man – Horace Faith/Teddy Davis (actually with The Discolettes) (Prod: Stan Beiderbeck/O.C.R [Orbach & Chambers Ltd]) (1978) [B SIDE ALSO ISSUED ON TROJAN LABEL TRO 9040B]

HOT ROD (PREFIX HR)

100   Walk The Hot Street/You Say You Don't Love Me – Carl Levy and The Cimarons/Peggy [McClarty] and The Cimarons (1970)

101   Remember Easter Monday/Pum Pum Lover – Peggy [McClarty] and Jimmy with The Cimarons/Carl Levy and The Cimarons (1970)

101   Dog Your Woman (aka 'Control Your Doggy')/I Shall Follow The Star – Patsy and Peggy [McClarty] with The Cimarons/Peggy [McClarty] and The Cimarons (1970) [DUPLICATE ISSUE ON BLANK LABEL ONLY – A SIDE ALSO ISSUED ON HR 107B AND B SIDE ALSO ISSUED ON HR 103A)

102   Why Why Why/Fistful Of Dollars – Betty Sinclair/Hot Rod All Stars (1970) [NOT ISSUED ON THIS NUMBER OR BY TROJAN. PUT OUT ON TORPEDO LABEL TOR 19 INSTEAD]

103   Gifted At The Top/I Shall Follow The Star – Peggy [McClarty] and The Cimarons/Carl Levy and The Cimarons (1970)

104   Skinhead Speaks His Mind/Carnaby Street – Hot Rod All Stars/Carl Levy and The Cimarons (1970)

105   Grandfather Clock/Kick Me Or I'll Kick You – The Cimarons (1970)

106   Prison Sentence/Darling I Need You – Winston James (actually Winston Groovy) and The Cimarons/Janet Ferron and The Cimarons (1970)

107   Strictly Invitation/Dog Your Woman – Patsy and Peggy [McClarty] (1970)

108   Beautiful World/Shocks Of A Drugs Man – Hot Rod All Stars (1970)

109 I Wish You Well/Impossible Love – Delroy Dunkley (actually Denzil Dennis)/
     Tony Nash and Delroy Dunkley (actually Denzil Dennis and Pat Rhoden)
     (1970)

110 Keep On Trying/Just Can't Do Without Your Love – Tony Nash (actually Pat
     Rhoden)/Winston James (actually Winston Groovy) (1970)

111 Leaving Everything/Psychedelic Bird – Josh [Roberts]/Hot Rod All Stars
     (1970)

112 NYT

113 I Don't Want To/I Don't Want To (Version 2) – The Merritts/Hot Rod All
     Stars (1970)

Note

All productions were by Hot Rod, aka Lambert Briscoe, operator of the Brixton-based
Hot Rod Sound System.

J-DAN LABEL (PREFIX JDN)

4400 Somebody's Baby/I Spy – Little Des [Desmond Riley] (1969)

4401 Cock Robin/Seven Zero – Ansel Collins/King Dennis (1970)

4402 Electric Shock/Black Robin – Music Doctors/King Dennis (1970)

4403 Bush Doctor/Lick Your Stick – Music Doctors (1970)

4404 Preaching Love/Iron Man – Music Doctors (actually with George Lee)/
     George Lee and Music Doctors (actually without George Lee) (1970)

4405 My Mother's Eyes/Gum Pot – The Soul Explosions (1970)

4406 NYT

4407 Johnny Dollar/Touch Of Poison – George Lee and Music Doctors/Music
     Doctors (1970)

4408 NYT

4409 NYT

4410 Can't Help From Crying/Can't Get Used To Losing You – The Israelites
     (1970)

4411 The Wild Bunch/Born To Be Strong – Music Doctors/Music Doctors
     (actually by The Israelites) (1970)

4412 Consider Me/You Walked Away – Roy Gee (1970)

4413 Try To Understand/I'd Rather Go Blind – Roy Gee (1970)

4414 In The Summertime/Foundation Track – Music Doctors (1970)

4415 I Want To Tell The World/Underground Man – The Mother's Sons/The
     Mother's Sons (actually by Music Doctors) (1970)

4416 I Don't Want No War/Third Note Swing – Boy Friday [Dandy] (1971)

4417 Doctor Dan/Discretion Version – Music Doctors/Boy Friday (1971) [ISSUED
     ON BLANK LABEL ONLY]

4418 Situation Version/Keep Tracking – Boy Friday [Dandy]/Our Band (1971)

4419 Free Man/Piano Twist – Boy Friday/Music Doctors (1971) [ISSUED ON
BLANK LABEL ONLY. B SIDE ALSO ISSUED ON BIG SHOT BI 587B]

Note

All tracks produced by Dandy except 4401, which was an Ansel Collins production.

JACKPOT (PREFIX JP)

700 Seven Letters/Too Bad – Derrick Morgan (Prod: Bunny Lee) (1969)

701 Dark End Of The Street/Apple Blossoms – Little Boy Blue (actually Pat
Kelly)/Mr Versatile (actually Lester Sterling) (Prod: Lee Perry/Edward 'Bunny'
Lee) (1969)

702 Having A Party/Devil's Disciples – Errol Dunkley/Mr Versatile (actually Lester
Sterling) (Prod: Edward 'Bunny' Lee) (1969)

703 Sweeten My Coffee (actually titled 'Then You Can Tell Me Goodbye')/Cherry
Pink – Wonder Boy (actually Slim Smith)/Mr Miller (probably by Bunny Lee)
(Prod: Edward 'Bunny' Lee) (1969)

704 Zapatoo The Tiger/Music House – Rolo Poley (actually Roland Alphonso
and unidentified male vocalist)/Rolo Poley (actually by Roland Alphonso)
(Prod: Edward 'Bunny' Lee) (1969)

705 Love Power/Since You Are Gone – Wonder Boy (actually Slim Smith)/Little
Boy Blue (actually Pat Kelly) (Prod: Edward 'Bunny' Lee/Lee Perry) (1969)

706 The Crimson Pirate/Moon Duck (actually 'Moon Dusk') – Peter Touch
(actually Peter Tosh) (Prod: Edward 'Bunny' Lee) (1969)

707 Feel It (aka 'Feel The Crumpet')/Kiss Me Quick – Mr Miller (possibly Bunny
Lee)/Mr Miller (actually by Keelyn Beckford) (Prod: Edward 'Bunny' Lee) (1969)

708 Funky Chicken/Funky Chicken Part 2 (actually 'Dallas Texas (Instrumental)')
– Winston Groovy/The Cimarons (Prod: Laurel Aitken) (1970)

709 Funny/Funny Version (actually unidentified instrumental) – Winston Groovy/
The Cimarons (Prod: Laurel Aitken) (1970)

710 Memory Of Don Drummond/Resting – Don Drummond Junior (actually by
Rico Rodriguez)/The Tobies (Prod: Charles 'Clancy' Collins) (1970)

711 Too Late/Late Night – Vincent McLeod/Sir Collins and The Earthquakes
(Prod: Charles 'Clancy' Collins) (1970)

712 Let's Fall In Love/Purple Moon – Claudette and The Cimarons/The Prophets
and The Cimarons (Prod: Grape) (1970)

713 Wood In The Fire/The Naked City – King Horror and The Cimarons (Prod:
Laurel Aitken) (1970)

714 Police/Honky Tonk Popcorn – King Horror/Pama Dice (Prod: Laurel Aitken)
(1970)

715   Bongo Man/Bear The Pussy – Pama Dice (Prod: Laurel Aitken) (1970)
       [PROBABLY UNISSUED]

716   Sin, Sun And Sex/Reggae Popcorn – Pama Dice (Prod: Laurel Aitken) (1970)

716   Police/Reggae Popcorn – Pama Dice (Prod: Laurel Aitken) (1970)
       [DUPLICATE ISSUE]

717   Pack Of Cards/Spread Joy – Nat Cole/Rita and Nat Cole (actually by Nat
       Cole and Sonny Binns) (Prod: Nat Cole) (1970)

718   Love Making/My Love (Part 1) (actually unidentified instrumental) – Rita
       (actually Rita Alston with Nat Cole and Sonny Binns)/Nat Cole (actually by
       Sonny Binns) (Prod: Nat Cole) (1970)

719   Riot/Boys And Girls – Moffat All Stars/The Impersonators (Prod: Melmouth
       Nelson) (1970)

720   NYT

721   NYT

722   Sugar Sugar/Sign Off – Nat Cole (actually by Winston Groovy)/Sonny Binns
       (Prod: Nat Cole) (1970)

723   The Wedding/Air Balloon – Roy Smith [Junior Smith] (both sides with The
       Cimarons) (Prod: Roy Smith [Junior Smith]) (1970)

724   If You Want Me Girl/Confusion – Roy Smith [Junior Smith] (Prod: Roy
       Smith) (1970) [UNISSUED]

725   NYT

726   NYT

727   Brotherly Love/Old Kent Road – Channel Five (actually by Martin Riley and
       The Uniques)/Channel Five (actually by Martin Riley) (Prod: Martin Riley)
       (1970)

728   Look Over Your Shoulder/The Kiss – Nora Dean and Verne (actually Veronica
       'Verne' Douglas)/Tommy McCook (Prod: Tommy McCook) (1970)

729   See You At Sunrise/Just Out Of Reach (Of My Two Empty Arms) – The
       Interns/Little Wonder (actually John Holt) (Prod: Edward 'Bunny' Lee) (1970)

730   Mr Chatterbox/Walk Through This World – The Interns (actually by Bob
       Marley and The Wailers)/Little Wonder (actually by Doreen Shaeffer) (Prod:
       Edward 'Bunny' Lee) (1970)

731   You Can Do It Too/All My Enemies Beware – The Twinkle Brothers/The
       Twinkle Brothers (actually by Eric Morris) (Prod: Edward 'Bunny' Lee) (1970)

732   Lonely Boy/Oo Boo – Errol The Champion (actually by Errol [Junior]
       English and The Champions) (Prod: Larry Lawrence) (1970) [A SIDE
       REISSUED ON JACKPOT JP 738A]

733   DJ's Choice/Can't Do Without It (actually titled 'Somebody Ought To
       Write A Book About It') – Winston Williams/Slim Smith (actually with The
       Uniques) (Prod: Edward 'Bunny' Lee) (1970)

734   I Just Don't Know What To Do With Myself/Lorna (actually titled 'Laura (What's He Got That I Ain't Got)') – Pat Kelly (Prod: Edward 'Bunny' Lee) (1970)

735   Get In The Groove/A Little Tear – Jeff Barnes/John Holt (Prod: Edward 'Bunny' Lee) (1970)

736   The Fastest Man Alive/Bloodshot Eyes – Dave Barker/Norman Grant (Prod: Edward 'Bunny' Lee) (1970)

737   NYT

738   Lonely Boy/All Of My Life – Errol [English] and The Champions/Tony [Sexton] and The Champions (Prod: Larry Lawrence) (1970) [A SIDE REISSUED FROM JACKPOT JP 732A]

739   NYT

740   Miss World/Take What You've Got – The Twinkle Brothers (Prod: Edward 'Bunny' Lee) (1970)

741   Sweet Young Thing/Grandma – The Twinkle Brothers (Prod: Edward 'Bunny' Lee) (1970)

742   Wet Version/I've Got To Get Away – Dave Barker (Prod: Edward 'Bunny' Lee) (1970)

743   The People's Choice/Let Me Go Girl – Winston Williams/Bobby James (actually by Bill Gentles) (Prod: Edward 'Bunny' Lee) (1970)

744   Top Of This World/Everybody Reggae – McBean Scott and The Champions/Larry Lawrence and The Champions (Prod: Larry Lawrence) (1970)

745   Girl Of My Dreams/On Broadway – Dave Barker (Prod: Edward 'Bunny' Lee) (1970)

746   The Same Song/Groovin' – Domino Johnson and The Champions (Prod: Larry Lawrence) (1970)

747   NYT

748   Cut Throat/Left The Water (actually 'You Left The Water Running') – Phil Pratt's All Stars/Ken Boothe (Prod: Phil Pratt) (1971) [B SIDE IS 1967 REISSUE]

749   NOT RELEASED – ISSUED ON SMASH SMA 2301]

750   The Truth Hurts/My Life Goes On (No More) – Ernest Wilson (Prod: Martin Riley) (1970) [A SIDE REISSUED ON JACKPOT JP 765B]

751   Sex Machine/You Left And Gone – The Aggrovators (actually with Dave Barker) (Prod: Edward 'Bunny' Lee) (1970)

752   Give Me Some Light/Don't Turn Your Back On Me – Dave Barker (Prod: Edward 'Bunny' Lee) (1971) [PROBABLY UNISSUED]

753   NOT ISSUED (RELEASED ON SMASH SMA 2307)

754   The Boy Was Mine/Unidentified – Maxine (actually TT Ross) (Prod: Edward 'Bunny' Lee) (1971) [UNISSUED]

755 Judge Aggro/Don't Rock The Boat – The Aggrovators/Satch [Ferdinand Dixon] (Prod: Edward 'Bunny' Lee) (1971) [PROBABLY UNISSUED]

756 NYT

757 Love Version/Ball Of Confusion – Winston Williams/Darker Shades Of Black (Prod: Edward 'Bunny' Lee) (1970)

758 War/People's Version – Darker Shades Of Black/Jeff Barnes (Prod: Edward 'Bunny' Lee) (1970)

759 I Won't Hold It Against You/King Of Hearts – David Crooks (actually Dave Barker)/Bobby James (Prod: Edward 'Bunny' Lee) (1970)

760 NYT

761 Hear My Heart (actually titled 'In My Heart')/Puppet On A String – Rob Walker (actually by Derrick Morgan) (Prod: Edward 'Bunny' Lee) (1971)

762 Midnight/Midnight Version – Lloyd [Clarke] and Doreen [Schaeffer]/Bunny Lee's All Stars (Prod: Edward 'Bunny' Lee) (1971)

763 Better Must Come/Better Must Come Version – Delroy Wilson/Bunny Lee All Stars (Prod: Edward 'Bunny' Lee) (1971)

764 Just For A Day/He Ain't Heavy, He's My Brother – Wonder Boy (actually Pat Kelly) (Prod: Edward 'Bunny' Lee) (1971)

765 Let Them Talk/The Truth Hurts – Ernest Wilson (Prod: Martin Riley) (1971) [B SIDE REISSUED FROM JACKPOT JP 750A]

766 My Desire/Bring It Up – The Soulettes (Prod: Bob Marley) (1971)

767 All Of Your Loving/Love Me – The Soulettes/Lloyd Clarke (Prod: Edward 'Bunny' Lee) (1971)

768 Do Your Own Thing/Talk About Love – The Twinkle Brothers/Wonder Boy (actually Pat Kelly) (Prod: Phil Pratt) (1971)

769 Cool Operator/I'm Yours – Delroy Wilson (Prod: Edward 'Bunny' Lee) (1971)

770 Try Again/Try Again Version – Delroy Wilson/The Aggrovators (Prod: Edward 'Bunny' Lee) (1971)

771 Double Attack/The Sniper – Lizzie and Delroy Wilson/The Aggrovators (Prod: Edward 'Bunny' Lee) (1971)

772 Stick By Me/It's A Pleasure – John Holt (Prod: Edward 'Bunny' Lee) (1971)

773 Jumping Jack/King Of The Track – Dennis Alcapone and John Holt/The Aggrovators (actually with Dennis Alcapone) (Prod: Edward 'Bunny' Lee) (1971)

774 It's A Jam In The Street/A Man Needs A Woman – John Holt (Prod: Edward 'Bunny' Lee) (1971)

775 Togetherness (Black And White)/Live Good – Dennis Alcapone and John Holt/Delroy Wilson (Prod: Edward 'Bunny' Lee) (1971)

776 Tell It Like It Is/Come Along – Dennis Alcapone/Delroy Wilson (Prod: Edward 'Bunny' Lee) (1971)

777 Miss Labba Labba/The Best Is Yet To Come – Twinkle Brothers (Prod: Three Sevens) (1971) [ISSUED ON BLANK LABEL ONLY – OFFICIAL RELEASE ON GREEN DOOR GD 4007]

778 Room Full Of Tears/unidentified track – Alton Ellis (Prod: Edward 'Bunny' Lee) (1971) [UNISSUED]

779 Keep Walking/Will You Still Love Me Tomorrow – Slim Smith (Prod: Edward 'Bunny' Lee) (1971)

780 Keep Your True Love Strong/Nice To Be Near – John Holt/Delroy Wilson (Prod: Edward 'Bunny' Lee) (1971)

781 Peace And Love/Who Is Your Brother? – Delroy Wilson/Jeff Barnes (Prod: Edward 'Bunny' Lee) (1971)

782 Nice To Be Near/Doing My Own Thing – Delroy Wilson (Prod: Edward 'Bunny' Lee) (1971) [UNISSUED. A SIDE RELEASED ON JP780B]

783 Oh Girl/The Clock – John Holt (Prod: Edward 'Bunny' Lee) (1971) [ISSUED ON BLANK LABEL ONLY]

784 Any More/Lost Love – John Holt (Prod: Edward 'Bunny' Lee) (1971)

785 NYT

786 I Need Your Loving/You Got What It Takes – Slim Smith (Prod: Edward 'Bunny' Lee) (1971)

787 Come On/Come On Version – The Cables (Prod: Edward 'Bunny' Lee) (1972)

788 Take Me Back/Where Do I Turn? – Slim Smith (Prod: Edward 'Bunny' Lee) (1972)

789 You're No Good/Rain From The Sky – Slim Smith (Prod: Edward 'Bunny' Lee) (1972)

790 Don't You Know/Riding For A Fall – John Holt (Prod: Edward 'Bunny' Lee) (1972)

791 The Mighty Organ/My Confession – Lascelles [Perkins] and Hortense [Ellis]/Stranger Cole (Prod: Edward 'Bunny' Lee) (1972)

792 Who Cares/Who Cares Version – Delroy Wilson/U Roy Junior with Bunny Lee's All Stars (Prod: Edward 'Bunny' Lee) (1972)

793 Let Them Talk/Bringing In The Guns – Derrick Morgan (Prod: Edward 'Bunny' Lee) (1972)

794 Won't Be This Way/Ain't No Love – Derrick Morgan (Prod: Edward 'Bunny' Lee) (1972)

795 The Same Old Song/Stay By Me – Delroy Wilson (Prod: Edward 'Bunny' Lee) (1972)

796 Play It Cool/King Of The Zozas – Alton Ellis/The Aggrovators (Prod: Edward 'Bunny' Lee) (1972)

797 Me Naw Run/All Night Long – Derrick Morgan (Prod: Edward 'Bunny' Lee) (1972)

798   Closer Together/Blinded By Love – Slim Smith (Prod: Edward 'Bunny' Lee)
        (1972)

799   Turning Point/Money Love – Slim Smith (Prod: Edward 'Bunny' Lee) (1972)

800   My Baby Is Gone/This Old Heart Of Mine – Delroy Wilson (Prod: Edward
        'Bunny' Lee) (1972) [UNISSUED. B SIDE RELEASED ON DOWNTOWN
        DT 496B INSTEAD]

801   The Minstrel (actually titled 'Queen And The Minstrel')/Put Yourself In My
        Place – Cornel Campbell (Prod: Edward 'Bunny' Lee) (1972)

802   Festival 10/Festival 10 Version – Derrick Morgan (Prod: Edward 'Bunny' Lee)
        (1972)

803   You'll Be Sorry/Green Grow The Lilacs – Dave Barker (Prod: Edward 'Bunny'
        Lee for Bush Productions) (1972)

804   Cheer Up/Loving You – Delroy Wilson (Prod: Edward 'Bunny' Lee for Bush
        Productions) (1972)

805   Guilty/Guilty Version – Ken Parker/The Aggrovators (Prod: Edward 'Bunny'
        Lee for Bush Productions) (1972)

806   Two Ton Gulleto/Gulleto Version – U Roy Junior (Prod: Edward 'Bunny' Lee
        for Bush Productions) (1972)

807   Looking Back/I'll Be There – John Holt (Prod: Edward 'Bunny' Lee for Bush
        Productions) (1972)

808   Cassius Clay/Love And Affection (actually 'I'm Gonna Make You Love Me') –
        Dennis Alcapone/Slim Smith (Prod: Edward 'Bunny' Lee) (1973)

809   Pity The Children/You're No Good – Cornel Campbell and The Eternals
        (Prod: Edward 'Bunny' Lee for Bush Productions) (1973)

810   Your Pretty Face/Your Pretty Face Version – Keble Drummond (Prod: Hugh
        Madden) (1973)

811   Ration/Things Not Easy – Joe Gibbs All Stars (actually by Bongo Herman
        and Bingy Bunny)/Joe Gibbs All Stars (actually by The Meditators) (Prod:
        Joel Gibson [Joe Gibbs]) (1973) [ALSO ISSUED ON SMASH (SMA 2331)
        WITH CORRECT CREDITS]

812   Justice To The People/Verse 2 – Lee Perry/The Upsetters (Prod: Lee Perry)
        (1973)

813   He Can't Spell/Acid Version – Dennis Brown/The Crystalites (Prod: Derrick
        Harriott) (1973)

814   Harry Hippy/Just One Kiss – Cornel Campbell (Prod: Edward 'Bunny' Lee)
        (1973)

Note

Although Jackpot was essentially the UK counterpart of Edward 'Bunny' Lee's label in
Jamaica, as can be seen from the listing a fair proportion of its output did not originate
from him.

JOE (PREFIX JRS)

1   Behold/Tea, Patty, Sex And Ganja – The Critics with The Nyah Shuffle/Sexy
        Frankie (1970)

2   Since I Met You Baby/Jughead – Paula Dean [Persis Jackson] and The Nyah
        Shuffle/Paula Dean [Persis Jackson] and The Nyah Shuffle (actually without
        Paula Dean) (1970)

3   She Caught The Train/Teahouse From Emperor Roscoe – Ray Martell/Pama
        Dice (1970)

4   The Thief/Dynamite Line – Joe Mansano/Joe's All Stars (1970) [ISSUED
        ON BLANK LABEL ONLY. REISSUED FROM DUKE LABEL (DU 51B)
        AND B SIDE REISSUED FROM DU 53B]

5   Trial Of Pama Dice/Jughead Returns Version 1 – Lloyd, [Pama] Dice and
        Mum with The Nyah Shuffle/The Nyah Shuffle (1970)

6   Son Of Alcapone/All My Enemies – Joe The Boss [Joe Mansano] (1970)

7   Small Change/Mind Your Business – Girlie/Girlie and Joe [Mansano] (1970)

8   People Are Running/Schooldays (incorrect title: probably 'Love Me Or Leave
        Me') – Pamela Brown/The Critics (actually by Pamela Brown) (1970)

9   Tony B's Theme/Skinhead Revolt – Joe's All Stars/Joe The Boss [Joe
        Mansano] (1970)

10   If Life Was A Thing (Money Could Buy)/Daisy Bothering – Joe The Boss [Joe
        Mansano]/Lloyd Kingpin and The Nyah Shuffle (1970)

11   Don't Play That Song/Just One Look – Delroy Williams and The Reaction/
        Boss All Stars (1970)

12   Spanish Harlem/People Get Ready – Joe's All Stars (1970) [ISSUED ON
        BLANK LABEL ONLY]

13   Joe's Song/Young And Strong Version 1 – Joe's All Stars/Joe The Boss [Joe
        Mansano] (1970) [PROBABLY ON BLANK LABEL ONLY]

14   Appeal Of Pama Dice/Young And Strong Version 2 – Lloyd, Mum and
        Barrister/Boss All Stars (1970)

15   Miss Doris's Rooster/Rooster Version – Girlie with Joe's All Stars and Rico
        Rodriguez/Rico Rodriguez and Joe's All Stars (1970) [ISSUED ON BLANK
        LABEL ONLY]

16   Lazarus/Brixton Is Free – Dice The Boss and Joe Mansano/Joe The Boss [Joe
        Mansano] and Rico Rodriguez (1970) [ISSUED ON BLANK LABEL ONLY]

17   The Informer/Cool It – Dice The Boss/Joe's All Stars (1970)

Note

All releases in this series were produced by Joe Mansano, who ran Joe's Record Shack
in Brixton's Granville Arcade. Also see the Duke label, which issued 11 singles with a
'Joe' label under its own DU Prefix. The numbers concerned are 23, 24, 28, 34, 41, 42,
50, 51, 52, 53 and 57.

JUMP UP (PREFIX JU)

540   Muhammed Ali/Undemocratic Rhodesia – Mr Calypson/Sampson The Lark
      (Prod: Ed Shaw) (1971)
541   Mr Walker/Mae Mae – Mighty Sparrow (Prod: Henry de Freitas) (1971)

MOODISC (PREFIX MU)

3501   Musically Red/Bratah – Winston Wright and Mudie's All Stars (1970)
3502   Back Door/Too Much Fire – Lloyd Charmers and Mudie's All Stars/Freddy
       McLean [Freddie McKay] (1970)
3503   Wha Who Wha Version/Wha Who Wha – Mudie's All Stars/GG Russell
       (actually by Count Sticky) (1970)
3504   On The Water/Cash Register – The Jolly Boys/Mudies All Stars (1970)
3505   I'll Run Away/Time Is The Master – Winston Shand/John Holt (1970)
3506   Christmas Joy/Now The Days Are Gone – Don Cornel (actually Cornel
       Campbell) and The Eternals (1970)
3507   Push Me In The Corner/Mudie's Madness – The Eternals/Mudie's All Stars (1971)
3508   Keep On Dancing/My Jealous Eyes – The Eternals/Hazel Wright (1971)
3509   Musical Pleasure/Hot Pop – I-Roy/Jo Jo Bennett (actually with Mudie's All
       Stars) (1971)
3510   Heart Don't Leap/Snow Bird – I-Roy and Dennis Walks/Dennis Walks and
       Mudie's All Stars (1971) [B SIDE REISSUED ON MOODISC MU 3514A]
3511   I'll Never Believe In You/Black Attack – The Dynamic Gang (actually by Bob
       Andy and Marcia Griffiths)/The Dynamic Gang (actually by Lloyd Willis and
       Mudie's All Stars) (1971)
3512   Let Me Tell You Boy/Let Me Tell You Boy (Version) – I-Roy and The Ebony
       Sisters/Mudie's All Stars (1971)
3513   It May Sound Silly/It May Sound Silly (Version) – John Holt/Mudie's All
       Stars (1971) [NOT ISSUED – RELEASED ON R&B DISCS' MOODISC
       IMPRINT]
3514   Snow Bird/Change The Tide – Jo Jo Bennett and Mudie's All Stars/Mudie's
       All Stars (1971) [NOT ISSUED]
3515   Whispering Drums/Give Me Some More Loving – Count Ossie and Mudie's
       All Stars/Slim Smith and The Uniques (1971) [NOT ISSUED – RELEASED
       ON R&B DISCS' MOODISC IMPRINT]

Note

All releases produced by Harry Mudie except MU 3511, which was a Sid Bucknor
production. It should be mentioned that there was a further series of Moodisc put out
by R&B Discs from November 1971, and a later one around 1975 put out by another
concern. The above listing, however, is the series put out by Trojan/B&C.

PRESSURE BEAT (PREFIX PB – BUT SEE BELOW)

5501   Honey, No Money/This Message To You – Niney and The Destroyers (actually
with Slim Smith)/The Inspirations (1970)

5502   Mad Rooster/As Far As I Can See (actually titled 'The Wicked Must Survive')
– Lloyd Willis/Niney and The Destroyers (actually by The Reggae Boys)
(1970)

5503   Walk By Day, Fly By Night/Unknown Tongue – The Reggae Boys/The
Destroyers (1970)

5504   News Flash/News Flash (Part 2) – Desi Young/The Destroyers (1970)

5505   Pressure Tonic/Machuki's – The Destroyers/The Destroyers (actually with
Count Machuki) (1970)

5506   Pussy Catch A Fire/Follow This Beat (actually 'Secret Weapon') – The
Soul Brothers/The Destroyers (actually by Ansel Collins) (1970) [B SIDE
REISSUED FROM AMALGAMATED AMG 832A]

5507   Jack Of My Trade/United We Stand – Lord Comic/Cynthia Richards
(actually with unidentified male vocalist) (1970)

5508   Ten Feet Tall (actually titled 'Wear You From The Ball')/Chapter Two (actually
titled 'Harmony Hall') – Lizzie/The Destroyers (actually by Nicky Thomas)
(1970)

5509   Them A Fi Get A Beatin'/Them A Fi Get A Beatin' (Version) – Peter Tosh/
Third and Fourth Generation (1972)

5510   Skanky Dog/Boney Dog – Winston Scotland/The Destroyers (1972)

5511   Hammering (Version)/Medicine Man – Nicky [Thomas] and Cat Campbell/
First Generation (1972)

5512   Yuh Wrong Fe Trouble Joshua/Joshua Row Us Home – Eddy Ford/Carey
[Johnson] and Lloyd [Young] (1972)

5513   Money In My Pocket/Money Love – Joe Gibbs and The Professionals
(actually by Dennis Brown)/Joe Gibbs and The Professionals (1972)

5514   Tipatone/Do It To Me – Joe Gibbs All Stars (actually by Keith Smiley) (1972)

5515   More Dub/More Dub (Version) – Johnny Lover/The Professionals (1973)

Note

All titles produced by Joe Gibbs [Joel Gibson]. Also, the first few issues were pressed
with a 'PR' rather than a 'PB' prefix, probably in error.

PYRAMID (TROJAN SERIES – PREFIX PYR)

7000   Money Never Built A Mountain/My World – The Tennors (Prod: Edward
'Bunny' Lee) (1973)

7001   Tip From The Prince/Fat Beef Skank – I-Roy/Dillinger (Prod: Tony
Robinson [Prince Tony]) (1973)

7002 Ba-Ba-Ri-Ba Skank/Buck And The Preacher Version – Dennis Alcapone and Lizzy/Tommy McCook All Stars (Prod: Arthur 'Duke' Reid) (1973)

7003 Truly/Cruising – Alton Ellis (Prod: Lloyd Coxsone [Lloyd Blackford]) (1973)

7004 Waxy Doodle/Go Away – Leo Graham (Prod: Leo Graham) (1973)

7005 Can You Keep A Secret?/Peter And Judas – Big Youth and Keith Hudson/Earl Flute and Horace Andy (Prod: Keith Hudson) (1973)

7006 I Could Never Love Another (After Loving You)/It Ain't Always What You Do – Brad Lundy (Prod: Sidney Crooks) (1974)

7007 Baby Don't Do It/You'll Never Know – The Now Generation (Prod: Federal) (1973)

7008 Belch It Off/Jack Horner – Dennis Alcapone (Prod: Sidney Crooks) (1974)

7009 New Situation/New Version – Rocking Horse (Prod: Lloyd Campbell) (1974)

7010 Great Messiah/Nana Nana – The Meditations (Prod: Alvin Ranglin) (1974)

7011 No Work, No Pay/Version – The Tellers (Prod: Rupie Edwards) (1974)

7012 Innocent People Cry/Innocent (Version) – Gregory Isaacs (actually with Freddy McKay)/GG All Stars (Prod: Alvin Ranglin) (1974)

7013 My Desire/Lemon Tree – Johnny Clarke (Prod: Edward 'Bunny' Lee) (1974)

7014 Butter Fe Fish/Bammie And Fish – Skin, Flesh and Bones (Prod: Dickie Wong) (1974) [PROBABLY ISSUED ON BLANK LABEL ONLY– OFFICIAL RELEASE ON HARRY J HJ 6670]

Q (PREFIX Q)

2200 Lavender Blue/Humpty Dumpty – Count Suckle (Prod: Count Suckle) (1970) [UNISSUED]

2201 Please Don't Go/Bread On The Table – Count Suckle with Freddie Notes and The Rudies (Prod: Count Suckle) (1970)

2202 NYT

2203 Tribute To Jimi Hendrix/Prove My Love To You – Jimmy Lindsay and The Beans (Prod: Freddie Notes) (1970)

2204 Moving Train/Sweet Louise – Hughie and Huyitis [The Rudies] (Prod: Freddie Notes) (1970) [UNISSUED]

RANDY'S (PREFIX RAN)

500 I'm The One, You're The One/End Us – Randy's All Stars (1970)

501 Pepper Pot/The Same Things – Randy's All Stars (actually with Count Machuki)/The Soul Twins (actually The Gaylads) (1970)

502 Dixie/Five Cents (actually 'A Lover's Question') – Randy's All Stars/Randy's All Stars (actually by Winston Samuels) (1970)

503 October/Time Out – Dave Barker/Randy's All Stars (1970)

504   Give Thanks/Get Ready (actually titled 'Rocking Chariot') – The Lyrics/
       Tommy McCook and Randy's All Stars (actually by The Generation Gap)
       (1970) [ISSUED ON BLANK LABEL ONLY. SEE ALSO RAN 511A]

505   Emperor Waltz/War – Randy's All Stars/Randy's All Stars (actually by Winston
       Cole and The Generation Gap) (1970) [B SIDE ALSO ISSUED ON RAN 517B]

506   Blue Danube Waltz/Together – Randy's All Stars/Delroy Wilson (1970)

507   Bridge Over Troubled Water/Waterfall – The Lyrics/Randy's All Stars (1970)

508   Want Man/Man Version – Nora Dean/Randy's All Stars (1970)

509   Me Want Girl/Girl (Version) – The Ethiopians/Randy's All Stars (1971)

510   True Man (aka 'Free Man')/Truthful (actually 'Tom's Version') – The
       Ethiopians/Randy's All Stars (actually by Herman Marquis) (1971) [B SIDE
       ALSO ISSUED ON SPINNING WHEEL SW 109B]

511   Give Thanks/Give (Version) – The Lyrics/Randy's All Stars (1971)

512   Mr Tom/Sad News – The Ethiopians and Randy's All Stars (actually
       unidentified male vocal group on A side) (1971)

513   NYT

514   Shake A Hand/Lick I Pipe – Jimmy London and The Impact All Stars/Carl
       Murphy and The Impact All Stars (1971)

515   Down By The Riverside/ Down By The Riverside Version – Keith and The
       Impact All Stars/Impact All Stars (1971)

516   Close To Me/Close To Me (Version) – Max Romeo/Impact All Stars (1971)
       [ISSUED ON BLANK LABEL ONLY]

517   Bridge Over Troubled Waters/War – Jimmy London and The Impact All Stars/
       Randy's All Stars (actually by Winston Cole and The Generation Gap) (1971)
       [B SIDE REISSUED FROM RAN 505B]

518   Hip Hip Hooray/Hip Hip Hooray Version – Jimmy London and The Impact
       All Stars/Impact All Stars (1971)

519   Go Back Version 4/Go Back Version 3 – Impact All Stars (1971) [UNISSUED]

520   A Little Love/A Little Love (Version) – Jimmy London and The Impact All
       Stars/Impact All Stars (1971)

521   It's Now Or Never/Now Or Never (Version) – Jimmy London/Impact All
       Stars (1972)

522   Hard Time/Change Your Ways – Rocking Horse (actually with The Impact All
       Stars) (1972)

523   King Of Babylon/Nebuchadnezzar – Junior Byles/The Upsetters (Prod: Lee
       Perry) (1972)

524   Stars/Stars (Version) – Lloyd Parks/Impact All Stars (actually by Dennis
       Alcapone) (1972)

525   Sing A Song Of Freedom/Song Of Freedom (Version) – The Freedom Group
       (actually with Max Romeo)/Impact All Stars (1972)

526   Cheater/Harvest In The East – Dennis Brown/Tommy McCook and The Impact All Stars (1972)

527   Jamaican Festival '72/Jamaican Festival '72 (Version) – Jimmy London and Rocking Horse/Impact All Stars (1972)

528   Meet Me At The Corner/Meet Me (Version) – Dennis Brown/Impact All Stars (1972) [SOME COPIES PLAY 'STARTING ALL OVER AGAIN (INSTRUMENTAL VERSION)' BY THE DYNAMITES AS PER ATTACK ATT 8035B]

529   Sweet Caroline/Caroline Version– C Donovan/Impact All Stars (1972)

530   Passion Love/Love Makes The World Go Round – The Melodians (Prod: Arthur 'Duke' Reid) (1972)

531   Kick The Bucket/I'm A Man Of My Word – Keith Poppin (Prod: Tony Robinson [Prince Tony]) (1973)

532   Froggie/Froggie (Version) – U Roy Junior /The Rhythm Rulers (Prod: Lloyd Campbell) (1973)

533   Don't Think About Me/Skin Him Alive – Horace Andy and Earl Flute/Dino Perkins (Prod: Keith Hudson) (1973)

534   Silver Platter/Jean You Change Everything – Keith Hudson and I-Roy/Keith Hudson (Prod: Keith Hudson) (1973)

535   I'm So Fed Up/I'm So Fed Up (Version) – Rocking Horse (1973)

536   Bedroom Mazurka/Version 2 – [Augustus] Pablo and Fay [Bennett]/The Crystalites (Prod: Derrick Harriott) (1973)

Note

All issues produced by either Vincent or Keith Chin for Randy's Productions unless otherwise indicated.

SMASH (PREFIX SMA)

2300   NYT (NUMBER POSSIBLY NOT USED)

2301   My Boy Lollipop/Everybody Needs Love – Maxine (actually TT Ross) (Prod: Edward 'Bunny' Lee) 1970

2302   Big Red Ball/Big Red Ball Version 2 – The Aggrovators (actually by Delroy Jones)/The Aggrovators (actually with Lloyd [Robinson] and Devon [Russell]) (Prod: Errol Thompson) (1970)

2303   My Heart Is Gone/My Heart Is Gone (Version) – John Holt/Phil Pratt's All Stars (Prod: Phil Pratt) (1970)

2304   Skanky/Skanky, Version 2 – Niney All Stars (actually by Leroy 'Horsemouth' Wallace and Niney)/Niney All Stars (Prod: Winston Holness [Niney]) (1970)

2305   I Had A Talk With My Woman/Life Is Not The Same Anymore – John Holt/ Maxine (actually TT Ross) (Prod: Edward 'Bunny' Lee) (1970)

2306   I Had A Talk With My Woman/I Had A Talk Version – John Holt/The Aggro Band (1970) (Prod: Edward 'Bunny' Lee) [UNISSUED]

2307   Stop Them/I Don't Care – Bill Gentles/Maxine (actually TT Ross) (Prod: Edward 'Bunny' Lee) (1970)

2308   NYT

2309   NYT

2310   NYT

2311   Don't Get Me Confused/Ball Of Confusion – Keith Hudson/D Smith (actually Dennis Alcapone) (Prod: Keith Hudson) (1970)

2312   One More Bottle Of Beer/Beer Version – The Aggrovators (actually by Dave Barker and The Upsetters)/The Aggrovators (actually by The Upsetters) (Prod: Lee Perry) (1970)

2313   Wake The Nation/One Thousand Tons Of Version – U Roy and Jeff Barnes/Jeff Barnes (actually with Roland Alphonso) (Prod: Edward 'Bunny' Lee) (1970)

2314   You Said It/Hot Sauce – Bobby James and Dave [Barker]/The Aggro Band (Prod: Edward 'Bunny' Lee) (1970)

2315   The Wizard (aka '33-66')/Sweet Like Candy – The Aggrovators (actually by Roland Alphonso)/The Aggro Band (actually with Don Tony Lee) (Prod: Edward 'Bunny' Lee) (1970)

2316   NYT

2317   I Am Trying/Trying Version – Delroy Wilson/Sir Collins' All Stars (Prod: Charles 'Clancy' Collins) (1970)

2318   Satisfaction/Satisfied Version – Delroy Wilson/Delroy Wilson and Alton Ellis (Prod: Charles 'Clancy' Collins) (1971)

2319   A Little Loving/Loving Version – Alton Ellis/Delroy Wilson (Prod: Charles 'Clancy' Collins) (1971)

2320   I'll Be There/Rude Boy Train – Alton Ellis/The Hi-Tals (Prod: Charles 'Clancy' Collins) (1971)

2321   Sir Collins' Special/Conqueror (actually titled 'Heart Of The Knights') – Collins All Stars (actually by Lester Sterling and Sir Collins)/Collins' All Stars (actually by Lennox Brown) (Prod: Charles 'Clancy' Collins/Sonia Pottinger) (1971) [B SIDE ALSO ISSUED ON HIGH NOTE HS 055A]

2322   Hard Life/Version Life – Merlene Webber/Collins' All Stars (Prod: Charles 'Clancy' Collins) (1971)

2323   What It Was/Chicken Thief – Delroy Wilson/Lloyd Clarke (Prod: Edward 'Bunny' Lee) (1971)

2324   Mother And Father Love/Mother Love Version – John Holt/The Aggrovators (Prod: Edward 'Bunny' Lee) (1971)

2325 Need No Whip/Grine Grine – Charlie Ace (Prod: Theo Beckford) (1971)

2326 Light Of Day/I Thought You Knew – Keith Hudson (Prod: Keith Hudson) (1973)

2327 Concentration/Version 2 – Dennis Brown/The Crystalites (Prod: Derrick Harriott) (1973)

2328 Soul Sister/Soul Sister (Version) – The Heptones/Impact All Stars (Prod: Lee Perry) (1973)

2329 Don't Break Your Promise/I've Been Admiring You – John Holt (Prod: Edward 'Bunny' Lee) (1973)

2330 Black Man Kingdom Come/Swing And Dine – The Gaytones (actually by The Melodians) (Prod: Sonia Pottinger) (1973) [B SIDE IS REISSUE FROM 1968]

2331 Things Not Easy/Ration – The Meditators/Bongo Herman and Bingy Bunny (Prod: Joel Gibson [Joe Gibbs]) (1973) [ALSO ISSUED ON JACKPOT JP WITH A AND B SIDES REVERSED AND WITH INCORRECT CREDITS]

2332 Hello My Little Queen/African Queen – Mickey Lee/Augustus Pablo (Prod: Joel Gibson [Joe Gibbs]) (1973)

2333 Rock And Cry/September Rose – Sugar Simone (Prod: Carlton Troutt) (1973)

2324 How You Gonna Get Control?/Dubbing Control – Bellfield/GG All Stars (Prod: Alvin Ranglin) (1973)

2335 I'm Just A Rover/Rover Version – You and I (actually by Bobby Davis) (Prod: Carlton Troutt) (1973)

2336 Trying To Wreck My Life/Live And Learn – Delroy Wilson (Prod: Edward 'Bunny' Lee) (1973)

2337 Magnificent Seven/Leggo Beast – I-Roy (Prod: Augustus 'Gussie' Clarke) (1973)

2338 Rose Of Sheron/Slip Out – I-Roy (Prod: Augustus 'Gussie' Clarke) (1973)

2339 Never Give Up/Fooling Me – Derrick Morgan (Prod: Edward 'Bunny' Lee) (1973)

2339 Straight To Jackson Head (You Are My Angel (Version))/You Are My Angel – The Aggrovators/The Aggrovators (actually by Horace Andy) (Prod: Edward 'Bunny' Lee) (1973) [DUPLICATE ISSUE]

SONG BIRD (PREFIX SB)

1001 Ling Tong Ting/Sweet Sweet – Lloyd Charmers/Lloyd Robinson (Prod: Winston Lowe) (1969) [A SIDE REISSUED ON HORSE HS 32B]

1002 Long About Now/Come See About Me – Bruce Ruffin and The Temptations (actually Bruce Ruffin and The Techniques)/Bruce Ruffin and The Temptations (actually by Lloyd Charmers and The Soul Leaders) (Prod: Lloyd Charmers) (1969) [B SIDE ALSO ISSUED ON DUKE DU 25B]

1003 Grooving Reggae/They Got To Move – Lloyd Charmers/Lloyd Robinson
(Prod: Lloyd Charmers) (1969) [UNISSUED]

1004 NYT

1005 Biddy Biddy/It's A Wonderful Time – The Eagles (Prod: Joe Sinclair) (1969)

1006 Rudam Bam/Prodigal Boy (actually titled 'Any Little Bit') – The Eagles/The
Crystals (actually by The Templets) (Prod: Joe Sinclair/Lloyd Charmers) (1969)

1007 In The Spirit/Duckey Luckey – Lloyd Charmers (Prod: Winston Lowe) (1969)

1008 Darling Please/I've Got Plans – Stranger Cole (Prod: Wilburn 'Stranger' Cole)
(1969)

1009 I've Been Loving You/Memphis Reggae – The Megatons (Prod: Jackson Jones)
(1969)

1010 Ging Gang Goolie/I'm Thirsty – The Megatons (Prod: Jackson Jones) (1969)

1011 The Clip/Little Miss Muffet – The Kingstonians/Tony (actually Tony Binns)
(1969)

1012 By The Time I Get To Phoenix/Heartbreak Girl – Noel Brown (1969)

1013 Riding For A Fall/I'm Not Begging – Derrick Harriott (1969)

1014 Sitting On Top/You Were Meant For Me – Derrick Harriott (1969)

1015 Musical Madness (Version 1)/Musical Madness (Version 2) – The Crystalites
(1970)

1016 NYT

1017 The Undertaker/Stop That Man – The Crystalites (1970)

1018 True Grit/True Grit Version 2 – Bongo Herman, Les [Chen] and The
Crystalites (1970)

1019 Singer Man/Singer Man, Version 2 – The Kingstonians/The Crystalites (1970)

1020 Lady Madonna/Ghost Rider – The Crystalites (1970) [B SIDE REISSUED
ON SB 1035B]

1021 Love I/Heavy Load – Glen Brown/The Crystalites (1970)

1022 Go Bye Bye/Laugh It Off – Derrick Harriott (1970)

1023 Come A Little Closer/Come A Little Closer (Version 2) – The Prunes
(actually with Eric Donaldson)/The Crystalites (1970)

1024 Isies/Isies (Version 2) – The Crystalites (1970)

1025 Stranger In Town/Stranger In Town (Version 2) – The Crystalites (1970) [B
SIDE REISSUED ON SB 1053B]

1026 I'm The One Who Loves You/Suffering In The Land – Clyde McPhatter and
The Rudies (Prod: Trojan) (1970) [UNISSUED]

1027 Use What You've Got/Only Yesterday – Clyde McPhatter and The Rudies
(Prod: Trojan) (1970) [UNISSUED]

1028 Message From A Blackman/Message From A Blackman (Version 2) – Derrick
Harriott (actually with The Chosen Few)/The Crystalites (1970)

1029   Psychedelic Train/Psychedelic Train (Part 2) – Derrick Harriott and The
        Chosen Few/Derrick Harriott and The Crystalites (1970)
1030   Sic Him Rover/Drop Pon – The Crystalites (1970) [B SIDE IS REISSUE
        FROM BIG SHOT BI 510B]
1031   Time Is Hard/Time Is Hard, Part 2 – The Chosen Few/The Crystalites (1970)
        [B SIDE REISSUED ON TROJAN TR 7040B]
1032   Going Back Home/Going Back Home Part 2 – The Chosen Few/The
        Crystalites (1970)
1033   No Man Is An Island/No Man Is An Island (Part 2) – Derrick Harriott/The
        Crystalites (1970)
1034   Overtaker (Version 1)/Overtaker (Version 2) – The Crystalites (1970)
1035   Undertaker's Burial/Ghost Rider – The Crystalites (1970) [B SIDE
        REISSUED FROM SB 1020B]
1036   Short Story (Version 1)/Short Story (Version 2) – The Crystalites (1970)
1037   NYT
1038   NYT
1039   Handful Of Friends/Handful Version – Pat Satchmo/The Crystalites (1970)
1040   No Baptism/Version 2 – The Ethiopians/The Crystalites (1970)
1041   Rumble Rumble/Rumble Version – The Kingstonians/The Crystalites (1970)
1042   Groovy Situation/The Crystal Groove (actually 'Lady Madonna') – Derrick
        Harriott/The Crystalites (1970) [A SIDE REISSUED ON TROJAN TR
        7887A. B SIDE REISSUED FROM SB 1020A]
1043   Psychedelic Train, Chapter 3/Groovy Situation, Version 2 – Derrick Harriott
        (actually by Ramon and The Crystalites)/The Crystalites (1970)
1044   Sesame Street/Sesame Version – Scotty and The Crystalites/The Crystalites
        (1970)
1045   Out There/Out There Version 2 – The Kingstonians/The Crystalites (1970)
1046   Why Can't I Touch You?/Touch You Version – The Chosen Few/The Inner
        Circle Band (1970)
1047   Good Ambition/Ambition Version – The Ethiopians/The Crystalites (1970)
1048   Hear That Train/Hear That Train (Version) – Tinga Stewart/The Crystalites
        (1970) [ISSUED ON BLANK LABEL ONLY]
1049   Riddle I This/Musical Chariot – Scotty and Derrick [Harriott]/Scotty and
        The Crystalites (1971)
1050   Home Sweet Home/Hail I – Bongo Herman and Les [Chen] (1970)
1051   Jam Rock Style/Rock Style Version – Scotty and The Crystalites/The
        Crystalites (1971)
1052   Candy/Candy Version – Derrick Harriott/The Crystalites (1971)
1053   Golden Chickens/Stranger Version – Ramon and The Crystalites/The
        Crystalites (1971) [B SIDE REISSUED FROM SB 1025B]

1054   Medicine Stick/Short Cut – Denzil Laing and The Crystalites/The Crystalites (1971)

1055   Lollipop Girl/Lollipop Version – Derrick Harriott/The Crystalites (1971)

1056   Penny For Your Song/Penny (Version) – Scotty/The Crystalites (1971)

1057   Earthly Sounds/Earthly Sounds Version – The Crystalites (actually with Hux Brown)/The Crystalites (1971)

1058   NYT

1059   What A Pain/Pain Version – The Ethiopians/The Crystalites (1971)

1060   Know Far I/Know Far I Version – Bongo Herman and Bunny/The Crystalites (1971)

1061   Shaft/Shaft Version – The Chosen Few (1971)

1062   Lot's Wife/Slave – The Ethiopians/Derrick Harriott (1971)

1063   Medley In Five (Part 1)/Medley In Five (Part 2) – Derrick Harriott (1971)

1064   Best Of Five (Part 1)/Best Of Five (Part 2) – The Ethiopians (1971)

1065   Have You Seen Her?/Have You Seen Her Version – Derrick Harriott/The Crystalites (1971)

1066   Salaam (Peace)/Scra-per – Bongo Herman, Les [Chen] and Bunny/The Crystalites (1971)

1067   Everybody's Just A Stall/Everybody (Version) – The Chosen Few/The Crystalites (1971)

1068   Over The River/River (Version) – Derrick Harriott/Derrick Harriott (actually by The Crystalites) (1972)

1069   We Are Praying/Praying (Version) – Bongo Herman and Bunny/The Crystalites (1972)

1070   Do Your Thing/Your Thing (Version) – The Chosen Few/The Crystalites (1972)

1071   Since I Lost My Baby/Baby (Version) – Derrick Harriott/Derrick Harriott (actually by The Crystalites) (1972)

1072   Trinity/Monkey Drop – The Crystalites (actually with Joe White)/Scotty (1972)

1073   Fat Boy/Boy Version – Bunny Brown (1972)

1074   Silhouettes/Silhouettes Version – Dennis Brown/The Crystalites (1972)

1075   Changing Times/Changing Times Version – Roman Stewart and Dave [Robinson]/The Crystalites (1972)

1076   NOT ISSUED

1077   NOT ISSUED

1078   Being In Love/Love Version – Derrick Harriott/Derrick Harriott (actually by The Crystalites) (1972) [REISSUED ON TROJAN TR 7970]

1079   Mash Up/Mash Up (Version) – The Diamonds/The Dynamites (1972)

1080   Clean Race/Version Train – Scotty and The Crystalites/The Crystalites (1972)

1081   Smokey Eyes/Smokey Version – Glen [Brown] and The Crystalites/The Crystalites (1972)

1082   People Make The World Go Round/People Make The World Go Round
        (Version) – Errol Brown and The Chosen Few/The Crystalites (1972)
1083   International Pum/Observer – Niney/Reggae Matic (Prod: Winston Holness
        [Niney]) (1972)
1084   Don't Rock The Boat/Rock Version – Derrick Harriott/Derrick Harriott
        (actually by The Crystalites) (1972)
1085   Lonely Woman/Lonely Woman Version – Horace Andy/The Crystalites (1973)
        [REISSUED ON HARRY J HJ 6699B WITHOUT HORNS]
1086   Dr Fud/La-Fud-Del-Skank – Fud and Del/Fud Christian All Stars (Prod: Fud
        Christian for La-Fud-Del) (1973)

Note

All releases produced by Derrick Harriott unless otherwise indicated.

SPINNING WHEEL (PREFIX SW)

100   Haunted House/Double Wheel – The Upsetters (Prod: Lee Perry) (1970)
101   The Miser/Do It Madly – The Upsetters/Chuck Junior (Prod: Lee Perry)
       (1970)
102   Choking Kind/Penny Wise (actually 'Penny Wise And Pound Foolish') – The
       Upsetters/Chuck Junior (Prod: Lee Perry) (1970)
103   Land Of Kinks/This Man – The Upsetters (actually with Hugh Hendricks)/
       The Upsetters (actually with Oniel Hall) (Prod: Lee Perry) (1970)
104   NYT
105   Bush Jacket/Soul Face – The In Crowd (Prod: Earl White) (1971)
106   My Sweet Lord/Devil's Lead Soup (Prod: The Rudies) (1971)
107   Soul For Sale/Bogusism – The Cimarons (Prod: Carl Levy) (1971)
108   Voice Of The People/People Version – Jimmy [Martin] Riley (Prod: Martin
       Riley) (1971)
109   Crying Every Night/Tom's Version – Tommy McCook and The Supersonics
       (actually by Stranger Cole)/Herman Marquis (Prod: Byron Smith) (1971) [B
       SIDE ALSO ISSUED ON RANDY'S RAN 510B]
110   Stupid Doctor/Groovin' In Style (Groovin' Out On Life) – Tommy McCook
       and The Supersonics/Rob Walker (actually by Ken Parker) (Prod: Byron
       Smith) (1971)

SUMMIT (PREFIX SUM)

8501   Everything Is Beautiful/Give Up – The Rockstones (actually by BB Seaton)/
        Beverley's All Stars (1970)
8502   Collie And Wine/Collie Version – Glenmore Brown [Glen Brown]/Beverley's
        All Stars (1970)

8503   Got To Get Away/Got To Get Away Version – Delroy Wilson/Beverley's All
        Stars (1970) [UNISSUED]
8504   All God's Children/All God's Children Version – Tony Brevett/Beverley's All
        Stars (1970) [UNISSUED]
8505   Walking In The Rain/Walking In The Rain (Part 2) – The Melodians/
        Beverley's All Stars (1970)
8506   Staircase Of Time/Staircase Of Time (Version) – Tony Brevett/Beverley's All
        Stars (1970)
8507   Blessed Be The Man/It's Gonna Take A Miracle – Ken Boothe (1970)
        [UNISSUED. B SIDE RELEASED ON TROJAN TR 7772A]
8508   Rivers Of Babylon/Babylon Version – The Melodians/Beverley's All Stars (1970)
8509   Bitterness Of Life/Ooh Child – Bruce Ruffin (1970)
8510   Peeping Tom/Peeping Tom Version – The Maytals/Beverley's All Stars (1970)
8511   Starvation/Starvation Version – The Pioneers/Beverley's All Stars (1970)
8512   It Took A Miracle/Miraculous Version – The Melodians/Beverley's All Stars
        (1971)
8513   Monkey Girl/Monkey Girl Version – The Maytals/Beverley's All Stars (1971)
8514   My Jamaican Girl/My Jamaican Girl Version 2 – The Gaylads/Beverley's All
        Stars (1971)
8515   Sounds Of Babylon/Second Babylon (Version) – Samuel The First [Philip
        Samuels]/Beverley's All Stars (1971)
8516   Candida/Are You Ready – Bruce Ruffin and Beverley's All Stars (1971)
8517   Get Ready/Get Ready Version 2 – The Pioneers/Beverley's All Stars (1971)
8518   I Wish It Could Be Peaceful Again/Peaceful Version – Ken Boothe/Beverley's
        All Stars (1971)
8519   Your Feeling And Mine/Your Feeling (Version) – Ken Boothe/Conscious
        Minds (1971) [UNISSUED]
8520   One Eye Enos/Enos version – The Maytals/Beverley's All Stars (1971)
8521   Knock Three Times/This Time I Won't Hurt You – Brent Dowe/The Gaylads
        (1971) [B SIDE ALSO ISSUED ON TROJAN TR 7738B]
8522   Come Ethiopians Come/Version 2 – The Melodians/Beverley's All Stars (1971)
8523   Bongo Man/Now I Know – James Chambers [Jimmy Cliff]/Ken Boothe
        (1971) [B SIDE REISSUED FROM TROJAN (TR 7772B]
8524   Free The People/Free The People (Version) – Bruce Downer (actually Bruce
        Ruffin)/Beverley's All Stars (1971)
8525   Put Your Hand In The Hand/Miracle Version (actually 'It's Gonna Take A
        Miracle (Version)') – Brent Dowe (actually with unidentified female vocalist)/
        Beverley's All Stars (1971) [FIRST PRESSING WITH 'SUM 8525B1' IN B
        SIDE RUNOUT)

8525   Put Your Hand In The Hand/Miracle Version (actually 'It Took A Miracle (Version)') – Brent Dowe (actually with unidentified female vocalist)/ Beverley's All Stars (1971) [SECOND PRESSING WITH 'SUM 8525B2' IN B SIDE RUNOUT]

8526   Stop The Train/Caution – The Wailers and Beverley's All Stars (1971)

8527   It's You/It's You (Version) – The Maytals/Beverley's All Stars (1971)

8528   Lady Of My Complexion/No Sad Song – The Pioneers (Prod: Sidney Crooks) (1971)

8529   Walk With Love/Walk With Love (Version) – The Maytals/Beverley's All Stars (1971)

8530   Freedom Train/Freedom Train (Version) – Brent Dowe/Beverley's All Stars (1971)

8531   Games People Play/Games People Play (Version) – The Melodians/Beverley's All Stars (1971) [UNISSUED]

8532   Rivers Of Babylon/My Life, My Love – The Melodians (1971) [WITHDRAWN FIRST PRESSING – HAS 'SUM 8532A1/A2' RESPECTIVELY IN RUNOUTS. A SIDE REISSUED FROM SUM 8508A]

8532   My Life, My Love/My Life, My Love (Version) – The Melodians/Beverley's All Stars (1971) [SECOND PRESSING – HAS 'SUM 8532 B1/SUM 8532 B2' RESPECTIVELY IN RUNOUTS]

8533   Never You Change/Never Change (Version) – The Maytals/Beverley's All Stars (1972)

8534   The Time Has Come/No Sins At All – The Melodians and Beverley's All Stars (1972) [HAS 'SUM 8534 B1' IN B SIDE RUNOUT]

8534   The Time Has Come/McIntosh – The Melodians/Beverley's All Stars (1972) [DUPLICATE ISSUE WITH 'SUM 8534 B2' IN B SIDE RUNOUT]

8535   Storybook Children/Gorgeous, Marvellous – Sidney, George and Jackie [The Pioneers] (1972)

8536   Thy Kingdom Come/Kingdom (Version) – The Maytals/Beverley's All Stars (1972)

8537   It Must Be True Love/True Love (Version) – The Maytals/Beverley's All Stars (1972)

8538   Haile Selassie/Old Man River – Mello and The Mellotones (Prod: Clancy Eccles for Bush Productions) (1972)

8539   Three Blind Mice/Mice Skank – Leo Graham/The Upsetters (Prod: Lee Perry) (1973)

8540   Memories By The Score/Scorer – Ansell Linkers [Ansell Cridland] and The Fud Christian All Stars/Fud Christian All Stars (Prod: Fud Christian for La-Fud-Del) (1973)

269

8541   Melody Maker/Uncover Me – Keith Hudson (Prod: Keith Hudson) (1973)

8542   A So We Stay (Money In Hand)/Scarface – Big Youth and Dennis Brown/
       Winston Scotland (Prod: Joel Gibson [Joe Gibbs]) (1973)

8543   Everyday Is The Same Kind Of Thing/Sweat Of Your Brow – Paulette
       [Williams]/Shorty Perry (Prod: Alvin Ranglin) (1973)

Note

All releases produced by Leslie Kong except where stated (8528 and last six issues).

TECHNIQUES (PREFIX TE)

900   Something Tender/Bewitch (aka 'Red Sunset') – Techniques All Stars (actually
      by Boris Gardner and The Love People)/Cannonball [Karl Bryan] (1970) [A
      SIDE REISSUED ON TE 920B UNDER DIFFERENT TITLE]

901   Double Barrel/Double Barrel (Version 2) – Dave [Barker] and Ansel Collins
      (1970)

902   War Boat/Mr Blue – The Sensations (1970)

903   Get Left (actually 'Get Left Version')/It's Your Thing – The Coons (actually by
      Techniques All Stars)/Alton Ellis (1970)

904   Lonely Man/I Feel Alive – The Techniques (1970)

905   I'll Be Waiting (actually titled 'I Don't Know Why I Love You')/Think You're
      Smart – Alton Ellis (actually by The Sensations)/The Techniques (1970)

906   Feel A Little Better (actually titled 'Peep In A Pot Of Fire')/You'll Get Left
      (Version) – The Coons (actually by The Techniques All Stars with Winston
      Wright) (1970)

907   Top Secret/Crazy Rhythm – Winston Wright (1970)

908   To The Other Woman/Woman (Version) – Hortense Ellis/Techniques All
      Stars (1971)

909   Jumping Jack/Point Blank – Rad Bryan/Ansel Collins (1971)

910   NYT

911   Unidentified/8.5 Special – unidentified artist/unidentified artist (1971)
      [LABEL FOR THIS RELEASE FEATURED ON SLEEVE OF *TROJAN
      STORY VOLUME 1* BUT EXISTENCE NOT CONFIRMED]

912   NYT

913   Nuclear Weapon/La La La – Ansel Collins/The Techniques All Stars (1971)

914   Monkey Spanner/Monkey Spanner (Version 2) – Dave [Barker] and Ansell
      Collins/Ansel Collins (1971) [B SIDE REISSUED ON TROJAN TR 7875B]

915   Karate/Doing Your Own Thing – Dave [Barker] and Ansel Collins (1971)

916   See And Blind/Rema Skank – Johnny Osbourne/Techniques All Stars (1972)
      [A SIDE REISSUED FROM BIG SHOT BI 549A]

917   High Explosion/High Explosion (Version) – Lloyd Young/Ansel Collins (1972)

918   Look Into Yourself/Yourself (Version) – Dennis Alcapone/Techniques All Stars (1972)

919   Promises/Promises (Version) – The Ethiopians/The Tivolies (1972)

920   Horns Of Paradise/Grass Root (aka 'Something Tender') – Trommy [Vin Gordon]/ Techniques All Stars (actually by Boris Gardner and The Love People) [B SIDE REISSUED FROM TE 900A UNDER DIFFERENT TITLE] (1973)

921   Mr Harry Skank/Tel Aviv Drums – Prince Jazzbo/Glen Brown (Prod: Glen Brown) (1973)

922   Woman Don't You Go Astray/Travelling Man – W [Winston] Riley/The Techniques (actually with Dave Barker) (1973)

923   Don't Throw Stones/Toughness (actually titled 'Lucifer') – Sidney Rogers and The Fighters/Sidney Rogers' Fighters (actually by Winston Wright) (Prod: Larry Lawrence) (1973) [ALSO ISSUED ON BIG SHOT BI 621]

924   That's When It Hurts/I'll Take You Home – The Silvertones (Prod: Lee Perry) (1973)

925   Just One Look/Sinner Man – Annette Clarke (Prod: Lee Perry) (1973)

926   Pauper And The King/Loving Pauper – I-Roy and Gregory Isaacs/Gregory Isaacs (Prod: Augustus 'Gussie' Clarke) (1973)

927   Rub It Down/Rub It Down (Version) – The Eagles/Tommy McCook All Stars (Prod: Arthur 'Duke' Reid) (1973)

928   Aunt Kereba (title probably incorrect)/Waterloo Rock (Version) (actually 'Aunt Kereba (Version)') – U Roy Junior/Don Reco (actually Rico Rodriguez and Lloyd Campbell's All Stars) (Prod: Lloyd Campbell) (1973)

929   Anywhere But Nowhere/Anywhere But Nowhere (Version) – K C White/ Impact All Stars (Prod: K C White) (1973)

930   Monkey Fashion/Medley Mood – I-Roy (Prod: Roy Cousins) (1973)

931   Tonight I'm Staying Here With You/Lady Love – Romey Picket (actually Ronnie Davis and The Tennors) (Prod: Edward 'Bunny' Lee) (1974)

Note

All tracks produced by Winston Riley except where indicated.

TREASURE ISLE (PREFIX TI)

7050   Skinhead Moon Stomp/Must Catch A Train – Symarip (Prod: Graeme Goodall for Philligree Productions) (1969) [A SIDE REISSUED ON TROJAN TRO 9062A]

7051   NYT

7052   Pop A Top/The Lion Speaks – Andy Capp/Rico [Rodriguez] (Prod: Lynford Anderson/Philligree) (1969)

7053 Boss Cocky/Musical True – Claudette/Live Shocks (Prod: Philligree) (1970)
[ISSUED ON BLANK LABEL ONLY. A SIDE CREDITED TO 'THE
RUDE GIRL' ON JAMAICAN ISSUE]

7054 Parson's Corner/Redeem – Symarip (Prod: Philligree) (1970)

7055 La Bella Jig/Holidays By The Sea- Symarip (Prod: Philligree) (1970)

7056 Hooked On A Feeling/Turn Round Twice – Boris Gardner/The Message
(Prod: Junior Chung/Philligree) (1970)

7057 NYT

7058 One Life To Live, One Love To Give/My Best Dress – Phyllis Dillon/Tommy
McCook and The Supersonics (1971)

7059 Drive Her Home/Version – Hopeton Lewis and U Roy/Tommy McCook
and The Supersonics (1971)

7060 To The Other Man/Stampede – Hopeton Lewis with Tommy McCook and
The Supersonics/Tommy McCook and The Supersonics (1971)

7061 Lets Build Our Dreams/Testify (Version) – John Holt with Tommy McCook
and The Supersonics/Tommy McCook and The Supersonics (1971)

7062 Behold/Way Back Home – U Roy with Tommy McCook and The
Supersonics (1971)

7063 Botheration/Mouth Trombone – Justin Hinds and The Dominoes with
Tommy McCook and The Supersonics/Vincent Hinds with Tommy McCook
and The Supersonics (1971)

7064 Everybody Bawlin'/Ain't That Loving You – U Roy and The Melodians with
Tommy McCook's All Stars/U Roy and Alton Ellis with Tommy McCook's
All Stars (1971)

7065 Sister Big Stuff/Black River – John Holt/Tommy McCook's All Stars (1971)

7066 Paragons Medley/Medley Version – John Holt (actually with The Paragons)/
Tommy McCook's All Stars (1971)

7067 Pirate/Depth Charge – The Ethiopians/Tommy McCook and The Soul
Syndicate (1971)

7068 Mighty Redeemer/Mighty Version – Justin Hinds/Duke Reid's All Stars (1972)

7069 The Great Woggie/Buttercup (Version) – Dennis Alcapone/Tommy McCook
and The Supersonics (1972)

7070 Midnight Confession/Midnight (Version) – Phyllis Dillon/Tommy McCook
and The Soul Syndicate (1972)

7071 Judgement Day/Version Day – Hopeton [Lewis] and Dennis [Alcapone]/Earl
Lindo and Tommy McCook and The Soul Syndicate (1972)

7072 Jungle Fever/Clean Up Woman – Cynthia Richards and The Soul Syndicate
(1972)

7073 Help Me Make It Through The Night/Help Me (Version) – Ken Parker/
Tommy McCook All Stars (1972)

7074 Wake Up Jamaica/Wake Up Jamaica (Version) – Dennis Alcapone (actually with Joya Landis)/Tommy McCook and The Supersonics (1973)

Note

Issues prior to 7050 were put out during the time when Treasure Isle was a subsidiary of Island Records and have not been included here for that reason. Those releases between 7050 and 7056 were put out during the time the label was administered by Graeme Goodall and the Doctor Bird group but have been included here for the sake of completeness. Numbers 7058 to 7074 inclusive were produced by Arthur 'Duke' Reid.

TROJAN (PREFIX TR)

FIRST SERIES (001–015)

001 Judge Sympathy/Never To Be Mine – Duke Reid (actually by The Freedom Singers and The Duke Reid All Stars)/Roland Alphonso (1967)
002 Fook Sang/Starry Night – Tony and Dennis/Tommy McCook (1967)
003 It's Raining/Sound Of Music – The Treetops (actually The Three Tops) (1967)
004 Ain't That Loving You/Comet Rock Steady – Alton Ellis and The Flames/ Alton Ellis and The Flames (actually by Tommy McCook and The Supersonics) (1967)
005 I Want To Be Loved By You/Tulips (actually titled 'Tulips And Heather') – Oliver St. Patrick and The Diamonds (actually Boris Gardner and Phyllis Dillon) (1967)
006 This Is A Lovely Way (actually titled '(This Is) A Lovely Way To Spend An Evening')/Things Of The Past (actually titled 'A Thing Of The Past') – Phyllis Dillon (1967)
007 Dedicated To You/Things I Said To You – The Jamaicans (1967)
008 NYT
009 Why Birds Follow Spring/Soul Rock – Alton Ellis and The Flames/Tommy McCook (actually with The Supersonics) (1967)
010 Love Is A Treasure/Zazuka – The Treasure Boys (actually by Freddy McKay)/ The Treasure Boys (actually by Tommy McCook and The Supersonics) (1967)
011 Loving Pauper/Sir Don – Dobby Dobson (actually with Tommy McCook and The Supersonics)/Tommy McCook and The Supersonics (1967)
012 NOT USED
013 NOT USED
014 NOT USED
015 Make Me Yours/We Have Happiness – Shirley Kay (actually Phyllis Dillon) (1967)

Note

All the above issues were produced by Arthur 'Duke' Reid.

TROJAN (600 SERIES)

601 Donkey Returns/Tribute To Sir K.B – Brother Dan All Stars (Prod: Brother Dan [Dandy]) (1968)

602 Our Love Will Last/Eastern Organ – The Jivers/Brother Dan All Stars (actually with Pat Rhoden) (Prod: Brother Dan [Dandy]) (1968)

603 Answer Me/Hold Pon Them – Owen Gray/Brother Dan All Stars (Prod: Brother Dan [Dandy]) (1968)

604 Wear My Crown/Down On The Beach – The Jivers (actually with Pat Rhoden) (Prod: Brother Dan [Dandy]) (1968)

605 Pony Ride/Baby You Send Me – Winston and Pat [Rhoden] (Prod: Brother Dan [Dandy]) (1968)

606 Woman Is Greedy/Endlessly – Pat Rhoden/Junior Smith [Roy Smith] (Prod: Brother Dan [Dandy]) (1968)

607 Read Up/Gallop – Brother Dan All Stars (Prod: Brother Dan [Dandy]) (1968)

608 Another Saturday Night/Bee's Knees – Brother Dan All Stars (Prod: Brother Dan [Dandy]) (1968)

609 Follow That Donkey/I Want To Rave – Brother Dan All Stars (Prod: Brother Dan [Dandy]) (1968) [ISSUED ON BLANK LABEL ONLY]

610 Bookie Man/More Love – The Race Fans/The Uniques (Prod: Lynford Anderson/Edward 'Bunny' Lee) (1968)

611 Spanish Harlem/If I Did Know (actually 'If I Didn't Know') – Val Bennett/ Roy Shirley (Prod: Lee Perry/Edward 'Bunny' Lee) (1968) [REPRESSED IN 1971 ON BROWN TROJAN LABEL]

612 Uncle Charlie/What A Botheration – The Mellotones/The Mellotones (actually by Lee Perry and The Upsetters) (Prod: Lee Perry) (1968) [B SIDE ALSO ISSUED ON DUKE DU 10A]

613 Tighten Up/Good Ambition – The Untouchables (actually by The Inspirations)/Roy Shirley (Prod: Lee Perry/Edward 'Bunny' Lee) (1968)

614 Donkey Train/Down By The Riverside – Denzil Dennis (Prod: Brother Dan [Dandy]) (1968)

615 Me Nah Worry/Hush Don't You Cry – Denzil Dennis (Prod: Brother Dan [Dandy]) (1968)

616 Place In The Sun/Handi-Cap – David Isaacs/The Upsetter All Stars (Prod: Lee Perry) (1968)

617 Stir It Up/This Train – The Wailers (Prod: Bob Marley) (1968)

618 The Toast/Kicks Out – Dandy (Prod: R Thompson [Dandy]) (1968)

619 Watch This Sound/Out Of Love (aka 'I'm The One That Love Forgot') – The Uniques (Prod: Winston Lowe) (1968)

620 Kansas City/Out The Light – Joya Landis (actually with Tommy McCook and The Supersonics) (Prod: Arthur 'Duke' Reid) (1968)

621 Rent Too High/Everytime (actually titled 'Ace Of Spades') – Glen Adams (actually by Ranny Williams)/Glen Adams (actually by Ranny Williams and George Regent) (Prod: George Regent) (1968)

622 Angel Of The Morning/Love Letters – Joya Landis (actually with Tommy McCook and The Supersonics)/Alton [Ellis] and Phyllis [Dillon] (Prod: Arthur 'Duke' Reid) (1968)

623 In Like Flint/Nobody's Business – The Good Guys/The Good Guys (actually with Ken Lazarus) (Prod: Byron Lee) (1968)

624 Soul Limbo/The Whistling Song – Byron Lee and The Dragonaires (Prod: Byron Lee) (1968)

625 Win Your Love/It's All In The Game – George A. Penny/Val Bennett (Prod: Lynford Anderson) (1968)

626 Fat Man/South Parkway Rock – Derrick Morgan/Val Bennett (Prod: Lynford Anderson) (1968)

627 Mix It Up/I'll Be Around – The Kingstonians (Prod: Karl 'JJ' Johnson) (1968)

628 No More Heartaches/I'll Follow You – The Beltones (Prod: Harry Johnson) (1968)

629 Sentence/You Crummy – Lee Perry/Danny [Simpson] and Lee [Perry] (Prod: Lee Perry) (1968)

630 I Can't Stand It/Trying To Reach My Goal – Alton Ellis with Tommy McCook and The Supersonics (Prod: Arthur 'Duke' Reid) (1968)

631 Mr Walker/Sunset Jump-up – Byron Lee and The Dragonaires/Byron Lee (Prod: Byron Lee) (1968)

632 Lovey Dovey/Grooving – Owen Gray (Prod: Brother Dan [Dandy]) (1968)

633 I'll Be Lonely/Second Fiddle – Jay and Joya (actually John Holt and Joya Landis with Tommy McCook and The Supersonics)/The Supersonics (Prod: Arthur 'Duke' Reid) (1968)

634 Love Up, Kiss Up/Labba Labba Reggae (actually 'Reggae (Lonely Goat Herd)') – The Termites/Alton Ellis (actually by the Tommy McCook and The Supersonics) (Prod: Arthur 'Duke' Reid) (1968)

635 Rudy The Red Nose Reindeer/White Christmas – Steam Shovel (Prod: Jim Simpson) (1968) [PRESSED ON 'BIG BEAR' LABEL]

636 Thunderstorm/Honey Love – King Cannonball [Karl Bryan]/Bert Walters (Prod: Lee Perry) (1968)

637 Time Marches On/Party Tonight – The Race Fans/The Silvertones (Prod: Lynford Anderson) (1968)

638 Dulcemania/Chinaman – Drumbago and The Dynamites/Clancy Eccles (Prod: Clancy Eccles) (1968)

639 Sweet Africa/Let Us Be Lovers – Clancy Eccles/Clancy Eccles (actually with Velma Jones) (Prod: Clancy Eccles) (1968)

275

640   Baby Baby/Barbara – Val Bennett (Prod: Lee Perry) (1968)

641   Moonlight Lover/I Love You True – Joya Landis (actually with Tommy
        McCook and The Supersonics) (Prod: Arthur 'Duke' Reid) (1968)

642   Breaking Up/Party Time – Tommy McCook (actually by Alton Ellis with
        Tommy McCook and The Supersonics) (Prod: Arthur 'Duke' Reid) (1968)

643   Tonight/Maybe Someday – John Holt with Tommy McCook and The
        Supersonics (Prod: Arthur 'Duke' Reid) (1968)

644   Uncle Desmond/Bronco (Ol' Man River) – Lee Perry (actually by The
        Mellotones)/Lee Perry (actually with The Upsetters and Sir Lord Comic)
        (Prod: Lee Perry) (1969) [REISSUED ON UPSETTER US 326A]

645   A-Yuh (actually 'Hey You')/The Love I Saw In You Was Just A Mirage – The
        Uniques (Prod: Winston Lowe) (1969)

646   Old Man Say/Promises – The Silverstars (Prod: Clancy Eccles) (1969)

647   Bangarang Crash/Rahtid – Clancy Eccles/The Dynamites (actually with
        Drumbago) (Prod: Clancy Eccles) (1969)

648   Constantinople/Deacon Son (actually 'Deacon Don') – Clancy Eccles (Prod:
        Clancy Eccles) (1969)

649   Demonstration/My Girl – Clancy Eccles/Val Bennett (Prod: Clancy Eccles)
        (1969)

650   I Can't Stop Loving You/Tell Me Darling – Owen Gray (Prod: Owen Gray)
        (1969) [UNISSUED – RELEASED ON BLUE CAT BS 156]

651   Love Is All I Had/Boys And Girls Reggae – Phyllis Dillon (Prod: Arthur
        'Duke' Reid) (1969)

652   You Should've Known Better/Third Figure – Justin Hinds and The
        Dominoes/Tommy McCook (actually with The Supersonics) (Prod: Arthur
        'Duke' Reid) (1969)

653   Out Of Sight/I Want You Closer – Danny Simpson (actually with Tommy
        McCook and The Supersonics)/John Holt (actually with Tommy McCook
        and The Supersonics) (Prod: Arthur 'Duke' Reid) (1969)

654   Hang 'Em High/Candy Lady – Richard Ace/[Hugh] Black and [George]
        Daley (Prod: Harry Johnson) (1969)

655   Things I Love/Since You've Been Gone – The Afrotones/Eric Fatter (actually
        by Keble Drummond) (Prod: Harry Johnson) (1969) [UNISSUED]

656   Sweet Chariot/Far Far Away – Max Romeo and The Hippy Boys (Prod: Max
        Romeo) (1969) [B SIDE ALSO ISSUED ON PAMA'S UNITY LABEL]

657   The Saint/Ease Me Up Officer – Tommy McCook (actually with The
        Supersonics)/Soul Ofrous (Prod: Arthur 'Duke' Reid) (1969)

658   Fattie Fattie/Last Call (aka 'Tribute To Drumbago') – Clancy Eccles/The
        Silverstars (actually by The Dynamites) (Prod: Clancy Eccles) (1969)

659 Dollars And Cents/Popcorn Reggae – Gladstone Adams (actually with The Treasure Isle Group)/Tommy McCook (actually with The Supersonics) (Prod: Arthur 'Duke' Reid) (1969)

660 Everybody Bawlin'/Kilowatt – The Melodians/Tommy McCook (actually with The Supersonics) (Prod: Arthur 'Duke' Reid) (1969)

661 Ali Baba/I'm Your Man – John Holt (actually with Tommy McCook and The Supersonics) (Prod: Arthur 'Duke' Reid) (1969)

662 Pick Out Me Eye (actually 'Dig Out Me Eye')/Think You Too Bad – The Royals (Prod: L Edwards) (1969)

663 Soul Scorcher/Lucky Boy – King Cannon [Karl Bryan]/Glen [Brown] and Dave [Barker] (Prod: Harry Johnson) (1969) [PRESSED WITH HARRY J LABEL]

664 Moon Is Playing A Trick (actually titled 'The Moon Is Playing Tricks On Me')/Soul Special – Trevor Shield/King Cannon [Karl Bryan] (Prod: Harry Johnson) (1969) [PRESSED WITH HARRY J LABEL]

665 Splender Splash/Please – The Jay Boys/Trevor Shield (Prod: Harry Johnson) (1969) [PRESSED WITH HARRY J LABEL]

666 Woman Capture Man/One (actually 'One Heart, One Love') – The Ethiopians (Prod: Karl 'JJ' Johnson) (1969)

667 Proud Mary/My Devotion – Tony King and The Hippy Boys (Prod: Bart Sanfilipo) (1969)

668 Love/The Whole Family Is Here – The Hippy Boys (actually with Max Romeo)/The Hippy Boys (Prod: Bart Sanfilipo) (1969)

669 Michael Row The Boat Ashore/Guess Who's Coming To Dinner – The Hippy Boys (actually with Max Romeo)/The Hippy Boys (Prod: Bart Sanfilipo) (1969)

670 Too Experienced/I Really Love You Baby – Owen Gray (Prod: Owen Gray) (1969)

671 Get On The Right Track/Moon Shot – Phyllis Dillon (actually with Hopeton Lewis)/ Tommy McCook (actually with The Supersonics) (Prod: Arthur 'Duke' Reid) (1969)

672 Long Shot Kick The Bucket/Jumping The Gun – The Pioneers/Rico [Rodriguez] (Prod: Leslie Kong/Dandy) (1969) [PRESSED WITH BOTH ALL-ORANGE AND ORANGE & WHITE LABELS. A SIDE REISSUED ON TROJAN TR 7968A AND TRO 9063A]

673 Red Ash/Bluebird – Cannonball [Karl] Bryan/The Silvertones (Prod: Arthur 'Duke' Reid) (1969)

674 What You Gonna Do Now/Have You Ever Been To Heaven – John Holt (Prod: Arthur 'Duke' Reid) (1969)

675   Liquidator/Festive Spirit (actually 'Feel It Festival Spirit') – Harry J All Stars
       (actually with Winston Wright)/Glen [Adams] and Dave [Barker] (actually
       by The Jamaicans) (Prod: Harry Johnson) (1969) [ON HARRY J LABEL:
       FIRST PRESSING. ALSO ISSUED ON TR 682A WITH CORRECT
       TITLE AND ARTIST CREDIT. A SIDE REISSUED ON TROJAN 9063B]

675   Liquidator/La La Always Stay (actually 'Rich In Love') – Harry J All Stars
       (actually with Winston Wright)/Glen [Adams] and Dave [Barker] (Prod: Harry
       Johnson) (1969) [ON HARRY J LABEL: SECOND PRESSING WITH
       DIFFERENT B SIDE. A SIDE REISSUED ON TROJAN TRO 9063B. B
       SIDE ALSO ISSUED ON TR 682B]

676   Take You For A Ride/I'm Coming Home – Girl Satchmo (actually with
       Tommy McCook and The Supersonics (Prod: Arthur 'Duke' Reid) (1969)

677   You Done Me Wrong/If This World Were Mine – Tyrone Davis (actually
       Tyrone Evans) (Prod: Arthur 'Duke' Reid) (1969)

678   Darling I Love You/Memory Of Don – Don Drummond Junior [Vin
       Gordon]/John Holt (Prod: Arthur 'Duke' Reid) (1969)

679   Ease Up/You Gonna Feel It – The Bleechers (Prod: Lee Perry) (1969)

680   Get Back/I'm Not For Sale – Anonymously Yours/Ernie Smith (Prod: Bart
       Sanfilipo) (1969)

681   It's Your Thing/'69 – Anonymously Yours/Anonymously Yours (actually by
       Wallace Wilson) (Prod: Bart Sanfilipo) (1969)

682/   Feel It Festival Spirit/La La Always Stay (actually 'Rich In Love') – The

675   Jamaicans/Glen [Adams] and Dave [Barker] (Prod: Harry Johnson) (1969)
       [PRESSED WITH GREEN/SILVER HARRY J LABEL. A SIDE ALSO
       ISSUED ON SECOND VARIATION OF TR 675 BUT WITH SLIGHTLY
       DIFFERENT TITLE CREDIT AND INCORRECT ARTIST CREDITS.
       B SIDE ALSO ISSUED ON FIRST VARIATION OF TR 675]

683   Double Shot/Gimme Gimme Gal (actually titled 'Banana Water') – Beverley's
       All Stars/Beverley's All Stars (actually by The Mellotones) (Prod: Leslie Kong)
       (1969)

684   NYT

685   Black Bud/Too Late – The Pioneers/The Pioneers (possibly by The
       Harmonisers) (Prod: Leslie Kong) (1969)

686   Lipstick On Your Collar/Tribute To Rameses – Phyllis Dillon (actually by
       Naomi Phillips)/Tommy McCook and The Supersonics (Prod: Arthur 'Duke'
       Reid) (1969)

687   NYT

688   You Had Your Chance/Wha' She Do Now – The Gaylads (Prod: Byron Lee/
       Lynford Anderson) (1969)

278

689   Sound Of Silence/Walk On By – St. Andrew's Girls Choir (actually by SPM [Sydne, Phillipa and Mary Ann]) (Prod: Byron Lee) (1969)

690   Wonderful World, Beautiful People/Hard Road To Travel – Jimmy Cliff (Prod: Leslie Kong and Jimmy Cliff) (1969)

691   Memphis Underground (Part 1)/Memphis Underground (Part 2) – The JJ All Stars (Prod: Karl 'JJ' Johnson) (1969)

692   Big Bamboo/King JA JA – Emile Straker and The Merrymen (Prod: George Benson) (1969) [1968 RECORDING REISSUED ON DUKE DU 113]

693   Put A Little Love In Your Heart/Jay Fever – Marcia Griffiths/The Jay Boys (actually with Karl Bryan) (Prod: Harry Johnson) (1969) [PRESSED WITH HARRY J LABEL. REISSUED ON HARRY J HJ 6613A WITH ADDED STRINGS]

694   Have Sympathy/Spyrone – John Holt/Harry J All Stars (Prod: Harry Johnson) (1969) [PRESSED WITH HARRY J LABEL]

695   Sweet Sensation/It's My Delight – The Melodians (Prod: Leslie Kong) (1969)

696   Got To Be Free/Situation – The Rulers (Prod: Karl 'JJ' Johnson) (1969)

697   Well Read (actually titled 'Well Dread')/Robert F Kennedy – The Ethiopians/ The Ethiopians (actually by The JJ All Stars) (Prod: Karl 'JJ' Johnson) (1969)

698   Poor Rameses/In Orbit – The Pioneers/Beverley's All Stars (Prod: Leslie Kong) (1969)

699   Night Of Love/Copy Cat – Ansel Collins/Derrick Morgan (Prod: Leslie Kong) (1969)

7700 SERIES

7700   One Way Love/No More Heartaches – The Coloured Raisins (Prod: Joe Sinclair) (1969) [SOME COPIES IN PICTURE SLEEVE]

7701   Moonlight Groover/Everyday Is Just A Holiday – Winston Wright (actually with Tommy McCook and The Supersonics)/The Sensations (actually with Tommy McCook and The Supersonics) (Prod: Arthur 'Duke' Reid) (1969)

7702   Wooden Heart/All My Life – John Holt (actually with Tommy McCook and The Supersonics) (Prod: Arthur 'Duke' Reid) (1969)

7703   There's A Fire/Last Time – The Gaylads (Prod: Leslie Kong) (1969)

7704   Dry Up Your Tears/One Way Street – Bruce Ruffin/Beverley's All Stars (Prod: Leslie Kong) (1969)

7705   Intensified Change/Marie – The Silvertones (Prod: Arthur 'Duke' Reid) (1969)

7706   Black Coffee/Heartaches – Tommy McCook and The Supersonics/Tommy McCook and The Supersonics (actually with Vic Taylor) (Prod: Arthur 'Duke' Reid) (1969) [B SIDE IS NOT 1967 CUT]

7707   Little Drummer Boy/Mary's Boy Child – The Merrymen (Prod: Emile
        Straker) (1969)

7708   I'll Need You Tomorrow/I'm Gonna Make It – The Kingstonians (Prod: Leslie
        Kong) (1969)

7709   Pressure Drop/Smoke Screen – The Maytals/Beverley's All Stars (Prod: Leslie
        Kong) (1969)

7710   Samfie Man/Mother Rittie – The Pioneers (Prod: Leslie Kong) (1969)

7711   Monkey Man/Night And Day – The Maytals (Prod: Leslie Kong) (1969)

7712   Cotton Dandy/Don't Get Weary – Ansel Collins/Carl Dawkins (Prod: Leslie
        Kong) (1969)

7713   Shanghai/Rome Wasn't Built In A Day (actually titled 'Honey Don't Go') –
        Freddie Notes and The Rudies/Freddie Notes and The Rudies (actually by
        Winston Francis and The Rudies) (Prod: Joe Sinclair) (1969)

7714   Lick It Back/Busy Bee – The Clarendonians/Beverley's All Stars (Prod: Leslie
        Kong) (1969)

7715   Moon Invader/You Gotta Love Me – Winston Wright and Tommy McCook/
        Radcliffe Ruffin and Tommy McCook (Prod: Arthur 'Duke' Reid) (1969)

7716   Why Baby Why/Keep My Love From Fading – Ken Boothe (Prod: Leslie
        Kong) (1969)

7717   Lock Jaw/My Desire – Tommy and The Upsetters (actually by Dave Barker
        with Tommy McCook and The Supersonics)/The Yard Brooms (actually with
        Tommy McCook and The Supersonics (Prod: Arthur 'Duke' Reid) (1969)

7718   Run Fattie/Hoola Bulla – The Slickers (Prod: Leslie Kong) (1969)

7719   Baby Don't Do It/Touchdown – The Clarendonians/Beverley's All Stars (Prod:
        Leslie Kong) (1969)

7720   A Day Seems So Long/Project – The Melodians/Beverley's All Stars (Prod:
        Leslie Kong) (1969)

7721   Wiggle Waggle/Jaga War – The Wanderers (Prod: Leslie Kong) (1969)

7722   Vietnam/She Does It Right – Jimmy Cliff (Prod: Leslie Kong and Larry
        Fallon/Leslie Kong) (1969) [PROMO COPIES IN PICTURE SLEEVE]

7723   Boss Festival/Lucky Side – The Pioneers (Prod: Leslie Kong) (1969)
        [UNISSUED – BLANK LABEL COPIES MAY EXIST]

7724   Rocco/Don't Tell Your Mama – Freddie Notes and The Rudies (Prod: Joe
        Sinclair) (1970) [ISSUED ON BLANK LABEL ONLY]

7725   Lucianna/I Really Like It – The Jubilee Stompers (Prod: Bryan Daley) (1969)

7726   Sweet And Dandy/54-46 – The Maytals (Prod: Leslie Kong) (1970) [B SIDE
        IS 1968 REISSUE FROM PYRAMID LABEL]

7726   Sweet And Dandy (actually plays 'Scare Him')/54-46 – The Maytals (Prod:
        Leslie Kong) (1970) [DUPLICATE ISSUE. B SIDE IS 1968 REISSUE
        FROM PYRAMID LABEL]

7727 Suffering/Crazy Elephant – Revelation/The Megatons [The Rudies] (Prod: Larry Fallon/Graeme Walker) (1970)

7728 Eldora/If It's Not True – Techniques All Stars/The Techniques (actually by Techniques All Stars) (Prod: Winston Riley) (1970)

7729 Moon Dust/Fat Cat – Beverley's All Stars (actually by Ansel Collins) (Prod: Leslie Kong) (1970)

7730 High Voltage/Version 3 – Ansel Collins and Beverley's All Stars (Prod: Leslie Kong) (1970)

7730 Monkey (Version 1)/Monkey (Version 2) – Ansel Collins and Beverley's All Stars (Prod: Leslie Kong) (1970) [DUPLICATE ISSUE WHICH PLAYS IDENTICAL TRACKS BUT UNDER DIFFERENT TITLES]

7731 Squeeze Up (Part 1)/Squeeze Up (Part 2) – Byron Lee and The Dragonaires (Prod: Byron Lee) (1970)

7732 Strong Man/Sentimental – The Hot Rod All Stars (Prod: Hot Rod [Lambert Briscoe]) (1970)

7733 Virgin Soldier/Brixton Reggae Festival – The Hot Rod All Stars/The Setters (actually by The Hot Rod All Stars) (Prod: Hot Rod [Lambert Briscoe]) (1970)

7734 Down On The Farm/Easy Street – Freddie Notes and The Rudies (Prod: Graeme Walker) (1970)

7735 Barbwire/Calypso Mama – Nora Dean/The Barons (Prod: Byron Smith) (1970)

7736 Birth Control/Love At First Sight – Byron Lee and The Dragonaires (Prod: Byron Lee) (1970)

7737 I'm The One/Who's Gonna Be Your Man – Bruce Ruffin (Prod: Leslie Kong) (1970)

7738 That's What Love Will Do/This Time I Won't Hurt You – The Gaylads (Prod: Leslie Kong) (1970) [B SIDE REISSUED ON SUMMIT LABEL SUM 8521B]

7739 Driven Back/Trouble Deh A Bush – The Pioneers (Prod: Leslie Kong) (1970)

7740 Show Me The Way/The Monster – Delroy Wilson/Beverley's All Stars (actually with unidentified DJ) (Prod: Leslie Kong) (1970)

7741 Bla, Bla, Bla/Reborn – The Maytals (Prod: Leslie Kong) (1970)

7742 Maybe Now/So Much Love – Joe White (Prod: Leslie Kong) (1970)

7743 Young, Gifted And Black/Moon Glow – The Gaylads/Beverley's All Stars (Prod: Leslie Kong) (1970)

7744 Mayfair/Enoch Power – Millie (actually with Symarip) (Prod: Eddie Wolfram for Philligree) (1970)

7745 Suffering In The Land/Come Into My Life – Jimmy Cliff (Prod: Leslie Kong and Jimmy Cliff) (1970)

7746 Simmer Down Quashie/Caranapo – The Pioneers (Prod: Leslie Kong) (1970)

7747   Bond In Bliss/Musical Scorcher – Byron Lee and The Dragonaires (actually with Winston Wright) (Prod: Byron Lee) (1970) [A SIDE REISSUED ON HORSE HOSS 56B]

7748   Family Man/Mellow Mood – The Upsetters (Prod: Bruce Anthony) (1970) [B SIDE REISSUED ON TROJAN TR 7823B]

7749   Capo/Mama Look (Monkey Man) – The Upsetters (Prod: Bruce Anthony) (1970)

7750   Love Of The Common People/Compass – Nicky Thomas/The Destroyers (Prod: Joel Gibson [Joe Gibbs]) (1970) [REISSUED ON TROJAN TRO 9067A]

7751   Popcorn Funky Reggae (title actually seems to be 'Reggae Chicken')/My Love (Part 1) – Rita Alston/Nat Cole (actually with Rita Alston) (Prod: Nat Cole) (1970)

7752   All Kinds Of Everything/All Kinds Of Everything (Instrumental Version) – Peggy [McLarty] with The Cimarons/Carl Levy with The Cimarons (Prod: Hot Rod [Lambert Briscoe]) (1970)

7753   Dynamic Pressure/Reggae Me Dis, Reggae Me Dat – Boris Gardner (Prod: Byron Lee) (1970)

7754   Party Time, Part 1 (Honeymoon)/Party Time, Part 2 (Mr Cox) – Bim, Bam and Clover (Prod: Randy's) (1970)

7755   Feel Alright/Telstar – The Pyramids (Prod: Bruce Anthony) (1970)

7756   Freedom Street/Freedom Version – Ken Boothe/Beverley's All Stars (Prod: Leslie Kong) (1970)

7757   Water Melon/She's My Scorcher – The Maytals (Prod: Leslie Kong) (1970)

7758   Al Capone/Kaiser Bill – [Emperor] Rosko (Prod: M Columbier) (1970) [SOME COPIES ISSUED IN PICTURE SLEEVE]

7759   Soul Shakedown Party/Soul Shakedown Version 2 – Bob Marley and The Wailers/Beverley's All Stars (Prod: Leslie Kong) (1970) [A SIDE REISSUED ON TROJAN TR 7911A]

7760   Battle Of The Giants/Message From Maria – The Pioneers (Prod: Leslie Kong) (1970)

7761   Julianne/We Five – Byron Lee and The Dragonaires (Prod: Byron Lee) (1970) [SOME COPIES IN PICTURE SLEEVE]

7762   ABC Reggae/Be Yours – The Rockstones (actually by The Gaylads)/Beverley's All Stars (Prod: Leslie Kong) (1970)

7763   Tell The Children The Truth/Something Is Wrong Somewhere – The Gaylads (Prod: Leslie Kong) (1970)

7764   Come Rock It With Me/Say Darling Say – The Melodians (Prod: Leslie Kong) (1970)

7765   Satisfaction/Things A Get Bad To Worse – Carl Dawkins/The Ethiopians
       (Prod: Karl 'JJ' Johnson) (1970) [A SIDE ISSUED ON DUKE DU 62A AS
       'THIS WORLD AND ME']

7766   Susie Is Sorrow/Don't Go – Horace Faith/Derrick Pepper (actually by Junior
       Smith) (Prod: Philip Swern and Johnny Arthey/Roy [Junior] Smith) (1970)

7767   You Can Get It If You Really Want/Be Aware – Jimmy Cliff (Prod: John Kelly
       for N.R.E Ltd) (1970)

7768   I'm Going To Get There/Kinky, Funky Reggae – Joe White/Rupie Edwards'
       All Stars (Prod: Rupie Edwards) (1970)

7769   Gave You My Love/Love Version – Delroy Wilson/Beverley's All Stars (Prod:
       Leslie Kong) (1970)

7770   To Sir With Love/Reggae Shuffle – The Pyramids (Prod: Bruce Anthony) (1970)

7771   Soul Sister/Soul Version – The Gaylads/Beverley's All Stars (Prod: Leslie Kong)
       (1970)

7772   It's Gonna Take A Miracle/Now I Know – Ken Boothe (Prod: Leslie Kong)
       (1970) [B SIDE REISSUED ON SUMMIT SUM 8523B]

7773   Sweeter She Is/Fire Fire – The Charmers/The Charmers (Prod: Lloyd
       Charmers/Byron Lee) (1970)

7774   Leaving Rome/In The Nude – Jo Jo Bennett and Mudie's All Stars (Prod:
       Harry Mudie) (1970)

7775   Meshwire/Darling Please Return – Winston Wright and Tommy McCook
       (actually with The Supersonics)/The Barons (Prod: Byron Smith) (1970)

7776   Cecilia/Stand Up – Bruce Ruffin/Beverley's All Stars (Prod: Leslie Kong) (1970)

7777   You Can Get It If You Really Want/Perseverence – Desmond Dekker (Prod:
       Leslie Kong and John Kelly for N.R.E Ltd/Leslie Kong) (1970)

7778   Everything Is Beautiful/Give Up – The Rockstones (actually by BB Seaton)/
       Beverley's All Stars (Prod: BB Seaton) (1970) [UNISSUED – RELEASED
       ON SUMMIT LABEL SUM 8501]

7779   It's All In The Game/Easy Come – The Rebels (Prod: Sidney Crooks) (1970)
       [A SIDE ISSUED ON PAMA'S GAS LABEL WITH MARTIN RILEY
       CREDIT]

7780   Drums Of Freedom/Drum Version – Ken Boothe/Beverley's All Stars (Prod:
       Leslie Kong) (1970)

7781   Money Day/Ska Ba Doo – The Pioneers (Prod: Leslie Kong) (1970) [A SIDE
       REISSUED ON TROJAN TR 7968B AND TRO 7995B]

7782   It's All In The Game/Version 2 – The Gaylads/Beverley's All Stars (Prod: Leslie
       Kong) (1970)

7783   ISSUED ON SUMMIT 8505

7784   NYT

7785   NYT

7786　Dr Lester/Sun, Moon And Stars – The Maytals (Prod: Leslie Kong) (1970)

7787　This Little Light/Lover – Ray Martell with The Cimarons and The Reactions/Ray Martell and The Cimarons (Prod: Al Barry and Philigree/Philigree) (1970)

7788　Oh Me Oh My/I Did It – Lloyd Charmers (Prod: Lloyd Charmers) (1970)

7789　NYT

7790　Black Pearl/Help Me Help Myself – Horace Faith (Prod: Philip Swern and Johnny Arthey for Pinpoint Record Productions/Philip Swern and Johnny Arthey) (1970)

7791　Montego Bay/Blue Mountain – Freddie Notes and The Rudies/The Rudies (Prod: Grape) (1970)

7792　Salt Of The Earth/Name Ring A Bell – The Cables (Prod: Harry Johnson) (1970)

7793　What Greater Love/Lady Love – Teddy Brown (Prod: Philip Swern and Johnny Arthey for Pinpoint Record Productions) (1970)

7794　Shamay Dray/Here – Draycopp (Prod: Best Production) (1970)

7795　I Need Your Sweet Inspiration/Everything Nice – The Pioneers (Prod: Leslie Kong) (1970)

7796　God Bless The Children/Red Eye – Nicky Thomas (Prod: Joel Gibson [Joe Gibbs]) (1970)

7797　Dancing In The Sun/Chick-a-Bow – Daniel In The Lion's Den (actually Carl Douglas and The Rudies)/The Lion's Den (actually The Rudies) (Prod: Des Bryan, Webster Shrowder and Joe Sinclair) (1970) [B SIDE REISSUED ON TROJAN TR 7866B]

7798　Patches/The Split – The Rudies (actually with Carl Douglas)/The Rudies (Prod: Swan) (1970)

7799　Fire And Rain/Cold And Lonely Night – The Gaylads (Prod: Leslie Kong) (1970)

7800　Take A Letter Maria/You're Coming Back – Dandy (Prod: Dandy) (1970) [A SIDE REISSUED ON TROJAN TRO 7994A]

7801　Honey Hush/Sunday Morning – Millie (Prod: Jimmy Cliff/Eddie Wolfram) (1970)

7802　The Song We Used To Sing/Get Up Little Suzie – Desmond Dekker (Prod: Leslie Kong and Jimmy Cliff/Leslie Kong and Warwick Lyn) (1970)

7803　All For You/All For You Part 2 (Instrumental) – The Pyramids (Prod: Bruce Anthony) (1971)

7804　You Got Me/2001 – Miller James (Prod: Philip Swern and Johnny Arthey for Pinpoint Record Productions) (1970) [DEMO COPIES IN TROJAN 'POP' SERIES]

7805 Stepping Out In The Lights/Beats There A Heart – Paul Tracy (Prod: Philip Swern and Johnny Arthey for Pinpoint Record Productions) (1970) [IN TROJAN 'POP' SERIES]

7806 Help Yourself/Why – Jimmy James and The Vagabonds (Prod: Phil Wainman for New Dawn Productions) (1970)

7807 If I Had A Hammer/Lonely Feelin' (actually titled 'No Sugar Tonight') – Nicky Thomas (Prod: Joel Gibson [Joe Gibbs]) (1970)

7808 54-46 Was My Number/54-46 Version 2 – The Maytals/Beverley's All Stars (Prod: Leslie Kong) (1970) [A SIDE IS NOT 1968 VERSION]

7809 Green Green Valley/Peace Of Mind (actually 'Peace In Your Mind') – Bob Andy (Prod: Clive Crawley/Harry Johnson) (1971) [B SIDE ALSO ISSUED ON HARRY J HJ 6612A]

7810 Walk A Mile In My Shoes/Reggae Rouser – Freddie Notes' Unity/Johnny Arthey's Reggae Strings (Prod: Philip Swern and Johnny Arthey for Pinpoint Record Productions) (1971)

7811 Rose Garden/Happiness Hasn't Hit Helen – Teddy Brown (Prod: Philip Swern and Johnny Arthey for Pinpoint Record Productions) (1971)

7812 Young, Gifted And Black (Bob [Andy] and Marcia [Griffiths])/Peace In Your Mind (Bob Andy)/Green Green Valley (Bob Andy)/We've Got To Get Ourselves Together (Bob [Andy] and Marcia [Griffiths]) (Prod: Harry Johnson/Harry Johnson/Clive Crawley/Harry Johnson) (1971) [EXTENDED PLAY IN PICTURE SLEEVE]

7813 Down In The Boondocks/Baby Make Out – Delroy Williams (Prod: Philip Swern and Johnny Arthey for Pinpoint Record Productions) (1971)

7814 Rain/Off Limits – Bruce Ruffin/Bruce Ruffin (actually by The Aquarians) (Prod: Herman Chin-Loy) (1971)

7814 Rain/Geronimo – Bruce Ruffin/Bruce Ruffin (actually by The Pyramids) (Prod: Herman Chin-Loy/Bruce Anthony) (1971) [SECOND PRESSING. B SIDE REISSUED FROM DUKE LABEL DU 80A]

7814 Rain/Stingo – Bruce Ruffin/Bruce Ruffin (actually by The Pyramids) (Prod: Herman Chin-Loy/Bruce Anthony) (1971) [THIRD PRESSING]

7815 Stand By Your Man/Credit Squeeze (aka 'Time Is Dread') – Merlene Webber/Clancy Eccles (Prod: Clancy Eccles) (1971)

7816 Same Old Fashioned Way/Out Of Many, One People – Dandy (Prod: R Thompson [Dandy]) (1971)

7817 I Shall Sing/Target (actually 'Musical Fight') – Jean (actually Judy Mowatt) and The Gaytones/The Gaytones (actually by The Crashers) (Prod: Sonia Pottinger) (1971) [A SIDE REISSUED ON HORSE HOSS 42A. B SIDE REISSUED FROM HIGH NOTE HS 037A]

7818 Pied Piper/Save Me – Bob [Andy] and Marcia [Griffiths] (Prod: Bob Andy) (1971)

7819 Thinking Of You/Thinking Of You Version – The Blues Busters/Byron Lee and The Dragonaires (Prod: Byron Lee) [UNISSUED – A SIDE ISSUED ON DYNAMIC DYN 408B INSTEAD]

7820 Black And White/Sand In Your Shoes – Greyhound (Prod: Dave Bloxham) (1971)

7821 One Woman/Save Me Version – Bob Andy/Bob Andy Band (Prod: Bob Andy) (1971) [A SIDE RESISSUED ON TROJAN TR 7840A AND HORSE HOSS 31A]

7822 Growing Up/Lovitis – Fabulous Flames (Prod: Clancy Eccles) (1971)

7823 Funky Strip/Mellow Mood – Charlie Boy (actually by Herman Chin-Loy)/ The Upsetters (Prod: Herman Chin-Loy and Dave Bloxham/Bruce Anthony) (1971) [B SIDE REISSUED FROM TROJAN TR 7748B]

7824 Mule Train/Mule Train Version – Count Prince Miller (Prod: Jackie Edwards) (1971)

7825 Let Your Yeah Be Yeah/More Love – The Pioneers (Prod: Jimmy Cliff and Sidney Crooks) (1971) [PROMO COPIES HAVE A SIDE ON BOTH SIDES]

7826 It's Too Late To Say That You're Sorry/Slow Rock – Laurel Aitken (Prod: Laurel Aitken) (1971) [EARLY PRESSINGS CREDIT A SIDE AS JUST 'IT'S TOO LATE']

7827 Walk The World Away/Senorita Rita – Teddy Brown (Prod: Philip Swern and Johnny Arthey for Pinpoint Record Productions) (1971)

7828 Salt Of The Earth/Salt Rock – Dandy/Dandy (actually by Ansel Collins) (Prod: R Thompson [Dandy]) (1971)

7829 NYT

7830 Tell It Like It Is/BBC – Nicky Thomas (Prod: Nicky Thomas) (1971)

7831 Hot Honolulu Night/Come Back Jane – Monsoon (Prod: Tic-Toc Music and Eddie Seago) (1971)

7832 One Big Happy Family/Heaven Child – Bruce Ruffin (Prod: Bruce Anthony) (1971)

7833 In Paradise/Take Me As I Am – Jackie Edwards and Julie Ann (actually Judy Mowatt)/Jackie Edwards (Prod: Edward 'Bunny' Lee) (1971)

7834 Follow The Leader/Funky Jamaica – Greyhound (Prod: Dave Bloxham) (1971)

7835 Jamaica/Sea Wave – Honey Boy/The Itals [The Cimarons] (Prod: Des Bryan and Webster Shrowder) (1971)

7836 Come On Girl/So Many Ways – Jackie Edwards (Prod: Count Prince Miller) (1971)

7837 Help Me Make It Through The Night/Reconsider Our Love – Joyce Bond (Prod: R Thompson-Mulby [Dandy]) (1971)

7838 Call Me Number One/Gypsy – The Aces (Prod: Barry Howard and Carl Blake [Carl Hall]) (1971)

7839 The Birds And The Bees/My Family – The Daytrippers (Prod: Santa Ponsa) (1971)

7840 One Woman/No Second Hand Love – Bob Andy (Prod: Bob Andy and Clive Crawley/Bob Andy) [REISSUED FROM TROJAN TR 7821A AND REISSUED ON HORSE HOSS 31A]

7841 NYT

7842 Hysteriacide/One Dream – Count Prince Miller (Prod: Count Prince Miller) (1971)

7843 NYT

7844 ISSUED ON TR 7876

7845 Those Good, Good Old Days/Pack Up Hang-ups – Jimmy Cliff (Prod: Jimmy Cliff) (1971)

7846 Give And Take/Pride And Passion – The Pioneers (Prod: Jimmy Cliff) (1971)

7847 Licking Stick/Live And Learn – Desmond Dekker (Prod: Leslie Kong and Desmond Dekker) (1971)

7848 Moon River/The Pressure Is Coming On – Greyhound (Prod: Dave Bloxham) (1971) [SINGLE-SIDED TEST PRESSING ON BLANK LABEL ONLY]

7848 Moon River/I've Been Trying/The Pressure Is Coming On – Greyhound (Prod: Dave Bloxham) (1971) [PRESSED AS TROJAN MAXI-SINGLE AND ON STANDARD BROWN 'SHIELD' LABEL. SOME COPIES IN PICTURE SLEEVE]

7849 Johnny Cool Man/Johnny Cool Man (Version) – The Maytals/Beverley's All Stars (Prod: Leslie Kong) (1971)

7850 Yesterday Man/I Can't Stand It – Nicky Thomas (Prod: Nicky Thomas and Clive Crawley/Nicky Thomas) (1972)

7851 Sex Machine/You Left And Gone – Dave Barker and The Aggrovators (Prod: Edward 'Bunny' Lee) (1971) [UNISSUED]

7852 Mother And Child Reunion/Corner Hop (aka 'Sweet Mademoiselle') – The Uniques (actually The Pioneers with The Cimarons)/The Uniques (actually by The Dynamites) (Prod: Bush/Clancy Eccles) (1972) [B SIDE REISSUED FROM GRAPE GR 3022A]

7853 I Am What I Am/Sky High – Greyhound (Prod: Dave Bloxham) (1972) [REISSUED ON TROJAN TR 7927]

7854   But I Do/I Don't Care – Bob [Andy] and Marcia [Griffiths] (Prod: Bob Andy/
       Bob Andy and Clive Crawley) (1972)

7855   You Don't Know Like I Know/Sometimes I'm Lonely – The Pioneers (Prod:
       Clive Crawley/Leslie Kong) (1972)

7856   For Your Precious Love/For Your Precious Love (Version) – Vic Taylor/Byron
       Lee and The Dragonaires (Prod: Dynamic Sounds) (1972)

7857   What Do You Wanna Make Those Eyes Eyes At Me For?/Suzanne Beware
       Of The Devil – Dandy (Prod: R Thompson [Dandy]) (1972) [FIRST
       PRESSING – WITHDRAWN]

7857   What Do You Wanna Make Those Eyes Eyes At Me For?/Talking About Sally
       – Dandy (Prod: R Thompson [Dandy]) (1972) [SECOND PRESSING]

7858   Just Because/Yes I Will – Danny Ray (Prod: Jackie Edwards) (1972) [A SIDE
       REISSUED ON TROJAN TRO 7993B]

7859   Pitta Patta/Litchfield Gardens – Ernie Smith (Prod: Federal Records) (1972)

7860   Roll Muddy River/Auntie Roachi – The Pioneers (Prod: Clive Crawley) (1972)

7861   I'll Take You There/Tropical Lament – The Deltones (Prod: Des Bryan,
       Webster Shrowder and Joe Sinclair) (1972)

7862   Suzanne Beware Of The Devil/Doing The Moonwalk – Nicky Thomas (Prod:
       Shady Tree [Dandy]/ Joel Gibson [Joe Gibbs]) (1972) [B SIDE ALSO ISSUED
       ON HORSE HOSS 29B]

7863   Star Trek/Concord – The Vulcans/The Vulcans (actually by The Prophets) (Prod:
       Bush) (1972) [B SIDE REISSUED FROM BIG SHOT BI 550B. SOME
       COPIES PLAY 'BACK A YARD' BY THE DELTONES ON B SIDE]

7864   Ebony Eyes/Version – The Chosen Few (Prod: Derrick Harriott) (1972)

7865   Louie Louie/Pressure Drop '72 – The Maytals (Prod: Chris Blackwell and
       Warwick Lyn) (1972)

7866   Lonely For Your Love/Chick A Bow – The Uniques [The Pioneers]/The
       Lion's Den (Prod: Bush) (1972) [B SIDE REISSUED FROM TROJAN TR
       7797B AND TR 7866B]

7867   Floating/I Troubles – Greyhound (Prod: Dave Bloxham) (1972)

7868   Come On Over To My Place/I'll Be Standing By – Jackie Robinson (Prod:
       Sidney Crooks) (1972)

7869   The World Needs Love/Destiny – The Pioneers (Prod: Sidney Crooks and
       Clive Crawley) (1972)

7870   Sugarloaf Hill/Baby Don't Wake Me – Del Davis (Prod: Clarence P Miller
       [Count Prince Miller]/Jackie Edwards (1972) [B SIDE REISSUED FROM
       BREAD BR 1105A]

7871   Julie On My Mind/Miss Black And Beautiful – Danny Ray (Prod: Jackie
       Edwards) (1972)

7872 Then He Kissed Me/All The Day Long – The Marvels (Prod: Clive Crawley)
(1972)

7873 Working On It Night And Day/Take A Look – The Aces (Prod: C Blake [Carl
Hall] And Barry Howard [Al Barry]) (1972)

7874 Pomps And Pride/Pomps And Pride (Part 2) – The Maytals (Prod: Dynamic
Sounds) (1972)

7875 Shocks Of Mighty/Monkey Spanner (Version) – Dave Barker and The
Upsetters/Dave [Barker] and Ansel Collins (Prod: Lee Perry/Winston Riley)
(1972) [A SIDE REISSUED FROM UPSETTER US 331A. B SIDE
REISSUED FROM TECHNIQUES TE 914B]

7876 It Gotta Be So/The First Time, For A Long Time – Desmond Dekker (Prod:
Shady Tree [Dandy] (1973)

7877 NYT

7878 Images Of You/I'll Be Waiting – Nicky Thomas (Prod: Joel Gibson [Joe
Gibbs]/Nicky Thomas) (1972) [UNISSUED. A SIDE ISSUED ON HORSE
HOSS 29A AND B SIDE ISSUED ON TROJAN TR 7885B]

7879 Time Hard/Fall In Love – George Dekker/Sidney, George and Jackie [The
Pioneers] (Prod: Sidney Crooks and Clive Crawley/Sidney Crooks) (1972)

7880 I Believe In Love/Habit – The Pioneers (Prod: Sidney Crooks and Clive Crawley/
Sidney Crooks) (1972) [PROMO COPIES EXIST WITH A SIDE ONLY]

7881 Reggae Christmas/Candy Man – The Gable Hall School Choir (Prod: John
Arthur [Johnny Arthey] for A.J.A Productions) (1972) [REISSUED ON
TROJAN TR 7943]

7882 Everybody Plays The Fool/You're A Big Girl Now – The Chosen Few (Prod:
Derrick Harriott) (1972) [B SIDE ALSO ISSUED ON GRAPE GR 3033A]

7883 White Christmas/My Love And I – Jackie Edwards (Prod: Jackie Edwards)
(1972) [PROMO COPIES HAVE A SIDE ON BOTH SIDES. REISSUE
FROM 1965]

7884 Hat Trick (actually 'Hot Trick')/Wet Vision – U Roy (Prod: Edward 'Bunny'
Lee) (1972)

7885 Have A Little Faith/I'll Be Waiting – Nicky Thomas (Prod: Joel Gibson [Joe
Gibbs]/Nicky Thomas) (1973) [B SIDE REISSUED FROM TROJAN TR
7878B AND REISSUED ON TRO 9026B AND HORSE HOSS 55B.
PROMO COPIES HAVE A SIDE ON BOTH SIDES]

7886 Nice Nice Time/Nice Nice Time Version – Zap Pow (Prod: Harry Johnson)
(1973) [PROMO COPIES HAVE A SIDE ON BOTH SIDES]

7887 Groovy Situation/The Loser – Derrick Harriott (Prod: Derrick Harriott)
(1973) [A SIDE REISSUED FROM SONG BIRD LABEL SB 1042A. B
SIDE IS REISSUE FROM 1967. PROMO COPIES PLAY A SIDE ON
BOTH SIDES]

7888   At The Discothèque/Step By Step – The Pioneers (Prod: Sidney Crooks, George Dekker and Jackie Robinson [The Pioneers]) (1973)

7889   What About You?/Come Beside Me – Pat Rhoden (Prod: Pat Rhoden) (1973)

7890   Check Out Yourself/Happy People – The Cimarons (Prod: R Thompson [Dandy] and Joe Sinclair/Joe Sinclair and Webster Shrowder) (1973)

7891   Ton-up Kids/Bandwagon – Dave [Barker] and Ansel Collins (Prod: Larry Lawrence) (1973)

7892   You Can't Buy My Love/The First Cut Is The Deepest – Donna Dawson [Ornell Hinds] (Prod: Sidney Crooks, George Dekker and Jackie Robinson [The Pioneers]) (1973)

7893   Is It Because I'm Black?/Black, Gold And Green – Ken Boothe (Prod: Lloyd Charmers) (1973) [REISSUED ON TROJAN TRO 9052B]

7894   Am I Black Enough For You?/Message From A Blackman – The Chosen Few/ The Chosen Few (actually with Derrick Harriott) (Prod: Derrick Harriott) (1973) [B SIDE IS REISSUE FROM SONG BIRD LABEL SB 1028A]

7895   Theme From 'Peyton Place'/Do What You Wanna Do – Jackie Edwards and The Now Generation/Jackie Edwards (Prod: Jackie Edwards) (1973)

7896   Keep Your Mouth Shut/Move Away – George Dekker/George Dekker Band (Prod: Sidney Crooks) (1973)

7897   Bad To Be Good/Smoking – The Pioneers (Prod: Sidney Crooks, George Dekker and Jackie Robinson [The Pioneers]) (1973)

7898   ISSUED ON TR 7899

7899   Big One/Oh She Is A Big Girl Now – Judge Dread (Prod: Des Bryan, Webster Shrowder and Joe Sinclair) (1973) [A AND B SIDES LATER FLIPPED]

7900   Way Over Yonder/Way Over Yonder (Version) – Judy Mowatt/Judy Mowatt (actually by The Gaytones) (Prod: Sonia Pottinger) (1973)

7901   The Whole World's Down On Me/For The Good Times – BB Seaton/Mikie Chung and The Now Generation (Prod: Lloyd Charmers) (1973)

7902   Reggae From The Ghetto/I'll Light Your Fire – John Holt (Prod: Mike Berry) (1973)

7903   I'm Gonna Get Married/How Can I Control You? – Danny Ray (Prod: Jackie Edwards) (1973)

7904   He's Got The Whole World In His Hands/Got To Get Away – The Marvels (Prod: Shady Tree [Dandy]) (1973)

7905   Molly/Dr Kitch – Judge Dread (Prod: Joe Sinclair) (1973) [PROMO COPIES HAVE A SIDE ON BOTH SIDES]

7906   A Little Bit Of Soap/Hit Me With Music – The Pioneers (Prod: Sidney Crooks, George Dekker and Jackie Robinson [The Pioneers]) (1973) [A SIDE REISSUED ON TROJAN TRO 9041A]

7907 Let's Get It On/Mother Mary – Ken Boothe/Lloyd Charmers (Prod: Lloyd
      Charmers) (1973)

7908 Pardon/Rub It Up – George Dekker (Prod: Sidney Crooks/Sidney Crooks,
      George Dekker and Jackie Robinson [The Pioneers]) (1974)

7909 Help Me Make It Through The Night/Tell Me Why – John Holt (Prod:
      Tony Ashfield) (1974) [SOME COPIES IN PICTURE SLEEVE AND
      PROMOTED AS DOUBLE A SIDE]

7910 It's The Way Nature Planned It/It's The Way Nature Planned It (Part 2) – Ken
      Boothe/The Charmers (Prod: Lloyd Charmers) (1974) [A SIDE REISSUED
      ON TROJAN TR 7960A]

7911 Soul Shakedown Party/Caution – Bob Marley and The Wailers (Prod: Leslie
      Kong) (1974) [A SIDE REISSUED FROM TR 7759A. B SIDE REISSUED
      FROM SUMMIT SUM 8526B]

7912 Emergency Call/Emergency Call Version – Judy Mowatt/Judy Mowatt
      (actually by The Gaytones) (Prod: Sonia Pottinger) (1974) [REISSUED
      FROM GAYFEET GS 207]

7913 I'm Gonna Knock On Your Door/Some Living, Some Dying – The Pioneers
      (Prod: Sidney Crooks) (1974)

7914 The Lord's Prayer/As Far As I'm Concerned – Annetta Jackson and Bobby
      Stephen (actually Ornell Hinds and Bobby Davis)/Des All Stars (Prod: Des
      Bryan and Webster Shrowder) (1974)

7915 Here I Am Baby/Tit For Tat – Al Brown and Skin, Flesh and Bones/Skin,
      Flesh and Bones (Prod: Dickie Wong) (1974)

7916 Play Me/Play Me (Version) – Marcia Griffiths/Lloyd Charmers (Prod: Lloyd
      Charmers) (1974)

7917 Ain't It A Beautiful Morning/Make Me Your Number One – Danny Ray
      (Prod: Shady Tree [Dandy]) (1974)

7918 You're My Future Wife/Do You Believe In Love? – Jackie Edwards (Prod:
      Jackie Edwards) (1974)

7919 Over The Rainbow/We Are Not The Same – The Cimarons (Prod: The
      Cimarons and Webster Shrowder) (1974) [A SIDE REISSUED ON TR 9038B]

7920 Everything I Own/Drum Song – Ken Boothe/Ken Boothe (actually by Willie
      Lindo and Charmers' Big Band) (Prod: Lloyd Charmers) (1974)

7921 Get On Your Feet/Love Is Here – The Marvels (Prod: Shady Tree [Dandy])
      (1974)

7922 If You're Ready, Come Go With Me/Parks' Version – Cynthia Richards/
      Cynthia Richards (actually by We The People Band) (Prod: Lloyd Parks) (1974)

7923 Honey Bee/Hot Blooded Man – The Pioneers (Prod: Sidney Crooks and
      Eddy Grant/Sidney Crooks) (1974) [TROJAN BLUE LABEL. PROMO
      COPIES HAVE A SIDE ON BOTH SIDES]

7924   I'd Love You To Want Me/I'm Dying For You – Ernie Smith (Prod: Jerome
        Francisque/Ernie Smith) (1974)

7925   Young, Gifted And Black/We Know – Bob [Andy] and Marcia [Griffiths]
        (Prod: Harry Johnson/Bob Andy) (1974) [REISSUED FROM HARRY J
        LABEL HJ 6605A. PROMO COPIES HAVE A SIDE ON BOTH SIDES]

7926   Mr Brown/Dracula – Bob Marley and The Wailers/The Upsetters (Prod: Lee
        Perry (1974) [BOTH SIDES REISSUED FROM UPSETTER LABEL US
        354. A SIDE REISSUED ON TROJAN TR 7979A. SOME COPIES PLAY
        'MR BROWN –VERSION' ON B SIDE]

7927   I Am What I Am/Sky High – Greyhound (Prod: Dave Bloxham) (1974)
        [REISSUED FROM TROJAN TR 7853]

7928   Back On The Scene/Newsboy – Junior English (Prod: Ellis Breary) (1974)

7929   Only A Child/Love Thy Neighbour – Nicky Thomas (Prod: Carlton Troutt/
        Nicky Thomas) (1974)

7930   You Can Get It If You Really Want/Reggae Time – The Cimarons (Prod:
        Trojan/The Cimarons) (1974)

7931   Jamaica Jerk-Off/Grandma Grandpa – The Pioneers (Prod: Sidney Crooks)
        (1974) [PROMOTED AS DOUBLE A SIDE]

7932   NYT

7933   You Make Me Feel Brand New/T.S.O.P – The Inner Circle (Prod: Tommy
        Cowan) (1974)

7934   Play De Music/Version – Tinga Stewart (Prod: Ernie Smith) (1974)

7935   I've Got To Go On Without You/I've Got To Go On Without You
        (Instrumental) – Al Brown/Skin, Flesh and Bones (Prod: Dickie Wong) (1974)

7936   Play Me/Going In Circles – Marcia [Griffiths] and Lloyd [Charmers]/
        Charmers' Band (actually by Bobby Blue [Bobby Davis]) (1974) [B SIDE
        REISSUED FROM DUKE DU 86A]

7937   Passing Strangers/Pick Yourself Up – The Marvels (Prod: R D Livingstone
        [Dandy]) (1974)

7938   Morning Side Of The Mountain/Riding My Bicycle – Danny Ray (Prod:
        Shady Tree [Dandy]) (1974)

7939   Sweet Number One/Tall Oak Tree – The Pioneers (Prod: Sidney Crooks)
        (1974)

7940   Everybody Plays The Fool/Hard Feeling (actually 'Time Is Hard (Part 2)')
        – The Chosen Few/The Chosen Few (actually by The Crystalites) (Prod:
        Derrick Harriott) (1974) [A SIDE REISSUED FROM TR 7882A. B SIDE
        REISSUED FROM SONG BIRD SB 1031B]

7941   This Is Reggae Music/Break Down The Barriers (Prod: Harry Johnson and
        Chris Blackwell) (1974)

7942 Code Of Love/I'm Lonely No More – Teddy Brown (Prod: Sidney Crooks) (1974)

7943 Reggae Christmas/Candy Man – The Gable Hall School Choir (Prod: John Arthur [Johnny Arthey] for A.J.A Productions) (1974) [REISSUED FROM TROJAN TR 7881]

7944 Crying Over You/Now You Can See Me Again (When Will I See You Again) – Ken Boothe (Prod: Lloyd Charmers) (1974)

7945 A Lover's Question/A Lover's Question (Question Sign) – Lloyd Charmers (Prod: Lloyd Charmers) (1974)

7946 Oh My My/Puppet And Clown – Winston Groovy (Prod: Sidney Crooks) (1974)

7947 Lola/Mama's Song – Nicky Thomas (Prod: Nicky Thomas/Joel Gibson [Joe Gibbs]) (1974) [B SIDE IS REISSUE FROM 1970]

7948 Road Block/Forward Jah Jah Children – Inner Circle (Prod: Tommy Cowan) (1975)

7949 Al Capone/Anna – Emperor Rosko/The Main Men (probably The Cimarons) (Prod: Alted [Judge Dread]) (1975) [REISSUED ON TR 9059]

7950 Got To Have You Baby/Got To Have You Baby (Part 2) – Lord Tanamo (Prod: Joseph Gordon [Lord Tanamo]) (1975)

7951 Bend Down Low/Sinner Man – Gregory Isaacs (Prod: Anna and Sidney Crooks) (1975)

7952 All For Jesus/Super Version – Ernie Smith (Prod: Richard Khouri and Ernie Smith for Federal Records) (1975)

7953 You Baby/Open The Door – John Holt (Prod: Tony Ashfield) (1975)

7954 Why Seek More/Why Seek More (Instrumental) – Dennis Brown/Dennis Brown (actually by The Observers) (Prod: Winston Holness [Niney]) (1975)

7955 I'm A Changed Man/I'm A Changed Man (Instrumental) – BB Seaton (Lloyd Charmers) (1975)

7956 Ram Goat Liver/Ram Goat Liver (Instrumental) – Pluto Shervington (Prod: XYZ/Togetherness Production) (1975) [REISSUED ON TROJAN TR 7978 AND TRO 9066]

7957 Midnight Train To Georgia/We Really Need Each Other – Teddy Brown (Prod: Steve Edgley and Phil Denys) (1975)

7958 Words (Are Impossible)/Bad Words – Cynthia [Schloss]/Now Generation All Stars (Prod: Winston Blake) (1975)

7959 Your Kiss Is Sweet/Judgement – Inner Circle (Prod: Tommy Cowan) (1975)

7960 It's The Way Nature Planned It/Sad And Lonely – Ken Boothe (Prod: Lloyd Charmers) (1975) [A SIDE REISSUED FROM TROJAN TR 7910A]

7961 Touch Me Baby/Gambling Ain't No Good – The Marvels (Prod: R D Livingstone and Shady Tree [Dandy]) (1975)

7962   I See You/Rainbow – Funky Brown (Prod: Paul Khouri for Federal Records) (1975)

7963   Key Card/Key Card (Instrumental) – Ernie Smith (Prod: Richard Khouri for Federal Records) (1975) [A SIDE REISSUED ON TR 9048B]

7964   Time Is Master Of Man/Read The News – Tito Simon (Prod: Keith Foster [Tito Simon]/Clancy Eccles) (1975) [B SIDE REISSUED ON TROJAN TRO 9002B AND ALSO ISSUED ON HORSE HOSS 125B]

7965   Can't Get Used To Losing You/Jane Anne – Danny Ray (Prod: Dandy and Shady Tree) (1975) [PROBABLY UNISSUED. A SIDE ISSUED ON TROJAN TRO 7993A]

7966   Let Go/Let Go (Instrumental) – Ken Boothe/C.H.A.R.M (Prod: Lloyd Charmers) (1975)

7967   For Your Love/For Your Love (Version) – Cynthia Richards (Prod: Cynthia Richards) (1975) [UNISSUED]

7968   Long Shot Kick The Bucket/Money Day – The Pioneers (Prod: Leslie Kong) (1975) [A SIDE REISSUED FROM TROJAN TR 672A AND REISSUED ON TRO 9063A. B SIDE REISSUED FROM TROJAN TR 7781A AND REISSUED ON TR 7968B AND TRO 7995B]

7969   Shaving Cream/Cream – Fabulous Five Inc. (Prod: Rahtid) (1975) [REISSUED ON TROJAN TRO 9047]

7970   Being In Love/I Told You So – Derrick Harriott/The Crystalites (Prod: Derrick Harriott) (1975) [A SIDE REISSUED FROM SONG BIRD SB 1078]

7971   Help Me/Running Over – Freddy McKay and Dansak (Prod: Sonny Binns and Trevor Starr) (1975)

7972   Wolf In Sheep's Clothing/Wolf Run (Version) – Big Youth (Prod: Manley Buchanan [Big Youth]) (1975)

7973   Eighteen With A Bullet/Eighteen With A Bullet (Version) – Derrick Harriott (Prod: Derrick Harriott) (1975)

7974   Baby Hang Up The Phone/I'll Be A Man – Lloyd Parks (Prod: Lloyd Parks) (1975) [B SIDE REISSUED FROM HARRY J HJ 6603B AND REISSUED ON TR 7985B]

7975   I'd Love You To Want Me/Morning Of My Life – John Holt (Prod: Tony Ashfield) (1976) [BOTH SIDES REISSUED FROM 1973]

7976   Run Johnny/Run Johnny (Version) – Lorna Bennett (Prod: Harry Johnson) (1976)

7977   Hit The Road Jack/Hit The Road Jack (Version) – Big Youth (Prod: Manley Buchanan [Big Youth]) (1976)

7978   Ram Goat Liver/Ram Goat Liver (Instrumental) – Pluto Shervington (Prod: XYZ/Togetherness Production) (1976) [REISSUED FROM TROJAN TR 7956 AND REISSUED ON TRO 9066]

7979 Mr Brown/Trenchtown Rock – Bob Marley and The Wailers (Prod: Lee Perry/Bob Marley) (1976) [A SIDE REISSUED FROM UPSETTER US 354A AND TROJAN TR 7926A. B SIDE REISSUED FROM GREEN DOOR GD 4005A]

7980 Ramblin' Man/Live The Life You Love – Gene Rondo (Prod: Keith Bonsoir) (1976)

7981 Why Do Fools Fall In Love/Dancing The Reggae – Derrick Harriott (Prod: Derrick Harriott) (1976) [A SIDE REISSUED FROM HARRY J LABEL HJ 6671]

7982 Ma Ma, Pa Pa/Manuel Road – Soul Syndicate (Prod: Harry Johnson) (1976)

7983 Wild Honey/If You Don't Know Me By Now – Zap Pow (Prod: Harry Johnson) (1976)

7984 Laugh And Grow Fat/I Like The Way (You Kiss And Hug Me) – Winston Groovy (Prod: Winston Groovy and Tony Hatch) (1976)

7985 The Wonder Of You/I'll Be Your Man – Lloyd Parks (Prod: Lloyd Parks) (1976) [B SIDE REISSUED FROM HARRY J HJ 6603B AND TR 7974B]

7986 Way Of Loving/Sweet Lorraine – Lloyd Miller (Prod: Lloyd Miller and Steve Wadey) (1976) [B SIDE REISSUED ON TR 9045B]

TROJAN (TRO SERIES – PREFIX TRO)

7987 I'll Take A Melody/Peace And Love – John Holt (Prod: John Holt and Keith Bonsoir/Keith Bonsoir and Tony Ashfield) (1976)

7988 What's Going On/Ten Against One – Big Youth (Prod: Manley Buchanan) (1976)

7989 Reverand Lee/The Other Woman – Lorna Bennett (Prod: Harry Johnson) (1976)

7990 Love Me For A Reason/Married Lady – Fab Five Inc. [Fabulous Five] (Prod: Fab Five) (1976) [A SIDE REISSUED ON TROJAN TRO 9047B]

7991 You'll Never Find Another Love Like Mine/Mr Bojangles – John Holt (Prod: Edward 'Bunny' Lee/Tony Ashfield) (1976)

7992 Jah Bring I Joy/Joyful Dub – Bobby Melody/Mighty Two (Prod: Joel Gibson [Joe Gibbs]) (1976)

7993 Can't Get Used To Losing You/Just Because – Danny Ray (Prod: Dandy and Shady Tree/Jackie Edwards) (1976) [A SIDE REISSUED FROM TROJAN TR 7965A. B SIDE REISSUED FROM TROJAN TR 7858A]

7994 Take A Letter Maria/Make Me Number One – Dandy (Prod: Dandy) (1976) [A SIDE REISSUED FROM TROJAN TR 7800A]

7995 My Special Prayer/Money Day – The Pioneers (Prod: Sidney Crooks) (1977) [B SIDE REISSUED FROM TROJAN TR 7781A AND TR 7968B]

7996   Run Away Pet/Version – Donna Hinds (Prod: Heavy Stone [Dandy]) (1977)

7997   NYT

7998   London/What Love Is – Nicky Thomas (Prod: Nicky Thomas) (1976)

7999   Soulful Lover Baby/Version – Floyd Lloyd [Seivreight] (Prod: Floyd Lloyd
        Seivreight and Harris [BB] Seaton) (1977)

TROJAN (TR 9000 SERIES)

9000   Heavy Manners/Version – Prince Far I (Prod: Joel Gibson [Joe Gibbs]) (1977)
        [ON LIGHTNING LABEL]

9001   Jah Jah Ital/Instrumental – Diego [Bobby Davis] and The Sons Of Jah (Prod:
        Trevor Starr and Bobby Davis) (1977)

9002   Oh Patricia/Read The News – Tito Simon (Prod: Tito Simon/Clancy Eccles)
        (1977) [REISSUED FROM HORSE HOSS 125. B SIDE ALSO ISSUED
        ON TROJAN TR 7964B]

9003   Silver Words/Speak Softly Love – Ken Boothe (Prod: Winston Holness
        [Niney]/Lloyd Charmers) (1977) [A SIDE REISSUED FROM GREEN
        DOOR GD 4053A]

9004   NYT

9005   Keep It Like It Is/Fattie Bum Bum Gone To Jail (actually 'Fattie Bum Bum
        Gone To Jail (Version)') – Louisa Marks/Laurel Aitken (actually with The
        Trojans) (Prod: Clement Bushay/Laurel Aitken) (1977) [B SIDE REISSUED
        FROM HORSE LABEL HOSS 111B]

9006   Bonanza Ska/Napoleon Solo – Carlos Malcolm and His Afro-Jamaican
        Rhythm/Lyn Taitt and The Jets (Prod: Carlos Malcolm/Federal Records)
        (1977) [REISSUES FROM 1966 AND 1967 RESPECTIVELY]

9007   Why Must You Cry/I Say Super Jaws (Instrumental) – Barry Biggs/The
        Trojans (Prod: Mickie Chung and Neville Hinds/Eddie Airey) (1977) [B SIDE
        REISSUED FROM HORSE LABEL HOSS 122B]

9008   Duppy Gunman/None Shall Escape The Judgement – Inner Circle (Prod:
        Tommy Cowan) (1977)

9009   Long Time/Version – Winston Fergus (Prod: Philip Cann) (1977) [ON
        LIGHTNING LABEL]

9010   African Woman/Version – Winston Fergus (Prod: Philip Cann) (1977) [ON
        LIGHTNING LABEL]

9011   Feel Like Making Love/Version – Elizabeth Archer and The Equators (Prod
        Philip Cann/Douglas/Carr) (1977) [ON LIGHTNING LABEL]

9012   Playboy/Choking Kind – Danny Ray (Prod: Jackie Edwards/Danny Ray)
        (1977) [SOME COPIES SHOW 'CHOKING KIND' AS A SIDE]

9013   African Dub/Version – The Silvertones (Prod: Jerry McCarthy) (1977) [ON
        'TROJAN ROCKERS' LABEL]

9014 My Twenty Eight/Version – Thunderball (Prod: Jerry McCarthy) (1977) [ON 'TROJAN ROCKERS' LABEL]

9015 What A Situation/Version – The Silvertones (Prod: Jerry McCarthy) (1977) [ON 'TROJAN ROCKERS' LABEL]

9016 Express Yourself/Rasshopper – Oddjob (Prod: Doug Gleave) (1977) [ON LIGHTNING LABEL: NOT REGGAE]

9017 Caribbean Way/Version – Lloyd Miller (Prod: Brian Carroll) (1977)

9018 Let's Get It While It's Hot/Ungrateful Baby – John Holt (Prod: Edward 'Bunny' Lee) (1977)

9019 Key Of Keys (actually titled 'I've Made Up My Mind')/Version – Michael Rose (actually by Enos McLeod)/The Mighty Two (Prod: Errol Thompson and Joel Gibson [Joe Gibbs]) (1977) [ON 'TROJAN ROCKERS' LABEL]

9020 I'll Be Free Some Day/Version – Candy Lewis [Candy McKenzie] (Prod: Clement Bushay) (1977)

9021 Can't Satisfy/Satisfied Version – Bagga Matumbi (Prod: Bevan Fagan) (1977) [ON 'TROJAN ROCKERS' LABEL]

9022 Jah Jah No New/Wailing Version – Lambert Douglas (Prod: C Francis) (1977) [ON 'TROJAN ROCKERS' LABEL]

9023 Happiness/Version – The Dingles (Prod: C Francis) (1977) [ON 'TROJAN ROCKERS' LABEL]

9024 When I Need You/Heavy Robbery – Owen Gray (Prod: Clement Bushay) (1977) [ON LIGHTNING LABEL]

9025 The Slave Trade/Roots – One Love (Prod: Bill Spencer) (1977) [ON LIGHTNING LABEL]

9026 Come Back Girl/I'll Be Waiting – Nicky Thomas (Prod: Tito Simon/Nicky Thomas) (1977) [B SIDE REISSUED FROM TROJAN TR 7878B AND 7885B AND HORSE HOSS 155B]

9027 Man In Me/After Tonight – Matumbi (Prod: Matumbi) (1977) [PROMOTED AS DOUBLE A SIDE]

9028 Nice And Easy/If You Need Me – Susan Cadogan (Prod: Lee Perry) (1977)

9029 You Are Mine/Strange Thoughts – Honey Boy (Prod: Keith Williams [Honey Boy]) (1977)

9030 Everybody's Talking/Only A Smile – John Holt (Prod: Edward 'Bunny' Lee) (1977) [SOME COPIES PLAY 'HOOLIGAN' ON B SIDE]

9031 NYT

9032 NYT

9033 Love Grows (Where My Rosemary Grows)/Two Timer – Lloyd Miller (Prod: Tito Simon) (1978)

9034 Right Road To Zion/Right Road To Dubland – The Jahlights (Prod: Bill Spencer) (1978)

9035 Pie In The Sky/Pie In The Sky (Version) – Eugene Paul (Prod: Tito Simon) (1978)

297

9036 Freedom Day/Love Don't Love Nobody – Ken Boothe (Prod: Lloyd
      Charmers) (1978)
9037 Rivers Of Babylon/Give The Children Food – The Melodians/Owen Gray
      (Prod: Leslie Kong/Clement Bushay) (1978) [A SIDE REISSUED FROM
      SUMMIT SUM 8508 AND 8532]
9038 Born Free/Over The Rainbow –Mighty Sparrow/The Cimarons (Prod: Byron
      Lee/The Cimarons and Webster Shrowder) (1978) [B SIDE REISSUED
      FROM TR 7919A]
9039 The Greatest Love Of All/ The Greatest Love Of All (Version) – Owen Gray/
      Jah Son (Prod: Clement Bushay) (1978)
9040 Let's Spend The Night Together/Heavy Reggae Man – Teddy [Davis] and The
      Discolettes (Prod: O.C.R [Orbach & Chambers Ltd]) (1978) [B SIDE ALSO
      ISSUED ON HORSE HOSS 158B]
9041 A Little Bit Of Soap/Over And Over – The Pioneers (Prod: Sidney Crooks,
      George Dekker and Jackie Robinson [The Pioneers]) (1978) [A SIDE
      REISSUED FROM TROJAN TR 7906A]
9042 Party Time/Sorry Harry – Dennis Alcapone (Prod: Sidney Crooks) (1978)
      [REISSUED FROM HARRY J LABEL HJ 6666 BUT WITH A AND B
      SIDES REVERSED]
9043 Riot In A Notting Hill/Anuma – The Pioneers (Prod: Sidney Crooks) (1978)
9044 Come Closer To Me/Sincerely – Jackie Edwards (Prod: Jackie Edwards/
      Edward 'Bunny' Lee) (1978)
9045 Who Dun it? (Muhammed Ali)/Sweet Lorraine – Lloyd Miller (Prod: Tito
      Simon) (1978) [B SIDE REISSUED FROM TR 7986B]
9046 Only A Fool Breaks His Own Heart/Maria – Mighty Sparrow (Prod: Byron
      Lee) (1978) [CALYPSO REISSUE FROM DUKE LABEL DU 114]
9047 Shaving Cream/Love Me For A Reason – Fab Five [Fabulous Five Inc] (Prod:
      Rahtid/Fab Five) (1978) [A SIDE REISSUED FROM TROJAN TR 7969A.
      B SIDE REISSUED FROM TROJAN TR 7990A]
9048 Duppy Gunman/Key Card – Ernie Smith (Prod: Ernie Smith/Richard
      Khouri for Federal Records) (1978) [A SIDE REISSUED FROM ATTACK
      ATT 8071A. B SIDE REISSUED FROM TR 7963A]
9049 NYT
9050 Tell The Children The Truth/Seeing Is Believing – Jimmy Riley (Prod: Jimmy
      Riley) (1978)
9051 ISSUED AS 12" 45 ONLY
9052 Who Gets Your Love?/Is It Because I'm Black – Ken Boothe (Prod: Phil Pratt/
      Lloyd Charmers) (1979) [B SIDE REISSUED FROM TROJAN TR 7893A]
9053 Barberman Bawling/Version – Well, Pleased and Satisfied (Prod: Paul Johnson)
      (1979)
9054 Just The Way You Are/Fancy Make-up – John Holt (Prod: Keith Bonsoir)
      (1979)

9055   Nothing Gained (From Loving You)/Can't Go Through With Life – Marie
        Pierre (Prod: Dennis Bovell) (1979) [B SIDE REISSUED ON TR 9057B]
9056   Let Me Down Easy/Wichita Lineman – Dennis Brown (Prod: Derrick
        Harriott) (1979)
9057   Walk Away/Nothing Gained (From Loving You) – Marie Pierre (Prod: Dennis
        Bovell) (1979) [B SIDE REISSUED FROM TR 9055A]
9058   Liquid Horns/The Liquidator – Vin Gordon and The Corner Shots/Junior
        and The Corner Shots (Prod: Fat Man [Ken Gordon]) (1979)
9059   Al Capone/Anna – Emperor Rosko/The Main Men (probably The Cimarons)
        (Prod: Alted [Judge Dread]) (1979) [REISSUED FROM TR 7949]
9060   Choose Me/Someone Else's Man – Marie Pierre (Prod: Dennis Bovell) (1979)
9061   ISSUED AS 12" 45 ONLY
9062   Skinhead Moonstomp/Skinhead Jamboree – Symarip (Prod: Graham Goodall
        for Philligree Productions) (1980) [A SIDE REISSUED FROM TREASURE
        ISLE TI 7050A]
9063   Long Shot Kick The Bucket/Liquidator – The Pioneers/Winston Wright
        and The Harry J All Stars (Prod: Leslie Kong/Harry Johnson) (1980) [A
        SIDE REISSUED FROM TROJAN TR 672A AND TR 7968A. B SIDE
        REISSUED FROM TR 675A]
9064   ISSUED AS 12" 45 ONLY
9065   Thank You Lord/Wisdom – Bob Marley and The Wailers (Prod: Bob Marley)
        (1981)
9066   Walk Away/Version – Marie Pierre (Prod: Dennis Bovell) (1981) [REISSUED
        FROM HORSE HOSS 157]
9066   Ram Goat Liver/Ram Goat Version – Pluto Shervington (Prod: XYZ/
        Togetherness Production) (1981) [REISSUED FROM TROJAN TR 7956
        AND TR 7978. DUPLICATE ISSUE ON THIS NUMBER]
9067   Love Of The Common People/Have A Little Faith – Nicky Thomas (Prod:
        Joel Gibson [Joe Gibbs]) (1980) [REISSUED FROM TROJAN TR 7750A
        AND TR 7885A RESPECTIVELY]
9068   ISSUED AS 12" 45 ONLY
9069   ISSUED AS 12" 45 ONLY
9070   ISSUED AS 12" 45 ONLY
9071   ISSUED AS 12" 45 ONLY
9072   ISSUED AS 12" 45 ONLY
9073   The Ten Commandments/Give It Up Michael – Judge Dread (Prod: Alted)
        (1983)
9074   Soul Shakedown Party/Caution – Bob Marley and The Wailers (Prod: Leslie
        Kong) (1981) [REISSUED FROM TROJAN TR 7911]
9075   Cherry Oh Baby/Please Don't Make Me Cry/Red Red Wine – Eric
        Donaldson/Winston Groovy/Tony Tribe (Prod: Edward 'Bunny' Lee/Winston
        Tucker [Groovy]/Dandy) (1984)

9076   54-46 Was My Number/Train To Skaville – The Maytals/The Ethiopians
        (Prod: Leslie Kong/Leebert Robinson) (1984)
9077   Too Much Love/Mr Bojangles – John Holt (Prod: Tony Ashfield) (1984) [B
        SIDE REISSUED FROM TR 7991B]
9078   Hippopotomous/007 – Desmond Dekker and The Aces (Prod: Leslie Kong)
        (1984)
9079   Sensi For Sale/Depression – Sandra Robinson (Prod: Ossie Ranks) (1985)
9080   Merry Christmas, Happy New Year/Return Of Django – Lee Perry and
        Sandra Robinson (Prod: Lee Perry) (1985) [B SIDE REISSUED FROM
        UPSETTER LABEL US 301A]
9081   ISSUED AS 12" 45 ONLY
9082   Sexy Lady/All Things Are Possible – Lee Perry and The Upsetters (Prod: Lee
        Perry) (1986)
9083   Papers/Frozen Moments – Alan Price (Prod: Alan Price) (1986) [NOT
        REGGAE]
9084   Do It Right/Opportunity – The Pioneers (Prod: Sidney Crooks) (1986)
9085   ISSUED AS 12" 45 ONLY
9086   ISSUED AS 12" 45 ONLY
9087   ISSUED AS 12" 45 ONLY
9088   You Make Me Feel Brand New/Elizabethan Reggae – Boris Gardner (Prod:
        Lloyd Charmers/Junior Chung) (1986) [B SIDE REISSUED FROM DUKE
        LABEL (DU 39A]
9089   Reggae Me/Shub In (Shebeen) – George Dekker (Prod: Sidney Crooks)
        (1986)
9090   Reggae In London City/My Woman – The Pioneers (Prod: Sidney Crooks)
        (1986)
9091   Heart Made Of Stone/Heart Made Of Stone (Version) – Audrey Hall (Prod:
        Edward 'Bunny' Lee and Joe Richards) (1986)
9092   Bring It On Home To Me/He'll Understand – Ken Boothe (Prod: Lloyd
        Charmers) (1986)
9093   ISSUED AS 12" 45 ONLY
9094   A Spaceman Came Travelling/My Oh My – John Holt (Prod: Edward 'Bunny'
        Lee and Joe Richards) (1986)
9095   Merry Christmas, Happy New Year/The Perry Christmas Dub – Lee Perry
        and Sandra Robinson (Prod: Lee Perry) (1986) [A SIDE REISSUED FROM
        TR 9080A]
9096   ISSUED AS 12" 45 ONLY
9097   Yodel Reggae/Yodel Dub – Leroy Gibbs (Prod: Desmond Rowe) (1987)
9098   ISSUED AS 12" 45 ONLY
9099   Do It Right/Honour Your Mother And Father – Desmond Dekker (Prod:
        Steve Grant and Delroy Williams) (1987)
9100   NOT ISSUED

9101 Wonderful World, Beautiful People/Licking Stick – Desmond Dekker (Prod: Steve Grant and Delroy Williams) (1987)

9102 NOT ISSUED

9103 You Can Get It If You Really Want/If You Can't Do The Time – Mr Bojangles (actually Delroy Williams) (Prod: Steve Grant and Delroy Williams) (1987)

TROJAN 12" SERIES (PREFIX TROT)

9051 Rock With Me Baby/Lady Love – John Holt (Prod: Edward 'Bunny' Lee) (1978)

9057 Walk Away/Nothing Gained (From Loving You) – Marie Pierre (Prod: Dennis Bovell) (1979)

9061 Skinhead Moon Stomp/Skinhead Jamboree/Fung Shu – Symarip (Prod: Graeme Goodall for Philligree Productions) (1979)

9063 Liquidator/Long Shot Kick The Bucket – Harry J All Stars (actually with Winston Wright)/The Pioneers (Prod: Harry Johnson/Leslie Kong) (1979)

9064 Herbsman Shuffle/Phantom/Next Corner/Vigorton 2 – King Stitt and Andy Capp/The Dynamites/King Stitt/King Stitt (Prod: Clancy Eccles) (1980)

9067 Love Of The Common People/Have A Little Faith – Nicky Thomas (Prod: Joel Gibson [Joe Gibbs]) (1980)

9068 Settle Down Girl/Settle Down Girl (Version) – Tristan Palmer (Prod: Linval Thompson) (1982)

9069 Ghetto-ology/Walking Through The Ghetto – Sugar Minott (Prod: Lincoln 'Sugar' Minott) (1982)

9070 Me Chat, You Rock/It's Me – U Brown (Prod: Hugh Brown) (1982)

9071 If I Didn't Want Your Loving/If I Didn't Want Your Loving (Version) – The Majesterians (Prod: Linval Thompson) (1983)

9072 The Iron Lady (Maggie May)/Mr Reagan, President Of The United States – Ranking Trevor (Prod: unidentified) (1983) [BADGED AS TROJAN 'SPECIAL']

9074 Soul Shakedown Party/Caution/Keep On Skanking – Bob Marley and The Wailers (Prod: Leslie Kong/Leslie Kong/Lee Perry) (1983)

9075 Cherry Oh Baby/Please Don't Make Me Cry/Red Red Wine/Many Rivers To Cross – Eric Donaldson/Winston Groovy/Tony Tribe/Jimmy Cliff (Prod: Edward 'Bunny' Lee/Winston Tucker [Winston Groovy]/Dandy/Leslie Kong) (1983)

9077 Too Much Love/Mr Bojangles/You'll Never Find Another Love Like Mine/Help Me Make It Through The Night – John Holt (Prod: Tony Ashfield/Tony Ashfield/Edward 'Bunny' Lee/Tony Ashfield) (1984)

9078 Hippopotomous/007 – Desmond Dekker and The Aces (Prod: Leslie Kong) (1984)

301

9079   Sensi For Sale (Part 1)/Boogie Mix (Part 2)/Depression/Life's Riddle/Boogie
        Mix – Sandra Robinson/The Tuff Tones/Sandra Robinson and The Tuff
        Tones/Dan Ambrassa and The Tuff Tones (Prod: Ossie Ranks) (1985)

9080   Merry Christmas, Happy New Year (The Perry Mix)/Merry Christmas,
        Happy New Year (The Crossover/Radio Mix)/Return Of Django (Original
        Version)/All Things Are Possible (Django '85) – Lee Perry and Sandra
        Robinson/Lee Perry and Sandra Robinson/The Upsetters/Lee Perry and The
        Upsetters (Prod: Lee Perry) (1985)

9081   Let It Play/Digital Style/Having Fun/Rastafari/Mafia History – Akenzie
        Stevens and The Tuff Tones/Winston Turner and The Tuff Tones/Winston Turner
        and The Tuff Tones/Isly Ren and The Tuff Tones (Prod: Ossie Ranks) (1985)

9085   Pirate/Pirate (Version)/Pirate (Original Version) – The Ethiopians (Prod:
        Leonard Dillon/Leonard Dillon/Arthur 'Duke' Reid) (1986)

9086   War Inna South Africa/Vocal Dub Version/Version – Killerman [Winston]
        Jarrett (Prod: Tony Shabazz and Patrick 'Scabba' Sutherland) (1986)

9087   If You Leave Me (aka 'Don't Stay Away')/ Jailhouse/Jailhouse (Version) – Private
        Tabby [Diamond] (Prod: Tony Shabazz and Patrick 'Scabba' Sutherland) (1986)

9091   Heart Made Of Stone/Heart Made Of Stone (Version)/It's Hard To Believe/
        It's Hard To Believe (Version) – Audrey Hall/Audrey Hall/Don Evans/Don
        Evans (Prod: Edward 'Bunny' Lee and Joe Richards) (1986)

9092   Bring It On Home To Me/He'll Understand – Ken Boothe (Prod: Lloyd
        Charmers) (1986)

9093   You're Everything To Me/You're Everything To Me (Version)/I'll Be Everything
        To You/I'll Be Everything To You (Instrumental) – John Holt and The Hit
        Squad/John Holt and The Hit Squad/June Powell and The Hit Squad/June
        Powell and The Hit Squad (Prod: Edward 'Bunny' Lee and Joe Richards) (1986)

9096   What Is Man/Joe Blake/Hangin' On/Pull Up '88 –Vivian Weathers (Prod:
        Vivian [Weathers], John and Jimmy) (1987)

9097   Yodel Reggae (Club Mix)/Yodel Reggae (Radio Mix)/Yodel Dub – Leroy
        Gibbs (Prod: Desmond Rowe) (1987)

9098   Israelites/Israelites (Live Version) – Desmond Dekker (Prod: Desmond Dekker
        and Delroy Williams) [EXISTENCE UNCONFIRMED]

TROJAN 12" (PREFIX TRD)

101A   Rock With Me Baby/Lady Love – John Holt (Prod: Edward 'Bunny' Lee) (1978)

TROJAN MAXI-SINGLES (PREFIX TRM – FIRST SERIES)

9000   Songs Of Peace/You Are The Best/We Can Make It – Bruce Ruffin (Prod:
        Bruce Anthony) (1971) [IN PICTURE SLEEVE]

9001   Chopsticks/I Got It/Put It On – The Deltones/The Low Bites/The Itals
        (Prod: Webster Shrowder, Des Bryan and Joe Sinclair for Bush Productions/
        Webster Shrowder, Des Bryan and Joe Sinclair for Swan Productions/Webster
        Shrowder, Des Bryan and Joe Sinclair for Swan Productions) (1972)
9002   The Liquidator/Return Of Django/Elizabethan Reggae – Harry J All Stars
        (actually with Winston Wright)/The Upsetters/Boris Gardner (Prod: Harry
        Johnson/Lee Perry/Junior Chung) (1972)
9003   Israelites/It Mek/007 – Desmond Dekker and The Aces (Prod: Leslie Kong/
        Leslie Kong and Graeme Goodall for Philligree Productions/Leslie Kong)
        (1972)
9004   Monkey Man/She's My Scorcher/One Eye Enos – The Maytals (Prod: Leslie
        Kong) (1972) [PROBABLY UNISSUED]
9005   Sweet Sensation/Rivers Of Babylon/It Took A Miracle – The Melodians
        (Prod: Leslie Kong) (1972) [PROBABLY UNISSUED]
9006   Are You Ready/Candida/Bitterness Of Life – Bruce Ruffin (Prod: Leslie
        Kong) (1972)
9007   NYT
9008   Guns Of Navarone/Bonanza Ska/Napoleon Solo – The Skatalites/Carlos
        Macolm and His Afro-Jamaican Rhythm/Lyn Taitt and The Jets (Prod:
        Coxsone Dodd/Carlos Malcolm)/Federal) (1972)
9009   Pickney Gal/Peace On The Land/Hippopotomous – Desmond Dekker (Prod:
        Leslie Kong) (1973)
9010   Phoenix City/El Pussy Cat/Guns Fever – Roland Alphonso and The Soul
        Brothers/Roland Alphonso and The Studio One Orchestra/Baba Brooks'
        Group (Prod: Coxsone Dodd/Coxsone Dodd/Arthur 'Duke' Reid) (1974)

TROJAN MAXI-SINGLES (PREFIX TRM – SECOND SERIES)

3001   Young, Gifted And Black/Private Number/Pied Piper – Bob [Andy] and
        Marcia [Griffiths] (Prod: Harry Johnson/Harry Johnson/Bob Andy) (1976)
3002   Double Barrel/Stone In Love With You/Monkey Spanner – Dave [Barker] and
        Ansell Collins/Dave Barker/Dave [Barker] and Ansel Collins (Prod: Winston
        Riley/Larry Lawrence/Winston Riley) (1976)
3003   Love Of The Common People/Have A Little Faith/Yesterday Man – Nicky
        Thomas (Prod: Joel Gibson [Joe Gibbs]/Joel Gibson [Joe Gibbs]/Nicky
        Thomas and Clive Crawley) (1976)
3004   The Liquidator/My Cherie Amour/Je'Taime – The Harry J All Stars (actually
        with Winston Wright) (Prod: Harry Johnson) (1976)
3005   Black And White/I Am What I Am/Moon River – Greyhound (Prod: Dave
        Bloxham) (1976)

3006   Let Your Yeah Be Yeah/Sweet Inspiration/I Hear You Knocking – The Pioneers
       (Prod: Jimmy Cliff and Sidney Crooks/Leslie Kong/Sidney Crooks) (1976)
3007   Phoenix City/Guns Of Navarone/Guns Fever – Roland Alphonso and The
       Soul Brothers/The Skatalites/Baba Brooks' Band (Prod: Coxsone Dodd/
       Coxsone Dodd/Arthur 'Duke' Reid) (1977)
3008   No One Day Love/What Good Is Life/One More Chance – Winston Groovy
       (Prod: Winston Tucker [Winston Groovy]) (1977)
3009   Israelites/It Mek/007 – Desmond Dekker and The Aces (Prod: Leslie
       Kong/Leslie Kong and Graeme Goodall for Philligree Productions/Leslie
       Kong) (1977) [REISSUE OF TRM 9003 FROM FIRST TROJAN MAXI
       SERIES]

TROJAN MAXI-SINGLES (PREFIX TMX)

4001   **Trojan Explosion**: Young, Gifted And Black/Black And White/Rivers Of
       Babylon/Ram Goat Liver – Bob [Andy] and Marcia [Griffiths]/Greyhound/
       The Melodians/Pluto Shervington (Prod: Harry Johnson/Dave Bloxham/
       Leslie Kong/XYZ and Togetherness) (1979)
4002   **Trojan Explosion:** Everything I Own/Song We Used To Sing/Montego
       Bay/You Can Get It If You Really Want – Ken Boothe/Desmond Dekker/
       Freddie Notes and The Rudies/Desmond Dekker (Prod: Lloyd Charmers/
       Leslie Kong and Jimmy Cliff/Grape/Leslie Kong and John Kelly for N.R.E
       Ltd) (1979)
4003   **Trojan Explosion:** Help Me Make It Through The Night/This Monday
       Morning Feeling/Black Pearl/Pied Piper – John Holt/Tito Simon/Horace
       Faith/Bob [Andy] and Marcia [Griffiths] (Prod: Tony Ashfield/Keith Foster
       [Tito Simon]/Philip Swern and Johnny Arthey for Pinpoint Record
       Productions/Bob Andy) (1979)
4004   **Trojan Explosion:** Israelites/Long Shot Kick The Bucket/Monkey Spanner/
       Love Of The Common People – Desmond Dekker and The Aces/The
       Pioneers/Dave [Barker] and Ansel Collins/Nicky Thomas (Prod: Leslie Kong/
       Leslie Kong/Winston Riley/Joel Gibson [Joe Gibbs]) (1979)
4005   **Trojan Explosion:** The Liquidator/Return Of Django/Elizabethan
       Serenade/It Mek – Harry J All Stars (actually with Winston Wright)/The
       Upsetters/Boris Gardner/Desmond Dekker and The Aces (Prod: Harry
       Johnson/Lee Perry/Junior Chung/Leslie Kong and Philigree) (1979)
4006   **Trojan Explosion:** Let Your Yeah Be Yeah/007/Double Barrel/Suzanne
       Beware Of The Devil – The Pioneers/Desmond Dekker and The Aces/Dave
       [Barker] and Ansell Collins/Dandy Livingstone (Prod: Jimmy Cliff and Sidney
       Crooks/Leslie Kong/ Shady Tree [Dandy]) (1979)

4007 **Trojan Explosion:** Skinhead Moon Stomp/Skinhead Jamboree/El Pussy
Cat/Guns Of Navarone – Symarip/Symarip/Roland Alphonso and The
Studio 1 Orchestra/The Skatalites (Prod: Graeme Goodall for Philligree
Productions/Graeme Goodall for Philligree Productions/Coxsone Dodd/
Coxsone Dodd) (1979)

4008 **Trojan Explosion:** Rudy, A Message To You/Tribute To The Prince/Big
City/Think About That – Dandy (Prod: Robert Thompson [Dandy]) (1979)

4009 **Skinhead Classics:** Train To Skaville/Monkey Man/Return Of Django/
Phoenix City – The Ethiopians/The Maytals/The Upsetters/Roland
Alphonso and The Soul Brothers (Prod: Leebert Robinson/Leslie Kong/Lee
Perry/Coxsone Dodd) (1979)

4010 **Trojan Expolosion:** Israelites/Monkey Spanner/It Mek/Side Show –
Desmond Dekker and The Aces/Dave [Barker] and Ansel Collins/Desmond
Dekker and The Aces/Barry Biggs (Prod: Leslie Kong/Winston Riley/Leslie
Kong and Graeme Goodall for Philligree Productions/Neville Hinds) (1979)

4011 **The Big One:** Big One/Big Six/Big Seven/Big Eight – Judge Dread (Prod:
Bush/Bush/Des Bryan, Webster Shrowder and Joe Sinclair/Des Bryan, Webster
Shrowder and Joe Sinclair) (1979)

4012 **Trojan Explosion – Reggae Instrumental Hits:** Tchaikovsky's Piano
Concerto No. 1/Take Five/Liquidator/Return Of Django – Neasden
Connection/Val Bennett/Harry J All Stars (actually with Winston Wright)/
The Upsetters (Prod: Shady Tree [Dandy]/Edward 'Bunny' Lee/Harry
Johnson/Lee Perry) (1979)

4013 **Skinhead Classics Volume 2:** Barbwire/Skinhead Moon Stomp/Wreck A
Buddy/54-46 Was My Number – Nora Dean/Symarip/The Soul Sisters/The
Maytals (Prod: Byron Smith/Graeme Goodall for Philligree Productions/Joel
Gibson [Joe Gibbs]/Leslie Kong) (1979)

4014 **Trojan Explosion:** Hurt So Good/Love Of The Common People/Crying
Over You/Moon River – Susan Cadogan/Nicky Thomas/Ken Boothe/
Greyhound (Prod: Lee Perry/Joel Gibson [Joe Gibbs]/Lloyd Charmers/Dave
Bloxham) (1979)

UPSETTER (PREFIX US)

300 Eight For Eight/You Know What I Mean – The Upsetters/The Inspirations
(1969) [INITIALLY INTENDED FOR RELEASE ON DUKE DU 11]

301 Return Of Django/Dollar In The Teeth – The Upsetters (1969)

302 Good Father/What A Situation – David Isaacs/Slim Smith (1969)

303 Ten To Twelve/People Funny Fi True – The Upsetters/Lee Perry (1969)

304 What A Price/How Can I Forget? – Busty Brown (1969)

305   I've Got Memories/I'm Leaving (actually 'Leaving On A Jet Plane') – David
        Isaacs (1969)

306   Mini Dress/Mad House – Winston Jarrett/Lee Perry (1969)

307   The Night Doctor/I'll Be Waiting – The Upsetters/The Termites (1969)

308   To Love Somebody/Farmers In The Den – Busty Brown/The Upsetters
        (actually by The Bleechers) (1969)

309   Kiddy-O/Endlessly – The Muskyteers (actually The Silvertones) (1969)

310   Man From MI5/Oh Lord – The Upsetters/The West Indians (1969)

311   He'll Have To Go/Since You're Gone – David Isaacs (1969)

312   Badam Bam/Medical Operation – The Ravers/The Upsetters (1969)

313   A Live Injection/Everything For Fun – The Upsetters/The Bleechers (1969)

314   Come Into My Parlour/Dry Your Tears – The Bleechers/The Mellotones
        (1969)

315   Cold Sweat/Pound Get A Blow – The Upsetters/The Upsetters (actually by
        The Soul Twins [Watty Burnett and Jimmy Nelson]) (1969)

316   Hello Dolly/King Of The Trombone (aka 'Tribute To A King') – Pat
        Satchmo/Busty Brown (1969)

317   The Vampire/The Upsetter – The Upsetters/The Bleechers (1969) [FIRST
        PRESSING WITH INCORRECT B SIDE TITLE CREDIT]

317   The Vampire/Check Him Out – The Upsetters/The Bleechers (1969)
        [SECOND PRESSING WITH CORRECT B SIDE TITLE CREDIT]

318   Soulful I/No Bread And Butter – The Upsetters/Milton Morris (1969)

319   Who To Tell/I Can't See Myself Crying About You – David Isaacs (actually by
        Bruce Bennett)/Busty Brown (1969)

320   Dirty Dozen/Crying Too Long – The Shadows (aka The Ravers, aka The
        Dukes) (1969)★

321   Stranger On The Shore/Drugs And Poison – The Upsetters (actually with Val
        Bennett)/The Upsetters (1969)

322   The Same Thing You Gave To Daddy/A Testimony – Nora Dean/Upsetter
        Pilgrims (1969)

323   The Same Thing/I Wear My Slanders (actually titled 'If You Don't Mind') –
        The Gaylads (1969)

324   Yakety Yak/Takio (actually 'The Takro') – The Upsetters (actually with Lee
        Perry) (1969)

325   Kill Them All/Soul Walk – The Upsetters (actually with Lee Perry)/The
        Upsetters (1970)

326   Bronco (Ol' Man River)/One Punch – The Upsetters (actually with Lee Perry
        and Sir Lord Comic)/The Upsetters (1970) [A SIDE REISSUED FROM
        TROJAN TR 644B]

327   Do You Like It/Touch Of Fire – Toots (actually Lee Perry)/The Upsetters (1970)

328   Consider Me (Version 1)/Consider Me (Version 2) – BB James (actually Busty
        Brown) (1970)

329   Melting Pot/Kinky Mood – The Heaters/The Upsetters (1970)

330   Spinning Wheel/Spinning Wheel Version 2 – Mel [Melanie Jonas] and Dave
        [Barker] (1970)

331   Shocks Of Mighty/Set Me Free – Dave Barker and The Upsetters (1970) [A
        SIDE REISSUED ON TROJAN TR 7875A]

332   Pick Folk Kinkiest/Na Na Hey Hey (Kiss Him Goodbye) – The Upsetters
        (1970)

333   Granny Show (Version 1)/Granny Show (Version 2) – The Upsetters (actually
        with Dave Barker) (1970)

334   Fire Fire/The Jumper – The Upsetters (1970)

335   The Pillow/Grooving – The Upsetters (1970)

336   Self-control/The Pill – The Upsetters (actually by Martin Riley and Fay
        Bennett)/The Upsetters (actually by Martin Riley) (1970) ##

337   Let It Be/Big Dog Bloxie – The Soulettes/The Upsetters (1970)

338   Fresh Up/Tooth Aches – The Upsetters (1970)

339   Thanks We Get/Hurry Up – The Upsetters (actually by The Versatiles) (1970)

340   My Cup/Son Of Thunder – Bob Marley and The Wailers/Lee Perry and The
        Upsetters (1970)

341   Blood Poison/Thunder Version – The Upsetters (1970) [UNISSUED]

342   Dreamland Version/Version Of Cup [My Cup Version] – The Upsetters (1970)
        [UNISSUED]

343   Sipreano/Ferry Boat (aka 'Give It Up')– The Upsetters (actually with Lee
        Perry)/The Upsetters (1970)

344   Some Sympathy/Tender Love – Dave Barker and The Upsetters /The
        Untouchables (1970)

345   Same Thing All Over/It's Over (Version) – The Untouchables/The Upsetters
        (1970)

346   Return Of The Vampire/Bigger Joke – The Upsetters (1970)

347   Sound Underground/Don't Let The Sun Catch You Crying – Dave Barker/
        Dave Barker (actually with The Wailers) (1970)

348   Duppy Conqueror/Justice – Bob Marley and The Wailers/The Upsetters
        (1970)

349   Upsetting Station (actually plays 'Duppy Conqueror')/Dig Your Grave – Bob
        Marley and The Wailers/The Upsetters (1970) [FIRST PRESSING WITH
        WRONG A SIDE: HAS MATRIX NUMBER US+349+A/US+349+B]

349   Upsetting Station/Dig Your Grave – The Upsetters (actually with Dave
        Barker)/The Upsetters (1970) [SECOND PRESSING WITH CORRECT
        SIDES]

350 Tight Spot/Knock On Wood – The Upsetters (actually with Dave Barker)/
     The Untouchables (1971)

351 NYT

352 Heart And Soul/Zig Zag – The Upsetters (1971)

353 Elusion/Big John Wayne – Teddy (actually with The Upsetters)/The Upsetters
     (1971)

354 Mr Brown/Dracula – Bob Marley and The Wailers/The Upsetters (1971)
     [BOTH SIDES REISSUED ON TROJAN TR 7926. A SIDE REISSUED
     ON TROJAN TR 7979A]

355 Confusion/Confusion Version – The Untouchables/The Upsetters (1971)

356 Kaya/Kaya Version – Bob Marley and The Wailers (1971) [UNISSUED]

357 Small Axe/All In One (Medley) – Bob Marley and The Wailers (1971)

358 Shocks '71/You've Got To Be Mine – Dave Barker (actually with Charlie
     Ace)/The Hurricanes (1971)

359 The Creeper/Creeping Version – Charlie Ace and The Upsetters/The
     Upsetters (1971)

360 NYT

361 Copasetic/All Africans (actually titled 'Don't Cross The Nation') – The
     Upsetters (actually with U Roy)/The Upsetters (actually by Little Roy) (1971)

362 Groove Me/Screw-Driver – Dave Barker/The Upsetters (1971)

363 You've Got To Be Mine/You've Got To Be Mine Version – The Hurricanes/
     The Upsetters (1971) [UNISSUED]

364 What A Confusion/Confusion Version 2 – Dave Barker (actually with Bunny
     Wailer)/The Upsetters (1971)

365 Earthquake/Place Called Africa – The Upsetters/Junior Byles (1971)

366 Run Up Your Mouth/Mouth Version – Rob Walker (actually by Stranger
     Cole)/The Upsetters (1971)

367 Never Had A Dream Come True/Dream Version – Glen Adams/The
     Upsetters (1971)

368 Picture On The Wall/Picture On The Wall Version – Rass [Carl] Dawkins and
     The Wailers/The Upsetters (1971)

369 More Axe/Axe Man – Bob Marley and The Wailers/The Upsetters (actually
     by Bongo Herman and Les Chen) (1971) [ISSUED ON BLANK LABEL
     ONLY. REISSUED ON UPSETTER US 372]

370 Dark Moon/You'll Be Sorry – The Upsetters/David Isaacs (1971)

371 Dreamland/Dream Version – The Wailers (actually by Bunny Wailer and The
     Upsetters)/The Upsetters (1971)

372 More Axe/Axe Man – Bob Marley and The Wailers/The Upsetters (actually
     by Bongo Herman and Les Chen) (1971) [REISSUED FROM UPSETTER
     US 369]

373   Well Dread/Well Dread Version 2 – The Upsetters (actually by Dennis
       Alcapone)/The Upsetters (1971)

374   Piece Of My Heart/Piece Version – Mahalia Saunders (actually Hortense
       Ellis)/The Upsetters (1971)

375   Earthquake (actually 'Earthquake Version')/Suspicious Minds – Hugh Roy
       (actually U Roy)/Mahalia Saunders (actually Hortense Ellis) (1971)

376   Give Me Power/More Power – The Stingers/The Upsetters and 3rd and 4th
       Generation (1971)

377   Alpha And Omega/Beat Down Babylon – Dennis Alcapone/Junior Byles (1971)

378   Example Part 1/Example Part 2 – Winston Wright and 3rd and 4th
       Generation/ The Upsetters with 3rd and 4th Generation (1971)

379   Mighty Cloud Of Joy/Mighty Cloud Version – Lloyd Parks/The Upsetters
       (1971)

380   Bet You Don't Know/Ring Of Fire (actually 'Babylon Chapter 5') – Chenley
       Duffus/The Upsetters (1972)

381   Wonder Man/There's A Place Called Africa (actually titled 'Africa Stand')
       – The Upsetters (actually with Dennis Alcapone and Dave Barker)/The
       Upsetters (actually by Dennis Alcapone) (1972)

382   Give Me Power Version 2/Public Enemy Number 1 – King Iwah and The
       Stingers/Max Romeo (1972)

383   Who Feels It/Chapter 2 – Prince Tallis and The Chalis/The Upsetters (1972)

384   Blackman's Time/Black Supreme – Neville Grant/Ansel Collins (1972)

385   French Connection/Chapter 2 – Lee Perry/The Upsetters (1972)

386   Babylon Burning/To Be A Lover (actually 'I Forgot To Be Your Lover') –
       Maxie [Romeo], Niney and Scratch/Chenley Duffus (1972)

387   Festival Da Da/Da Da – The Upsetters/Junior Byles (1972)

388   Master Key/Key Hole – Dennis Alcapone/The Upsetters (1972)

389   Back Biter/Back Biter (Version) – Dennis Alcapone and Lee Perry/The
       Upsetters (1972)

390   Whiplash/Whiplash Part 2 – Wesley Germs [Wesley Martin]/The Upsetters
       (1972)

391   Natty Natty/Natty Version – Reggie Lewis (actually Alva Lewis)/Alva Lewis
       and The Upsetters (1972)

392   Keep On Moving/African Herbsman – Bob Marley and The Wailers (1972)

393   Crummy People (actually titled 'One Love, One Heart')/Moving Version –
       The Upsetters (actually by The Righteous Flames)/Big Youth (1972)

394   Water Pump/Pumping (Version) – The Upsetters (actually with Lee Perry)
       (1972)

395   Preacher Man/Preacher (Version) – The Stingers/The Upsetters (actually with
       The Stingers) (1972)

396   Puss-See-Hole/I Wanna Be Loved★★ – The Upsetters (actually with Lee
       Perry)/Winston Groovy (1972)

397   Jungle Lion/Freak Out Skank – Lee Perry and The Upsetters/The Upsetters
       (1973)

398   Cow Thief Skank/7 and Three Quarters Skank – The Upsetters (actually with
       Charlie Ace) (1973)

399   News Flash/Flashing Echo – Leo Graham/Leo Graham and The Upsetters
       (1973)

400   Stranger On The Shore/John Devour – David Isaacs/Dillinger (1973)

Note

All tracks produced by Lee Perry except ★ which were Bobby Aitken productions,
which were Martin Riley productions, and ★★ which was a Winston Groovy production.

TROJAN PRE-RELEASES: BDS, BZX, GPW, JWL AND TMX MATRICES

For a time, Trojan issued blank label 45s in limited quantities using several separate
matrices which were available through Muzik City shops at premium prices on a 'pre-
release' and highly exclusive basis.

The identifying numbers used for each release in the various matrix series would
ultimately be printed on the label of the corresponding 45 when it was officially (i.e.
given full label status) released on a Trojan label. So, for example (citing a quite well-
known single), John Holt and Joya Landis's 'I'll Be Lonely' paired with Tommy
McCook's 'Second Fiddle' was available first as a TMX matrix blank label release
(TMX 3 and TMX 4 printed in the run-outs respectively). The same two sides later
gained an official release on Trojan's main label as TR 633 with the TMX matrices
noted in small print underneath the main catalogue number.

The vast majority of these blank label issues did see full release on one or other
Trojan labels, either as 45s or as album tracks, but there were some that didn't, and
it is these that are often hugely rare. It's apparent that some that never saw release
were issued on Pama (like Tony King's 'Don't Cry Daddy', or the Viceroys' 'Come
On Over' for example), and this may have been part of a waiting game to see who
would put the track out first (and two identical releases by different companies would
inevitably see profits split). In the case of Lee Perry, it's clear that Trojan had so much
of his music it wouldn't have known which of it should be officially released, resulting
in sides like 'Slow Motion' (all three versions) only ever being available on TMX
blanks at, possibly, no more than 99 copies a time. Either way, even finding a GPW
blank of a relatively easy to find Trojan 45 like Jackie Edwards and Judy Mowatt's 'In
Paradise' would take some serious hunting down.

The pre-release series were relatively fleeting, with TMX having by far the biggest
output and lasting until around November 1970. All dates listed in brackets indicate the
year in which each recording was mastered by Trojan.

BDS SERIES (FOR DANDY/BROTHER DAN PRODUCTIONS)

BDS 1   Run Come Have Fun – Dandy (Prod: Dandy) (1968)

BDS 2   Unidentified (Prod: Dandy) (1968) [A SIDE INCLUDED ON TROJAN
         ALBUM TRL 2 ('DANDY RETURNS')]

BDS 4   Tribute To The Prince – Dandy (Prod: Dandy) (1968)

BDS 3   The Race Is On – Dandy (Prod: Dandy) (1968) [TRACKS INCLUDED
         ON TROJAN ALBUM TRL 2 ('DANDY RETURNS')]

BDS 6   Dance To The Music – Downtown All Stars (Prod: Dandy) (1968)

BDS 5   Everybody Feel Good – Brother Dan All Stars (Prod: Dandy) (1968) [B
         SIDE ISSUED ON DOWNTOWN DT 426A]

BDS 7   Move Your Mule – Dandy (Prod: Dandy) (1968)

BDS 8   You're Not The Same Girl – Dandy (Prod: Dandy) (1968) [A SIDE
         ISSUED ON DOWNTOWN DT 401A. B SIDE INCLUDED ON
         TROJAN ALBUM TRL 2 ('DANDY RETURNS')]

BDS 9   NYT

BDS 11   All I Have To Do Is Dream – Denzil [Dennis] and Pat [Rhoden] (Prod:
         Dandy) (1968) Sincerely – Denzil [Dennis] and Pat [Rhoden] (Prod:
         Dandy) (1968) [ISSUED AS DOWNTOWN DT 403]

BDS 10   Come Back Girl – Dandy (Prod: Dandy) (1968)

BDS 14   Shake Me Wake Me – Dandy (Prod: Dandy) (1968) [ISSUED AS
         DOWNTOWN DT 402]

BDS 16   Move Your Mule – Dandy (Prod: Dandy) (1968)

BDS 12   Reggae Me This – Dandy (Prod: Dandy) (1968) [ISSUED AS
         DOWNTOWN DT 401. SEE ALSO BDS 7]

BDS 13   Tell Me Darling Dandy (Prod: Dandy) (1968)

BDS 15   Cool Hand Luke – Brother Dan All Stars (Prod: Dandy) (1968) [ISSUED
         AS DOWNTOWN DT 404]

BDS   NYT
17–23

BDS 30   I Second That Emotion – Audrey [Hall] and The Dreamers (Prod: Dandy)
         (1968)

BDS 35   Dear Love – The Dreamers (Prod: Dandy) (1968) [ISSUED AS
         DOWNTOWN DT 408]

BDS 32   Pushwood – Mr Most [Dandy] (Prod: Dandy) (1968)

BDS 31   Reggae Train – Mr Most [Dandy] (Prod: Dandy) (1968) [ISSUED AS
         DOWNTOWN DT 409]

BDS 33   Sweet Chariot – The Dreamers (Prod: Dandy) (1968)

BDS 25   Let's Go Downtown – The Dreamers (Prod: Dandy) (1968) [ISSUED AS
         DOWNTOWN DT 407]

BDS 36   Reggae In Your Jeggae – Dandy (Prod: Dandy) (1969)

BDS 24   Reggae Shuffle – The Dreamers (Prod: Dandy) (1969) [ISSUED AS
          DOWNTOWN DT 410]

BDS 26,
27, 28, 29
AND 34
NYT

BZX SERIES

This has been a particularly contentious list to compile as Trojan's inventory of the titles
was on a rolling basis when in fact it wasn't necessarily the case that every 45 was issued
with consecutive numbers on either side. The pattern started to change with BZX 23,
which was backed with BZX 25 and not 24 as might have been predicted. So, there
has had to be an element of guesswork on what pairings actually made up both sides
of a single. Generally, these have been based around what might have been released as
both sides of a labelled/officially released 45, and marrying up sides that came from a
particular producer.

Also, it can be seen that some sides in this series were issued by Island in the period
just after Trojan/B&C became a business in its own right in July 1968. These had
probably already been slated for release by Island before the changeover.

BZX 1   Chattie Chattie – Junior Soul (Prod: Derrick Harriott) (1968)
BZX 2   Magic Touch – Junior Soul (Prod: Derrick Harriott) (1968) [ISSUED AS
         BIG SHOT BI 503]
BZX 3   Standing In – Derrick Harriott (Prod: Derrick Harriott) (1968)
BZX 4   Bumble Bee – The Crystalites (Prod: Derrick Harriott) (1968) [ISSUED
         AS BIG SHOT BI 505]
BZX 5   NYT
BZX 6   NYT
BZX 7   If You Can't Be Good Be Careful – The Gaylettes (Prod: Ken Khouri for
         Federal Records) (1968)
BZX 8   Something About My Man – The Gaylettes (Prod: Lynford Anderson)
         (1968) [ISSUED AS BIG SHOT BI 502]
BZX 9   My Argument – Lloyd Charmers (Prod: H Robinson) (1968)
BZX 10   Foey Man – George Dekker (Prod: H Robinson) (1968) [NEITHER
         SIDE ISSUED ON ANY TROJAN LABEL – BOTH SIDES
         RELEASED ON ISLAND WI 3158 AND TRACKS PROBABLY
         PROVIDED TO THE COMPANY BY EDWARD 'BUNNY' LEE]
BZX 11   The Prodigal Returns (aka 'I'm Going Home') – Errol Dunkley (Prod:
         Edward 'Bunny' Lee) (1968)

BZX 12   Nursery Rhyme Rock Steady – Errol Dunkley (Prod: Edward 'Bunny'
          Lee) (1968) [NEITHER SIDE ISSUED ON ANY TROJAN LABEL]
BZX 13   NYT
BZX 14   NYT
BZX 15   NYT
BZX 16   NYT
BZX 17   Forest Gate Rock – Lester Sterling (Prod: Edward 'Bunny' Lee) (1968)
BZX 18   It Might As Well Be Spring – Val Bennett (Edward 'Bunny' Lee) (1968)
          [ISSUED ON BIG SHOT BI 507A AND BI 506B RESPECTIVELY]
BZX 19   Unidentified
BZX 20   Shower Of Rain – Derrick Morgan (Prod: Edward 'Bunny' Lee) (1968) [B
          SIDE ISSUED ON BIG SHOT BI 506A]
BZX 21   NYT BUT POSSIBLY OTHER SIDE OF BZX 24
BZX 23   Hold You Jack – Derrick Morgan (Prod: Edward 'Bunny' Lee) (1968)
BZX 25   One Morning In May – Derrick Morgan (Prod: Edward 'Bunny' Lee)
          (1968) [NEITHER SIDE ISSUED ON ANY TROJAN LABEL – BOTH
          SIDES RELEASED ON ISLAND WI 3159]
BZX 24   Too Bad – Derrick Morgan (Prod: Edward 'Bunny' Lee) (1968)
BZX ??   Unidentified [A SIDE ISSUED ON JACKPOT JP 700B]
BZX 26   It's Reggae Time – Don Tony Lee (Prod: Edward 'Bunny' Lee) (1968)
BZX 22   The Clamp Is On – Errol Dunkley (Prod: Edward 'Bunny' Lee) (1968)
          [NEITHER SIDE ISSUED ON ANY TROJAN LABEL – BOTH
          SIDES RELEASED ON ISLAND LABEL WI 3160]
BZX 27   My Baby – The Harmonians (Prod: Albert Gene Murphy) (1968)
BZX 29   Gonna Make It – Cliff Smith (Prod: Albert Gene Murphy) (1968) [A
          SIDE ISSUED ON BIG SHOT BI 517B. B SIDE NOT ISSUED ON
          ANY TROJAN LABEL]
BZX 28   Reggae Girl – The Tennors (Prod: Albert Gene Murphy) (1968)
BZX 30   Donkey Trot – Clive All Stars (Prod: Albert Gene Murphy) (1968) [BOTH
          SIDES ISSUED AS BIG SHOT BI 501]
BZX 31   In Like Flint – The Good Guys (Prod: Byron Lee) (1968)
BZX 32   Nobody's Business – The Good Guys (actually with Ken Lazarus) (Prod:
          Byron Lee) (1968) [BOTH SIDES ISSUED AS TROJAN TR 623]
BZX 33   Power Cut – Abby Adams and His Boys (Prod: Edward 'Bunny' Lee)
          (1968)
BZX 34   Robin Hood Rides Again – Abby Adams and His Boys (Prod: Edward
          'Bunny Lee') (1968) [A SIDE NOT ISSUED ON ANY TROJAN
          LABEL. B SIDE ISSUED ON ISLAND WIP 6051B]
BZX 35   The Big Race – Lord Power (Prod: Harry Johnson) (1968)

BZX 36   More Callaloo- Lord Power (Prod: Harry Johnson) (1968) [NEITHER
         SIDE ISSUED ON ANY TROJAN LABEL. BOTH SIDES RELEASED
         ON PAMA'S ESCORT SUBSIDIARY]

BZX 37   NYT

BZX 38   Another Lonely Night – Derrick Harriott (Prod: Derrick Harriott) (1968)

BZX 39   Been So Long – Derrick Harriott (Prod: Derrick Harriott) (1968)
         [BOTH SIDES ISSUED AS BIG SHOT BI 511]

BZX 40   NYT

BZX 41   NYT

BZX 42   Sufferer – The Kingstonians (Prod: Derrick Harriott) (1968)

BZX 43   Kiss A Little Finger – The Kingstonians (Prod: Derrick Harriott) (1968)
         [BOTH SIDES ISSUED AS BIG SHOT BI 508]

BZX 44   John Jones – Rudy Mills (Prod: Derrick Harriott) (1968)

BZX 45   Place Called Happiness – Rudy Mills (Prod: Derrick Harriott) (1968)
         [BOTH SIDES ISSUED AS BIG SHOT BI 509]

BZX 46   NYT

BZX 47   Biafra – The Crystalites (Prod: Derrick Harriott) (1968)

BZX 48   Drop Pon – The Crystalites (Prod: Derrick Harriott) (1968) [BOTH
         SIDES ISSUED AS BIG SHOT BI 510]

BZX 49   NYT

BZX 50   NYT

BZX 51   Worries A Yard – The Versatiles (Prod: Lee Perry and Enid Barnett) (1969)

BZX 52   Hound Dog Special – Val Bennett (Prod: Lee Perry and Enid Barnett)
         (1969) [BOTH SIDES ISSUED AS BIG SHOT BI 520]

BZX 53   Suzy Wong – Keelyn Beckford (Prod: Enid Barnett) (1969)

BZX 54   Deebo – The Swinging Kings (Prod: Enid Barnett) (1969) [BOTH SIDES
         ISSUED AS BIG SHOT BI 521]

BZX 55   Son Of A Preacher Man – The Gaylettes (Prod: Ken Lazarus and Richard
         Khouri for Federal Records) (1969)

BZX 56   That's How Strong My Love Is – The Gaylettes (Prod: Ken Lazarus and
         Richard Khouri for Federal Records) (1969) [BOTH SIDES ISSUED AS
         BIG SHOT BI 516]

BZX 57   NYT

BZX 58   NYT

BZX 59   NYT

BZX 60   Deportation – Eric 'Monty' Morris (Prod: Albert Gene Murphy) (1969)

BZX 63   Say I'm Back (aka 'He Is Back') – Eric 'Monty' Morris (Prod: Albert Gene
         Murphy) (1969) [BOTH SIDES ISSUED AS BIG SHOT BI 513]

BZX 61   You're No Good – The Tennors (Prod: Albert Gene Murphy) (1969)

BZX 62   Do The Reggae – The Tennors (Prod: Albert Gene Murphy) (1969) [BOTH SIDES ISSUED AS BIG SHOT BI 514]

BZX 64   NYT (BUT POSSIBLY OTHER SIDE OF BZX 59)

BZX 65   Another Scorcher – Jackie Bernard and The Tennors (Prod: Albert Gene Murphy) (1969)

BZX 66   My Baby – The Harmonians (Prod: Albert Gene Murphy) (1969) [BOTH SIDES ISSUED AS BIG SHOT BI 517. B SIDE ALSO ISSUED ON BZX 27]

BZX 68   Parapinto – Karl Bryan and Johnny Moore (Prod: Albert Gene Murphy) (1969)

BZX 67   Cool Hand Luke – Karl Bryan and Johnny Moore (Prod: Albert Gene Murphy) (1969) [BOTH SIDES ISSUED AS BIG SHOT BI 518]

GPW SERIES

GPW stands for Graeme P Walker, one of the main men at Trojan/B&C around 1970/71.

GPW 1   Confusion – The Untouchables (Prod: Lee Perry) (1971)

GPW 2   Confusion Version – The Upsetters (Prod: Lee Perry) (1971) [ISSUED AS UPSETTER US 355]

GPW 3   Elusion – Teddy (Prod: Lee Perry) (1971)

GPW 4   Big John Wayne – The Upsetters (Prod: Lee Perry) (1971) [ISSUED AS UPSETTER US 353]

GPW 5   Mr Brown – Bob Marley and The Wailers (Prod: Lee Perry) (1971)

GPW 6   Dracula – The Upsetters (Prod: Lee Perry) (1971) [ISSUED AS UPSETTER US 354]

GPW 7   Kaya – Bob Marley and The Wailers (Prod: Lee Perry) (1971)

GPW 8   Kaya Version – Bob Marley and The Wailers (Prod: Lee Perry) (1971) [UNISSUED, AS WAS THE CASE WITH ITS COUNTERPART ON UPSETTER US 356]

GPW 9   Heavy Load – Carl Dawkins (Prod: Lee Perry) (1971) Unidentified – unidentified (Prod: Lee Perry) (1971)

GPW 10   Got To Be Mine/Down The Road – The Hurricanes/The Upsetters (Prod: Lee Perry) (1971) [A SIDE ISSUED ON UPSETTER US 358B. B SIDE POSSIBLY GPW 11]

GPW 11   NYT [SEE ALSO GPW 10]

GPW 12   Small Axe/Unidentified – Bob Marley and The Wailers/unidentified (Prod: Lee Perry) (1971) [A SIDE ISSUED ON UPSETTER US 357A]

GPW 13   White Christmas/My Love And I – Jackie Edwards (Prod: Jackie Edwards) (1971) [ISSUED ON TROJAN TR 7883]

GPW 14   NYT
GPW 15   NYT
GPW 16   NYT
GPW 17   NYT
GPW 18   NYT
GPW 19   NYT
GPW 20   NYT
GPW 21   NYT
GPW 22   NYT
GPW 23   NYT
GPW 24   NYT
GPW 25   NYT
GPW 26   NYT
GPW 27   NYT
GPW 28   NYT
GPW 29   NYT
GPW 30   NYT
GPW 31   NYT
GPW 32   Message To The Ungodly/Isaiah Version – Niney and The Observers (Prod:
          Winston Holness [Niney]) (1971) [ISSUED AS BIG SHOT BI 586]
GPW 33   The Gardener/Version – Julie Anne [Judy Mowatt]/The Professionals
          (Prod; Joel Gibson [Joe Gibbs]) (1971) [A SIDE ISSUED ON TROJAN
          LP TBL 183 ('HEPTONES AND THEIR FRIENDS MEET THE NOW
          GENERATION')]
GPW 34   Dreamland/Dream Version – The Wailers/The Upsetters (Prod: Lee Perry)
          (1971) [ISSUED AS UPSETTER US 371]
GPW 35   NYT
GPW 36   Hello Mother/Rod Of Correction Version – The Dynamites (Prod:
          Clancy Eccles) (1971) [A SIDE ISSUED ON CLANDISC CLA 237A.
          B SIDE ISSUED ON CLANDISC CLA 233B]
GPW 37   Cotton Comes To Harlem/Harlem Version – Winston Wright and The
          Crystalites/The Crystalites (Prod: Derrick Harriott) (1971) [NOT
          ISSUED ON ANY TROJAN LABEL]
GPW 38   Take Me As I Am/In Paradise – Jackie Edwards/Jackie Edwards and Julie
          Anne [Judy Mowatt] (Prod: Edward 'Bunny' Lee) (1971) [ISSUED AS
          TROJAN TR 7833]
GPW 39   Walk With Love/Walk With Love (Version) – The Maytals/Beverley's All
          Stars (Prod: Leslie Kong) (1971) [ISSUED AS SUMMIT SUM 8529]
GPW 40   NYT

GPW 41 Pick Your Choice/The Road To Zion – Niney and The Observers (Prod: Winston Holness [Niney]) (1971) [NOT ISSUED ON ANY TROJAN LABEL]

GPW 42 Musical Revolution/Trouble (Take 2) – Charlie Ace/The Green Busters (Prod: Theo Beckford) (1971) [NOT ISSUED ON ANY TROJAN LABEL]

GPW 43 Give You All My Love/Trouble (Take 1) – The Green Busters (Prod: Theo Beckford) (1971) [NOT ISSUED ON ANY TROJAN LABEL]

GPW 44 Teacher, Teacher/Teacher, Teacher Version – The Maytals/Beverley's All Stars (Prod: Leslie Kong) (1971) [NOT ISSUED ON ANY TROJAN LABEL]

GPW 45 Poor Chubby/Better Days – Junior Byles/Carlton and The Shoes (Prod: Lee Perry) (1971) [A SIDE ISSUED ON TROJAN LP TRL 52 (JUNIOR BYLES' 'BEAT DOWN BABYLON'). B SIDE ISSUED ON BREAD BR 1111B]

GPW 46 Brand New Secondhand/Secondhand (Version) – Peter Tosh and The Wailers/The Upsetters (Prod: Lee Perry) (1971) [NOT ISSUED ON ANY TROJAN LABEL]

GPW 47 My Girl/Coming Again – Busty Brown (unconfirmed)/Junior Byles (Prod: Lee Perry) (1971) [A SIDE NOT ISSUED ON ANY TROJAN LABEL. B SIDE ISSUED ON TROJAN LP TRL 52 (JUNIOR BYLES' 'BEAT DOWN BABYLON')]

GPW 48 Walking The Street/Jah Is Mighty – The Hurricanes/Bob Marley (Prod: Lee Perry) (1971) [NOT ISSUED ON ANY TROJAN LABEL]

GPW 49 Jump And Rail/Trying My Faith – The Bleechers/The Stags (possibly The Versatiles) (Prod: Lee Perry/Bush Productions) (1971) [A SIDE NOT ISSUED ON ANY TROJAN LABEL. B SIDE ISSUED ON EXPLOSION EX 2066B]

GPW 50 Come On Over/River To Cross – The Viceroys (Prod: Lee Perry) (1971) [NOT ISSUED ON ANY TROJAN LABEL. BOTH SIDES RELEASED ON PAMA'S BULLET LABEL (BU 450A AND BU 453B RESPECTIVELY)]

GPW 51 NYT

GPW 52 NYT

GPW 53 Bongo Man Rise/Remember – The Maytones/Roy and Bim (Prod: Alvin Ranglin) (1971) [ISSUED ON GG LABEL AS GG 4525]

GPW 54 King Of Glory/Stretch Forth Thy Hand – Dennis Alcapone/Prince Huntley (Prod: Alvin Ranglin) (1971) [ISSUED ON GG LABEL AS GG 4526]

GPW 55 Closer Together/Closer Together (Version) – Gregory Isaacs/Rupie Edwards' All Stars (Prod: Rupie Edwards) (1971) [NOT ISSUED ON ANY TROJAN LABEL]

GPW 56   Know Far I/Know Far I Version – Bongo Herman and Bunny/The
          Crystalites (Prod: Derrick Harriott) (1971) [ISSUED AS SONG BIRD SB
          1060]

GPW 57   Mister Big Stuff/Mister Big Stuff (Version) – The Crepsoles/The
          Aquarians (Prod: Herman Chin-Loy) (1971) [NOT ISSUED ON ANY
          TROJAN LABEL]

GPW 58   Bye Bye Love/Valley Of The Dolls – The Fabulous Shoemakers/Roy and
          Dizzy (actually Roy Richards and Johnny Moore) (Prod: Fud Christian for
          La-Fud-Del) (1971) [NOT ISSUED ON ANY TROJAN LABEL]

GPW 59   Miss Annie Oh/Version – Nora Dean/Fud Christian All Stars (Prod: Fud
          Christian for La-Fud-Del) (1971) [NOT ISSUED ON ANY TROJAN
          LABEL]

GPW 60   High And Dry/Love Is Blue/Moon River/Peace And Love – Greyhound
          (Prod: Dave Bloxham) (1971) [MAXI-SINGLE. ALL TRACKS ISSUED
          ON TROJAN LP TRL 27 ('BLACK AND WHITE')]

GPW 61   Don't Cry Daddy/I Like It – Tony King and The Hippy Boys/Tony
          King (actually by The Hippy Boys) (Prod: Ranny Williams) (1970) [NOT
          ISSUED ON ANY TROJAN LABEL: RELEASED ON PAMA'S GAS
          SUBSIDIARY GAS 156]

GPW 62   Love Of The Common People/The Dragon's Net – Eric Donaldson/The
          Dragonaires (actually with Denzil Laing) (Prod: Dynamic Sounds) (1971)
          [ISSUED AS DYNAMIC DYN 423]

GPW 63   NYT

GPW 64   NYT

GPW 65   NYT

GPW 66   NYT

GPW 67   NYT

GPW 68   Strange World/Unidentified – Bob [Andy] and Marcia [Griffiths] (Prod:
          Bob Andy) (1971) [NOT ISSUED ON ANY TROJAN LABEL]

GPW 69   NYT

GPW 70   NYT

GPW 71   NYT

GPW 72   NYT

GPW 73   NYT

GPW 74   NYT

GPW 75   Strong Man Medley/Stronger Version – Monty Malibu (unconfirmed)/
          The Observers (Prod: Winston Holness [Niney]) (1971) [NOT ISSUED
          ON ANY TROJAN LABEL]

GPW 76   Best Of Five (Part 1)/Best Of Five (Part 2) – The Ethiopians (1971) (Prod:
          Derrick Harriott) (1971) [ISSUED AS SONG BIRD SB 1064]

GPW 77 Java/Java Version 2 – Augustus Pablo and The Impact All Stars (Prod: Vincent Chin for Randy's) (1971) [A SIDE ISSUED ON TROJAN LP TBL 182 ('VERSION TO VERSION ')]

GPW 78 Present In School/Walking Stick – Cat Campbell/Philip Samuel (Prod: Alvin Ranglin) (1971) [TRACKS ISSUED ON TROJAN LP TBL 176 ('REGGAE REGGAE VOLUME 2')

GPW 79 A Love Like Yours/Just Keep It Up – John Holt (Prod: Alvin Ranglin) (1971) [ISSUED ON GG'S LABEL AS GG 4529]

GPW 80 Rosemarie/Version – Scotty/The Crystalites (Prod: Derrick Harriott) (1971) [A SIDE ISSUED ON TROJAN LP TRL 33 (SCOTTY'S 'SCHOOL DAYS')]

GPW 81 Have You Seen Her?/Have You Seen Her Version – Derrick Harriott/The Crystalites (Prod: Derrick Harriott) (1971) [ISSUED AS SONG BIRD SB 1065]

GPW 82 Milk And Honey/Israel Want To Be Free – Dennis Alcapone/The Ethiopians (Prod: Alvin Ranglin) (1971) [A SIDE INCLUDED ON TROJAN LP TBL 176 ('REGGAE REGGAE VOLUME 2'). B SIDE ISSUED ON GGs LABEL GG 4533B]

GPW 83 Hits Medley/Bad To Be Good – The Pioneers (Prod: Sidney Crooks/ Sidney Crooks, Jackie Robinson and George Dekker [The Pioneers]) (1971) [A SIDE NOT ISSUED ON ANY TROJAN LABEL. B SIDE ISSUED ON 7897A]

JLW SERIES

Only two issues, both produced by Joe Sinclair. The matrix may possibly have stood for 'Joe White Label'.

JWL 1 Behold/Thunderball – The Setters/Des All Stars [Ken Elliott and The Cimarons] (1974) [A SIDE ISSUED ON TROJAN COMPILATION '20 TIGHTEN UPs' (TRLS 90). B SIDE ISSUED ON HARRY J HJ 6674B]

JWL 2 Wide Awake In A Dream/P.E.O 111 – The Setters/Des All Stars [Ken Elliott and The Cimarons] [A SIDE ISSUED ON TROJAN COMPILATION '20 TIGHTEN UPs' (TRLS 90). B SIDE ISSUED ON ATTACK ATT 8067B]

TMX SERIES

Note

Probably standing for 'Trojan Matrix', this was another of Trojan's special blank label 'pre-release' series and the one that spanned the most releases. Again, like BZX it's been a bit of a nightmare trying to allocate many of them to their exact couplings. The vast bulk of them did actually see official release across Trojan and its subsidiary labels as 45s, but some (like TMX 1/2) weren't.

TMX 1	Mary Poppins – Tommy McCook and The Supersonics with Danny Simpson (Prod: Arthur' Duke' Reid) (1968)
TMX 2	If You See Jane – The Yardbrooms (Prod: Arthur 'Duke'Reid) (1968) [A SIDE ISSUED ON TROJAN LP TRL 6 ('HERE COMES THE DUKE'). B SIDE NOT ISSUED ON ANY TROJAN LABEL]
TMX 3	I'll Be Lonely – John Holt and Joya Landis (Prod: Arthur 'Duke' Reid) (1968)
TMX 4	Second Fiddle – Tommy McCook and The Supersonics (Prod: Arthur 'Duke' Reid) (1968) [ISSUED AS TROJAN TR 633]
TMX 5	NYT
TMX 6	NYT
TMX 7	NYT
TMX 8	I Wish It Would Rain – The Techniques (Prod: Arthur 'Duke' Reid) (1968)
TMX 9	There Comes A Time – The Techniques (Prod: Arthur 'Duke' Reid) (1968) [ISSUED AS DUKE DU 1]
TMX 10	NYT
TMX 11	Soul Remedy – Tommy McCook and The Supersonics (Prod: Arthur 'Duke' Reid) (1968) [B SIDE ISSUED ON TROJAN LP TRL 6 ('HERE COMES THE DUKE')]
TMX 12	Love Up, Kiss Up – The Termites (Prod: Arthur 'Duke' Reid) (1968)
TMX 13	Those Guys – The Sensations (Prod: Arthur 'Duke' Reid) (1968) [A SIDE ISSUED ON TROJAN TR 634A. B SIDE ISSUED ON DUKE DU 2A]
TMX 14	I'll Never Fall In Love Again – The Sensations (Prod: Arthur 'Duke' Reid) (1968)
TMX 15	True True True – Ken Parker (Prod: Arthur 'Duke' Reid) (1968) [A SIDE ISSUED ON DUKE DU 2B. B SIDE ISSUED ON TROJAN LP TRL 6 ('HERE COMES THE DUKE')]
TMX 16	NYT
TMX 17	Reggae (Lonely Goat Herd) – Tommy McCook and The Supersonics (Prod: Arthur 'Duke' Reid) (1968) [B SIDE ISSUED ON TROJAN TR 634B]
TMX 18	NYT
TMX 19	NYT
TMX 20	NYT
TMX 21	I Wear His Ring – Phyllis Dillon (Prod: Arthur 'Duke' Reid) (1968)
TMX 22	Don't Touch Me Tomato – Phyllis Dillon (Prod: Arthur 'Duke' Reid) (1968) [ISSUED AS TREASURE ISLE TI 7041

TMX 23   Dulcemania – Drumbago and The Dynamites (Prod: Clancy Eccles) (1968)

TMX 24   Chinaman – Clancy Eccles (Prod: Clancy Eccles) (1968) [ISSUED AS
          TROJAN TR 638]

TMX 25   Sweet Africa –Val Bennett and The Dynamites (Prod: Clancy Eccles)
          (1968)

TMX 26   Let Us Be Lovers –Velma Jones and Clancy Eccles (Prod: Clancy Eccles)
          (1968) [ISSUED AS TROJAN TR 639]

TMX 27   Mix It Up –The Kingstonians (Prod: Karl 'JJ' Johnson) (1968)

TMX 28   I'll Be Around –The Kingstonians (Prod: Karl 'JJ' Johnson) (1968)
          [ISSUED AS TROJAN TR 627]

TMX 29   I'll Make It Up – Carl Dawkins (Prod: Karl 'JJ' Johnson) (1968)

TMX 30   One Dollar Of Music – JJ All Stars (Prod: Karl 'JJ' Johnson) (1968)
          [ISSUED AS DUKE DU 3]

TMX 31   NYT

TMX 32   NYT

TMX 33   Fat Man – Derrick Morgan (Prod: Lynford Anderson) (1968)

TMX 34   South Parkway Rock –Val Bennett (Prod: Lynford Anderson) (1968)
          [ISSUED AS TROJAN TR 626]

TMX 35   Thunderstorm – Burt Walters (Prod: Lynford Anderson) (1968)

TMX 36   Honey Love – Burt Walters (Prod: Lynford Anderson) (1968) [ISSUED
          AS TROJAN TR 636]

TMX 37   Party Tonight –The Silvertones (Prod: Lynford Anderson) (1968)

TMX 38   Time Marches On –The Race Fans (Prod: Lynford Anderson) (1968)
          [ISSUED AS TROJAN TR 637 BUT WITH A AND B SIDES
          REVERSED]

TMX 39   Win Your Love – George A. Penny (Prod: Lynford Anderson) (1968)

TMX 40   It's All In The Game –Val Bennett (Prod: Lynford Anderson) (1968)
          [ISSUED AS TROJAN TR 625]

TMX 41   You Crummy – Lee Perry (Prod: Lee Perry) (1968)

TMX 42   Sentence – Danny [Simpson] and Lee [Perry] (Prod: Lee Perry) (1968)
          [ISSUED AS TROJAN TR 629]

TMX 43   Soul Limbo – Byron Lee and The Dragonaires (Prod: Byron Lee) (1968)

TMX 44   The Whistling Song – Byron Lee and The Dragonaires (Prod: Byron Lee)
          (1968) [ISSUED AS TROJAN TR 624]

TMX 45   Baby Baby –Val Bennett (Prod: Lee Perry) (1968)

TMX 46   Barbara –Val Bennett (Prod: Lee Perry) (1968) [ISSUED AS TROJAN
          TR 640]

TMX 47   Farmer's In The Den –The Bleechers (Prod: Lee Perry) (1968)

TMX 48   I'm Coming Home – unidentified artist [A SIDE ISSUED ON
          UPSETTER US 308B]

TMX 49   Mother Hen – The Harmonisers (Prod: Joel Gibson [Joe Gibbs]) (1968)

TMX 50   Chastise Them – Winston Sinclair (Prod: Joel Gibson [Joe Gibbs]) (1968)
          [UNCONFIRMED] [ISSUED IN 1969 AS DUKE DU 32]

TMX 51   Uncle Desmond – Lee Perry (Prod: Lee Perry) (1968)

TMX 52   Bronco (Ol' Man River) – Lee Perry and The Upsetters with Sir Lord
          Comic (Prod: Lee Perry) (1968) [ISSUED AS TROJAN TR 644]

TMX 53   Left With A Broken Heart – The Paragons (Prod: Winston Riley) (1968)

TMX 54   I've Got To Get Away – The Paragons (Prod: Winston Riley) (1968)
          [ISSUED AS DUKE DU 7]

TMX 55   Freedom Sound – The Afrotones (Prod: Harry Johnson) (1968)

TMX 56   Easy Sound – The Jay Boys (Prod: Harry Johnson) (1968)
          [UNCONFIRMED] [ISSUED IN 1969 AS DUKE DU 19]

TMX 57   Happy Time – Keble Drummond (Prod: Harry Johnson) (1968)

TMX 58   Smashville – The Jay Boys (Prod: Harry Johnson) (1968) [ISSUED AS
          DUKE DU 4]

TMX 59   Lavender Blue – Lloyd Robinson (Prod: Harry Johnson) (1968)

TMX 60   Cuss Cuss – Lloyd Robinson (Prod: Harry Johnson) (1968) [ISSUED AS
          DUKE DU 5 BUT WITH A AND B SIDES REVERSED]

TMX 61   Easy Sound – The Jay Boys (Prod: Harry Johnson) (1968)

TMX 62   Candy Lady – [Hugh] Black and [George] Daley (Prod: Harry Johnson)
          (1968) [A SIDE ISSUED ON DUKE DU 19B IN 1969. B SIDE
          ISSUED ON TROJAN TR 654B IN 1969]

TMX 63   NYT

TMX 64   A Man Of My Word – The Techniques (Prod: Winston Riley) (1968)

TMX 65   The Time Has Come – The Techniques (Prod: Winston Riley) (1968)
          [ISSUED AS DUKE DU 6]

TMX 66   Tou're My Everything – The Techniques (Prod: Winston Riley) (1968)

TMX 67   What Am I To Do – The Techniques (Prod: Winston Riley) (1968)
          [ISSUED AS DUKE DU 22 IN 1969 BUT WITH A AND B SIDES
          REVERSED]

TMX 68   NYT

TMX 69   NYT

TMX 70   You Know What I Mean – The Inspirations (Prod: Lee Perry) (1968)

TMX 71   Unidentified [A SIDE ISSUED IN 1969 ON UPSETTER US 300B]

TMX 72   Dollar In The Teeth – The Upsetters (Prod: Lee Perry) (1968)

TMX 73   Return Of Django – The Upsetters (Prod: Lee Perry) (1968) [ISSUED
          AS UPSETTER US 301 IN 1969 BUT WITH A AND B SIDES
          REVERSED]

TMX 74   Mini Dress – Winston Jarrett (Prod: Lee Perry) (1968)

TMX 75   Mad House – Lee Perry (Prod: Lee Perry) (1968) [ISSUED AS
          UPSETTER US 306 IN 1969]
TMX 76   Stand By Me – The Inspirations (Prod: Lee Perry) (1968)
TMX 77   Unidentified [A SIDE ISSUED IN 1969 ON DUKE DU 10B]
TMX 78   Moonlight Lover – Joya Landis with Tommy McCook and The
          Supersonics (Prod: Arthur 'Duke' Reid) (1969)
TMX 79   I Love You True – Joya Landis with Tommy McCook and The
          Supersonics (Trojan) (Prod: Arthur 'Duke' Reid) (1969) [ISSUED IN
          1969 AS TROJAN TR 641]
TMX 80   Eight For Eight – The Upsetters (Prod: Lee Perry) (1969) [ISSUED IN
          1969 ON UPSETTER US 300A]
TMX 81   Breaking Up – Alton Ellis with Tommy McCook and The Supersonics
          (Prod: Arthur 'Duke' Reid) (1968)
TMX 82   Party Time – Alton Ellis with Tommy McCook and The Supersonics
          (Prod: Arthur 'Duke' Reid) (1968) [ISSUED AS TROJAN TR 642]
TMX 83   Tonight – John Holt with Tommy McCook and The Supersonics (Prod:
          Arthur 'Duke' Reid) (1968)
TMX 84   Maybe Someday – John Holt with Tommy McCook and The Supersonics
          (Prod: Arthur 'Duke' Reid) (1968) [ISSUED AS TROJAN TR 643]
TMX 85   Penny Reel – Whistling Willie [Neville Willoughby] (Prod: Neville
          Willoughby) (1969)
TMX 86   Soul Tonic – Whistling Willie [Neville Willoughby] (Prod: Neville
          Willoughby) (1969) [ISSUED AS DUKE DU 8]
TMX 87   Good Father – David Isaacs (Prod: Lee Perry) (1969)
TMX 88   What A Situation – Slim Smith (Lee Perry) (1969) [ISSUED AS
          UPSETTER US 302]
TMX 89   What A Botheration – Lee Perry and The Upsetters (Prod: Lee Perry)
          (1969)
TMX 90   I'll Be Waiting – The Termites (Prod: Lee Perry) (1969) [A SIDE
          ISSUED ON TROJAN TR 612B AND DUKE DU 10A. B SIDE
          ISSUED ON UPSETTER US 307B]
TMX 91   Big Boy – Ranny Williams and The Hippy Boys (Prod: Ranny Williams)
          (1969)
TMX 92   Theme From 'A Summer Place' – Ranny Williams and The Hippy Boys
          (Prod: Ranny Williams) (1969) [NOT ISSUED ON ANY TROJAN
          LABEL. RELEASED ON PAMA'S BULLET SUBSIDIARY WITH A
          AND B SIDES REVERSED]
TMX 93   Seven Letters – Derrick Morgan (Prod: Edward 'Bunny' Lee) (1969)
          [ISSUED ON JACKPOT JP 700A. POSSIBLE LINK HERE WITH
          BZX 24?]

TMX 94   Cut Down Your Speed – The Ethiopians (Prod: Lee Perry) (1969)

TMX 95   Not Me – The Ethiopians (Prod: Lee Perry) (1969) [UNCONFIRMED. NOT ISSUED ON ANY TROJAN LABEL. RELEASED ON DOCTOR BIRD IN 1968]

TMX 96   The Love I Saw In You Was Just A Mirage – The Uniques (Prod: Winston Lowe) (1969)

TMX 97   Hey You – The Uniques (Prod: Winston Lowe) (1969) [ISSUED AS TROJAN TR 645 BUT WITH A AND B SIDES REVERSED]

TMX 98   Soul Pipe – King Cannon [Karl Bryan] with Anderson's All Stars (Prod: Lynford Anderson) (1969)

TMX 99   Overproof – King Cannon [Karl Bryan] with Anderson's All Stars (Prod: Lynford Anderson) (1969) [ISSUED AS DUKE DU 13]

TMX 100   Constantinople – Clancy Eccles (Prod: Clancy Eccles) (1969)

TMX 101   Demonstration – Val Bennett (Prod: Clancy Eccles) (1969) [A SIDE ISSUED ON TROJAN TR 648A. B SIDE ISSUED ON TROJAN TR 649A]

TMX 102   Deacon Don – Clancy Eccles (Prod: Clancy Eccles) (1969)

TMX 103   My Girl – Clancy Eccles (Prod: Clancy Eccles) (1969) [A SIDE ISSUED ON TROJAN TR 648B. B SIDE ISSUED ON TROJAN TR 49B]

TMX 104   Old Man Say – The Silver Stars (Prod: Clancy Eccles) (1969)

TMX 105   Promises – The Silver Stars (Prod: Clancy Eccles) (1969) [ISSUED AS TROJAN TR 648]

TMX 106   Bangarang Crash – Clancy Eccles (Prod: Clancy Eccles) (1969)

TMX 107   Rahtid – The Dynamites (Prod: Clancy Eccles) (1969) [ISSUED AS TROJAN TR 647]

TMX 108   Auntie Lulu – Clancy Eccles (Prod: Clancy Eccles) (1969)

TMX 109   Don't Brag, Don't Boast – Clancy Eccles (Prod: Clancy Eccles) (1969) [ISSUED AS DUKE DU 8]

TMX 110   I Can't Stop Loving You – Owen Gray (Prod: Owen Gray) (1969)

TMX 111   Reggae Dance – Owen Gray (Prod: Owen Gray) (1969) [A SIDE ISSUED ON BLUE CAT BS 156A. B SIDE ISSUED ON DUKE DU 12A]

TMX 112   Tell Me Darling – Owen Gray (Prod: Owen Gray) (1969)

TMX 113   I Know – Owen Gray (Prod: Owen Gray) (1969) [A SIDE ISSUED ON BLUE CAT BS 156B. B SIDE ISSUED ON DUKE DU 12B]

TMX 114   What A Price – Busty Brown (Prod: Lee Perry) (1969)

TMX 115   How Can I Forget – Busty Brown (Prod: Lee Perry) (1969) [ISSUED AS UPSETTER US 304]

TMX 116   Ten To Twelve – The Upsetters (Prod: Lee Perry) (1969)

TMX 117   People Funny Fi True – Lee Perry (Prod: Lee Perry) (1969) [ISSUED AS UPSETTER US 303]

TMX 118   I've Got Memories – David Isaacs (Prod: Lee Perry) (1969)

TMX 119   Leaving On A Jet Plane – David Isaacs (Prod: Lee Perry) (1969)
          [ISSUED AS UPSETTER US 305]

TMX 120   Diana – Alton Ellis (Prod: Arthur 'Duke' Reid) (1969)

TMX 121   Personality – Alton Ellis (Prod: Arthur 'Duke' Reid) (1969) [ISSUED AS
          DUKE DU 14]

TMX 122   Love Is All I Had – Phyllis Dillon (Prod: Arthur 'Duke' Reid) (1969)

TMX 123   Boys And Girls Reggae – Phyllis Dillon (Prod: Arthur 'Duke' Reid)
          (1969) [ISSUED AS TROJAN TR 651]

TMX 124   You Should Have Known Better – Justin Hinds and The Dominoes
          (Prod: Arthur 'Duke' Reid) (1969)

TMX 125   Third Figure – Tommy McCook and The Supersonics (Prod: Arthur
          'Duke' Reid) (1969) [ISSUED AS TROJAN TR 652]

TMX 126   Out Of Sight – Danny Simpson with Tommy McCook and The
          Supersonics (Prod: Arthur 'Duke' Reid) (1969)

TMX 127   I Want You Closer – John Holt (Prod: Arthur 'Duke' Reid) (1969)
          [ISSUED AS TROJAN TR 653]

TMX 128   Forever – The Uniques (Prod: Winston Lowe) (1969)

TMX 129   Cuyah – Lloyd Tyrell [Lloyd Charmers] (Prod: Winston Lowe) (1969)
          [ISSUED AS DUKE DU 15 BUT WITH A AND B SIDES REVERSED]

TMX 130   NYT

TMX 131   NYT

TMX 132   NYT

TMX 133   NYT

TMX 134   Home Without You – The Beltones (Prod: Harry Johnson) (1969)

TMX 135   Why Pretend – The Beltones (Prod: Harry Johnson) (1969) [ISSUED AS
          DUKE DU 17]

TMX 136   Life – Roy Shirley (Prod: Karl 'JJ' Johnson) (1969)

TMX 137   I Like Your Smile – Roy Shirley (Prod: Karl 'JJ' Johnson) (1969)
          [ISSUED AS DUKE DU 18]

TMX 138   NYT

TMX 139   NYT

TMX 140   Hang 'Em High – Richard Ace (Prod: Harry Johnson) (1969)

TMX 141   Candy Lady – [Hugh] Black and George [Daley] (Prod: Harry Johnson)
          (1969) [UNCONFIRMED] [A SIDE ISSUED AS TROJAN TR 654A.
          B SIDE LIKELY TO HAVE BEEN ISSUED ON TR 654B]

TMX 142   Suffering Stink – Band Of Mercy and Salvation (Prod: Coxsone Dodd
          for Disclick) (1969)

TMX 143   The Break – Winston Francis (Prod: Coxsone Dodd for Disclick) (1969)
          [ISSUED AS DUKE DU 20]

TMX 144   Never My Love – Boris Gardner and The Love People (Prod: Sam
          Mitchell) (1969)

TMX 145   The Bold One – Boris Gardner and The Love People (Prod: Sam
          Mitchell) (1969) [ISSUED AS DUKE DU 21]

TMX 146   Sweet Chariot – Max Romeo and The Hippy Boys (Prod: Max Romeo)
          (1969)

TMX 147   Far Far Away – Max Romeo and The Hippy Boys (Prod: Max Romeo)
          (1969) [ISSUED AS TROJAN TR 656. B SIDE ALSO RELEASED ON
          PAMA'S UNITY LABEL]

TMX 148   NYT

TMX 149   NYT

TMX 150   NYT

TMX 151   NYT

TMX 152   The Saint – Tommy McCook and The Supersonics (Prod: Arthur 'Duke'
          Reid) (1969)

TMX 153   Ease Me Up Officer – Soul Ofrous (Prod: Arthur 'Duke' Reid) (1969)
          [ISSUED AS TROJAN TR 657]

TMX 154   Fattie Fattie – Clancy Eccles (Prod: Clancy Eccles) (1969)

TMX 155   Last Call (aka 'Tribute To Drumbago') – The Silver Stars (Prod: Clancy
          Eccles) (1969) [ISSUED AS TROJAN TR 658]

TMX 156   Friends And Lovers Forever – Patti La Donne (Prod: Joe Mansano) (1969)

TMX 157   Hot Line – Joe's All Stars (Prod: Joe Mansano) (1969) [ISSUED AS
          DUKE DU 23 (JOE LABEL)]

TMX 158   Hey Jude – Joe's All Stars (Prod: Joe Mansano) (1969)

TMX 159   Musical Feet – Joe's All Stars (Prod: Joe Mansano) (1969) [ISSUED AS
          DUKE DU 24 (JOE LABEL)]

TMX 160   Battle Cry Of Biafra – Joe's All Stars (Prod: Joe Mansano) (1969)

TMX 161   Funky Reggae, Part 1 – Joe's All Stars (Prod: Joe Mansano) (1969)
          [ISSUED AS DUKE DU 28 (JOE LABEL)]

TMX 162   Five To Five – Lloyd Charmers and The Hippy Boys (Prod: Winston
          Lowe) (1969)

TMX 163   Come See About Me – The Soul Stirrers (Prod: Lloyd Charmers) (1969)
          [ISSUED AS DUKE DU 25. B SIDE ALSO ISSUED ON SONG
          BIRD SB 1002B]

TMX 164   Hear Ya – The Scorchers (Prod: Karl 'JJ' Johnson) (1969)

TMX 165   Live Life – The Vibrators (Prod: Karl 'JJ' Johnson) (1969) [ISSUED AS
          DUKE DU 26]

TMX 166   Glad Your Living – Stranger Cole (Prod: Karl 'JJ' Johnson) (1969)

TMX 167   Help Wanted – Stranger Cole (Prod: Karl 'JJ' Johnson) (1969) [ISSUED
          AS DUKE DU 27)

TMX 168   The Night Doctor – The Upsetters (Prod: Lee Perry) (1969)

TMX 169   To Love Somebody – Busty Brown (Prod: Lee Perry) (1969) [A SIDE ISSUED ON UPSETTER US 307A. B SIDE ISSUED ON UPSETTER US 308A]

TMX 170   Everybody Bawling – The Melodians (Prod: Arthur 'Duke' Reid) (1969)

TMX 171   Kilowatt – Tommy McCook and The Supersonics (Prod: Arthur 'Duke' Reid) (1969) [ISSUED AS TROJAN TR 660]

TMX 172   Ali Baba – John Holt with Tommy McCook and The Supersonics (Prod: Arthur 'Duke' Reid) (1969)

TMX 173   I'm Your Man – John Holt with Tommy McCook and The Supersonics (Prod: Arthur 'Duke' Reid) (1969) [ISSUED AS TROJAN 661]

TMX 174   Dig Out Me Eye – The Royals (Prod: L Edwards) (1969)

TMX 175   Think You Too Bad – The Royals (Prod: L Edwards) (1969) [ISSUED AS TROJAN TR 662]

TMX 176   Dollars And Cents – Gladstone Adams (actually with the Treasure Isle Group) (Prod: Arthur 'Duke' Reid) (1969)

TMX 177   Popcorn Reggae – Tommy McCook and The Supersonics (Prod: Arthur 'Duke' Reid) (1969) [ISSUED AS TROJAN TR 659]

TMX 178   NYT

TMX 179   NYT

TMX 180   NYT

TMX 181   NYT

TMX 182   NYT

TMX 183   NYT

TMX 184   NYT

TMX 185   NYT

TMX 186   NYT

TMX 187   NYT

TMX 188   NYT

TMX 189   NYT

TMX 190   Big Boy – Ranny Williams and The Hippy Boys (Prod: Ranny Williams) (1969)

TMX 191   Too Late – The Harmonisers (Prod: Ranny Williams) (1969) [A SIDE ISSUED ON TMX 91 AND PAMA'S BULLET LABEL. B SIDE ISSUED AS TROJAN TR 685B – CREDITED TO THE PIONEERS]

TMX 192   Sweet Things We Used To Do – The Harmonisers (Prod: Ranny Williams) (1969)

TMX 193   House On Fire – The Harmonisers (Prod: Ranny Williams) (1969) [NEITHER SIDE ISSUED ON ANY TROJAN LABEL]

TMX 194   Hog In A Mi Minte – Winston Shand and The Hippy Boys (Prod: Ranny Williams) (1969)

TMX 195   Dick Stiff And Shine – George Anthony (Prod: Ranny Williams) (1969) [A SIDE NOT ISSUED ON ANY TROJAN LABEL BUT RELEASED ON PAMA'S BULLET SUBSIDIARY. B SIDE NOT ISSUED ON ANY TROJAN LABEL]

TMX 196   Never Gonna Give You Up – The Royals (Prod: L Edwards) (1969)

TMX 197   Don't Mix Me Up – The Royals (Prod: L Edwards) (1969) [ISSUED AS DUKE DU 29]

TMX 198   NYT

TMX 199   NYT

TMX 200   Man From MI5 – The Upsetters (Prod: Lee Perry) (1969)

TMX 201   Dry Up Your Tears – The Mellotones (Prod: Lee Perry) (1969) [A SIDE ISSUED ON UPSETTER US 310A. B SIDE ISSUED ON UPSETTER US 314B]

TMX 202   Oh Lord – The West Indians (Prod: Lee Perry) (1969)

TMX 203   Come Into My Parlour – The Bleechers (Prod: Lee Perry) (1969) [A SIDE ISSUED ON UPSETTER US 310B. A SIDE ISSUED ON UPSETTER US 314A]

TMX 204   Everything For Fun – The Bleechers (Prod: Lee Perry) (1969)

TMX 205   A Live Injection – The Upsetters (Prod: Lee Perry) (1969) [ISSUED AS UPSETTER US 313 BUT WITH A AND B SIDES REVERSED]

TMX 206   Soulful I – The Upsetters (Prod: Lee Perry) (1969)

TMX 207   No Bread And Butter – Milton Morris (Prod: Lee Perry) (1969) [ISSUED AS UPSETTER US 318]

TMX 208   Medical Operation – The Upsetters (Prod: Lee Perry) (1969)

TMX 209   Badam Bam – The Ravers (Prod: Lee Perry) (1969) [ISSUED AS UPSETTER US 312 BUT WITH A AND B SIDES REVERSED]

TMX 210   Thunderball – The Upsetters (Prod: Lee Perry) (1969)

TMX 211   NYT [A SIDE ISSUED ON TROJAN LP 'THE UPSETTER' (TTL 13)]

TMX 212   Kiddy-o – The Muskyteers [The Silvertones] (Prod: Lee Perry) (1969)

TMX 213   Endlessly – The Muskyteers [The Silvertones] (Prod: Lee Perry) (1969) [ISSUED AS UPSETTER US 309]

TMX 214   What Is Wrong With You – The Bleechers (Prod: Lee Perry) (1969)

TMX 215   Tidal Wave – The Upsetters (Prod: Lee Perry) (1969) [A SIDE UNISSUED ON ANY TROJAN LABEL. B SIDE ISSUED ON TROJAN LP 'THE UPSETTER' (TTL 13)]

TMX 216   NYT

TMX 217   He'll Have To Go – David Isaacs (Prod: Lee Perry) (1969)

TMX 218   Since You Are Gone – David Isaacs (Prod: Lee Perry) (1969) [ISSUED
          AS UPSETTER US 311]
TMX 219   NYT
TMX 220   NYT
TMX 221   NYT
TMX 222   NYT
TMX 223   NYT
TMX 224   NYT
TMX 225   Because You're Mine – Les Foster (Prod: Les Foster) (1969)
TMX 226   Do It Nice – Les Foster (Prod: Les Foster) (1969) [ISSUED AS BIG
          SHOT BI 522 BUT WITH A AND B SIDES REVERSED]
TMX 227   Windy, Part 2 – The Saints (Prod: Les Foster) (1969)
TMX 228   NYT [A SIDE ISSUED ON BIG SHOT BI 522B]
TMX 229   Windy, Part 1 – The Saints (Prod: Les Foster) (1969)
TMX 230   NYT [A SIDE ISSUED ON BIG SHOT BI 522A]
TMX 231   John Public – The Dynamites (Prod: Clancy Eccles) (1969)
TMX 232   I Don't Care – The Dingle Brothers (Prod: Clancy Eccles) (1969) [A
          SIDE ISSUED ON DUKE DU 30B. B SIDE ISSUED ON DUKE DU
          31A]
TMX 233   Shoo Be Doo – Clancy Eccles (Prod: Clancy Eccles) (1969)
TMX 234   Fire Corner – King Stitt (Prod: Clancy Eccles) (1969) [A SIDE ISSUED
          ON DUKE DU 31B. B SIDE ISSUED ON DUKE DU 30A]
TMX 235   I've Tried Before – The Impersonators (Prod: Melmouth Nelson) (1969)
TMX 236   Make It Easy On Yourself – The Impersonators (Prod: Melmouth Nelson)
          (1969) [SCHEDULED FOR RELEASE ON BIG SHOT BI 524 WITH
          A AND B SIDES REVERSED BUT PROBABLY UNISSUED]
TMX 237   You Belong To My Heart – The Demons (Prod: Melmouth Nelson) (1969)
TMX 238   Bless You – The Demons (Prod: Melmouth Nelson) (1969) [ISSUED AS
          BIG SHOT BI 523]
TMX 239   NYT
TMX 240   NYT
TMX 241   Who To Tell – Bruce Bennett (Prod: Lee Perry) (1969)
          [UNCONFIRMED]
TMX 242   I Can't See Myself Crying About You – Busty Brown (Prod: Lee
          Perry) (1969) [DEPENDING ON A SIDE, THIS MAY HAVE BEEN
          RELEASED AS UPSETTER US 319]
TMX 243   Woman Capture Man – The Ethiopians (Prod: Karl 'JJ' Johnson) (1969)
TMX 244   One Heart, One Love – The Ethiopians (Prod: Karl 'JJ' Johnson) (1969)
          [ISSUED AS TROJAN TR 666]
TMX 245   NYT

TMX 246   NYT

TMX 247   Proud Mary – Tony King and The Hippy Boys (Prod: Bart Sanfilipo)
           (1969)

TMX 248   My Devotion – Tony King and The Hippy Boys (Prod: Bart Sanfilipo)
           (1969) [ISSUED AS TROJAN TR 667]

TMX 249   The Whole Family Is Here – The Hippy Boys (Prod: Bart Sanfilipo) (1969)

TMX 250   Love – Max Romeo and The Hippy Boys (Prod: Bart Sanfilipo)
           (1969) [ISSUED AS TROJAN TR 668 BUT WITH A AND B SIDES
           REVERSED]

TMX 251   Michael Row The Boat Ashore – Max Romeo and The Hippy Boys
           (Prod: Bart Sanfilipo) (1969)

TMX 252   Guess Who Is Coming To Dinner – The Hippy Boys (Prod: Bart
           Sanfilipo) (1969) [ISSUED AS TROJAN TR 669]

TMX 253   Chastise Them – Winston Sinclair (Prod: Joel Gibson [Joe Gibbs]) (1969)
           [ISSUED ON DUKE DU 32B BUT UNCONFIRMED – NOT
           CLEAR WHAT OTHER SIDE WOULD HAVE BEEN]

TMX 254   Apple Blossoms – Lester Sterling (Prod: Edward 'Bunny' Lee) (1969)

TMX 255   Devil's Disciple – Lester Sterling (Prod: Edward 'Bunny' Lee) (1969)
           [A SIDE ISSUED ON JACKPOT JP 701B. B SIDE ISSUED ON
           JACKPOT JP 702B]

TMX 256   Having A Party – Errol Dunkley (Prod: Edward 'Bunny' Lee) (1969)

TMX 257   NYT [A SIDE ISSUED ON JACKPOT JP 702A]

TMX 258   Love Power – Slim Smith (Prod: Edward 'Bunny' Lee) (1969)

TMX 259   Since You Are Gone – Pat Kelly (Prod: Lee Perry) (1969) [ISSUED AS
           JACKPOT JP 705]

TMX 260   Too Experienced – Owen Gray (Prod: Owen Gray) (1969)

TMX 261   I Really Love You Baby – Owen Gray (Prod: Owen Gray) (1969)
           [ISSUED AS TROJAN TR 670]

TMX 262   Dark End Of The Street – Pat Kelly (Prod: Lee Perry) (1969)

TMX 263   Cherry Pink – possibly by Bunny Lee (Prod: Edward 'Bunny' Lee) (1969)
           [A SIDE ISSUED ON JACKPOT JP 701A. B SIDE ISSUED ON
           JACKPOT JP 703B]

TMX 264   Then You Can Tell Me Goodbye – Slim Smith (Prod: Edward
           'Bunny' Lee) (1969) [ISSUED ON JACKPOT JP 703A BUT
           UNCONFIRMED – NOT CLEAR WHAT OTHER SIDE WOULD
           HAVE BEEN]

TMX 265   Music House – Roland Alphonso (Prod: Edward 'Bunny' Lee) (1969)

TMX 266   Zapatoo The Tiger – Roland Alphonso and unidentified male vocalist
           (Prod: Edward 'Bunny' Lee) (1969) [ISSUED AS JACKPOT JP 704 BUT
           WITH A AND B SIDES REVERSED]

TMX 267   Seven Lonely Days – Owen Gray (Prod: Owen Gray) (1969)

TMX 268   He Didn't Love You Like I Do – Owen Gray (Prod: Owen Gray) (1969)
          [ISSUED AS DUKE DU 33]

TMX 269   Long Shot Kick The Bucket – The Pioneers (Prod: Leslie Kong) (1969)
          [ISSUED ON TROJAN TR 672A BUT UNCONFIRMED – NOT
          CLEAR WHAT OTHER SIDE WOULD HAVE BEEN]

TMX 270   Too Experienced – Owen Gray (Prod: Owen Gray) (1969)

TMX 271   I Really Love You Baby – Owen Gray (Prod: Owen Gray) (1969)
          [ISSUED AS TROJAN TR 670]

TMX 271   Get On The Right Track – Phyllis Dillon and Hopeton Lewis (Prod:
          Arthur 'Duke' Reid) (1969) [UNCONFIRMED – THERE LOOKS
          TO BE TWO TMX 271s]

TMX 272   Moon Shot – Tommy McCook and The Supersonics (Prod: Arthur
          'Duke' Reid) (1969) [ISSUED AS TROJAN TR 671]

TMX 273   NYT

TMX 274   Stagger Lee – Anonymously Yours (Prod: Bart Sanfilipo) (1969)

TMX 275   Dream Baby – Anonymously Yours (Prod: Bart Sanfilipo) (1969)
          [ISSUED AS DUKE DU 38 BUT WITH A AND B SIDES
          REVERSED]

TMX 276   Itch – Anonymously Yours (Prod: Bart Sanfilipo) (1969)

TMX 277   Organism – Anonymously Yours (Prod: Bart Sanfilipo) (1969) [ISSUED
          AS DUKE DU 40 BUT WITH A AND B SIDES REVERSED]

TMX 278   NYT

TMX 279   NYT

TMX 280   Red Ash – Cannonball [Karl] Bryan (Prod: Arthur 'Duke' Reid) (1969)

TMX 281   Blue Bird – The Silvertones (Prod: Arthur 'Duke' Reid) (1969) [ISSUED
          AS TROJAN TR 673]

TMX 282   If This World Were Mine – Tyrone Evans (Prod: Arthur 'Duke' Reid)
          (1969)

TMX 283   You Done Me Wrong – Tyrone Evans (Prod: Arthur 'Duke' Reid) (1969)
          [ISSUED AS TROJAN TR 677]

TMX 284   Lipstick On You Collar – Naomi Phillips (Prod: Arthur 'Duke' Reid) (1969)

TMX 285   Tribute To Rameses – Tommy McCook and The Supersonics (Prod:
          Arthur 'Duke' Reid) (1969) [ISSUED AS TROJAN TR 686]

TMX 286   What You Gonna Do Now? – John Holt (Prod: Arthur 'Duke' Reid)
          (1969)

TMX 287   Have You Ever Been To Heaven? – John Holt (Prod: Arthur 'Duke' Reid)
          (1969) [ISSUED AS TROJAN TR 674]

TMX 288   Everybody Bawlin' – Don Drummond Junior [Vincent Gordon] (Prod:
          Arthur 'Duke' Reid) (1969)

TMX 289   Come Look Here – The Silvertones (Prod: Arthur 'Duke' Reid) (1969)
          [ISSUED AS DUKE DU 37]
TMX 290   Darling I Love You – John Holt (Prod: Arthur 'Duke' Reid) (1969)
TMX 291   Memory Of Don – Don Drummond Junior [Vin Gordon] (1969)
          [ISSUED AS TROJAN TR 678]
TMX 292   Soul Serenade – Winston Wright with Byron Lee and The Dragonaires
          (Prod: Byron Lee) (1969)
TMX 293   Elizabethan Reggae – Boris Gardner (Prod: Junior Chung) (1969)
          [ISSUED AS SECOND PRESSING OF DUKE DU 39]
TMX 294   The Hustler – Junior Murvin (Prod: Derrick Harriott) (1969)
TMX 295   Magic Touch – Junior Murvin (Prod: Derrick Harriott) (1969) [A SIDE
          ISSUED ON BIG SHOT BI 527A. B SIDE ISSUED ON BIG SHOT
          BI 503A AND BI 527B]
TMX 296   NYT
TMX 297   NYT
TMX 298   Nice Nice – The Kingstonians (Prod: Derrick Harriott) (1969)
TMX 299   I'll Be Around – The Kingstonians (Prod: Derrick Harriott) (1969)
          [ISSUED AS BIG SHOT BI 526A]
TMX 300   NYT
TMX 301   NYT
TMX 302   Bigger Boss – Ansel Collins (actually with Count Sticky) (Prod: Karl 'JJ'
          Johnson) (1969)
TMX 303   My Girl – The Ethiopians (Prod: Karl 'JJ' Johnson) (1969) [ISSUED AS
          DUKE DU 35]
TMX 304   Mr Tambourine Man – Ken Boothe (Prod: Keith Hudson) (1969)
TMX 305   Old Fashioned Way – Ken Boothe (Prod: Keith Hudson) (1969)
          [ISSUED AS BIG SHOT BI 528]
TMX 306   Safari – Lloyd Charmers (Prod: Winston Lowe) (1969)
TMX 307   Last Laugh – Lloyd Charmers (Prod: Winston Lowe) (1969) [ISSUED AS
          DUKE DU 36]
TMX 308   In The Spirit – Lloyd Charmers (Prod: Winston Lowe) (1969)
TMX 309   Duckey Luckey – Lloyd Charmers (Prod: Winston Lowe) (1969)
          [ISSUED AS SONG BIRD SB 1007]
TMX 310   Jumping The Gun – Rico Rodriguez (Prod: Dandy) (1969)
TMX 311   Chicken Lickin' (aka 'Night Fall') – The Hippy Boys (Prod: Sonia
          Pottinger) (1969) [A SIDE ISSUED AS TROJAN TR 672B (BUT SEE
          ALSO TMX 269). B SIDE ISSUED ON HIGH NOTE HS 30A]
TMX 312   Dracula, Prince Of Darkness – King Horror (Prod: Joe Mansano) (1969)
TMX 313   Honky – Joe's All Stars (Prod: Joe Mansano) (1969) [ISSUED AS DUKE
          DU 34 (JOE LABEL)]

TMX 314   Liquidator – Winston Wright and Harry J's All Stars (Prod: Harry
Johnson) (1969)

TMX 315   Feel It Festive Spirit – The Jamaicans (Prod: Harry Johnson) (1969)
[ISSUED AS TROJAN TR 675 (HARRY J LABEL): FIRST
PRESSING. B SIDE ALSO ISSUED ON TROJAN TR 682]

TMX 316   Take You For A Ride – Girl Satchmo with Tommy McCook and The
Supersonics (Prod: Arthur 'Duke' Reid) (1969)

TMX 317   I'm Coming Home – Girl Satchmo with Tommy McCook and The
Supersonics (Prod: Arthur 'Duke' Reid) (1969) [ISSUED AS TROJAN
TR 676]

TMX 318   Get Back – Anonymously Yours (Prod: Bart Sanfilipo) (1969)

TMX 319   I'm Not for Sale – Ernie Smith (Prod: Bart Sanfilipo) (1969) [ISSUED
AS TROJAN TR 680]

TMX 320   '69 – Wallace Wilson (Prod: Bart Sanfilipo) (1969)

TMX 321   It's Your Thing – Anonymously Yours (Prod: Bart Sanfilipo) (1969)
[ISSUED AS TROJAN TR 681 BUT WITH A AND B SIDES
REVERSED]

TMX 322   Higher And Higher – Josh [Roberts] (Prod: Joe Mansano) (1969)

TMX 323   African Meeting – Girlie and Jomo [Denzil Dennis] (Prod: Joe Mansano)
(1969) [ISSUED AS DUKE DU 42 (JOE LABEL) BUT WITH A AND
B SIDES REVERSED]

TMX 324   The Judge – Josh [Roberts] (Prod: Joe Mansano) (1969)

TMX 325   Soul Of Joe – Ron (Prod: Joe Mansano) (1969) [ISSUED AS DUKE
DU 41 (JOE LABEL)]

TMX 326   Ease Up – The Bleechers (Prod: Lee Perry) (1969)

TMX 327   You Gonna Feel It – The Bleechers (Prod: Lee Perry) (1969) [ISSUED
AS TROJAN TR 679]

TMX 328   Cold Sweat – The Upsetters (Prod: Lee Perry) (1969)

TMX 329   Pound Get A Blow – The Bleechers (Prod: Lee Perry) (1969) [ISSUED
AS UPSETTER US 315]

TMX 330   Check Him Out – The Bleechers (Prod: Lee Perry) (1969)

TMX 331   Who To Tell – Bruce Bennett (Prod: Lee Perry) (1969) [A SIDE ISSUED
ON UPSETTER US 317 (SECOND PRESSING). B SIDE ISSUED
ON UPSETTER US 319A]

TMX 332   Hello Dolly – Pat Satchmo (Prod: Lee Perry) (1969)

TMX 333   King Of The Trombone (aka 'Tribute To A King') – Busty Brown (Prod:
Lee Perry) (1969) [ISSUED AS UPSETTER US 316]

TMX 334   Feel It Festive Spirit – The Jamaicans (Prod: Harry Johnson) (1969) [ISSUED
AS TROJAN TR 675A (HARRY J LABEL): FIRST PRESSING. ALSO
ISSUED ON TROJAN TR 682. SEE ALSO TMX 315B]

TMX 335   NYT

TMX 336   Rich In Love – Glen [Adams] and Dave [Barker] (Prod: Harry Johnson)
(1969) [ISSUED ON TROJAN (HARRY J LABEL) TR 675B:
SECOND PRESSING]

TMX 337   Extension 303 (aka 'Confidential') – Lloyd Charmers and The Hippy
Boys (Prod: Lloyd Charmers) (1969)

TMX 338   Brixton (aka 'Soul Of England') – The Jokers (Prod: Lloyd Charmers)
(1969) [NEITHER SIDE ISSUED ON ANY TROJAN LABEL:
RELEASED ON PAMA'S CAMEL AND ESCORT SUBSIDIARIES
RESPECTIVELY]

TMX 339   Sweet Sweet (aka 'Real Real') – Lloyd Robinson (Prod: Winston Lowe)
(1969)

TMX 340   African Zulu – Lloyd Charmers and The Hippy Boys (Prod: Lloyd
Charmers and Herman Chin-Loy) (1969) [A SIDE ISSUED ON
SONG BIRD SB 1001A. B SIDE UNRELEASED ON ANY TROJAN
LABEL: RELEASED ON PAMA'S PUNCH SUBSIDIARY AND THE
'HOUSE IN SESSION' COMPILATION (SECO 25)]

TMX 341   Eko-Craft – Lloyd Charmers and The Hippy Boys (Prod: Lloyd
Charmers) (1969)

TMX 342   House In Session – Tommy Cowan with Lloyd Charmers and The Hippy
Boys (Prod: Lloyd Charmers) 1969 [NEITHER SIDE ISSUED ON
ANY TROJAN LABEL: B SIDE RELEASED ON PAMA'S 'HOUSE
IN SESSION' COMPILATION (SECO 25)]

TMX 343   Black Bud – The Pioneers (Prod: Leslie Kong) (1969) [ISSUED ON
TROJAN TR 685A]

TMX 344   Come See About Me – The Soul Stirrers (Prod: Lloyd Charmers)
(1969)

TMX 345   NYT [A SIDE ISSUED ON SONG BIRD SB 1002B AND DUKE
DU 25B. SEE ALSO TMX 163]

TMX 346   NYT

TMX 347   NYT

TMX 348   Who Yeah – King Stitt (Prod: Clancy Eccles) (1969)

TMX 349   Mr Midnight (Skokiaan) – The Dynamites (Prod: Clancy Eccles) (1969)
[ISSUED AS CLANDISC CLA 203]

TMX 350   Dollar Train – Clancy Eccles and The Dynamites (Prod: Clancy Eccles)
(1969)

TMX 351   The World Needs Loving – Clancy Eccles and The Dynamites (Prod:
Clancy Eccles) (1969) [ISSUED AS CLANDISC CLA 201 BUT WITH
A AND B SIDES REVERSED]

TMX 352   On The Street – King Stitt (Prod: Clancy Eccles) (1969)

TMX 353   Mount Zion – Clancy Eccles and The Dynamites (Prod: Clancy Eccles) (1969) [A SIDE ISSUED ON CLANDISC CLA 203B. B SIDE ISSUED ON CLANDISC CLA 202B]

TMX 354   Vigorton Two – King Stitt (Prod: Clancy Eccles) (1969)

TMX 355   Foolish Fool – Cynthia Richards (Prod: Clancy Eccles) (1969) [A SIDE ISSUED ON CLANDISC CLA 202A. B SIDE ISSUED ON CLANDISC CLA 203A and CLA 220A]

TMX 356   NYT

TMX 357   Rudam Bam – The Eagles (Prod: Joe Sinclair) (1969) [ISSUED ON SONG BIRD SB 1006A]

TMX 358   Biddy Biddy – The Eagles (Prod: Joe Sinclair) (1969)

TMX 359   It's A Wonderful Time – The Eagles (Prod: Joe Sinclair) (1969) [ISSUED AS SONG BIRD SB 1005]

TMX 360   NYT

TMX 361   NYT

TMX 362   Any Little Bit – The Templets (Prod: Lloyd Charmers) (1969) [ISSUED ON SONG BIRD SB 1006B]

TMX 363   NYT

TMX 364   NYT

TMX 365   NYT

TMX 366   NYT

TMX 367   NYT

TMX 368   NYT

TMX 369   Soul Power – Barrington Sadler (Prod: Clancy Eccles) (1969)

TMX 370   Rub It Down – Barrington Sadler (Prod: Clancy Eccles) (1969) [ISSUED AS CLANDISC CLA 204]

TMX 371   NYT

TMX 372   NYT

TMX 373   The Vampire – The Upsetters (Prod: Lee Perry) (1969)

TMX 374   Dirty Dozen – The Shadows (Prod: Bobby Aitken) (1969) [A SIDE ISSUED ON UPSETTER US 317A. B SIDE ISSUED ON UPSETTER US 320A]

TMX 375   Crying Too Long – The Shadows (aka The Ravers, aka The Dukes) (Prod: Bobby Aitken) (1969)

TMX 376   Stranger On The Shore – Val Bennett and The Upsetters (Prod: Lee Perry) (1969) [A SIDE ISSUED ON UPSETTER US 320B. B SIDE ISSUED ON UPSETTER US 321A]

TMX 377   Drugs And Poison – The Upsetters (Prod: Lee Perry) (1969) [ISSUED ON UPSETTER US 321B. COULD POSSIBLY ALSO EXIST COUPLED WITH TMX 321A]

TMX 378   The Same Thing You Gave To Daddy – Nora Dean (Prod: Lee Perry) (1969)

TMX 379   A Testimony – The Upsetter Pilgrims (Prod: Lee Perry) (1969) [ISSUED AS UPSETTER US 322]

TMX 380   The Same Things – The Gaylads (Prod: Lee Perry) (1969)

TMX 381   If You Don't Mind – The Gaylads (Prod: Lee Perry) (1969) [ISSUED AS UPSETTER US 323]

TMX 382   NYT

TMX 383   NYT

TMX 384   NYT

TMX 385   NYT

TMX 386   Double Shot – Beverley's All Stars (Prod: Leslie Kong) (1969)

TMX 387   Banana Water – The Mellotones (Prod: Leslie Kong) (1969) [ISSUED AS TROJAN TR 683]

TMX 388   The Crimson Pirate – Peter Tosh (Prod: Edward 'Bunny' Lee) (1969)

TMX 389   Moon Dusk – Peter Tosh (Prod: Edward 'Bunny' Lee) (1969) [ISSUED AS JACKPOT JP 706]

TMX 390   Kiss Me Quick – Keelyn Beckford (Prod: Edward 'Bunny' Lee) (1969)

TMX 391   Feel It (aka 'Feel The Crumpet') – Mr Miller (possibly Bunny Lee) (Prod: Edward 'Bunny' Lee) (1969) [ISSUED AS JACKPOT JP 707 BUT WITH A AND B SIDES REVERSED]

TMX 392   Wonderful World, Beautiful People – Jimmy Cliff (Prod: Leslie Kong and Jimmy Cliff) (1969)

TMX 393   Hard Road To Travel – Jimmy Cliff (Prod: Leslie Kong and Jimmy Cliff) (1969) [ISSUED AS TROJAN TR 690]

TMX 394   This Old Man – Sylvan Morris (Prod: Hawk) (1969)

TMX 395   Sweeter Than Honey – Sylvan Morris (Prod: Hawk) (1969) [A SIDE ISSUED ON BIG SHOT BI 533A. B SIDE ISSUED ON BIG SHOT BI 532A]

TMX 396   When The Morning Comes – Sylvan Morris (Prod: Hawk) (1969)

TMX 397   Son Of Reggae – Sylvan Morris (Prod: Hawk) (1969) [A SIDE ISSUED ON BIG SHOT BI 533B. B SIDE ISSUED ON BIG SHOT BI 532B]

TMX 398   NYT

TMX 399   NYT

TMX 400   Bye Bye Love – The Dials (Prod: Charles 'Clancy' Collins) (1969)

TMX 401   It's Love – The Dials (Prod: Charles 'Clancy' Collins) (1969) [ISSUED AS DUKE DU 48]

TMX 402   Love Is A Treasure – The Dials (Prod: Charles 'Clancy' Collins) (1969)

TMX 403   I Want To Be – The Black Diamonds (Prod: Charles 'Clancy' Collins) (1969) [ISSUED AS DUKE DU 49]

TMX 404   NYT

TMX 405   NYT

TMX 406   I Want To Be Loved – Sir Collins and The Black Diamonds (Prod: Charles 'Clancy' Collins) (1969)

TMX 407   Black Panther – Sir Collins and The Black Diamonds (Prod: Charles 'Clancy' Collins) (1969) [ISSUED AS DUKE DU 46 BUT WITH A AND B SIDES REVERSED]

TMX 408   Black Diamonds – Sir Collins and The Black Diamonds (Prod: Charles 'Clancy' Collins) (1969)

TMX 409   I Remember – The Black Diamonds (Prod: Charles 'Clancy' Collins) (1969) [ISSUED AS DUKE DU 47]

TMX 410   Bond In Bliss – Byron Lee and The Dragonaires (Prod: Byron Lee) (1969) [ISSUED ON DUKE DU 39A (FIRST PRESSING), TROJAN TR 7747A AND HORSE HOSS 56B]

TMX 411   NYT

TMX 412   NYT

TMX 413   NYT

TMX 414   NYT

TMX 415   Read The News – Tito Simon (Prod: Joe Mansano) (1969)

TMX 416   It's Not Impossible – Tito Simon (Prod: Joe Mansano) (1969) [A SIDE ISSUED ON DUKE DU 57B (JOE LABEL). B SIDE ISSUED ON DUKE DU 53A (JOE LABEL)]

TMX 417   Reggae On The Shore – Joe's All Stars (Prod: Joe Mansano) (1969)

TMX 418   Brixton Cat, Big And Fat – Dice The Boss (Prod: Joe Mansano) (1969) [A SIDE ISSUED ON DUKE DU 52B (JOE LABEL). B SIDE ISSUED ON DUKE DU 50A (JOE LABEL)]

TMX 419   The Thief – Joe Mansano (Prod: Joe Mansano) (1969)

TMX 420   Dynamite Line – Joe's All Stars (Prod: Joe Mansano) (1969) [A SIDE ISSUED ON DUKE DU 51B (JOE LABEL). B SIDE ISSUED ON DUKE DU 53B (JOE LABEL)]

TMX 421   Your Boss DJ – Dice The Boss (Prod: Joe Mansano) (1969)

TMX 422   But Officer – Dice The Boss (Prod: Joe Mansano) (1969) [A SIDE ISSUED ON DUKE DU 57A (JOE LABEL). B SIDE ISSUED ON DUKE DU 52A (JOE LABEL)]

TMX 423   Solitude – Joe's All Stars (Prod: Joe Mansano) (1969)

TMX 424   Gun The Man Down – Dice The Boss (Prod: Joe Mansano) (1969) [A SIDE ISSUED ON DUKE DU 50B (JOE LABEL). B SIDE ISSUED ON DUKE DU 51A (JOE LABEL)]

TMX 425   Simmering – The Earthquakes (Prod: Charles 'Clancy' Collins) (1969)

TMX 426   Earthquake – Sir Collins and The Earthquakes (Prod: Charles 'Clancy' Collins) (1969) [ISSUED AS DUKE DU 56 BUT WITH A AND B SIDES REVERSED]

TMX 427   I Can't Stop Loving You – The Earthquakes (Prod: Charles 'Clancy' Collins) (1969)

TMX 428   Muriel – Sir Collins and The Earthquakes (Prod: Charles 'Clancy' Collins) (1969) [ISSUED AS DUKE DU 54 BUT WITH A AND B SIDES REVERSED]

TMX 429   Brother Moses – Sir Collins and The Earthquakes (Prod: Charles 'Clancy' Collins) (1969)

TMX 430   Funny Familiar Forgotten Feelings – Sir Collins and The Earthquakes (Prod: Charles 'Clancy' Collins) (1969) [ISSUED AS DUKE DU 55 BUT WITH A AND B SIDES REVERSED]

TMX 431   Hot Shot – Boris Gardner and The Love People (Prod: Winston Riley) (1969)

TMX 432   Watch This Music – Boris Gardner and The Love People (Prod: Winston Riley) (1969) [ISSUED AS BIG SHOT BI 539]

TMX 433   Memories Of Love – Boris Gardner and The Love People (Prod: Winston Riley) (1969)

TMX 434   Sweet Soul Special – Boris Gardner and The Love People (Prod: Winston Riley) (1969) [ISSUED AS BIG SHOT BI 537 BUT WITH A AND B SIDE REVERSED]

TMX 435   Something Tender (aka 'Grass Root') – Techniques All Stars (Prod: Winston Riley) (1969)

TMX 436   See And Blind (Version) (aka 'Rema Skank') – Techniques All Stars (Prod: Winston Riley) (1969) [A SIDE ISSUED ON TECHNIQUES TE 900A AND TE 920B UNDER DIFFERENT TITLES. B SIDE ISSUED ON TECHNIQUES TE 916B]

TMX 437   Darkness – Ansel Collins and The Love People (Prod: Winston Riley) (1969)

TMX 438   Lamb Chops – Ansel Collins and The Love People (Prod: Winston Riley) (1969) [ISSUED AS BIG SHOT BI 538]

TMX 439   NYT

TMX 440   Just One Smile – The Sensations (Prod: Winston Riley) (1969) [ISSUED ON DUKE DU 60B]

TMX 441   The Workman Song – The Sensations (Prod: Winston Riley) (1969) [NOT ISSUED ON ANY TROJAN LABEL]

TMX 442   Silhouettes – The Sensations (Prod: Winston Riley) (1969) [NOT ISSUED ON ANY TROJAN LABEL]

338

TMX 443   I Never Knew (Make Believe) – The Escorts (Prod: Winston Riley)
          (1969) [NOT ISSUED ON ANY TROJAN LABEL]
TMX 444   Where Were You – The Sensations (Prod: Winston Riley) (1969)
          [ISSUED ON DUKE DU 60A]
TMX 445   Mother Nature – The Escorts (Prod: Winston Riley) (1969) [ISSUED
          ON BIG SHOT BI 535B]
TMX 446   I Know A Girl (aka 'She's Gonna Marry Me') – The Shades (Prod:
          Winston Riley) (1969) [NOT ISSUED ON ANY TROJAN LABEL]
TMX 447   I'm So Afraid Of Love – The Sensations (Prod: Winston Riley) (1969)
          [ISSUED ON BIG SHOT BI 535A]
TMX 448   He Who Keepeth His Mouth – Johnny Osbourne and The Sensations
          (Prod: Winston Riley) (1969)
TMX 449   One Day (You'll Need My Kiss) – Johnny Osbourne and The Sensations
          (Prod: Winston Riley) (1969) [ISSUED AS BIG SHOT BI 536]
TMX 450   Bewitch (aka 'Red Sunset') – Karl Bryan (Prod: Winston Riley) (1969)
          [ISSUED ON TECHNIQUES TE 900B]
TMX 451   I'll Need You Tomorrow – The Kingstonians (Prod: Leslie Kong)
          (1969)
TMX 452   I'm Gonna Make It – The Kingstonians (Prod: Leslie Kong) (1969)
          [ISSUED AS TROJAN TR 7708]
TMX 453   NYT
TMX 454   NYT
TMX 455   NYT
TMX 456   NYT
TMX 457   NYT
TMX 458   NYT
TMX 459   I've Been Loving You – The Megatons (Prod: Jackson Jones) (1969)
TMX 460   Memphis Reggae – The Megatons (Prod: Jackson Jones) (1969)
          [ISSUED AS SONG BIRD SB 1009]
TMX 461   Ging Gang Goolie – The Megatons (Prod: Jackson Jones) (1969)
TMX 462   I'm Thirsty – The Megatons (Prod: Jackson Jones) (1969) [ISSUED AS
          SONGBIRD SB 1010]
TMX 463   Darling Please – Stranger Cole (Prod: Wilburn 'Stranger' Cole) (1969)
TMX 464   I've Got Plans – Stranger Cole (Prod: Wilburn 'Stranger' Cole) (1969)
          [ISSUED AS SONG BIRD SB 1008]
TMX 465   Dirty Dog – Amor Vivi (Prod: Vivian Comma [Vee Coma]) (1969)
TMX 466   Round And Round The Moon – (Prod: Vivian Comma [Vee Coma])
          (1969) [ISSUED AS BIG SHOT BI 534]
TMX 467   Leaving Me Standing – Winston Groovy (Prod: Laurel Aitken) (1969)

TMX 468   Little Girl – Winston Groovy (Prod: Laurel Aitken) (1969) [ISSUED AS
           GRAPE GR 3005]
TMX 469   The Hole – King Horror (Prod: Laurel Aitken) (1969)
TMX 470   Merry Xmas – Winston Groovy (Prod: Laurel Aitken) (1969)
           [A SIDE ISSUED ON GRAPE GR 3006A. B SIDE ISSUED ON
           GRAPE GR 3008A]
TMX 471   Lochness Monster – King Horror and Rico Rodriguez (Prod: Laurel
           Aitken) (1969)
TMX 472   Zion I – The Visions (Prod: Winston Riley) (1969) [ISSUED AS
           GRAPE GR 3007]
TMX 473   Lover Come Back – Lloyd Deslandes and The Mellotones (Prod: Lloyd
           Deslandes) (1969)
TMX 474   I Am Lonely – Barry Bailey (Prod: Lloyd Deslandes) (1969) [A SIDE
           ISSUED ON GRAPE GR 3006B. A SIDE ISSUED ON GRAPE
           GR 3008B]
TMX 475   NYT
TMX 476   NYT
TMX 477   NYT
TMX 478   NYT
TMX 479   NYT
TMX 480   NYT
TMX 481   NYT
TMX 482   NYT
TMX 483   NYT
TMX 484   NYT
TMX 485   NYT
TMX 486   NYT
TMX 487   NYT
TMX 488   NYT
TMX 489   NYT
TMX 490   NYT
TMX 491   NYT
TMX 492   NYT
TMX 493   NYT
TMX 494   NYT
TMX 495   NYT
TMX 496   NYT
TMX 497   NYT
TMX 498   NYT
TMX 499   NYT

TMX 500 Slow Motion (Version 1) – The Upsetters (Prod: Lee Perry) (1970)
TMX 501 Slow Motion (Version 2) – The Upsetters (Prod: Lee Perry) (1970)
         [NEITHER SIDE ISSUED ON ANY TROJAN LABEL]
TMX 502 Slow Motion (Version 3) – The Upsetters (Prod: Lee Perry) (1970)
TMX 503 Love Me Baby – The Upsetters (Prod: Lee Perry) (1970) [NEITHER
         SIDE ISSUED ON ANY TROJAN LABEL]
TMX 504 Bad Thief – The Upsetters (Prod: Lee Perry) (1970)
TMX 505 Take A Sip – The Upsetters (Prod: Lee Perry) (1970) [NEITHER SIDE
         ISSUED ON ANY TROJAN LABEL]
TMX 506 I Want To Thank You – The Upsetters (Prod: Lee Perry) (1970)
TMX 507 Wax It – The Upsetters (Prod: Lee Perry) (1970) [A SIDE ISSUED
         ON TROJAN'S 'SCRATCH THE UPSETTER AGAIN'
         COMPILATION LP (TTL 28). B SIDE NOT ISSUED ON ANY
         TROJAN LABEL]
TMX 508 Hurry Up – The Versatiles (Prod: Lee Perry) (1970)
TMX 509 Val Blows – Val Bennett and The Upsetters (Prod: Lee Perry) (1970)
         [A SIDE ISSUED ON UPSETTER US 339B. B SIDE NOT ISSUED
         ON ANY TROJAN LABEL]
TMX 510 Too Gravalitious (Organ Version) – The Upsetters (Prod: Lee Perry)
         (1970)
TMX 511 Unidentified title – unidentified artist (Prod: Lee Perry) (1970)
         [NEITHER SIDE ISSUED ON ANY TROJAN LABEL]
TMX 512 Tooth Aches – The Upsetters (Prod: Lee Perry) (1970)
TMX 513 Ferry Boat (aka 'Give It Up') – The Upsetters (Prod: Lee Perry) (1970)
         [A SIDE ISSUED ON UPSETTER US 338B. B SIDE ISSUED ON
         UPSETTER US 343B]
TMX 514 OK Corral – U Roy and The Upsetters (Prod: Lee Perry) (1970)
TMX 515 Move And Groove – Count Sticky (Prod: Lee Perry) (1970) [NEITHER
         SIDE ISSUED ON ANY TROJAN LABEL]
TMX 516 Bush Tea – Lee Perry (Prod: Lee Perry) (1970)
TMX 517 Sellasie Serenade – Lee Perry (Prod: Lee Perry) (1970) [NEITHER
         SIDE ISSUED ON ANY TROJAN LABEL]
TMX 518 No Gwow (actually 'No Gwan') – The Upsetters (Prod: Lee Perry)
         (1970)
TMX 519 Lead Line – The Upsetters (Prod: Lee Perry) (1970) [NEITHER SIDE
         ISSUED ON ANY TROJAN LABEL]
TMX 520 NYT
TMX 521 NYT
TMX 522 NYT
TMX 523 NYT

TMX 524   Squeeze Up (Part 1) – Byron Lee and The Dragonaires (Prod: Byron Lee) (1970)

TMX 525   Squeeze Up (Part 2) – Byron Lee and The Dragonaires (Prod: Byron Lee) (1970) [ISSUED AS TROJAN TR 7731]

TMX 526   NYT

TMX 527   NYT

TMX 528   NYT

TMX 529   NYT

TMX 530   Rocco – Freddie Notes and The Rudies (Prod: Joe Sinclair) (1970) [ISSUED ON TROJAN TR 7724A (BLANK LABEL)]

TMX 531   The Bull – Freddie Notes and The Rudies (Prod: Joe Sinclair) (1970)

TMX 532   The River Ben Come Up – Freddie Notes and The Rudies (Prod: Joe Sinclair) (1970) [ISSUED AS DUKE DU 63]

TMX 533   Don't Tell Your Mama – Freddie Notes and The Rudies (Prod: Joe Sinclair) (1970)

TMX 534   Rude Exodus – Freddie Notes and The Rudies (Prod: Joe Sinclair) (1970) [A SIDE ISSUED ON TROJAN TR 7724B (BLANK LABEL). B SIDE ISSUED ON FREDDIE NOTES AND THE RUDIES' 'MONTEGO BAY' LP (TBL 152)]

TMX 535   Down On The Farm – Freddie Notes and The Rudies (Prod: Graeme Walker) (1970)

TMX 536   It Came From Out Of The Sky – Freddie Notes and The Rudies (Prod: Freddie Notes, Graeme Walker and The Rudies) (1970) [A SIDE ISSUED ON TROJAN TR 7734A. B SIDE ISSUED ON B&C LABEL CB 125A AND FREDDIE NOTES AND THE RUDIES' 'MONTEGO BAY' LP (TBL 152)]

TMX 537   Chicken Scratch – Count Suckle with Freddie Notes and The Rudies (Prod: Count Suckle) (1970)

TMX 538   Nationality – The Rudies (Prod: Joe Sinclair) (1970) [A SIDE ISSUED ON DUKE DU 68B. B SIDE NOT ISSUED ON ANY TROJAN LABEL]

TMX 539   Chicken Inn – Freddie Notes and The Rudies (Prod: Joe Sinclair) (1970)

TMX 540   I Don't Want To Keep Up With The Jones's – Freddie Notes and The Rudies (Prod: Joe Sinclair) (1970) [A SIDE ISSUED ON DUKE DU 68A. B SIDE ISSUED ON FREDDIE NOTES AND THE RUDIES' 'UNITY' LP (TBL 109)]

TMX 541   Pick Folk Kinkiest – The Upsetters (Prod: Lee Perry) (1970)

TMX 542   Na Na Hey Hey (Kiss Him Goodbye) – The Upsetters (Prod: Lee Perry) (1970) [ISSUED AS UPSETTER US 332]

TMX 543   Fire Fire – The Upsetters (Prod: Lee Perry) (1970)

TMX 544   The Jumper – The Upsetters (Prod: Lee Perry) (1970) [ISSUED AS UPSETTER US 334]

TMX 545   The Pillow – The Upsetters (Prod: Lee Perry) (1970)

TMX 546   Grooving – The Upsetters (Prod: Lee Perry) (1970) [ISSUED AS UPSETTER US 335]

TMX 547   Granny Show (Version 1) – Dave Barker and The Upsetters (Prod: Lee Perry) (1970)

TMX 548   Granny Show (Version 2) – Dave Barker and The Upsetters (Prod: Lee Perry) (1970) [ISSUED AS UPSETTER US 333]

TMX 549   This Man – O'Neil Hall (Prod: Lee Perry) (1970)

TMX 550   Double Wheel – The Upsetters (Prod: Lee Perry) (1970) [A SIDE ISSUED ON SPINNING WHEEL SW 103B. B SIDE ISSUED ON SPINNING WHEEL SW 100B]

TMX 551   Haunted House – The Upsetters (Prod: Lee Perry) (1970)

TMX 552   Land Of Kinks – The Upsetters (Prod: Lee Perry) (1970) [A SIDE ISSUED ON SPINNING WHEEL SW 100A. B SIDE ISSUED ON SPINNING WHEEL SW 103A]

TMX 553   The Miser – The Upsetters (Prod: Lee Perry) (1970)

TMX 554   Choking Kind – The Upsetters (Prod: Lee Perry) (1970) [A SIDE ISSUED ON SPINNING WHEEL SW 101A. B SIDE ISSUED ON SPINNING WHEEL SW 102A]

TMX 555   Do It Madly – Chuck Junior (Prod: Lee Perry) (1970)

TMX 556   Penny Wise And Pound Foolish – Chuck Junior (Prod: Lee Perry) (1970) [A SIDE ISSUED ON SPINNING WHEEL SW 101B. B SIDE ISSUED ON SPINNING WHEEL SW 102B]

TMX 557   Blood Poison – The Upsetters (Prod: Lee Perry) (1970)

TMX 558   Double Sip – The Upsetters (Prod: Lee Perry) (1970) [A SIDE ISSUED ON UPSETTER US 341A. B SIDE NOT ISSUED ON ANY TROJAN LABEL]

TMX 559   Kangaroo Hop – The Upsetters (Prod: Lee Perry) (1970)

TMX 560   Never Found Me A Girl – David Isaacs and The Upsetters (Prod: Lee Perry) (1970) [NEITHER SIDE ISSUED ON ANY TROJAN LABEL. B SIDE ISSUED ON PAMA LP 'CLINT EASTWOOD' (PSP 1014)]

TMX 561   Once In My Life – Errol English [Junior English] (Prod: Larry Lawrence) (1970)

TMX 562   In A Cottage In A Wood – Errol English [Junior English] (Prod: Larry Lawrence) (1970) [ISSUED AS BIG SHOT BI 548]

TMX 563   Love Is Pure – Errol English [Junior English] (Prod: Larry Lawrence) (1970)

TMX 564   I Don't Want To Love You – Errol English [Junior English] (Prod: Larry
           Lawrence) (1970) [ISSUED AS BIG SHOT BI 547 BUT WITH A AND
           B SIDES REVERSED]

TMX 565   NYT

TMX 566   Prison Sentence – Winston James [Winston Groovy] and The Cimarons
           (Prod: Hot Rod [Lambert Briscoe]) (1970)

TMX 567   The Black Scorpion – Winston James [Winston Groovy] and The
           Cimarons (Prod: Hot Rod [Lambert Briscoe]) (1970) [A SIDE ISSUED
           ON HOT ROD HR 106A. B SIDE NOT ISSUED ON ANY
           TROJAN LABEL]

TMX 568   Dry Dream – Betty Sinclair and The Hot Rod All Stars (Prod: Hot Rod
           [Lambert Briscoe]) (1970)

TMX 569   Honey I Love You – Betty Sinclair and The Hot Rod All Stars (Prod: Hot
           Rod [Lambert Briscoe]) (1970) [NEITHER SIDE ISSUED ON ANY
           TROJAN LABEL]

TMX 570   Just Can't Do Without Your Love – Winston James [Winston Groovy]
           (Prod: Hot Rod [Lambert Briscoe]) (1970)

TMX 571   Trouble Down Road – Hot Rod All Stars (Prod: Hot Rod [Lambert
           Briscoe]) (1970) [A SIDE ISSUED ON HOT ROD HR 110B. B SIDE
           NOT ISSUED ON ANY TROJAN LABEL]

TMX 572   Mayfair – Millie and Simaryp (Prod: Eddie Wolfram for Philligree) (1970)

TMX 573   Enoch Power – Millie and Simaryp (Prod: Eddie Wolfram for Philligree)
           (1970) [ISSUED AS TROJAN TR 7744]

TMX 574   Come Into My Life – Jimmy Cliff (Prod: Leslie Kong and Jimmy Cliff)
           (1970)

TMX 575   Suffering In The Land – Jimmy Cliff (Prod: Leslie Kong and Jimmy Cliff)
           (1970) [ISSUED AS TROJAN TR 7745 BUT WITH A AND B SIDES
           REVERSED]

TMX 576   NYT

TMX 577   Blood Poison – The Upsetters (Prod: Lee Perry) (1970)
           [UNCONFIRMED. SEE ALSO TMX TMX 557A]

TMX 578   NYT

TMX 579   This Man – O'Neil Hall (Prod: Lee Perry) (1970) [UNCONFIRMED.
           SEE ALSO TMX 549A]

TMX 580   NYT

TMX 581   NYT

TMX 582   Promises – Cynthia Richards (Prod: Clancy Eccles) (1970)

TMX 583   Real Sweet – Clancy Eccles and The Dynamites (Prod: Clancy Eccles)
           (1970) [ISSUED AS CLANDISC CLA 211. A SIDE ALSO ISSUED
           ON CLANDISC CLA 216B]

TMX 584   Black Beret – The Dynamites (Prod: Clancy Eccles) (1970)

TMX 585   Phantom – The Dynamites (Prod: Clancy Eccles) (1970) [A SIDE
ISSUED ON CLANDISC CLA 212A. B SIDE ISSUED ON
CLANDISC CLA 213A]

TMX 586   Africa – Clancy Eccles and The Dynamites (Prod: Clancy Eccles) (1970)

TMX 587   Africa Part 2 – Clancy Eccles and The Dynamites (Prod: Clancy Eccles)
(1970) [ISSUED AS CLANDISC CLA 214]

TMX 588   See Me – Earl George (Prod: Clancy Eccles) (1970)

TMX 589   Love Me Tender – Barry [Barrington Clarke] and The Affections (Prod:
Clancy Eccles) (1970) [A SIDE ISSUED ON CLANDISC CLA 215A.
B SIDE ISSUED ON CLANDISC CLA 212B]

TMX 590   Can't Wait – Cynthia Richards (Prod: Clancy Eccles) (1970)

TMX 591   Promises – Cynthia Richards (Prod: Clancy Eccles) (1970) [A SIDE
ISSUED ON CLANDISC CLA 216A. B SIDE ISSUED ON
CLANDISC CLA 211A AND 216B. SEE ALSO TMX 582A]

TMX 592   Sounds Of '70 – King Stitt with Clancy Eccles and The Dynamites
(Prod: Clancy Eccles) (1970)

TMX 593   Zion We Want To Go – The Westmorelites (Prod: Clancy Eccles) (1970)
[A SIDE ISSUED ON CLANDISC CLA 215B. B SIDE ISSUED ON
CLANDISC CLA 217A]

TMX 594   Revival – The Dynamites (Prod: Clancy Eccles) (1970)

TMX 595   Skank Me – Barry [Barrington Clarke] and The Affections (Prod: Clancy
Eccles) (1970) [A SIDE ISSUED ON CLANDISC CLA 217B. B SIDE
ISSUED ON CLANDISC CLA 213B]

TMX 596   Single Girl – Silkie Davis [TT Ross] (Prod: Les Foster) (1970)

TMX 597   NYT [A SIDE ISSUED ON DUKE DU 104A]

TMX 598   Together We'll Be – Les Foster (Prod: Les Foster) (1970)

TMX 599   NYT [A SIDE ISSUED ON DUKE DU 104B. IT MAY ALSO
POSSIBLY HAVE BEEN COUPLED WITH TMX 596]

TMX 600   NYT

TMX 601   NYT

TMX 602   NYT

TMX 603   NYT

TMX 604   I Need Your Sweet Inspiration – The Pioneers (Prod: Leslie Kong) (1970)

TMX 605   Israel – The Maytals (Prod: Leslie Kong) (1970) [A SIDE ISSUED ON
TROJAN TR 7795A. B SIDE NOT ISSUED ON ANY TROJAN
LABEL]

Trojan Albums Overview

In essence, Trojan Records used three main prefix systems to identify their album releases. Also over the course of time Trojan released albums on eight-track cartridge, cassette and compact disc.

The three prefix systems were TTL, the budget-price album range that sold for 14/6d (771/2p); TBL, which retailed at 19/11d (99p); and the prestige TRL(S) series that initially sold at 29/11d (£1.49) before climbing to the dizzy price of £1.99 by the middle of the 1970s. As mentioned elsewhere, Dandy launched both the TRL and TBL series in 1968, while the TTL series first saw action with the best-selling *Tighten Up* in 1969.

The TRL series was intended for prestige releases, mainly licensed in from Jamaican producers, with the later 'S' being added to the prefix indicating the recordings were in stereo, although quite a number of early TRL(S) albums have conflicting prefixes with the sleeve and label at odds with each other, as to whether the recording is in stereo or not. By late 1972, all TRL releases were in stereo – at least in theory – and could more or less accurately bear the S suffix, which continued until Trojan's takeover by Sanctuary in 2001.

A number of the early TRL albums appeared in the UK with American printed sleeves over-stickered with the Trojan catalogue number, while the vinyl disc was the normal Trojan UK pressing. These were the product of Byron Lee and his Dynamic recording set-up in Jamaica. An album such as TRL8 *Sparrow Meets The Dragon* is found in a high quality US gatefold sleeve over-stickered, as is TRL28 *Reggae Splashdown* from bandleader Byron Lee, which comes in a single sleeve design. These albums would be counterparts to existing albums in Jamaica, so the need to construct a new sleeve would be minimal, when the album was issued by Trojan in the UK. Particularly when, according to Rob Bell, Byron Lee's albums did not sell in large quantities, so Trojan would want to keep the production costs to a minimum.

The more wealthy Jamaican producers, such as Byron Lee, who had close ties with Trojan, purchased the sleeves in America due to the far higher quality of print and construction. He would then send the sleeves to London with an album master tape, to be used by Trojan, replacing the Jamaican catalogue number with their own, via a sticker, as nothing else needed altering for the UK issue. Trojan would also print extra sleeves for an album release and export them to Jamaica for use with the locally pressed disc.

The TBL prefix series started slightly after the TRL and was intended as a range of budget-priced albums. After the first album in 1968, the series issued four albums the following year and only really got into its stride with the success Trojan were having both in the national charts and with the strong sales generated by the new skinhead audience.

These facts are reflected in the high number of various artists series issued, like *Tighten Up*, *Club Reggae* and *Reggae Chartbusters*, which all collect together many chart hits alongside more 'ethnic' material popular in the clubs.

The early 1970s DJ records' popularity was reflected in the *Version to Version* and *Version Galore* series, which capture some of the finest recordings of that genre, while albums such as *Foolish Fool* and *Herbsman Reggae* underlined the sound of producer Clancy Eccles, and *The Undertaker* sold well, highlighting Derrick Harriott's Crystalites band.

The skinhead market was identified as a growth area and was particularly well catered for in 1970, with top names like The Maytals, Kingstonians and the ubiquitous Harry J All Stars all having their work issued on TBL albums. Many sold well into the West Indian community as well, although Symarip's *Skinhead Moonstomp* was definitely angled straight at the new youth market. The TBL series was dropped in 1973.

Illustrating Trojan's somewhat inconsistent approach to releasing material, alternative versions of some early Trojan LPs can be found. Bob Marley's *Soul Rebels* album saw two pressings, initially appearing on Upsetter, albeit with the standard matrix number, and then a second pressing using the same number on the main Trojan label. Dave and Ansel Collins' *Double Barrel* album also saw two pressings, both utilising the Trojan matrix TBL162 –

initial copies were pressed using the Trojan version of producer Winston Riley's Techniques label, while slightly later the release was transferred to the main Trojan label.

The TTL series started in 1969 and issued bargain-priced collections, including *Tighten Up* and *Duke Reid Golden Hits*. Single artists were represented by albums such as *This Is Desmond Dekker* from the number one hit maker, and Derrick Morgan's *Seven Letters* collection. *Red Red Wine* cast the spotlight on Dandy's UK productions and was particularly boosted by Tony Tribe's national chart hit from which the album took its name. Original copies were pressed on the Downtown label while retaining the Trojan matrix, with slightly later pressings appearing on the normal Trojan label. All the sleeves showed a Downtown logo but retained the Trojan numbering. Similarly for Reco's *Blow Your Horn* LP, which found initial release on Downtown before being moved to the main Trojan imprint.

A whole host of attractive albums were issued, including producer Harry 'J' Johnson's work on *No More Heartaches*, Lloyd Charmers' work on *Reggae Is Tight* and Lee Perry's debut album for Trojan, *The Upsetter*. The bulk of the first 35 issues were first-rate, with a few retrospective albums offered alongside contemporary work, notably the *Guns Of Navarone* ska collection, the *Ride Your Donkey* ska and rocksteady set and the *You Left Me Standing* compilation, essentially a best-of set featuring mid-'60s music from the Rio label. These LPs were the precursors of the revive albums that would bring Trojan back to prominence in the late '80s and early '90s.

After this initial burst of activity, the TTL series was confined mainly to out of date work, much of it originating from the Island label of the early to mid 1960's. Titles included Derrick Morgan's *Forward March*, a ska collection from 1963, *Keith And Enid Sing*, a collection of sentimental early-1960s ballads, and *Club Ska Volume One*, which had an original issue date of 1967, as *Club Ska '67*, again via Island on its WIRL imprint. Many of the titles were illustrated on the reverse of the TTL series albums. An extraordinary piece of cut-and-paste was executed on the *Club Ska* sleeve illustration, as the title is moved to the centre of the album and the '67' felt-penned over.

Several of the albums listed as TTL reissues that originated from the Island catalogue have never surfaced, such as Derrick Harriott, *Best Of Volume Two* and *Duke Reid Rock's Steady*. Whether they did find any form of release, possibly only to white label test-press, remains to be seen, although after such a length of time it would be thought that any titles that were going to turn up would have done so by now. Rob Bell recalls that they all reached at least the mastering stage.

The final TTL release was TTL58. It was a live recording from the Electric Living Trade Fair in Brighton, and featured The Pioneers on one side and Byron Lee and The Dragonaires on the other. *Caribbean Festival* was a limited edition promotional album issued in collaboration with the Electricity Council. The sleeve was a wrap-around paper affair with no joining at the top and bottom making it very vulnerable for the album simply to slide straight out of its cover. Judging by the number of copies that still appear, although a promotional item, the press run must have been in the thousands rather than a couple of hundred.

Tighten Up Volume Two and *Red Red Wine* were both originally to be issued on the Island label with different track listings and sleeves to the normal TTL releases. A track listing exists showing the alternative *Red Red Wine*, but beyond that and their inclusion in an Island catalogue nothing has ever been seen of these mysterious releases.

Beyond the normal TTL, TBL and TRL numbering systems Trojan issued triple albums such as *The Trojan Story* on TALL1 in a fold-over wallet-style sleeve, then repackaged it as a box set and renumbered it TALL100. Other triple album box sets followed all using the TALL prefix. Any double albums, the first of which was Desmond Dekker's *Double Dekker*, were prefixed TRLD and came in gatefold sleeves except Desmond's set which came in a standard cover.

Lee Perry, exceptionally, was granted his own prefix PERRY for the three triple box sets devoted to his work which Trojan assembled in the '80s. This unique accolade shows how collectable Scratch's music had become by that time.

Trojan also licensed recordings to mainstream budget labels such as Hallmark and MFP (Music For Pleasure), who no doubt were eager to cash in on the reggae boom of the early 1970s. These albums would be compiled from current or former hit records and packaged with the obligatory tasty West Indian young lady on the sleeve. Easily the best of these collections is *Reggae Party* on MFP from 1970, which consists of 12 top rate Leslie Kong-produced tracks, the majority of which had been originally released on Trojan related labels. With a price sticker of 49p and none of the recordings being older than 18 months, the set was an absolute snip for the enthusiast.

DISCOGRAPHICAL ODDITIES

TRL15 *Absolutely* by The Uniques vocal group exists both as a normal issue and as a Jamaican press using the Trojan metal stampers on the Splash label. In both instances the sleeve is a standard UK issue. Marley and Co's *Soul Rebels* (TBL126) from 1970 can also be found as a Jamaican-pressed Upsetter label in a UK sleeve. Once again the UK-manufactured metal stampers have been used bearing the Trojan matrix numbers.

It is known that Lee Perry would take the superior UK-manufactured metal stampers back to Kingston for the Jamaican pressings of his albums.

TBL1 45 issued as *Tighten Up Volume Three*, was also used for *That Wonderful Sound* from singer Dobby Dobson. This had the same track listing as a Pama Records album release, although a different sleeve. It was possibly deleted when Pama issued theirs, since very few copies have surfaced on Trojan.

TRL1 7 *I Need You* from Dandy and Audrey was briefly issued on the pink-coloured Island label with a different sleeve. It had an Island catalogue number with the Trojan one in brackets.

Copies of TRL38 *Vic Taylor Does It His Way* from 1972 occasionally appear on an olive green Dynamic label as well as the standard Trojan imprint.

Tighten Up Volume Five. There are three pressings of this album: 1) with Peter Tosh's 'Memphis' in place of 'Duppy Conqueror'; 2) with 'Know Far I' appearing twice, and 3) the conventional issue with the tracks as listed.

Jackpot of Hits (Amalgamated). There was another pressing with only 11 tracks (omitting 'Good Time Rock'). Probably this was because there are two pressing faults on the normal 12 track issue ('Catch The Beat' and 'Just Like A River'), so Trojan remastered it but left off the last track in error.

The Inspirations, *Reggae Fever* also included tracks by Ken Parker and Lloyd Willis so it could not be considered as exclusively Inspirations material.

Sufferer by The Kingstonians: the track 'Easy Ride Reggae' is by the Crystalites.

Man From Carolina by The GG All Stars: the track 'Gold On Your Dress' is by The Slickers and 'Chariot Without A Horse' is by Nyah Hunter and The GG All Stars.

Reggae Reggae Volume Two: unconfirmed if this was supposed to be Vol 2 of *Reggae Reggae Reggae* (TBL 130).

Reggae Power Volume Two: there is a miscredit on 'Sylvia's Mother' which is the Eric Donaldson cut, not the version by John Jones (which was supposed to have been issued on Attack). Also there is no Vol 1 of this, unless one was pressed but not put out. Of course there is the *Reggae Power* single-artist album by The Ethiopians, so possibly there was a mix-up with one or the other album titles – this seems likely as there is no track titled *Reggae Power* on The Ethiopians set.

Herbsman Reggae, The Dynamites: 'See Me' is by Earl Lawrence (Earl George), not Larry Lawrence.

Music House Volume Two: 'Beef Balls & Gravy' is the same as 'Bawling Baby' on a Pama Bullet single. 'Black Is Togetherness' is the same as 'Black Is Black' by Martin Riley, also on a Pama Bullet single. 'I Wish Someone' is the same as 'I Wish' by Basil Gail – yet again on a Pama Bullet single! ('I Wish' is also on the *Bob Marley and Friends* Trojan box set credited to Glen Adams.)

Music House Volume Three: 'Molly' is by Lord Creator (Kentrick Patrick).

Tighten Up Volume Seven: unknown singer on 'Be Faithful Darling' – not Clancy Eccles as credited. 'I'm Feeling Lonely' is by Vernon Buckley solo rather than his vocal group The Maytones.

There are a number of gaps in all the numbering systems; some were never issued and a few have yet to be confirmed as having been pressed.

Trojan Albums Discography

1968-93

AMALGAMATED (PREFIX AMGLP) *(Month stated when known)*

2001	Fly Away To Glory – Al Stewart and The Marvetts (Prod: Joe Gibbs)	1968
2002	Explosive Rocksteady – Various Artists (Prod: Joe Gibbs)	1968
2003	Greetings From The Pioneers – The Pioneers (Prod: Joe Gibbs)	1968

AMALGAMATED (PREFIX CSP)

3	Jackpot Of Hits – Various Artists (Prod: Joe Gibbs)	1969

ATTACK (PREFIX ATLP)

FIRST SERIES

1001	The Heptones and Friends Volume 2 – Various Artists (Prod: Joe Gibbs)	1973
1002	Wake Up Jamaica – Dennis Alcapone (unissued)	
1003	Darling Ooh! – Errol Dunkley (Prod: Sonia Pottinger/Various)	1973
1004	Green Mango – Tommy McCook and Bobby Ellis (Prod: Winston Riley)	1973
1005	Belch It Off – Dennis Alcapone (Prod: Sidney Crooks)	1974
1006	U Roy – U Roy (prod Arthur 'Duke' Reid)	1974
1007	Tommy McCook – Tommy McCook/Various (Prod: Arthur 'Duke' Reid)	1974
1008	Musical Consortium – Various Artists (Prod: Sidney Crooks)	1974
1009	Officially – Lloyd Parks (Prod: Lloyd Parks)	1974
1010	A Love I Can Feel – John Holt (Prod: Clement Seymour Dodd)	1974
1011	Big Bamboo Sample – Various Artists (Prod: Clement Seymour Dodd)	1974
1012	Rave On Brother – Various Artists (Prod: Clement Seymour Dodd)	1974
1013	Picture On The Wall – Freddie McKay (Prod: Clement Seymour Dodd)	1974

1014	Natty Dub – The Aggrovators (Prod: Edward 'Bunny' Lee)	1975
1015	Enter Into His Gates With Praise – Johnny Clarke (Prod: Edward 'Bunny' Lee)	1975
1016	Feel So Good – Derrick Morgan (Prod: Edward 'Bunny' Lee)	1975
1017	Dubbing With The Observer – Niney and King Tubby (Prod: Winston 'Niney' Holness)	1975

SECOND SERIES

101	Various – Sufferer's Choice (Prod: Various)	1988
102	The Original Man – Andrew Tosh (Prod: Andrew Tosh)	1988
103	Do The Reggae, 1966–70 – The Maytals (Prod: Leslie Kong)	1988
104	Shocks Of Mighty, 1969–74 – Lee Perry and Friends (Prod: Lee Perry)	1988
105	Enter His Gates With Praise – Johnny Clarke (Prod: Edward 'Bunny' Lee)	1989
106	Johnny In The Echo Chamber: Dubwise Selection, 1975–1976 – The Aggrovators (Prod: Edward 'Bunny' Lee)	1989
107	Don't Trouble Trouble – Johnny Clarke (Prod: Edward 'Bunny' Lee)	1989
108	Public Jestering – Lee Perry and Friends (Prod: Lee Perry)	1990
109	Put On Your Best Dress, 1967–1968 – Various Artists (Prod: Sonia Pottinger)	1990
110	Dub Justice – The Aggrovators (Prod: Edward 'Bunny' Lee)	1990
111	Dub Jackpot – The Aggrovators and King Tubby's (Prod: Edward 'Bunny' Lee)	1990
112	Roots Reggae – Various Artists (Prod: Various)	1991
113	Reggae Attack – Various Artists (Prod: Various)	1990
114	Sufferer – The Kingstonians (Prod: Derrick Harrriott)	1991
115	Be Thankful (sampler) – Various Artists (Prod: Various)	1991
116	Darling Ooh – Errol Dunkley (Prod: Sonia Pottinger/Various)	1991

BIG SHOT (PREFIX BBTL)

3000	Reggae Girl – Various Artists (Prod: Albert Gene Murphy)	1968
4000	Live It Up – Various Artists (Prod: Various)	1968
4001	Once More – Various Artists (Prod: Various)	1968

BIG SHOT (PREFIX BILP)

101	Top Of The Ladder – Clancy Eccles/Various Artists (Prod: Clancy Eccles)	1973
102	Captivity–Delroy Wilson (Prod: Edward 'Bunny' Lee)	1973
103	Ready Or Not – Johnny Osbourne/Various Artists (Prod: Winston Riley)	1973
104	Turntable Reggae – Various Artists (Prod: Edward 'Bunny' Lee)	1973

BLUE CAT (PREFIX BCL)

| 1 | Jamaican Memories – Various Artists (Prod: Various) | 1968 |

HIGH NOTE (PREFIX BSLP)

5001	ABC Rocksteady – The Original Orchestra (Prod: Sonia Pottinger)	1968
5002	Dancing Down Orange Street – Various Artists (Prod: Sonia Pottinger)	1968
5005	Reggae With The Hippy Boys – The Hippy Boys (Prod: Sonia Pottinger)	1969

HORSE (PREFIX HRLP)

701	Images Of You – Nicky Thomas (Prod: Various)	1973
702	Just Tito Simon – Tito Simon (Prod: Clancy Eccles/Joe Sinclair)	1973
703	Blackbird Singing – Rosalyn Sweat and The Paragons (Prod: Arthur 'Duke' Reid)	1973
704	Hit Picks – Various Artists (Prod: Rupie Edwards)	1974
705	Atlantic One – Various Artists (Prod: Alvin Ranglin)	1974
706	Cookin' – Tommy McCook and The Aggrovators (Prod: Edward 'Bunny' Lee)	1975
707	The Great Junior English – Junior English (Ellis Breary)	1976
708	Still In Love With You – Alton Ellis (Prod: Alton Ellis/Various)	1977

TROJAN (PREFIX TTL)

1	Tighten Up – Various Artists (Prod: Various)	1969
2	Not issued	
3	Not issued	
4	This Is Desmond Dekker – Desmond Dekker (Prod: Leslie Kong)	4.69
5	Seven Letters – Derrick Morgan (Prod: Various)	1969
6	Not issued	
7	Tighten Up Volume 2 – Various Artists (Prod: Various)	1969
8	Duke Reid Golden Hits – Various Artists (Prod: Arthur 'Duke' Reid)	1969
9	You Left Me Standing – Various Artists (Prod: Various)	1969
10	Reggae Power – The Ethiopians (Prod: Karl 'JJ' Johnson)	1969
11	Red Red Wine – Various Artists (Prod: Various) (issued on Downtown label)	1969
12	Blow Your Horn – Reco and The Rudies (Prod: Robert Thompson [Dandy])	1969
13	The Upsetter – Lee Perry/Various Artists (Prod: Lee Perry)	1969
14	No More Heartaches – Various Artists (Prod: Harry Johnson)	1969
15	Independent Jamaica – Various Artists (Prod: Various)	1969
16	Guns Of Navarone – Various Artists (Prod: Various)	1969

17	Millie and Her Boyfriends – Millie Small/Various (Prod: Various)	1969
18	Ride Your Donkey – Various Artists (Prod: Various)	1969
19	Not issued	
20	Not issued	
21	Fire Corner – Clancy Eccles/Various Artists (Prod: Clancy Eccles) (issued on Clandisc label)	1969
22	Freedom – Clancy Eccles/Various Artists (Prod: Clancy Eccles) (issued on Clandisc label)	1969
23	Memorial – Don Drummond/Various Artists (Prod: Arthur 'Duke' Reid)	1969
24	Reggae With Soul – Owen Gray (Prod: Owen Gray)	1969
25	Reggae Is Tight – Lloyd Charmers (Prod: Lloyd Charmers for Winston Lowe)	1969
26	Dandy Your Musical Doctor – Dandy and The Music Doctors (Prod: Robert Thompson [Dandy]) (issued on Downtown label)	2.70
27	Reggae Fever – Inspirations (Prod: Joe Gibbs) (issued on Amalgamated label)	1970
28	Scratch The Upsetter Again – Lee Perry and The Upsetters (Prod: Lee Perry)	1970
29	Come Back Darling – Johnny Osbourne and The Sensations (Prod: Winston Riley)	2.70
30	Reggae Charm – Lloyd Charmers and The Dragonaires (Prod: Lloyd Charmers/Byron Lee)	1970
31	Moonlight Groover – Various Artists (Prod: Arthur 'Duke' Reid)	1970
32	Tighten Up Volume 3 – Various Artists (Prod: Various)	1970
33	Not issued	
34	What Am I To Do – Various Artists (Prod: Harry Johnson)	1970
35	Version Galore – U Roy (Prod: Arthur 'Duke' Reid) (scheduled but not issued)	
36	Hard Road To Travel – Jimmy Cliff (Prod: Jimmy Cliff)	1970
37	Keith and Enid Sing – Keith and Enid (Prod: Chris Blackwell)	1970
38	Forward March – Derrick Morgan (Prod: Leslie Kong)	1970
39	The Silver Stars – The Silver Stars (Prod: WIRL) (possibly unissued)	1970
40	The Most Of – Jackie Edwards (Prod: Leslie Kong) (possibly unissued)	1970
41	Dr Kitch – Various Artists (Prod: Various)	1970
42	Behold – The Blues Busters (Prod: Byron Lee/Ronnie Nasralla)	1970
43	The Best Of – Derrick Harriott (Prod: Derrick Harriott) (possibly unissued)	1970
44	Kiss Me Neck – Charlie Hyatt (Prod: Island) (possibly unissued)	1970
45	Come On Home – Jackie Edwards (Prod: Island) (possibly unissued)	1970
46	By Demand – Jackie Edwards (Prod: Island) (possibly unissued)	1970

47	Pledging My Love – Millie and Jackie Edwards (Prod: Island) (possibly unissued)	1970
48	Club Ska Volume 1 – Various Artists (Prod: Various)	1970
49	The Best Of – Millie Small (Prod: Various)	10.70
50	Derrick Harriott's Rock Steady Party – Various Artists (Prod: Derrick Harriott) (possibly unissued)	1970
51	Club Ska Volume 2 – Various Artists (Prod: Various) (possibly unissued)	1970
52	The Best Of Jackie Edwards and Millie (Prod: Various)	1970
53	Duke Reid Rock's Steady – Various Artists (Prod: Arthur 'Duke' Reid) (possibly unissued)	1970
54	Club Rock Steady – Various Artists (Prod: Various) (possibly unissued)	1970
55	The Best Of Derrick Harriott, Volume 2 – Derrick Harriott (Prod: Derrick Harriott) (possibly unissued)	1970
56	Treasure Chest – The Merry Men (Prod: WIRL) (possibly unissued)	1970
57	Premature Golden Sands – Jackie Edwards (Prod: Jimmy Miller and Chris Blackwell)	1970
58	Caribbean Music Fair – Pioneers/Byron Lee and Dragonaires (Prod: Leslie Kong/Byron Lee)	1971
59	Not issued	
60	Not issued	
61	Not issued	
62	Not issued	
63	Not issued	
64	Not issued	
65	Soul Revolution Volume 2 – Bob Marley and The Wailers (Prod: Lee Perry) (scheduled but not issued)	
66	The Good, The Bad And The Upsetters – The Upsetters (Prod: Lee Perry) (scheduled but not issued)	

TROJAN (PREFIX TBL)

101	Let's Catch The Beat – Brother Dan All Stars (Prod: Robert Thompson [Dandy])	1968
102	Skinhead Moonstomp – Symarip (Prod: Philigree)	4.70
103	Long Shot – The Pioneers (Prod: Leslie Kong)	4.70
104	Liquidator – Harry J All Stars (Prod: Harry Johnson) (issued on Harry J label)	1969
105	Reggae Chart Busters – Various Artists (Prod: Various)	4.70
106	Brixton Cat – Joe's All Stars (Prod: Joe Mansano)	1969
107	Monkey Man – The Maytals (Prod: Leslie Kong)	1970
108	Time Will Tell – Millie (Prod: Philigree)	1970

109	Unity – Freddie Notes and The Rudies (Prod: Joe SindairfTrojan)	9.70
110	Reggae Blast Off – Byron Lee and The Dragonaires (Prod: Byron Lee)	1970
111	Greater Jamaica – Various Artists (Prod: Arthur 'Duke' Reid)	1970
112	Woman Capture Man – The Ethiopians (Prod: Karl 'JJ' Johnson)	1970
113	Sufferer – The Kingstonians (Prod: Derrick Harriott)	1970
114	The Undertaker – The Crystalites (Prod: Derrick Harriott)	1970
115	Reggae Flight 404 – Various Artists (Prod: Alvin Ranglin)	4.70
116	Red Red Wine Volume 2 – Various Artists (Prod: Robert Thompson [Dandy]) (issued on Downtown label)	9.70
117	Reggae In The Summertime – The Music Doctors (Prod: Robert Thompson [Dandy])	9.70
118	Morning Side Of The Mountain – Dandy and Audrey (Prod: Robert Thompson [Dandy]) (issued on Downtown label)	9.70
119	The Good The Bad and The Upsetters – The Upsetters (Prod: Bruce Anthony)	4.70
120	Tighten Up – Various Artists (Prod: Various) (reissue of TTL1)	1973
121	Reggae Happening – Boris Gardiner (Prod: Boris Gardiner)	9.70
122	Young Gifted and Black – Bob and Marcia (Prod: Harry Johnson)	1970
123	Foolish Fool – Cynthia Richards/Various Artists (Prod: Clancy Eccles) (issued on Clandisc label)	1970
124	Herbsman Reggae – Various Artists (Prod: Clancy Eccles) (issued on Clandisc label)	1970
125	Eastwood Rides Again – Lee Perry/Upsetters (Prod: Lee Perry) (issued on Upsetter label)	1970
126	Soul Rebels – Bob Marley and The Wailers (Prod: Lee Perry) (issued on Upsetter label)	1970
127	Prisoner Of Love – Dave Barker and The Upsetters (Prod: Lee Perry) (issued on Upsetter label)	1970
128	Hot Shots Of Reggae – Various Artists (Prod: Leslie Kong)	9.70
129	Man From Carolina – Various Artists (Prod: Alvin Ranglin) (issued on GG label)	11.70
130	Reggae Reggae Reggae – Various Artists (Prod: Various)	9.70
131	Who You Gonna Run To – Various Artists (Prod: Winston Riley) (probably unissued)	1970
132	Mudie's Mood – Rhythm Rulers/Various Artists (Prod: Harry Mudie)	1970
132	Tighten Up Volume 2 – Various Artists (Prod: Various) (reissue of TTL7) (issued on Moodisc label)	1973
133	Groovy Jo – Jo Jo Bennett and Mudie's All Stars (Prod: Harry Mudie) (issued on Moodisc label)	1970
134	Not issued	

135	Lochness Monster – Various Artists (Prod: Various)	11.70
136	Queen Of The World – Various Artists (Prod: Bush)	1970
137	Funky Chicken – Various Artists (Prod: Various)	1970
138	Stay A Little Bit Longer – Delano Stewart (Prod: Sonia Pottinger)	1970
139	Battle Of The Giants – The Pioneers (Prod: Leslie Kong)	9.70
140	King Size Reggae – Various Artists (Prod: Leslie Kong)	1970
141	Psychedelic Reggae – Derrick Harriott & Crystalites (Prod: Derrick Harriott)	1970
142	You Can't Wine – Various Artists (Prod: Rupie Edwards)	1970
143	Love Of The Common People – Nicky Thomas (Prod: Joe Gibbs)	11.70
144	Reggae Movement – Various Artists (Prod: Harry Johnson) (issued on Harry J label)	1970
145	That Wonderful Sound – Dobby Dobson (Prod: Rupie Edwards)	1970
145	Tighten Up Volume 3 – Various Artists (Prod: Various) (reissue of TTL32 with altered sleeve)	10.70
146	You Can Get It If You Really Want – Desmond Dekker (Prod: Leslie Kong)	11.70
147	Reggae Chartbusters Volume 2 – Various Artists (Prod: Various)	1970
148	Not issued	
149	On My Way – Gene Rondo (Prod: Gene Rondo)	1970
150	Not issued	
151	Reggae Steady Go – Various Artists (Prod: Various)	1970
152	Montego Bay – Freddie Notes and The Rudies (Prod: Joe Sinclair/Trojan)	1970
153	This Is Desmond Dekker – Desmond Dekker (Prod: Leslie Kong) (reissue of TTL4)	1973
154	Keith and Enid Sing – Keith and Enid (Prod: Chris Blackwell) (reissue of TTL 37)	
155	The Best Of – Jackie Edwards and Millie (Prod: Island) (reissue of TTL 52)	1973
156	Premature Golden Sands – Jackie Edwards (Prod: Island) (reissue of TTL57)	1973
157	Not issued	
158	Not issued	
159	Club Reggae – Various Artists (Prod: Various)	1971
160	Issued as TBL 161	
161	Version Galore – U Roy (Prod: Arthur 'Duke' Reid)	1971
162	Double Barrel – Dave and Ansel Collins (Prod: Winston Riley) (issued on Techniques label)	1971
163	Tighten Up Volume 4 – Various Artists (Prod: Various)	1971
164	Club Reggae Volume 2 – Various Artists (Prod: Various)	1971

165	Tighten Up Volume 5 – Various Artists (Prod: Various)	1971
166	Africa's Blood – Various Artists (Prod: Lee Perry)	1971
167	Bartle Axe – Various Artists (Prod: Lee Perry)	1972
168	Not issued	
169	Reggae Chartbusters Volume 3 – Various Artists (Prod: Various)	1971
170	Music House – Various Artists (Prod: Bush)	1971
171	Caribbean Dance Festival – Various Artists (Prod: Various)	1971
172	Trojan Reggae Party – Various Artists (Prod: Robert Thompson (Dandy])	1971
173	Not issued	
174	Miss Labba Labba – Various Artists (Prod: Various for Bush)	1971
175	Version Galore Volume 2 – Dennis Alcapone and U Roy (Prod: Various)	1972
176	Reggae Reggae Volume 2 – Various Artists (Prod: Various)	1972
177	Music House Volume 2 – Various Artists (Prod: Various for Bush)	1972
178	Club Reggae Volume 3 – Various Artists (Prod: Various)	1972
179	Not issued	
180	Trojan's Greatest Hits – Various Artists (Prod: Various)	1972
181	Reggae Jamaica – Various Artists (Prod: Various)	1972
182	Version To Version – Various Artists (Prod: Various)	1972
183	The Heptones and Friends – Various Artists (Prod: Joe Gibbs)	1972
184	Pledging My Love – John Holt (Prod: Edward 'Bunny' Lee)	1972
185	Tighten Up Volume 6 – Various Artists (Prod: Various)	1972
186	Just A Dream – Slim Smith (Prod: Edward 'Bunny' Lee)	1972
187	Guns Don't Argue – Dennis Alcapone (Prod: Edward 'Bunny' Lee)	1972
188	Club Reggae Volume 4 – Various Artists (Prod: Various)	1972
189	Reggae Power Volume 2 – Various Artists (Prod: Various)	1972
190	Trojan's Greatest Hits Volume 2 – Various Artists (Prod: Various)	1972
191	16 Dynamic Hits – Various Artists (Prod: Various for Dynamic)	1.73
192	Music House Volume 3 – Various Artists (Prod: Various)	1972
193	Reggae Jamaica Volume 2 – Various Artists (Prod: Various)	1973
194	Not issued	
195	Rhythm Shower – The Upsetters (Prod: Lee Perry) (scheduled but not issued)	
196	Tighten Up Volume 7 – Various Artists (Prod: Various)	1973
197	You Are My Angel – Horace Andy (Prod: Edward 'Bunny' Lee)	1973
198	Memorial – Slim Smith (Prod: Edward 'Bunny' Lee)	1973
199	Cornel Campbell – Cornell Campbell (Prod: Edward 'Bunny' Lee)	1973
200	Version Galore Volume 3 – Various Artists (Prod: Various)	1973
201	Charmers In Session – Various Artists (Prod: Lloyd Chamers)	1973
202	Not issued	
203	Pipeline – Various Artists (Prod: Alvin Ranglin)	1973

204	Reggae Jamaica Volume 3 – Various Artists (Prod: Various)	1973
205	Club Reggae Volume 5 – Various Artists (Prod: Various)	1973
206	Version To Version Volume 3 – Various Artists (Prod: Various)	1973
207	Tighten Up Volume 8 – Various Artists (Prod: Various)	1973
208	Trojan's Greatest Hits Volume 3 – Various Artists (Prod: Various)	1973
209	16 Dynamic Hits Volume 2 – Various Artists (Prod: Various for Dynamic)	1973
210	Early Years – Slim Smith (Prod: Edward 'Bunny' Lee) (scheduled but not issued)	
211	Tighten Up Volume 9 – Various Artists (Prod: Various) (scheduled but not issued)	

TROJAN (PREFIX TRL/TRLS)

1	Follow That Donkey – Brother Dan All Stars (Prod: Robert Thompson [Dandy])	1968
2	Dandy Returns – Dandy (Prod: Robert Thompson [Dandy])	1968
3	Soul Of Jamaica – Various Artists (Prod: Arthur 'Duke' Reid)	1968
4	Sand and Steel – Rising Sun Steel Band (Prod: WIRL)	1968
5	Rock Steady Explosion – Byron Lee & The Dragonaires (Prod: Byron Lee)	1968
6	Here Comes The Duke – Various Artists (Prod: Arthur 'Duke' Reid)	1968
7	Top Of The Ladder – Byron Lee and The Dragonaires (Prod: Byron Lee) (scheduled but not issued)	
8	Sparrow Meets Dragon – Mighty Sparrow and Byron Lee (Prod: Byron Lee)	1969
9	Not issued	
10	Not issued	
11	This Is Antigua – Hells Gate Steel Band (Prod: WIRL)	1969
12	Not issued	
13	Not issued	
14	Not issued	
15	Absolutely – The Uniques (Prod: Lloyd Charmers for Winston Lowe)	1969
16	Jimmy Cliff – Jimmy Cliff (Prod: Leslie Kong)	12.69
17	I Need You – Dandy and Audrey (Prod: Robert Thompson [Dandy]) (issued on Downtown label)	1969
18	Reggae – Byron Lee and The Dragonaires (Prod: Byron Lee)	2.70
19	Return Of Django – Lee Perry/Upsetters (Prod: Lee Perry) (issued on Upsetter label)	1.70
20	Not issued	
21	Not issued	
22	Not issued	

23	Rain – Bruce Ruffin (Prod: Herman Chin Loy/Leslie Kong/Bruce Anthony)	1971
24	Yeah! – The Pioneers (Prod: The Pioneers/Jimmy Cliff)	1971
25	Tell It Like It Is – Nicky Thomas (Prod: Nicky Thomas)	1972
26	Pied Piper – Bob and Marcia (Prod: Keith Anderson [Bob Andy])	1971
27	Black and White – Greyhound (Prod: Dave Bloxham/Greyhound/ Graham Walker)	2.72
28	Reggay Splashdown – Byron Lee and The Dragonaires (Prod: Byron Lee)	1971
29	Not issued	
30	Not issued	
31	Not issued	
32	Not issued	
33	School Days – Scotty (Prod: Derrick Harriott)	1971
34	Not issued	
35	Not issued	
36	Grooving Out On Life – Hopeton Lewis (Prod: Neville Hinds for Dynamic)	1972
37	Still In Chains – John Holt (Prod: Edward 'Bunny' Lee)	1972
38	Vic Taylor Does It His Way – Vic Taylor (Prod: Neville Hinds for Dynamic)	1972
39	Bridge Over Troubled Water – Jimmy London (Prod: Vincent Chin)	1972
40	Reggay Hot Cool and Easy – Byron Lee and The Dragonaires (Prod: Neville Hinds for Dynamic)	1972
41	One Life To Live – Phyllis Dillon (Prod: Arthur 'Duke' Reid)	1972
42	Eric Donaldson – Eric Donaldson (Prod: Edward 'Bunny' Lee/Dynamic)	1972
43	Holt – John Holt (Prod: Edward 'Bunny' Lee)	1972
44	Better Must Come – Delroy Wilson (Prod: Edward 'Bunny' Lee)	1972
45	Dandy Livingstone – Dandy Livingstone (Prod: Robert Thompson [Dandy])	1972
46	Greyhound – Greyhound (Prod: Dave Bloxham) (scheduled but not issued)	
47	I Do Love You – Jackie Edwards (Prod: Jackie Edwards)	1972
48	I Believe In Love – The Pioneers (Prod: The Pioneers)	1972
49	Hotter Then Ever – Mighty Sparrow (Prod: Byron Lee)	1972
50	Slatyam Stoot – Toots and The Maytals (Prod: Warrick Lyn) (scheduled but not issued)	
51	From Bam Bam To Cherry Oh Baby – Various Artists (Prod: Various)	1972
52	Beat Down Babylon – Junior Byles (Prod: Lee Perry)	1972
53	Star Trek – The Vulcans (Prod: Joe Sinclair, Bunny Lee, Webster Shrowder and Des Bryan)	1972

54	Reggae Strings – Johnny Arthey Orchestra (Prod: Johnny Arthey)	1972
55	The Further You Look – John Holt (Prod: Tony Ashfield)	1972
56	Hit After Hit – The Chosen Few (Prod: Derrick Harriott)	1973
57	Super Hits – Dennis Brown (Prod: Derrick Harriott)	1973
58	Black Gold and Green – Ken Boothe (Prod: Lloyd Charmers)	1973
59	Thin Line Between Love And Hate – BB Seaton (Prod: Lloyd Charmers)	1973
60	Dreadmania – Judge Dread (Prod: Bush)	1973
61	Screaming Target – Big Youth (Prod: Augustus Clarke)	1973
62	African Herbsman – Bob Marley and The Wailers (Prod: Lee Perry/ Bob Marley)	1973
63	Presenting – I-Roy (Prod: Augustus ClarkeNarious)	1973
64	Freedom Feeling – The Pioneers (Prod: The Pioneers)	1973
65	From The Roots – The Maytals (Prod: Leslie Kong)	1973
66	Soulful Reggae – Various Artists (Prod: Various)	1973
67	The Marvels – The Marvels (Prod: Robert Thompson and A Hinds for Shady Tree)	1973
68	Not issued	
69	Silver Bullets – The Silvertones (Prod: Lee Perry)	1973
70	Double Seven – Lee Perry/Upsetters/Various Artists (Prod: Lee Perry)	1973
71	Hell and Sorrow – I-Roy (Prod: Roy Reid [I-Roy])	1973
72	Double Dekker – Desmond Dekker (Prod: Leslie Kong) (scheduled but not issued)	
73	Not issued	
74	Soul To Soul DJ's Choice – Dennis Alcapone and Lizzy (Prod: Arthur 'Duke' Reid)	1973
75	1,000 Volts Of Holt – John Holt (Prod: Tony Ashfield)	1973
76	Build Me Up – Brent Dowe (Prod: Sonia Pottinger)	1974
77	Sparrow Power – Mighty Sparrow (Prod: Slinger Francisco)	1974
78	For The Good Times – Now Generation (Prod: J Franscique)	1974
79	Life Is For Living – Ernie Smith (Prod: Lloyd Charmers)	1974
80	Jimmy Brown – Ken Parker (Prod: Arthur 'Duke' Reid/Ken Parker)	1974
81	20 Explosive Reggae Hits – Various Artists (Prod: Various)	1974
82	Hit Me With Music – Various Artists (Prod: Various)	1974
83	Let's Get It On – Ken Boothe (Prod: Lloyd Charmers)	1974
84	The Same One – Danny Ray (Prod: Various for Shady Tree)	1974
85	Dusty Roads – John Holt (Prod: Tony Ashfield and Mike Berry)	1974
86	The Best Of Lloyd Charmers – Various Artists (Prod: Lloyd Charmers)	1974
87	In Time – The Cimarons (Prod: Webster Shrowder for Kush)	1974
88	Presenting – Winston Groovy (Prod: Sidney Crooks)	1974

89	Rasta Revolution – Bob Marley and The Wailers (Prod: Lee Perry)	1974
90	20 Tighten Ups – Various Artists (Prod: Various)	1974
91	Many Moods Of I-Roy – I-Roy (Prod: Roy Reid [I-Roy])	1974
92	Reggae Strings Volume 2 – Johnny Arthey Orchestra (Prod: Johnny Arthey)	1974
93	Rock The Boat – Inner Circle (Prod: Tommy Cowan)	1974
94	Sweet Bitter Love – Marcia Griffiths (Prod: Lloyd Charmers)	1974
95	Everything I Own – Ken Boothe (Prod: Lloyd Charmers)	1974
96	Moody And Blue – Lloyd Charmers (Prod: Lloyd Charmers) (scheduled but not issued)	
97	Club Reggae – Various Artists (Prod: Various)	1974
98	I'm Gonna Knock On Your Door – The Pioneers (Prod: Sidney Crooks)	1974
99	Here I Am Baby – Al Brown (Prod: Geoffrey Chung)	12.74
100	Working Class 'Ero – Judge Dread (Prod: Bush)	1974
101	Original Reggae Hits – Various Artists (Prod: Various)	6.74
102	In Person – Gregory Isaacs (Prod: Alvin Ranglin)	1975
103	Peace And Love – Dadawah (Ras Michael) (Prod: Lloyd Charmers)	3.75
104	This Is Reggae Music – Various Artists (Prod: Various)	3.75
105	Not issued	
106	Everybody Plays The Fool – The Chosen Few (Prod: 'Prince' Tony Robinson)	3.75
107	Just Dennis – Dennis Brown (Prod: Winston 'Niney' Holness)	5.75
108	This Monday Morning Feeling – Tito Simon (Prod: Clancy Eccles/Joe Sinclair/Keith Foster)	3.75
109	Girl In The Morning – Lloyd Parks (Prod: Lloyd Parks)	1975
110	Live At The Turntable Club – Various Artists (Prod: Winston 'Niney' Holness)	1975
111	20 Tighten Ups Volume 2 – Various Artists (Prod: Various)	1975
112	Ja Gan – Leslie Butler (artist in fact Joe White) (Prod: Harry Johnson)	1975
113	Nyahbinghi – Ras Michael & Sons Of Negus (Prod: Tommy Cowan)	1975
114	Blame It On The Sun – Inner Circle (Prod: Tommy Cowan)	5.75
115	Ital Dub – Augustus Pablo (Prod: Tommy Cowan and Warrick Lyn)	5.75
116	Greatest Reggae Hits – Derrick Harriott (Prod: Derrick Harriott)	1975
117	Speak Softly – Barrington Spence (Prod: 'Prince' Tony Robinson)	1975
118	Original Reggae Hot Shots – Various Artists (Prod: Leslie Kong)	1975
119	Not issued	
120	Freedom Street – Ken Boothe (Prod: Leslie Kong)	1975
121	All I Have Is Love – Gregory Isaacs (Prod: Sidney Crooks)	1976
122	Susan Cadogan – Hurt So Good (Prod: Lee Perry)	1976
123	Natty Cultural Dread – Big Youth (Prod: Manley Buchanan [Big Youth])	1976

124	In The Ghetto – Dave and Ansel Collins (Prod: Larry Lawrence)	1976
125	Strange Thoughts – Honey Boy (Prod: Keith Williams [Honey Boy])	1976
126	Loving You – Lloyd Parks (Prod: Lloyd Parks)	1976
127	Greatest Reggae Hits – Various Artists (Prod: Various)	1976
128	Cool Rasta – The Heptones (Prod: Harry Johnson)	1976
129	My Jamaican Girl – The Fab Five (Prod: Harry Johnson)	1976
130	Revolution – Zap Pow (Prod: Harry Johnson)	1976
131	In Miami – The Chosen Few (Prod: King Sporty [Noel Williams])	1976
132	Tribute To The Emperor – Ras Michael and Sons Of Negus (Prod: Jazzbo Abubaka)	1976
133	Dreadlocks Affair – Jah Woosh (Prod: Neville Beckford Jah Woosh])	1976
134	2,000 Volts Of Holt – John Holt (Prod: Keith Bonsoir/Tony Asfield/ John Holt)	1976
135	DJ Round Up – Various Artists (Prod: Various)	1976
136	The Best Of – Barbara Jones (Prod: Alvin Ranglin)	1976
137	Hit The Road Jack – Big Youth (Prod: Manley Buchanan [Big Youth])	1976
138	Sarra I – Lizzard (Prod: Clive Hunt [Lizzard])	1976
139	Fire And Bullets – Owen Gray (Prod: Owen Gray)	1977
140	Personal Choice – Various Artists (Prod: Various)	1977
141	Stars Of The Seventies – Various Artists (Prod: Various)	1977
142	Barry Biggs & Inner Circle – Barry Biggs and Inner Circle (Prod: Byron Lee/Tommy Cowan)	1977
143	3,000 Volts Of Holt – John Holt (Prod: Edward 'Bunny' Lee)	1977
144	Roll On Muddy River – The Pioneers (Prod: Various)	1977
145	The Best Of – Matumbi (Prod: Dennis Bovell)	1977
146	16 Greatest Reggae Hits – Various Artists (Prod: Various)	1977
147	Roots Of Holt – John Holt (Prod: Jo Jo Hookim/Bunny Lee/John Holt)	1977
148	Blood Brothers – Ken Boothe (Prod: Lloyd Charmers)	1978
149	Reggae Rock – Various Artists (Prod: Various)	1978
150	Dreams Of Own Gray – Owen Gray (Prod: Owen Gray)	1978
151	I Love Marijuana – Linval Thompson (Prod: Linval Thompson)	1978
152	African Princess – Big Joe (Prod: Linval Thompson)	1978
153	Negrea Love Dub – Revolutionaries (Prod: Linval Thompson)	1978
154	Sweet 16 Hits – Desmond Dekker (Prod: Leslie Kong)	1978
155	The Groovy Collection – Winston Groovy (Prod: Winston Tucker [Groovy])	1978
156	Pusher Man – The Pioneers (Prod: Sidney Crooks)	1978
157	Religious Dread – Jah Woosh (Prod: Neville Beckford Uah Woosh])	1978
158	Sincerely – Jackie Edwards (Prod: Jackie Edwards and Bunny Lee)	1978

159	Peace And Love – Mighty Sparrow (Prod: Slinger Francisco)	1978
160	Holt Goes Disco – John Holt (Prod: John Holt and The Now Team)	1978
161	Just A Country Boy – John Holt (Prod: Edward 'Bunny' Lee)	1978
162	Only A Fool – Mighty Sparrow (Prod: Mark Arthurworrey)	1978
163	Let It Go On – John Holt (Prod: John Holt)	1978
164	Who Gets Your Love – Ken Boothe (Prod: Phil Pratt/Bunny Lee/ Lloyd Charmers)	1978
165	Never Get To Zion – Pancho Alphonso and Revolutionaries (Prod: Pancho Alphonso)	1978
166	The One Eyed Giant – King Sighter (Prod: Phil Pratt)	1978
167	Tell The Youths The Truth – Jimmy Riley (Prod: Jimmy Riley)	1979
168	16 Irie Reggae Rockers – Various Artists (Prod: Various)	1979
169	Outlaw Dub – The Revolutionaries (Prod: Linval Thompson)	1979
170	Rock In The Ghetto – Trinity (Prod: Linval Thompson)	1979
171	The Best Of – Toots and The Maytals (Prod: Leslie Kong/Warrick Lyn)	1979
172	Greatest Reggae Hits – The Pioneers (Prod: Various)	1979
173	Ghetto-Ology – Sugar Minott (Prod: Lincoln 'Sugar' Minott)	1979
174	Kamikazi Dub – Prince Jammy (Prod: Prince Jammy)	1979
175	Free From Sin – Prince Far I (Prod: Prince Far I)	1979
176	20 Reggae Blockbusters – Various Artists (Prod: Various)	1979
177	Love Affair – Marie Pierre (Prod: Dennis Bovell)	1979
178	Dread At The Controls – Mikey Dread (Prod: Mikey 'Dread' Campbell)	1979
179	Darling Ooh! – Errol Dunkley (Prod: Sonia Pottinger/Various)	1979
180	Creation Rockers Volume 1 – Various Artists (Prod: Various)	1979
181	Creation Rockers Volume 2 – Various Artists (Prod: Various)	1979
182	Creation Rockers Volume 3 – Various Artists (Prod: Various)	1979
183	Creation Rockers Volume 4 – Various Artists (Prod: Various)	1979
184	Creation Rockers Volume 5 – Various Artists (Prod: Various)	1979
185	Creation Rockers Volume 6 – Various Artists (Prod: Various)	1979
186	Black Ash Dub – Sly (Dunbar) and The Revolutinaries (Prod: Jah Thomas)	1980
187	Skinhead Moonstomp – Symarip (Prod: Philligree) (reissue of TBL102 with new sleeve)	1980
188	Monkey Business – Various Artists (Prod: Various)	1980
189	Every Day Skank (The Best Of) – Big Youth (Prod: Various)	1980
190	Jamaican Heroes – Prince Far I (Prod: Prince Far I [Michael Williams])	1980
191	Cool Pon Your Corner – Barry Brown (Prod: Barry Brown)	1980
192	20 Golden Love Songs – John Holt (Prod: Various)	1980
193	A1 Dub – The Morwells (Prod: Maurice Wellington)	1980

194	Dub It In A Dance – Ranking Joe (Prod: 'Ranking' Joe Jackson)	1980
195	The Upsetter Collection – Lee Perry/Upsetters/Various Artists (Prod: Lee Perry)	1981
196	The Early Years – Gregory Isaacs (Prod: Alvin Ranglin/Winston 'Niney' Holness/Sidney Crooks)	1981
197	Money In My Pocket – Dennis Brown (Prod: Various)	1981
198	Songs For Midnight Lovers – Derrick Harriott (Prod: Derrick Harriott)	1981
199	The Best Of Beverley's – Various Artists (Prod: Leslie Kong)	1982
200	Melodica Melodies – Various Artists (Prod: Various)	1981
201	Funky Kingston – Toots and The Maytals (Prod: Warrick Lyn)	1981
202	In The Dark – Toots and The Maytals (Prod: Warrick Lyn)	1981
203	Disarmament – Ras Michael and Sons Of Negus (Prod: Ras Michael [George Henry])	1981
204	Voice Of Thunder – Prince Far I (Prod: Prince Far I [Michael Williams])	1981
205	Cry Tuff – Prince Far I (Prod: Prince Far I [Michael Williams])	1981
206	Gems From Treasure Isle – Various Artists (Prod: Arthur 'Duke' Reid)	1982
207	Tighten Up Volume 2 – Various Artists (Prod: Various)	1982
208	We Must Unite – The Viceroys (Prod: Linval Thompson)	1982
209	Poor Man Style – Barrington Levy (Prod: Linval Thompson)	1982
210	Scientist and Jammy Fight Back – The Roots Radics Band (Prod: Prince Jammy)	1982
211	Ravers Party – U Brown (prod Hugh Brown)	1982
212	Revelation – Ras Michael and Sons Of Negus (Prod: Ras Michael [George Henry])	1982
213	Mix Up – Reggae George (Prod: Prince Far I [Michael Williams])	1982
214	Musical History – Prince Far I (Prod: Prince Far I [Michael Williams])	1983
215	Settle Down Girl – Tristan Palma (Prod: Linval Thompson)	1983
216	One Of A Kind – Charlie Chaplin (Prod: Roy Cousins)	1983
217	Not issued	
218	Not issued	
219	The Royals Collection – The Royals (Prod: Roy Cousins)	1983
220	Not issued	
221	In The Beginning – Bob Marley and The Wailers (Prod: Various)	1983
222	20 Reggae Classics – Various Artists (Prod: Various)	1984
223	For Lovers And Dancers – John Holt (Prod: John Holt and The Roots Radics Band)	1984
224	20 Reggae Classics Volume 2 – Various Artists (Prod: Various)	1984
225	A Love I Can Feel – John Holt (Prod: Clement Seymour Dodd)	1985
226	Original Reggae Hit Sound – Desmond Dekker and The Aces (Prod: Leslie Kong)	1985

227	Battle Of Armageddon – Lee Perry (Prod: Lee Perry)	1986
228	Original Reggae Hit Sound – The Ethiopians (Prod: Various)	1986
229	The Dynamic Duo – Audrey Hall and Don Evans (Prod: Edward 'Bunny' Lee and Don Evans)	1986
230	The Reggae Christmas Hits Album – John Holt (Prod: Edward 'Bunny' Lee)	1986
231	16 Dynamic Reggae Hits – Various Artists (Prod: Edward 'Bunny' Lee and Joe Richards)	1986
232	Greatest Hits Volume 1 – Frankie Jones (Prod: Edward 'Bunny' Lee)	1986
233	Sarge – Delroy Wilson (Prod: Lloyd Charmers)	1986
234	Lovers Paradise – Ken Parker (Prod: Lloyd Charmers) (scheduled but unissued)	
235	Sweet Memories – Lloyd Charmers (Prod: Lloyd Charmers) (scheduled but unissued)	
236	Sweet Memories Volume 2 – Lloyd Charmers (Prod: Lloyd Charmers) (scheduled but unissued)	
237	Sweet Memories Volume 3 – Lloyd Charmers (Prod: Lloyd Charmers) (scheduled but unissued)	
238	The Exit – Dennis Brown (Prod: Prince Jammy)	1986
239	Perfidia – Pam Hall (scheduled but unissued)	
240	Taxi Gang Versus Purple Man – Sly and Robbie (Prod: Edward 'Bunny' Lee) (scheduled but unissued)	
241	Best Of Live – Dillinger (Prod: Webster Shrowder and Larry Sevitt)	1988
242	Not issued	
243	This Is Augustus Pablo – Augustus Pablo (Prod: Clive Chin) (scheduled but unissued)	
244	Not issued	
245	Not issued	
246	Trojan Explosion – Various Artists (Prod: Various)	1987
247	Not issued	
248	Not issued	
249	The Ken Boothe Collection – Ken Boothe (Prod: Various)	1987
250	Not issued	
251	Classic – Junior Soul (Prod: Willie Lindo)	1987
252	Not issued	
253	Beat Down Babylon (The Upsetter Years) – Junior Byles (Prod: Lee Perry)	1987
254	Give Me Power – Lee Perry/Various Artists (Prod: Lee Perry)	1988
255	Keep On Coming Through The Door – Various Artists (Prod: Various)	1988
256	20 Reggae Classics Volume 3 – Various Artists (Prod: Various)	1988

257	Blow Mr Hornsman – Various Artists (Prod: Various)	1988
258	Studio Kinda Cloudy – Keith Hudson/Various Artists (Prod: Keith Hudson)	1988
259	Music Is My Occupation – Various Artists (Prod: Arthur 'Duke' Reid)	1988
260	Dance Crasher – Various Artists (Prod: Various)	1988
261	The Reggae Train – Joe Gibbs/Various Artists (Prod: Joe Gibbs)	1988
262	Fattie Fattie – Clancy Eccles/Various Artists (Prod: Clancy Eccles)	1988
263	Blood and Fire – Niney/Various Artists (Prod: Winston 'Niney' Holness)	1988
264	Unbelievable Sounds – Scotty (Prod: Derrick Harriott/Various)	1988
265	Ba Ba Boom – Duke Reid/Various Artists (Prod: Arthur 'Duke' Reid)	1988
266	Let Me Tell You Boy – Harry Mudie/Various Artists (Prod: Harry Mudie)	1988
267	Step Softly – Derrick Harriott/Various Artists (Prod: Derrick Harriott)	1988
268	With A Flick Of My Musical Wrist – U Roy/Various Artists (Prod: Various)	1988
269	When Will Better Come – Junior Byles (Prod: Lee Perry/Winston 'Niney' Holness) 1988	
270	Jumping With Mr Lee – Bunnie Lee/Various Artists (Prod: Edward 'Bunny' Lee) 1989	
271	Hold Me Strong – Various Artists (Prod: Various)	1989
272	My Voice Is Insured For Half A Million Dollars – Dennis Alcapone (Prod: Various)	1989
273	Bring The Cushie – Niney/Various Artists (Prod: Winston 'Niney' Holness)	1989
274	Birth Of Ska – Various Artists (Prod: Arthur 'Duke' Reid)	1989
275	Shuffling On Bond Street – Various Artists (Prod: Arthur 'Duke' Reid)	1989
276	Now This Is What I and I Call Version – Various Artists (Prod: Edward 'Bunny' Lee)	1989
277	They Talk About Love – Various Artists (Prod: Phil Pratt) (scheduled but unissued)	
278	Version Like Rain – Lee Perry/Various Artists (Prod: Lee Perry)	1990
279	It's Rocking Time – Various Artists (Prod: Arthur 'Duke' Reid)	1990
280	Ire Feelings: Chapter and Version – Rupie Edwards/Various Artists (Prod: Rupie Edwards)	1990
281	Let There Be Version – Rupie Edwards (Prod: Rupie Edwards)	1990
282	My Time Is The Right Time – Alton Ellis (Prod: Various) (scheduled but unissued)	
283	The Magnificent 14 – Various Artists (Prod: Various)	1990
284	20 Reggae Classics Volume 4 – Various Artists (Prod: Various)	1990
285	Celebration – Leon D (Delroy) Williams (Prod: Delroy Williams)	1990
286	Just My Imagination – Various Artists (Prod: Various)	1990

287	Dance All Night – Various Artists (Prod: Various)	1991
288	Doing The Moonwalk – Nicky Thomas (Prod: Joe Gibbs/Nicky Thomas)	1991
289	I Shall Sing – Various Artists (Prod: Various)	1991
290	Babylon A Fall Down – Various Artists (Prod: Various)	1991
291	Solid Gold – Various Artists (Prod: Various)	1991
292	King Of Ska – Desmond Dekker (Prod: Delroy Williams and Desmond Dekker)	1991
293	Solid Gold Volume 2 – Various Artists (Prod: Various)	1991
294	Yesterday – Various Artists (Prod: Various)	1991
295	Solid Gold Volume 3 – Various Artists (Prod: Various)	1991
296	We Chat You Rock – Jah Woosh and I-Roy (Prod: Neville Beckford Jah Woosh]/Roy Reid [I-Roy])	1991
297	Out Of Many The Upsetter – Various Artists (Prod: Lee Perry)	1991
298	Tears Of A Clown – Various Artists (Prod: Various)	1991
299	My Best Girl Wears My Crown – The Paragons (Prod: Arthur 'Duke' Reid)	1992
300	I Am The Ruler – Derrick Morgan (Prod: Various)	1992
301	Music Like Dirt – Desmond Dekker (Prod: Leslie Kong)	1992
302	Solid Gold Volume 4 – Various Artists (Prod: Various)	1992
303	Rain From The Skies – Slim Smith (Prod: Edward 'Bunny' Lee)	1992
304	Tougher Than Tough – Various Artists (Prod: Various)	1992
305	Adults Only – Various Artists (Prod: Various)	1992
306	Not issued	
307	Not issued	
308	Adults Only Volume 2 – Various Artists (Prod: Various)	1992
309	Not issued	
310	Not issued	
311	Dock Of The Bay – Various Artists (Prod: Various)	1992
312	The World Goes Ska – The Ethiopians (Prod: Various)	1992
324	King Of Kings – Desmond Dekker and The Specials (Prod: Roger Lomas)	1993
328	Midnight Train To Georgia – Various Artists (Prod: Various)	1993

TROJAN REGGAE SUNSPLASH ALBUMS (PREFIX TRLS)

8901	Live At Reggae Sunsplash – Toots and The Maytals (only issued on cassette)	1982
8902	Not issued	
8903	Not issued	
8904	Live At Reggae Sunsplash – Day One – Various (only issued on cassette)	1982

8905	Live At Reggae Sunsplash – Big Youth	1982
8906	Live At Reggae Sunsplash – Eek A Mouse plus Michigan and Smiley	1982
8907	Since I Throw The Comb Away – Live At Reggae Sunsplash – The Twinkle Brothers	1982

LOWBITE ALBUMS (PREFIX LOW)

| 01 | Censored – Lloydie and The Lowbites | 1970 |
| 02 | Censored Volume 2 – Lloydie and The Lowbites (unissued) | |

TROJAN ALBUM (PREFIX TRJC)

| 100 | Unlimited – Jimmy Cliff | 1990 |

TROJAN ALBUMS (PREFIX TRPT)

| 100 | Bush Doctor – Peter Tosh | |
| 101 | Mystic Man – Peter Tosh | |

TROJAN ALBUM (PREFIX TMLP)

| 1 | Tight Rock – Various Artists | 1977 |

TROJAN ALBUM (PREFIX TRBLP)

| 1 | The Trojan Sound – Various Artists | 1974 |

TROJAN SAMPLER ALBUMS (PREFIX TRS)

| 1 | Out Of Many, One – Jamaican Music, 1962 to 1975 – Various Artists | |
| 2 | Out Of Many, One – Jamaican Music, Part 2 – Various Artists | |

TROJAN DOUBLE ALBUMS (PREFIX TRLD)

401	Double Dekker – Desmond Dekker	1973
402	The Trojan Story – Various Artists	1976
403	Rebel Music – Various Artists	1979
404	Officially, Live And Rare – Desmond Dekker	1987
405	Not issued	
406	Soul Revolution Parts 1 & 2 – Bob Marley and The Wailers	1988
407	Skinhead Classics – Various Artists	1988
408	Musical Fever, 1967–68 – Clement Dodd/Various Artists (Prod: Clement Seymour Dodd)	1989
409	King Tubby's Special '73/'76 – Various Artists	1989
410	Wake The Town And Tell The People – U Roy (scheduled but unissued)	

411	Reggae Phenomenon – Big Youth	1990
412	Return Of The Liquidator – Harry J/Various Artists	1991
413	Celebration – Various Artists	1992

TROJAN DOUBLE ALBUM (PREFIX BYD)

| BYD 1 Reggae Phenomenon – Big Youth | 1977 |

TROJAN TRIPLE ALBUMS (PREFIX TALL)

1	The Trojan Story – Various Artists	1972
100	The Trojan Story – Various Artists	1980
200	The Trojan Story Volume 2 – Various Artists	1982
300	The Tighten Up Box Set – Various Artists	1988
400	In Memoriam – Bob Marley and The Wailers	1991
500	Bob Marley and The Story Of Reggae – Various Artists	1992

TROJAN TRIPLE ALBUMS (PREFIX PERRY)

1	The Upsetter Box Set – Various Artists	1985
2	Open The Gates – Various Artists	1989
3	Build The Ark – Various Artists	1990

MOONCREST LP (PREFIX CREST) – REGGAE RELEASE ONLY

| 5 | Conscious – Dandy Livingstone (prod Robert Thompson) | 1973 |

ACTION (PREFIX ACT) – SOUL RELEASES ONLY

4500	Give Me One More Chance/Get It – Wilmer (Alexander) and The Dukes	9.68
4501	Competition Ain't Nothing/Three Way Love – Little Carl Carlton	1968
4502	Dancing Man/Later For Tomorrow – Ernie K-Doe	1968
4503	Grab Your Clothes And Get On Out/No Love At All – Minnie Epperson	1968
4504	Got To Get Myself Together/Darling Depend On Me – Buddy Ace	1968
4505	Oh Baby Mine/Working On Your Game – OV Wright	1968
4506	Earthquake/How Long – Al 'TNT' Braggs	10.68
4507	Tore Up/I Get So Tired – Harmonica Fats	1968
4508	Shine It On/Things Are Looking Better – Vernon Garrett	1968
4509	Baby I Eed Your Love/Try It Again – Bobby Williams	1968
4510	Tell Him No/Throw Away The Key – The Bell Brothers	1968
4511	I'll Forget You/Be My Aby – John Roberts	1968
4512	Gotta Pack My Bag/How Sweet You Are – Ernie K-Doe	1968

4513	Here I Am In Love Again/I'm Tired Of You – Brothers Two	1968
4514	Drums, 1 Guitar/Why Don't They Leave Us Alone – Carl Carlton	1968
4515	People Make The World Go Round/Hard To Forget – Roosevelt Grier	12.68
4516	Omar Khayyam/Tomorrow – Rubaiyats	1968
4517	Call On You/The Woodsman – Chuck Trois and The Amazing Maze	1968
4518	Young Boy Blues/You Were Meant For Me – Eddie 'Buster' Forehand	1969
4519	So Anna Just Love Me/Boogaloo No 3 – Roy Lee Johnson	1969
4520	You Got A Deal/Say You'll Never – Alice Clark	1969
4521	Not released	
4522	What Kind Of A Lady/You're Gonna Miss Me – Dee Dee Sharp	1969
4523	Slow Drag/So Glad I'm Yours – The Intruders	1969
4524	Rockin' In The Same Old Boat/Wouldn't You Rather – Bobby Bland	1969
4525	Don't Make The Good Girls Go Bad/Your Love Is All I Need – Della Humphrey	1969
4526	I'm A Good Man/I Like What You Do To Me – Al 'TNT' Braggs	1969
4527	I Want Everyone To Know/Gonna Forget About You – OV Wright	1969
4528	Baby What You Want Me To Do (Parts 1 And 2) – Little Richard	1969
4529	You're Everything/Our Love Will Grow – Norman Johnson and The Showmen	1969
4530	Hot Tamales (Parts 1 And 2) – The Prime Mates	1969
4531	Save It/This Love Was Meant To Be – Melvin Davis	1969
4532	Make Me Yours/What Am I Living For – ZZ Hill	1969
4533	Ain't No Reason For Girls To Be Lonely (Parts 1 And 2) – Bobby Marchan	1969
4534	Stuff/You Gotta Come Through – Jeanette Williams	1969
4535	Ride Your Pony/Trouble With My Lover – Betty Harris	1969
4536	Shing-A-Ling Stroll/Don't Kick The Teenagers Around – Eddie Wilson	1969
4537	Look At Mary Wonder/Bad For Each Other – Carl Carlton	1969
4538	Got To Get To Know You/Baby I'm On My Way – Bobby Bland	1969
4539	Baby Do The Philly Dog/Mine Exclusively – The Olympics	1969
4540	Don't Hurt Me No More/Get Yourself Together – Al Greene	1969
4541	That's In The Past/I Can't Get Over You – Brenda and The Tabulations	1969
4542	Slipping Away/Half A Love – Barbara Mason	1969
4543	Is There Anything Better Than Making Love/New Love – Fantastic Johnny C	1969
4544	Hide Out/Jolly Joe – Hideaways	1969
4545	Take It Baby/In Paradise – Norman Johnson and The Showmen	1969

4546	He's Got A Blessing/Rockin' A Weary Land – The Wash Hopson Singers 1969	
4547	I Love You/I Surrender – Eddie Holman	1969
4548	Share Your Love With Me/Honey Child – Bobby Bland	1969
4549	She Shot A Hole In My Soul/We're Gonna Hate Ourselves – Clifford Curry	1969
4550	Black Gal/Frog Legs – Clifton Chenier	1969
4551	I Can't Save It/I Can Take Care Of Myself – Gene Chandler	1969
4552	I Can't Stop You/LA Stomp – The Performers	1969
4553	Chains Of Love/Ask Me About Nothing But The Blues – Bobby Bland	1969
4554	Not released	
4555	Get Out In The Street/It Must Be Love – Eddie Wilson	1970
4556	I'll Do A Little Bit More/Same Old Thing – Olympics	1970
4557	Hound Dog/I Can Feel A Heartbeat – Jeanette Williams	1970

ACTION (PREFIX ACT)

SECOND SERIES

4601	You're Everything/Our Love Will Grow – Norman Johnson and The Showmen	10.71
4602	Rae – Do It/Crying Clown – Billy Sha	1971
4603	That's A Bad Thing To Know/All In Your Mind – The Bobbettes	1971
4604	I'm In Love With You/Married Lady – Bobby Patterson	1972
4605	Why Didn't You Let Me Know/What Life Is All About – The Hoagy Lands	1972
4606	Born To Make You Cry/Thunder Road – Kim Fowley	1972
4607	Sign Of The Crab/May The Best Man Win – Joe S. Maxey	1972
4608	Women's Lib/ – Buster Pearson (Prod: Buster Pearson)	1973
4609	Check Your Bucket (Parts 1 And 2) – Eddie Bo	1973
4610	Soul Makossa (Parts 1 And 2) – Gaytones (Prod: Sonia Pottinger)	1973
4611	Sticky Fingers – (Parts 1 And 2) – Jamaica Band (Prod: M Wesley and D Paramour)	1973
4612	Big Funk/Pretty Woman – Buster Pearson Band (Prod: Buster Pearson) (NB: Five Star's dad)	1973
4613	Get It While You Can/Amen – Wilbert Harrison	1973
4614	Super Sweet Girl Of Mine/Set Your Mind Free – Five Miles Out	1973
4615	I'll Go Out And Getcha Part 1/Part 2 – Stanley	1973
4616	Just Keep On Truckin'/Never Can Say Goodbye – Backyard Heavies	1973
4617	I Found Myself/Don't Forget About Me – Mill Edwards	1973
4618	My Sweet Baby/Henry Ralph – Esquires	1973

4619	Soul Of A Black Man/Reap What You Sow – Aaron McNeil	1973
4620	Black, Foxy Woman/God Bless The Children – Chuck Armstrong (Prod: King Sporty)	1973
4621	Rock Springs Railroad Station/Endless Confusion -Tom Green	1973
4622	I Want To Make It With You (Parts 1 And 2) – Bobbi Houston (Prod: King Sporty)	1974
4623	Funky Butter/Wondering – Chosen Few (Prod: King Sporty)	1974
4624	Get Some/Plan For The Man – Wee Willie (Armour) and The Winners	1974

SPECIAL ISSUE

People/Action promo 45 (V/A, Action label 1 side, People the other)

B&C SINGLES (PREFIX CB) – SOUL RELEASES ONLY

101	Freedom Train/That's The Way Love Turned Out For Me – James Carr	1969
102	Dancing Everywhere/Baby It's Over – Bob and Earl	1969
104	Spinning Wheel/Like I Used To Do – Horace Faith (Prod: Stan Biederbeck)	1969
105	Whether It's Right Or Wrong/Baby I'm Satisfied – Jackie Lee and Dolores Hall	1969
106	Denver/Tell Me – Clyde McPhatter	1969

MIAMI (PREFIX MIA)

401	Night And Day/Funky Buttercup – The Chosen Few (Prod: Noel Williams aka King Sporty)	1976
402	Thinking Of You/Dancing Mood – King Sporty (Prod: Noel Williams aka King Sporty)	1976
403	Morning, Noon And Night/Fighting Time – Dean Lewinson (Prod: Ralph Adu)	1976
404	Help Yourself/Why – Jimmy James and The Vagabonds (Prod: Phil Wainman for Dawn Productions)	1975
405	Sweet Temptation/Sugar M,Y Love – The Love Dimension (Prod: Berek Nemeceb)	1976
406	Don't It Feel Good/Watcha Do To Me – City Lights (Prod: Mack Fleming)	1976
407	This Old Man/Always Friends – The Playgrouns (Prod: Rupert Holmes)	1976
408	Reggae Rock Road/Reggae Rock Road (Version) – King Sporty (Prod: Noel Williams aka King Sporty)	1976

PEOPLE (PREFIX PEO)

101	Forever/Baby Let Me Get Close To You – Baby Washington and Don Gardner	1973
102	Lonely Days Lonely Nights/I'm So Proud Of You – Don Downing	1973
103	Dynamite Explodes/Bring It On Home – Gentle Persuasion	1973
104	Get On Board/Get On Board (Instrumental) – Wee Three	1973
105	Just Can't Get You Out Of My Mind/You're Just A Dream – Baby Washington	1973
106	Who Is She And What Is She To You/If Loving You Is Wrong – Della Reese	1974
107	I've Got To Get Away/Can't Get Over You – Baby Washington	1974
108	Dream World/The Miracle-Don Downing	1974
109	/I'll Take You There/Cisco Kid – Reuben Wilson	1974
110	Stick Up/Who Do You Think You Are – Krissie K	1974
111	Running In And Out Of My Life/Highway – Westside (Matumbi)	1974
112	Stretchin' Out/Don't Tell Your Mama – Doris Troy	1974
113	She Called Me Baby/Signed Sealed And Delivered – J Kelly and The Premiers	1974
114	NYT	
115	The Hostage/Let's Work Together Now – Donna Summer	1974
116	I Don't Know What You Got (Parts 1 And 2) – Wee Willie and The Winners	1974
117	NYT	
118	In The Pocket/Everybody Loves A Winner – Brothers	1975

ACTION LPS (PREFIX ACLP)

6001	Boogaloo Down Broadway – Fantastic Johnny C	1969
6002	Oh How lt Hurts – Barbara Mason	1969
6003	Dry Your Eyes – Brenda and The Tabulations	1969
6004	A Whole Lotta Soul – ZZ Hill	1969
6005	Various Artists – Action Packed Soul	1969
6006	A Piece Of Gold – Bobby Bland	1969
6007	Soul Perfection – Betty Harris	1969
6008	Back Up Train – Al Greene	1969
6009	Various Artists – These Kind Of Blues	1969
6010	Live On Stage – Gene Chandler	1969
6011	Down In Virginia – Jimmy Reed	1969

ACTION MID-PRICE LP (PREFIX ACMP)

| 100 | Bottle Up And Go – Eddie 'Guitar' Burns (Prod: Jim Simpson for Big Bear Records) | 1972 |

B&C BUDGET-PRICED LP (PREFIX BCB)

| 1 | Bob and Earl – Bob and Earl | 1969 |

PEOPLE LPS (PREFIX PLEO)

1	Cisco Kid – Reuben Wilson	1973
2	NYT	
3	Dawn Of A New Day – O'Donel Levy and Larry Willis	1974
4	You Don't Have To Be Black To Love The Blues – Junior Parker	1974
5	Sweet Sister Funk – Ramon Morris	1974
6	NYT	
7	Let Me In Your Life – Della Reese Carmen McRae	1974
8	Sundance – Chick Corea	1974
9	NYT	
10	American Pie – Groove Holmes	1974
11	Fly Dude (Advertised With This Number) – Jimmy McGriff	1974
12	Madame Foo Foo – Dakota Staton	1974
12	Stretching Out – Doris Troy (prod by Dandy)	1974
13	Lay Some Loving On Me – Baby Washington and Don Gardner	1974
14	Fly Dude – Jimmy McGriff (existence unsubstantiated)	1974
15	NYT	
16	NYT	
17	Friday 13th, Cook Ciunty Jail – Jimmy McGriff and Lucky Thompson	1974
18	Love Ain't Nothing But A Business Going On – Junior Parker	1974
19	Let's Stay Together – Jimmy McGriff	1974
20	The Sweet Life – Reuben Wilson	1974
21	NYT	
22	NYT	
23	NYT	
24	Super Sweet Soul – Various Artists	1975
25	Disco Soul – The Brothers/Various Artists	1975

PEOPLE DOUBLE LP (PREFIX PLEO)

| 501 | Black And Blues – Jimmy McGriff | 1974 |

Index

Printed in the United States
By Bookmasters